ALSO BY BOB OATES

Rams: The Inside Story
Roman Gabriel: Player of the Year

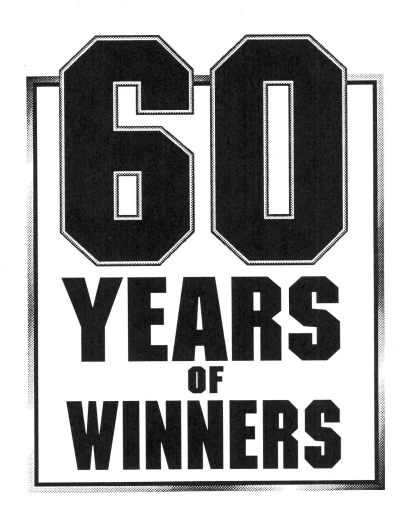

A Sportswriter's Look at Champions of the Century

BOB OATES

GRANGER PRESS

Granger Press
104 North Cromwell
Fairfield, Iowa 52556

Copyright © 1996 by Bob Oates
All rights reserved.

Library of Congress
Cataloging-in-Publication Data

Oates, Bob.
SIXTY YEARS OF WINNERS:
A Sportswriter's Look at Champions of the Century

1. Sports Journalism.   2. Sports
3. Football—American.   I. Title
96-77587   1996

CIP

ISBN 0-9653692-3-4

Copy editing by Martha Bright
Typography by Robert M. Oates, Jr.
Cover designed by David Bordow

For
Christopher Oates and
Andrew Oates and
Their Grandchildren

You ask me why I think newspapers essential, why they must be free, and honest. When the people are well informed, they can be trusted.

Inform and educate the whole mass of people. There is no other way to attack the great destroyer of mankind, ignorance.

CRUSADE *against ignorance.*

As for myself, I had rather be shut up in a very modest cottage, with my books and my family, dining on simple food, and letting the world roll on as it liked, than to occupy the most splendid post which any human power can give.

— from the letters of
THOMAS JEFFERSON

Foreword

Spectator sports on their vast modern scale are a twentieth-century phenomenon. There was relatively little public interest in athletic teams anywhere before the 1920s, when, for the first time, large crowds gathered regularly to watch Babe Ruth and other baseball players and Red Grange and other football players. And it was as a 1920s youngster — with, already, a deep-seated interest in newspapers — that I began attending the major league events in my neighborhood: Big Ten football games.

Accordingly, if this is the century that introduced extensive organized athletic activity to massed groups of witnesses, I have been part of it most of the way.

From the mid-1930s to the mid-1990s, during my first sixty years as a sportswriter, I wrote the newspaper stories that follow in these pages. A sequel is now projected: "The Second Sixty Years." I have found a job I like.

One aim of the present volume is to show how a metropolitan sportswriter put in most of the years of the twentieth century. There is nothing definitive here, and little that is chronological. This is simply a selection of the newspaper stories I most enjoyed creating in the days and nights of six absorbing decades. They were written, most of them, for the Los Angeles Times, the Los Angeles Examiner, or the Herald-Examiner. Some were abridged and edited for other publications. And I must say that although it's an open question whether sportswriters contribute in any way to the general society, I have liked everything about the life and effort involved except, of course, composing first drafts.

A second reason for assembling these articles is to document the results of a lifetime focus on winners — sixty years of winners. The premise is that in a major league activity, the will to achieve doesn't lead automatically to achievement. Winning doesn't just happen. To me, the most appealing aspect of any game resolves to a question: "What did you do to win?"

I have never voluntarily entered a losers' locker room. Even though some of the nation's finest writers insist that losers are the best story, an inference that leads them to specialize in heartbreak, turmoil, gossip and scandal — the fruit of human frailty — I continue to specialize narrowly in success. And I submit that what counts most with newspaper readers is the striving for success: the endeavor by groups of exceedingly talented athletes and their leaders to compete with sustained excellence in continuous pressure.

Not that I'm touting my way to anyone else, and not that I have anything against losers. Some of my best friends are losers. It just happens that my interest is in how winners win.

When I changed base from South Dakota to Southern California in the 1930s, it was my good luck to arrive in the heyday of newspapers at a time that might have been, despite depression and war, the heyday of American civilization. The country's population was then an optimum, manageable one hundred twenty-five million. And in the most livable of America's pre-World War II cities, my first California affiliate, the Los Angeles Examiner, was thought of by area editors and reporters as the finest of the city's five daily papers.

A quarter century later, the Examiner was still that when, for budgetary reasons, it was folded into the Herald-Examiner. Subsequently, after a capital-labor rupture paralyzed the Herald-Examiner, I accepted an offer from the Times just in time to participate in the most dramatic newspaper adventure of the century, the Otis Chandler renaissance in Los Angeles.

Always a financial success, the Times, for many decades, had been a disappointment as a newspaper. Chandler, a Southern California native whose family had owned the paper for generations, meant to change that. And, taking charge in the 1960s, he did. During a twenty-year run as a hands-on publisher, consistently showing the strength and ability to get what he wanted, Chandler established himself as the foremost journalist of his time.

The turning point for the Times was his decision to cover the world. Understanding that there can be but limited interest in local news and minor activities in a sprawling community as amorphous as Los Angeles, Chandler built the largest circulation in America with staffs of national, Washington and foreign writers second to none.

For everyone at the Times in those years, that was the best time to be a journalist in the history of journalism, or so it seemed, and still seems, to me. In 1960, Chandler had come in with two goals — to create America's best newspaper and to make it the most profitable of all newspapers — and he worked toward these ambitious goals with so much ingenuity and energy that for awhile in the 1970s, he hit both at the same time. And there I was: a reporter with a special interest in winners suddenly representing a newspaper that was the biggest winner of them all. To track such a happening at first hand, and to be part of it myself, was endlessly stimulating.

My part was unique. From Chandler's editors came, year after year, assignments of unprecedented scope for a sports reporter. I went from beat writer covering the local pro football club to a position that then existed on no other paper — national pro and college football writer — while serving simultaneously as the Times' most frequently published long-feature reporter. Traveling the nation, and on to Europe, writing some of the lengthiest feature-style articles ever printed in a daily newspaper, I had a first-class assignment in a first-class organization during the great days of first-class travel before deregulation.

A severe downswing for newspapers didn't then seem possible — couldn't be imagined — but unhappily, it is here. In the America of the 1990s, the population, by comparison with that of the 1930s, is unmanageable — having more than doubled — yet newspaper readership steadily dwindles. For this is the era of television and computers; and the trends, nationwide, are seemingly irreversible: many, many, many more people but fewer readers, fewer advertisers, fewer papers with fewer pages, and fewer reporters. In Los Angeles alone, of the ten or twelve newspapers that were alive earlier in the century, the Times is the single survivor.

The novel reality of the 1920s — spectators in vast numbers for Ruth, Grange, and their successors — has become an American way of life in an age when, incongruously, there are so many fewer to write about it. Journalists today see the twenty-first century dimly if at all, and I can only vouch for one thing. For an individual who for sixty years has asked for nothing more nor less than a career as a newspaper writer, the twentieth has been some century.

Marina del Rey, Calif. BOB OATES.
October, 1996.

Contents

Foreword *9*

Introduction *A Writer's Life 17*

PART 1 PEOPLE *49*

I ROCKNE *Golden Age Superstar 51*

    Dorais to Rockne *60*   Rockne's Last Game *64*
    George Gipp *62*   The Four Horsemen *65*

II DIALOGUE *Conversations with Champions 71*

    Stan Musial *73*   Doc Kearns *96*
    Dick Daugherty *75*   Ginger Drysdale *97*
    Dorothy Poynton *76*   Dr. Frank Ryan *99*
    Tony Bettenhausen *78*   Walter O'Malley *101*
    Bobby Thomson *80*   Tom Mack *104*
    Raymond Berry *82*   Dick Butkus *106*
    Roger Craig *83*   Don Sutton *108*
    Hugh McElhenny *85*   Merlin Olsen *110*
    Danny Goodman *86*   Mike Marshall *112*
    Parry O'Brien *88*   Davey Lopes *114*
    John Roseboro *89*   Manny Mota *116*
    Frank Selvy *94*   Fred Dryer *119*

III SPORTSMEN *The Men Behind the Games 123*

    John Madden *124*   Charlie O. Finley *150*
    O.A. (Bum) Phillips *132*   James Naismith *158*
    Gene Upshaw *137*   Al Davis *164*
    Bobby Knight *144*   Bobby Bowden *170*

IV ATHLETES *Profiles of Champions 175*

    Ben Hogan *176*   O.J. Simpson *198*
    Bobby Riggs *181*   Paul Hornung *204*
    Bronko Nagurski *187*   Hank Aaron *210*
    Jimmy Clark *193*   Arnold Palmer *213*

PART 2 FOOTBALL 225

V THE BEAT *A Football Writer's Seven-Day Week* 227

Second-Day Story 228
The Ram Pro-File 230
Next Opponent 232
Voice of the People 234
Q&A With a Star 236
Game-Day Advance 238
Game Story 239

VI THE GAME *Seven Decades of Game Stories* 243

1936: Dutch Clark 246
1949: Bob Waterfield 248
1955: Otto Graham 250
1964: Jack Kemp 252
1967: Bart Starr 255
1973: Rae & Swann 258
1982: Joe Montana 261
1993: Steve Young 264

VII LEADERS *A Game of Coaches and Quarterbacks* 267

George Halas 269
Ram Champions 273
  Jumbo 273
  Hamp 278
John Unitas 280
Paul Brown 281
Shotgun Pioneers 285
  Kilmer on Hickey 286
  Clark Shaughnessy 287
Vince Lombardi 290
  Fears on Lombardi 294
  Wood on Lombardi 295
George Allen 297
Joe Namath 300
Sammy Baugh 305
George Blanda 307
Woody Hayes 312
John Robinson 315

VIII THE TEAM *San Francisco 49ers: Best of Century* 319

The Champions 319
Joe Montana 326
Eddie DeBartolo 333
Bill Walsh 337

IX REASONING *The Analysis Dimension* 343

Gillman Wins 344
Allen Wins Promptly 345
Middle Linebackers 347
Power versus Veer 350
The Option Problem 355
How Stars Differ 357
Analyzing the Super Bowls:
'84 Raiders over Redskins 360
'87 Giants over Broncos 362
'93 Cowboys over Bills 366
'96 Cowboys over Steelers 372

PART 3 MEDLEY *375*

X EUROPE *A Matchless Summer* 377

    Ancient Greece *378*
    Sports in Vienna *386*
    Climbing the Eiger *390*
    Heidelberg Dueling *394*

    Soccer in London *400*
    Eton College Sports *404*
    A Welsh Superstar *409*
    Scotland Hunting *413*

XI FITNESS *And Recreation* 419

    California Fox Hunt *419*
    Risk is Essential *425*
    Wilderness Survival *427*
    How to Be Faster *433*

    How to Be Quicker *436*
    Reach for the Gin *439*
    How to Fight Stress *442*
    Pros Don't Choke *443*

XII 1981 *It Was Another Good Year* 445

    Jim Plunkett *446*
    Raiders Win XV *452*
    Inside XV *454*
    Hubbell's Screwball *455*
    Tommy Lasorda *459*
    A Century of Football 462
      Walter Camp *469*
      Flying Wedge *471*
      The Single Wing *472*
      The NFL Evolution *474*
      All-Time Team *475*

    Joe DiMaggio *476*
    Hacksaw Reynolds *482*
    Ronnie Lott *485*
    Dan Reeves *488*

    The Biggest Winners
      A.A. Stagg Has 314 *494*
      The Bear Has 307 *496*
      Now the Bear Has 315 *500*

PART 3 *continued*

XIII JOURNALS *And Journalists* 503

    Sports Illustrated: In the Ess-Eye of the Beholder *504*
    Traveling Headline Writer: On the Job in London *512*

XIV CAMPUS *Never Saw One I Didn't Like* 519

    Seminole, Oklahoma *521*
    USC: Football Winner *527*
    Georgia *529*
    Texas versus Oklahoma *532*
    Wisconsin *536*
    University of Chicago *539*
    Football at Dartmouth *544*
    Stanford: Excellence *549*
    USC: Academic Winner *553*

XV COMMENT *In My Opinion* 557

    Three Subjects
        Examiner *558*
        Herald-Examiner *560*
        Times *562*
    More Shorts
        Dodgers *564*
        Cold Weather *565*
        Cousin Larry *566*
        Super Bowl *567*
    The Essay
        Identity Conflict *568*
        Owners Beat Union *570*
        No World Series *572*

    Long Commentary
        Michael Jordan *575*
        Hey, Coach, Sit Down *581*

    What Kind of
    Century Was It?
        Hall of Fame *587*
        Top Ten Athletes *588*
        Ten Biggest Days *592*

INTRODUCTION

There is singularly nothing that makes a difference . . .
except that each generation
has something different at which they are all looking. . . .
By this I mean that otherwise they are all alike.
— GERTRUDE STEIN.

The most outrageous newspaper scandal California has known shocked the West one day in the 1930s when a state legislator, naming eleven Los Angeles sportswriters, said they took racetrack money. Three sports editors and eight others, he disclosed, were all on the payroll of the most prosperous sporting enterprise in the vicinity, a race track in Tijuana, Mexico.

Of the double-dippers, one was the sports editor of the Herald-Express. One, sports editor of the Evening News, also represented the old Daily News. Three were Los Angeles Times sportswriters, illustrating the comparative prominence of that paper. And six, including the sports editor, were Los Angeles Examiner sportswriters.

In the turbulence of the Great Depression, after the conspirators confessed, newspaper jobs suddenly opened for ten young aspirants who had been living, until then, on odd-job income ranging up to $3 or $4 a week. The eleventh opening was lost when the Evening News stubbornly declined to fire a man who, the publisher said, was just trying to better himself.

The Examiner, in the Los Angeles of that day, was obviously the consummate venue. Though at the time I was disturbingly underemployed, I didn't even consider the Times. But when I got to the Examiner office that April morning, four of the six positions had already been taken, and another candidate, Gus Vignolle, hat in hand, was talking to the new sports editor. The prize was $25 a week, the Newspaper Guild's entry-level wage in the 1930s. And Vignolle won his a few minutes before I won mine.

In an era when newspaper assignments were dictated largely by seniority, Vignolle was offered his choice of the last two available sports beats, pro football and bowling. And after thinking it over carefully, he chose bowling.

So it was that pro football chose me.

In the 1930s that meant, in Southern California, the minor-league Los Angeles Bulldogs and Hollywood Bears. Super Bowl I, which in the 1990s seems so far in the past, was then far in the future. But I was on my way.

As a newspaper reporter for the last sixty years, I remain troubled by one story I can't investigate. It is frustrating to realize that I can never learn how in former centuries, my grandparents and their forefathers put in their time from year to year and day to day — at work and at play. What I most want to know about all persons, from athletes to ancestors, is, simply, how they live their lives. If, as it seems, I can't talk with my great great grandparents about that, I can at least talk now about my own life and century with the select few I'd most like to know in future centuries: my great great grandchildren.

Speaking as a present-tense person, I agree that the realities of yesterday and tomorrow are never easy to determine. Composer Paul Bowles has said, "There's no such thing as the future. . . . I remember the past as one remembers a landscape, an unchanging landscape. . . . I live in the present."

In sports, clearly, today's title contenders matter most — not yesterday's champions — at least to me. Nor is nostalgia useful. But history is.

They tell me that starting about age three, I hustled out to get the morning paper on the front lawn every day, rain or shine. That was in Aberdeen, South Dakota, where my earliest recollection is sitting on the front steps at dawn one summer day inspecting the page-one pictures and headlines in a fresh new copy of the Aberdeen Morning American. I wasn't yet in kindergarten.

My father subscribed to four newspapers, the Morning American, Aberdeen Evening News, Minneapolis Journal and New York Times. And by the time I was in Simmons Junior High, I was reading them all. One day I hurried home from school, sat down with the newspapers, and began copying front-page stories word for word with an old black pencil

— asking myself after each paragraph why the reporter wrote the story the way he did.

My industry surprised my mother, who at all times showed a compassionate interest in her four sons. I was the oldest. And watching me scribble that afternoon, she asked what I was up to. I said: "I'm practicing to be a reporter for the Times."

She said: "Writers these days have to write on a typewriter."

So she invested in a second-hand Underwood and asked my father to bring home an instruction book. Every morning after breakfast, my mother read up on that day's lesson, always staying one lesson ahead of me. And she taught me to operate a typewriter in a short burst of intensive afternoon classes, although, to the end of her life, she couldn't type herself.

Many years later, after five years of college and five on a metropolitan newspaper, I was classified by the U.S. Army not as a historian or public relations specialist but as a typist. My mother would have loved that.

Although I have spent my life writing sports, mostly football, my primary interest has always been not sports but newspapers. There are, as I have learned, a lot of fascinating ways to pass the time on a newspaper. I neither aimed for nor ruled out the sports section, either as a young adult in California or as a boy in South Dakota, where I opened with seventeen years in Aberdeen and finished with four years at Yankton College. But I've never avoided sports. My games as a schoolboy were football and tennis, each indifferently played. My high school tennis partner was a classmate named Wally Hay, and one year the most talked-about headline in the Morning American, where I worked summers, was: "Hay and Oates Win State Title."

Aberdeen was a railroad town. The second largest city in the state, home to eighteen thousand of us, it was served by four railroad lines. And I still recall with sorrow the morning I stood across the way from the Great Northern depot and learned that I'd never have the throwing accuracy to be a quarterback, or even a pitcher.

That day I'd been invited out by a group of older boys to participate in a popular local sport, throwing rocks at the hoboes who often rode trains through town. When I got there, a slow-moving coal train was rumbling by, and dozens of migratory hoboes were running along the tops of the cars, dodging rocks, and aiming handfuls of coal at my friends. Angrily, I fired back, but couldn't hit the broad side of a railroad car. Only later did I learn that the leaders of the rock throwers were just out there to stimulate a shower of coal, which they carefully loaded up and carried home.

In that crowd of Aberdeen kids, three were sons of the Lutheran minister, a St. Olaf College alumnus who named his boys Matthew, Mark and Luke. The congregation waited impatiently to hear if the minister's fourth child would also be a boy. It was, and he named him Olaf.

Northeastern South Dakota in my time was a flat godforsaken windswept prairie, but Aberdeen itself was recognized for miles around as an oasis of pleasant parks, tall trees, attractive residences, and friendly residents. And it still is. The weather is South Dakota's only problem — monotonously fierce summer heat; long, freezing winters — but the people there rise above it somehow, managing to be both upbeat and public-spirited. In the last years of the nineteenth century, not far removed from the pioneer era, they taxed themselves heavily to distribute colleges throughout a state that is still thinly populated.

In all, those old South Dakotans built seven tax-supported colleges and universities, and the one they placed in Aberdeen, known now as Northern State University, employed my father for a quarter century as financial vice president. My father was a neat, stocky, self-educated Iowan — born William Maclay Oates — who in his first Aberdeen years met and married a college student named Idah Armstrong, a pretty farmer's daughter from Illinois. In earlier generations, their families had lived in Wales and England, respectively, although, among her forebears, my mother counted Scotch-Irish and Spanish people, too.

My father, an amateur singer, was also the best public speaker in Aberdeen. The crowd for his annual sermon at the Methodist Episcopal Church was always one of the two largest of the year, matched only by the Easter Sunday turnout. The crowds for his annual high school speech were so large that students and alumni stood three and four deep in back and along the sides of a big assembly hall. Though my father always had a message, they came, I'm sure, to hear his funny lines and jokes. He told us one day about the time when, at a party, he sang "Carry Me Back to Old Virginia." Noticing afterward that a young woman was in tears, he asked her, tenderly, "Are you a Virginian?" Looking up at him, she sobbed, "No, I'm a musician."

When I was in high school, my father made $300 a month, a not-bad Depression salary. He and the president were the school's two highest-paid employees. To this day, my father's portrait hangs in his old office along with pictures of the six others who have succeeded him.

I'd like to see some pictures of *his* father, Henry Oates, but they don't exist. Reportedly named for nineteenth-century Senator Henry Clay, my grandfather was a small-town Wisconsin hardware merchant who came home for dinner one noon and, as my father told the story, advised the family that the city council had voted wet that morning. That meant beer, wine and liquor were legal again after a ten-year prohibition. My grandmother, who had helped found the Women's Christian Temperance Union, said: "We're moving, Henry."

Said grandfather: "I'm selling the store this afternoon."

And he did, buying another hardware store in a dry township close by. And when that town voted wet, he moved again. All told, my father used to say, his family lived in nine little towns in Wisconsin and Iowa before he was fourteen years old, when Henry settled down for good in an Iowa River town that is *still* dry, Iowa Falls.

That's all I know about my grandparents except that they obviously pushed their points of view effectively. For, at all times, my father warmly embraced their morals and conservative attitudes, and, arriving in South Dakota, began a lifelong fight against tobacco and alcohol. He only had two vices himself, reading newspapers and driving new cars.

MINNEAPOLIS

The best football in my neighborhood during the years when I was growing up was played by the Big Ten team at Minnesota, whose stadium stood exactly 312 miles due east of the big old barn my family had in Aberdeen behind our big old house at 913 South Jay Street.

I measured the road myself one October Friday.

My father always parked the family automobile in that barn. He was an indefatigable motoring buff who, after trading in a horse for his first car, took a joy ride around town every night of every year for the rest of his life. And that dark Friday morning, looking forward to the long drive to Minneapolis, he backed the car out of the barn at 4:15 for a twelve-hour trip — on the dusty, pockmarked gravel roads of those days — to see the glamorous Golden Gophers.

Before or since, I have seldom known a more magical weekend. To begin with, my father left my brother William and me on our own for the first time that Friday night at the Minneapolis YMCA, a cheerful new building, while he and my mother moved on to the staid old Curtis Hotel. The next morning, we drove to the stadium hours early, my father bravely steering through the heavy streetcar and motorcar traffic of a football Saturday in Minneapolis. After parking at the stadium, still moving with enthusiasm, he even got out the lunch. He was, possibly, the first tailgater.

That was an era when the Minnesota team always seemed to be getting better and better — Bernie Bierman was shortly to coach the Golden Gophers to four national championships — and for a pre-teen boy, it was breathtaking that sunny Saturday afternoon to experience, for the first time, the show that is college football. The star was a huge Minnesota fullback who also played tackle, Bronko Nagurski.

Piling it on, my parents treated us that night to a double feature in Minneapolis' newest movie palace, which, between films, turned a spotlight alternately on a mighty organ and a stage show with a name band led by Duke Ellington. Though it would make us late arriving home, we spent Sunday morning at my father's favorite church, Hennepin Avenue Methodist, then the most magnificent in the Midwest. For Sunday dinner, we were in my father's favorite dining room, the YMCA cafeteria.

Afterward, as he headed the car home, I was all but overcome by a fit of sadness. It was so painful leaving Minneapolis behind, after watching Minnesota beat Iowa as the centerpiece of a storied weekend in the first big city I'd seen, that I made a silent promise to myself: I'll never do this again. The excitement of the trip wasn't worth the agony of withdrawal.

It was a promise I couldn't keep — my father carried us along on one fabulous Minneapolis football excursion after another through high school. But the memory of that painful first departure is still vivid — along with the memory of the first game: that enchanting introduction to big league football. One unbreakable thread of my life was in place.

And I remain grateful that my father was so fond of football that he would go far out of his way to keep up with the nearest big-time team at a time when, in a small, remote, provincial town, nobody else seemed to care.

South Dakota

For two disparate reasons, the 1930s Depression, as I experienced it during those early years in South Dakota, wasn't the trial to me personally that it was to many others. First, my father invested in a new car every year, without exception. Second, Aberdeen and Yankton were both large enough for good daily papers.

Starting not long after the invention of the horseless carriage, my father began picking up a new two-door Chevrolet sedan each spring, trading the old one in for the next model at a yearly cost of about $250, or nearly a month's salary.

And every night an hour or so after dinner, he lifted his heavy gold watch out of its resting place in his vest, clicked it open, looked at it and said: "Let's go, boys." As we raced for the car, we were only thinking about two things, popcorn and ice cream. For each evening, during our forty-five minute ride about Aberdeen, we each had to choose between a five-cent sack of popcorn and a five-cent ice cream cone. After mashed potatoes, those are my two favorite dishes, and having to choose between them — when my father stopped at the store on Main Street — was the toughest decision I had to make every day of my life in Aberdeen.

One spring night as my father put the car back in the barn, he said I could have it Friday for the junior prom. And that opened still another window on the world. I discovered that girls love new cars, too.

For a school kid, it doesn't get much better than a new car every year.

In those days I also found that my early interest in journalism was still growing. One year I published my own newspaper, The Boy Scout Times. A print-shop fan at Aberdeen's Central High, I got The Times out once a month, printing each issue on a small hand press. I also set the type myself. Dipping into the print shop's large wooden cases of loose metal letters, I set every stick by hand, piece by piece, the way Gutenberg did it. In the idiom of the country editors of a distant day, most of my material was actually written *at the case*.

During the summer after my sophomore year in high school, advancing my newspaper career, I stepped in as a vacation pinch hitter for reporters at the Morning American and Evening News. In retrospect, the first day was routine, but I walked the beat proudly, calling at the mayor's office, railroad stations, courthouse, and, at noon, the Lions Club. The trip yielded one priceless item: Sinclair Lewis, who wrote "Main Street," would be passing through town a day later, and might be glimpsed when the Milwaukee train stopped at the Main Street station. For that time and place, front-page stuff.

In the American-News editorial department, the workday began at 7 a.m. But no one I knew left a wake-up call in those years in Aberdeen, where the railroad lines angled out in all directions. At dawn, your alarm clock was the distant whistling of the switch engines. That was the age of steam; and in any little Midwestern town you could also tell the temperature each morning, without getting out of bed, by the pitch of the steam-engine whistles. On a summer morning in Aberdeen, the train's high notes made 100 or above seem likely, but on winter days the pitch fell drastically. The deeper the whistle, the colder it was outside. On winter mornings, you knew by the hoarseness of the sound whether you'd need to gird for the half-mile walk to work or school with three pair of long johns, or just two.

Every year, though, soon enough, it was much too hot in South Dakota for long underwear, or even short. On summer days, it cooled off only at Enemy Swim Lake, sixty miles northeast of Aberdeen, where I spent an idyllic week or two annually in Boy Scout camp. One summer, my patrol won the state knot-tying championship, largely due, as I've often said, to the clever way I could throw a clove hitch. The next year, on hikes in the shade of the nature trail, I learned to identify twenty-three kinds of birds. That qualified me for the coveted prize known as the bird-study merit badge — and for an essay prize that fall in an English class.

I liked everything about high school — the teachers, the parties, the lake, the birds, the newspaper office, the football trips, my dad's new cars. High school in South Dakota was for me a three-year run of good times.

College was even better.

A southeastern South Dakota private school with an enrollment of four hundred, the Yankton College I knew in the 1930s was a handsome collection of old brick buildings and residence halls in a park on an eminence named Observatory Hill.

From the front steps of the observatory itself — which had a seven-inch refracting telescope, the Dakotas' largest — you could see nearly all of Yankton as it spread out and down to the Missouri River two miles away. A tree-crowned community of seven thousand, Yankton, named for an Indian tribe, was once the capital of Dakota Territory. It was the state's leading river town, having begun as a steamboat stop.

In time, I was to catch on downtown as a reporter for the Yankton Daily Press & Dakotan. But on the hill, there was also a good college paper; and as a campus editor one year, having fun with a tabloid-size weekly, I learned about the impact that big pictures make on newspaper readers. On that occasion I scheduled a photo of the homecoming queen for the front page — for the entire page, that is, except for the headlines above and a column of news to one side. When the printer downtown balked, demanding $13 extra for such a large engraving, I telephoned the queen's father in Spearfish, South Dakota, and asked if the project would be worth $13 to him. He sounded thrilled. I got a lot of comment on the page. And the next day, I got his check for $13.

Although Yankton won that homecoming game, the football team was usually a disappointment at a school that registered top of the line in three other ways, academically, socially and culturally.

Academically, before our class got there, Yankton College was already known for its Rhodes Scholars, seven of them, more than the combined total produced by the nineteen other state and private colleges and universities of the two Dakotas.

Socially, one Yankton attraction was the Saturday-night dance. And for me, the first dance, in my first week away at college, remains the most memorable. The best dancer there that night was a slim beautiful freshman, a state debate champion, age sixteen. Her name, I soon learned, was Marjory Collins, whom her family called Marnie. I learned by asking her. I also asked her to marry me, and eight years later she did. Still the most important person in my life, Marnie was the first winner I was to know well. Golden-natured, unpretentious, and greatly gifted, she won the national extemporaneous speaking championship for Yankton College the spring that students from Stanford and Alabama finished second and third. In our senior year, long before females were politically acceptable in most precincts, Marnie was elected student-body president — the first woman at our college to hold that office. To this moment, she's the only woman I've met who has everything.

Culturally, there were two very good things about Yankton College. One was my date. Marnie liked the things I did. The other was the variety. One night, the school even brought in the Imperial Russian Symphony Orchestra, which was a hit right up until it surprised everyone with its final number, "Hail Yankton College." As we all jumped to our feet, the musicians missed a bar or two. We didn't learn until later that our music school, commissioned long ago to produce a college anthem, had instead freshened up an old marching song, the Russian national anthem.

Culturally, also, Yankton College was distinguished by an outdoor theater, the Garden Terrace, which had been built without seats on a large tree-shaded lawn sloping gradually down to a stage with a permanent roofed balcony for "Romeo and Juliet." On spring nights when the theater was dark, that balcony, as seen dimly in the moonlight, has proved inspirational over the years to generations of Yankton College women. A classmate, Lawrence Brewster, counted forty-one couples there one warm evening, with room for many more. One boy always brought his radio, connected it to a socket on stage, and tuned in the name bands — Benny Goodman, Earl (Father) Hines, the Dorsey brothers — playing marvelously from remote locations throughout the nation. It was almost as much fun when it snowed.

One year at the Garden Terrace Theater, I had a speaking part in a Shakespeare play, "The Tempest." Marnie was proud of me, I noticed, even though it was just a one-word part. With the passage of the years, unhappily, I have drawn a blank. For the life of me, I can't remember that word.

I do remember that nearly every evening after rehearsals, a group of us, as few as four and as many as nine, gathered in Dave Bates' room at Look Hall to play poker. Our game was no-limit poker, the only card game worth a man's time besides contract bridge. In the 1930s, the ante was a penny or two, and seven cents was a good-sized bet, but you could make them pay two or three times that, or more, to see your cards, if that's the way you felt about it.

By that year, I was also on the staff of the Press & Dakotan, a six-day daily. Holding my first full-time newspaper job while also attending college, I earned $10 a week as city editor on a four-man news staff. It was an active period for me — daytime job, afternoon classes, play rehearsals, and card games long into the night — but never dull.

The two-mile hike up and down the hill to the P&D office was a bother only when the wind blew hard, which was almost every day, so my father loaned me the money to buy my first car, a 1928 Whippet. In that depressed year, it was one of only two cars privately owned by Yankton College students. One night when the weather was unseasonably warm for November, I decided to leave it out overnight in front of my home away from home, a campus rooming house known as the House of Warren; and I still recall with dismay that the next morning, from my upstairs window, I couldn't find the old Whippet. In an all-white landscape, it was completely buried in the snow that had started falling after midnight.

That, nonetheless, was only the beginning of a wonderful winter, if you like South Dakota winters, and I usually did. The weather was so cold in one stretch that the college closed down classes for a week, meaning that the poker game that time lasted seven days.

Count me among those who as a rule enjoyed the change of seasons in South Dakota. The summers, though everlastingly hot, were just right for the long hitch-hiking trips I sometimes made in high school and later as a college student before joining the P&D full-time. On such trips, every twenty-four hours, one needs a place to sleep — and in summer weather, my choice was usually the back seat of a parked car. At 10 p.m. or so, walking down a dark street, if I deduced that someone's car might remain there overnight, I crawled in and went to bed. As a hitchhiker, the only time I ever slept in a real bed was at a world's fair in Chicago, where, at the model House of Tomorrow, I slipped into a closet one night while they closed up, then stretched out for eight hours in the master bedroom.

INTRODUCTION

I think of that period of time — roughly the interval between the two world wars — as a relatively crime-free window in U.S. history, perhaps the only one. Climbing into a stranger's car today could get you shot. And it was often that dangerous in the old Wild West. But in the America of the 1930s and into the '40s, crime seemed to be out of style, leading many citizens to leave the doors of their cars and houses continuously unlocked. Most people lived in small towns then — in a United States with half the population of the overcrowded 1990s — and hardly anyone ever confronted any criminal except a bootlegger.

In such an environment, on my most extended hitch-hiking tour, I was on the road for two months the summer after my freshman year at Yankton. Heading first for Niagara Falls, New York, and Atlantic City, New Jersey, I doubled back all the way to California and invaded both Canada and Mexico on an excursion that carried me into more than half of the American states. And the drivers who stopped to pick me up seemed no more afraid of me than I was of them. On the first day alone, two of my chauffeurs were women, one a seventeen-year-old high school student who, before turning off for her home up near Duluth, left me standing on the highway. There a friendly woman in her seventies, driving a new car, stopped and carried me on for another hundred miles.

That night as usual, I walked into a restaurant — this one was in Blue Earth, Minnesota — and volunteered to spend an hour or two as a dishwasher in exchange for dinner. Few restaurateurs that summer turned me down. On the entire see-America trip, after starting out with $10 cash, I spent but $9.49. Breakfast was frequently a five-cent quart of milk.

There was law trouble only in Pittsburgh, where I was captured by the police one morning and jailed for most of the day. I was on the roof of a tall building that time, one of Pittsburgh's tallest; and following my usual practice in big cities, I was examining the downtown area when the police closed in, guns drawn. There had been a robbery a week earlier, and the thief had been last seen on my roof.

Sitting in a jail cell that afternoon, I had nothing to read but my girlfriend's letters, which, at my urging, she had been sending general delivery from time to time. Opening one of them again, I suddenly realized that I had picked that letter up in a Washington, D.C., post office on the very day of the great Pittsburgh robbery. I was innocent! I could prove it! And after banging on the jail cell bars, I did. Marnie had saved me again.

Not until the late summer ahead of my senior year at Yankton College — long after the end of my career as a hitchhiker — did I face another serious personal crisis. A P&D old-timer by then but still the newspaper's junior employee, I was required to start work at 7 a.m. for the most important assignment of the entire day in South Dakota journalism: turning on the Associated Press receivers. The AP began ticking out the news at that hour, creating a major conflict with life at a small school. The Yankton College subjects I needed to graduate on schedule (history, economics and political science) were only offered in 7:40 or 8:40 classes — the critical working hours on any afternoon paper.

The dilemma — work or graduate — has confronted many others, but that didn't make it easier for me. Nor did it help much that I had a campus job offer: editor of the school paper. The money was comparable — by then I was making $18 a week as both city editor and sports editor on what had become a three-man P&D staff. But the college paper was only a weekly, and I was already a daily newspaperman. One night in the last week before classwork resumed, I spent the entire night on my feet, pacing and thinking the problem through, and making pro and con lists. As an editor-reporter on a daily paper, I now had what I'd always wanted. But since first grade, my parents had been pushing me toward college. A day never went by without a reminder of some kind from my father that the only civilized people were college graduates. And shortly after dawn, I decided to give the P&D a week's notice. Two weeks would have been more civilized, but I only saw that later.

My departure in those circumstances foreclosed a return to the Press & Dakotan after graduation. I had been replaced on a small staff, the new guy was proving out, and there was no place for me. In that crisis, happily, I had an option. My coast-to-coast hitch-hiking expedition had left me with the certain knowledge that as a place to live and work, Los Angeles was incomparably far ahead of whatever was second in America.

More to the point, that's where Marnie was headed. Her home until then had been in Tyndall, South Dakota, where she grew up in the care of her grandparents. When her father, a Los Angeles dentist named Cecil Hickman Collins, urged her to go west — and drove back to Yankton with his new wife to retrieve her — she made the heart-wrenching decision to leave her childhood home. Had she stayed, I'd have stayed, and we might still be running the Tyndall paper, then and now a weekly.

For the California migration, I was ready with an improved vehicle. Flush with newspaper and poker earnings, I had traded in the 1928 Whippet for a 1927 Ford roadster, which, in the middle-1930s, was still one of the two sportiest cars in Yankton. The other was the banker's Duesenberg. The 1927 models were the first Model A Fords, and mine had both a rumble seat and a radio, one of the few car radios in the county at that time if not the state.

All the way to Los Angeles, the crowd of three in the front seat included two large Yankton College football players, Pete Hurtig and Maurice Rundell. Our luggage was in the rumble seat, and my mother's priceless Underwood typewriter was on the floor. In California, Pete and I became charter members of the Yankton College Contract Bridge Club of Los Angeles, which after sixty years is still in business.

CALIFORNIA

Before television changed the country, five Los Angeles newspapers, competing energetically for 1930s circulation, brought out numbers of new editions every day. In sports at that time, the majors were all still eastern leagues; but in both football and baseball, the Pacific Coast had the nation's fastest minors. And on game days, as a result, the newspapers printed even more editions than usual.

It seemed clear enough that, for the first game I covered as a Los Angeles football writer, I would need a spotter to help get me through all the deadlines on time. The Examiner had hired me on the strength of my South Dakota experience as a reporter and sports editor — but this wasn't Yankton versus Spearfish. The spotter I had in mind was the national speaking champion from Yankton College — if she would accept my invitation. She would. And as the game began in old Gilmore Stadium, home of the Pacific Coast League's champion Hollywood Bears, I sat down between Marnie and a Western Union operator.

On one side, Marnie kept telling me what was going on. And on the other side, the Morse code operator, reading over my shoulder, and never waiting for me to finish any sentence on the old Underwood, kept telling the Examiner office what I was writing. He was using a telegraph key like the ones you see at railroad stations in old Western movies. And the whole game passed through me to him from Marnie without, I swear, my knowing much about it.

Even so, the finished product was pretty well written, I thought, looking over the game story at breakfast the next day. Thus I wasn't surprised when the sports editor hurried up to me as I walked into the office.

"Hi," I said nonchalantly.

"Congratulations," he said, beaming. "You didn't miss a deadline."

At my request, Marnie stayed around. She was still helping me at the Coliseum from time to time after the Cleveland Rams became the Los Angeles Rams in 1946 as the first pro club to move West.

Otherwise at the Examiner, in those first California years, I was trying to bridge the gap between papers with circulations of four thousand in Yankton and four hundred thousand in Los Angeles, and I was finding a few differences. There were never any newsroom signs or banners, for instance, at the Yankton P&D. The first day I saw the inside of the Examiner office, a huge sign crossed the newsroom, wall to wall, carrying three questions in large red type on a white background. To the left, the first read: "Is It Accurate?" In the middle, the next question, in much larger type, asked: "Is It Clear?" The final question, in really large words, demanded: "Is It Interesting?"

The bottom line was: "William Randolph Hearst." And those were his priorities, although, if you made it interesting enough, he tended to ignore the first two.

Working for him the last dozen years of his life, I could see that the Examiner was his favorite of the twenty-six Hearst papers in what was then by far the largest U.S. newspaper chain. His love for Los Angeles was built into the stylish Examiner building, which is still a national landmark at Eleventh and Broadway, and which he topped with a penthouse for himself. Along the east side of the building at street level, large plate glass windows faced Broadway for a half block. And behind those windows, Hearst placed the massive Examiner presses, which, printing Sunday supplements for half of the country's Hearst papers, rolled magnificently for most of every day. Those presses were the best show in town. One morning, the streetcars couldn't get through the cars and buses dropping off school children to see a real newspaper.

Hearst's interest in sports news was, however, minimal. So ours was the most cramped department on the editorial floor. The three youngest sportswriters all shared one desk, where my personal allotment was two small drawers. One day I was searching for a pencil there when I got a memo from the managing editor with a printed notation: "From the desk of Raymond T. Van Ettisch." And that gave me an idea for my own stationery. My printed notation read: "From the drawers of Bob Oates."

During my first year at the Examiner, I worked the first 325 days consecutively. After they paid me for a five-day week, I went back on days off to learn about metropolitan newspapers. By the mid-1940s, from the day the Rams set up shop in Los Angeles, I was both the Ram beat writer, writing stories and columns from every town in the National Football League, and assistant sports director. For obscure reasons, we then had, instead of a sports editor, a sports director, Ben Woolbert.

Sitting in for him on his days off, I decided to specialize as a photo editor for two reasons: Since experimenting with oversized photos in college, pictures have always been my second interest, professionally, and they were W.R. Hearst's *only* sports interest.

On the afternoon of my first USC-Notre Dame game at the Coliseum, I had eight staff cameramen out there, strange as that was, at the time, in sports journalism. After hurrying back to the Examiner office in the fourth quarter, I first selected a one-per-second sequence of photos of the day's big play — photos taken from high in the stands with a long-lens *magic eye* camera. Then I threw out all but the four best of the day's big action pictures — leaving at least three photographers entirely unrepresented. One picture consumed half the front page. The others consumed page three. The big-picture concept was a newspaper rarity a half century ago, and I heard one day that the first time W.R. saw that edition, he reacted with a smile.

In recent years, sequence pictures and picture pages have fallen out of favor with newspaper editors, who reason that they can't compete on that level with TV — but I don't think they're right about that. TV pictures are transitory. Newspaper pictures are *there*. They helped W.R. Hearst build an empire.

I was in direct communication with him only once. On one of my early days at the Examiner, after a late-afternoon deadline, I happened to be almost alone on the editorial floor, probably examining my drawers, when the editorial operator called to say she had Mr. Hearst on the line from San Simeon.

I said: "Yes, Mr. Hearst."

He said: "I want you to look up something for me, young man. What's the name of the third stomach of a cow?"

I had a quick mental picture of Hearst at his desk writing another stern anti-Roosevelt farm-policy editorial, but all I said was something like, excuse me? He repeated the request, and I promised to get back to him, very, very soon.

First, though, I walked over and asked the operator: "Who was that man?"

She looked at me for a moment, then said: "Who do you think? Get moving."

So I rushed to the encyclopedias, found the word, double-checked the spelling in several places, and within ten minutes, proudly, I placed the call.

I said: "About that word, Mr. Hearst."

And I spelled it out carefully.

There was nothing but silence on the other end. The line seemed to have gone dead. Finally, I asked: "Are you still there, sir?"

He said: "Yes, I'm here. But it doesn't fit."

Nervously, I asked: "Doesn't fit what, sir?"

That prompted him to tell me that he was working a crossword puzzle — and not just any crossword puzzle. He confessed that he had been stumped — this man with twenty-six newspapers and a bunch of national magazines — by a puzzle in a rival paper, the L. A. Times.

As a circulation-builder, the Times, I knew, was then having a crossword-puzzle contest, with a first prize of $10,000. I'd also heard that Hearst's own newspapers were in trouble financially — that W.R. might not ride out the Depression. He *needed* that $10,000, and I'd let him down.

I promised to try harder.

That evening I braced nearly every Examiner employee who was a known crossword-puzzle addict. And at last one of our cartoonists told me that his father had it, had a lock on the $10,000. In the name of the Examiner, and the financial well-being of the Hearst empire, not to mention my financial future, and his, I begged the young artist to call home and get the word. Eventually, reluctantly, he did.

"I think we've got it," I told Hearst.

He wrote it down and said, "Thank you, young man," and hung up.

I never learned if he won. All I heard was that when our people sent in his entry, they used a false name.

The Examiner, a morning paper, survived Hearst (who lived into the 1950s) by only ten years. His children shortsightedly abandoned the morning market in 1962 and merged us into an afternoon paper called the Herald-Examiner, although, as the highest newsroom executives at the Times conceded privately then and later, the Examiner was still the best paper in town. Simultaneously, the owners of the Times, living up to their end of the deal, closed their afternoon paper, realizing, before others did, that televised evening news was already replacing afternoon papers.

Doubling as Ram beat writer and assistant sports editor of the Herald-Examiner in what was, abruptly, a two-newspaper town, I got up every morning asking myself the same question: "What can I do to beat the Times today?" I had been comparing daily journalism tactics and procedures since the year in South Dakota when, not yet old enough for school, I began reading my father's four newspapers. And now, ignoring speculation that the Herald-Examiner was doomed, I concentrated as an editor on three things: colorfully made-up pages, large action pictures, and the day's biggest news stories — to the exclusion of other stories.

We started by stressing horizontally laid-out pages, building on a design scheme with which I was familiar. As a junior editor, I had invented horizontal makeup. At least, I had never seen it anywhere in our large supply of exchange papers until, one day in the 1930s, the Examiner advanced me to a low-priority job as sports editor of the Sunday *bulldog* edition — the one printed the Friday before. That was when I discarded the vertical-makeup system and began presenting most stories in packages three to ten inches deep and three to eight columns wide under multiple-column headlines. The drill elsewhere in the world then and for years afterward was a mix of vertical stories, dribbling down the page in single columns, as, on its front page, the Wall Street Journal does it to this day.

By the middle 1960s, our front-page goal in every Herald-Examiner sports section was two big stories with two banner headlines above the fold — much as USA Today does it now. The reasoning: Give the reader an immediate choice of two special stories by suggesting, with bold horizontal makeup, that they're special. In the rest of our sports section, most other stories were also placed under multiple-column headlines, a practice that is now common; but in those days we felt the excitement of pioneers.

Despite limited space at the Herald-Examiner, we also displayed our action pictures prominently on the first two or three pages much as Sports Illustrated, with a great deal more space, has done it in recent years.

Our third scheme was to confine our coverage basically to major news and daily features on all the major beats, particularly football and baseball. Rather than throw away space on minor sports and neighborhood news, we catered to the interests of the largest sports constituency in Los Angeles, big league fans. We reasoned that the second interest of a Dodger fan isn't high school baseball, or hunting and fishing, but rather the San Francisco Giants or other major league ballclubs. High school fans, we knew, could read their neighborhood papers, of which Southern California has scores. As for hunters, they'd rather hunt than read.

The big league sports fan could turn only to us for focused, in-depth big-story coverage.

This plan proved doable largely because of the cooperation of the page-one sports columnist, Melvin Durslag, and the sports editor, Bud Furillo. As a highly skilled columnist, Durslag contributed humor, apt commentaries and timeliness. And to a news executive, his extraordinary timing was central. You could display Durslag's often inspired material when the story was hot.

Furillo, the most supportive of Hearst sports editors, provided sound angles and good coverage on big stories. Whenever a single story dominated the day's news, a heavyweight fight, say, or a decisive World Series game, we could, and usually did, feature the Durslag and Furillo columns both on page one, along with large action photos, all (in the old eight-column days) under eight-column banner headlines.

In content and presentation, those mid-1960s Herald-Examiner sports pages were, I still believe, the best in sixty years of U.S. sports. They helped keep us comparable with the Times in total circulation in an era when the morning-paper advantage was everywhere and everyday getting more pronounced.

And so at the Herald-Examiner I achieved editorially what in all my years as a newspaper student, going back to the Aberdeen days, I had hoped and wanted to do. After a quarter century-plus on Hearst papers, my career as an editor-reporter climaxed in those last years before a strike-lockout shot the Herald-Examiner down.

But I've been lucky: There was to be another and even more satisfying climax at the Los Angeles Times, where in a new and distinctly different role — as a national-assignment news-and-feature sportswriter — I've spent another rewarding quarter century-plus.

In the late 1960s, the Times sent for me when the Herald-Examiner crumbled. I was grateful but waited six months in the vain hope that Hearst's children would call off the strike-lockout. Finally, not wanting to miss a football season, I moved along.

I began at the Times as I had begun at the Examiner: working every day. For 159 consecutive mornings that first year my pro football stories were in the Times.

Though by now the biggest paper in the West, it had never been highly thought of by Los Angeles journalists — even those at the Times — except as a business institution. It had always made money. But with Otis Chandler in full charge as publisher, and with Bill Thomas heading the newsroom as one of the nation's great editors, the Times not only overcame its dreary past but quickly shot to first in America in excellence as well as net income.

The editorial budget rose proportionately; and though I continued to cover the Rams, the editors sent me out on more and more national stories.

INTRODUCTION   35

During the decade that arrived in 1970, no newspaper in the world made room for longer pieces on a greater variety of subjects than those in the Times. And as my job description grew to encompass more sports and more states, my assignments were increasingly surprising and stimulating.

Coincidentally, the 1970s might have been the heyday of sports.

The Pittsburgh Steelers, whose players were the most physically talented in football history, fielded their four Super Bowl champions in the 1970s, when the best modern baseball team, the Oakland A's, won three consecutive World Series titles. The Los Angeles Lakers won their unprecedented thirty-three consecutive NBA games in that decade and the UCLA basketball team astonishingly won a record eighty-eight consecutive college games. At USC, college football's all-time best team, the 1979 Trojans, sent twelve first-round draft choices to the NFL. Individually, Muhammad Ali became the world's greatest-ever fighter in the 1970s, when Reggie Jackson once hit four World Series home runs with four consecutive swings. It all climaxed scant weeks into the decade of the '80s with what has been called the biggest sports event yet, the Winter Olympics triumph of America over a seemingly unbeatable Soviet hockey team.

Those were years when, from one month to the next, traveling for the Times was making my job continuously engrossing. Life on the road was like a party. There was, for example, the afternoon of a Los Angeles-bound flight from New York — a 1970s jet trip that was in most ways typical of all the others in that decade — when cocktails and hors d'oeuvres were, as usual, brought out at 5 p.m. Two flight attendants were always in the first-class section in those days — along with three or four passengers, rarely more — and this time three other travelers and I were up there to get the front-cabin treatment: five-course dinners served on white tablecloths with distinctive dishware, silverware, and glassware and, for each course, appropriate wines.

But the thing I remember most about that trip was none of that. The most memorable thing was the personal tribute I got from the other passengers when we were about two hours out of New York. I had spent those hours steadily typing an early draft of a long Times story on a noisy old portable typewriter; and when the cocktail hour began, as I leaned over to set the typewriter on the floor, the three others in first class all stood and applauded.

By contrast, one of those Eastern assignments — in an early year of the computer revolution — led to the most devastating trauma I've had at the Times. On a Tuesday morning, they called me in, handed over a small gray box — which turned out to be a word processor — and said I'd have to use it from then on, starting Sunday at the football game in Philadelphia. Sports Columnist Charles Maher, who also got his first computer that day, talked back. "*Anything* that makes writing harder is a bad idea," Maher said; and though I didn't protest, I agreed.

So that week I took two tools to Philadelphia — my old portable typewriter and my new computer — and because on out-of-town assignments I am always a sightseer, I had both with me that Sunday morning when I toured Independence Hall. I think of the Declaration of Independence, which was signed there in 1776, as man's greatest single literary production. A framed copy of the Declaration hangs on one of my living-room walls, as it has for forty-five years; and I never miss a chance to revisit the place where Jefferson submitted the original. It was inconvenient — absurd, really — to walk among the inkwells of two hundred years ago carrying a typewriter and a computer, plus a briefcase; but on the morning of a football game, it's my practice never to let my tools out of my sight.

And that afternoon, covering the New York Giants versus the Philadelphia Eagles, I wrote the game story on the portable typewriter as usual. Then, laboriously, I typed the whole thing into my computer, and, miraculously pushing the right modem buttons, managed to fire it off to Los Angeles on a telephone wire. I felt sorry for the Western Union operator who was in the row just ahead of me. A skilled, accurate craftsman, she had for years dispatched most of my copy from Philadelphia. Now as she sat there with nothing to do, I thought I saw a tear in her eye. I know there was one in mine.

By the 1990s, distressingly, the festiveness had gone out of travel. Airline deregulation had led to overcrowded airports, overcrowded airplanes, fewer flight attendants, fewer flights, and, in the abominable hub-city era, the obligation to stop in Dallas, and perhaps St. Louis, in order to move from Los Angeles to Cleveland. The Times since the early 1980s, moreover, provoked like all newspapers by financial worries, has put its employees in the economy section of every airplane, forsaking Otis Chandler's standing instructions, which were: Regardless of destination (Sacramento? New York? London?), Times writers always go first class.

The change, however, has never affected either the Times as a product or me as a contributor. In late years, as my work base shifted again, I settled in as the go-to writer whenever the editors asked for in-depth stories on any subject. Though continuing as a football analyst, I have specialized for most of every year in the kind of magazine-length material that has been reproduced here and there in Parts One and Three of this book. In the 1950s and 1960s, I had often averaged a story a day. By the 1990s I was averaging — except in the football season — one story a month. My friends, assuming that I had twenty-nine days a month off, envisioned me at my computer on the thirtieth, working like hell around the clock.

On the whole, it's easier to write newspaper stories once a day than once a month; but the difference to me is meaningless. For sixty years, my approach to assignments has been the same in every newspaper office: Why not do what the editors want? W.R. Hearst wanted big pictures. The Yankton P&D wanted the wires turned on at 7 a.m. At the Times, Otis Chandler and Bill Thomas and Bill Shirley and Bill Dwyre wanted three-thousand-word stories. I'm a newspaperman. Why not?

BALDWIN HILLS

In a country with fifteen hundred daily newspapers, ten sportswriters have been there to cover each of the first thirty Super Bowl games. As one of the ten, I most distinctly remember an early Super Bowl day in New Orleans. The game site in those years, before the rise of the Louisiana Superdome, was Tulane Stadium, and I've always enjoyed the walk to Tulane through the Garden District. That day, however, the weather was wintry for New Orleans, close to freezing, so I rode the St. Charles Avenue streetcar instead, climbing in out of the biting cold.

Somehow, in an open press box, we all lived through the game. Then, heading back to the press hotel near the French Quarter, I hitched a ride with a New York writer who habitually travels in rental cars. Thus in an accounting era when the hotel bill went directly to the newspaper's auditors, my only out-of-pocket expense all day was the streetcar. And when I got back to Los Angeles, I sent in the smallest one-day expense-account total in Times history, as I learned later: fifteen cents.

If that turns a spotlight on the cost of living in New Orleans, at least in the 1970s, it also says something about my personal lifestyle inclinations. And lifestyle, whether the individual is famous, unfamous, or infamous, is a particular interest of mine.

Were I to have a conversation with my forebears, what I'd most like to know is not only how they spent their years but also their days and hours. Were I to converse with my descendants, here are a few of the things I might tell them:

When on the move, I prefer to walk rather than ride anything (except sailboats). I'll take streetcars or cable cars over taxis or limousines or rentals — and I never fly if there's time for an overnight train. One of the great things about covering the Rams in the 1940s was the ride to San Francisco in a night-train berth on Southern Pacific's luxurious old Lark. What's the hurry?

In general, as those preferences may indicate, the philosophy I endorse is as simple as it is unoriginal: You're only here once. Every day is Christmas. Live the life you love. And the best things in life are free.

For me, the three most enjoyable days of every year have always been Christmas, the first day of vacation, and the first day of football practice, but I have never particularly looked forward to any of them or to anything else, even weekends or holidays or parties. There's no such thing as the future. I'll take today.

I'd have retired long ago, I know, if alarm clocks had played any role in my life. I still feel the damage that, on college mornings, wake-up calls did to my nervous system. But since then, I haven't had to set an alarm. At home in the Baldwin Hills area of Los Angeles, my daily routine has for decades begun the same way. It starts whenever I wake up, which is usually when the birds start calling outside.

And because a simple routine helps a writer, I get to work right away, following the lead of Novelist James Michener, who told me one time that because he could happily fritter away the morning hours, he had the morning paper delivered at noon.

I simply decline to look at the Times until Marnie gets up at 8 or 9 and sets it out with breakfast. For fifty years, every other morning, we've had bacon and eggs and waffles with the morning paper. The rest are cereal days. Back at the computer after some upper-body exercise sweeping the patio, I work until lunch at 2. The afternoon is for research-related activities. I prefer not to write after lunch except in a press box.

In the late afternoon of nearly every day, we hike for thirty minutes or so, walking nearby through tree and meadow in what for us is the most attractive residential park in Los Angeles, the Baldwin Hills Village Green. During most of my years at the old Examiner, where I worked at the office four days a week, I did my hiking downtown, pacing the surrounding streets; but in subsequent decades, I have visited the downtown office an average of but once a week.

In the late, late afternoon, continuing the simple life, I manufacture a couple of dry martinis (his and hers). On workdays as well as days off, the best two hours of every day are the breakfast and cocktail hours with my wife. For cocktail-time entertainment, I put on big-band phonograph records and listen to the only form of popular music that has ever combined great musical skill with harmonious richness of sound. There is also a fire in the fireplace nearly every night we're home from October to late June. Though incompetent in most handcraft situations, I have with some effort learned to do three difficult things with style: build a fire, program the video cassette recorder, and, on big-breakfast days, open the tomato juice.

My dinner-hour preference is a VCR movie, one I've previously taped. The multiply talented five-star chef I married sets out dinner on small tray tables in the living room, after which we finish the movie — or a taped installment of NYPD Blue — before I resume my lifelong second career as a dishwasher about 9 p.m. Then I turn in with a book. I am one of those who read two books at the same time, in my case usually fiction and history.

For variety, two or three times a week, we head out in the late afternoon for live jazz by the musicians playing in one or another of Southern California's best small groups. Monday is dinner-dance night at the Alpine Village Inn twenty-five minutes down the freeway. The orchestra there is directed by Tracy Wells, who leads one of the last of the active big swing bands: five trumpets, four trombones, five reeds, four rhythm. The Wells sound is an updated reprise of the best there was a half century ago in the Peacock Court at my favorite San Francisco hotel, the Mark Hopkins, or in the Madhattan Room of the Hotel Pennsylvania in New York. My notion of the finest in entertainment is still, after all these years, a dinner-dance. Or, but only at home, a movie.

All this, I'm sure, doesn't sound like heaven on earth to everyone. I'm confident that many others could wish for something more than four trombones or a walk in the park or a computer screen that stares back six or seven hours a day. But for me, I have to say, somebody laid it out right.

Home base for this simple life (as my great great grandchildren may want to know) is the house we've lived in for an even fifty years. As Jefferson said, let the world roll on. Ours is a three-bedroom cottage that I found when, during my 1940s days at the Examiner, it was under construction. I picked it out for its functional design and westside location. The salesman said the Baldwin Hills area is twenty minutes from everywhere; but in the subsequent freeway era, it has proved to be less than that to Los Angeles International Airport, to the Hollywood Bowl, to the Times office downtown, and to the beach or Marina del Rey.

I deliberately chose a house without a breakfast nook or kitchen table.

Instead, daytimes, we headquarter in our small dining room, where my wife's desk is the dining-room table. In her primary role for many years, she has been a private investor, a nearly full-time position. Financially, the soundest instruction I've had came from the 1930s football coach of the Hollywood Bears, a multimillionaire who said anyone can be a multimillionaire. "Budget and invest," he said. From her dining-room chair, my wife's view through sliding glass doors is of our brick-floored patio, where, exercising a prejudice against concrete surfaces, I laid the bricks myself forty-nine years ago.

Close by, two of our bedrooms are furnished as compact libraries. And on workdays in the smaller of these rooms, I unpack the portable word processor — which succeeded generations of portable typewriters — set it up on the rolling library table I designed three decades ago, and create an instant newspaper office that looks out on a Baldwin Hills forest.

In our living room, Marnie's grand piano stands in one corner. Against an opposite wall we've placed our classic 1960s Packard-Bell entertainment center — seven feet broad, three feet high, solid maple — with a sliding panel across the television screen. It's been with us for thirty years. Our old phonograph records, as they revolve at some thirty-three revolutions per minute, still sound as if the big bands are in the room with us. The Packard Bell also plays my new compact discs and cassette tapes.

Behind our house, our back yard, a hundred feet deep, seventy feet wide, is ringed by shrubs and trees, including a massive avocado tree. Our sons played football there. Our grandsons play soccer. The playing field is private: A wall fourteen feet high, more than a half mile in length, edges our property in back. In front, our street ends in a traffic-free cul-de-sac.

This neighborhood retreat is wholly unlike the flatlands of a typical big-city residential area. To the south of us, it's a one-mile walk to the top of our hill, where the ocean gleams in the distance in the afternoon sunlight. And to the west of us, just across the street, another of the Baldwin Hills rises, tree-covered, out of our neighbors' back yards.

From a jet landing on the north runway of the Los Angeles airport, you can see the Baldwin Hills, which are just to your right. From a jet taking off from the same runway, you can see, also off to the right, our sailboat at Marina del Rey. It's a thirty-four-foot Hunter sloop that we own with our son and his wife, Steve and Susanne, and two friends of ours, Kirk and Beverly Busby. I picked it out because it has three cabins that close off, aft, main and fore. I frequently go aboard to run the word processor but can't sail the boat myself. We use it mostly as a beach house. Steve and Kirk are the seamen; and once in awhile, they take us to Catalina

Island. Otherwise, the *Delfin* is a very quiet place to write. Every day is Christmas.

The area that includes our neighborhood and our marina has our kind of weather, cool days and sunny afternoons. The California climate is widely misunderstood, even by Californians. If you live more than a half dozen miles from the ocean, you might as well be spending the summer months in South Dakota or Texas. By contrast, mornings are often chilly and overcast in the Baldwin Hills, conducive to work, and the prevailing early-afternoon west wind off the ocean pushes the smog east each day. Air-conditioning is unnecessary. When in previous decades the air-conditioning went out in our cars, we didn't bother to get the units repaired.

You do need cars in Southern California. And we've had ours so long they're now both classics. Marnie drives a carefully maintained black 1961 Thunderbird convertible, the one that looks like a twin-engine rocket ship. Mine is a light green 1967 Mustang convertible. I like the cars I like, but I didn't inherit my father's new-car passion. I also have a problem with the appearance of the 1990s models, which seem to be burrowing their noses into the road. We don't drive much anyway.

About the only place Marnie goes is to the tennis courts at Marina del Rey. She plays at the California Yacht Club, where her game, paddle tennis, is something like tennis on a half-size court. It was my game also until I went down with a rotator-cuff tear in 1994. Not that we ever excelled as athletes. Once a year, on the average, Marnie can beat one of the women's champions, Joan Swanson or Jackie Leebody. And I distinctly remember the day that I beat the men's champion, Dick Dulgarian, whose backhand is internationally feared.

For Baldwin Hills residents, one good thing about Marina del Rey is that it's a short drive from home. But elsewhere in California, as motorists, my wife and I don't necessarily confine ourselves to our ancient cars. If the trip we're planning can't be made in two hours, round trip, we pick up a rental and enjoy, several times a year, a new car with new gadgets: my father's old thrill. We are also in a lot of new cars on my out-of-town assignments, when, if it's a trip of a week or more, Marnie always flies along with me. Since the invention of the cassette tape deck, I have never rented a car anywhere without one. A privilege of life in the late twentieth century is being able to move around with one's own music exclusively, land, sea or air. On city streets, there's nothing like big-band music to drown out the rock or rap in the next car.

Marnie and I have taken holiday trips in new automobiles at least once in each of the last fifty years, although, in all that time, we've only owned five cars. For awhile before investing in our present convertibles, we drove similar his and hers 1950 Pontiacs, a rust-colored hardtop coupe and a black convertible. The coupe was the motor industry's first hardtop and, when we bought it new in 1950, the most beautiful car on the road. Our first purchase, an eternity ago, was a battleship gray 1939 Chevrolet four-door that had everything but a tape deck, which you didn't need in those days. The Los Angeles radio stations *all* played big-band jazz.

FAMILIA

Not so long ago, as it certainly seems, the central people in my life were my sons. And day in and out, to my wife and me, they're still central in our thoughts. As she says, they are, both of them, well-built and good-looking. And both exceed six feet two as the tallest members of either of our families (which is a tribute, I think, to Marnie's studies in the science of pre- and post-natal nutrition). Both were also good high school football players. One year at Dorsey, in one of the city's toughest football leagues, Bob was All-Southern League quarterback,

But as young men at the University of Southern California, both chose to move in other directions.

Bob has been a writer and college professor since he led his USC class for three and a half years, when he graduated with a grade-point average of 4.0, straight A. His UCLA M.A. is in history. He lives with his wife, Patricia, in Fairfield, Iowa, where they're both on the faculty of Maharishi International University. I agree with the influential former NFL publisher, David Boss, that Bob is the country's best-ever football writer. Of his twelve books, half are on sports subjects — including "A Matter of Style," the definitive book on the art of forward passing, which he wrote with Hall of Fame Quarterback Joe Namath — and half are on people or topics related to the Transcendental Meditation® program.

Steve is Dr. Stephen Oates, a widely respected dentist with offices in Manhattan Beach and Fountain Valley, California, and patients from places as far away as Chicago. His Manhattan Beach office building, which is a block from the ocean on Manhattan Avenue, is an architectural design winner. A USC D.D.S., Steve, who designed the building himself, lives nearby with his wife, Susanne, formerly of Frosakull, Sweden, and their sons, Christopher and Andrew, who, both of them, are bright, bilingual, and a lot of fun. Steve and Susanne have a vacation home in Sweden. Steve is the type who can do anything well, and in the Los Angeles South Bay area these days, in his American Youth Soccer Association district, he is the chief referee.

In the 1930s and '40s, there were four brothers who came out of South Dakota to live in four sections of the country. The first to move, I was followed by William, who went to Harvard for bachelor's and doctoral degrees. Formerly headmaster of St. Paul's School in New Hampshire, William resides now in Kennebunkport, Maine. The next to move, Jim, formerly chief financial officer of Container Corporation of America, is a University of Chicago M.B.A. He still lives in Chicago. The youngest of the four, my late brother Dick of New York, went from Cornell College in Iowa, of which he was a graduate, to IBM, which called him a programming genius.

William's sons are William (Billy), Jim and Tom, who all still live in the East. And in the Boston area, Billy and Jim organize the family's national celebrations along with Billy's wife, the interior designer Elizabeth (Muffy), and Jim's wife, the architect Judy Oates.

In my wife's family are her sister-in-law, Mrs. Richard Collins (who is known as Josephine or Tutty) and daughters Melinda Norris, Marnie Olmstead and Grace (Gady) Bramlet. My wife's other niece is Patricia Grigg.

These are agreeable people, all of them; but in terms of reunions, the family has a problem. In a big country, we live all over it.

THE PRESS

On an early morning in a 1930s South Dakota newspaper office, looking up from my typewriter, I noticed that one of the older reporters was absent. "Where's Charles today?" I asked.

"He had to take the day off," the editor said. "Alice called in sick."

Alice must be Charles' wife, I thought at first. Then I remembered: Alice was one of the linotype operators in our back shop. She was an indispensable employee, the only operator in the building who could read Charles' handwriting. On her day off, he had to take a day off.

"I wish Charles would learn to run a typewriter," the editor grumbled.

But he never did. A good reporter when sober, he was one of the last of a now-extinct species: the tramp newspapermen who moved from city to city in the early years of the century, carrying their own quills or pens and pencils, and occasionally their own ink, from one newspaper office to the next.

So I've seen it all: quills, pencils, typewriters, and computers. And through it all, the press has been, for me, an important avocation as well as vocation. My lifestyle can be simple because my principal focus, my occupation, has also been an inexhaustible source of stimulation and entertainment. I am interested in anything and everything about newspapers, or about writing for newspapers, or about writing in general.

In any form, the art of parlaying just the right sentences into just the right paragraphs, using just the right words, is, as writers keep telling people, a notably perplexing and challenging occupation. And, I say, anyone who has mastered it has done something. It was a sad day not too many years ago when I heard that Tennessee Williams had given up playwriting. Some critics believe that Williams in his prime could say more in two or three sentences, and say it better, than any other writer of the century; and when he quit, he could still write. He said it was opening nights he couldn't stand. The suspense — the possibility that he might have created a failure — was killing him. Other writers, looking at the string of words on their computer screens, can identify with that.

Writing for periodicals makes for a life of two dimensions. Half of it is research or reporting. That usually means watching other people at work or at play and talking to them about what they do, which is a pleasant vocation, one of my favorite ways to pass the time. The other half of the job, the writing, is by contrast torturous. Former New York Writer Red Smith in fact called his workroom the torture chamber. And for me the first draft is the vertical-face mountain; if I can somehow main-force my way up that cliff, the rewrites and cuts are usually downhill.

Because the profession is so arduous, I'm always interested in what time of day writers do their work. Balzac, uniquely, could write anytime, night or day. Mozart wrote music only from midnight to 5 a.m. Sixteenth President Lincoln, who at his best was probably the best writer of English since Shakespeare, spent his days telling jokes to cabinet members and office seekers, then sat down and, long into the evening, wrote his most important documents and messages. That's the hard way. Michener's way is easier: up with the birds and start hitting keys.

Of the profession of journalism, after a lifetime in its pursuit, I also hold some definite opinions. Prime among them: In an era of slumping circulations, the way to win and keep big-city newspaper readers, I'm increasingly convinced, is with a single-minded focus on major stories, whether local or regional, or across the nation, or around the world. The people in every American metropolis, it seems self-evident, have more interest in the United States Supreme Court, for example, than in any state's supreme court, and, with rare exceptions, more interest in state courts than municipal courts. Only two sets of Los Angeles journalists in this century — the group in Herald-Examiner sports in the mid-1960s and, shortly thereafter, the leaders of the Times — have realized (and capitalized on the realization) that neighborhood news and fringe topics lead to few subscribers for big-city, general-circulation dailies. With a premise that all the world's a stage, Times Publisher Otis Chandler and his editor, Bill Thomas, attained, in the 1970s, heights of acceptance and profitability never before reached by journalists. What they demonstrated was an understanding that the general reader — lured by the big story — is the true constituency of a metropolitan newspaper.

Ironically, as newspaper circulation continues to fall, the prevailing U.S. journalistic flaw is that suburban editors are over-covering major news while metropolitan editors over-cover small-time news.

Here are some other priorities, prescriptions, and views of the press:
• I value day-in day-out reliability and consistency of excellence above all other newspaper qualities. In a publication issued 365 mornings a year, the everyday reader is not well served by journalists who chase the numerous one-day prizes of their craft. The journalistic challenge is to show up every day with your best work.
• The preeminent newsroom executives of my first sixty years have been Thomas of the Times and Ben Bradlee of the Washington Post, who, along with the most effective of the sports editors I have worked with, Bill Dwyre of the Times, tell me that the single thing they like best about journalism is actively supervising the developments in a rare, ongoing blockbuster story. As an old editor, I can't disagree with that; as a writer, though, I am most content when working on any story, any day. I have enjoyed covering all the Super Bowl football games so far; but on the day of an exhibition game, that's the newspaper assignment I covet.
• I have never had a friend on any sports team or in any sports organization. In fraternization, I feel sure, conflicts of interest are unavoidable. A sports reporter or editor should be a man without a country and without sports-team or sports-institution intimates. The ideal relationship between any newspaper employee and any potential news source in any field is one of mutual respect.
• For the same reasons, publishers should in my view strictly limit the cash value of Christmas presents and other gifts for newspaper people to an even twenty cents. I've seen junior editors corrupted by bottles of bourbon.
• When confident that a news source is not telling the truth, I never quote him directly. If that hurts my stories sometimes, I have at least denied one forum to a liar.

- In a first reference to any person I'm writing about, or quoting, I insist on making an appropriate identification. The fact that a newspaper writer is aware that a given individual is a shortstop — or wide receiver, coach or U.S. congressman — is no guarantee that the readers know. It can only annoy them to be unsure.
- I can't remember when I wasn't a feminist, but this is a personal viewpoint that has rarely shown up in my work. My chief regrets are that I didn't spend a year in Paris as a twenty-year-old Herald-Tribune staff writer; that I didn't spend my twenty-first year as a Ringling Brothers publicist; that I haven't yet produced a big-band record with Steve Allen as the pianist and arranger, and that I've had so few assignments on women's sports. I think of former tennis Champion Billie Jean King as the nation's most engaging sports personality of recent decades, male or female, and she and I have visited several times, but I've never had a King assignment.
- For expedient reasons that might not be valid, I have throughout this book used the words he and his when I might just as well have said she and hers. It slows things down to keep repeating he or she and his or hers, but each time that's what I mean.
- When asked, I recommend journalism school to all media candidates. At the urging of Bob Lochner, then executive sports editor of the San Francisco Chronicle, I took a master's degree in journalism at UCLA. And later I taught that subject for two years in the UCLA English Department.
- Even so, it's my view that the surest road to newspaper employment is simply to volunteer, as an unsalaried intern, to answer copy-desk telephones. I didn't learn that in time to profit by it — and today it might not apply everywhere — but one thing is still true of all newspaper people: They hate to answer the telephone.
- Of the many sports beats on a modern metropolitan newspaper, the most challenging, I'd say, is the NFL beat. It's also the most interesting.
- Nonetheless, in my opinion, the general-assignment sports reporter has the best job on any newspaper. There are three other kinds of newspaper writers — beat specialists, rewrite specialists, and writers of columns or commentaries — and two kinds of editors: copy editors and supervisors. And across the years in Los Angeles, I've worked at all six trades, and hugely enjoyed them all. But beat people have too many responsibilities, rewrite people not enough, column work is too restrictive, and editing too far from the action. The general-assignment reporter, by comparison, works in a blissful world of wide-ranging subject matter and changing and often elastic deadlines.
- Of all newspaper responsibilities, regularly producing a column is

toughest. To be accountable for even a monthly column, as Columnist Eric Sevareid said, is like making love to a nymphomaniac: As soon as you're done, you've got to start all over again.

• Several years ago in his final newspaper column, Sevareid, describing what he'd been up to all his life as both writer and television commentator, identified himself as an elucidator. Among the others ranking with Sevareid as the surest and most incisive elucidators of my time are Adlai Stevenson, James Reston, Walter Lippmann, and, as a radio broadcaster, Vin Scully. Even though an attempt to interpret or elucidate can evoke charges of didacticism, it seems a reasonable aspiration for any communicator, including a sports reporter. I feel sure that most readers are receptive when, on topics that interest them, the critical points are made plain.

• The optimal way to write anything is with a light touch — thus acknowledging that almost everyone out there in a despairing world yearns to laugh. But it is equally correct to say that all comedians have a conspicuously low batting average — even those with a great natural gift for the comic. And so, early on, I set a different goal for myself: to be as clear and specific as possible in every sentence while using a minimum of clichés. That isn't easy, either. There's no easy way.

But for sixty years I've loved the trying.

As Gertrude Stein said, every generation looks at something different. When my great great grandkids ask what I was doing with my time when I wasn't listening to the big bands, tell them I spent it watching words take shape.

OATES.

PART 1 PEOPLE

My newspaper assignments have for many years brought me into contact with some of the world's finest athletes and others in sports, leading to results that, depending on the preferences of the assignment editors, have been of different kinds:

• In some instances, the editors I have worked with sought magazine-length profiles. The in-house word for such an assignment is *look*. As in: Take another look at Ben Hogan.

• In other instances, the requirement has been either an interview or question-and-answer discussion, sometimes magazine-length, sometimes newspaper-column length.

These are all represented in the four chapters of this volume which constitute Part One.

Champions tend to differ one from another in extraordinary ways; and in these stories, I have aimed to stress their differences, to bring out each individual's unique approach to success. Among those with whom I visit on these pages, there is, indeed, but one common denominator. They all have what it takes to win.

I

ROCKNE

During the Knute Rockne decade, the Notre Dame football team he coached was a famous winner. That was in the 1920s, when the college team I followed, Minnesota, was also a winner. But sportswriters get to meet a lot of nice losers, too; and it wasn't until the central years of the twentieth century that I made a career decision to spend more time with champions than losers.

It was a decision reached in the early California incumbency of the Los Angeles Rams, who, during two memorable stretches, knew seven years of winning and seven years of losing — paralleling, numerically, the famous Biblical intervals. And as the reporter responsible in those days for Ram coverage in the Los Angeles Examiner, I saw, for the first time, how hard it is to win and how easy to lose — and how easy to blame and disparage and denounce losers. And after awhile, I decided that defaming the unsuccessful isn't for me.

Knocking is just too simple. Too depressing. Too uninformative and, all too frequently, too uninformed.

As a sports reporter you have choices. Why not spend your time with

Rockne, Arnold Palmer, Stan Musial, Joe Namath, Gene Upshaw, Bobby Knight, John Madden and the other champions in this book? The reasoning is uncomplicated: You learn more, and feel better, talking to winners than knocking losers.

Journalism now offers, however, many sportswriters with wholly different views. On most of today's newspapers, whenever there is even a perception of human failure or weakness on any ballclub, there are writers who hurry to their word processors and open fire, hitting targets that are as diverse as teams, leagues, athletes, leaders, communities, and events. Everything is in their sights now.

And I'll concede that focusing on failures or perceived failures instead of champions — using language that evokes pity or revulsion — can be of interest to a certain kind of reader. It could even be of some small service sociologically, helping to illuminate what many think of as the essential tragedy of the human condition. But it holds no appeal for me.

The achievements of the dramatic Rockne era are more to my taste. Of the four Americans who most obviously dominated their time in the twentieth century, three were U.S. presidents — Franklin Roosevelt, Dwight Eisenhower and John Kennedy — and the fourth, quite possibly, was Knute Rockne.

In the 1920s, when the nation's presidents were less charismatic, most of the American people were familiar with the face, shape and voice of Rockne, who, as a magnetic winner, was a daily presence on radio and in the theater newsreels. Those were the new technological marvels of that decade, comparable to television and computers at a later date, and Rockne was the sports star most in demand.

Then at age forty-three, stunning the country, he died in 1931 in one of the world's first commercial airline tragedies.

As the fiftieth anniversary of that crash approached, I set out in 1981 to reconstruct Rockne and his times — the heady post-war world when, as the first football coach to become a national celebrity, he kicked off a century of sports. Correspondingly, the story I wrote about him kicks off this book. It was the longest single-author feature the Los Angeles Times had until then printed, parlaying so many words in the main story and related stories that our editors added a page to the sports section for the overflow. Later when our promotion department people were publicizing the in-depth coverage of the Times with advertisements in Eastern papers, they led off the series with full-page reprints of the Rockne feature in the New York Times and Wall Street Journal. I can't swear the story was worth all that exposure; but now that I've gotten to know him, I'm sure Rockne was.

In the package here are sidebars on his greatest player, George Gipp, and, among others, his most celebrated backfield, the Four Horsemen.

1. The Rockne Years

SOUTH BEND, Ind. March 31, 1981.

For most people, big news stories have the power to freeze an event in memory. Thus, many who have forgotten much that happened in 1941, 1963 or even 1980 can readily recall where they were and what they were up to when they heard about Pearl Harbor or the murders of John Kennedy and John Lennon.

For football fans a bit older, the shock they couldn't get over came on March 31, 1931. On that day fifty years ago an airplane crashed in Kansas to end it all for the greatest football coach of his time, perhaps of any time, Knute Rockne of Notre Dame.

Very early in the age of commercial air travel, it all ended so very soon for Rockne, who that spring was forty-three. At the summit of an unparalleled career, he died just weeks after completing his fifth undefeated and untied season in thirteen years at Notre Dame with a 27-0 upset victory over USC. Playing some of the nation's strongest schedules, his teams had lost only twelve games in those thirteen years and won 105, with five ties. After five decades, his winning percentage, .897, is still football's all-time record, college or pro, among those coaching ten years or more.

Yet in a fast-moving century, even the most celebrated names, after four or five decades, tend to fade. To most sports fans today, Knute Kenneth Rockne is a legend if that. The America of 1981 is as far removed from the living Rockne as his generation was from the American Civil War. The other day when a reporter asked three Californians in their thirties if they knew about a man named Rockne, each answered tentatively. "He gave great halftime speeches," said one. "There was a movie about him," another recalled. The third asked: "Isn't he the hunchback of Notre Dame?"

Rockne wasn't handsome, but he wasn't a hunchback, and he was a lot more than a legend who made speeches and inspired movies. Those who remember him and his era, or those who have studied the early twentieth century in America, rank Rockne with the leaders of the 1920s in any field. Though a high school dropout, he was a brilliant chemist who graduated magna cum laude from Notre Dame. At age thirty, after beginning as the track coach there, he took over the football team in 1918 just as the curtain was going up on what was to be called the Golden Age of Sports — which coincided with what also was known as the Flapper Era, and, as well, the Era of Wonderful Nonsense. It could have been all of that. World War I was just over, and for prosperous America in 1918, looking into a gleaming future, anything at all seemed possible.

Thirteen years later, at the dawn of a tragically different American experience known as the Great Depression, the dramatic end for Rockne brought down the last curtain on the golden age of Babe Ruth, Jack Dempsey, Red Grange and the other sports personalities of the Roaring Twenties, not to forget the historians: Will Rogers, Grantland Rice and, among others, F. Scott Fitzgerald. The day after the crash in Kansas, in his Los Angeles Times column, Rogers wrote: "It takes a mighty big calamity to shake this country all at once, but you did it, Knute. You did it."

II

Rockne was the first American celebrity to perish in a commercial airline disaster; and in his time, few celebrities were more widely known. Born in Norway, an immigrant obliged to learn a new language in the public schools of Chicago, he had become, in the years before Winston Churchill and Franklin Roosevelt and Adlai Stevenson, one of the world's most effective communicators in English. It was the heyday of newsreels and radio broadcasts, and by 1931 Rockne's was an instantly recognized face and voice in most American communities. The voice in particular was as familiar as those of the most prominent other personalities of that day, including Actor-Philosopher-Writer Rogers, Tenor Enrico Caruso, and Crooner Rudy Vallee. A contemporary writer, Jerry Brondfield, remembering Rockne, observed: "Nobody used the human voice with more startling and unforgettable emphasis. It was flat, nasal, metallic. Each word emerged as though coated with brass."

To have that voice suddenly stilled in a great accident, at the very peak of the man's extraordinary and heavily publicized career, and at such a comparatively young age, threw a pall over the country.

The first thought of many was for Rockne's means of transportation. What, they asked, was he doing in an airplane? Though he was an enthusiastic flyer, commercial air travel was so unusual in 1931 that Rockne had to take a train from Chicago to Kansas City to catch the Los Angeles plane that March morning. A frequent Los Angeles visitor, he had contracted to make a football demonstration movie in Hollywood.

On 3/31/31, at 0930, Transcontinental-Western's Flight 599 was scheduled to depart Kansas City rain or shine. A year-old, eight-passenger, tri-motor Fokker, it left on time with two pilots and six passengers. Fifty years ago on 599, there were already two no-shows. The primitive airliner flew immediately into a storm, picked up a load of ice, and lost momentum, falling into a wheat field. There were no explosions, no fires, no survivors. Rockne's body was retrieved by a Kansas farmer. The nearest village: Bazaar.

"It is out of the question to consider the airplane itself defective," designer Anthony Fokker said at the inquest. "I inspected it personally, two days (earlier), and found it in perfect condition."

The national impact of Rockne's spectacular life and violent death made his funeral week one of America's most emotional between Lincoln's in 1865 and Roosevelt's in 1945. More than sixteen hundred of the nation's seventeen hundred daily papers carried Rockne editorials that week. The funeral procession from his modest South Bend home to Notre Dame's stately Sacred Heart church — a replica of a medieval French Gothic cathedral — was witnessed by an estimated hundred thousand persons lining the streets of a city of about eighty-five thousand. Some two hundred Rockne players who had moved along to careers as college and high school coaches — twenty-three of them college football head coaches — returned for the funeral.

Rockne was gone. "But he still lives," the Reverend Edmund P. Joyce, Notre Dame's executive vice president, said on March 31, 1956 — twenty-five years later, twenty-five years ago. "Knute Rockne is still a vibrant living force at this university because of the powerful personal influence he exerted over so many Notre Dame men."

Among others. So many others.

III

A football fan who never knew him said recently: "One thing about Rockne is that he looked like a coach and sounded like a coach. Even his name sounded like a coach's name." To historian Brondfield, "Rockne proved that not all Vikings are blond, tall and lithe. He was only five feet eight and weighed 160 dumpy, irregular pounds. His pumpkin-shaped head was balding, and he was deeply furrowed above the eyes. His nose, broken at least three times, was the wayward feature of a preliminary boy who never made the main event. But then there was that famous Rockne smile — a broad, rippling, lopsided smile soaked in warmth and charm. And there was that voice. . . ." To Sportswriter Grantland Rice, who knew everybody, "Rockne was a man of great force, deep charm and an amazing personality. I have never known anyone quite his equal in this respect."

Sartorially, Rockne was a bum, coaching in baggy pants and torn sweatshirts. Even when dressed for a night out, he usually resembled (as someone said of someone else) an unmade bed. But in 1951, some six or seven decades after football was first played, and twenty years after he died, Rockne was the runaway winner of an Associated Press poll for all-time coach. He had 526 votes to 127 for Pop Warner and 89 for Amos Alonzo Stagg.

Rockne's influence on the America of then and today has been if anything underestimated. His is now the country's most popular sport, and, though foreign-born, he did more to make this distinctively American game nationally important than anyone (or anything else) except television.

Before Rockne, football was a kind of provincial pastime. It developed fierce rivalries, but most were within the Ivy League and selected other precincts. The so-called National Football League was then a parochial eastern league. College football was a sport with one bowl game and few intersectionals. Into this void, Rockne moved resourcefully in the 1920s. He was the first to schedule annual intersectionals — from Georgia and the Southeast to New York (when Army was a football power) and on to Chicago and Los Angeles. He went after the best teams that would play him in any part of the country.

This was something brand new. No other team, in any sport, had ever set out to compete regularly on a national stage, certainly no other major league baseball or basketball or pro football team. And no one else did until long after, when, somewhat reluctantly, the mid-century NFL moved West.

Also undervalued is Rockne's role in promoting his university. His teams had the country talking. Most Americans, reacting intensely, seemed to be either for or against the small Catholic boys school in rural Indiana. A contemporary newspaper observer, Paul Gallico, wrote years later: "With the skyrocketing of Notre Dame out of the West (sic) hundreds of thousands of people who had never been to college or near any campus identified themselves with the school with the wonderful sobriquet, 'Fighting Irish.'"

And hundreds of thousands didn't, rooting hard against the Irish.

Gallico on the Notre Dame-Army series: "New York was never before or since so sweetly gay as it was when Rock brought his boys to town and the city was electric with excitement." Or as Chicago Writer Bill Gleason summed up: "In the '20s and '30s, before TV, most sports fans could only read about the stars. They never came to *their* town. Rockne was the first national hero to get around — almost everywhere — close enough to touch."

IV

People closely involved with or fully informed about Rockne in the teen years and early 1920s in Indiana were aware that he didn't burst out of nothingness. As a Notre Dame undergraduate, he was possibly the school's most energetic student ever. He did all this:
• Played the flute in the Notre Dame symphony orchestra, playing in every concert, and almost every rehearsal.
• Took a major role in every school play of his four years.
• Wrote regularly for the student newspaper and yearbook.
• Fought semiprofessionally (at 145 pounds) in club smokers in downtown South Bend and in Elkhart. His second was Quarterback Gus Dorais.
• Worked his way through school, first as a janitor and then as a chemistry assistant to Professor Julius A. Nieuwland, whose discoveries led to synthetic rubber. From time to time, Rockne himself made some of the minor tests for these discoveries.
• Went out for the varsity sports in season, setting a school record for the indoor pole vault (12-4) and making Walter Camp's All-American football team as a third-string end.
• Reached the finals of the Notre Dame marbles tournament as a junior.
• Considered himself primarily a student, and graduated with grades averaging 90.52 (on a scale of 100). In some of the tougher subjects, he was well over 90. As a freshman he had a 99 in bacteriology and 97 in chemistry, as a junior 98 in English, and as a senior 94 in philosophy and 98 in human anatomy.

What all this indicated, of course, was a high degree of energy and intelligence, the two things all supremely successful people seem to have in common. "Rock could have been anything," says Edward W. (Moose) Krause, the school's veteran athletic director. "He had the brains, energy and personality to do anything he chose to do."

He chose football, then demonstrated that the work required to create five undefeated football teams in thirteen years wasn't enough for a restless genius. As head coach of the Fighting Irish, these were some of the other things he did simultaneously:
• During his first four years in charge, including the year of his first

national championship, Rockne worked without assistants and at the same time served as Notre Dame's athletic director, trainer, doctor, equipment manager, track coach, intramural sports director, business manager, ticket director and chemistry instructor.

• Drawing on his medical and anatomical knowledge, he designed all the equipment his players wore from their shoulder pads down. He also designed the Notre Dame uniform and was the first to put his players in sleek, streamlined, satin-and-silk pants (before streamline was in the dictionary). He wanted a smaller target for opposing tacklers, and, as a scientist, he wanted to cut down wind resistance, increasing speed.

• Seemingly inexhaustible, Rockne toured the Midwest making public speeches both in season and out, many of them sales speeches for a car manufacturer, Studebaker, which paid him more than he got from Notre Dame, a lot more.

• As another sideline, in the midst of his last season, he opened a stock brokerage firm in South Bend.

• He wrote a nationally syndicated newspaper column three times a week.

• He wrote several books, one a volume of juvenile fiction. (To speculation that some of this might have been ghosted, there are a couple of rejoinders: he was accustomed to working on three or four things at once, and the prose isn't that good.)

• He was a dedicated family man and gardener who for years raised much of the family's food, "and who otherwise spent hours with his four children," one friend said.

• In one November week in 1929 he coached two football teams simultaneously, preparing Notre Dame for Northwestern Saturday, and the Notre Dame all-stars for a benefit game Sunday.

• To the delight of subsequent football generations, Rockne was also the principal designer of Notre Dame Stadium, where his final team played the 1930 season, and which after fifty years remains a nearly ideal stadium for its size (49,000 seats, all Notre Dame could then afford). Although Rockne was a track expert with track roots before he became interested in football, he knew better than to clutter up a stadium with a running track — the bane of most stadiums built about that time, and later. Says one historian: "It's inconceivable that a less than perfect sports stadium could ever have been built here in Rockne's time."

• On the practice field, Rockne was a teaching coach who, after perfecting each blocking technique personally, got down in the dirt and instructed his players himself. Said one of them, Rip Miller: "Because

Rock only weighed about 155, he had to make a study of blocking angles and leverages. And he got right in there, without pads, smacking into us, hitting us with a shoulder, hip, upper arms, everything that was legal. He'd yell: 'Come on, now, I won't hurt you!'"

V

The energy and intelligence that drove Rockne were possibly in his genes. His grandfather and great grandfather were for years blacksmiths near Voss, Norway, a picture-postcard resort town on a lake near the North Sea. Knute was born there on March 4, 1888. His given name is pronounced Canute in Norway but usually Nute here. His father Lars was a machinist who created and also built horse-drawn carriages. When he sold several to Kaiser Wilhelm of Germany, Lars Rockne was encouraged to enter one in the 1891 World Fair in Chicago, where he won the grand prize. This encouraged him to send for his family, which detoured Knute to the Rose Bowl from a probable trip to the World Cup.

The gainer, in addition to Notre Dame, was American football, in which, in his lifetime, Rockne was best known to the strategists of the game for two innovations: shock troops and the Notre Dame shift. In using a full team of second-stringers at the start of most games (he called them shock troops) he was anticipating two platoons — a football refinement that was still decades away. At the same time he was giving bunches of players game experience and sweater letters, improving morale.

The Notre Dame shift, in which all four backs were in motion at the snap, was a tactic of such precision and grace that it was compared to a New York chorus line. In truth, Rockne, a stage fan, was rumored to have got the inspiration watching Broadway's long-legged, closely-synchronized female dancers. When his opponents couldn't handle his version of the chorus line, they persuaded the rules board to legislate against it. Hence the present rule requiring all backs except one to come to a one-second halt before the snap of the ball.

The rule change didn't slow him down. For, philosophically, defying most other practitioners in a power era, Rockne preferred light, fast, smart players, even on the line of scrimmage. Using a pony-size backfield, a gang known as the Four Horsemen, he sprinted past Stanford in the 1925 Rose Bowl.

Throughout his coaching career, Rockne preferred to deceive rather than run over opposing players. His goal at all times was to misguide opponents as to the real strength of the Notre Dame team. He loved to talk about the time when, as a Notre Dame receiver, after first limping around the field to fool the other team's defensive backs, he raced away to catch a big touchdown pass. Later he was to fool, and rout, USC with a speedy fullback wearing the uniform number of a slow fullback. In short, Rockne was football's original first Great Deceiver, antedating Al Davis, George Allen and other winners who have operated the same way.

Rockne also held a modern view of passing, which he believed is about half of football, speaking not numerically but strategically. He insisted, however, that football is a man's game, that the winner wins physically first. You must beat them running the ball, he said, although it is the threat of the pass — the fact that you've passed successfully before and can again, and will again — that makes a sound offense.

Those who knew him say invariably that as a football coach, Rockne was first and last a cheerleader — as was Vince Lombardi, among others, years later. Football is that kind of game. And so the legends properly accent Rockne's halftime speeches as the definitive explanation for his achievements. He couldn't have moved 1980s football players with 1920s oratory, perhaps, but since they still have to be moved, he would have found a way.

2. Dorais to Rockne

SOUTH BEND, Ind.: March 31, 1981.

The game that changed football the most — making it basically what it is today — was played in November, 1913, at West Point, New York, where the Cadets lost to the Fighting Irish, 35-13, in the first-ever Army-Notre Dame game. Quarterback Gus Dorais completed fourteen of seventeen passes that day, most of them to Notre Dame's captain and left end, Knute Rockne, for 243 yards, a total that surprised college football people as much as it impressed them.

Previously, football as a sport had been more like tug o' war. Since Dorais and Rockne in 1913, it has been a game of passes as well as runs.

Passing was legal before 1913 — it just wasn't the thing to do. Indeed, between 1906 and 1912, the rules of football specified that a pass could be legally completed only if it crossed the line of scrimmage not more than five yards to the left or right of center, and not more than twenty yards downfield. To help the officials in their calculations, the field was chalk-lined vertically as well as horizontally into a maze of five-yard squares. And although the grids disappeared sixty-seven years ago, it has been called a gridiron ever since.

In the early 1900s, passing had been legalized only under the gun of an

American president, Theodore Roosevelt, who threatened to abolish the sport if football players kept getting killed. But then as now, most coaches, overwhelmingly conservative, feared the pass, and insisted on numerous deterrents. The grids were plainly an asinine manifestation of this, and so were two new rules:

- An incomplete pass, like a fumble, could be *recovered by the defense* (unless an offensive man had touched it).
- A completed pass into the end zone *didn't count.* It was ruled a touchback, not a touchdown, and the other team was awarded the ball.

One consequence of all this conservative meddling was that passes, for years, were infrequent. Even in 1912, after the five- and twenty-yard gridiron restraints were removed from the rulebook because they were impossible to enforce, the coaches wouldn't throw.

Football was still a game of running and kicking almost exclusively when Dorais and Rockne, theorizing that passing seemed at times more intelligent, went into the summer of 1913 — the summer before their senior year at Notre Dame. They spent it at a Lake Erie resort waiting on tables and inventing football's first pass offense. It was an era when players often did more coaching than coaches — but creating the rudimentary first tactics and strategy of passing was no easy thing. Dorais had to learn how to throw a spiral with what was then an awkwardly shaped fat ball. And Rockne had to learn how to catch it with extended hands while in stride. There was nobody to teach any of this. In every former year, if the football were thrown at all, it was caught in the stomach or chest like a medicine ball.

The 1913 Fighting Irish had a new coach, Jesse Harper, who, doubtless at the urging of the devious Captain Rockne, used the new pass offense sparingly through their first three games, walloping teams like South Dakota without it. Not until November did they open up at West Point to rout Army, too, in the game that brought two new phenomena to national attention: Notre Dame and pass offense. The New York Times got the point immediately, carrying this headline the next morning: "Notre Dame Open Play Amazes Army." Said the Times writer: "The Westerners (sic) flashed the most sensational football ever seen in the East." That was the region where American football was born and nurtured, in the proud Ivy League and other old schools.

Army also got the point immediately. The Cadet coach, one Charley Daley, put in an embryonic pass offense to win the *big* game a week later, beating Navy's fine ball-running team to end the Army season with only one defeat — to the team that changed football.

3. George Gipp: As Good as His Legend

SOUTH BEND, Ind.: March 31, 1981.

Was anyone at Notre Dame more important than Knute Rockne — in Rockne's time? It's hard to believe, but one guy apparently was. The established star in 1920, when Rockne, thirty-two, had been a head coach for only two years, was a senior running back named George Gipp, who pronounced his last name with a hard g, as in gosh.

Ending a brilliant four-year college football career, the 1920 Gipp averaged 8.1 yards carrying the ball, still the Notre Dame record, on the way to what would have been almost certain Heisman Trophy recognition if the trophy had been awarded that early in the century. Instead, there was then something of an official All-American team — as selected by Walter Camp, a Far Easterner who chose mostly Far Easterners — and Camp, who thought of Gipp as a Westerner, made him his 1920 fullback, the first Notre Dame All-American.

Before the year was out, Rockne was to say, "Football will never again see Gipp's equal, as a player or a person." Was he all that? Where does the legend leave off and the man begin? Nobody really knows. Despite Gipp's prominence in South Bend, he was never interviewed by any newspaper reporter. He was never even quoted in a locker-room story. That was a very different media era, and hence every fact about 1920 football can be challenged.

It is with inferences that Gipp has to be reconstructed, and to use that method is to envision a classic triple-threat football player — an athlete who, from at least the twenty-five or thirty-yard line, was a constant threat to score with a run, pass or dropkick.

One inference is that Gipp was a superior kicker. He handled all the kicking for Rockne as both punter and dropkicker at a time when field goals could be scored with either dropkicks or placekicks. And the legend has Gipp dropkicking the ball sixty-two yards in a freshman game. Take twenty yards off the legend and it's still pretty good. In 1920, Gipp drop-kicked nine field goals, the Notre Dame record for fifty-seven years until 1973, when ex-Ram placekicker Bob Thomas matched him.

A second inference is that Gipp was a good passer. As the running back who took most of the direct passes from the 1920 center in Rockne's single-wing backfield — the famous Notre Dame box — Gipp was also the team's primary forward passer. The legend says that on his longest touchdown completion, the ball was in the air fifty-five yards. Take a few yards off the legend and it's still pretty remarkable with the pumpkin they threw in those days. For three years, Gipp led Notre Dame in passing. And as a senior, heaving the pumpkin at will, he completed thirty of sixty-two, not great, but better than most passers of his day.

The final inference is that Gipp was most valuable when carrying the ball. To have averaged 8.1 yards as a running back — in football's push-and-pull era — the 1920 Gipp must have been a terror, setting up his passes and dropkicks with a lot of big runs. It was an assignment for which he had the size. At six feet even and 180 pounds, he was one of the four biggest men on the team, heavier than most linemen, and the biggest back Rockne ever had except for Marty Brill (190) in the 1930 season, Rockne's last.

In historical terms, Gipp (1895-1920) lived and died an elusive figure. Son of a Congregational minister in Laurium, Michigan, Gipp drove a taxi after high school, and, like Rockne, was already an old man in his twenties when he first saw Notre Dame. Coincidentally, both laid out four years before college, Rockne as a Chicago postal clerk. In the last tragic coincidence, both died young, at the peak of their careers.

Four years older than his classmates, Gipp preferred to live off campus, and the legends have him gambling at cards and in pool halls weekdays, and nights, until Thursday, when you could usually count on him at football practice. It's in the record that unlike Rockne, he was no scholar. Academic problems in the spring of 1920 cost Gipp the captaincy that had been awarded by his teammates.

The evidence suggests that coaching a player as big, gifted and honored as Gipp permanently changed Rockne. Never again did a single person star for this coach. The prominence of the 1924 backfield known as the Four Horsemen — whose four principals shared the headlines with one another and therefore with Rockne — does not seem accidental.

Gipp's shocking death in the December of his twenty-fifth year — the greatest year of his life — wrenched the campus like no other until March 31, 1931, when Rockne went at forty-three. Before costing him his life, a strep throat ending in pneumonia cost Gipp a chance (in Notre Dame's last two games) to become a 1,000-yard gainer in 1920, when he had 827 yards in his first seven games. Not for another fifty-six years did any Notre Dame man reach 1,000.

Whether on his death bed Gipp actually asked his coach to tell a Notre Dame team someday to win one for the Gipper is a secret that Rockne, a dedicated psychologist, took to the grave. The clippings tell us that Gipp played his best games against Army — he never lost to Army — and when Rockne used the Gipper story, it was to win an Army game that doubtless couldn't have been won any other way in Rockne's worst-ever season.

Legends are one thing, the record another, and Gipp's place in the hearts of the Notre Dame men of his time can be reconstructed from a poem that appeared anonymously in the issue of the campus paper that carried his obituary:

> *O Lady, you have taken of our best*
> *To make a playmate for the Seraphim;*
> *There on the wide, sweet campus of the blest*
> *Be good to him.*

4. Rockne's Last Game

SOUTH BEND, Ind.: March 31, 1981.

Knute Rockne never knew it, but he saved the best for last. He went out winning. In his finest game, Notre Dame upset USC, 27-0, at the Los Angeles Coliseum on December 6, 1930 — the last day Rockne ever coached. That was some twelve weeks before the forty-third anniversary of his birth and fifteen weeks before he died.

It was his tenth straight win that year and nineteenth straight in two years. The last to beat Rockne was USC, which creamed him at the Coliseum in 1928, 27-14, two weeks after his weakest Notre Dame team (5-4) had "won one for the Gipper" against Army at Yankee Stadium, 12-6.

Going into the 1930 Notre Dame game, the Trojans had overwhelmed UCLA, 52-0; Stanford, 41-12; Cal, 74-0, and Washington, 32-0. The Fighting Irish went in undefeated but had lost their fullback, Joe Savoldi, their most useful performer. In a year when the fathers could kick a player off the team, and out of school, a Catholic boys school, for suing his wife for divorce, they did. They hadn't even known Savoldi was married. At the time, and for years thereafter, they had a rule that married students couldn't play ball for Notre Dame.

Although losing Savoldi jolted Rockne, he was more than a match for the crisis, visualizing and then carrying through two shrewd pieces of deception that entirely fooled USC — which at his death stood 1-4 against Notre Dame and has never caught up. First, on a stopover in Arizona, he called a rare early-morning drill, then sneakily told the hotel operator to cancel all wake-up messages to his players. When they wandered out an hour late, Rockne, at his tongue-lashing best, tore into them for their tardiness, whipping the team into a frenzy. Next, at gametime, Rockne dressed his fastest fullback, Bucky O'Connor, in the uniform of the slow-moving reserve who had been announced as Savoldi's replacement, and O'Connor ran wild.

"It was Notre Dame's greatest victory of all time over USC," Braven Dyer wrote in the Times eighteen years later, meaning the art form, not the score. And fifty years later, it still is.

5. The Four Horsemen

SOUTH BEND, Ind.: Oct. 24, 1982.

During college football's fourth season after World War I, four sophomore athletes became the Four Horsemen of Notre Dame. This is the sixtieth anniversary of the season they were first outlined against a blue-gray October sky. Halfback Jim Crowley, the last survivor, went into and then out of a hospital in Pennsylvania this month — fighting off a heart attack — to stir the memories again of the dwindling handful who saw him play.

It was in the Roaring Twenties that the Four Horsemen played at Notre Dame, Crowley combining with Elmer Layden, Don Miller and Harry Stuhldreher in the most celebrated backfield ever. And their place as number one has been assured for the ages by tactical changes in the game that have made four-man backfields obsolete. But they're all gone now, all but Sleepy Jim Crowley, who always was the hardest to bring down.

Crowley, now eighty, played left halfback in the group first called the Four Horsemen by Sportswriter Grantland Rice. Their coach was Knute Rockne, who, sixty years ago this month, had the vision to combine them as sophomores though their average weight was under 160. The best all-sophomore backfield football has had, and, pound for pound, the greatest backfield of them all, the horsemen came together during Notre Dame's 1922 season when Layden was reassigned to fullback. At the time, he weighed 160. The halfbacks, Miller and Crowley, weighed 150 and 158. The five-foot-seven quarterback, Stuhldreher, came in at 148.

Even in the 1920s, in an era of smaller Americans, there had never been so much football talent in such a small package. And now, of course, in the age of the weight lifters, it won't happen again. The Four Horsemen will remain forever unique.

They helped Notre Dame win the national championship in the season of Rockne's only Rose Bowl appearance, an undefeated season. In all, the Fighting Irish played thirty games with Layden, Crowley, Miller and Stuhldreher, and lost only to one team, Nebraska, losing twice (by a touchdown each time in 1922 and 1923) before turning on the Huskers in 1924, 34-6. When asked to name the game he recalls most vividly, Crowley instantly replied: "The 1923 Nebraska game." (Score Nebraska 14, Notre Dame 7.) Commenting, Raider Owner Al Davis said: "Champions only remember the ones they lose."

There are too many of the others.

The 1924 Notre Dame team, featuring Crowley and his classmates as college seniors, was football's first to travel from coast to coast meeting all comers — from Army to Nebraska to Stanford — and because the backs were more famous than the linemen, who had become known as the Seven Mules, Rockne had to work to keep matters in perspective. One day he asked the players to vote secretly on who was more important to Notre Dame, the horsemen or the mules, and later he called press conference to announce: "The mules won, 7 to 4."

Rockne also separated the players on Notre Dame's special trains, assigning linemen to lower berths and backs to uppers. This didn't sit so well with the backs, particularly Stuhldreher, the feisty little quarterback. Interviewed one day in Chicago, he was asked: "What makes the Four Horsemen so agile?" Said Stuhldreher: "Getting in and out of upper berths."

Agile athletes pleased Rockne the most. He didn't especially prize strength or power in offensive football, preferring three other values, quickness, deception, and perfect timing. Hence, the horsemen were ideal Rockne backs, light enough and gifted enough to play the game his way — swirling around each other in the backfield while handing and passing the ball back and forth. Rockne was thirty-seven years old the season Notre Dame played in the Rose Bowl, and he was to know better backs in the six years of life that remained to him, but none that suited him so well. "Our timing was spiritual as well as physical," halfback Miller, later a lawyer, once remarked. "Lord, how we meshed."

As football players, the Four Horsemen were each a little different, unified only by their size. The fastest was Layden, whom Rockne called the most unusual fullback in football. "He pierced a line with sheer speed," Rockne said. The right half, Miller, was the breakaway threat, shiftier than Layden. At quarterback, Stuhldreher was cocky, self-assured, ambitious, a wise signal caller and good enough passer. In short, said Rockne, he was "a typical Notre Dame quarterback." The left half, Crowley, was the most modern runner of the four, a clever cutback runner who, as he said the other day, liked to "break back against the grain." As a group, they couldn't play with today's football players, but in 1924 they couldn't lose.

II

Casual sports fans noting that Notre Dame scored four touchdowns in the 1925 Rose Bowl to win over Stanford, 27-10, may have concluded that it was a wipeout. And in a sense, it was. Stanford, except on the scoreboard, wiped out Notre Dame. As Fullback Ernie Nevers outran the Four Horsemen combined, Stanford outgained Notre Dame, 298 yards to 179. The Irish made only seven first downs (to seventeen for Stanford) and completed only three passes (against eleven by Stanford). The longest sustained drive by the Four Horsemen measured thirty-two yards. At the time, Nevers was the best-known and possibly best player in the country, more famous than an Illinois junior, Red Grange. But the 1925 Rose Bowl game was a defensive game. The decisive clutch plays were defensive plays, and there were many of them, and the Irish made them all.

A principal difference was that Layden rose to the occasion with possibly the greatest all-around game ever played in the old bowl. Another difference was that there were four Horsemen and only one Nevers. In a two-way era (everybody on the field played both offense and defense), the four Irish backs were by far the four quickest people in sight. "The Four Horsemen were better defensive than offensive players," Rockne once said, and so, in a 1920s defensive game, they prevailed.

Of Layden's three touchdowns, two were scored while he was playing defense. Intercepting two passes, he ran both back immense distances, going sixty-five yards for one touchdown, and then seventy. A faulty twenty-two-yard Stanford punt set Layden up for his other touchdown, which he scored on a short fullback run. Providing still a fourth touchdown for the winning team, Stanford obligingly fumbled.

The game's turning point came in the second half after a long, scoreless Stanford drive ended at the Notre Dame one-foot line. On Stanford's last play of that series, Nevers scored, they said in the press box, but the officials blew it. A moment later, standing inches in from the end line, Layden punted the ball back nearly ninety yards — eighty-two from the line of scrimmage — to the Stanford eighteen-yard line, where it bounced out of bounds.

"That was the ballgame," Stuhldreher said afterward.

III

As an offensive unit, the Four Horsemen can be graded as no more than one of the best in the first 101 years of American football. The most influential, converting the game into the present T-Formation era, was Stanford's 1940 backfield: Kmetovic, Standlee, Gallarneau and Albert. A few years later, Army Coach Red Blaik had one of the great ones: Davis, Blanchard, McWilliams and Tucker. The best some of us have seen was a mid-century pro backfield in San Francisco: McElhenny, Perry, Johnson and Tittle. In 1929, one of the anonymous poets that always seem to be hanging around Notre Dame immortalized yet another backfield that many Irish fans in the late Twenties called best ever:

> *Is it the ghost of the Four Horsemen that ranges the field*
> *Advancing the pigskin to scoring position?*
> *But no! Those mad shadows that mass for the kill*
> *Are Elder, Carideo, Mullins and Brill.*

More likely, Notre Dame was stronger yet in Rockne's last season, 1930, when Schwartz replaced Elder. But for romance, the Four Horsemen will always be first. There has never been another team like theirs. From the ranks of those who played for Rockne in the Four Horsemen era came head coaches for ten major college teams (Alabama, North Carolina, South Carolina, Fordham, Purdue, Navy, Notre Dame, Wisconsin, Villanova, Duquesne) and other college teams as well as four pro teams (Cleveland, Pittsburgh, Los Angeles and the old Chicago Rockets). The center, Adam Walsh, was the first head coach of the Los Angeles Rams and a respectable winner. Stuhldreher also won for awhile but ran out of luck at Wisconsin in 1948, inspiring the first of college football's grossly insulting signs, a huge "Goodbye, Harry" banner that was draped in front of the Wisconsin rooting section one otherwise brilliant fall afternoon.

Crowley, who coached both college and pro clubs, remains a close student of football. Looking back nearly three quarters of a century, he described USC's O. J. Simpson as the best running back he's seen. He named Army's Glenn Davis next and then the big, powerful Stanford fullback he met in the Rose Bowl, Ernie Nevers. In those days, however, Crowley said, he underestimated the impact that was being made by the Four Horsemen. "If we'd lost a game in 1924, I don't think we'd be remembered," he said. But they finished 10-0. And so the memory of what they did has merged neatly with Rice's imagery.

POSTSCRIPT

It was perhaps the most widely talked about sports story ever written. Grantland Rice, who could mix metaphors with anybody, began a 1924 football report with these words:

"Outlined against a blue-gray October sky, the Four Horsemen rode again. In dramatic lore they are known as Famine, Pestilence, Destruction and Death. These are only aliases. Their real names are Stuhldreher, Miller, Crowley and Layden. They formed the crest of the South Bend cyclone before which another fighting Army football team was swept over the precipice at the Polo Grounds yesterday afternoon, as 55,000 spectators peered down on the bewildering panorama spread on the green plain below.

"A cyclone can't be snared," Rice continued confidently. "It may be surrounded, but somewhere it breaks through to keep going. When the cyclone starts from South Bend, where the candle lights still gleam through the Indiana sycamores, those in the way must take to storm cellars at top speed. Yesterday the cyclone struck again, as Notre Dame beat Army, 13 to 7, with a set of backfield stars that ripped and crashed through a strong Army defense with more speed and power than the warring cadets could meet."

This rhetoric in the old New York Tribune was to make five people famous, including Rice, who, his associates said, had the bent if not the talent of a poet. The "dramatic lore" of his second sentence alludes to a World War I novel, "The Four Horsemen of the Apocalypse," by Spanish Writer Vicente Blasco Ibanez. It was made into a movie starring Rudolph Valentino.

In the fifteenth century, German painter Albrecht Durer's conception of "The Four Horsemen of the Apocalypse" had illustrated the book of Revelation (or Apocalypse) in a famous edition of the Bible, of which it is the last book. Rice, a religious man, may have seen that, too. Rice followed Ibanez in naming the horsemen Famine, Pestilence, Destruction and Death. In the Bible they are Conquest, Slaughter, Famine and Death. All typify war, to which football is often compared.

The fact that there are four riders in Revelation was a break for Rice. Four is a poetic word, like seven and eleven. The Apocalypse, as ascribed to the apostle John, is full of such words. But this time, to pump air into the myth of football's four horsemen, Rice needed some help from Notre Dame's publicity people, who hired four horses to immortalize their riders in a famous picture made the day after publication of Rice's story. That image immortalized Rice, too, as the poet who came up with the most lasting of the contrived surnames of sports, doubtless the most recognizable, possibly even the most fitting. To this day in football, when you have the talent, you have the horses.

II

DIALOGUE

After three decades as a football beat writer, I once calculated that I was involved in twenty-one hundred sit-down, one-on-one interviews with players, coaches and others in sports. For, as a way to make contact in a newspaper between a news source and a reader, the question-and-answer interview, it has always seemed to me, is the most effective.

As a device it's nothing new — in fact, the Q&A interview is, in print, approximately as old as Gutenberg — but in the concept as it existed when I came into journalism, I thought some fundamental changes would help.

And so, avoiding the stiff and informational approach that had been everywhere favored earlier, I have since the 1930s aimed for a conversational tone that would engage readers in visits with celebrated persons. The goal is to give them the sensation of sitting down over coffee with people they'd like to know. Other newspapers and magazines, including Playboy, have in more recent years used a similar approach.

One disappointment after all this time is that I never got a chance to interview one of the world's great winners, Isaac Newton, who at twenty-seven was a full professor of mathematics at Trinity College, Cambridge. Before calling on Sir Isaac in 1669, I would have compiled about fifty questions starting with the kind I like to get into right away: What was your father's occupation? Why were you sitting under an apple tree that day? What do falling apples have to do with Saturn's orbit?

Now we'll never have his answers.

Specifically, in any interview with a competitor in any field, what I want to find out is, first, the pattern of traits, thought patterns, background facts, priorities and personal ambitions that make him what he is and, second, his approach in detail to his particular job.

In press conferences, I have learned, there are many interviewing styles. My way is to continually rephrase the questions I want answered, following up, if need be, with suggestions like, What do you mean by that? or, What's an example of that from your experience? A man's first reply in any significant or controversial area is often [1] evasive or [2] a warm-up answer. In the finished piece, I may use only his third or fourth answer — and I'm sure I'll use only a fraction of the dialogue.

In all kinds of interviewing, these, it seems to me, are the other things that matter:

• I make it a fixed rule to avoid questions that can be answered yes or no, for, in any newspaper, one-word answers hardly advance the story. Instead of inquiring, Did you do that? I ask, Why did you do that? If he didn't do it, let him say he didn't.

• Though some critics of media interviewers deplore what they call the soft approach, I'm not much concerned by the distinction between hard and soft questions. I'm not impressed with journalists who feel they must skewer their prey. What I'm after is not a confrontation but a discussion.

• I never accept the assessment: "That's a stupid question." Most often, such a response is simply a way to avoid the question; and at football games particularly, standing in a locker room afterward — before anyone has seen the movies or tapes — most coaches and players have no more idea of what happened than an observant reporter. My belief is that if, as an accredited newspaperman, I ask a question, they, as public figures, should respond with answers, not lectures.

• I've found that ignorance — real or assumed — is no bar to effective questioning. To the contrary, it is usually an advantage. The least effective interviewers are those who seek to impress a news source with what they think are important comments of their own — thus appropriating the spotlight while stepping between the audience and the person being interviewed. Let the expert be the expert. The reporter's role is to listen and to ask the questions that will allow him, and the similarly uninformed audience, to understand. In a written interview, the comments I interject are mainly for change of pace.

• One goal in every interview is to leave no significant question unanswered. For that reason, interview-preparation time often exceeds interview time.

In the following collection of conversations, most were written as sports columns for the Examiner and Herald-Examiner. Times interviews are longer and somewhat different.

1. Stan Musial, First Base

IN APRIL, 1958, baseball's first year in Los Angeles, with the game squeezed lopsided into a football stadium, everything was new and fresh and exciting. My object in the paper was to help site an old game in a new community; and Stan Musial, universally styled Stan the Man, was a good source.

LOS ANGELES: April 28, 1958.

You are in First Baseman Stan Musial's cell in the St. Louis Cardinals dressing room under the western slope of the Coliseum. The Man is stretched out on a wooden bench, his head on a folded white towel. He looks and acts tired — after nine innings of baseball.

Newspapermen pass in and out like doctors making their morning rounds. The writers are used to interviewing beat-up football players in this place; one asks Musial what makes baseball so exhausting.

"One ballgame is not too exhausting," The Man says. "Neither are two or three or a dozen of them. It's the long season that wears you out. It's playing every day — and night and day — that gets you. It's the strain, in other words, not the exercise."

The interviewer is not convinced. He persists, reopening the subject of football, and football's physical drudgery, as Musial rises and tugs wearily at the buttons of his jersey, opening it slowly. You notice that Musial's shoulders are bent into a permanent stoop — doubtless the result of two thousand days and nights of baseball in the famous Musial crouch. "How many games," Stan asks, "do football players play a year? Ten? Fifteen? I'm not saying football isn't strenuous — but nothing is as strenuous as a 154-game baseball season."

Musial isn't really the case example of the point he's making. Now thirty-seven, he has outlasted all of the professional football players —

even the quarterbacks — who were active when he started with the Cardinals in the early 1940s. He is at pains to explain that. "Baseball," he says, "is a game you can play as long as you still have two things — desire and the ability to concentrate. It's concentration that comes hardest of all."

And this is exhausting?

"The most. You can't relax for a second. If the pitcher has a fastball, or even if he hasn't, you have to give him your undivided attention every second. The effect of this on the nervous system is cumulative. At the end of every game I'm beat."

How often do you unwind a bit and swing at a bad ball?

"Never in a park like the Coliseum, if I can help it. Once in awhile in Ebbets Field or the Polo Grounds, I used to go for a pitch that was a few inches out of the strike zone. Frankly, the short fences there were too much of a temptation."

As I recall, your record is better against the Dodgers in Ebbets Field than in St. Louis or anywhere. How do you account for that?

"The right-field fence in Brooklyn was made for a left-hand hitter. Ask Duke Snider [the Dodger center fielder]. He's still in mourning. But that's only part of it. The fans are different there. They're exciting. I just felt like hitting in Brooklyn."

They say that of all the people in baseball except Snider, you are the saddest to see the Dodgers in the Coliseum, where the short left field is balanced by deep fences in right.

"It's too early to tell about that. The fences were closer in Brooklyn, but the fans seem just as excited here. The way I look at it, an enthusiastic crowd stimulates all ballplayers, not just the home team."

How are you changing your batting style for the Coliseum after so many successful seasons in Brooklyn?

"Only in one way. I'll wait for strikes here, I hope. No bad balls. You can adjust to any park. The Coliseum isn't the best in baseball, but I'll say this. They aren't going to break any baseball records in the Coliseum. It isn't that bad. Besides, the pitchers won't let you."

How much better are pitchers today than when you broke in?

"They're no better, and no worse. That goes for the batters, too. I hear about the new records that are set all the time in other sports; but the ability of ballplayers, as far as I can tell, is almost exactly what it was in 1941. In all that time, only one player has changed."

Who?

"Me. I'm getting a little tired."

2. Dick Daugherty, Linebacker

FOOTBALL HAS changed consistently and considerably since the day in 1946 when the Rams brought the NFL to Los Angeles. There was an enormous gap just between 1951, the Rams' only NFL title-winning season, and seven years later — largely because the Ram coach in 1958 was Sid Gillman, one of the first of the scientific football leaders. The report here is from Dick Daugherty, a guard and linebacker, who was always a perceptive source.

LOS ANGELES: Nov. 18, 1958.

Of the 1958 Rams, Dick Daugherty alone wears the black-and-gold 1951 watch, the trophy of the only world championship the Rams have won for Los Angeles. The attrition of but seven years has wiped out all thirty-four of Daugherty's associates of those exciting days. "It would be amusing to bring the old pros back for one week on this club," says Daugherty, a twenty-nine-year-old linebacker. "They would think somebody invented a new game. A football career used to be fun seven days a week — with two fast hours of practice a day, and parties every night except Saturday. It's only fun now on Sunday afternoons. The rest of the time we're businessmen — on the job at 9 o'clock, home at 5:30 or 6."

How did the Rams get ready for a game in 1951 with only two hours of work each day?

"We didn't spend much time on movies," Daugherty says. "Instead of exchanging movies with the other teams, we sent scouts to every game, and all we had to do was look over the scouting report. It didn't take long. Suppose I was going up against Ray Bray of the Bears. The report on Bray would give me this information: 'Been in the league seven years, one of the toughest guys in the league, will knock your hat off and step on your a face.' I could digest a report like that by noon on Tuesday and take the rest of the week off."

What kind of scouting reports do you get today?

"We get the report on a screen. This year, for instance, we had the movies of three different Bear games, and we ran them back and forth, over and over. The Bears still have guys who will step on your face, but now we see exactly how they go about it."

Why does it take a week to get through a horror movie?

"Everything takes longer today. A football practice in the old days was a lark. It required no mental effort compared to practices today. In a typical week in 1951, we spent half our time running through every offensive play we had. We spent the rest of the time polishing up the only two defenses we had. We could have done this in our sleep. In fact, I often did."

How would you describe the difference today?

"We make an original approach today to each new game. We concentrate on just a small percentage of the plays we're capable of operating, and we vary them specifically to fit the other team's weaknesses. Preparing for a football game now is a full-time thinking job, and the biggest change has come on defense. Today, we have at least two hundred possible defenses, compared to the two we had in 1951."

How do you think Bob Waterfield [who won championships for the Rams in 1945, in Cleveland, and in 1951] would have done as a quarterback against two hundred defenses?

"Bob was a quarterback who would have thought of something. I remember one day in Chicago when we couldn't move the Bears with the plays we'd been practicing every blasted morning for five months. Bob improvised in the huddle. He turned to [Receiver] Tom Fears and said, 'Listen, Fears, if Connor goes out wide with you this time, I'll send Towler through the hole he leaves. If Connor says in the line, I'll throw you a quick one. Be ready for anything.' Connor went with Fears, and Towler went for a touchdown. Now, that's exactly the way we do things in 1958, except we don't improvise in the huddle. We prepare special plays like that all week."

What else was different in 1951 football?

"The coaches' idea of mental preparation in those years was a memory test. Before every game, we had to memorize the names and numbers of all the players on the other side. If you missed one number, it was an automatic fine."

That was Jumbo Joe Stydahar's first year as a head coach, and I remember there were a lot of fines.

"I think Tom Fears still holds the all-time record. Tom had one argument with Stydahar that went on for fifteen minutes. And every time Tom shouted something, Jumbo raised the price. Jumbo won the argument by rounding out the fine at an even one thousand dollars."

What was the original crime?

"Tom had been one minute late for practice."

3. Dorothy Poynton, Olympic Diver

NEWSPAPERS LOVE promotions, and they keep trying to get their writers to help out. My practice has been to assist the promotion departments unfailingly, if not cheerfully, and at the same time come up with the most readable columns possible. Before a 1959 travel show, I remember, I used much more of my time finding a valid subject to write about than I spent visiting with Dorothy Poynton and writing it combined.

LOS ANGELES: Jan. 21, 1959.

At the Examiner's Sports, Vacation and Travel Show February 15-21, those who pass by the Celebrities Booth at the Sports Arena could well find themselves in a conversation with Dorothy Poynton, the Olympic diver. A pert, trim champion with nice legs, Dorothy is an authority on murder.

"Drowning is nothing but murder," she says. "No American boy or girl above the age of twenty-four months should ever die in a swimming pool. Of course, it will happen many times this year. But when you read these tragic stories of a child's death by drowning, remember this: It shouldn't have happened. Someone is guilty of murder."

Any youngster can be taught to swim at the age of two, says Dorothy, whose Los Angeles career as a swimming teacher at the Dorothy Poynton Aquatic Club has been a natural sequel to her career as a diver. A twelve-year-old prodigy on America's 1928 Olympic team at Amsterdam, she went on to win the world's platform diving championship twice, in the 1932 Games at Los Angeles and in 1936 at Berlin.

"The greatest responsibility," she says, "that any parent has to his child — in this city of swimming pools — is to provide him with swimming lessons."

But I understand that some people just can't learn — no matter how many lessons they take.

"That's an old wives' tale," says Dorothy. "It's just absurd. In the eight years that I've operated this school, everyone has learned to swim who has stayed with me for eight weeks of lessons."

I'm sure you're excluding two-year-old kids.

"Not so. I have made good on every guarantee to teach any two-year-old boy or girl to swim across the pool in eight weeks. Do you know the average age of the Los Angeles children who toddle into our pools and drown these days?"

I don't believe I've ever seen such a survey.

"Most of them are between three and four, closer to three. What a tragedy. They could have been swimming for more than a year."

What safety precautions do you recommend?

"Let's say you live in a neighborhood without swimming pools, and suddenly someone up the street puts one in. The first thing you should do, if you have a child of two or older, is take him to a qualified teacher for lessons. It's more important than paying taxes or going to church."

It would seem that children would be safer if everyone with a pool fenced it in.

"No fence is reliable. The only real security is knowing how to swim. The responsibility for the safety of a child belongs entirely to his parents."

As it happens, my wife and I are both good swimmers. Why can't we teach our children ourselves?

"There is only one chance in thousands that you will have the patience to stick with it. The point is this: In the Los Angeles area, your youngsters should learn as soon as they are physically able — which means within about two months of their second birthday. It takes a qualified teacher to instruct them that fast."

Now, when you use the word swim in connection with youngsters, surely, you don't mean the Australian crawl.

"No, I mean the dog-paddle. Children should be five or six before they tackle the Australian crawl. The dog-paddle, you know, is the greatest stroke in swimming. Basically, it's the same stroke as treading water — and the way you save your life when you fall in a pool or the ocean is to tread water. I'll bet you'd never guess how many Americans can't tread water."

About half?

"The statistics are alarming. More than ninety per cent of the people in this country can't swim at all. They never even learned to dog-paddle, or tread water. Adults know the danger, of course. Kids don't. You can't keep a parent from drowning himself but you should try to keep him from drowning his child."

4. Tony Bettenhausen, Race Driver

A DISPROPORTIONATE number of race drivers were killed on race tracks in the mid-century years because of unsafe equipment. In a 1990s car, Tony Bettenhausen, a safe driver, would most likely have survived his practice-lap accident in Indianapolis. He didn't worry about it even in 1959, when he had two years to live.

LOS ANGELES: Feb. 2, 1959.

The best automobile driver in the country is a stocky, energetic, forty-three-year-old Illinois farmer who has one blue eye, one gray eye, three jobs and two hobbies. This is Tony Bettenhausen, who races cars, raises beans and sells sparkplugs.

"I am kept on the move by two exciting hobbies," says Bettenhausen, who as American's national champion big-car driver will be a starter in the Pomona Grand Prix March 7-8.

And what are these hobbies of yours?

"Making money," says Bettenhausen, "and spending it."

Which one takes the most time?

"Spending it. Every year it gets tougher. Soy beans are very popular these days, and I've got 518 acres of soy beans at Tinley Park."

Then why don't you stay there instead of racing around the country?

"I would like to do that, but as an occupation, farming is too dangerous. If I stayed there the year around, my life wouldn't be worth a nickel. The accident rate on farms and ranches is higher than in any other American vocation."

Are you implying that it's safer to race automobiles than raise soy beans?

"I'm not implying it. I'm saying it."

This statement requires some evidence.

"All right. I'll tell you about my father. He homesteaded my place at Tinley Park half a century ago. He was a good farmer, and a good father, raising nine children. I was the ninth. When I was thirteen months old, a horse kicked dad in the head, and killed him. I don't remember my dad, of course, but I've never forgotten what happened to him."

How many times have you been shaken like that by an accident in a race?

"Well, there are hazards in racing, but they have never seemed important to me. They can be controlled. All you need to be a living, winning driver are quick reflexes, mechanical ability, and a good level mind."

And courage?

"Not necessary."

I would think that it is.

"What I mean is that it is relatively unimportant whether a race driver has guts or whether he's something of a chicken. I've known all kinds, and good ones. Guts is something you need on a battlefield. Racing is a business, not a battle."

How do chickens get along in a big Indianapolis race?

"They do fine if they've got a good thinking head. They do better, in fact, than a gutsy kid who has less mechanical ability or slower reflexes or a smaller mind."

Speaking as a survivor of twenty-one years in racing, how many of these fearless kids are causing all the accidents in racing today?

"Few if any. Every driver who can officially qualify for a sanctioned race is an excellent driver, regardless of age or anything. The biggest cause of accidents and almost the only cause is faulty equipment."

I've heard that was true in Bill Vukovich's last race a couple of years ago.

"I think everyone is pretty well agreed now that Vukovich was a victim of the fact that the front axle snapped on Roger Ward's car."

I thought Vukovich was the best driver in the country, present company excepted. And you were on the track at Indianapolis when it happened. What crossed your mind?

"I thought, what God-awful luck. Here's a great man in the right place at the wrong time."

It would certainly seem that there is more opportunity for such a tragic accident in a race than on a farm in Illinois.

"I think the business of living is hazardous. In your own home, you can be in the right place at the wrong time if an airplane drops on your head. It happens all the time."

But the accident odds are higher at Indianapolis.

"No, they're not. You're at Indianapolis one day a year. You're at home 350 days a year. I'll take those odds."

5. Bobby Thomson, Outfielder

ONE OF the benefits of a job as a sportswriter is that you can look up and draw out an athlete who accomplished some rather awesome feat. Bobby Thomson fits in that category. Nobody ever did anything more momentous to a ball.

LOS ANGELES: July 25, 1959.

On a late afternoon at the Coliseum this week, Bobby Thomson of the Chicago Cubs squinted at the close-in but very high screen in left field and said: "My hit probably would have caught the top bar of that thing, but it never would have gone over."

Thomson, a new Cub outfielder, was reviewing the most dramatic base hit of modern times, his three-run homer which won the 1951 pennant for the New York Giants over the Brooklyn Dodgers, 5-4, in the ninth inning of the last day of a three-day playoff. "It would have been no more than a long single in the Coliseum," he said, turning back the clock. "But it was an easy home run in the Polo Grounds."

What if anything happened that day to ease the pressure on you in the hottest spot there can be in baseball?

"I have always felt that the injury to [Outfielder] Don Mueller set me up," he said.

How do you figure that?

"If you'll remember, [First Baseman] Whitey Lockman's double finished [Dodger Pitcher] Don Newcombe. It drove in [Shortstop] Al Dark to make the score 4-2, but Mueller hurt himself sliding into third. I was the next man up, and I was worrying about him instead of me when we all ran down there. I had time to settle my nerves while the Dodgers brought in Ralph Branca to pitch to me."

What did you say to yourself when you squared away against Branca?

"I kept mumbling, 'Wait for the ball, watch the ball, wait for it, watch it.'"

There were two out and two on. What was the count on the last pitch of the 157th game of the season?

"Branca had a strike on me. I took a good one. I don't know why. The next pitch was a fastball, high and inside. Today, I'd probably pop it up. But that was the year I hit them high and inside."

How would you describe your feelings when the ball dropped into the lower deck for a home run?

"To tell the truth, I had a hard time shaking a lost feeling that bothered me all day. Newk had mowed us down in the eighth. They had us 4-1 in the ninth. When our last turn came, all I could think was, 'It's all over.' We had been thirteen and a half games behind the Dodgers in August, we had almost pulled the impossible, but now we were through. I never felt worse in my life then I did in that ninth inning. Afterwards, well, you can't get used to a miracle the minute it happens."

When did you begin getting used to it?

"The next day. I got a long night letter from a lady in Rochester. She said, 'You don't know me but I am eighty-two years old. I watched you on TV, Mr. Thomson. When you took your last bats in the ninth inning, I got down on these old knees and prayed for you. You must be a nice man because my prayers were answered."

I assume that other wires and letters made your mail rather heavy that winter.

"I had trouble answering all of it. One character wanted to sue me. He said he gave up in the ninth, and went to take a bath. He heard the home run on the radio while he was climbing in, and got so excited he fell down in the bathtub and broke his wrist. He thought I should pay for it."

As you may recall, coast-to-coast TV was new in L.A. that week. What did you hear from California?

"A guy told me that he was in his office watching me bat when his wife's lawyer called to say she was divorcing him. He's a Giant fan, and he said it was the only time he ever got two good breaks the same minute."

Whatever happened to the ball that went for the home run?

"As a matter of fact, a fan met me at the gate at Yankee Stadium the next day and gave it to me. A souvenir like that is worth two World Series tickets, so I went inside to get them. When I got there, seventeen other fans were standing in line, and every last one of them had the home run ball. If they all saw the Series — and I hope they did — they paid their way in."

6. Raymond Berry, Receiver

THIS PLAYER made more out of less than any athlete of my time. Though a Hall of Famer, his legs were uneven, his back a wreck, his fingers askew, and his eyes a joke. But he owned third down.

BALTIMORE: Dec. 10, 1959.

Raymond Berry is a slender, near-sighted, crooked-backed Texan who plays football for the Baltimore Colts and practices football by the hour. Asked what he works on, Berry says: "As an offensive end, the payoff for me is getting my hands on the ball, and holding it. So I have a daily hand drill that's the most important thing I do in practice. Although I've been playing this game for quite a few years, I've found that I can't do such a simple thing as catch a football unless I work at it regularly."

During these drills, what are you specifically trying to achieve?

"My objective," Berry says, "is one hundred per cent concentration on the two parts of the job: watching the ball into my hands, and getting it under my arm fast."

When you're working on this, what is [Quarterback John] Unitas practicing?

"I don't rightly know, because I never use the regular passer in practice. Our practice goals are so different that it would get Unitas into bad habits if he worked with me. In a practice situation, his goal is to throw good passes, and mine is to catch bad ones. I ask the fellow who works with me — it's usually Billy Pricer, the fullback — to throw the ball over my head, on my shoes, behind me, and everywhere else. What I'm doing with Pricer is simulating the tail end of a pattern when I might have to move away from where Unitas expects me, or Unitas might be rushed into less than a perfect throw."

Is Pricer any threat to Unitas?

"Billy has a good arm. He stands twenty-five yards away and slams it in. We work with a backstop to block overthrows because part of the time, I turn my back to him. He fires at one of my ears, and hollers, 'Ball.'" For what period of time do you actually work with Unitas at practice each day?

"It's a matter of seconds, not minutes. We're lucky if we get in twenty minutes a week. A pro team is trained and polished not during the week but at training camp. It doesn't matter how tired you get in July when you're not playing games. But when the season starts, overwork is the worst thing you can do. The trouble with even one day of overwork during the week is that you can't recover by the weekend. At least seventy-five per cent of the job of catching passes is done by the legs."

Getting under the ball?

"Footwork, yes, but also the spring. It takes a good spring to get a lot of balls, and when your legs are tired, you don't have the pep for it. You drop more balls when you're tired."

"You dropped one the other day. What did Unitas say?

"He said, 'Pricer can play quarterback for this club, Berry, but what's he going to use for receivers?'"

7. Roger Craig, Pitcher

FROM HIS rookie year as a pitcher through his career as a manager, the thoughtful Roger Craig was always worth listening to, so I put myself in position to listen to him often. As a Dodger he was forever experimenting with new pitches, and in his time he invented a few — including, much later than the day I talked to him for this story, the split-finger fastball.

LOS ANGELES: May 17, 1960.

Because the National League's 1960 pennant will be won and lost in the last half of the season — after Dodger Pitcher Roger Craig returns — he was asked the other day to review his curious 1959 record. A 6-7 loser at triple-A Spokane, Roger became an 11-5 winner when he came up to the Dodgers. Which of these two pitchers will we see when their fractured collarbone mends?

"I can win for any ballclub that has a sound infield," says Craig, a friendly, twenty-nine-year-old Carolinian whose frankness is never mistaken for excessive vanity by those around him. "I'm an infield pitcher. If I have a great infield, I'm a successful pitcher. If they're so-so, I'm so-so. You can give me any three outfielders who know what to do with the bat."

How much did infield breakdowns have to do with your ordinary record last year at Spokane?

"Put it this way," Craig puts it. "In the minor leagues, I was a minor league pitcher. Their infielders are just not as quick or agile as major leaguers. Triple-A infielders just miss on the double play that big leaguers make. As a low-ball, control pitcher without too much swift, I need a big league defense to win."

And the Dodger defense is pretty good.

"The best in baseball. I walked onto a club with the four best infielders in either league: Maury Wills, Charlie Neal, Gil Hodges and Jim Gilliam."

Exactly what does a group like that do for you?

"First, they know I throw strikes, they know I throw breaking balls, they know what to look for, so they get in position to make the play. Second, they have the genius to make the play. I'm good for them, too. A control pitcher like me makes a great infield look great. When a control pitcher is on the mound, the infield is always on its toes. It's harder to play for a fastball pitcher who walks a lot of guys. The infield gets lazy. They're not ready for every pitch."

Now, in the old days, you were a fastball pitcher yourself. How much do you mourn for those times?

"Only to this extent. I wish I knew then what I know now. I was just a thrower then. I didn't learn how to pitch until I hurt my arm. The trouble with a stuff pitcher is that he only has his stuff two-thirds of the time. Once in every three days, he won't have his curve, or his fastball won't move. Nobody knows why, but it happens to all of them. But take a control pitcher. Nothing goes wrong with him. An upset stomach doesn't upset his knowledge of the batters."

I suppose that in this second pitching career of yours, you rely mostly on sliders.

"Sliders and sinkers, thrown low. That's why my infield is so busy."

What variety of sliders do you have?

"I use two positions, and several speeds. The slider is the best pitch in baseball. Actually, it's two pitches in one. It comes up like a fastball, and slides away like a little curve. It breaks over and down a bit, away from a right-hand batter and into a left-hand batter. On a corner, it's tough to hit."

How much does your slider break?

"Eight inches or so, sometimes a foot."

How big is the break on [Dodger Pitcher] Sandy Koufax's curve?

"Over two feet. He has to throw it at the batter to get it over. [Giant Pitcher] Sam Jones throws *behind* the batter."

Some say that such a pitch is better than a slider.

"I don't think so. The hitter can pick up a curve faster, and any time a good hitter knows what's coming, they've got it made. Of course, a good curveballer on a big night can hardly be touched."

Is that bad?

"I'm not against strikeouts, but this is a team game. Why not share the load with the infield?"

8. Hugh McElhenny, Halfback

THEY CALLED him Hustlin' Hugh, and there are many who still think of him as the finest broken-field running back, ever, because he played football the way Walter Mitty would do it — even celebrating his touchdowns with a flash that brought in the era of the spikers. Somehow, it was more fun when McElhenny did it.

SAN FRANCISCO: Oct. 1, 1960.

When Hugh McElhenny turned pro nine years ago, there were forty-five or fifty other halfbacks in the National Football League. Today, McElhenny and Frank Gifford are the sole survivors of the halfback generation that carried the ball for pro teams in 1952. "It's sort of a Last Man's Club," says McElhenny, the lively San Francisco extrovert who will next be seen in the Ram-49er telecast from Kezar Stadium Sunday. "They tell me Big Daddy Lipscomb is surprised there are any of us left."

What accounts for the rapid turnover of running backs in pro football?

"Halfbacks are always moving full steam when they get hit," McElhenny says. "Linemen take a beating, too, but it's a quieter beating — like taking six-inch punches all night in a fight. Halfbacks take haymakers. They're knocked out of football in about three years on the average."

How have you managed to last three times as long?

"I've heard that I'm plain lucky. [Fullback] Joe Perry says it's because I never threw a block in eight years. Take your choice."

The ability to move fast is one of your strongest points. What's the importance of speed to a running back?

"I'd say balance is more important. By balance, I mean a feel for running. The ability to bounce around and keep going. I'll give you an example. In our game last year, [Ram Halfback] Ollie Matson was hit squarely on the five-yard line. He shivered and shook there for a second, looked the guy in the eye, and walked into the end zone."

How does your style differ from that?

"I don't know what kind of a style I've got. I've never thought about it."

What is it that you do think about when you have the ball?

"Nothing. I just feel my way along. My mind is a complete blank, except I do know the destination."

Suppose a tackler shows up. Don't you give some thought to the best way to get around him?

"No, sir, none. It's just like someone shining a bright light in my face. Naturally, I jump. I jump away. I'm not going to stand there and stare at the light."

9. Danny Goodman, Concessionaire

OF THE things that go on every night at the ballpark, some are hats and caps. They're sold right there. It takes more than ballplayers, umpires, and fans to make a ballgame.

LOS ANGELES: April 15, 1961.

The Los Angeles baseball fan wouldn't be where he is today, it's often said, if it hadn't been for Abner Doubleday, Walter O'Malley, and Danny Goodman. In order, Abner gave him a game, Walter brought him a team, and Danny sold him his cap, scorecard, pennant, bugle, shirt and transistor radio.

Goodman is the Dodger concessionaire who revolutionized baseball, adding eighty items to an inventory which used to consist, almost entirely, of hot dogs. "Take radios," says Danny. "Everybody knows that no Dodger fan would be without one. But did you ever stop to think about the poor guys that forgot to bring theirs?"

Not to worry. Goodman to the rescue.

"Just last night," he says, "a young couple ran out of the Coliseum to one of our booths in the first inning, and the girl said: 'This big handsome lunk left our transistor home in the bathroom. I hope you sell radios here, because if you don't, we're going right back to the house and hear [Dodger Broadcaster] Vin Scully.' We sell more radios that way."

What else is selling fast this season?

"We're very big in hats and caps," Goodman says. "This is what I would call a hats-and-caps town. In fact, we have to design a new hat every year to keep up with the demand. I think I could hold a job with any Paris designer."

What happens to last year's unsold hats?

"That's where we're a horse up on Paris. All of our old hats are still moving. The first year at the Coliseum, you remember, we had a white plastic helmet. Then we introduced a straw with a ribbon. And last year we came with a yodeler's hat with feathers. They're all still popular along with the new 1961 number, the beret."

How do you road-test hats? Or do you just take a chance they'll sell?

"I spend hours at schools, boys clubs and playgrounds testing everything in our inventory. I have found that in L.A., if a kid will take a present free, it will sell. If it isn't going to sell, he isn't about to take it free."

What sorts of suggestions do the kids give you?

"They suggested we sell blue jeans — Dodger style — and predicted a big sale. They were right."

You must have *some* dogs that don't sell.

"We had trouble with the whole World Series line we put in last year after winning the 1959 Series. People were embarrassed to look at Dodger World Champion novelties when they're team was in third or fourth place. And an embarrassed guy won't buy. You could set the world on fire with the world-champion cigaret lighters we stored in the attic."

Later this year, perhaps, the picture will change enough to resume the sale of this merchandise.

"I sincerely hope so. A lighter is a durable item, fortunately. Which reminds me that when I started out in this business, the first big concession I got was the popsickle concession at an auto race. I bought three thousand popsickles and stored them in a big ice truck overnight. The next morning when I opened the door, I had three thousand sticks. The guy next door had the hot-dog concession, and he burned charcoal all night."

Was this in Los Angeles?

"No, in Baltimore. I had been living in Milwaukee, but when I decided to go into the concession game I had to leave town. I was thirteen years old, and the Milwaukee truant officer knew me on sight. This makes my thirty-sixth year in the same business."

What attracted you to it in the first place?

"After my father died when I was eleven, I worked two summers at the Milwaukee ballpark for my meals — hot dogs and popcorn."

In your first thirty-six years, did you come across anyone you consider your favorite customer?

"Yes, Walter O'Malley. He buys one of everything. I feel certain that Walter is the only cigar smoker still firing up with our world-champion lighter."

10. Parry O'Brien, Shot-Putter

DURING THE years when Olympic Establishment people, along with others in track and field, were pretending that an amateur athlete is an amateur athlete, I never missed a chance to show that their activities were unfair, discriminatory, and hugely harmful to the athletes. The battle has now been largely won — most top Olympic athletes in training can support themselves full-time through appearance fees and endorsements. But thirty-five years ago, few were helping them win the fight. A prominent 1960s athlete puts the argument in cold-war terms.

LOS ANGELES: May 25, 1961.

The world tends to judge Russia and America on their prestige in two fields — space and sport — in the opinion of Parry O'Brien, the Beverly Hills banker who has traveled 360,000 miles in ten years advancing the science of shot-putting. Therefore, he fears that the recent feats of American astronauts may be shielding the U.S. public from the truth that the sport gap is widening at the same time that the space gap is closing.

O'Brien is due at Moscow for the USA-USSR meet in July. But he may not go. His reasons — together with a summary of the large differences today between the Russian and American approach to athletics — are included in an exclusive survey for The Los Angeles Examiner by the veteran Olympian, who was the first human to put the shot sixty feet. The parallels Parry draws:

• Only one of the two nations is actually preparing for this summer's meeting.

USSR: "The Russian track team," says O'Brien, "went into hard training as a group one month ago at an athletic base on the Black Sea."

USA: "Americans," he says, "except for those in college, are still on their civilian jobs, and will remain at their desks until they depart for Moscow."

• Only one of the two teams is on salary.

USSR: "When the Russian athletes left their civilian jobs last month, they were replaced by workers with similar abilities. The athletes are continuing on the same income they had when relieved, and will keep it until they return to their regular jobs."

USA: "The Americans who compete in Moscow will not be paid, of course. Those of us who are out of college, married, and employed have the option of taking part on our vacation time. I am undecided at this point whether to use my vacation for this purpose. During the 1959 Soviet-

American meet in Philadelphia, I spent Friday here at the bank, flew East Friday night, competed Saturday, and flew home Sunday."

• Only one nation supervises the conditioning and developing of its athletes.

USSR: "At their Black Sea camp, the Soviet athletes are working full time under Russia's top coaches."

USA: "Americans are spare-time athletes. After a day at the office, we fight the traffic to a playground for a hasty workout, minus supervision. However, it is true that our government officials did one thing for us. They gave us an extra hour for practice — when they authorized daylight saving."

• Philosophically, the two nations have irreconcilable views of amateurism.

USSR: "An athlete is an athlete — neither amateur nor professional."

USA: "Our concept of amateurism, imposed by [Olympic Leader] Avery Brundage, is antiquated, unnecessary, and dangerous, the more so because the world thinks it's foolish."

• The everyday sports routine differs in the two nations.

USSR: "In Moscow, there are more than two hundred athletic clubs competing in track and field. There are that many and more in rugby and other sports."

USA: "In Los Angeles, the Striders are the only such club competing in track and field. Furthermore, on the grade school and high school level, there is little or no encouragement for the Olympic sports, the very sports that get the concentration in Moscow from kindergarten up."

• Civilian participation.

USSR: "In Moscow, all workers take two breathers every day, morning and afternoon, for the purpose of supervised exercise."

USA: "In Los Angeles every day, we take two coffee breaks."

11. John Roseboro, Catcher

THE DODGER catcher through the California glory years of Shortstop Maury Wills, their most underrated position player, and Hall of Fame Pitcher Sandy Koufax was John Roseboro, who, in a hipster's, jazz-oriented conversational style, had something special to say on nearly every topic. I'd have interviewed him every week if I could have made it look like working.

LOS ANGELES: June 10, 1961.
John Roseboro's June hitting streak has helped the Dodgers prolong what Outfielder Wally Moon started in April and May. But nobody

really expects catchers to hit. What you want them to do is take charge — and as a take-charge catcher, John has become one of the better ones of his generation. Among his skills is verbal communication, a la Roseboro, as he demonstrates in this definition: "A take-charge ballplayer is a cat who can make everybody think."

A mellow-voiced, twenty-eight-year-old, stocky six-footer whose organs of sight, large, warm and expressive, have been fenced by a major league mask for five seasons, Roseboro adds, softly, "In this dodge, you want the whole gang to think — our pitchers, our infielders, and their hitters."

Their hitters?

"Them above all, dad," he says. "Thinking is the worst thing you can do at the plate. A good hitter is a guy who has brainwashed himself. He only has two ideas: 'Watch the ball. Hit it.' Our job is to make those devils think of something else."

How do you do that?

"One way is to shake off a lot of signs. If we gave him the fire on the last pitch and want to burn another one by him, we'll shake off a few — and maybe he'll set for a curve. And while we're waiting and shaking, maybe [Dodger Coach] Leo Durocher will yell at him. Leo has been very helpful this year."

Does Durocher ever try to rattle [Giant Outfielder] Willie Mays?

"Old Folks Mays? You know it. Last week, Leo rattled him pretty good. Mays overheard Leo telling me Friday night in a loud whisper, 'Don't forget, now, knock him down.' In the three-game series, Old Folks got one RBI. Four times, when he was up there, Leo shouted: 'Here it comes.'"

Otherwise, as a catcher, how does John Roseboro evaluate his disposition and temperament for the work of taking charge?

"I don't stomp around and cuss the pitchers like [former Catcher] Roy Campanella used to. I don't dominate the pitcher because I'm not made up that way. But I know everything about every one of our pitchers, and that's the main thing. I ride 'em in a subtle way."

What are the circumstances in which you will leave your station for a visit with the pitcher?

"Our men are the best in the league, but they have three faults, generally. They forget to bend their back when they throw a curve. They lose their temper. And they throw too fast. So naturally we confer."

What about the fielders? Do you take the responsibility for shifting them around?

"I signal [Manager] Walt Alston, and he moves them. When a catcher tells Maury Wills to move, he moves a step. When the manager tells him, he moves three steps."

SAN FRANCISCO: June 17, 1961.
Making out a job description for the job, what should be included besides the ability to take charge? What does it take to be a big league catcher?

John Roseboro's answer: "Two hands, two feet, a good attitude, good morals, and experience. The biggest difference between the bigs and Class D is experience. In fact, that's the biggest difference between some catchers in the major leagues and the Little Leagues."

Are you perhaps exaggerating?

"Check it out sometime. Check the action of a Little Leaguer. Shut your eyes and think of [Milwaukee Catcher] Del Crandall. Catching is about the same everywhere — like weddings. All you need is a diamond."

So why is there a scarcity of good catchers?

"How many people would set out to be a catcher — and stay with it? I mean, how many in their right minds? Maybe one or two prospects out of hundreds. The kids I played with in my hometown, Ashland, Ohio, they weren't about to squat down and take the fat end of the bat on their chin. Most children believe they can hit, or learn to hit."

Later on when they find out they can't, why don't they take up catching?

"It's too late then, daddy, it's too late. Any man over twenty-one can get to the majors if he's caught the ball every day of his life since the sixth grade. But if you waste your childhood in center field, you don't build up any experience handling pitchers and learning the other stuff."

In your case, by the time you reached high school, were you the best all-around player on your team?

"I've never been the best player on any team that's had me yet, and it's beginning to look as if that honor will escape me. There were a lot of upstanding citizens in Ashland who did more with a bat than I could. The two guys I knocked around with all my life, both of them were better hitters than I was."

What ballclubs did they sign with?

"None, they quit school and went into the iron foundry. They were smart kids, but they liked the idea of a fast buck. They got married, and settled into a routine of work and babies. More work and more babies. From what I've seen, the world is full of major league ballplayers who got married at seventeen or eighteen and went to work in shops or driving trucks."

If experience makes the difference in catching, how much can you improve your skills in the offseason?

"I wouldn't know. I never get behind the plate if it isn't necessary. A man catching batting practice can split three fingers in five minutes. More than ever, the batsmen are trying to go to the opposite field these days, and while they're trying, they foul everything back into the only right hand I'm probably ever going to have. Foul tips are the one thing that keep a catcher from enjoying a better life than President Johnson."

How many foul tips can you expect in a game?

"The average is one bleeder and two stingers. When I walk out there today for the first pitch, I can count on it that sometime, somehow, somewhere, I'm going to take one good solid shot in the finger. The only thing I don't know is which finger. It gets to be kind of a game, like guessing what the dealer has in blackjack."

Are foul tips worse than collisions at home plate?

"Oh, my, yes. A tag play is a lot of fun if you're aggressive. All you have to do is get the ball first and go after the guy. Sometimes there's a little bump, of course, if he comes in while I'm reaching for the ball, but one foul tip helps me forget a dozen bumps."

I seem to recall, however, that you've been injured occasionally while blocking the plate.

"Yes, it is true that I have had some trouble with my teeth. In fact, one time I lost nine of them at one crack. I was playing winter ball in Venezuela, and the base runner came down from third with his elbow at half mast and took out my uppers. But a year or so later, things evened up. I was catching the bullpen in the Coliseum. There was a wild left-hander on the mound, and he let go when I wasn't looking and took out my lowers."

LOS ANGELES: June 24, 1961.

A baseball fan wrote in the other day to ask if a spitball pitch can be identified or recognized when he's watching a game on television.

John Roseboro's answer: "Sure, and that's a right smart place to be when they're throwing it."

What are its characteristics?

"The spitball reminds me of a drunk passing out suddenly, and sprawling to the floor. You might say it's loaded. I don't mean that you can recognize it all the time on television, or even at the game. But suppose you see a pitch that is coming in waist high, and then all of a sudden it's groveling on the ground. Nobody in baseball has a sinker that good. Nobody."

For the catcher, is it as tough to handle as, say, the knuckleball?

"It isn't too hard to handle — when you know it's coming. Personally, I relish the spitball if I'm working on it with a glove. I know the hitter isn't going to touch it, and that leaves me free to attend to the ball."

For the hitter, what's the problem?

"The main problem is that you don't know when it's coming. A loaded ball is an illegal pitch — anyway I hear people say it's illegal — so it isn't thrown as often as it was in the old days when there were quite a few good spitball hitters. Today, nobody hits it good, because it's hard to guess when a guy like [Milwaukee Pitcher] Lew Burdette will load one or decide to offer you something legal."

Of the young throwers on the Dodger staff, who offers the best spitball?

"Our fellows? The Dodgers? We wouldn't do that, friend. It's illegal."

All right, then, try this: Of the Los Angeles pitchers, who has the most variety?

"When I sit and think of a young man with a lot of pitches, my thoughts always go out to John Podres. John has the variety — and don't forget Don Drysdale. Don keeps hitters guessing, too."

Ignoring the spitball for now, do you feel more pressure catching a fastball specialist or a curveballer?

"Let's put it another way. I'd rather go out to the park on the day when a man with a good curve is getting it over. Sandy Koufax is the shining example in the league this year. When all is said and done, major league baseball is a war of curves. You've got to hit that pitch to stay with the group. And if you can throw it, man, you've got it made."

Have you ever been frightened by a pitcher?

"The first day I caught Drysdale was the worst day of my life. He still scares me. His fastball will either rise or dip, and only the ball knows which. If Drysdale had the same easy temperament in a game that he has off the field, he'd be leading the league. A winning pitcher is a guy who lives in a little world between total relaxation and total determination to win. And Drysdale is still blindly determined to win. It's an excellent fault, but it is a fault."

How much pleasure do you get from handling winners like these, helping them get better?

"It's fun, but that's not why I'm doing this gig. Like everybody else, I'm just here to hit. If I had my druthers, I'd never take another foul tip in my life. The place to play this game is out in the pasture. It's no upset that all these kids coming up, if they can hit, they join the herd. All they have to take charge of out there is a fly ball."

Does the pounding a catcher takes every day take some of the joy out of hitting?

"Nothing takes the joy out of swinging a bat. That's the part that everybody loves, hurt or not. I never let them bat for me if I can help it. When it's my turn to hit, dad, I'd rather do it myself."

12. Frank Selvy, Guard

THE FOLLOWING column was my last for the old Los Angeles Examiner. In my work room at home, I was finishing the final paragraphs when the office called with an order to rush it in for the first edition, which was also the final edition. A day later, the morning Examiner folded into the afternoon Herald-Express to become the afternoon Herald-Examiner.

LOS ANGELES: Jan. 7, 1962.

Many years ago, many strange things happened to Frank Selvy, the basketball player whose finesse as a Los Angeles Laker floor man this season has helped achieve a phenomenon in this part of California: a winning team. Born on election night, 1932, he was named Franklin Delano Selvy. When next heard from, FDS was scoring a hundred points for Furman University — in one game — the all-time American record. Later he married Miss Arkansas, then dropped from sight again.

Year in and out, Selvy kicked around the National Basketball Association, throwing in two or three field goals a night for Baltimore, Milwaukee, St. Louis, New York, Minneapolis, or Syracuse. Often, it took him a full year to accumulate as many points as he had once scored in forty minutes.

This winter, overnight, Selvy returned from exile, and all at once he has become a major factor in the Lakers' title bid, abruptly reversing the trend of his career. "The reason," he says, "is a little matter of fifteen minutes a game. The difference between a good player and a guy who plays bad is whether he's in there for thirty minutes or so, every time, or only ten or fifteen. I always had it. I wasn't playing."

How would [Center] Wilt Chamberlain do as a fifteen-minute man?

"No better than anybody else," says Franklin Delano, who, he hopes, will play a good thirty minutes this afternoon against the Boston Celtics at the Sports Arena. "He'd lose his confidence, too, to say nothing of his timing. Those are the things that go out the window when you sit on a bench watching the others enjoy themselves. Take timing. When you aren't in there much, you find that you're just a hair off on your shots. On a pass, you release the ball a split second late, or soon. That's what killed me."

Why concern yourself with confidence? Doesn't every NBA veteran assume he's one of the world's chosen handful?

"It's like Stan Musial told me one time in St. Louis. No pro athlete ever knows for sure how good he is. We all have self-doubts. When you're playing, your confidence keeps going up — although just a bit at a time. When you're not playing, it goes down fast. I got so I was afraid to take any shot except a layup."

Even now, you don't shoot much. What's holding you back now?

"Don't you think I'd look a little silly going for the basket all the time on a team with Elgin Baylor and Jerry West? I simply believe the best shooters should shoot."

You still hold the NCAA record for average — forty-one points a game. A lot of great college players haven't come close to that. It tells us something about you.

"It tells us that I was the best shooter on that team. The next guy was practically as good, but not quite, so I insisted on shooting all the time. The only thing I feel I really know about basketball is that the best men should take every possible shot. It's a matter of percentage. I'm not the best shooter on the Lakers."

Still, you once scored a hundred points in one game. How does any basketball player do that?

"I hogged the ball. I took three shots from the center of the floor that night, with Furman men open under the basket, and made every one."

How do you compensate now for the loss of prestige you once had at Furman as the big man?

"I think everybody is happiest who finds out what he does best, and works his head off to perfect it."

What do you do best now?

"I'm pretty good at several things: the driving layup, the good fake, that first quick step, and the long step that starts you through. I'm happy about that — and one thing more. When I go home, there's a cute blonde waiting for me. Not everybody is married to a Miss Arkansas."

13. Doc Kearns, Fight Manager

FOR THE next several years, my interview columns, including this early one with a veteran boxing character, were written for the Herald-Examiner. It's a question whether, in the present century, the United States has produced a brighter manager of fighters than Doc Kearns, who rose to fame with a heavyweight champion, Jack Dempsey. In a famous controversy, Kearns broke with Dempsey simply because he thought marriage would undermine and abbreviate the champion's career, which it did. Kearns was a Diamond Jim Brady type whose only noticeable hobby was spending money. By the time I caught up with him, he was managing Archie Moore, the artist, philosopher and light-heavyweight champion who fought Cassius Clay for the heavyweight title at age forty-plus.

LOS ANGELES: Jan. 14, 1962.

During his fifty-seven years as a fight manager, Jack [Doc] Kearns says he has known fifty-seven varieties of fighters — plus Archie Moore, who is under Doc's sponsorship now. "I had twelve champions before Archie," says Kearns, a lean, dapper reformed playboy who managed former Heavyweight Champion Jack Dempsey forty years ago. "And some of them never went to bed before midnight. Archie's habits are slightly different. He gets up at midnight."

What for?

"He's a big writer," says Kearns, "and that's when he does his writing. I'll be eighty in August, but Archie isn't much more than fifty. He thinks nothing of calling me up at 1 or 2 o'clock in the morning, and reading me a page from a movie he's writing, or a verse from his latest song."

How often did Dempsey bother you with such problems?

"Dempsey only did one thing that bothered me in all the time I knew him. He got married."

Why are you opposed to marriage?

"I was opposed to his marrying Estelle Taylor, that's all. Everything was different after that."

What was it precisely that led to the breakup of your relationship with Dempsey?

"I was at a party in Los Angeles one night in 1926 when I got a call from Mexico. The operator says, 'The champ wants to talk to you.' Jack comes on the line and says, 'Hi, Doc, I want you to meet the wife.' He handed the phone to Estelle, I guess. I don't know. I hung up on her."

Why didn't either you or Dempsey attempt to patch up the quarrel?

"Jack and I never quarreled. We've never had an argument in our life, and that's the truth. He just changed managers. I had him when he was winning. Estelle managed him against Jim Tunney."

How much money did you make in the Dempsey years?

"Jack figures we took in over twenty million dollars gross. When we split, he still had more than three million — which was three million more than me. I had fifty per cent of Dempsey, and after a fight he went to bed with his fifty per cent. I went out on the town with mine."

How much did you spend in those years?

"I don't know. I didn't quit drinking until I was sixty."

After a half century in boxing, which of your talents or achievements are you proudest of?

"My long suit was spending money. Most guys don't know how to spend it, even when they got it. Diamond Jim Brady, for instance, always gave a girl a bracelet when he took her to dinner, and that was a good start. But he didn't know how to tip, or how much to leave. And sometimes he ordered direct from the menu. Brady was a bum spender and a bum host."

Speak to us about your way.

"I'm referring to the bootleg era now, you know. It was nothing like today's generation of small-timers. I usually walked in tipping with $50 bills. Then I ordered wine all around, everybody in the house, and if possible I stirred up two or three fights. Everybody in the room knew Kearns was there."

Financially, how does Archie Moore measure up to your standards?

"We get along fine. We won't defend for less than a hundred thousand dollars. Besides, we've been the best in the world since 1958, when we beat Yvon Durelle in Canada. Remember how Durelle kept knocking us down in the first round?"

Vaguely.

"After he did it again in the fifth, I wouldn't let Archie sit down. I made him stand up and wave to his wife. Durelle thought Archie was waving at him, and it took the heart out of him. That's how we win."

Did you and Archie do the town afterward?

"I did. He went home and wrote a song."

14. Ginger Drysdale, Baseball Wife

THROUGHOUT Don Drysdale's career as a Dodger pitcher, I visited frequently with him and his wife Ginger. Three decades after this interview first appeared as a Herald-Examiner sports column, it probably seems sexist to some critics, but I've kept it as an example of the sort of thing that appealed to 1960s editors — and also to me. The visit at Dodger Stadium and my typewritten report afterward constituted a workday [in a five-day week] that was interrupted only by Swiss steak and white wine in the press dining room.

LOS ANGELES: May 6, 1964.

Ginger Drysdale discloses that plans are afoot for a new family program on television. The stars, she warns, are tonight's pitcher, his wife, and the Drysdale heiress, Kelly, age five. "Don looks very nice in cowboy clothes," Ginger reports. "And he knows how to ride a horse. But at this point in the planning, we don't know exactly what form the television series will take. A ballplayer and his family get involved in so many crazy real-life situations that there is all kinds of material."

What situations?

"Well," says Ginger, "there was the time in 1958 that the Herald-Examiner city desk sent a photographer to a Dodger game to do a picture story called, 'Girl Meets the Dodgers.' That was the first season of major league ball at the Coliseum, and I thought it was a very cute idea, especially when the city editor asked me to be the girl in the pictures. And that's how I met Big D. In fact, it was the first time I ever heard of him."

Weren't you a baseball fan in those days?

"Oh, yes, I was a Cardinal fan, and Stan Musial was my idol. I had to buy a Dodger yearbook to find out what position Drysdale plays."

He pitches.

"Yes, but not very well unless I cook just the right meal for him at 3:30 in the afternoon before the game. You'd be surprised at some of the superstitions ballplayers have, and one of them is food. Two years ago, we had the best steak money can buy when Don won his first start. Naturally, we had steak every afternoon after that, and Don won twenty-four more, and our butcher was driving a Cadillac along with the home run hitters."

Why did you quit serving steak last year?

"I didn't quit. I was very careful to do everything the same way. So many shakes of salt, so many shakes of pepper, and so on. But, unfortunately, it has never been definitely proved that a superstition will work two years in a row. So we had to start experimenting, and Don would win one and lose one, until finally, this year, just the other night, I thought of hamburger. It was a stroke of genius, really. Don won easily. I know very well that our butcher went out to the park that night and rooted for the Giants, but it won't do him any good. We're a hamburger family this year."

In addition to taking charge of the Drysdale barbecues, how do you help him win?

"For one thing, I never miss a game. Suppose I stayed home some night and Don won. He wouldn't let me go again until he lost, and the way he's pitching now, that might be years. Then there was the time in 1962 I wore white pants. You know about white pants. You only wear them once. But Don won and won, and I had to wear those pants and the same white blouse every night. I was a mess. The Dodgers eventually lost the playoff, but that was entirely the fault of Gertie Wills [Shortstop Maury's wife]."

What did Gertie do?

"The day we won, she wore the prettiest suit you ever saw, but she changed it the next day, and us girls have always felt that Gertie lost the 1962 pennant."

What ambitions do you have for the 1964 pennant?

"If my hamburgers can't do it, I have another bright idea. You know Kelly and I would do anything for Don. I'll suggest dinner out every day."

15. Dr. Frank Ryan, Quarterback

THIS WAS the player who beat Baltimore Quarterback John Unitas in one of the most surprising NFL championship games yet played, a title game I covered, as usual in those days, for the Herald-Examiner. In an Ohio gale, Unitas called a strangely conservative game during the thirty minutes he had the wind. When Frank Ryan had it, he came out throwing — and that's what routed the Colts, 27-0. Several days before the game, Ryan, who also won his mathematics Ph.D. that year, delivered the kind of prediction that made Joe Namath famous only four years later. An era later.

CLEVELAND: Dec. 16, 1964.

When in July, 1962, the Rams gave up on Quarterback Frank Ryan after four seasons, he told the Herald-Examiner that the Los Angeles coaches were "premature." Said Ryan at that time: "It takes seven years to make a pro football quarterback."

At age twenty-eight, Ryan is just about on schedule. This is his seventh season in the NFL, he has earned his way into the championship round, and against the Baltimore Colts here December 27 he'll be fighting John Unitas for the title. "I'll win," Frank says flatly.

A trim, scholarly chess player who will join the Rice Institute faculty as a math professor next month, the Cleveland Browns passer continues: "We have more offense than Baltimore has. Ours is a bit more conservative, which should fit this weather, and it's a better-balanced offense than Baltimore's."

What about the quarterbacks? I hear people saying that the Colts have an edge at that position.

"Paraphrasing Sid Gillman, I haven't see the Baltimore movies yet. But I do know that I'm a better quarterback than I used to be in Los Angeles. I've learned to make plays that I could never make out there. Did you see the Giant game on TV Saturday?"

Yes.

"One of our big plays that day was the long pass to [Wide Receiver] Paul Warfield just before the half. It was sort of a broken-pattern operation. Paul was running what we call a double-out. He was supposed to go ten yards and out, then ten more and out again. But he broke it off after the first leg and kept going deep because he had his man beat. It surprised me so much that if it had happened in Los Angeles three years ago, I'd have eaten the ball. But I've learned now that the receivers can't always do what they're supposed to do. I stood in and threw. I must say that it wasn't a very good pass, but it got there."

In that same game, the play you used the most was a quick pass to Warfield or sometimes [Wide Receiver] Gary Collins slanting in. How can you work that against Baltimore's zone defense?

"I'm not prepared to answer that question yet. We'll talk after the game. In general, you fit the pass to the defense, of course. The Giants were giving us that pattern — a quick seven-yard slant-in. Warfield runs it like a veteran, and he's very fast, but the Colts may give us something else. With the coaching we have here, we think we can adjust to any defense. It's much better coaching than I had in Los Angeles."

Those were slow years with the Rams, no matter who the coach was. But what have they done to you in Cleveland that Ram staffs couldn't accomplish?

"In Cleveland, they coach me. In Los Angeles, they assumed that I was a passer — and that if I didn't deliver, it was because I just wasn't good enough. One of the biggest fallacies in football is that passing can't be taught. They teach it here."

How do they do that?

"Coach [Blanton] Collier breaks the job down to fundamentals, and he criticizes me in detail when I'm the least bit off in execution. The way he explains passing, it's a three-step procedure. First, you get set. Second, pick out a target. Third, drill the ball with authority. Several times a game, Coach Collier may have to remind me. He will say: 'You threw that one off balance. Watch it.' Or: 'It looked to me like you just threw that in the general vicinity of Big Jim. Pick him out and drill him.' Or: 'You were twirling the string that time, Frank. Drill it.' That's coaching."

During the week, how much do you work with Collier on strategy?

"It works this way in the Collier system. [Offensive Coach] Dub Jones and I do most of the planning. I take the movies home three times a week, so does Dub, then we get together. We weed out the plays from our basic offense that won't go against the defense we're playing, and maybe we'll make some additions."

How much does the night work cut into the time you ought to be using for your Ph.D. dissertation?

"Very little, the writing is just about finished."

When do you get the degree, and have you settled on a title for the dissertation?

"I'm set for the degree in June, but starting in February I'll be teaching a senior mathematics course at Rice. From now on, I'll spend the off-season on the faculty there. My hardest job right now is putting a definitive title on the dissertation. All I can tell you is the mathematics field it deals with."

Then tell me.

"It deals with asymptotic sets of functions holomorphic in the unit circle."

16. Walter O'Malley, Dodger Owner

AFTER MOVING to the Times, I wrote fewer Q&A pieces but more on baseball subjects. This one is with the man who brought baseball West, who built Dodger Stadium, and who also put together many unusual teams that won many pennants and World Series championships by emphasizing only two ways of playing the game: speed and defense. As owner of the Dodgers, Walter O'Malley never spent much money on hitters. "The best hitters," he told me, "disappoint you seven times out of ten." O'Malley was a big man, a big thinker and a big talker who, uniquely among the rich in sports and elsewhere, actually believed his talk about free enterprise.

LOS ANGELES: Feb. 18, 1969.

Overlooking the playing field of Dodger Stadium, Walter F. O'Malley is in his office setting fire to a thirty-five-cent cigar. Then he smiles pensively and says he has decided to make a change in the organization.

O'Malley's twelfth — and last — year as president of the Los Angeles ballclub will begin Saturday, he says, when he boards the Dodger jet for Florida and a new season of spring training.

"The other day I signed up for Medicare," he confides. "And the Medicare people handed me the biggest surprise I've had since Sandy Koufax retired. They billed me for $12. Shows you how easy it is to make mistakes. I always thought *they* paid *you*."

Could it be that the government is just trying to get something back after giving you Chavez Ravine?

"That, my friend, is a misconception," says O'Malley, who will be succeeded next year by his son Peter. "In fact, there are many misconceptions about us. Now that I'm getting ready to step up, as they say, to board chairman, let's put some of the record straight. First, this isn't Chavez Ravine."

It isn't? What is it?

"On the maps it's Goat Hill," says O'Malley. "Chavez Ravine is the next ravine over."

But they did give it to you.

"They did not," he says. "We bought this land."

For how much?

"We bought it by swapping Wrigley Field, including the real estate. That was our first California investment, back in 1957. Those who really know me are aware that it is out of character for me to ask for a subsidy."

Or a stadium?

"That's right: The Dodgers own the only privately-financed baseball stadium built in this country in the last forty-five years. The public's money is in all of the other new ballparks."

Still, the land-grab story persists. What accounts for the misperception?

"The public has an appetite for gossip and there are those in the media who cater to it. Negative arguments are easier and more sensational than facts. Roscoe McGowen of the New York Times, who retired some time ago, was the last of the baseball reporters who wrote about baseball. Today, everybody has to have a slant or angle."

One angle is that O'Malley is one of the most ruthless individuals in Los Angeles. This is part of your image.

"Nobody is a knight in shining armor. I'll admit to a weakness in my approach. I have been high-handed at times. I have a temper, and when irritated I can tell people off."

What people?

"I have told a few mayors where to go — and other politicians. One of the biggest mistakes I made when I came west was taking western politicians at their word. I had been informed that a western politician was a hearty, candid fellow whose handshake was his bond. I learned otherwise — about some of those with whom I dealt — and my reaction is responsible for that word you used: image."

It is a bit naive, maybe, to think of western people as greatly different from New Yorkers.

"At the least, I didn't expect a double-cross. But it's all over now. When they took the Dodgers to the voters of Los Angeles, and we won the referendum, the picture was clarified. We are grateful to the majority of citizens who voted with us. Our motto is, 'Don't be a sore winner.'"

Los Angeles, in fact, has become your oyster.

"In a manner of speaking. You must realize that we're open eighty days a year and pay taxes three hundred and sixty-five. I don't think Dodger Stadium will be here a hundred years from today. The tax bill makes this increasingly unlikely."

What is the size of your tax bill?

"Off the record, I paid exactly [several hundred thousand dollars] in taxes last year. That would buy a few cigars."

It must be gratifying to you that Dodger Stadium has become one of the city's great tourist attractions.

"Oh, it is. Buses drop off loads of visitors here every day. They lean down and touch the grass, and walk out to the mound where Don Drysdale stands in those Vaseline commercials. And I have to hope that many of those visitors will come back. But as the years go along, we're judged more and more as a baseball team."

You're saying that Los Angeles is no better and no worse than other baseball cities.

"No, I'm not saying that. It is obviously much better. The combination of the Los Angeles community and the Dodger organization has made this the greatest city in baseball. We have fourteen thousand tickets sold by the time the season starts. We're the only ballclub in the country with that kind of support. In other sports, they sell season tickets for seven or ten games, or perhaps twenty or forty games. Our season-ticket holders buy all eighty-one games, and fourteen thousand is some kind of support."

Indicating some kind of prosperity as usual.

"Don't forget, we haven't raised ticket prices since we opened the stadium."

Is it possible that you have been too busy running the National League? It is even said that O'Malley runs baseball.

"I have abdicated to the new commissioner."

You're jesting.

"Sure, this is just another misconception. There's no more truth to this rumor than in the yarn that Los Angeles gave us Chavez Ravine."

Goat Hill.

"Either one."

There must be something to the charge that you ran baseball for the last two commissioners.

"There isn't much, but I'll tell you how the rumor started. When I came into baseball, I sold my railroad. I sold my advertising agency. I gave up my law practice, and devoted all my time to baseball. Other owners have kept their former businesses. They haven't had the time to serve on committees. I've been on so many committees for so long that I became identified with every baseball decision — the bad ones, anyway."

Suppose you were asked to prove that you have just been a member of these committees — not running them.

"All you have to do is look at the record. If I had been the commissioner, we never would have lost control of the players this spring. We wouldn't have all these divisional playoffs. In fact, we'd have three leagues, not four divisions. We wouldn't have the rookie draft. That is socialistic, and I'm for free enterprise. For instance, I'm against subsidizing baseball. We are big enough to build and own our own ballparks."

Is it true that only ten or eleven other families have owned Chavez Ravine?

"Only five, actually. The other six owners were two counties, a pueblo, a state, a country and the city. The King of Spain took possession first — in 1769. We're two hundred years old today."

17. Tom Mack, Pro Bowl Guard

MORE THAN any other Los Angeles pro, Tom Mack was a businessman-football player. A gifted and proud competitor, he made a business of football while using football to set himself up in business. And, all these years later, he's still with the same corporation, Bechtel.

FULLERTON, Calif.: July 12, 1971.

Tom Mack, the Rams' consistent Pro Bowl guard who in the preseason picks is starting to make All-Pro as usual again this summer, signed for 1971-72 here Sunday, accepting a contract that almost any quarterback would have been proud of six or eight years ago. "Offensive guards," says Mack, "are finally getting what they're worth."

How much?

"I'm sorry," he says, "but my attorney won't let me tell you."

How does the size of a pro's salary affect the way he plays?

"Few things mean more. If two guys have about the same ability, the best-paid player tends to play better."

Some people expect a real pro to put out as hard as he can every time.

"Sure, a real pro will give you one hundred per cent in every game, regardless of whether he's underpaid. But that's not what I'm saying. My point is that salary is about the most important ingredient in a man's self-confidence. A player puts the same value on his ability that the club has. Let's say you have a veteran who, by comparison with others in his position around the league, is worth $40,000. And let's say he has a penny-pinching general manager who gets him to sign for $30,000. In this case, you can look for him to play more like a $30,000 man than a $40,000 man."

Why?

"If your club doesn't respect you enough to pay you what you're worth, there's no way to keep your confidence up. Subconsciously, you believe the club may be right, and that you're not as good as you think you are. Your performance inevitably suffers."

What does an individual football player use for a yardstick in evaluating his own ability?

"Well, in the case of offensive guards, the first thing is the new respect that offensive guards as a class have these days in the league. We aren't as famous yet as defensive linemen, but we're getting there — thanks to instant replay. Before TV had instant replay, the only players anybody ever saw in a football game were the quarterbacks, running backs, and receivers. The rest of us were just spear-carriers — just part of the background."

The coaches must have known who was valuable and who wasn't.

"Yes, but why pay big money to an offensive guard if he's just part of the background? Suddenly, with instant replay, everybody in the world can see that there really are eleven men on a football team, and that offensive guards are as essential as quarterbacks. People still look at the man with the ball the first time around, but on instant replay they are forced to see the rest of us."

What do you think when you watch yourself in one of those isolated TV scenes?

"Invariably I'm messing up. I mean, I'm always blocking the wrong guy, or doing something else wrong. But that doesn't matter. What does matter is that I'm wiping somebody out — showing the world that an offensive guard has a big job to do. Who knows or cares if I'm mistakenly wiping out the safetyman instead of the cornerman? The only reason I'm on instant replay is that I've blocked somebody, anybody, and so brought great distinction to every offensive guard in the league."

And more money?

"Ah, yes, that, too."

You've been getting more and more publicity personally. Does this help your game or hurt it?

"It's a problem in one way. Your opponents get up for a game against a man who plays in Pro Bowls and makes all-star teams. But it works for you because it provides a challenge. You feel you've got to live up to the label, so you play harder. On balance, I'd rather have the challenge."

How important is experience to your success — in football *or* business.

"That's a big reason I went with Bechtel years before I retired from the Rams. I wasn't after the money, I wanted to be in it. Let me tell you how important experience is. A lot of people think Vince Lombardi was the best coach of all-time — but back in 1960, he lost the first championship game he was ever in. Norm Van Brocklin — an old quarterback — beat him."

Van Brocklin was protected by what two guards?

"Who knows? That was before instant replay."

18. Dick Butkus, Linebacker

DICK BUTKUS is what God had in mind when he invented football's trench warfare.

LOS ANGELES: Jan. 17, 1972.

You are spending an hour with Dick Butkus, without whom there hasn't been a Pro Bowl game since George Allen drafted him four years ago for the Chicago Bears. Butkus is one of three middle linebackers who are usually grouped as the best in football.

"I keep reading more about the other two," he says, referring to Tommy Nobis of Atlanta and Ray Nitschke of Green Bay, "and I don't mind too much except I get tired reading the same old two things."

What two things?

"They say," Butkus reports, "that Nitschke has the experience and that Nobis has the potential — and I don't know what that leaves for old number fifty-one. Well, I'll go with the fifty-one kid."

Is that someone we know?

"That's me," says Butkus, who at twenty-five was voted first-team All-Pro by the AFL and NFL writers at the Super Bowl last week.

Why are you putting the knock on Nobis and Nitschke?

"You know me better than that. I've always said Nobis does a fairly good job for a new expansion team. And Nitschke was my idol when I was growing up in Chicago."

But not now?

"I'm sure I'd still like him fine if he played a different position. I was honored to be categorized with him during my rookie year in the league, but things are different now. There's no way to play this game without first convincing yourself that you're the greatest player in the world at your position."

Among other things, at 248 pounds, you're bigger than the others, and George Allen says the main defensive trend is to larger linebackers. Why?

"A pro team is limited today in the defenses it can use if it doesn't have a big middle linebacker who can move. You have to get around like a defensive back in some defenses. In other alignments, you have to get up in the line and hit like a defensive tackle. Any 250-pound offensive guard in the league today has the advantage over any light linebacker, no matter how good the backer."

What's the best part of playing your position on a football team?

"The middle linebacker meets all the most interesting people. On one play you meet a center, or a guard, and on the next a tackle, or a tight end — or even a fullback. And best of all, you meet a lot of nice quarterbacks."

They say blitzing the quarterback is the most rewarding play a linebacker can make.

"It's the most rewarding and also the trickiest. The blitz is not a well-understood play. After a blitz works and the quarterback is lying there, and maybe the game is turned around, we're asked why we don't go in all the time. The answer is mathematical."

Too many blockers?

"And too few linebackers. The offense starts with five linemen for sure, plus the tight end maybe — and if the quarterback guesses right, two backs. That's eight blockers. We have a four-man defensive line and three linebackers."

What's the answer?

"The maximum blitz. Baltimore shoots nine men sometimes. But that doesn't always work, either. There have been a lot of one-sided games this winter. The offense is ahead of the defense now."

You are playing in your fourth straight Pro Bowl. Do you think of this as a privilege or a duty?

"It's a great honor. I keep it in mind all year. I read about Nobis and Nitschke, and I think about the Pro Bowl."

19. Don Sutton, Pitcher

BOTH AS athlete and communicator, this athlete has distinguished himself in the sport he likes best.

LOS ANGELES: May 18, 1972.

Don Sutton, 5-0, comes off the road today looking forward to two things, breakfast at home and tonight's game at Dodger Stadium. The new ace of a strong Dodger staff and a man with an improbable 0.52 ERA this year, Sutton, twenty-seven, has matured suddenly as one of the National League's most effective pitchers.

He is 21-6 in his last twenty-seven decisions.

"It's great to be home," he says. "I used to enjoy breakfast on the road, but not any more. Everybody sits there in the dining room and stares at me."

What do you have for breakfast?

"Ham and eggs, wheat toast, and fifty-eight pills," says Sutton. "I wouldn't be where I am now without fifty-eight pills a day and a screwball."

What led you in those directions?

"I decided last spring that I'd have to do something radical, so I looked up four experts, a nutritionist, a physical therapist, a physical conditioning specialist and pitching Coach Red Adams. I listened to all of them and added two pitches, the screwball and a shorter, harder curveball. The nutritionist recommended the pills."

What's in them?

"Everything from vitamin C to lecithin."

What's lecithin?

"I don't know, but he recommended it."

What, generally, are you trying to do with all these pills?

"Well, a number of them are food supplements. I take extra protein, calcium, all the vitamins, things like that. The nutritionists say an athlete is like a Cadillac. You don't burn regular fuel in a Cadillac. The idea is simply that pitchers can use more fuel than less active persons."

So when you go in to breakfast now, you say, fill'er up.

"Yes, but I carry my own vitamins. I make up a packet every day and after ordering breakfast, I eat the fifty-eight pills with a spoon. It takes a few minutes, and the people sitting around me can't believe it. My roommate says we're going to be raided some morning."

You seem to be stronger now that you're on all that stuff.

"I think so, too. My strength hasn't jumped by a power of ten, but it's convincing enough to get [Pitcher] Claude Osteen on the same diet. I noticed the other morning that Osteen is up to thirty-seven pills already."

The rest of your new diet probably includes organic food.

"No, just plain substantial food: steaks and salads but no sweets or sauces and not much coffee."

How much has the nutritional improvement had to do with your success as a pitcher in the last twelve months?

"It's hard to measure. All the changes I've made since last May are responsible — I mean the changes in my daily life and baseball routine. But I don't know if one thing helped more than another. One big improvement was recommended by my physical therapist. He told me to quit putting ice packs on my arm after pitching. I'd been doing it because Sandy Koufax did it, but what's good for one pitcher is not necessarily good for another. As they say in physical therapy, 'Nature abhors a sudden change.' I stopped the swelling with the ice pack, all right, but it was a bad remedy because it constricted the muscles."

Until last May, your baseball problem was inconsistency, a good game today, a bomb tomorrow. What's helped the most in that department?

"The thing that made me understand the inconsistency was a movie. Red Adams and I compared films of my pitching last year with movies taken in 1966 [Sutton's second in organized ball, when he made National League Rookie Pitcher of the Year]. We found that I was pitching from the side, putting strain on the elbow, instead of coming over the top. Movies are where you start when you're in a slump."

How did you decide to add the screwball?

"I had been experimenting with it for three years, and when I got so I could control it I put it in, along with a new hard curve [slider]. So last year I became a four-pitch pitcher, and that made an amazing difference. Until then I had been a two-pitch pitcher, basically, which is all right if you can throw them both for strikes. But on the days when I didn't have my good curve, they waited and sat on my fastball. I realized I had two choices. I could learn another pitch or lead the world in home run balls."

You've never even had the great fastball, to tell you the truth. Until last year, Sutton was mainly a curveball specialist. Why throw curves?

"That was the first pitch I learned as a kid, and I could already control it when I was twelve years old. The man who taught me was my sixth-grade teacher in Clio, Alabama, where we lived on a farm. His name is Henry Roper, and he used to pitch in the Giant chain. After school the winter before I was twelve, he taught me how to spin the curveball and get it over. He stressed control, and I got by on his formula for fifteen years including five in the majors — just throwing curves and spotting the fastball."

So Henry Roper has had a significant impact. How influential was Sandy Koufax in your life?

"I'll always think of Sandy as the epitome of the professional athlete."

What does that mean to you?

"To give a hundred per cent on the mound and to remember that what a pitcher does off the mound is critical, too. Sandy believed strongly in relaxing between innings. He'd say: 'Watch the other guys, take an interest in them, forget the last inning, it's over, it will never come back.' He never liked to replay an inning or a game. Sandy's secret was that he always looked ahead."

As a baseball fan, Don, what pitcher do you prefer to watch?

"If I can only take one, it would be Tom Seaver from the sixth inning on with a 1-0 lead. He completely overpowers the other team in that situation, like Koufax used to."

Yet your style is not much like Seaver or Koufax, either one.

"There is no one best way to pitch. That's the main plank in my philosophy. The Dodgers have ten kinds of pitchers, and they have a pitching couch who knows it. Adams' strength is that he refines rather than indoctrinates."

How does it feel to be number one on such an exceptional staff?

"After games I see more reporters than I used to, two or three more. Of course, I'm not the only pitcher who's been 5-0 in May. I have to stay with my daily 58."

20. Merlin Olsen, Defensive Tackle

ONE OF the last of my many interviews with Merlin Olsen summed up much of the philosophy that made him a Hall of Fame defensive lineman for fourteen years. I've never known a pro athlete who more thoroughly understood the mental aspects of his sport.

LOS ANGELES: Aug. 3, 1973.

Merlin Olsen is known to his peers as the most consistent football player in the game's history. He has been voted into eleven Pro Bowls in eleven years as a defensive tackle for Los Angeles. During Olsen's era, there have been five Ram head coaches — a new one about every two years — and they've all said the same thing: He's never had a bad season, a bad game, hardly ever a bad play.

"The key to consistency of performance is concentration," says Olsen, who opens a new season tonight at the Coliseum against Dallas in the annual Times Game. "I've probably held my ability to concentrate over a longer period of time than some athletes."

What do you concentrate on?

"Each game at the beginning of each new play, I think of it as the most important play of the year," he says. "I go into it as if the game depends on it. If you have any lapses, you start to slide immediately, and you may not even be ready next week."

In a lopsided game, how do you convince yourself that a fourth-quarter play is important?

"I don't think about the preceding play or the following play or anything else. I approach every play as if it's an individual, distinct incident — a complete little game of its own. I consider a new play to be not only a separate situation but a new challenge. This doesn't mean I play perfect football on every play — but I try."

That's a daunting challenge.

"The first thing I learned as a rookie is that if you don't completely involve yourself in every play, you suddenly find you've lost it. If you take it easy for ten minutes, it takes a long time to get it back, sometimes a week or two. Like everything else, concentrating is a habit."

How do you get into that kind of habit?

"After each play, I start thinking about the next play, using a simple little system. First, I tell myself the down and distance, then our position on the field, then I mentally review the tempo of the game. After those three things, I recall what I know — or what I've learned during the week — about what the other team likes to do in this particular situation. Then I clear all of those things out of my mind, and prepare myself for the play."

Why tell yourself the down and distance and then forget it?

"It's like putting material into a computer. The significant difference between the human mind and a computer is that a computer can't be distracted. And that's what I'm trying to achieve. I want to eliminate everything that could be distracting. When the play starts, computers don't guess, and I don't want to guess, either. I'm reacting. I know the two or three things the other team likes to do in every situation, and as the play develops I'm cued by what they do to react to what they do."

When you talk to yourself, what sort of thing do you say?

"Just the most obvious things. If it's third and twelve, I'm thinking, 'Off on the ball. Get to the quarterback.' If it's fourth and one on our five-yard line, I think, "Off on the ball, hold them.' You should always begin by reminding yourself to go with the snap. The only thing that comes ahead of that is the correct stance."

How much does concentration have to do with longevity?

"Longevity starts with love of the game. Second, you have to develop concentration until it's a habit. Athletes differ, of course, but those who can sustain their concentration last longer than others. And third, good coaching helps."

What football player in your time has been able to concentrate most effectively?

"[Baltimore Quarterback] John Unitas. And the thing that gives Unitas his concentration is his courage. He's the bravest man I've known in football. Out of the corner of his eye, Unitas may see you coming, and I swear that when he does, he holds that ball a split second longer than he really needs to — just to let you know he isn't afraid of any man. Then he throws it on the button."

[Ram Defensive End] Deacon Jones weighs 255. He stands six feet five. Unitas is 196 and six feet one — and thirty-four years old. How can Unitas even think of getting involved in such an uneven match?

"He is a quarterback. No position in football requires more ability. No position in any sport is even remotely as hard to play. NFL quarterbacks are the greatest athletes in America today."

21. Mike Marshall, Relief Pitcher

A SPIKY loner, Mike Marshall played his own game in his own style. He played it very well, and his thinking emphasizes that baseball is a team game in only the most tenuous ways. In 1974, the year of our interview, Marshall appeared in a hard-to-believe 106 Dodger games and finished 83. Those are both still major league records. He also won the Cy Young award that season as the National League's leading pitcher.

LOS ANGELES: Feb. 10, 1974.

Mike Marshall, the Dodgers' new right-handed relief pitcher who came from Montreal in the Willie Davis trade, may shortly be recognized as California's most unusual athlete. Here are some of the reasons:

• He thinks winning is overrated. As a ballplayer, Marshall, thirty-one, is a nonconformist with a different goal: to pitch well. "Nothing matters to me," he says, "but competing against the hitters. The victory is in the competition — not the result."

• He prefers college classrooms to major league ballparks. This is

Marshall's fourteenth year in baseball and fifteenth year as a student at Michigan State University, where he earned a B.A. in 1965 and an M.S. in 1967. Now finishing his Ph.D. course work there, Marshall also has taught at Michigan State since 1966. His subject is kinesiology [the study of human anatomical movement].

• Marshall's academic interest is human growth and development. His field is physiological psychology and he is writing his doctoral thesis on "Maturation at Adolescence in Males."

• His research has led him to conclude that he can pitch in all 162 Dodger games this year. In any case he felt underworked last year when he appeared in a league-record ninety-two games, saving thirty-one in a 14-11 season in which he finished second in the Cy Young Award voting and first among National League pitchers in the MVP voting.

• As a relief specialist, Marshall, when summoned, jogs from bullpen to mound. "If they bunt on the first pitch," he says "my legs are ready."

His interest in baseball has little to do with winning games or trophies.

"It's based on other things," Marshall says.

What things?

"Individual competition, mainly," he says. "Major League baseball gives me an opportunity to compete against the best in the world."

Why is that more rewarding than winning?

"I measure my performance on how well I do, not on the score. If Willie Stargell gets the game-winning hit, I'll still feel I've won if I threw him a very good pitch and he hit it anyway. I'll know I did the best I could."

Suppose it's the ninth inning of a close game and you're asked to walk the other team's best hitter. Surely that gives you a sense of relief.

"No, I'd rather pitch him tough to see if I can get an out by getting him to make a mistake. I keep a precise book on every hitter — in writing. To me, the rest of the game is incidental. If I could get guys like Stargell to drop by Michigan State and go one-on-one with me, I'd never have to play in a National League game."

Would you give Stargell your autograph if he asked for it?

"I think it's demeaning to both parties when one person seeks an autograph from another. A man who leads the league in hitting or pitching is just a man who plays baseball well. I don't like to perpetuate the myth that he's important."

What's your philosophy on Little League baseball? As a student of kinesiology and pitching, you're doubtless a model for kids who may hurt their arms throwing curves and screwballs.

"Before the age of fifteen, no boy should pitch more than the equivalent of two innings a week, in my opinion. My suggestion for pre-fifteen baseball, in fact, is that everybody switch positions every inning. And I recommend two-out innings. That way they can learn all the skills without subjecting themselves to the trauma of injury from overuse of certain muscles."

With everybody pitching an inning, you might be creating an army of relief pitchers.

"It's an honorable profession."

But is it a long-lived profession? Many relievers seem to burn out early.

"A power pitcher — anybody who throws hard most of the time — has a shorter career, starters or relief pitchers. A relief man who relies on control and finesse can go on a long time."

Even if he pitches frequently?

"The idea that a pitcher should throw regularly is supported by research. The body tends to atrophy at lower levels of use. This has been shown in cardiovascular tests, and the principle applies to any muscle. To retain a high level of efficiency you have to practice regularly. That means a pitcher has to keep pitching."

On a staff with nine or ten pretty good pitchers, regular work is sometimes hard to arrange.

"If so, to keep in shape I'll pitch batting practice or throw on the side. I did that at Montreal when they couldn't get me in the game."

Between appearances in ninety-two games you pitched on the sideline?

"Throughout the season."

22. Davey Lopes, Second Baseman

THE DODGERS have employed two famous thieves, Shortstop Maury Wills, who reinvented base-stealing in the early 1960s, and Davey Lopes, another infielder who, fifteen years later, taught schoolkids how to do it.

MESA, Ariz.: Jan. 19, 1975.

Davey Lopes, the Dodger second baseman who graduated from Washburn College in Topeka, Kansas, has been going to school again this winter. This one is a baseball school in Mesa, where he also teaches. "There's a lot to learn," says Lopes, a converted outfielder who finished second to Lou Brock in stolen bases last season. "And the kind of thing I want to know more about is the double-play pivot. And bunting. The kind of thing I feel I can teach myself is stealing."

Lopes at twenty-eight is a pleasant fellow, short, stocky, smooth and spirited — a take-charge type, potentially, for the Dodgers. "There are two reasons to steal," he says. "I mean there are two reasons why it is better to win stealing than hitting. First, the fans like it. They're really interested in base-running. It's the most action in baseball. And second, it puts pressure on the pitcher, the catcher and the infield. Just being on base, a good runner takes away from the other team's game."

Why do baseball fans like base runners better than hitters?

"A stolen base is an act of aggression," says Lopes, "and the public likes aggressive people — daring people. Maury Wills proved that. Maury's philosophy is that success in baseball depends on how daring you are. The way he popularized base-stealing, Maury demonstrated he's one of the few great innovators or style changers baseball has had."

During lectures on running bases, what do you say about him?

"I remind them that Maury deliberately created a new thing in baseball — the sport where nothing new was supposedly possible. Early in his career, he wasn't a big stealer. He just saw an opportunity and went to work on it."

How does a good runner take away from the other team's game just by being on base?

"The pitcher can't devote all his attention to the hitter. He tends to get edgy and is more prone to balk or throw wild. The guy at the plate will get a lot of fastballs. The pitcher wants to get rid of the ball quickly."

What else do you tell young students of base running?

"Be aggressive. If you're picked off, don't worry about it. Come back next time and try again. And never hesitate. It had to be Ty Cobb or some other base runner who first said: 'He who hesitates is lost.' The only way to learn to steal is by trial and error. You've got to do it over and over, and hang the mistakes. Getting picked off once in a while isn't bad if you learn from it."

Is stealing third base harder or easier than stealing second?

"It's more of a challenge and more daring, and it's also more fun. Of course, stealing second is more essential. It's more important to be in scoring position. Baseball is a game of getting people to second base. So you have to play the percentages carefully on stealing third."

What are the percentages?

"Before attempting to go to third, you better be eighty-five to ninety per cent sure of getting there. To steal second, a seventy per cent chance is good enough. Most guys feel the job is done if they get to second, but the really big thrill is stealing third. It is exceeded only by the embarrassment when you fail."

23. Manny Mota, Pinch Hitter

PINCH HITTERS are people, too. Here's an example of a winner who thought through his specialty in every particular and from every standpoint and who can interest me just talking about it.

LOS ANGELES: June 29, 1976.

The home dugout at Dodger Stadium is a place where Manager Walt Alston and his thirty-eight-year-old pinch hitter, Manny Mota, are like a pair of bookends. They sit at the extreme left and right sides of the bench holding up the Dodgers. By the eighth inning, it is usually clear to Mota whether he'll be asked to run out and hold up the Dodgers at the plate.

Usually, he is only needed when a late-inning hit will be the difference between winning and losing. Therefore, he only appears in about one out of three or four games. When Alston calls, Mota goes out and swings, makes a hit or an out, and returns to the bench.

That's half his job for the week. The other half is to go out and do the same thing once more later in the week.

Mota passed a milestone Sunday with his hundredth career pinch hit. Alston: "It's the toughest job in baseball. The game is always on the line for us and Manny — or else he wouldn't be in there. The pressure is incredible. I don't see how he does it."

How do you do it, Manny?

"I don't think about the pressure," he says. "This is my job, and I think about the job."

What do you think about?

"I watch every move their pitchers make — the guy on the mound and the pitcher throwing in the bullpen. I want to know what they're doing different. Maybe they haven't got their best pitch tonight. Maybe it's better than usual. People who concentrate one hundred per cent aren't ever nervous. Haven't you noticed that? How can you be nervous if you're concentrating? Concentration is the only chance I've got. I think about my job."

So thinking keeps the pressure off. And moving keeps him loose. Mota's whole life — except for a rare trip to the plate — is thinking and moving around in the shadows of the dugout. Never taking his eyes off the pitcher, he stands up, bat in hand, and runs a few steps in place, or takes a brisk, short walk, or, between innings, still holding the bat, jogs up and down the runway leading to the locker room indoors.

"Concentration and relaxation," he says. "Those are the big things in hitting. If your muscles are loose, they'll do what you tell them to do. Then if your mind is on nothing but the job, you've got everything going for you, mind and muscles. That's why it's important to hold the bat all through the game. The bat is as much a part of me as my hands. I carry it to help keep me relaxed. You've got to relax your hands to hit a baseball right. And if you're always carrying a bat, you're always relaxed. It gets to be a habit."

The Mota formula has made him the most productive pinch hitter in baseball. He is the only active major leaguer with as many as a hundred pinch hits. His hundredth Sunday was, as usual, a key hit for the Dodgers.

Mota has six pinch hits this year in twenty high-pressure at bats [.300]. He entered the season batting .301 as a Dodger pinch hitter. In the history of baseball, only four pinch hitters are over .300 lifetime, Frenchy Bordagaray, .312; Tommy Davis, .307; Frankie Baumholtz, .307, and Red Schoendienst, .303. Alston: "Consistent pinch hitters are the rarest birds in the game. A guy who can pinch hit anywhere near .300 is a gem."

Only four are ahead of Mota in lifetime pinch hits, Smokey Burgess, 144; Jerry Lynch, 116; Red Lucas, 114, and Gates Brown, 107 — all retired.

So specialized is Mota's job that he is considered one of the best of all time although, last year, he got only ten hits for the Dodgers. The most pinch hits he has ever had in one year were fifteen — and that total, in 1974, made him the all-time single-season Dodger record-holder since 1890.

Alston thinks there are two reasons why most ballplayers don't succeed as pinch hitters — one psychological and one physical. "They feel they have to play regularly," he says. "And if they don't, they're discontent. You have to be content to hit well. Second, if they're not playing regularly, they simply don't see enough pitches to get their timing down."

Mota has sustained a long, deliberate effort to minimize these particular handicaps. He believes, first, that a hitter can make up for not playing regularly by studying the pitchers and keeping active. Second, he works on his timing continually by taking extra batting practice.

"I've always wanted to play regularly," Mota says, "but you don't have to bat against a pitcher to know what you're up against. You'll know if you watch every pitch he throws on the mound or in the bullpen. You also watch how your hitters react to each pitcher. You know what your hitters can do, so how they swing against a pitcher shows what *he* is doing."

As for extra batting practice, it takes two forms for Mota. "Twice a week, I get in five or ten minutes of extra hitting with the hitting coach," he says. "I do that to make sure I haven't picked up any bad habits. The only reason a good hitter stops hitting is he has picked up a bad habit. The other thing I do, three nights a week, is go inside and hit a hundred balls at the indoor batting cage. I do that just to see the ball, to work on my concentration."

You hit in there by yourself?

"And I don't just hit," he says, "I pretend. On the first ball I'll pretend there's a man on first and I have to hit behind the runner. Then I'll say to myself, there's a man on second and nobody out, and I've got to move him over. On the next pitch, I'll pretend there's a man on third and one out, and I've got to hit a fly ball. In batting practice I never go up and just swing away. I always think of a game situation."

At the plate in Dodger Stadium, Mota bats against batting practice pitchers almost exclusively, meaning he seldom sees a ball thrown with major league velocity. Non-regulars always grumble about this, citing it as a reason for unsuccessful pinch hitting. "All you have to do is keep it in mind," says Mota. "You tell yourself you've got to be ready to adjust to a man throwing faster."

Mota occasionally hits into a double play, as he did in Cincinnati on the last road trip when, if the ball had found a hole, the Dodgers probably would have won. "There's more luck in baseball than most people realize," he says. "you've got to be lucky to keep the ball away from five gloves [including the pitcher's]. A pinch hitter gets fewer chances to be lucky than a regular. So he's got to be luckier yet."

Alston: "All you expect of any pinch hitter is for him to hit the ball hard. What you want him to do is make contact. A certain number of balls are going to be hit at an infielder, but if a pinch hitter has hit it hard, he's done all you can ask him to do. I judge him only on that."

Mota thinks his longevity as a ballplayer — fifteen years in the major leagues — is partially due to the invention of television.

"I play with the videotape all the time," he says. "The day after a game in which I've been used as a pinch hitter, the first thing I do when I get to the park is go to the videotape machine and see how I swung the bat. If I made out, I can see it was because I did something wrong. It's so easy to do something wrong, pull your arm back, move your head, stride too far out [over the plate] or something. I don't think anybody in the world gets more chances to do something wrong than hitters. In the Dominican, I have my own videotape. I hit all winter and watch myself all the time. One bad habit can put you out of baseball."

Asked to describe the second thing he does each day at Dodger Stadium, Mota says:

"I beat [Third Baseman] Ron Cey playing casino. He's terrible."

24. Fred Dryer, Defensive End

THREE THINGS about this All-Pro illuminate him. He was, first, a great football player. Second, of all the athletes I've known, he has shown the most aptitude for acting roles in Hollywood and television. And he has a lively approach to life.

LOS ANGELES: Oct. 11, 1981.

Fred Dryer, the old pro who has begun a new life as a Hollywood actor, closed the door on his last career with no regrets. Of his time in the NFL — in which he played 174 consecutive games as a 228-pound defensive lineman, most recently as a Ram — he says he "lived a fantasy for thirteen years.

"In the back of my mind," Dryer says, "I knew from the first that as great as it was — and it was so great, so exciting, so rewarding — it was all slipping away. The lucky part for me was to be successful within the fantasy, starting the first day."

How did it start?

"In New York City," he says. "Up from San Diego State. Walking around the big city in a New York Giants windbreaker, tasting the excitement, smelling it, living it. To be twenty-one years old, a first draft choice, and introduced at Yankee Stadium as the starter for an NFL team — that was every football player's dream. I loved those days."

Was it as enjoyable in 1972 coming to Los Angeles?

"Hell, yes, this is home. I grew up with the Rams. Going out into the world, making it, coming back to play for my team, that's like writing down the things you want, and they all come true."

What's it like, being a pro football player?

"It's a continuously self-gratifying feeling. For awhile, you think everyone on earth is interested in what you're doing. When you grow out of that, you still keep asking yourself, why am I so lucky? The ending is never pleasant, and for me the Rams made it ugly. But I'm not going to let that stain my memory. For thirteen years I lived a fantasy that was chock full of life and dreams come true — emotionally, physically, spiritually.

You know, of course, that it isn't going to last. There's a part of you, way down deep inside, that is always uneasy about that. And it does end so fast. It all went by in a heartbeat."

What's the best thing about an NFL career?

"It keeps you young. You're getting old, but you feel as young as ever. You're stockpiling memories — and later, your memories do a great deal to keep you young within yourself. Pro football is a mysterious, monstrous subculture, a self-contained fragment of society. Yet it is *the* society when you're living it. The NFL is like a gigantic bus station. You feel like a character in a book, and all the people you meet and know are the other characters."

Who was the most interesting character you met?

"Well, Tommy Prothro was one of them. When I first came to the Rams, Prothro was the coach, so I got to spend one training camp without a curfew."

How did you spend it?

"We tested it right along, [Receiver] Lance Rentzel and I. At times I was so tired, I could hardly go out again the next night. I remember once just before midnight when Lance banged on my door and said: 'Let's go.' I said: 'Not tonight, man, Hollywood can wait. I'm asleep.' He said: 'You can sleep tomorrow at practice.' So I got dressed, and we walked right out the front door, and there was Prothro, having a cigaret with an assistant coach. I cringed, but Lance kept us marching along to his car. And as he pulled out from the curb, I looked back. There was Prothro on the sidewalk, following us. I couldn't think of anything to say to him, so I waved — and he waved back."

Most of those who played for Prothro say he was the most unusual coach they ever knew.

"I respect him a lot for daring to be so unconventional in such an inbred society as pro football. The best time we had during two-a-day practices one July started at lunch one noon when Prothro got up to make a speech. He said: 'We've been working pretty hard, men' — we hadn't, but nobody argued with him — 'so why don't we all go to the beach today?' For a good fifteen or twenty seconds, there wasn't a sound. Everybody was stunned. Then everybody got up at once and stamped for the door. I thought I had it made, but didn't quite get there, and got knocked down and trampled in the rush. It was the only time I was injured all year. The funny thing was, when I finally got outside, my car wouldn't start. The battery or something was dead. I was under the car, cursing, and everyone else had driven away, when Prothro strolled by. He leaned over, put his hands on his knees, looked down at me, and said: 'Dryah, you're losin' the bettah paht of the day.'"

Calling your attention now to some other NFL characters: Who's the best player you saw in your thirteen years, excluding the Rams?

"That would have to be Dick Butkus. Nobody ever beat up on a running back like Dick Butkus did. When Larry Smith was a halfback with the Rams, I remember we warned him one year not to run upright in the Chicago game. He didn't listen to us — and for a week after we played the Bears, Larry couldn't wear a helmet. His forehead swelled out so much after Butkus worked him over that he couldn't get a helmet on."

Who else do you think of?

"Gale Sayers was the best running back of my time. I never saw Jim Brown, but Sayers has to be right there with him. He's the most electrifying runner I ever tried to tackle. The best quarterback is Terry Bradshaw. I don't want to take away from Joe Namath and others, but Bradshaw and [New Orleans Quarterback] Archie Manning affected my life adversely more than anybody."

Of all the characters in your life, Rams and non-Rams, who do you think of first when you're asked to name the one greatest football player.

"I think of [Ram Defensive Tackle] Merlin Olsen first."

Who would you say best epitomized pro football in your day?

"That was [Ram Defensive End] Jack Youngblood. It takes a special kind of person to play pro football — after the first game, everyone plays hurt for six months — and that requires a rare kind of devotion. But Jack Youngblood is the only player I ever knew who would, and did, play a football game on a broken leg."

How did you get along with [Ram Coach] Chuck Knox?

The only thing I didn't like about Knox was that he kept telling me, over and over, You'll have to prove yourself this week. Although my playing weight was 228 — I was the lightest lineman in the league — I thought I should be judged on performance, not size. Performance and consistency. Starting my rookie year, I played every game until they wouldn't pay me this year. That's 174 straight."

I looked it up the other day. Of the 11,700 who have played pro football since the NFL was organized in 1920, you stand twenty-eighth in consecutive games. How can one do that at your size?

"I gained a lot of strength from my fantasy. For thirteen years I saw myself playing brilliant football in the NFL as a 228-pound defensive end. You'll probably never see another lineman that small. I was the last of an era."

III

SPORTSMEN

The newspaper stories in this chapter are either profiles of or interviews with a basketball coach, a baseball genius, a television analyst and some of the other sportsmen I have known. These people are, most of them, *worth* knowing. But they aren't here for that reason. They're here because, in their very competitive world, they have excelled.

Several of the champions America has produced in this century *aren't* worth knowing, arguably. Some seem instead to be disagreeable and/or dishonorable. But one thing can be said of all of them: Like politicians, CEO's, entertainers and America's other major league winners, and, indeed, like all the rest of us, they live in a free country. Every winner (and any loser) can choose to be a civic slacker or a cipher as a parent or an ignoramus as a poet or all three — or worse.

Yet why should that matter deeply to any person who isn't personally involved? A champion isn't necessarily anything more than a specialist. Why think of champions as role models? Think of them as what they are: athletic experts who, in their fields of specialization — extremely difficult fields that are of great interest to many — have learned to excel in unthinkable pressures that seldom burden the rest of us.

A champion doesn't have to be acclaimed or flattered or even complimented, as far as I'm concerned. I'm not here to laud winners, just, if possible, to understand them.

One link between two of the sports leaders in this chapter is that although both achieved greatly, both would make any list of the twentieth century's most underrated and under-reported citizens. They are James Naismith, the inventor of basketball, and former Oakland A's Owner Charlie O. Finley, who single-handedly built a three-year World Series winner, an individual accomplishment unprecedented in baseball.

Although Finley was the closest thing to a sports genius this nation has produced, the favorite Finley talk-show topic all these years has been his off-center personality. He didn't even achieve acceptance in Oakland, where — in the years when the A's were winning a record five consecutive American League division championships — Raider exhibition games got more space and a better play in the newspapers than A's games in the pennant-racing days of August.

Naismith, by contrast, has strangely just been ignored. Perhaps nothing but electricity, television and air conditioning has changed America more in this century than basketball, the activity that reigns in the wintertime leisure hours of almost every town and neighborhood in the country. The basketball hoop over the garage door is now endemic. You almost never see football goal posts in the driveway.

And you *never* see Naismith's picture.

Making partial atonement, I'd like to reintroduce him here in a chapter that begins with a ride on John Madden's train.

1. John Madden: Coach Conquers New World

OF THE newspaper and magazine writers who have toured the country with John Madden since he left coaching for television, I was the first. In those days, before Pat Haden came along to finally give him some competition, Madden was off by himself as a TV analyst — and as an Amtrak traveler. And I leaped at the opportunity to work while riding a train. In more recent years, Madden has moved about in a customized bus, although I suspect that if trains went everywhere on the hour, every hour, he would still be aboard. During his Amtrak days, he needed a car and driver to catch a train that might be distant hundreds of miles. The convenience of a bus is a given. Madden's is always waiting for him at the press box elevator. But he does have one serious problem now: instead of relaxing on a train, he has to ride a bus.

ABOARD the Sunset Limited: Dec. 15, 1982.
The idlers in the club car of an Amtrak railroad train include a stout, big-faced former football coach named John Madden, who retired three years ago at forty-two to become a television analyst. As the train rushes along, there is a lot of talk, day and night, about sports and television. And in the midst of it all, there is a question for Madden about his aptitude for a new career in broadcasting after so many years in athletics. His reply surprises his companions.

"For twenty-five years or more," he says, "what I've tried to do — what I've learned to do — is look at anything and say a few words about it."

"Anything?" he is asked.

"Anything or anybody," he says. "I practice all the time."

"Say something about this," a fellow traveler suggests, pointing to one of the swivel chairs facing the club-car window.

"It was made by someone who wasn't an American," Madden says smoothly, starting a commentary of about fifteen seconds. "When they designed this car, comfort wasn't a consideration. . . . There are seats for two people in a space that's about right for one. . . . The ash trays are inaccessible. . . . They should have just copied the old club car chairs."

No one but a chronically nosy individual — or one with a profound interest in the world around him — would think that deeply about a chair. An individual in the latter group, Thomas Jefferson, once said: "Not a blade of grass shoots up that is not of interest to me." Confirming his own catholic tastes, Madden says he wasn't aiming for TV or any other line of work in the early years when his curiosity drove him into a novel hobby.

As an exercise in serendipity, however, his job as a football analyst requires Madden only to make brief comments about "anything that pops up on the screen," or so he tells his fellow loungers over the faint soprano notes of the Sunset Limited whistle. In his judgment, his job is comparable to that of a photo caption writer on a newspaper. "All I really do is talk about pictures," he says. "There are a hundred people down there (on the sidelines and the field), but the camera only closes on a handful at any one time, and it could focus anywhere."

It could even focus on the moon, and one night this year it did. Madden's director, television veteran Sandy Grossman, was choosing from a half dozen mostly football scenes in Texas Stadium when he abruptly filled the screen with a live picture of the moon. "I wonder if they'll ever play football up there," Madden remarked, as if the scene had been rehearsed. It hadn't, Grossman insists — except in the sense that

Madden, in reality, has been in rehearsal most of his life, although he never suspected it until recently.

"I have always been a people watcher," he tells the passengers on the swaying club car. "I can't remember when I didn't look at a man or a woman — everybody — and make up little stories about them in my mind." On TV these days the difference is that he doesn't have to make things up — just relay what he knows or what he's heard in short bursts, fifteen seconds ideally. There is only a half minute between plays in pro games, and the other announcers have to talk, too.

Madden's strange mastery of a strange art form has done two things for him. It has made him possibly the most popular conversationalist on the railroads of America, which he rides to every game, traveling more than a hundred thousand miles a year as Amtrak's number-one customer. And it has made him television's top football analyst or color man — and even, some believe, the best of all sports announcers. The most widely known TV sports personality, Howard Cosell, brings the most excitement to a game, in the opinion of many. But Madden, a different type, recently became the first color man to win the industry's prestigious Golden Mike award.

It can truthfully be said of Madden — as of most radio and TV announcers — that he talks too much. Still, no other football man on radio or TV so well combines the informative or technical aspects of this difficult work with the entertaining. He is deliberately technical.

"That's what people want," he says. "I mean they want technical information if it's understandable. The guy who did the most to prove that was the doctor (Dennis O'Leary) who came on television a couple of years ago when Ronald Reagan was shot. His subject was complex surgery, but he used drawings and descriptive terms to make the whole thing clear. I told my wife if a doctor can explain surgery, a football coach should be able to explain a game." And soon thereafter, frankly imitating Dr. O'Leary, Madden was using drawings himself, scribbling Xs and Os directly on his instant-replay slate.

The quality that makes him able to do this rapidly and accurately is his extraordinary vision. Whereas most football spectators watch only the man with the ball, Madden seems to watch almost everybody. "When a play starts after the center's snap," he says, "I can sit in the press box and tell you what all twenty-two players are doing." That seems impossible. All? "I may miss somebody now and then," he says, "but not often."

How does he do it? "The key is knowing which specialists are on the field," he says, "and being aware of each player's strengths and weaknesses. First, as the play starts, I look at the offensive formation and place the offensive players in my mind with a coach's code words — east or west, left or right, I or slot, and so on. Then I look at the defense to see where the offense is heading — where the hole should be if they run, or where the quarterback should throw the ball if the defense is giving them something."

What Madden means is that as a TV commentator, he's still anticipating with a coach's mentality. As the center puts the ball in the quarterback's hands, the movement of every player is briefly etched in Madden's head, helping him follow the play, as it develops, the way he once followed each play as a coach. "If it's an important play," he says, "I think the fans want to know why it worked or why it didn't."

So he tells them, speaking unaffectedly, using up another fourteen or fifteen seconds, as if he were sitting around an Amtrak club car.

II

It has never been easy to walk down the aisle of a passenger car on a moving train, and, lord knows, it isn't easy on today's roadbeds. To maintain one's balance, one must walk rapidly, legs wide apart, hands raised like an offensive lineman's to grab anything or anybody if the train lurches. And here comes John Madden. Rolling left and right with the sway of the train, bound for the dining car, he is taking big, fast steps, legs apart, hands up. A massive but stooped figure, Madden comes on like an ax murderer.

By 1970s football fans, he is remembered as a bulging, arm-flapping redhead. Striding about the field aggressively, he was larger than most football players — and at six feet four and 270, he still is. And the dark red hair is still unruly, as if combed with his ax.

He is dressed for the road in jeans, old tennis shoes and a T-shirt with blue horizontal stripes accentuating the obvious, namely, that this is one immense man. On his left hand, fittingly, he wears an immense present from his wife — a ring that shouts "100" in flashing diamonds. This identifies Madden as the only coach who ever led an NFL team to a hundred wins in ten years. The day he coached a Super Bowl champion is recalled in another mass of diamonds on a right-hand finger.

Three years after navigating the 1976 Raiders past Minnesota that afternoon in Super Bowl XI, Madden lost his enthusiasm for coaching. He retired for that reason. And three years after retiring, he has become the nation's most dedicated train freak. A claustrophobic disposition put Madden on the rails. The world's largest airplanes are too small for him, too confined. He could put up with air travel as a football coach (it was coaching he tired of, not flying) because one can move around on charter jets visiting with one's friends. "But in a commercial plane," he says, "there's no place to go except the bathroom. And how many times can you go to the bathroom?"

He never found out. On a commercial flight shortly after his departure from the Raiders, he panicked before the plane even left the ground. Sweating, eyes glazed, he struggled to his feet and shouted, "Let me out of here." They did, and he never went back.

Like other victims of claustrophobia, Madden also panics slightly in small cars, elevators and TV booths. His problems on a recent trip to Dallas were typical. Arriving at the game, he and partner Pat Summerall walked together into Texas Stadium, where the press elevator and an escalator are on opposite sides of the main lobby. There they parted, Summerall taking the elevator, Madden even objecting to the escalator. Asking them to please stop it, he walked up the escalator steps.

Together again in the press box, Summerall and Madden soon parted again, Summerall walking down to the field, where, like most announcers, he likes to mingle with the coaches and club owners while their teams warm up. In the CBS booth, Madden paced around like a caged lion. He'd resign if he had to fight his way down through the crowd just to see a football coach. Just being in the ballpark was bad enough. He was glad to get back to the train.

He likes everything about trains: the motion of the cars, the clatter of the wheels, the little bedrooms, the big windows and the changing landscape, the changing cast of characters, the lifestyle. He relaxes totally on a train, blending into the scene, sleeping until noon or later, working (on his files and charts) when the spirit moves him, talking the night away in the club car as, on some trips, a bright moon crosses slowly from port windows to starboard. He puts in six months a year on the road, August to January, making, in all that time, only two or three quick stops at his home in Pleasanton, near Oakland, when an assignment takes him to California.

He travels like a circus travels. After a game in Atlanta he entrains for New York, where he works a day or two, then takes a train to Detroit. Returning to New York, his headquarters during the football season, he soon boards a train for Minneapolis. Logistically, the difference between him and other football announcers is that they spend an hour or two getting to an assignment and he spends a day or two.

On a train, he takes a geography student's interest in the countryside. When the conductor or somebody announces Lordsburg, New Mexico,

Madden looks out the window and beams. "How many people," he asks, "know what New Mexico looks like?" Recalling his first trip to Denver, he asks: "How many people have sat all day and watched Wyoming?"

At Lordsburg, the kids who run up to him, both about ten years old, produce a pencil and get his autograph before running off. They're back moments later, just before the train rolls out to the timeless shout, "All aboard." "Now what?" Madden asks pleasantly, one foot on the boarding ladder. "My dad won't believe this," the taller boy says, pointing to Madden's autograph. "He'll want to call you up. Would you write your phone number under your name?" Madden feigns displeasure. "Get along with you," he is saying as his home away from home rolls on.

His life on trains isn't the healthiest. It's hard to exercise. There isn't much to do but sit and read or talk and smoke cigarets, and that's how Madden puts in half the year, usually pulling on a diet cola, even at dinner. Nutritionally, Amtrak is an Indianapolis coffee shop with white tablecloths and canned vegetables, but if you like it, this *is* a great life.

III

At 1:30 in the afternoon, as the Sunset Limited races through a little Texas town, Madden's bedroom door is still closed. He had turned in at 3 a.m. after discussing new surgical techniques and the effects of cortisone on the scapula joints with an M.D. from Glendale. On an Amtrak sleeping car, the first-class bedrooms are all on one side, leaving room for a narrow aisle on the other. There are windows on the aisle and, therefore, passengers bumping along past Madden's door could (and some did) watch Texas rolling bleakly by outside.

If they gave a thought to the big man behind the door (and some did), they doubtless figured he was still in the sack, although it wasn't literally true. He was studying. During the football season, Madden spends much of the midweek reading up on the teams he'll be talking about Sunday. And for doing that, he ranks the Amtrak environment as unmatched.

"You can do it anywhere, but a train is ideal," he says. "There's no mail, no telephones, no interruptions. It's just you and the track. You close the door, and close out the world. I come aboard with suitcases full of every scrap of information I can find on the teams coming up. And when I get off, the best stuff is all in my head."

He takes no written notes to games because he has "total recall of the things I'd like to recall." What he wants is a better filing system. "I bought a home computer this year," he says, "one with an excellent printout capability. And I'll soon have everything in there — the twenty-eight media guides, some clippings, and all the other notes, quotes and anecdotes. When I get on the train next year I'll take along the printouts. That will make the job easier and more scientific."

At his Pleasanton home — a California ranch-style tract house he's owned for many years — he plans to run the computer himself with help from his wife Virginia and two sons. For Madden, the offseason is work time. During the regular season, Virginia videotapes all the network games so John can play them back in the offseason, adding new commentaries. Fifteen-second commentaries, of course.

Madden has spent most of his life in California's Bay Area, where Pleasanton isn't that far from his boyhood home in Daly City. Son of an Irish auto mechanic, he was the baby in a house with two older sisters. His boyhood friend, USC Coach John Robinson, "is like a brother," he says. At Cal Poly San Luis Obispo, Madden played football and, he says, "met Virginia." She tells a different story. "I don't know why John says that," Virginia says. "We met in a bar. Harry's. At Plano Beach."

According to Virginia, John is a man of few interests. "His hobbies," she says, "are poker, people and working with the mentally handicapped." Pausing to think about this, she adds: "He is a very compassionate person."

Except, others say, when he is playing poker. A quarter century ago, according to Madden, he worked his way through college helping an older kid promote poker games. And thus blessed, he usually wins the neighborhood games in Pleasanton.

"To win," he says, "you've got to make more out of your cards than the other guys make out of theirs. Secondly, you can't force mediocre cards. A loser in poker is a guy who wants to dance every dance." The other Pleasanton card players are an airline pilot, banker, barber, real estate developer and highway patrolman. Madden bought into their cul de sac early in his career with the Raiders, whose head coach he became in 1969 (at age thirty-two) at the dawn of a California real estate boom.

Property investments with various owners of the Raiders left him, if not actually rich, comfortable enough to contemplate retiring at forty. He stuck it out for two more years for strictly statistical reasons. Coaching records are based on a minimum of ten years as a head coach and, as an admirer of former Green Bay Coach Vince Lombardi, he wanted to top Lombardi in games won. He went on to finish 103-32-7 (.763) to Lombardi's 96-34-6 (.738). The Madden percentage is the NFL's highest, all time.

IV

Talking about sports announcers recently, a rival network executive said: "John Madden is the most knowledgeable expert on the air."

And he doesn't just know football. He also seems to know more about TV than many TV veterans. Those watching CBS put together the Summerall-Madden broadcasts have noted that Madden often appears to be in charge of the production. Some testimony:

- Before a recent game, when the players walked out from the sidelines for their pro-union solidarity handshakes, Madden turned to a cameraman and said, "Are you getting this?"
- When the Dallas coach first walked out, Madden told a director: "Tom Landry has a new hat. We can get close (closeup) on that."
- During a timeout, after one of his associates had erred on a minor matter, Madden made a short speech to the crew reminiscent of his coaching days when the Raiders were behind at halftime. "I'd like to coin a phrase right here," he said mildly. "When you start to accept mediocrity, the best you will ever be is mediocre."

If this was a rebuke to a professional who was a television regular when Madden was still on the sideline, the explanation is the ambition and competitiveness that drove him to the top in football. He wants national-championship recognition every year both for himself and his network team. "And not just the recognition," he says. "I mean to be the best actually, every time out, preseason, regular season, postseason.

On the air, Madden's play-by-play colleague, Summerall, a one-time Russian history major at Arkansas, is more professional than Madden — indeed he is the most professional of the ex-athletes — whereas Madden sounds like a player or coach. And this, Madden says, is the way he wants it. "I think you can get by in radio and TV if you remember to be yourself," he says. "The key to the whole thing is to be natural. When we're on, I talk and act as if I were talking with my quarterback or my wife."

His passion for naturalness and openness takes him in several directions. For one thing, he never uses the ubiquitous phrase, "off the record," and doesn't like to hear it. Coaches who think they're speaking privately with Madden wind up speaking to the nation. Nor does he talk about "skill positions," a phrase that has become an unpleasant cliché. "What do the other guys play?" he asks. "Unskilled positions?" At home, studying, Madden never listens to a Madden tape. "I wouldn't like myself, and I'd want to make some changes," he says. "How many snapshots do you like of yourself? Doing things like changing the pitch of your voice makes you a phony."

Finally, on the road, he never calls room service, preferring to sit with the crowds in hotel coffee shops and dining rooms. "Room service," he says, "makes you a recluse."

And how could a recluse see America on Amtrak?

2. O.A. (Bum) Phillips, Country Philosopher

THE NFL'S most dramatic home-and-home series matched Pittsburgh and Houston during the years when the Steelers were winning four Super Bowl trophies. "Pittsburgh has ten blue chippers on offense alone," Hall of Famer Tom Fears told me one day. "Houston only has one [Earl Campbell] on their whole team." But Houston also had Bum Phillipps.

ROSHARON, Tex.: Nov. 20, 1986.

Thirty-one miles straight south of the Astrodome, where the Houston Oilers are playing football this day, O.A. (Bum) Phillips has been building an oat bin since sunup. With the help of three neighbors, he will have it nicely pounded into place before supper time. "Man cain't build an oat bin in a day, he should find some other way to make a livin'," he says.

There was a time when Phillips, now sixty-three, spent his Sundays at the Astrodome, where he coached the Oilers for six years. He's the only winner they've had there in the last quarter century. He hasn't seen them play, though, since they fired him in 1980, except once, when he was coaching the New Orleans Saints.

And he hasn't seen a football game, anywhere, since he quit the Saints just a year ago. A month was then remaining of the thirty-seventh and last season that Phillips spent in football. "It ain't that I hate football," he says. "It ain't that at all. I love football more than anythin' else in this world except horses and my wife. But I'm too busy nowadays for football. Maybe there's times I see the second half of the Monday night game, but since I got this place five months ago, I been workin' seven, eight, nine days a week, and lovin' it all."

This place is the two-thousand-acre Oak Tree Ranch, which he has leased from an oil-rich friend. The lease will take him into the 1990s and, he trusts, beyond. Phillips put in many long days searching for such a place, and when he found it, he says, he knew instinctively that this is where he wants to spend the rest of his life.

About halfway between Houston and the Gulf of Mexico, the ranch steams and shimmers in the humidity of some of the hottest, flattest land south of North Dakota. There are five hundred Phillips cows, a dozen horses, and thousands of low-growing oak trees on the property, plus three little ranch houses and ten or twelve barns, sheds and other buildings. The help lives on the ranch. Phillips lives with his wife nineteen miles up the Houston road in Dewalt, an old Houston suburb.

"Ranchin' is one of the only two things I ever wanted to do," says the man called Bum, the name he's gone by since the 1920s, when a baby sister couldn't pronounce brother. "That, and coachin' football. No fishin' for me. No golfin'. Just horses and football. And when I let up a bit, dominoes."

II

In his new life as a rancher, the people that a famous NFL coach gets to know are all that Phillips really misses about football. "The day I took over the New Orleans Saints (in 1981) was one of the most excitin' days of my life," he says. "They had fifteen hundred people at a booster luncheon, and every last one of them wanted to be my friend."

One of the fifteen hundred was the priest who delivered the invocation that is an invariable component of football in the South, at games, luncheons, whatever. "It was a powerful prayer," Phillips remembers. "The priest said: 'Oh, lord, when Israel was in trouble, you sent them three wise men from the East. I hope you know what you're doing now, dear lord, sending us one bum from the West.'"

Remembering that moment, the happy rancher grins a little, but instead of the dais on which he once sat as the toast of New Orleans, Bum Phillips is sitting on a tractor now in a desolate Texas field. Otherwise, he looks much as he did in, say, Pittsburgh a decade ago, when the Oilers were playing there in a series of memorable games. The big face is a little fuller and older now, and there's a bit more to the stomach than there used to be. But the big Texas Stetson could be the one he used to wear on the sidelines at Three Rivers Stadium. The jeans also could be the same. And the old cowboy boots doubtless *are* the same.

One thing is new, the white shirt with the modest inscription on one sleeve, "New Orleans Saints." He wouldn't have worn that during the heart-stopping Steeler-Oiler games of the 1970s, when, as he remarked one day in an apt phrase that has taken root in the language, "The road to the Super Bowl runs through Pittsburgh."

Then as now, Houston and Pittsburgh played in the same division, and it was Phillips' misfortune to come up with his best teams in the years when the Steelers were a shade better and going to the Super Bowl all the time. Phillips had Running Back Earl Campbell at his peak when the

Steelers had Quarterback Terry Bradshaw at his, and each year, for four years consecutively, they split their home-and-home series. In championship games, though, as NFL fans know, the great passer beats the great runner every time. For Phillips, the road to the Super Bowl always stopped in Pittsburgh.

"You got to remember that a lot of fellers never get that far," he says, with a touch of pride.

The pride is well founded. Phillips was well thought of, and well rewarded, in the NFL. He was working for $600,000 a year in New Orleans when, with four games left, he abruptly stepped down fifty-one weeks ago today. At the moment he left, the Saints, bound by a long-term contract, owed him a bundle — every dollar guaranteed. "I walked out on all of it," Phillips says. "I walked away from a million three — actually a million, three-hundred fifty thousand. When I told (club Owner) Tom Benson that I was leavin', I told him he didn't owe me a penny. I don't think Tom would've fired me, ever, but even if he had, I wouldn't've let him pay me. Way I see it, a man don't earn it, it don't belong to him."

Eleven years ago, Phillips says, he told Oiler Owner Bud Adams the same thing. "When he hired me, I said, 'Someday you'll fire me, Mr. Adams, but don't worry about it, you won't owe me a damn penny.'" An even six years after that pledge, Adams frivolously got out the ax although Phillips had led the Oilers to consecutive 11-5 seasons following a 10-6 season. Without Phillips, the Oilers slumped instantly, and in no time were down to 2-14 and 3-13. So far this season, they are 2-9. "I only said one thing when Bud Adams fired me," Phillips recalls. "I thanked him for six good years and told him, 'We're even.' I've always said there's only two kinds of coaches — them that's been fired, and them that's goin' to get fired."

Phillips' final NFL season in 1985 was a painful one. He departed with a 4-8 record. His son Wade, who took over, finished 1-3.

"I'd decided (before the season) to make that my last year in football," says Bum, who was a college lineman at Stephen F. Austin forty-odd years ago. "When it got to where I couldn't get to .500, I thought somebody else should take a shot. Sure, I could've used the million dollars, but I wasn't desperate. This is a league that has a great retirement plan for coaches. When you coach as long as I did (fifteen years in the NFL) and if you make as much as I did in your last five years, you earn the maximum, and the maximum ain't bad. Under their retirement plan, they'll be payin' me $90,000 a year for the rest of my life. Man cain't make it on $90,000, his livin' expenses are too high."

III

The difference between Phillips' town and some of the other little towns on the flatlands along the gulf is that Rosharon has a stop-and-go light, reportedly the envy of Sandy Point, and even Guy, Texas. Although no other vehicle is anywhere in sight, Phillips waits for the green light before turning left and heading north. He's driving a late-model red pickup truck that boasts many of the comforts of civilization, things like power windows and a cassette player. Carrying his music with him, Phillips puts on a country tape. He never listens to the radio. "I don't need the news," he remarks idly, turning the volume down a bit. "If they have a war, I figure someone will tell me."

The music reminds him of his early days in Beaumont, Texas, where his father, an auto mechanic, ran a dairy on the side. "Ain't much fun milkin' cows 367 days a year, twice a day," he says. "Way it is now, my calves nurse 'em." In childhood, Phillips, an inconspicuous member of a large family, had two role models, his grandfathers, who both lived well on giant Texas ranches. A century ago, one grandfather was a cattle driver on the old Chisholm Trail, which ran from San Antonio to the railhead in Abilene, Kansas.

"Them were the days," Phillips says.

Nineteen minutes up the road from the Oak Tree Ranch, Phillips turns into the driveway of his Dewalt residence, which he put up on a ten-acre lakeside plot when he was still coaching the Oilers. He first shows a visitor the little private lake. "I built it and stocked it (with fish) before I built the house," he says.

The dedicated angler in the Phillips family is Bum's wife, Helen. Because it's a twelve- or fifteen-minute walk around their lake, she uses a motorized golf cart equipped with a bait tank. "She fishes from the cart all the time, but she's no good at untangling lines," says Bum. "So I go along with her when I can, and watch her fish. I like that, 'cause she's a fine-looking woman. 'Course, I wouldn't've married any other kind."

All told, there are seven women in Phillips' life, including five married daughters. A small bumper sticker on Bum's pickup truck discloses the whereabouts of the other daughter, who is twenty. The sticker reads, "I am a TAM Dad." TAM is Texas A&M.

Inside his spreading ranch-type house there's a pleasing view of Lake Phillips from a living room about the size of the main dining room in a luxury hotel. A long, curving bar seats twenty-six, including, sometimes, all seven grandchildren. A domino table has a place of honor in front of the picture windows. "This is the first year I ever had time to play in the Texas state domino tournament," Phillips says. "But I ain't goin' to enter that again. They won't let you talk in them tournaments. You cain't say a word, and bee-essin' is half the fun of dominoes."

Phillips' big-screen TV is connected to a big satellite dish outside. "My wife sees all the Eagle games," he says. "Our son Wade is the defensive coordinator for Buddy Ryan."

Monitoring his wife instead of the screen, Bum is beginning to suspect that she prefers football to horses and the other baggage of ranch life. "I heard her on the phone one night," he says. "She was talkin' about the old days in New Orleans, an' she was sayin', 'The only place I ever went was a football game. And now he don't even take me there.'"

She drives a Mercedes. It's parked next to Bum's truck as he walks back outside to inspect the orchard that shades their house — the pear, peach, plum, fig and pecan trees he planted fifteen years ago. "A squirrel got all the pecans again this year," he says sadly. "Feller told me he'd loan me a gun to shoot the squirrel with, but after thinkin' it over, I said, 'No, thanks.' I told him that I'd go to the store and buy my pecans. That way I'll have some pecans and the squirrel, both."

IV

The one restaurant in Rosharon is more like a small coffee shop, with a few old wooden tables set out here and there. After ordering a hamburger, Phillips leans back as a young stranger carrying a camera walks up. "Recognized you the minute you come in," the young man drawls. "I'd sure love to have your picture. Mind if this guy takes you and I together?"

Phillips replies cheerfully: "My pleasure."

He is still a favorite of Southern sports fans and reporters, and also football players, particularly an old Hall of Famer named Earl Campbell. Having retired from football a very rich man, Campbell boards his horse at Phillips' ranch. "Last year, Earl asked me if he could keep it here two days," Phillips says. "Well, that ol' horse is still here. My barn, my feed. There's no one I like any better than Earl, but confidentially, he's a little close with his loose change. I never worried about Earl on drugs. You have to buy it, and he ain't goin' to buy it.'"

The economics of ranching are such that Campbell's money wouldn't help much even if he paid his way at Oak Tree. "This ain't a big-money business," Phillips says. "Everybody goes broke ranchin', eventually. The good thing about it is that if you play your dominoes right, it does take a long time. It takes longer to go broke on a ranch than almost anywheres else in America."

He leases, instead of buying, in order to stretch his cash reserves. "There's just no way to come out even these days raisin' cattle on land you own yourself," he says. "You cain't make the interest payments and come out."

If there's no money in it, why do it? Phillips thinks about this for an instant, then says: "I like to fool with horses, and watch things grow. On a ranch, you can see what you're accomplishin'. It's like coachin' football. Everythin' sets right out there in front of you. For fun I like to ride cuttin' horses. I raise 'em and train 'em and ride 'em, and you cain't do that in town."

And what are cutting horses? "You and your horse cut a calf out of a herd," Phillips says. "In a cuttin' horse contest, you got two and a half minutes to do your thing — make your horse behave just right while he's goin' after the calf. It's a great sport."

In this weather?

"This is beautiful weather," Phillips says. "I cain't stand snow and sleet and ice. They remind me of Pittsburgh."

In Texas, it's the neighbors who make life a joy in the ranch country, Phillips says. Neighbors are, among other things, the south Texas labor force. They come from miles around to help one another build, say, a new barn. "Man here cain't afford to hire much help," he says. "So we scratch each other's back. Take this here oat bin. Three neighbors and me put it up in ten hours. 'Course, only two of us were doin' much work. Two of us were laughin' an' tellin' jokes and drinkin' a hell of a lot of beer."

3. Gene Upshaw, All-Pro Labor Leader

WHEN THE full history of the hard, long drive for respectable working conditions in America is in the books, it seems probable that former Los Angeles Raiders All-Pro Gene Upshaw will rank as one of the century's most influential labor leaders — in or out of sports. On one big day, Upshaw killed his union in order to save it. *That*, certainly, made him stand out in the labor field. A Hall of Fame athlete, he has been a winner since his first game.

WASHINGTON, D. C.: June 12, 1993.

Gene Upshaw, the labor leader who ran the campaign that won free agency for pro football this year, was both captain and player rep of the Raiders during their winning era. And recalling those heady days, his former teammates say they've never known a more inspirational leader than the old pro who has spent the last ten of his forty-seven years struggling against the National Football League's twenty-eight club owners.

At the team meeting that made the most enduring impression on the Raiders, Upshaw, then a veteran Pro Bowl guard, stood up a week before one Super Bowl game, and told the coaches: "I've heard that you want a curfew starting Friday night, but we're changing that. We're starting the curfew tonight."

Then he glared around the room to see if anyone disagreed. Nobody did — not even the club's most famous playboys — and presently, the well-rested Raiders won the game. "Gene knew he could do that because he always knows what football players are thinking," Richard Berthelsen, his chief counsel, says.

That, in fact, is what Upshaw is all about. During his Hall of Fame career, he made it a point to maintain a close personal relationship with everyone else in pro ball — even rookies. "I think he was the only NFL player who ever knew every other player in the league," an aide, Doug Allen, says.

Upshaw's other priority, Allen adds, is, "Winning."

As a winner, he began as a pulling guard. Employed by the 1967-82 Raiders in two cities, Oakland and Los Angeles, Upshaw played the game with concentrated aggression. "Pulling to lead a sweep was my play," he says. "Receivers want catches. Defensive linemen want sacks. I got my satisfaction pulling out of the line to lead a running back sweeping around end. That's a play that comes down, at the end, to just me and one man. If I block him clean, we're going to make a long gain. If I miss him, we don't get a yard. So my goal was to crush him."

Upshaw in his playing days disapproved of any other way to proceed. He remembers with mild disdain the cute blocking schemes used in Miami by the offensive line of the Larry Csonka-era Dolphins — blockers who tricked defensive players as often as they blocked them head-on. "I couldn't believe the junk blocking that line got away with," Upshaw says. "They called it misdirection. Misdirection, hell. On the Raiders, you blew your man off the ball, or they got someone who could."

But the world looks different to a labor leader — particularly a pro football labor leader. You can't blow a rich bunch of club owners off the ball — they're much too tough for that — and Upshaw showed the flexibility to adjust.

He won with misdirection.

II

To beat the NFL this year, Upshaw needed, above all, the continuing support of the players, whose inclination for years has been to see themselves as brilliant, talented individual contractors, not union members. Somehow, in the crunch, Upshaw kept their support and prevailed. "Gene is a born politician. We used to call him Governor," says his former Raider roommate, Art Shell, who coaches the club now. Says Allen, the NFLPA's assistant executive director: "I remember the day that Gene went down a list of nearly a thousand players and told me how each of them differed (on a controversial matter)."

If that sounds impossible, consider a little thing that Upshaw did earlier this year, when, returning to his Washington office, he picked up forty-seven telephone messages — from his lawyers, his wife, friends, co-workers, newspaper reporters, Commissioner Paul Tagliabue, and one player, Freeman McNeil. Stacking the messages on his desk in order of priority, he called McNeil first. "In this shop," Upshaw says, "nobody comes before a player."

With that commitment, Upshaw in recent months has achieved smartly in three historic ways:

• As an AFL-CIO vice president, he has become one of the most powerful labor leaders in America. Says Southern California AFL-CIO chief Bill Robertson: "Our three bright lights are Richard Trumka of the Mine Workers, Ron Carey of the Teamsters and Upshaw."

• As one of hundreds who have fought the NFL over the years, Upshaw has become the first to bring the rich and mighty old league to its knees. Pro football's club owners, united and unbending, had held off free agency for three-quarters of a century before Upshaw dropped them this year — in the courts and then at the bargaining table — freeing hundreds of players.

• Upshaw has emerged, finally, as one of a small handful of Americans who have found extraordinary success in two prominent, very different fields. Of the thousands who have played pro football since Red Grange, Upshaw is one of only 165 in the Hall of Fame. And of the thousands who have led labor unions since Samuel Gompers, Upshaw is one of the few spectacular winners.

Says Commissioner Tagliabue: "The explanation is that Gene has shown the same level of ability at the NFLPA that he showed on the field."

III

It was less than six years ago that Upshaw and his players, taking one blow after another from the owners of NFL clubs, hit bottom. To begin with, the owners broke an NFLPA strike with what they called replacements and the players called scabs. Then, after the NFLPA voted to end that strike in time for the sixth weekend of a torn season, the owners decided to teach the players another lesson, locking them out — without pay — for still another week. "The owners rubbed their noses in it," says former Commissioner Pete Rozelle.

Finally, a few months later, a U.S. Appeals Court ruled that although a 1982 bargaining agreement had lapsed, the players' union was still bound by its provisions. Spectacularly one-sided, this decision meant that there was no reason for the owners to deal with the union again — and most of them never meant to.

Depressed but unyielding, Upshaw called his staff together in Washington the next morning to consider a new game plan. In his view, he had four options. He could (1) sign with the owners on their terms and resume the NFLPA's age-old bargaining for incidental perks, such as more meal money. He could (2) start another court case in a different district and hope for a better result. He could (3) resign. Or he could (4) run a misdirection play, disbanding the NFLPA. Union commitments to the owners, made in 1982, would no longer be valid if there were no union.

In the end, astounding some associates, he adopted (4).

"If the owners can ignore us for as long as we're a union, then we won't be a union anymore," Upshaw said, making one of the century's most dramatic and far-reaching labor decisions.

The surprise action stirred many doubters — few unions ever willingly decertify — but it is regarded today as one of the century's boldest moves by a union leader. "It was brilliant strategy," Robertson says from his AFL-CIO office.

Rozelle, who wasn't involved in the negotiations, says: "To my knowledge, the owners had never considered a situation where the union would cease to exist. Under labor law, they could have stonewalled Upshaw indefinitely. Decertification changed everything."

What it changed the most was the courtroom status of the players. Left alone to face the owners as individuals, they became, instantaneously, free agents. Since the players no longer had their union, the owners could no longer use the old agreement with that union as a shield against antitrust allegations. Freeman McNeil and other players whose contracts had expired, shopping themselves around the league, got no offers, then used this obvious collusion by the owners as the basis for an antitrust suit.

And in a series of legal proceedings in Judge David Doty's district court in Minneapolis, judge and jury both ruled for the players. Suddenly, it was the owners who faced the hard choices. They could either (1) risk their net worth in antitrust cases, (2) accept total free agency with no draft of college players, or (3) crawl back to Upshaw and make a deal. In the end, they adopted (3), whereupon he certified the union once again.

Upshaw watchers say, however, that it wasn't all quite as easy as it sounds now. His game plan wasn't unanimously popular in the NFLPA — and in any case, keeping millionaire athletes in line is never easy. "Our strategy wouldn't have succeeded without Upshaw," Berthelsen says. "Winning took all the personal leadership and courage that Gene could muster."

The NFL in its long fight against Upshaw fought him with everything it had. For one thing, needing an agreement from a union of some kind to justify their annual collusion in the player draft, the owners continuously sought to overthrow him. In three instances, they strongly backed three former players who had set out to organize pliant new unions. Moreover, at a time when Upshaw commanded the loyalty of ninety-three per cent of his membership, NFL executives repeatedly said, "The player sentiment I hear most often is, 'Save us from our union.'"

Most threatening of all — and most mean-spirited — the owners struck at Upshaw's revenue base: the NFLPA's licensing arrangements for trading cards and other products. They offered large cash sums to players who would abandon the NFLPA and sign exclusive licensing permits with the league.

Union people say that during the most bitter stages of the big fight, the public was generally unaware of just how rocky the road was for Upshaw. Three potholes were particularly deep:

• To begin with, as the leader of a football players' union, he was negotiating with uniformly prosperous club owners who could have resisted a settlement indefinitely. Indeed, without some key Upshaw compromises, they would be resisting still.

• The NFL's club owners were, in addition, some of the toughest individuals who have ever owned sports teams. They had invariably fought every other NFLPA leader — and until this year, they had invariably won.

• A majority of the owners had said publicly, and frequently, that they would oppose player free agency forever. Thus, more than their money was at stake, and more than their will. Repeatedly, they had committed themselves in public — putting their pride on the line.

The effect of all this was to put Upshaw's career on the line. The union had so much at stake that if the owners had won, Upshaw, almost certainly, would have been forced out. "But he didn't waver once,"

Berthelsen says. "Weaker people would have settled sooner, for less. Gene's leadership was decisive."

IV

On Texas' gulf coast, Kingsville, population twenty-five thousand, is the big town between Corpus Christi and Brownsville. And, once, Upshaw knew Kingsville well. Thirty years ago, the oldest of three sons of an oil field roustabout, he hitchhiked the twenty-four miles from his birthplace at Robstown to start a new life there at Texas A&I. "My father gave me $75 and sent me off to get an education," Upshaw says. "He also wanted me to play college baseball, and hopefully sign a pro baseball contract sometime."

But on the way to baseball practice one day, Eugene Thurman Upshaw II stopped to watch football practice. And soon the football coach came over to ask him why he was just standing there. When Upshaw showed some interest, "he gave me a uniform, and three days later gave me a scholarship," the union leader recalls.

At Texas A&I, he began as a six-footer weighing 205 pounds. "I grew to six-five and 260 in one semester," he says. "That's five pounds more than I weigh today." Still big enough now to deal as an equal with active players, Upshaw, who runs and lifts weights to stay in shape, looks, acts and seems younger than his years. He is apparently a born leader. "You could always talk to Gene," Rozelle says. "He handled himself very well."

Upshaw, who lives in Great Falls, Virginia, with his wife, Gerri, and their two sons — an older son is in college in Florida — remembers that he had his first brush with the outside world during the college bowl season of 1966-67, his last year at Texas A&I. "I was an unknown from an unknown school when they invited me to the Senior Bowl," he says. "I played with guys who had never heard of either me or Texas A&I, but it was a thrill to play with the best players of my generation: Bubba Smith, Gene Washington, Bob Griese, Steve Spurrier, Floyd Little, Mel Farr, Nick Eddy, George Webster, Alan Page."

Six months later, Upshaw was invited to a bigger show, the Chicago All-Star game. New venue, same players. And one day Griese and Little called a players-only meeting. By then, the unknown from the unknown school was everybody's friend. He was elected captain, unanimously. "I'm sure he was a humane captain," the AFL-CIO's Robertson says. "Gene is a man of common decency who doesn't try to intimidate people. He has the sense of compassion that the great labor leaders all have."

In his management style, his associates say, Upshaw is unpretending, open-handed and open-minded. "I don't think of myself as a (labor boss)," he says. "My philosophy is that the NFLPA only has one boss: the players. I have a great lawyer, Dick Berthelsen, and a great assistant, Doug Allen, and I'd be a fool not to give them the flexibility to be as creative as they've shown they can be."

An employee who watched Upshaw visiting with a letter carrier at the NFLPA building one day says: "Gene is the only one I know who treats everybody the same." That is a result, no doubt, of Upshaw's background. "My earliest memory is picking cotton in the Texas heat," he says. "My brothers and I were out in the fields every day, from dawn to night, well into our teens. You don't feel like pushing people around when you remember the years you spent tearing up your hands picking cotton."

v

During his playing career, Upshaw's former teammates and opponents say, he built himself into one of the most reliable blockers in league history. And so in a Raider huddle one day, when Quarterback Ken Stabler seemed stumped for a third-down call, Fullback Mark van Eeghen spoke up. "Let's take it down Highway 63," he recommended. Said Stabler: "Great idea. Let's go."

For sixteen years, 63 was Upshaw's uniform number — and Highway 63 was the area that Upshaw cleared on sweeps ahead of his running backs. And as usual that time, he swept the other team's cornerback away. First down.

Only one other thing about Upshaw was perhaps as influential in defining him as a player. And that was his studied determination not to take his talent for granted. "Every year when I headed for training camp, I never had a job, the way I figured it," he says. "I always went in fighting for a starting position."

He has run the NFLPA about the same way, fighting for his job every morning, striving for peace in his time. And when a peaceful solution was reached this year, Upshaw was applauded, understandably, by most NFLPA members.

By some, though, he was second-guessed for one major decision: He agreed to a cap on player salaries that will settle in eventually at fifty-eight per cent of most NFL revenues. Salaries that would in time have gone through the roof have apparently been blocked for at least the rest of this century.

Accordingly, some players are complaining, mostly players who don't understand that there's a significant signing-bonus loophole in what has been inaccurately termed a "hard" cap. Their goal was total free agency, with no brakes whatever on spending by the owners, and some highly-placed NFL stars are publicly taking out their frustrations on Upshaw.

He talks back like a statesman. "Total free agency would have been unhealthy for the players as well as the owners," he says, mentioning the need for a draft to maintain competitive balance. "Our union and the league both made major compromises in a win-win situation. The NFLPA wants the NFL to be successful. We're all better off if both sides are making a lot of money."

That attitude, as conciliatory as it is enlightened, is a match for the creativity and raw courage Upshaw showed during the negotiations. The combination has led neutral critics to maintain that Upshaw clearly deserves the notices he's getting, the recognition as the most successful labor boss in sports history. His legacy is that, for better or worse, the league will never be the same.

4. Bobby Knight Stirs Up the Hoosiers

FROM THE age of thirty, basketball Coach Bobby Knight has been a major league winner. Along the way, he has done some controversial things; and in company with such other winners as George Allen, Al Davis, and Woody Hayes, he has been a media outcast — even outlaw in the reckoning of some reporters. But I'm not overwhelmed with curiosity about Knight's techniques as a chair-thrower. What I went to Indiana to see him about in 1976 was how he wins basketball games. Eventually he won every one that year, including the NCAA title game. In the long intervals between his outrageous acts, Knight, who answers these days to both Bob and Bobby, plainly does some things right.

> *Gloriana, Frangipana,*
> *E'er to her be true!*
> *She's the pride of Indiana,*
> *Hail to old IU.*
> — INDIANA UNIVERSITY
> ALMA MATER

BLOOMINGTON, Ind.: March 5, 1976.
If the recent history of college basketball belonged to UCLA, the immediate future could belong to Indiana. Since the retirement of John Wooden, sixty-four, his heir has seemed to be the Indiana University wonderkid, Bobby Knight, thirty-five. Nobody today, in any case,

compares with Knight, whose Indiana Hoosiers have won more regular-season games consecutively (fifty-six) than any other basketball team in the history of his conference.

In the seventy-eighth year of the Big Ten, this is Knight's fifth season at this university, and he has now coached four straight Big Ten champions.

Before Knight, IU had won only thirty-four of its last eighty-four conference starts, and, after that long drought, they're living it up here again in the heartland of American basketball. On game days, the state legislature adjourns early, day or night, to make the first tipoff. Indianapolis clubs, men's and women's alike, meet only on Knight's nights off. Movie theaters are all but deserted when the Hoosiers play. (Home games are all televised live by at least one Indiana station and sometimes by six or seven.) And next day, old friends greet each other not with "Good morning," but "We're number one."

Although it isn't true that basketball was invented in Indiana, it took root here early, and has always seemed the best way to spend an Indiana winter. But here as elsewhere, rabid interest in basketball depends on games won, and there was little that was rabid about those who followed the Hoosiers during the slump that lasted from the 1950s through the '60s and into the '70s.

The frenzy of the Knight era, accordingly, is two things. It is a fusion of old Hoosier basketball interest — nationally recognized, but lately dormant — with the excitement provided by a gifted new coach.

II

Bobby Knight, as he appears to all comers, is a tough, blunt, smart loner — as candid as he is unbending. Born a hundred and fifty years too late, he belongs on the Indiana frontier with the original Hoosiers, the pioneers who got things going in this state. He is (or could be) the alert, reclusive old Hoosier on Indiana's 1976 license plates. In an interview, he suggests the following for his headstone: "He was honest, and he kissed no man's ass."

Asked to expand on that thought, Knight says: "I can't think of a more fitting epitaph. It isn't my way to pat someone on the back in public and cut their heart out in the next room. I know I turn a lot of people off, but it's difficult for me ever to be anything but straightforward."

The only human qualities he seems to admire are courage and integrity. He has admitted that he doesn't like people. And he has said that he dislikes women particularly "because of their insincerity." When the subject comes up again, the young coach blurts out: "How many persons can you really count on, women *or* men? Think back over your lifetime. Most people are not only unreliable, they cheat."

Knight doesn't drink or smoke, and he kicks reporters out of his office if they light up. He also agrees with Byron that he is "never less alone than when alone." The Knight hobbies are those of the classic introvert, fishing and reading. "I don't get any pleasure out of being around a bunch of people I don't know," he says. "Cocktail parties are impossible for me to take, especially the inane chatter of so many women. The kind of thing I enjoy is being somewhere, anywhere, by myself."

He is saying all this quietly, matter of factly, on a game day in his office, a comfortable, red-carpeted room on coaches' row in Assembly Hall. It is late afternoon, and as his players rest, Knight retreats to his desk to answer his mail and a few questions. One on one with an out-of-town interviewer, he is personable and accommodating, a big man in a yellow sweater, a bigger, more youthful model of California's Governor Jerry Brown.

Not long removed from his boyhood, Knight says his idols have been Thomas Edison, George Washington, Ted Williams, Woody Hayes, Pete Rose and John Havlicek. "I like their dedication," he says. "Williams' ambition was to have people say as he walked down the street: 'There goes the greatest hitter who ever lived.' He's my kind."

III

At a recent Hoosier basketball game in Bloomington, where the issue was never in doubt, the cheerleaders went wild, along with the crowd, after every free throw. By the last play of the game, when Indiana beat Iowa by an even twenty points (!) with its final layup, 101-81, everybody was limp. The 17,691 spectators, 1,023 over capacity, had erupted with a dozen standing ovations, including two just for the coach.

Throughout the game, Knight was up and down as usual, lecturing the officials and his players indiscriminately. His floor-side deportment, which non-Indiana fans find so offensive, obviously pleases most Indiana fans, who watch him closely. He is part of the show. A striking, animated figure in his customary game-night uniform (bright polyester jacket, dark pants, tie loosened at the throat), Knight, who is six feet five, spent the entire Iowa game individually coaching somebody, player or referee. He was on his feet twenty-nine times in the first half alone to eighteen for Iowa coach Lute Olson, who, the Iowa writers said, was "much more active than usual."

At almost every break, Knight was out on the floor with his arm around a player, yelling in his ear. When the ball was in play, Knight could only stand and shout instructions. When he couldn't make himself heard, he sent in a substitute, and sat the exiting player down — correcting him on the spot before allowing him to return. It looked more like an Indiana practice than a game. Few basketball coaches, and none in football, coach so much when the game is on.

Knight finished each conversation the same way, with a swinging pat to the player's rump. On one occasion, when he seemed particularly upset with sophomore Wayne Radford, the pat was more of a spank — sending a surprisingly loud murmur through the big crowd. Looking up, startled, Knight made it a point to call Radford over again a moment later, and this time he let him off with a tap.

The attitude of the Indiana players to their coach was one of patient obedience or submission, almost subservience. They weren't taller (nor did they seem to be athletically better) than Iowa's, but all had been handpicked in recent years by Knight, who plainly recruits talent of a particular type. His word for what he seeks: "coachable." Translation: no trouble-making free thinkers need apply.

This is a coach who is sure he has the answers. And what he wants are players who want Knight's answers. Plainly, there are still enough such athletes around for a five-man sport, at least in Indiana.

IV

On the day after the game, in unseasonably warm weather, the Hoosier victory was replayed at length downtown by Bloomington's businessmen and professional men. In front of their shops and offices, they stood in shirt sleeves talking in the welcome sunshine that flooded the four wide streets surrounding the old domed courthouse here in Bloomington Square. This is the financial heart of Hoosierdom.

A typical Midwest college town (except for the square), Bloomington has more big trees and fewer big buildings than most. Otherwise, the downtown area is a place of generally neat but characterless shops and stores. The wooded Indiana University campus sprawls over half of the city, the half east of College Street, whose proliferation of fast-food dispensaries identifies the area immediately as a college community. Most of the seventy-five thousand who live in Bloomington attend the university or work there or are married to people who do. More than thirty-two thousand are full-time students.

Laid out on 1,850 mostly flat acres, IU is distinguished mainly by its forests. There are so many college buildings and residence halls separated by so many trees on so many streets that the university operates its own fleet of full-size city buses. Those riding or walking under the trees look much like California college students, the boys in jeans and long hair, the girls in long hair and jeans. Their sweaters and shoes are a little heavier here, and at night they wear mittens. But as in California, the only girls who look like girls are the cheerleaders, and the only boys who look like boys are the athletes.

Indiana's athletic plant stands on a former cattle pasture north of the main campus. The dominant structure is a fifty-two-thousand-seat football stadium built fifteen years ago. This is separated by a parking lot from the new basketball headquarters in Assembly Hall. The Hall was completed in 1972 — and that seemed like a good time to bring in a new coach.

For although IU has been playing basketball since 1901, it has been less successful than you would expect of a state university in the nation's basketball hotbed. Before Knight, there were only two productive IU eras, those of Everett Dean, who finished .571 in the Big Ten, and Branch McCracken, .644. By contrast, in the same conference, Knight is over .850 — with only ten defeats in five years.

The man who turned things around for Indiana is not, however, a native. Knight is from Ohio, where his father was a railroad man and his mother a thirty-eight-year-old schoolteacher when he was born in 1940. At Ohio State twenty years later, he played on an NCAA champion and three Big Ten champions, then joined the U.S. Army, which sent him to West Point. He was twenty-four when he became head coach at Army, where in six years he was 6-0 over Navy and 102-50 overall.

With his blonde wife, Nancy, and two sons, Knight lives on three wooded acres at the edge of Bloomington in a neighborhood of $100,000 to $150,000 houses. His $34,000 salary is believed to be less than a third of his annual income, most of which derives from TV, speeches, endorsements and a lucrative summer basketball school. He says he will "never coach" pro basketball. The critics who compare Knight to Woody Hayes believe he'd fail in the NBA because, as one said, "older athletes won't put up with his dictatorial methods."

Citing his bluntness and ruthlessness, Knight's critics point to the Michigan game this year when he grabbed one of his players — sophomore Jim Wisman, who had made two consecutive mistakes — and pulled him off the floor by his shirt. The scene was recorded by an Indiana photographer and made newspapers all over the country.

On Knight's squad the effect was minimal (the Hoosiers went on winning as usual) but the incident started a war with a prominent local newspaper, the Indianapolis Star, that isn't over yet. When the Star covered the top half of its front page with two pictures of the incident, Knight was enraged. "I doubt if anything in the last five years has meant more to this state than this basketball team," he said coldly, "and this was the first time we'd ever been out there on page one."

Thereupon he devoted a part of his television program to an attack on the Star, which, after fencing awhile with the many angry Hoosier fans who kept tying up its switchboard, responded by printing Knight's unlisted telephone number. "Don't call us," said Sports Editor Bob Collins, one of Indiana's best-read humorists, "call him."

Knight, still peeved, refers to that as another cheap shot. "It sure was," Collins agrees merrily.

Characteristically, Knight came out of the fight ahead. First, he subtly extricated himself from an unflattering mess with a player, shifting the public's attention to a journalistic scapegoat. Second, he hardened his position as a man of strength and courage who will fight anybody, even a powerful newspaper. Everyone knows that now.

V

On the basketball floor in this era, Indiana players are as feisty as their leader, but they're no longer the "Hurryin' Hoosiers" of the old legends. Knight is a defensive coach who favors a set offense and a game of movement. On the occasions when the Hoosiers pass the ball twenty times before laying it in, they discover, upon laying an eye on the bench, that Knight is seated, content, maybe even smiling, and doubtless dreaming his championship dream.

There are those who say he isn't a great basketball coach. What he has mastered is a way to dominate a five-man team as if there were five Bobby Knights out there. More than most basketball teams in any era, the Hoosiers seem to be the literal extension of their coach. Indiana forward Scott May, a six-foot-seven All-American, puts it like this: "The only way I know is to work. There's really not any time for the night life or the girls for me. Maybe I've missed some things in college life because of basketball, but I don't regret it a bit."

Then there's the case of Jim Wisman, the player Knight hauled off by the shirt. "He made me a promise after that," Wisman says, winking. "He promised he'd get me a break-away shirt."

The feud Knight carried on with a newspaper and its executives after the Wisman incident hasn't extended to the working press. "A reporter has to make a living same as I do," he says. Thus, unlike some coaches, he regularly opens his locker room to sportswriters. "It's part of a player's education to talk to the press," says Knight, indicating a faith in his players that other coaches lack. At UCLA, Wooden infuriated working reporters by keeping them away from, among others, his star player, Lew Alcindor (later Kareem Abdul Jabbar) — a policy that helped make Wooden one of the least publicized of all big winners.

At Indiana, no doubt, Knight's secret is that he trusts his players because he only recruits those he can trust. He gets that kind with a unique recruiting system. On his team it isn't the coaches but the players who have the last word on whether a given prospect gets a basketball scholarship. "When we bring in a kid for a visit," Knight says, "we always have our players go out with him, to dinner, or perhaps a movie. If they turn him down, that's it. We don't recruit him." Last summer when they turned down an all-state prep star that Knight was sure he wanted, the boy was packed off within the hour.

Pressed to define the kind of athletes who have made Indiana University number one, Knight thinks a moment. When he answers, he ignores all athletic considerations. "We recruit players who don't make jerks of themselves," he says.

5. Charlie O. Finley: Baseball's Greatest Leader

BASEBALL HAS fallen in the popularity polls in recent years, slipping well behind football, but it wouldn't have happened if the game's leaders had named Charlie O. Finley commissioner. He was too abrasive for them, but he was the smartest of the bunch.

LA PORTE, Ind.: July 7, 1987.

One summer in the 1970s when Charlie O. Finley owned the Oakland A's, his best player, Reggie Jackson, stopped hitting home runs during a long batting slump that pained Finley as much as Jackson. Finally, reasoning that he needed Jackson to win another World Series, Finley called him in.

Defiant, Jackson asked, "You want something?"

"Yes, Reggie," the owner replied patiently. "I'm going to tell you what your problems are. Your big problem — you're not going to like this, Reggie — you think you're God. And you're all wrong about that," Finley continued, his voice rising. "*I'm* God."

Years later, Jackson said: "I'll always believe he meant it."

There isn't much doubt that Finley, who at sixty-nine still runs an insurance business in Chicago and lives on an Indiana farm, owned baseball's largest ego in the era when his club won three straight World Series in 1972-73-74. Then as now a big, restless, abrasive dictator type with white hair and bushy eyebrows, Finley had talked himself into believing that he knew a great deal more about baseball than anyone else. And he probably did. Even considering the people who built the old New York Yankees — baseball committee types, mostly — this guy might have been the greatest of all baseball executives. "But nobody realizes it," a former employee, George Costa, says, speaking from Oakland, where he is director of stadium operations. "Charlie O. is the most underrated winner of all time."

The facts: Finley's team is the only one that ever won five consecutive divisional titles. His is the only club — aside from the Yankees — that ever won as many as three consecutive World Series. His living monuments today are (1) designated hitters, that American League abomination, and (2), much more impressively, World Series night games and World Series weekend openers.

Even more significant, in any evaluation of Finley's impact on baseball, is the way it all ended for him in Oakland. It wasn't Finley's doing. It wasn't Finley who messed up. He was the classic case of a great man in the wrong place at the wrong time.

To begin with, Finley had been a maverick owner. Coming into baseball as a one-man gang, he made himself the master of a game long dominated by the big, glossy organizations, the Yankees, Dodgers, St. Louis Cardinals and others. And his beloved ballclub, the mid-1970s Oakland Athletics (or A's), with a hammerlock on their sport, seemed headed for a long run at the top when Finley was suddenly overtaken and crushed by an unforeseen sequence of revolutionary procedural changes in the game. "For sure, the old firebrand wasn't beaten on the field," says one of his high school classmates, Tom Harmon, the Michigan All-American.

In fact, Finley was only beaten by the weight of the four great, game-altering forces of the 1970s: arbitration, free agency, central scouting and the college player draft. As any sports student can see, those mighty forces have remade baseball entirely from what it was in its first century, rebuilding it into a game indulged in by millionaire players playing for multimillionaire owners.

In the days when Finley emerged as the maker of Oakland's World Series champions, he was well off but hardly wealthy, the possessor of a neat little fortune that he had dredged up selling insurance. He could win when the game was table-stakes, but not when it was no-limit. Not in Oakland — a football town where the A's only filled the stadium on Hot Pants Night. Thus the bitter end for Charlie Finley, whose story could be seen as a Greek tragedy if the leading character weren't so Irish.

At the time that Finley bought into baseball twenty years ago, there had been no basic alterations in the rules and regulations and by-laws of baseball for three quarters of a century. He played and won by the same rules that governed the Yankee committees in the years when they were winning four and five World Series in clusters. These rules included an inflexible reserve clause and other restrictions on player movement that had enslaved the help in every baseball generation since the beginning more than a hundred years ago.

Finley was in his fifties in his big decade, the 1970s, and his grasp of major league baseball, as played since 1884, was so sure-handed that none could match him. Then, in the middle of the game, baseball changed the rules on him. Under the old rules, he could have won for, conceivably, another twenty years. Under the new rules — which require big money for free agents and for the players succeeding in arbitration suits — he couldn't win at all.

The landmark date was 1973, when baseball's club owners took an absurdly stupid view of their little world. After beating back Outfielder Curt Flood in a major antitrust case, the owners, flushed with victory, agreed thoughtlessly, fatuously, to install a system of arbitration with their players. Not long thereafter, Finley became the first victim. The A's had only just won their third straight World Series when Finley lost his best pitcher, Jim (Catfish) Hunter, to an arbitrator's decision. "We got to the 1975 playoffs without Catfish," Finley says, recalling the A's fifth straight division-winning season. "We got there. We couldn't go on."

It misses the point to suggest that Finley may have been at fault in the Hunter case. The point is that he was the first smart baseball man who had to tell it to an arbitrator. The old Yankees were never in danger of losing Joe DiMaggio to arbitration. They could never have lost Lefty Gomez or Yogi Berra. Yet in less than two years, Finley lost not only Hunter but the bulk of his extraordinary team to the new rules of the game. Free agency — a phrase that Babe Ruth never heard — cost the A's such World Series stars as Jackson, Sal Bando, Joe Rudi, Rollie Fingers, Ken Holtzman and Bert Campaneris, among others.

The draft completed the destruction of the A's, who, like the old Yankees, had been put together by clever bush-beating scouts — in this case by Finley himself, mainly. Although the draft technically began in 1965, Finley's competition wasn't smart enough to hurt him with it until central scouting arrived to do the headwork for everybody in the 1970s.

The 1966 draft had been typical. To begin with, Finley, as usual, had identified the year's number-one prospect, a lad named Reggie Jackson. But the New York Mets, drafting first, chose one Steve Chilcott, a catcher who has yet to play a big league game. Then Finley drafted Jackson, capitalizing on the kind of blunder that can no longer be made by the Mets, or anyone else, in the age of central scouting.

"The draft was the beginning of the end of free enterprise," Finley says.

And of Finley.

I sacrificed my wife to the A's.
— FINLEY

In a hotel dining room, the waiter appears in due course at Finley's table and starts taking orders. "I'd like the prime rib," his companion says. Finley, sizing up the waiter, says, "I'd like to see the chef." And with that, the three-time World Series winner is off for the kitchen. Returning a few minutes later, he explains: "It's easy to screw up Lake Superior whitefish. I always tell the cooks what to do."

It was in that spirit that he ran his ballclub, and he still runs his life that way. He is a tyrant. He is a gourmet. And also a gourmet chef. "Today, my two hobbies are cooking and eating," says Finley, who looks it. And, happily for him, he can spend much of his time on a farm, where he raises most of the entrees: Blue Channel catfish, chicken, wild duck, even deer.

A La Porte, Indiana, ornament, the farm, in a manner of speaking, saved his life. When the A's and his marriage crashed at the same time ten years ago, the farm became an outlet for Finley's astounding energy. He doesn't, be advised, ride any tractors, but he has a heck of a lot to say to the men who do.

He came to this end down a strange road. One of three children of a Birmingham steel worker, Charlie worked with his dad in the mills for many years after the family moved to Gary, Indiana. On the side, he managed semi-pro baseball teams and sold insurance, putting away a few dollars before marrying his high school sweetheart. They were to have seven children.

Pretty conventional stuff, you say, but there's more:

• In his twenties, when Charlie fell ill and went into a sanitarium for two years with tuberculosis, his wife kept body and soul and the children together with a job as a proofreader on a Gary newspaper.

• In his thirties, when Charlie recovered, he used his newly acquired knowledge of the medical business to become a millionaire overnight by selling group disability insurance to doctors.

• So at forty-two, he had the money and nerve to buy the worst team in baseball, the old Kansas City A's, for $1.9 million.

• He struggled in Kansas City for seven years, then moved and began struggling in Oakland. "It's a long way up when you see it from the absolute bottom," he says. "You can't possibly average more than one or two new World Series-quality players a year. It takes a long, long time to reach the top."

He was fifty-three when he got there, but after winning his first divisional title in 1971 he knew he could stay there. "When you get the foundation right, hard work will keep you going," he says. "All you need to win baseball games forever is one good, new acquisition a season."

That's all — he means — in a world without arbitrators. At fifty-seven, they beat him. Then his wife left him. She has since remarried. "I sacrificed my wife to the A's," Finley says. "Had I not been such a baseball workaholic, I'd have my family with me today."

His last move in Oakland was to sell the A's — for $12 million — but he got to keep only a little of that for himself. "For tax reasons, Charlie had put two-thirds of the club in the names of his wife and children," says his Chicago banker, Fred Sack. "And they wouldn't give it back. They outfoxed him and kept it all. All Charlie got was one-third, less taxes."

In an acrid postscript, the judge awarded Finley's wife the largest of his two farms — the 1,200-acre, $500,000 spread edging the west side of La Porte. From king of the hill, Finley had fallen to the bottom.

That barn over there set him back a million dollars.
— ROLAND KUHN, La Porte, Ind., contractor.

No one can predict what any man will do in heartbreaking adversity. Depressed but still fighting, Finley drove across town and threw himself into his other farm, a 640-acre north-side spread. Picturesquely, it rolls along both sides of Highway 35, a stone's throw from Pine Lake. First off, Finley converted the house into a white-pillared Southern mansion.

Branching out, he next commissioned a large, unique painting of Reggie Jackson. Actually, it's more than a painting. It's a stained-glass window, with Jackson at bat, nearly life size, in radiant color. Then he ordered several other magnificent stained-glass windows. Finley is particularly fond of one that is an enlarged full-color reproduction of a 1975 Time magazine cover. It features Finley, no less, in a big green hat.

The painted windows would be strange enough if they were in his ten-room mansion, which was built in 1860 by a friend of Abraham Lincoln's. Instead, they're on the exterior walls of Finley's barn — a barn with stained glass windows.

It is, unquestionably, the craziest barn in Indiana, and no doubt the most expensive. It set the owner back an estimated $1 million in a county where you can put up a real nice barn for $25,000. In the melancholy aftermath of his estrangement from baseball and family, Finley poured much of his time and resources into the construction of this curious building, which, in addition to garish windows, has a big front porch. It's a lengthy, cool porch furnished with no fewer than six old-fashioned swings. On any given Sunday, Finley goes out to the barn and swings in the one with the most breeze and best view of Pine Lake.

Not to stint the upstairs, Finley put a ballroom in the barn's hayloft, complete with a grand piano for the pianists who come in with the big jazz bands to play from time to time. And, perched above the ballroom, on the barn's top floor, there is a fully furnished press box with a sweeping view of much of Finley's acreage. Above the press box, he has installed a gold-roofed bell tower. The bell rings at suppertime.

Downstairs, the stalls for the horses are each tastefully lined in one or another of five kinds of solid hardwood: oak, maple, walnut, birch or cherry. The hardwood is all at least two inches thick. The tack room in a corner is lined in two inches of mahogany. Why a walnut stall? "If you were a horse, wouldn't you want a nice place to stay?" Finley says. Why a press box on a farm? "I always wanted my own," he says. Near the hayloft, there is even a master bedroom with all the amenities, including what Finley defines as a shower for two. "He asked us to design and construct the barn," says an old friend, La Porte Contractor Roland Kuhn, whose son Steve is an architect.

The day they reported with the completed blueprints, Finley took one look and said: "This is just what I wanted, Rollie. But, let's see, I think we should make this wall here twenty feet longer. And while we're at it, let's put a kitchen in the tack room. And move the tack room there."

Smiling, Steve Kuhn slowly tore up the blueprints. "I don't think we'll be needing these, Mr. Finley," he said.

And building a barn for the ages, Finley, who in baseball had been his own general manager, served the construction crew as his own architect. Nobody who knows him would have expected anything else.

> *Charlie is living three or four years*
> *ahead of his time. Other owners are just not as sharp.*
> — JIM (CATFISH) HUNTER, A's pitcher, 1973.

One year during the All-Star break, Charlie Finley, promoting his newest idea, orange-colored baseballs, moved about the USA with a platoon of costumed Playboy bunnies. Wearing A's caps and high heels, the young women distributed samples and speculated earnestly that baseball would have more action with an orange ball because it would be easier to see and hit.

At the All-Star Game, one bunny even brought a gaudy orange baseball to a prominent spectator, Secretary of State Henry Kissinger. But first, the Secret Service people tapped the ball, shook it, bit it, and listened to it closely to make sure it wasn't ticking. When Kissinger had it at last, he stood up, and, as the nearest bunny smiled proudly, tipped his hat to Finley.

As an idea, the orange ball is still bottled up somewhere in the commissioner's cellar. But Kissinger is by no means the only sports fan who has — or who *should* have — tipped his hat to Finley. "Charlie's night-game idea has made it possible for thousands of working men to see the World Series every year," says one of them, a Gary banker, Jack Morfee. "People tell you he did it to get more TV money for baseball — but I know better. I know him. His dad worked next to my dad in the steel mills for thirty years. Charlie was thinking of those guys — the guys who can never get away to see daytime baseball."

Finley's arsenal of farsighted ideas combined with his studied flamboyance — hiring bunnies and mules and badgering players, commissioners, sportswriters and other owners — helped create a public image of him that is partially true. As many writers in Finley's time charged, he thought of himself as a deity who could routinely insult or humiliate anyone. But that is far from the whole truth about Finley. And worse, it obscures the main truth: that in his mastery of the art and science of baseball — in Oakland, of all places — Finley proved to be a near-genius.

If there's a Hall of Fame somewhere that will have him, he'll honor it.

To be sure, luck was a factor in the rise of the A's, as it always is in such instances, but it wasn't luck that took Finley in the early 1960s to the Macon, Georgia, home of a high school pitcher named John (Blue Moon) Odom. Making friends with the Odom family, Finley accepted their invitation to stay overnight, and the next day, adding to his reputation as a gourmet chef, he prepared and set out a big chicken dinner for the whole gang.

"There was also a Boston Red Sox scout there that week," Finley remembers. "Blue Moon's mother gave him one room and me the other. And I fed him, too."

But that's all the Red Sox got. It was the A's who got Odom, a frequent big-game winner for Finley thereafter.

In that era he also discovered and reeled in Catfish Hunter, who was to become the A's biggest winner. One winter, Finley moved into the Hunter home in Hertford, North Carolina, to stay a night or two during the Carolina state high school tournament. "Nicest curveball I'd ever seen from a high school arm," says Finley, who, in the pre-draft era, combined salesmanship with an eye for talent to build the team of the 1970s.

Among other young, true free agents he and his scouts found and signed in similar ways — in those last productive years before the draft — were Infielders Bert Campaneris and Dick Green, Outfielder Joe Rudi, Catcher Gene Tenace and Pitcher Rollie Fingers, each eventually a star on World Series teams. Moreover, in the early years of the draft, before central scouting, the A's found such players as Third Baseman Sal Bando in the sixth round and Pitcher Vida Blue in the second.

Strangely, that information has never been widely acknowledged by baseball's wealthier and more conventional club owners and executives. Despising Finley for one reason or another, they have mostly tried to ignore him. One exception, Frank Lane, the veteran trader-winner, once said: "Finley's a no-good s.o.b. . . . but he has made himself a thorough student of player talent. He calls all the shots (on the A's) and he's become a damn good manager. . . . That's right, I said manager."

He started early.

"I managed my first sandlot team when I was twelve," Finley says, "and I played semipro ball until I was thirty-two, and that's more than it takes to learn all there is to learn about baseball. I've sat in the stands with grandmothers who know baseball. That isn't the secret. The secret is having the courage to make a decision."

To many people, courage often seems more like arrogance. One of Finley's Chicago friends, Banker Fred Sack, remembers that in Oakland one day, he was shocked by the players' attitude toward the owner.

Walking with Finley through the A's locker room after a 1973 defeat, Sack sensed hostility in every face. "It was like walking among enemies," he says. "But for the first time, I realized that he criticized them on purpose. It was a motivation technique. He knew baseball so well that he knew exactly what they'd done wrong that day. They didn't want to hear it, but he had the courage to tell them anyway. And the next day they went out and took it out on Charlie. Every time they hit a home run, they were swinging at Charlie's head."

As Finley remembers it: "I got along well with the guys I wanted on my teams. The only arguments we ever had were over money." The players, looking back, see it about the same way. Few knock him. Tenace: "He was a hell of a general manager." Jackson: "He changed the game as no one else has."

Finley, it's clear now, was born twenty years too late. One of the two or three most effective sportsmen of all time, he was operating in an era that wouldn't tolerate baseball's slave drivers much longer. Nobody ever knew more about the old game — baseball's reserve-clause game — than he did. But the rules that made millionaires of his players made a farmer of Charlie Finley.

6. James Naismith Invents Basketball

IT SEEMS like I've known James Naismith all my life. Although I never met him, I can't remember when I wasn't impressed that a game as deceptively simple, as deceptively sophisticated, and as much fun to play as basketball emerged from the brain of one person. In the 1920s in Aberdeen, South Dakota, there was nothing else to do when it was too cold to skate, which was nearly every day from late fall until April. I also agree with Naismith that for sports fans, basketball is the least interesting spectator sport.

SPRINGFIELD, Mass.: March 29, 1988.

The year before James Naismith invented basketball in a gymnasium here ninety-seven winters ago, he was a twenty-nine-year-old college student who went out for football and played center. His coach that fall was a new young teacher, Amos Alonzo Stagg.

In time, Naismith was to become a medical doctor; but this was 1890, and as a student he only wore three hats. He was an ordained Presbyterian minister, a physical training specialist, and, putting on another hat — the first football helmet — he was a star lineman who played in football's first indoor game, against Yale, at New York's Madison Square Garden.

He invented the helmet himself.

Canadian born and a resident of Canada his first twenty-eight years, Naismith, who loved all contact sports, thoroughly enjoyed the life of an American football player. He just couldn't understand why Alonzo Stagg wanted him at center. So one day, as Naismith noted in a book he wrote at age eighty-five, three years before he died, he asked the coach for an explanation. Stagg told him: "Jim, I play you at center because you can do the meanest things in the most gentlemanly manner."

Plainly, Naismith played to win. It was the story of his athletic career. It follows that when he got around to creating a new sport, he created a winner — a game that was to join tennis and soccer as one of the three most widely played in the world. Today more Americans are into basketball than any other sport — by many thousand when you count pro, playground, college, high school and other players, young and old, male and female.

In total attendance, too, basketball ranks first among all U.S. games. "The crowds always surprised him," Naismith's grandson, Civil Engineer James P. Naismith, said the other day from Texas. "He would never have believed the Final Four could become one of the biggest spectacles in the world. He thought a game was something to be played, not seen."

Naismith was, in fact, a physical fitness nut who originated basketball in response to what might have been the first student protest movement on an American campus: the 1891 revolt against the boredom of compulsory gym classes at his school. Founded in 1885 as the School for Christian Workers, it is known now as Springfield College. The school's campus, as it appears to the 1988 visitor, stretches pleasantly along the shores of tree-lined Lake Massasoit, where, in all, there are two attractions: the college and the nearby Naismith Memorial Basketball Hall of Fame, which is celebrating its twentieth anniversary at Springfield in this year that the Final Four is celebrating its fiftieth anniversary at Kansas City.

Basketball is not much older. In 1991, the world's youngest big-time game will observe the centennial of an invention that was unprecedented in these unique respects:

• Of America's major sports, basketball was, and remains, the only intrinsic American game. The nation's other pastimes all evolved slowly from sports played in other lands.

Football, for instance, is rooted in soccer, whose beginnings are unclear. Baseball, often credited to Abner Doubleday in 1839, was played earlier than that and almost certainly evolved from the old English game of rounders. Hockey is a variation of field hockey, which was played in ancient Greece, and no doubt earlier, elsewhere. Tennis was the original sport of kings, probably French kings. Golf, long associated with Scotland, most likely grew out of a game taken there by the conquering Romans, or it might have begun in Sweden. And so on. Excepting only basketball, all grew haphazardly, over a period of many decades, in some instances over centuries.

• In 1891, by contrast, basketball was deliberately made in America by one man in one brief time period — about twenty-four hours.

Before Naismith, every interesting American game had been geared to the outdoors, leaving naught for the athletically inclined person to do — either outside or inside — when the wind chill factor made even an afternoon walk unbearable. Since Naismith, the difference that basketball has made to the United States is incalculable. Basketball is everywhere today, in every town and school, in nearly every neighborhood. And no one has ever been able to improve on it, or even match it, as an indoor game.

Accordingly, 127 years after he was born near Bennie's Corners, Ontario, Naismith continues to be the most underrated figure in modern sports. Considering what this naturalized American has meant to the America of any long winter, his was the greatest invention by any individual in sports history.

The achievement was, nonetheless, consistent with a man who had what it takes to excel in theology and medicine as well as sports. A farm boy orphaned at age eight, Naismith had displayed his venturesome nature as early as grade school, when, one winter afternoon, he took a horse-drawn sleigh out on an errand for his guardian, Peter Young, an uncle. Seeing a shortcut across what seemed to be a frozen river, Naismith unexpectedly drove the horses onto thin ice, where they crashed through and foundered in the deep water. At the risk of his life, the youngster jumped in and loosened the reins, then pulled first one horse and then the other to safety. "(As) I sat down on the bank to rest a minute, I turned to see if the horses were all right," Naismith reported many years later. "My uncle was standing back in the trees, watching me."

So the boy wasn't alone after all. But he had thought he was alone, and he had acted boldly — and effectively — on his own. It was a confidence-building lesson that he never forgot.

II

Possibly the most remarkable thing about basketball is that it was scientifically created. Each essential of the game was systematically thought out by Naismith before the first tipoff, including the tipoff itself and even the height of the basket, which he decided to place an even ten feet above the floor — where it has remained. Of Naismith's thirteen original rules, twelve, astonishingly, are still applicable.

In the beginning, there was nothing but a need for a new game, and in the 1890s the need was most urgently felt at Springfield. As a school for sports-minded YMCA workers, Springfield, specializing in a new field, had enrolled the nation's largest congregation of gym teachers and coaches, who were all experienced in calisthenics, gymnastics, apparatus exercises and related indoor activities, and who, therefore, were tired of them all. Instead, they wanted to play a game. All fall they had played football. All spring they would play baseball. Now, with snow a foot deep outside, they wanted somebody to give them a comparably entertaining game that could be played all winter — indoors.

The college first asked its two most experienced teachers to solve the problem. When they failed, the job was handed to the institution's newest and youngest teacher, Jim Naismith, age thirty. Thus was basketball created as a school assignment. The inventor, changing professions, had moved from Canada to America only the year before. He had come to Springfield for a physical education degree. Within twelve months he was on the faculty, and in December, 1891, he was given two weeks to work up a satisfactory indoor game before the Christmas holidays.

During the next thirteen days, with only Sundays off, Naismith made one effort after another to interest the school's students in the modifications he devised for them in children's games, sailors' games, football games, lacrosse and others. All were pretty good adaptations. All failed to amuse the class.

And on the fourteenth day, Naismith created basketball.

If he couldn't update an old game, working alone in his small office near the school gym, he would come up with a new one. Years later, in speeches and magazine articles, and a somewhat unsatisfactory book, he described the invention process, step by step:

First, reminding himself that most games were played with a ball, Naismith reasoned that he would have to choose between a small ball of the sort used in baseball or tennis and a larger football or soccer ball. Second, for a game for the masses, he ruled out small balls because in each instance — from baseball or golf to hockey and lacrosse — a stick or racket was required. And skill in wielding such an implement must be developed. "The game we sought would be played by many," he said. "Therefore, it must be easy to learn." Thus, third, he would use either a football or soccer ball. He told himself he would decide that later.

Fourth, Naismith ranked the games he had played in the order of their appeal, placing rugby football first. But on an indoor floor, he knew, the physical contact essential to rugby couldn't be allowed. Though he had decided on a rugby-sized ball, he seemed otherwise to have reached a dead end. Fifth, realizing suddenly that tackling could be outlawed by merely outlawing ballcarrying, Naismith came to a turning-point conclusion. In his new game, he would prohibit running with the ball. This might have been the most revolutionary decision by anyone in sports since 1823, when, at Rugby School in England, a soccer player had made exactly the opposite decision — running with a soccer ball to create rugby. Sixth, Naismith perceived that passing would have to be extensive to compensate for the prohibition on running. Thus he legalized throwing the ball in any direction. This was another revolutionary change for the times — although, a few years later, it prompted football to legalize passing.

Seventh, meditating at his desk, Naismith sought an objective for the players besides passing the ball around. This, the creation of a scoring play, was the most difficult aspect of his invention. In the other sports he had analyzed, the objective was to propel a ball across a goal line or kick it over goal posts or knock it over the fence or into a receptacle. These all demanded both strength and accuracy. But in an indoor game, he reasoned, the premium should be almost entirely on accuracy. Strength would lead to the contact and roughness he was trying to avoid. He wanted a scoring play that would require comparatively little muscle. So he outlawed kicking or smashing the ball with one's fist, and waited for another burst of inspiration.

Eighth, keeping accuracy in mind, Naismith finally broke new sports ground intellectually with his most original conception. He would place little boxes at either end of the gym, each about eighteen inches square, and compel the players to throw the ball in an accurate arc to get it into the boxes. When it stayed in, it would count as a goal. Ninth, experimenting briefly, he discovered that scoring boxes appealed most strongly to the defense. Every defensive player with a goalkeeper's mind — meaning most defensive players — wished simply to stand near the box and prevent all shots on goal. The boxes had to go somewhere else. And there was only one way to go — up — well above the players' heads.

Tenth, taking another look at the various balls that were laid out on his office floor, "I realized that (the football) was shaped so that it might be carried in the arms," Naismith reported later. "There was to be no carrying of the ball in this new game, so I walked over, picked up the soccer ball, and started in search of (some receptacles to throw it into)."

The school janitor, asked if he could help, told the inventor: "I haven't any more boxes, but I'll tell you what I do have. I have two old peach baskets down in the store room."

And so boxball became basketball when Naismith nailed the peach baskets to the walls, nailing them ten feet up.

III

Eventually, the ball was enlarged slightly. But otherwise, incredibly, there were hardly any loose ends to tidy up.

One of the few was the closed-bottom basket. It is a commentary on the rigidity of the human mind that five years after basketball had been invented — and four years after it had spread throughout the United States — somebody still had to take the ball out of the basket after every field goal and free throw. By that time, Naismith had lost interest in his game, and had moved on to other pursuits. The peach baskets were also gone. But the peach basket mind-set remained. Some teams persuaded friends or passers-by to stand on ladders next to the baskets and lift the ball out by hand. And shortly, equipment companies were competing with one another, building baskets that had pull-down chains. The chain temporarily opened the bottom of the basket, releasing the ball. The game was so much fun, however, that it survived all this nonsense until somebody finally thought of the obvious: cut the bottoms off the baskets.

In those days, running tracks circled many gymnasiums, considerably above the floor, and the baskets were usually nailed to the outside walls of the running tracks. One night a particularly imaginative team put one of its substitute players up there, next to the basket, and whenever the ball got close, he tapped it in. This led to another change, the backboard, whose purpose was to put the game out of reach of upstairs substitutes. It also brought in the bank shot.

In still another refinement, running with the ball came back into the sport — but only when the ball was dribbled. Eventually, dribbling became a science of its own; but Naismith had anticipated even that by permitting the ball to be dropped or bounced and caught before it was passed.

He had also anticipated a wealth of players per side. Basketball, in fact, was a game with nine-man teams for several years — for a quaint reason. In the particular gym class that Naismith had taught on the fourteenth day, there were eighteen students. Not wishing to bench anybody, he divided them in half. On each team, he delegated three forwards, three centers and three guards. Not until 1897, six years after its invention, did basketball officially become a five-man game.

Not even the inventor, in twenty-four hours of anguish, could think of everything.

IV

The grandchild who knew him best, Margaret Stanley Lewis, remembers James Naismith as a bright-eyed, erect, muscular man of medium height who promoted physical exercise so avidly that he had the build of a wrestler. He habitually wore a big mustache that turned from black to white over the years. "He was a very human man," Lewis said from her ranch near Westcliff, Colorado. "He was gentle of manner, and gentle-voiced. Nobody ever heard him use a swear word. He lived the life he wanted his family to live, and he always made time for his friends."

He had finished grafting basketball onto America before he left for medical school at Denver after spending only four of his eighty-eight years at the scene of the invention, Massachusetts. A husband and father, he became a med student at thirty-four in 1894 and a doctor at thirty-eight. "He never practiced medicine, just as he never held a pastorate," his grandson, James, said from Corpus Christi, Texas. "He studied anatomy to help him understand and help young men."

After the uncommonly eventful decades of the first half of his life, Naismith settled serenely into the second half at the University of Kansas, where for decade after decade he was the director of physical education — a position he left only to battle prostitution for a year or two in World War I. "That was in France," his grandson said. "He was a volunteer YMCA worker over there in his fifties."

As American soldiers picked up their overnight passes and headed for the delights of Paris, Naismith would stand by the gate and shout, cheerfully, "Hey, guys, we've got boxing here tonight — six great bouts. Stick around." According to a wholly unconfirmed and probably apocryphal report, that stopped some of them. "Doing it that way was typical of him," his grandson said. "He didn't just lecture you on venereal disease. He gave you an alternative."

In 1891, for the snowbound boys of Massachusetts, basketball had been the big alternative. But, curiously, Naismith never cared much for the game he created. "He only played in two games in his life," his grandson said. "And he was never a basketball fan. He was a doer, not a watcher."

7. Al Davis: A Fighter Who'll Fight Anybody

WHEN AL DAVIS moved the Raider football team from the Oakland Coliseum to the Los Angeles Coliseum in the early 1980s, he was one of the most controversial people in sports. And nothing has changed. One recent day, he even moved back to Oakland. His perceived flaws have brought a lot of heavy criticism to Davis, as they have to Bobby Knight, George Allen and others, but my interest is in Davis the three-time Super Bowl winner. His attitude in one of his darkest hours, when, en route to both Los Angeles and the Pro Football Hall of Fame, he was in limbo, is revealed in the following.

PALM SPRINGS, Calif.: March 14, 1980.

Long before he took command of the Oakland Raiders seventeen years ago, Al Davis appeared to be, above all, three things: maverick, fighter, and winner. He walked alone. He would fight anybody. And he usually won. Today, after three decades in football, Davis has never seemed so alone, nor has he ever been in such a fight. But this time, a Davis win is plainly less than a sure thing.

For, taking himself to an extreme that even Al Davis couldn't have foreseen until lately, he has picked *this* fight with one of the richest and most powerful institutions in sports, the National Football League. As one of the twenty-eight club owners, he holds NFL membership himself. Which means that in the struggle to move the Raiders to Los Angeles, he has twenty-seven opponents. Make that twenty-eight. The leader of the opposition is the commissioner, Pete Rozelle.

This week as the conflict spreads to the desert, where the NFL is in annual convention, it is clear that Davis has emerged as one of the boldest and most singular of the nation's free-enterprise individualists. Few other competitors in any field have ever shown the temerity and awesome self-assurance to fight so hard and long at a risk so large and final. There is a possibility that by pressing his crusade into another year, Davis could lose a franchise worth upward of $30 million. In the uncertain judicial climate of the day, there is even a chance that Oakland's suddenly concerned statesmen will prevail in their bid for eminent domain seizure, in which case control of the team would pass to their city. There is at least a chance that in "flouting the (NFL) constitution," in the words of his opponents, Davis has forfeited the right to go on owning an NFL team.

It is even possible that, for ignoring an Oakland judge's restraining order, he could get some jail time for contempt of court.

What kind of person would take such risks? Why is the NFL's most notorious eccentric so determined to get to Los Angeles? One answer comes from Davis himself. "To me, life is two things," he says. "It's challenge and creativity. That's what America is. That's what it's about. You go out and make your mark in life."

He has obviously made his mark on the NFL. Having pushed the commissioner and the other owners into a corner with his Los Angeles romance, he has become, in their reckoning, an outlaw. Ostensibly in violation of a new NFL rule, he contracted to move to Los Angeles before getting the league's endorsement. The vote against him was 22-0, with six abstentions — including Davis'.

Typically, the NFL's action didn't make a dent in Davis' ardor for the Los Angeles Coliseum, which the Rams abandoned this year for a refuge in Anaheim. "I predicted we wouldn't get the vote," he says, writing it off. "But I'm more interested than ever in Los Angeles as a place for the Raiders. Number one, I'm very impressed with the people we're working with there — (Labor Leader) Bill Robertson and the others. They seem to be on the level. The people I have to deal with in Oakland are a bunch of bastards."

Davis' determination to move on is rooted in the challenge posed by the Los Angeles community, or so he says. Although in the long run he could earn more money in Los Angeles than Oakland, he swears the fiscal incentives are secondary. "There has obviously been something wrong between the Rams and the city," he says. "Attendance figures show. . . . Anyhow, I'm intrigued by the opportunity. I want to see if we can go in and turn it around. I want to turn Los Angeles into the number one football town in the nation. I want to get them in a frenzy, you know what I mean?"

Davis often speaks in incomplete sentences, and he often inserts meaningless phrases, but his meaning is seldom unclear, particularly when referring to himself. "Up to now, I've had it all," he says. "I've been an assistant coach, head coach, commissioner (of the once-rival American Football League) and club owner. What seems different or difficult for others is kind of normal for me, know what I . . . ? I'd like to go down to Los Angeles and see if we can create the best organization in football — maybe the world. What's outrageous about . . . ? That's the way I feel."

II

It can be safely assumed that no other NFL owner has ever been maverick enough or fighter enough or audacious enough to feel that way, or in any case talk that way. Yet through a controversial career, Davis has been infamous for all that, along with, to be sure, a reputation for deviousness — plus a knack for winning.

At twenty-one, a graduate of Syracuse and at work on his first job as line coach at Adelphi University, he was writing magazine articles about the science of offensive football, foretelling a future as one of the two NFL owners (the other is George Halas) who know the most about the game. At twenty-nine, as an assistant coach at USC, he recruited so aggressively — inaugurating the era of Eastern imports — that the NCAA cracked down, imposing sanctions. Investigators alleged, and he agreed, that Davis had used his own money to buy a plane ticket for a Pennsylvania quarterback. Characteristically, he explains: "I didn't know they had a rule against it." Then he adds: "That was the turning point of my life. If it hadn't happened, I'd probably still be a college coach."

Instead, at thirty, he landed in pro ball to stay, brought in as an assistant by Sid Gillman, coach of the then Los Angeles Chargers. Three years later in Oakland, Davis at thirty-three became the youngest head coach and general manager in football. Turning around a chronic loser in five years, he changed a 1-13 team into a 13-1 team. Both technically sound and progressive, the Raiders have ever after been known for high morale — the "pride and poise" Davis sought from the first — and for their ability to throw long passes effectively, even when other teams were mostly running it.

At thirty-six, as the AFL's last commissioner, Davis recruited NFL quarterbacks and other stars so aggressively and expensively that the leagues made peace within seven weeks, ending a war that had lasted six years. To this day, others still claim credit for the peace. But to the war correspondents who at the time were closest to the front, Davis' generalship was decisive.

So, at thirty-seven, he was invited back to Oakland as the youngest owner in the league. Without putting up a dollar, he got control of the franchise as managing general partner, eventually paying for a ten per cent interest, he says, out of his share of club earnings. In his forties, in Oakland courtrooms, he was fighting again — beating his most prominent partner, Wayne Valley, the man who had brought him to Oakland in the first place. They differed on who, that time, was the devious one, but with Valley's departure, Davis increased his club holdings to twenty-five per cent. The rest is still in the hands of other Oakland businessmen.

Finally, at fifty, Davis is in the biggest fight of his life, one often described as Davis versus NFL. He sees it as Davis versus Rozelle. "I'm not unresponsible for the . . . ," he begins tentatively. "But the other man (Rozelle) is more responsible. The owners were just dragged along. I honestly wish there were a way for Rozelle to win and for me to move to Los Angeles. That would be the best for the league. To me, this isn't a game. Honestly, I don't give a damn if he wins in court. All I want is what every other owner has had the right to do — play their home games wherever they want to. Most of them have moved — at least once — to different towns and stadiums."

III

On one memorable occasion early in his Oakland career, Davis was on the road as a talent hunter the afternoon he ran into a Dallas Cowboys vice president, Gil Brandt, in a hotel men's room. All week, both had been tracking the same large group of Midwest college players — Davis for the AFL, Brandt for NFL teams — and although Davis is probably the league's most gifted personnel scout, he never relies wholly on his brains when he can get additional help. So he stood around until Brandt was inextricably occupied in the bathroom, whereupon he strolled out, and raced for a house phone.

"This is Gil Brandt," Davis told the telephone operator. "I'm tired and don't want to be disturbed. Please don't put any calls through to my room until morning."

"Yes, Mr. Brandt," the operator replied, and, with uncommon efficiency, broke all contact between the Dallas executive and the players and agents he expected to hear from that night.

Asked about the story, which was widely current in the war years, Davis, smiling, says, "You know I wouldn't do anything like that."

Says his mentor, former Coach Gillman, a Davis admirer, "Oh, he's a sly fox. He even looks like a sly fox."

Others see something else when they examine the owner of the would-be Los Angeles Raiders. A Sports Illustrated writer describes him as "a tall, good-looking man with powerful arms and shoulders that he keeps hard by lifting weights in his cellar." To a New York writer, Davis is "a harmless-looking All-American boy from Brooklyn." And a Bay Area reporter seems haunted by "the tinted, steel-rimmed glasses which increase the pinched appearance of his narrow face."

There is some truth in all these observations, and also in the opinion of a woman reporter that Davis looks better than he photographs. A six-footer weighing 188 — those were also his college dimensions — he is known as the best dresser among NFL owners, or at least the flashiest. And he is at pains to keep that reputation. His shirts are all custom-made in Beverly Hills by Jack Varney.

On the day of the 22-0 vote at the NFL meetings, Davis appeared in white from neck to toe except for a loosely woven, lightweight black jacket over his frilly, ruffled white shirt. The transparency of the jacket made it look silver and black — the club's colors, chosen long ago. Colorblind, he loves black and *either* white or silver. In Palm Springs, still more silver flashed on Davis' left wrist — it's a diamond bracelet — and he wore diamond rings on both hands. One commemorates a Super Bowl win. The other, a three-diamond ring, was his father's.

One day later, turning out in a black velour warmup suit, Davis met an interviewer on the patio of his ground-floor suite. In every Raider team hotel, coast to coast, he invariably rooms on the ground floor, where it's an easy out in a fire, or earthquake. His accommodation here overlooks the hotel's elegant artificial lake, which, on sunny mornings, reflects the west-of-Palm Springs mountain range that is the best thing about this desert. In this peaceful setting, Davis doesn't look like the man who, in the words of yet another writer, is "a devious, ingenious genius." Confronted with that description, he says, "I'll take it." Asked why, he says, "It's complimentary. You don't have to be devious, maybe, but it helps. They've said of every great leader of my time that he's devious — from Roosevelt and Churchill to Eisenhower, Kissinger and Mao."

Among a man's heroes, it is said, is the man he'd like to be.

The truth is that nothing seems quite usual about football man Davis — from his pass offense to his personal life. And, speaking of that, he says, "I couldn't be with my wife the night our son was born." This obviously still worries him, perhaps even drives him. "I was busy coaching football at the Citadel when she gave birth," he continues, sadly. "I never saw the boy the first week of his life. I regret it deeply — I love them both — I couldn't be there." A friend has said: "If you know what he thinks of his wife and son, you *know* what he thinks of football."

Davis' wife Carol, whom he calls Carolee, now recovering from serious illness, has been his softening influence. "We met when I was coaching at Adelphi," he says. "I was a kid. She was a super kid, a man's girl, a little wild. She knew sports, she was smart, she was well versed in the things that were.... She was my kind of woman." Before they were married, he says, "I told her what football meant to me. I told her only two things could take me away from football: life and death."

He meant her life or his death. And when Carol fell desperately ill last fall, another side of Al Davis was exposed. He gave up football. For many weeks, he had no contact, at all, with the Oakland Raiders. As his associates noted at the time — when, from every state in the union, friends called — Carol's husband spent his days and evenings at the hospital, and he went directly home each night, leaving the Raiders to proceed as best they could, which, for awhile, wasn't very well, and which, to Davis, didn't seem to matter in the slightest. Carol was to recover almost miraculously, and this week he brought her to the desert.

As confirmed Californians, they have lived for two decades in Oakland, which is a long way from Davis' boyhood home. Born in Brockton, Massachusetts, he spent his early years in Brooklyn, where his father was a well-to-do businessman. In his youth, Al didn't see himself in any of his father's businesses. He opted for a sports career, instead, inspired in part by another Brockton lad, former Heavyweight Champion Rocky Marciano. He still regards Marciano as "one of the three great competitors" he's seen — along with baseball Hall of Famer Jackie Robinson and former Raider Quarterback George Blanda. He calls Muhammad Ali "the greatest athlete of all time."

Years ago, his father was one of the first to see the maverick in Al Davis. In the NFL, Detroit Lions Owner William Clay Ford was one of the first to see the fighter. That was in the early years of NFL-AFL warfare, when the Raiders and Lions, choosing in different leagues, made two common choices in the same draft. To save bidding costs, Davis proposed one day that he and Ford divide the choices, "one for you, one for me." Ford declined. Thereupon, Davis signed both.

Winning — beating the NFL — was easy for Davis in those days. Now that he is himself a member of this exclusive club, it's harder — for even a devious, ingenious genius.

8. Bobby Bowden Likes to Throw It

ON THE way to a football game in Miami some time ago, I stopped briefly at Florida State to take a look at a college coach whose winning ways were causing a commotion in the Southeast. In the years since then, Bobby Bowden has become the most successful bowl-game coach of all time with an NCAA-record eleven straight wins and a bowl-game winning percentage of .816 to Joe Paterno's .673 and Bear Bryant's .552.

TALLAHASSEE, Fla.: Sept. 9, 1983.

Bobby Bowden, the football coach who turned Florida State University's losers into a winner, has been called the most eminent citizen of Tallahassee, the state capital. "The governor is a poor second," the alumni like to say. Bowden was even popular, for a while, at his last stop, West Virginia. But when he finished under .500 for the only time in six years at Morgantown — after four consecutive winning seasons — the townspeople hanged him in effigy.

For Bowden, that was a learning experience. "I learned I'd better not do that again," he says, laughing about it now.

Jovial, high-spirited, outgoing, Bowden seems the wrong sort to hang in effigy, even if he lost every game. But it's made an impression. "You never forget it when they run you up a tree," he says, still smiling. "My children could hardly stand it. They'd come home at night and say, 'Daddy is still up there in that old tree.' Finally, one of my assistant coaches went out and cut it down, and I'm here to tell you, I've kept hiring that man. He has a job for life."

On the Florida State team, no doubt. For at Tallahassee, shaken by his West Virginia experience, Bowden has made the most sensible contractual agreement in football. Every morning when he gets up, he has a new five-year contract with the Seminoles. They must pay him for five full seasons (more than $600,000) if they ever fire him. The hitch is that if Bowden ever leaves for a better job, *he* must pay Florida State $600,000, and what coach can come up with that kind of money? Not Bowden, certainly. As indulgent as most extroverts, he has always provided the best for his family.

His contract has discouraged, among others, at least one university that went after him, LSU, along with at least one pro club, the new Jacksonville franchise in the United States Football League. At the same time, to the huge benefit of football fans in these precincts, the arrangement has encouraged Bowden to develop one of the most entertaining offensive teams in college football without worrying about interceptions and the other unfortunate consequences of a lively passing game.

A sign in his office reads: "I firmly believe that man's finest hour, his greatest fulfillment to all he holds dear, is that moment when he has worked his heart out in a good cause and lies exhausted on the field of battle . . . victorious." This is the spirit that unites Bowden to other winners. But unlike the ball-control winners, Bowden wants to do it in style. His objective is to put a team on the field that can do everything — run every kind of offensive play and throw every pass.

"We'll throw it wherever it is," he says when asked to sum up his offensive strategy. "They have to defend every corner of the field."

Unlike the game's legion of conservative coaches, Bowden starts most plays by dropping his quarterback straight back. "Our goal is to score every time," he says. "I don't want to punt — I hate to punt — I want the ball. And to move it, you have to throw it. We're as likely to throw on our goal line as theirs — more likely. From our goal line we have 109 yards to pass in. From theirs, only eleven. It's much harder to throw down there. We work more on our first-and-goal pass offense than any thing else we do."

II

At fifty-three, Bobby Bowden is a younger, pudgier, more puckish Bum Phillips without the hat and boots — as friendly as Phillips, as popular with the media, but bubblier. Everyone who knows him calls him a joy to be around. Like many old football players, Bowden, who stands, at most, five feet ten, is always fighting the battle of the bulge, and always joking about it. "I go up and down like a balloon, losing twenty pounds, gaining twenty," he says. His vice is food. "I've got no prejudices," he says. "I'll eat anything."

He no longer smokes, but his favorite toys are the long unlit cigars he bites into from time to time morning, noon and night. Sitting at his desk in a day-long growth of whiskers, saggy-eyed, usually smiling, looking up at a visitor through half-glasses, he appears to be, if not Bum Phillips, a 1980s Benjamin Franklin.

There are days when Bowden is at work at 4 a.m. "I don't set an alarm clock but I start to work whenever I wake up," he says. "Some nights I go home, and I just can't wait for sleep to be over. Just so I can go out and begin the next day." A lifelong Baptist and still a lay preacher whose sermons have been heard in many churches in the South, Bowden once told a Tallahassee sports editor, Bill McGrotha, "When I was young, people used to tell me I ought to be a minister. But I never felt like I was called. It was more like I was called to coaching."

It happened in Birmingham, where, son of a realtor, Bowden was born next to a football field. "From our front door," he says, "you could kick the ball through the goal posts." That was at Woodlawn High School, which he attended before making Little All-American as a quarterback at Birmingham's Howard University, now Samford. Actually, like any Alabama prep sensation, Bowden had gone to Alabama first. But he had left a girl back in Birmingham and couldn't stand to be without her. Asked why he didn't marry the girl, a five-foot-two brunette cheerleader, and take her to Tuscaloosa with him, Bowden says: "She was still in high school. When I did marry her, Ann was only sixteen. I was nineteen."

They have four sons, two daughters. "My sister also has six children," he says. "Every time we had one, they had one — within a month of us every time. Then we both had operations and that's all that's kept me from starving. For thirty-five years I've been head over heels in love."

His sons all played football on Bowden teams and three of them later coached on his staff. One is now the wide receiver coach at Duke, another is head coach at Salem and the third is on the Salem staff. One daughter is married to a football coach and the other to a football player. "And last Saturday all six of us got beat," Bowden says. "My wife cried all day, then wiped her tears and called them all up. 'Don't let this get you down, dear,' she said, over and over. 'Remember, it happened to Daddy, too.' Oh, that was a morbid scene, I tell you. Morbid."

Looking suddenly serious, Bowden remembers his oldest son, a college professor with a Ph.D. in religion. "The black sheep," he says.

III

The Bowdens live on a Tallahassee golf course in a big house that "we're still paying for," he says. The house is a mob scene at family reunions with children, grandchildren, cousins and second cousins.

They all like to come to Tallahassee, a pleasant upper Florida town with Spanish moss dripping from the oak and pecan trees. There are only two industries in Tallahassee, education and government, and the population is around a hundred thousand when the university and legislature are both in session, much less than half that in the hot summers.

Florida State, which began as a women's school and has been a football-playing university only since 1947, spreads around on the hills of the only rolling countryside of an otherwise depressingly flat state. In one of the American Indian languages, Tallahassee means seven hills. The campus has a traditional, somewhat sleepy, Deep South look. At Gainesville, by contrast, the University of Florida is faster paced and more modern with a brick-and-glass look.

Nobody at Florida State seems to like anyone at Florida, which is about a hundred miles east and fifty miles south. A traveler asking directions to Gainesville is told to "go east until you smell it and south until you step in it." Later when a Florida professor was advised of this message and asked for comment, he said, heatedly, "That's our line. They stole it like they steal everything else."

Bowden seems somewhat removed from all this acrimony. When he isn't coaching, he plays golf, his only other passion. "Golf has helped my football," he says. "It's taught me patience and that you're never out of it. I've seen the pressure you can put on somebody by playing well, and that works in football, too."

IV

On his first day at Florida State, Bowden took charge of a Florida State team that had gone 4-29 in its last three years. The Seminoles in Bowden's seven seasons, counting the rebuilding seasons, are 59-22 (.728) — and so they're proud of him in Tallahassee, the more so because of his success on the road. Despite rigorous out-of-town schedules, Bowden, as a Florida State coach, is 1-1 at Nebraska, 2-0 at Ohio State, 1-0 at Notre Dame, and 4-1 at LSU.

An early 1970s Florida State athletic director, Clay Stapleton, gave Bowden that opportunity, dreaming up difficult out-of-town schedules to make some money for the university's athletic department, which was then nearly bankrupt. Though Stapleton held the job only a year or so, he lined up seventy-two games with teams in the nation's top ten "on their terms, and in their towns," as he once said.

Thus, two years ago, Bowden found himself scheduled against five powers on consecutive Saturdays, on their terms, and in their towns: Lincoln, Nebraska; Columbus, Ohio; South Bend, Indiana; Pittsburgh; and Baton Rouge, Louisiana. "I'd have quit before the season," he says, "if I hadn't had this danged contract."

Astonishingly, he won three of the five, and since then he has never looked back, proceeding to compile a Florida State road record of 29-14. And any way you look at it, that's better than a hanging.

IV

ATHLETES

Skilled athletes keep the world of competitive sports alive. And from time to time, I have run into some of the twentieth century's most skilled in most sports. So this is a chapter of mostly retrospective pieces about a few of the great athletes I have known.

In the analysis and evaluation of athletes, major league or minor, one differential should be mentioned: the distinction between skill and ability. In any human activity, ability is innate. Skill is acquired, reflecting dedication and other essential qualities.

For a good long career, ability, plainly, is an indispensable. Most of the people in this chapter, and elsewhere in the book, have had a lot of it. At the same time it's true that on almost every school team in America, there are athletes with intrinsic but unrefined and never-to-be-discovered big league ability. Only those with the determination to develop appropriate skills break out and move up.

It follows that, for the newspaperman, the things most worth examining are the athlete's skill level — mental as well as physical — and the qualities that alter it: the extent of his dedication, ambition, and, most valuable of all, will to conquer. All that is what I try to get at in visits with any athlete and in research into his life and environment. It's either explicit or implied in much of what I like to do.

1. Ben Hogan, the Man Who Came to Practice

AS A WINNER, Golfer Ben Hogan was a character in the most benevolent meaning of the word. No other competitor in any sport was ever more continuously uptight or humorless or dedicated to a single mission: improving himself as a competitor. And few ever overcame so much to accomplish so much. In the last sixty years, I haven't known any winner who could match Hogan for variety of adversity.

FORT WORTH, Tex.: June 19, 1988.

For years, the very name, Ben Hogan, made strong men tremble — the strong men who pioneered tournament golf. Before and after World War II; before and after the 1949 auto accident that nearly killed him; before Arnold Palmer and Jack Nicklaus — and after Bobby Jones — Texas' Ben Hogan was the most feared competitor in golf. They called him the Hawk. And they knew that even on their best days, the Hawk would probably get them anyhow. He once won the Masters, the U.S. Open, and the British Open the same year. That was long ago, more than three decades ago. Has the Hawk flown away?

No chance. At seventy-five, Hogan was found this summer where he started sixty-five years ago. On a golf course in Texas. Practicing his tee shots, practicing his irons, even his putts. And loving it all. "When I'm not playing, I like to practice," he says. "To me, practicing has always been half the fun."

Golf in the United States originated just twenty-five years before Hogan was born. And by mid-century, he was, at the least, Player of his Time. Most golfers, in fact, continue to rank him in the century's top five with Jones, Nicklaus, Palmer and Walter Hagen. "Nicklaus and Palmer made golf pay off," says Hogan, a high school dropout who made his fortune as a businessman manufacturing golf clubs here with five hundred employees. "That's the difference between them and the rest of us."

It's one difference. Other differences were and are more personal. As a golfer, and as a person, Hogan, in the words of one or another of the newspaper reporters of his day, was cold, calculating, distant, antisocial, uncooperative, preoccupied, and obsessive in a drive for perfection. "His forbidding manner ground down the opposition," one writer said. "To look at him was to shiver in the bones." When tournament Golfer Al

Geiberger was asked what it was like to play with Hogan, he said: "It was spooky."

No one ever said that about Arnold Palmer.

For a participant in an arduous vocation, the Hawk was a small one. Slender and small-boned, he weighed no more than 135 pounds as a champion and stood not much more than five feet eight. So it wasn't his bulk that awed them, it was the Hogan manner, the Hogan look. He unnerved rivals and reporters alike with the steady, unsmiling, icy approach of a professional gambler. The contemporary celebrity he most resembled was the model Hollywood mobster, George Raft.

These days, Hogan has added a few pounds and subtracted some hair, but he's still fit, erect, and direct of manner, still neat and formal in a summer sport coat and slacks. The carefully knotted tie is blue, the spectacles gold-rimmed. He has finally quit smoking, yielding a year ago after an appendectomy. Texas-born and bred, never willingly absent from Texas, he has been married to the same woman for fifty-three years. "Valerie is a Fort Worth girl," golfer Jimmy Demaret, Ben's friend, once said. "She met Ben at the ripe old age of twelve, and they've been inseparable ever since. They have no children, and live for each other."

In the old days when you could pin Ben down out of sight of a golf course — which wasn't often — he was usually a cordial enough interview, and so he remains. In his handsome wood-paneled office, seated behind a leather-topped desk in front of a large oil portrait of Valerie, he is still a pleasant enough companion. He wasn't, he insists, a born golfer. "There's no such thing as a born golfer, a born anything," he says. "Any duffer can shoot in the seventies if he applies himself properly. Practicing is the necessary thing. Playing is just an anticlimax."

A long, lovely afternoon of golf? Anticlimax? To Hogan, it was. The other players just got in his way. It was the game that challenged him.

II

As a professional golfer, Hogan was a late starter who didn't win his first tournament until he was twenty-eight. By then, he had been trying for ten years. He won his first U.S. Open at thirty-six. By contrast, Bobby Jones, who also won four U.S. Opens, *retired* at twenty-eight.

After Hogan got the hang of it, though, he played like a champion almost every time out. Winless until 1940, Hogan won three straight tournaments that year, and thereafter he won in bunches, suggesting that he was a self-made champion who until his late twenties had everything but self-confidence. A great but erratic pitcher who suddenly starts winning at twenty-eight is usually a man who has developed everything but control, which is to say confidence, and golf can be like that. Reinforcing the thought that Hogan was an uncommonly competitive, self-made champion, he kept his career going until the year he turned sixty, when he entered his last tournament the last year he was on the mainstream tour.

The summit year for Hogan was 1953, when he activated two dreams, winning the U.S. Open for the fourth time and opening his own manufacturing firm. Having launched the Ben Hogan Company with a partner, he was proud of the new clubs they manufactured that first year — at a start-up cost of $150,000 — until he tried them out. "It was obvious that they weren't up to my standards," he says quietly. "I had approved the model, but we were training new people, and the clubs were badly made. I said: 'These can't go out.' Orders were coming in like crazy, but we never shipped any of those clubs. I took them out back one day and broke them all, one by one."

As a result, in his first venture as a businessman, Hogan ate $150,000. "Actually, I ate more than that," he says. "My partner had wanted to ship those clubs — he couldn't see anything wrong with them — and I had to buy him out."

If that is the attitude of a perfectionist, it is perfection that Hogan has always sought, in either business or golf. At his office one morning, he talked about the night of a haunting dream. He dreamed that he started a round with seventeen consecutive holes in one. "Then at the eighteenth, the tee shot lipped out," he says. "It woke me up. I was madder than hell."

Hogan's restless search for perfection has been a consequence, no doubt, of the struggles of his early years. His father was a blacksmith who suffered from ill health and financial reverses. Giving up one night, he shot himself to death in his living room before an audience of one, a youngster named Royal.

Royal is Ben's older brother.

At nine, Ben was selling newspapers at a train station in downtown Fort Worth. At ten, changing careers, he began supporting himself as a caddie.

Perhaps no other champion of the century can match Hogan for repeated adversity. Never really big enough to be a champion, fatherless in his school years, he was a child of an infamous long grind: the Great Depression. Then World War II caught him at thirty-one and interrupted his golf career during the nearly three years he served as an Army officer. And next, at thirty-seven, Hogan almost died on a Texas highway in the head-on collision that knocked him out of golf for another year.

The accident left him with injuries that hurt his game ever after, though his determination to ignore them led him to become even more successful. He had won only one U.S. Open before breaking his pelvis, a rib or two, a collarbone, and an ankle bone in the 1949 crash. He came back to win three of the next four Opens, in 1950, '51 and '53.

Hogan had one other big problem that hurt the worst: He was born without authentic championship ability. He was born to be one of the duffers he speaks of — the golfers who by practicing correctly on weekends, and occasionally at midweek, can learn to shoot in the seventies.

He fooled them by playing and practicing twelve hours a day, every day.

Then, one night, he took a few putts and swings in his hotel room before going to bed, and that started another Hogan tradition. He began doing that *every* night. Finally, crawling dead-tired into bed at last, he visualized his game for another hour or two — often playing a full eighteen holes.

Byron Nelson, the champion who grew up with Hogan, put it this way: "Nobody had to work as hard to play golf as Ben. Nobody."

III

Hogan's powers of concentration were not the least of his game. They might in fact have been most of it. Tournament Golfer George Fazio once said that he could never forget the eagle two he made one day when paired with Hogan. The gallery, which had come to see the Hawk, broke into a long cheer for Fazio that was heard as far away as the clubhouse. But not, apparently, by Hogan, who as usual was grimly focusing on his own game. At the next tee, picking up his scorecard to record his opponent's score, Hogan asked: "What did you have on that last hole, George?"

On the tour in those days, no one was more competitive, then or ever. Tournament Golfer Tony Penna talks about the time he played with Hogan in a four-ball match at Minneapolis, where the Hawk asked his partner to serve as captain. Flattered, Penna says, "That meant I'd decide on conceding any putts." At an early hole, taking his responsibilities seriously, Penna knocked away a putt of several inches by one of their opponents. Hogan was livid. "You can't give anybody a putt that long," he railed. "You're not the captain anymore!"

There were times on the tour when Hogan was so charged up that he could hardly sleep. Nelson, who occasionally roomed with him in the early years when they lived on doughnuts and hamburgers, tells about the night that a strange noise awakened him. He jumped out of bed apprehensively, fearing that a pack of rats had invaded their cheap room. Not until he hunted around closely did Nelson discover the truth. "It was only Ben gnashing his teeth," he says.

The competitive stress that nudged Hogan throughout his career paid off handsomely. He won sixty-three times on the U.S. tour. In his six years at the top, 1948-53, he won seven major tournaments: two Masters, four U.S. Opens and the only British Open he played. He also won two PGA championships, in 1946 and '48, when the PGA was a match play event. From 1942 to 1956, Hogan was first or second six times in the U.S. Open and first or second six times in the Masters, although he spent three of those fifteen years in the Army and most of another in the hospital.

Only a scientist, perhaps, could have done all that, and to Hogan golf was an onerous if gratifying science. He approached every phase of the game with the care of a medical researcher. If Jones was golf's greatest artist, Hogan was its greatest scientist.

Harvie Ward, who often played with him, once recalled the day that he came upon Hogan examining a carton of new golf balls with a magnifying glass. After studying them at length, the Hawk kept a few, but threw most into his shag bag. Asked why he had discarded so many, Hogan said: "Some of the dimples have too much paint in them."

In his book, "Five Lessons: The Modern Fundamentals of Golf," Hogan compares the gallery's reaction with his own at the 1950 Open when, at the seventy-second hole, his two-hundred-yard two-iron shot stopped forty feet from the cup, helping him into the playoff, which he won. The crowd saw it as an inspired pressure shot. To Hogan, it was nothing more than another example of what a man can do when his practice objective every day and night is a correct, powerful, repeating swing. "I didn't hit that shot then," he observed. "I'd been practicing that shot since I was twelve years old."

Asked about it now, Hogan says: "There are invariably four or five key shots in any tournament. Normally, they are the long iron shots. So you take a good long look at the course before the tournament. You find out what you'll especially need that week — and you practice that. You have to practice the right things."

Thus, Hogan was the first to make a habit of practicing each day after finishing a tournament round. "That's the best time because you remember what you just played," he says. "You can see where you haven't practiced hard enough."

This dedication shocked Hogan's rivals, who admired him almost as much as they feared him. Once when New York Writer Dave Anderson asked Golfer Tommy Bolt to compare Nicklaus and Hogan, Bolt said that he had seen Nicklaus go watch Hogan practice, but he had never seen Hogan go watch Nicklaus practice.

Over the years in American sports, there have been others as ambitious as the Hawk — but none with quite the same ambition. "Hogan didn't come into golf just to win titles," Golf magazine's Charles Price said one day. "He came into the game to prove to himself and others how well it could be played, by anyone, anywhere."

Anyone, anywhere — at any age. A compulsive competitor, Hogan, until age sixty, wouldn't quit — though he won only twice in his last eighteen years on the tour. Why quit when practicing is half the fun?

2. Bobby Riggs: Life of a Hustler

CHAMPIONS come in all sizes. Winning seems to be unrelated to height and weight for those who are either inspired by their lack of physical stature or who ignore it. As a tennis champion, Bobby Riggs was often the smallest seeded player in sight, but no one was quicker, and no one had more heart. Near the end of Riggs' life, Times Sports Editor Bill Dwyre asked for this piece, reasoning sensibly that a man should get to enjoy his own memorial. The last time I saw him, Riggs said he did.

ENCINITAS, Calif.: April 15, 1995.

When Attorney F. Lee Bailey was starring in a 1970s television series, he once summoned former Wimbledon tennis Champion Bobby Riggs as a witness. Strapping a lie-detector on Riggs, and standing over him menacingly, Bailey asked: "Did you throw that match to Billie Jean King?"

The witness, a noted gambler and hustler, responded evenly: "I did not."

And that surprised many viewers. For, at the Houston Astrodome, in a 1973 battle of the sexes — planned by Riggs himself to demonstrate male superiority — he instead inspired, in defeat, widespread skepticism and disbelief. Only five months earlier, hadn't Riggs, then fifty-five, drubbed the world's number one-ranked women's player, Margaret Court? He had. Hadn't Riggs, a noted male chauvinist, vowed to dominate King, twenty-nine, a renowned feminist? He had.

Number two King took him on anyway. And on national television, before a record tennis crowd of 30,472, she took Riggs in straight sets, 6-4, 6-3, 6-3.

To many, that had the look of Part One in a hustle. In Part Two, they figured, he'd win a bundle. But it didn't happen: King wouldn't play him again. And talking about it now, Riggs, confirming the testimony of Bailey's lie-detector experts, says: "You know I'm a male chauvinist. You know I'm a hustler. Billie Jean just caught me on a bad day."

Today, Riggs, a Church of Christ preacher's son who lives here on the ocean, is in failing health. He has finally given up hustling. At seventy-seven, he is seeing doctors now instead of tennis players and golfers. For the last three months, he has been unable to play either of the games that have been his life for most of his life. "Health-wise, I've broken down," he says. But as a friend notes, Riggs carries misfortune well.

On a sunny day at his beach house, visiting casually with pals and neighbors, he still resembles an aging contemporary, Actor Mickey Rooney. A big-time athlete for a half century, Riggs still cuts a small but trim figure, 140 pounds, five feet seven plus. He still wears those round-rimmed glasses. He still has his sense of humor. And, moving about the premises to do for guests, he still walks like a duck — a clever, cocky duck, to be sure.

A neighbor guesses indeed that Riggs seems ready for at least nine holes. "No, sir, you can't tell a book by its cover," the old champion warns, shaking his head, then adding that he is already at work on epitaphs. One is: "He Served More Aces Than They Did." But that, he fears, is "kind of deceptive because I never had many aces — I was just harder to ace than the other guy." Also under consideration: "He Had His Ups and Downs, but He Won His Share." That's closer, although he suspects that when he can't quite get to the last drop shot, the final ode to Riggs will be in six words:

"He Put Women on the Map."

II

If Riggs in his competitive years lacked the size and muscle of other winners, he was nonetheless a big winner. He was a national tennis champion in the 1930s and world pro champion in the '40s. And he will be remembered, he hopes, for those and the many other achievements that are shortly to be celebrated again in the tennis museum he is planning nearby.

Yet he has spent the last quarter century another way, happily hustling bets on himself on golf courses and tennis courts. And it is for that unique career, his friends say, that Riggs seems to be best known today. He has made a fortune betting on himself. Who started him in that direction?

He says it was Hall of Fame Ballplayer Hank Greenberg. As Riggs tells it, the big, hard-hitting Detroit Tiger and the little, weak-hitting tennis champion were sitting around an exclusive men's club one afternoon discussing the other members, who, Riggs complained, wouldn't bet with him. Standing on their constitutional rights, they declined to be hustled.

"Tell you what, Bobby," said Greenberg. "Put a park bench in the middle of your court, and if one of those rich guys runs you into it, it's their point." Said Riggs: "Great idea, I'll do it."

But some fine-tuning was soon needed. Jumping a bench ruined his timing — and his bank account. Refining Greenberg's idea, he replaced the bench with three or four wooden chairs. Or, warming up to the possibilities, he played his wealthy friends when he had a patch over one eye, or when carrying an umbrella or a pail of water, or while roller skating. Or while leading his dog on a leash — or a lion.

In no time, he won a lot of their money, and on tours he won more in stadiums and arenas. And, he says, he has decided to put some of it into the new Bobby Riggs Tennis Museum in Cardiff-by-the-Sea, adjoining the Bobby Riggs Tennis Club, which is owned by a friend, Lornie Kuhle.

"Look for the tennis racket I used against Billy Jean," says Riggs. "It might be there. Then again, I might have thrown it in the ocean."

III

For most of his first seventy-six years, Riggs confides, he lived a charmed, lucky life, playing tennis or golf or both all day, almost every day. And every time, he wagered on himself to win. "The bigger the bet, the better I played," he says.

Until nightfall, when he usually read a book a night, usually a mystery, Riggs, who was twice divorced, only made time for sports — unless it rained. Then he played cards all day. "The best poker game is seven-card stud, high-low-splits," he says. "I mean it's the best if you don't have to declare high or low, and can win it all with a low straight."

As a gambling man, that's what he likes best, winning it all.

His friend, Kuhle, remembers one rare day when the little champion couldn't scare up a fellow gambler for anything — tennis, golf, gin, or even dominoes. "He went home and brought back his wife Priscilla," Kuhle says. "She told him: 'I'll keep you company — I'll go around the golf course with you — but I don't want to play.'" He said: "That's okay, I'll play two balls, yours and mine. His and hers."

They agreed on $50 a hole, and on a typically lucky round for Bobby, he won $750, which made his day. "And Priscilla paid him," says Kuhle.

IV

Few good athletes have ever enjoyed more than one successful career. F. Scott Fitzgerald wasn't overstating by much when he said, in a somewhat different context, "There are no second acts in American lives." If few prominent athletes have even doubled as prominent coaches, it's a fact that even fewer have gone on to succeed in business — as former Los Angeles Times Publisher Otis Chandler did after his days as a world-class shot putter at Stanford. And still fewer have made it in television, as former NFL Halfback Frank Gifford has. But for almost all — including NFL Union Leader Gene Upshaw, the former All-Pro — the maximum seems to be two careers.

All except Bobby Riggs. Astonishingly, Riggs has enjoyed not two, or three, but four big careers.

To begin with, as a tennis player, he was the amateur champion in the era when that was a synonym for world champion. At Forest Hills, New York, Riggs, twenty-one, won the U.S. championship in 1939, when, before joining the U.S. Navy, he also won at Wimbledon in all three divisions: singles, doubles, and mixed doubles. "No one else ever won the triple crown their first year there," he says.

In a storied second career, Riggs became the world professional champion after World War II just as pro tennis was on the rise. To get there, he had to beat a much better player, Don Budge, who was probably the game's best between Bill Tilden and John McEnroe. "Budge was kind of lazy," Riggs says. "When I was a Navy seaman, he was an Army lieutenant, and I knew he would play around with all those officers instead of practicing. For three years as a tennis instructor, I worked on beating Budge every day I was in the South Pacific. And the biggest thrill I've had was beating him in the finals for the 1946 pro championship." The score was 6-3, 6-1, 6-1.

His third career began when he couldn't beat the next challenger, Jack Kramer, who suggested, perceptively, that what Riggs was really meant for was promoting. And in a tricky business, Riggs made a bundle as a promoter, most conspicuously in the Riggs-King match, for which he held TV and residual rights. On a winner-take-all night, "I paid Billie Jean $100,000," he says. "But *my* payoff lasted five years. I made a million and a half."

Riggs' fourth career — as a hustler — has been "the most fun of all," he says, remembering a strange day in Tennessee. In a tennis match with the Grand Ole Opry's Minnie Pearl — in the county where Riggs' grandfather went to war as a Confederate Army cavalryman — she insisted on a handicap of forty kitchen chairs. Although Pearl's serves arrived in a service box that, by agreement, had been left clear, there were so many chairs in the rest of the court that Riggs, playing his normal soft-shot game, blew $100 in a one-set match. The score was 6-0, Pearl.

Afterward, a challenger came down out of the stands seeking the same handicap. Riggs said no. The guy said: "How about a side bet of $1,000." Riggs said yes. And, suddenly, the forty chairs were irrelevant. Riggs' hard serves proved unreturnable — as did his suddenly hard service returns. The score was 6-0, Riggs.

"The all-time hustle," he says.

V

Riggs recalls that he first bet on himself at age twelve, when his first game was marbles. Tennis was then a distant second, in large part because his family couldn't afford a tennis racket. "But nothing is forever," his brother John, eighty-four, says.

John remembers that one day during Bobby's reign as the marbles champion of Lincoln Heights, a Los Angeles area, he won every marble in the possession of a thirteen-year-old who lived nearby — even his shooter. When the kid said he wanted them returned — and when he offered, in exchange, his sister's new tennis racket, Bobby agreed. Finally, a racket of his very own in hand, he was in position to start another career — but not yet. "The next day I went out and won the marbles back," he says.

Bobby was the youngest of seven in the family of a fundamentalist minister, Gideon Riggs. "He was a good father. But he frowned on card-playing and drinking," Bobby says. "Also dancing, and even organ music, and especially gambling." Hence, Gideon, who was fifty when Bobby was born, often expressed displeasure with the youngest of his six sons, though learning to take pride in him when he began winning as a teen-ager at the Los Angeles Tennis Club.

Older members remember that after Bobby's first tournament victory there, Gideon, who was then nearly blind, stood outside beaming and accepting congratulations and shaking everyone's hand. "Just like coming out of church," Bobby says.

That day, of course, Bobby had bet on himself to win. From the first day, he says, he bet on every tennis match he was ever in. That isn't hard to do, he found, in London, where bookmaking is legal. And although he tried for better odds, he could only get three to one, he says, on Riggs to win Wimbledon in 1939. Deciding to make a three-way parlay, the best he could get was six to one and then twelve to one in doubles and mixed doubles. So he put up 100 pounds, about $500 in that era, and let it ride.

The parlay paid off at 21,600 pounds — or $108,000.

"The war was coming," he said. "I stashed it in a safety-deposit box."

VI

As a tennis champion, where does Riggs rank? Not at the top, surely, but not far behind, either. Those who have followed his career report that from thirteen to seventy-six — from the amateurs to the seniors and beyond — Riggs was always the world's best tennis player for his age.

His friend Pancho Segura, the former tennis champion, attributes Riggs' success to the simple but decisive fact that he always led his opponent in fewest unforced errors. Or as Riggs says: "I once played amateur tournament tennis six months without double-faulting." Segura adds: "Bobby has nerves of steel."

Former football Coach Sid Gillman, watching Riggs hit golf balls on their home course, La Costa, learned that long ago. One day when Riggs was playing with a new member, Gillman noticed that the other guy suddenly picked up the ball and threw it toward the green. "I couldn't believe it until they told me Bobby had arranged the game himself," Gillman says. "They were playing nine holes, and he had given the guy two throws a hole." And, Gillman enthuses, "Bobby won."

Throwing the ball can be an equalizer, Riggs says, disclosing: "One time I told Arnold Palmer that I'd play him eighteen holes, for any amount, if he'd give me one throw a hole." Palmer thought it over for five or six seconds, then refused. "Arnie doesn't like to lose," Riggs says.

As every gambler knows, hustlers are sometimes trapped in a miscalculation, and, looking back, Riggs agrees that in 1973 he underestimated Billie Jean King. Before their match, reminding Texas sports fans that he was a male chauvinist pig, he sought to psych her out by forming a Chauvinist Pig Club. "We had a booth accepting new members at $10 a head," he says.

King wouldn't psych. "I knew he had made a mistake when he, a fifty-five-year-old man, agreed to three out of five sets with *me*," she says, speaking this week from Chicago.

At the Astrodome, King had herself carried in by four big, heavily-muscled athletes, who, upstaging Riggs, bore her on a litter like Cleopatra's. And as they set her down, she stepped off like a queen, nodding curtly, and handing Riggs an exquisitely wrapped box. When he opened it, a little pig jumped out.

So King was one up before the match began. And she didn't need five sets, taking him in three. But if Riggs is looking for epitaphs, here's one: With chutzpah and style, he took almost everyone else.

3. Bronko Nagurski: Football's First Big Winner

OF THE athletes who have stirred America during the twentieth century, Bronko Nagurski joined Red Grange and Sammy Baugh in the first wave of pro football players. Each symbolized something different, but the Nagurski career was strangest. Known as the game's most powerful runner, far more powerful than Grange, he equaled Baugh in championships won passing — two each.

INTERNATIONAL FALLS, Minn.: Aug. 21, 1983.

A winner named Bronko Nagurski, the huge fullback who led the Chicago Bears to victory in the National Football League's first championship game fifty years ago, may have been the greatest football player of all time. In any case, he is so identified in his hometown here in the far north of Minnesota, where the leading hotel, a new Holiday Inn, opened a Bronko Nagurski Room last July. A tinted, life-size Nagurski photo was unveiled when the room, a banquet hall, was dedicated, and everybody was there — almost everybody in Kouchiching County, that is — except Nagurski, who refused to come. "That's Bronko," a friend said the other day. "He's a shy one. Always has been."

At seventy-four, Nagurski lives with his wife, the former Eileen Kane, on the Canadian border at nearby Rainy Lake, which is four miles up the Rainy River from International Falls (population 6,940). Their modest cottage hard by the lake, where they raised six children, is the one they moved into when Bronko was playing three positions — tackle and linebacker as well as fullback — for the 1930s Bears.

Numerous Kanes and Nagurskis still live in this area, which is alternately a winter wonderland and a domain of brief, joyous summers, and last year they held a family reunion, with Bronko and Eileen as guests of honor. Eileen was there, but Bronko, of course, wouldn't come. "He's almost reclusive," Dave Siegel, a reporter for the International Falls Daily Journal, said. "We've been trying to get an updated file picture of Nagurski for ten years, and we hung around the reunion all day, but no luck."

He was easier to shoot in the 1930s, when, at one time or another, almost every Chicago cameraman caught Nagurski ferrying an opponent or two across the goal line on his back. For five decades his name has symbolized the raw power, the brute force of football. To this day, they point out the brick wall in Chicago that Nagurski cracked when he ran into it carrying a football one fall afternoon in Wrigley Field. Scoring the winning touchdown in that game — at the south end of a cramped field where the end zone was only nine yards deep — Nagurski stomped on two opponents, leaving one unconscious and the other with a broken shoulder. Then he collided with a goal post and spun into the wall, which stopped him at last. Picking himself up, he told a teammate, "That last guy hit pretty hard."

At an NFL game years later, when former Quarterback Fran Tarkenton asked him about that day, Nagurski remembered everything but fracturing the wall. "But I've seen the crack myself," Tarkenton said. "Oh, c'mon now," Nagurski said. "No human could crack a brick wall."

No human, maybe. But Nagurski had super-human strength. Everybody who played in that era says so. He was the first big NFL winner, and he's the one they talk about the most whenever oldtimers get together, as they did this month in Canton, Ohio, home of the Pro Football Hall of Fame. "I saw Nagurski for the first time when I was an NFL rookie," said Don Hutson, who has ranked as one of football's top two or three receivers, all-time, since his All-Pro days at Green Bay. "At Alabama, I'd been known as a good defensive end, so I played Nagurski the way I'd play a Georgia fullback. On first down they gave him the ball, and he ran straight over me. I mean he ran me down and kept going without breaking stride."

Arch-rival Green Bay Fullback-Linebacker Clark Hinkle remembers: "He was the most bruising runner ever. The first time I tackled Nagurski, I had to have five stitches in my face. My biggest thrill in football was the day he announced his retirement."

At Canton, Hutson was joined eventually by no fewer than four other all-timers — Center Mel Hein, Guard Dr. Dan Fortmann, Halfback Johnny Blood (McNally), and, of all people, Bronko Nagurski himself. Hutson and Blood lured Bronko out of International Falls, Hein said, by putting pressure on Eileen Nagurski, somehow persuading her to fly in with the Recluse of Rainy Lake. It isn't true that he hadn't left his lakeside cottage for twenty years, but he hadn't left it often, and his appearance at Canton made the show for old-time fans.

Hein, the New York Giants' Hall of Fame center, was asked how the Hutson-Blood connection could get Nagurski all the way to Canton when the International Falls people can't get him downtown. "In the last few years, Hutson and the rest of us have called on Bronko at the lake," Hein said. "He knows what we look like, and we know what he looks like now. So he doesn't mind being around us. But I think he's embarrassed to show himself in public at International Falls. He'd rather they remember him as he used to be, as he used to look, when he had his strength — when he was tough and trim, and awesomely vigorous."

II

He's lost a lot of the vigor, no doubt about that, but Nagurski is still spunky, still aggressive, still forthright. Braced by a visiting reporter one day, he was asked if he sometimes wears his Hall of Fame ring. Pointing one massive but arthritically gnarled hand at the other, he said: "I can't get it on any more, but I still carry it around with me." And, reaching deep into a front pants pocket, he brought it out and showed it happily as a bride — a size nineteen and a half ring. It was the largest player's ring ever made until well into the Super Bowl era, when the 300-pounders arrived to dismantle all the records.

Fact is, much of Nagurski is still a match for many of today's biggest NFL people. He still has those massive arms and wrists. His collar size is nineteen. He had ballooned to 300 himself until taking some of it off last winter. Fifty years ago, in an era of 175-pound linemen and 165-pound backs, he packed 225 pounds on a six-foot-two-inch frame. That made him one or two sizes bigger than the other players. And he was rock hard. "Running into Bronko was like getting an electric shock," a former teammate, Red Grange, said.

As introverted as ever, Nagurski seems genuinely distressed by personal questions. When a reporter asked him how fast he was in 1933, he grinned and said, "Fast enough." Asked about his dimensions, he said, "I was big enough." Later, he also said he was strong enough. He'll talk some about football, but not much about himself. His preference is to let the old records talk.

They have plenty to say. As a 1930-37 running back, Nagurski gained more than three thousand yards against NFL teams and averaged 4.4 — an excellent number for a fullback in a day that was long before the big-play era. Simultaneously, as a sixty-minute regular, he was also excelling as an offensive tackle, defensive tackle, and linebacker. "Most versatile football player ever," his college coach, Doc Spears, said of Nagurski, who came to fame at the University of Minnesota in the years when some of us first saw him in 1927-29. "He could be All-America at any position."

He was, in fact, a consensus All-American at two positions, tackle and fullback — the only football player yet with that distinction.

Still, in a depressed time, his income never reflected his skills. As he reminded Chicago reporters later: "The first contract I signed with (Bear Owner-Coach George Halas) was for $5,000. Even though I had a good year, my salary was cut to $4,500 my second year. The Depression was on, and the club was losing money. I got $3,700 my third year with the Bears, and that's where my salary stayed. They finally upped it to $5,000 again in 1937 when I talked about retiring. But when I asked for $6,000 in 1938, they turned me down. I went home figuring they'd call me, but they never did."

So in 1938, in the prime of his career, age twenty-nine, Nagurski slipped away to the obscurity of Rainy Lake, emerging only to wrestle occasionally at county fairs — a lucrative pastime he hated — and to play one wartime season with the Bears in 1943. He was then thirty-five. Significantly, they won the NFL championship again that season — their third in Nagurski's years. It may also be significant that in the forty years since 1943, the Bears — minus Nagurski — have won but two more championships.

III

In International Falls, just across the border from Canada, there is a liquor store on an historic site at Third Avenue and Third Street. Until fifteen years ago, when he retired from the business world, Bronko Nagurski pumped gas on that corner. He bought a Pure Oil station there after leaving the Bears, and, in a long-gone American era when service stations were service stations, he worked the place alone, coming out to fill your tank himself, whether it was ninety above or ninety below.

It was more often the latter.

For this is the chilly attic of America.

The people of greater International Falls don't, however, seem to mind, as, celebrating the winter, they barge around on the coldest days of the year. They love the town's designation — Ice Box of the Nation — and they take pride in hearing that theirs is the coldest weather in the U.S.

Among those admiring the place have been four generations of Nagurskis, beginning with Bronko's parents, who for years ran a mom-and-pop grocery store at Ninth Avenue and Eighth Street. They had migrated from the Ukraine to the village of Rainy River, Canada, where Bronko was born into a family that was to include two boys and two girls. He was four when they moved across the river to America, where, early on, he acquired what has been termed the most intimidating name in sports. When playmates couldn't pronounce his given name, Bronislau, they started calling him Bronko. A violinist might prefer Bronislau, but in football, as an opponent said, the very name of the man, Bronko Nagurski, struck a note of terror.

Four and a half miles out of International Falls, going north, the scent is of pine trees and wood-burning fireplaces as you come first to the old fullback's extensive vegetable garden. It stretches a half block along the lakeshore road. And behind the garden, snug in a wooded acre or two, stands the little Nagurski cottage with its wide green front lawn that sweeps some thirty-five yards down to the lake. The lone sound is from a Boise Cascade lumber train whistling in the distance.

The conversation piece in the little entry hall is another life-size color photo of Nagurski running the ball.

He hasn't seen the inside of a football stadium in years, he said, although he still keeps up on television, watching the Bears and other teams regularly. He said the modern Bears have a tendency to rely too heavily on their best running back. "They overworked Gale Sayers," he said, "and they've overworked Walter Payton. The Bears would be better with more balance." The implication was that they were better balanced in their championship seasons in the 1930s, so Nagurski was asked how often he carried the ball in a typical pro game. "Ten or twelve times," he said after thinking about it for a moment. "Of course, in those days, we had to play defense, too. We had to save something for that. But I think fifteen carries is about right for a running back."

Though it's hard to believe Nagurski built his workhorse reputation carrying the ball only ten or twelve times a game, he's a reliable source, obviously. His knees aren't what they once were but his mind is. And he's had a lot of time at Rainy Lake to remember.

IV

If anyone had thought of it, Super Bowl would have been a good name for the NFL's first championship game. It was the event of the year in 1933, when the fourteen-year-old league was first split into Eastern and Western divisions. A Christmas-Week attraction in Chicago's Wrigley Field, the '33 title game set the Eastern-Champion New York Giants against the Bears, best of the West. And it showcased Bronko Nagurski, the first of the MVPs in the league's long title series.

To score the two decisive touchdowns of a 23-21 spectacular, rarely matched in the later, less exciting, more prominent Super Bowl era, Nagurski threw the ball. He only faked the plunges that worried 1930s defensive teams the most. Both times, as he thundered toward the line of scrimmage, the powerful fullback straightened up, jumped like a basketball player, and passed the ball with enough touch and accuracy to get touchdowns on eight- and thirty-three-yard plays. Before he delivered the longer of these passes in the fourth quarter, the Giants had moved into a 21-16 lead. They never led again.

Asked about the two winning plays, Nagurski said, simply, "I wasn't much passer."

For him, that game was the second milestone event in football's emerging age of air. Twelve months earlier, with a pass to Grange, Nagurski had won a specially arranged one-game playoff for the 1932 league championship against the old Portsmouth Spartans. In those days, the ball could only be lawfully launched from a point at least five yards behind the line, and Portsmouth protested, unsuccessfully, that Nagurski's pass was illegal. The controversy persuaded the NFL to legalize passes from any point in the backfield beginning in 1933. Revealingly, the Bears won the title game that year only because they had developed a new weapon — and had seen it engraved in the rule book — the fake-run, play-action pass (as thrown by Nagurski).

New York Center-Linebacker Hein recalls that in the championship game, on Nagurski's two touchdown-pass plays, the possibility that he might carry the ball froze the Giant defense. "Bronko was the toughest fullback I ever met," Hein said. "If you hit him low, he'd run over you. When you hit him high, he'd knock you down, and then run over you."

Thus, the irony of Nagurski is that although his passing is responsible for his place in history as a winner, everybody talks about the other Bronko, the ballcarrier. They still tell Nagurski stories at high school banquets in the Midwest, laughing about the day that the Pittsburgh Steelers' special car derailed with a sickening jolt on their train trip home from a defeat in Chicago's Wrigley Field. "Run for your lives," Pittsburgh Coach Forrest (Jap) Douds shouted. "Nagurski is still after you!"

A quarter century following his retirement, Nagurski attended the annual dinner meeting of the Baseball Writers Association of America in New York, where he was the guest of the New York chapter, and where there was the usual polite applause for every baseball all-star introduced. Then, according to a reporter who was there, "The man on the dais said: 'And let's pay tribute to a visitor from another sport, Bronko Nagurski.'" Instantly, everyone was on his feet, necks craned for a glimpse of the burly Giant-killer with the size nineteen collar and the size nineteen and one-half ring finger. An applause meter would have given Nagurski the unanimous decision for the night, people said. For the century, maybe.

4. Jimmy Clark, Boy Champion

ANNIVERSARY DATES are both important to a newspaper and hard to remember. It was already April 5, 1988, when one of Jimmy Clark's friends called the office to remind our editors that Clark had taken his last ride just twenty years earlier, on April 7, 1968. In a very brief conversation with the Times' senior assistant sports editor, Mike Kupper, I recommended a later publication date, reminding him that stories of this importance require a research period of two or three weeks. He reminded me that the Times is a daily paper.

LOS ANGELES: April 7, 1988.

When Jimmy Clark died in his race car twenty years ago today — at age thirty-two — he was probably the world's best driver. Some people in racing called him the best of all time, and some still do, though it's hard to prove. In the different eras of auto racing, there have been too many other great drivers, starting with Tazio Nuvolari and Barney Oldfield. Later, A.J. Foyt and Al Unser Sr. each won the Indianapolis 500 four times. Juan Manuel Fangio won five world championships in four kinds of cars. And Jackie Stewart eventually broke most of Clark's records before climbing out at thirty-four, when he had the wit to stay out.

Clark, called the most famous Scot since Robert Burns, could have retired, too.

He talked about it. He had done everything, had everything. Born wealthy, Clark was the heir to two sizable, prosperous farms in Scotland, and his constant companion was London Model Sally Stokes. Small, blonde and outgoing, she was also his timekeeper, and she came with him when Clark, the small, dark and introverted champion, raced in the United States, where he was known as the Flying Scot. He had every reason to give up racing, everything but the will. Instead, Clark:

• Became the first Grand Prix driver to win twenty-five world championship races.

• Won the world driving title in 1963 and again in 1965, and at twenty-nine, in the midst of the 1965 season, became the first to double as Indy 500 champion and Formula One champion.

• Helped end the Offenhauser monopoly at Indianapolis, where he started the industry's rear-engine revolution when he won in a Ford-powered Lotus.

And he did it all so soon. He was, comparatively, so young. Most Indy drivers are thirty-two or more. Fangio was thirty-eight when he *began* his spectacular European career. At twenty-seven, Clark had become the youngest Grand Prix world champion, the youngest and, whenever he was racing, one of the happiest to be doing just that. And five years later, on the last day of his life, he was delighted to be out on another track, this one at Hockenheim, West Germany.

It was a Formula Two race, which in motor sports is to Formula One as the minors are to the majors in baseball. It was his first ride at notorious Hockenheim, then one of the world's most dangerous speedways. Ominously, the day was gloomy, rainy, foreboding.

Nearing a bend in the road, Clark, running eighth with sixteen laps to go, was all by himself. The bend is known as Shrimps Head Curve. It's a long, flat-out turn, and Clark, the first to average 150 m.p.h. as an Indianapolis winner, was going 170 m.p.h. when he approached it. He apparently never let up, and never got through. "Suddenly, Jim's car broke out," said the nearest driver, Chris Irwin of Britain, who was sprinting along 250 yards behind. "It looked like something mechanical."

Losing control, Clark zigged, zagged and somersaulted broadside into the forest that bordered the autodrome, wrapping the car's front end one way around a tree, and the rear end the other way. Wreckage rained over a 140-yard radius. Clark died instantly.

What did it all prove?

Some pointed to the irony of a champion's end in a Formula Two race. Others focused on a need for the safety measures that might have saved him — some tree removal there, for example, or more adequate roadside barricades, some of which are now in place. Still others talked of the tragedy of his death as a youth, when he was thought of as one of the world's most eligible bachelors. "I won't make her a widow," he had often said of Sally Stokes. "It isn't right, I tell you, I won't wed and drive."

That was a promise he kept.

II

Dan Gurney was the American race driver who had been closest to Clark, although a Glasgow taxi driver didn't recognize him when Gurney landed in Scotland twenty years ago this week. "Chirnside," Gurney said as he stepped into the cab. "Chirnside!" the taxi driver exploded. "That's clean across the country." Said Gurney: "Please take me there. I have to say goodbye to a friend." He was just in time. Of the many who attended Clark's funeral, Gurney had come the farthest, six thousand miles.

"Jimmy was a person who inspired that kind of devotion," says Mrs. Edouard Swart of Palos Verdes. She is the former Sally Stokes of Woodford, Essex and London, who years ago married another race driver from

Britain. He is now a businessman in the United States. "Everyone who was around Jimmy very much says the same things about him," she says. "He was kind, loyal and lots of fun. Strangers didn't always see that because he was a very private person. Few knew him well. I could count on one hand the ones he knew well."

Times Arts Critic Charles Champlin, who as a Time magazine reporter met Clark twenty-five years ago, says, "He didn't say two words if one would do, and wouldn't say one if he could get by with silence." Champlin remembers that the Flying Scot only had one change of expression: "He sometimes looked even more solemn than at other times."

To fellow race drivers, Clark was, however, a stimulating figure. "Jimmy was a great inspiration to me," says Mario Andretti, the Indianapolis rookie of the year in 1965 when Clark won. "There are still times I ask myself how Jimmy would have tackled this or that."

For one thing, Clark was the first to successfully move back and forth from Formula One to Indy car racing, setting the example for a select few, Andretti among them. "The way he performed from continent to continent has always given me strength," Andretti says. "In his quiet way, he moved a lot of people."

In fact, he still moves one follower at Hockenheim, where the race track, minus the trees that once made it a snare, is now the site of the German Grand Prix. On the day of the race there each year, a magnificent wreath of fresh flowers always appears on the embankment where Clark's car somersaulted into the forest. "They tell me that a German girl puts them there," Andretti says. "They say she is Utta Fausel, the photographer. I've won at Hockenheim. I've seen the flowers. Such devotion — after all these years."

III

In Scotland, too, they remember. They still drop by the churchyard in the Berwickshire village of Chirnside where Clark was buried that April day in 1968. He had been born nearby, at his father's farm, Edington Mains, on March 4, 1936. The Clark place is a fifteen-hundred-acre sheep farm, itself a little old village of barns and cottages. The dominating structure to every visitor is the great, gray stone mansion where Clark, youngest of five children, lived with his parents and four sisters when he was beginning life as a gentleman shepherd.

At eight he was in a tractor, at ten he was racing around the farm in a jalopy, and at seventeen he began to race his own cars, even though he always seemed too frail and sensitive for the hot, raucous machinery.

A nonsmoker and light drinker, Clark was regularly in a shirt and tie when he wasn't in a car. His favorite pronoun, everybody says, was we, not I. Or he would say, as he did after winning at Indianapolis, "I was just one link in a chain."

To Gurney, Clark was *the* link. "Jimmy dominated his era," Gurney says. "He could rise to any challenge, he was consistently tough, and he could beat you in any kind of car. He was the standard. I lost a great deal personally when Jimmy died. I didn't get much kick out of any win if there wasn't a driver of that class in the race."

Gurney, the only active racing figure who has succeeded single-handedly in Formula One, won the 1967 Belgian Grand Prix in a car and with an engine he designed and produced himself. But, he insists, he would chuck everything to have Clark's skills. "Jimmy was the top of the line," Gurney says.

IV

Big-screen, closed-circuit television was the new thing in the 1960s when, for a few years, much of America saw the Indianapolis 500 live at theaters and arenas. Thus Clark's radical new race car, the rear-engine Lotus, made an instant American impact in 1965 the day the Flying Scot finished first at Indy. In the most famous head start of his career, riding in the front row between Foyt and Gurney, Clark came out of the pace lap with a breathtaking rush. And as his sleek little Lotus screamed into the first turn far in front, the collective oooooh here at the Sports Arena, where thousands saw it on theater-size screens, dissolved into a roar.

"What a car," the fans shouted.

Shortly thereafter, when Clark skidded into a 360-degree spin and, somehow, sped on, they shouted, "What a driver."

And it was all true. As a combination, car and driver, both imports, were making U.S. history.

The car had been designed and built by a former British race driver named Colin Chapman, a genius type who had two unconcealed beliefs. He believed in himself, and he believed that conventional race cars were much too heavy. So he kept asking, where can I lose weight?

There was, really, only one place, and it seemed ridiculous to consider cutting there. Cars need frames, don't they? At first, Chapman agreed. But the more he thought about it, the more he wondered. And in the end, he built a monocoque car. The word means that the car's body was itself the frame. Keeping an eye on American rules, Chapman was able to bring an Indy car in at 1,270 pounds — a bare ten pounds over the minimum.

Only a very talented jockey could handle a steed so frail, the designer knew, and he knew one of those, too. Much earlier, when Chapman was thirty and going nowhere as a driver, he had finished first at a small track in the South of England though he was aware that he had run an indifferent race. A rookie named Jimmy Clark, then twenty-two, finished a close second that day driving a beautiful race in an indifferent car. Chapman realized it. He had built both cars himself.

Immediately, he understood that if he could put Clark in his seat, they'd have something. A fuel-injected Ford V-8 racing plant completed the package. "Those two made a unique combination — Colin with his ingenuity and Jimmy with his skills," Andretti says. "They quieted all the skeptics. The new technology, that car, that driver, were a turning point at Indy."

Others drew other conclusions, charging that Chapman's new technology was too much — that his cars were too light. It is Gurney's view that Chapman, who died of a heart attack at fifty-four in 1982, sometimes sacrificed safety for speed. "Chapman was in charge at Lotus," he says. "Their designs all had his approval — and they did get a faster car. But they paid a price for it, and the price was a more fragile car. They found a way to go faster — with lighter machines — but they lacked an extra margin of strength." Referring to Clark's fatal accident at Hockenheim, Gurney says: "That was typical of what Jimmy had to put up with on that team. The Lotus cars had more than their share of design failures, mechanical failures."

Clark, however, was a team player. He was also the ace of the Lotus staff, and that year the factory had a shot at the world Formula Two championship. He was obliging the factory that spring day at Hockenheim, then a new track, although the decision to race Hockenheim wasn't entirely Lotus' fault. There were plenty of Formula Two sites in Britain. It was Clark's fault that he passed them all up. A Redondo Beach admirer, Deke Houlgate, says: "It was the only mistake Jimmy ever made in ten years as a driver."

A mistake. A dangerous track in a forest. And a car with few safety features. In the 1960s, there weren't even roll bars on race cars. Seat belts had only recently seemed necessary, nor were the helmets of the '60s much protection. Clark's car was shattered, leaving no trace of the accident's cause.

Six years after the accident, after reviewing all the evidence for the "Encyclopedia of Auto Racing Greats," Robert Cutter and Bob Fendell wrote: "Exactly what happened is not known. But the consensus seems to rest on mechanical failure rather than driver error or the off (rainy) track."

With or without evidence, that April in the rain, no one who knew Clark could have concluded otherwise.

5. O.J. Simpson in a Former Life

THE TRAGEDY that took two young lives in O.J. Simpson's neighborhood in June, 1994, has, despite his acquittal, left him a murderer in the minds of many Americans, forever changing him, and changing America as well. The shock to those who knew Simpson when he was a uniquely gifted artist — a man who could play football with a distinction seldom before or since realized — is that in his playing years he displayed, in addition to his physical brilliance, a generous and solicitous character rare among sports superstars. He was not only the best player on his teams, but also the best liked, and his teammates played hard to make him look good. The Simpson of 1996 is the protagonist in an ongoing tragedy, and it is chastening to remember the heights from which he fell.

BUFFALO, N.Y.: Sept. 27, 1974.

Everything about O.J. Simpson seems big league: the way he runs, the way he talks, the way he makes friends and movies and money. And the way he lives. The first to gain two thousand yards in a football suit — in one calendar year — Simpson lives with his wife Marguerite and their two children in a stately new ten-room, two-story English Tudor house that sits on a large lot in a small new Buffalo suburb full of trees, streams, big green lawns and other big new houses.

And Simpson seems fond of the rural peace and quiet, especially when, on a clear, cold morning, a football game has left him aching in every muscle. At breakfast, moving very slowly, he serves orange juice and Sanka, and watches a leaf drop. "Who wouldn't enjoy the woods and open spaces around here?" he asks. "In the West, everybody has a fence that tells you this is my property, this is your property. The East is friendlier. You don't see any fences here. And better than that, in thirty seconds you can be alone in wooded country. Just looking at these woods makes you feel like Huckleberry Finn."

A big man in a brown bathrobe, Simpson smiles. It's a pleasant smile that says, "I like everybody."

The 1968 Heisman Trophy winner mentions his four-year-old son and continues: "Last week I took Jason snake hunting. He came in one day with his eyes big talking about a boa constrictor he saw on television, and I asked him, 'Want to go catch a snake?' We got a Baggie out of the kitchen and a big stick, and went on a safari across the street. Came back empty-handed, but we saw frogs that can jump a six-foot stream, and we sat down next to the biggest toad I've ever seen. Big as a football."

Elsewhere in this county these days, people spend less time watching frogs and toads than discussing O.J., but that's also O.K. with O.J., who in Buffalo, whether running a football or hunting snakes, is no longer Orange Juice. He is merely the Juice, as in electricity. His offensive line is called the Electric Company because, in the words of All-Conference Guard Reggie McKenzie, "We turn on the Juice."

Last night in the first home game of the year, they turned him on for a 6.5-yard average and seventy-eight yards in less than a half, when Simpson left with a minor injury. After the Bills won, upsetting Oakland, 21-20, everybody figured Simpson was a prophet. For he's been saying that this is a Super Bowl team. From a pulpit as the NFL's best running back — as well as most popular Bill and the most visible individual in the city — he has been trying to talk his team into the title. And it could be that by sheer force of personality, he has already built the Bills into a contender. Some fans are beginning to say so. There are even some Bills who say so.

II

Twelve noon. That's the doorbell. It penetrates every room of the Simpsons' house, a full-blown Westminster chime that sounds like a grandfather clock. The car pool has come to pick O.J. up for football practice, Reggie McKenzie driving, Ahmad Rashad riding shotgun. Tomorrow, it's Simpson's turn at the wheel. A passenger today, he has turned himself out in an orange outfit — with jeans to match — and when he hits the car, everybody, remembering Oakland, is smiling. "You're up early," says Rashad, who a few hours ago caught two touchdowns in two minutes to beat the Raiders. Says O.J.: "I haven't been to sleep yet."

After the excitement of a night game, Marguerite had confided earlier, O.J. never can sleep.

The car pool hears the latest about the Simpson daughter, Arnella, five, as O.J. says: "When we got home at 3:30, Marguerite said, 'There's no way I can get up to get Arnella off to school this morning.' I said, 'Don't worry, baby, I'll be up.' I got her some breakfast while she got ready, and she looked like a million when the school bus came."

In McKenzie's bus, a black Mercedes, Simpson slumps in the back seat for the half-hour ride to work as the talk turns to tonight's team party. As part of his role as the club's self-installed cheerleader, Simpson rounds up the Bills one or two nights a week for beer, cards, music and small talk. Togetherness. Let's beat (fill in name of opponent). Attendance isn't compulsory, but the crowd usually equals the club roster count.

"Whist tonight at the team trip," O.J. says happily. He is an excellent card player.

"Where's it at?" McKenzie asks.

"Mulligan's," O.J. replies, naming a Buffalo night club. "Bring money."

As McKenzie turns onto another throughway, rain suddenly lashes the windshield. "I know it's September already, but I hope the snow holds off a little while," Simpson says. "Once the snow is on the ground, a football team can't get in that hard work."

A visiting passenger asks: Is Buffalo weather tough on a Californian? Says Simpson: "I think of cold weather as a good thing, a very good thing. It gives our football club the advantage. I don't know if you've noticed, but the top two teams in our division play in extreme climates, Miami hot, Buffalo cold. And physically, Miami's players are better off. It's harder for us to get rid of aches and pains. But psychologically, Buffalo is the place to play. Our weather worries the other teams. And it toughens up our team. The Bills always play better late in the season. Remember that."

III

Movietime. The Bills are in a team meeting, dissecting the filmed version of the Oakland game. And while the players are sequestered, there is a moment to reflect on what Simpson has become as a football player — in his seventh season in the pros — and on how he compares against the many others who have played his game. And to put it abruptly, it seems possible at this time to conclude that this is the most accomplished running back the game has known, better than Jim Brown, better than Gale Sayers.

More than that, he is the most accomplished football player some of us have seen yet at any position, although, to be sure, such comparisons are as difficult as they are subjective.

Three things set Simpson apart.

One: He is the only football player ever acknowledged to be, first, the best running back in college football and, then, the NFL's best running back. Since the origin of sports, he's the only Heisman Trophy winner who has also won the Hickock belt as America's number-one professional athlete.

Two: Indescribable as a stylist, Simpson is something of a combination of Brown and Sayers, who until the other day ranked one-two in the minds of most critics. Carrying the ball, Simpson, like Sayers, can make full-speed right-angle cuts. And he can do it faster — at 9.4 speed — with almost Brown's breakaway power. Simpson at USC was on the 440-yard relay team that still holds the world record.

Three: By disposition, Simpson is the most dedicated and determined team player of all the great running backs. None of the great runners before him — surely not Bronko Nagurski nor Hugh McElhenny nor Jim Brown — ever attempted to psychologically recreate a football team. At Buffalo, Simpson discovered early on that, in an eleven-man sport, he needed ten other dedicated souls to help him do what he knew he could do as a matchless running back. And to do it — to build a showcase for his talent — he has, among other things, shamelessly advertised the Bills as a good football team, clearly expecting them to live up to his billing.

He has, they say, willed a little sophomore quarterback, Joe Ferguson, into a winner — by continuously identifying him as a winner — and he has willed the offensive line into a power by calling it powerful. Moreover, when questioned by an old acquaintance from Los Angeles, Simpson makes no attempt to hide this strategy. "There's a close ratio between recognition and production in football or anything else," he says. "The more recognition you get, the more you want to put out."

So this is Simpson's mission for the 1970s: to lift Buffalo into the Super Bowl with his talent, his fidelity, and an uncommon personality. The Bills are starting from a long way back, particularly on defense, but Simpson has already achieved uniquely in one respect. Whereas, before him, a single athlete has occasionally made a good team great — as Joe Namath did, and as Kareem Abdul-Jabbar did — O.J. is the first to make a lousy team good.

IV

Late afternoon. The Bills have finished for the day; Simpson has time to talk, and he's willing to take the time. Newspaper people have ranked him as the most considerate of news sources since his first game at USC. Standing in the locker room after a game in which he has played either well or passably, or worse, he answers routine questions from any accredited reporter patiently, politely, forthrightly, and almost interminably. "I want them to get the story right," he says. "A long time ago, I learned from Kareem Abdul-Jabbar to say exactly what you mean. Don't leave anything to an individual's interpretation."

How does one learn that from Kareem?

"I saw him interviewed once," Simpson says, "and I knew what he meant when he said there are a lot of insincere, superficial people in Los Angeles. I feel that way myself. But when it came out in the media, Kareem was quoted as saying that Los Angeles is a phony town. It isn't, and he didn't say it, but it came out that way. Since then, I've tried to be precise."

Speaking precisely, why do you think it's necessary to seek applause for highly paid major league athletes?

"If the quote star is a regular guy who takes an interest, the sky's the limit in this business. Pro football is like a forty-seven man relay race. No other sport needs half that many guys pulling together. One sure way to get such a big group going is for an O.J. or Joe Namath to make sure guys like McKenzie aren't overlooked. Sports fans think I know something about football — and as a matter of fact, I do."

Calling on that expertise, what would you say first if you were invited to speak on the mechanics of running a football?

"I'd say that in football today, there are two kinds of great running backs, the sidesteppers and the challengers. I'm a sidestepper. I never challenge a great defensive player. I never let him hit me square, and if I can avoid him altogether, I do. I study the films during the week, and on the field I always look for the baddest dude on the other team. I get it in my mind he's never going to hit me. My favorite tacklers are the little cornerbacks and safetymen. I run at those guys, and sidestep the linemen."

What runner would deliberately run into a lineman?

"The thing that makes Larry Brown great is his courage, his desire. Larry will challenge anybody, and he isn't as big as I am. One year he took such a beating he couldn't play the last two games. That's the only way I won the league running championship that time."

What if it's third and one and Dick Butkus is standing in the hole?

"Larry will take Butkus on if necessary and I won't. Larry is always going head-over-heels. How often do you see O.J. on his head? My game is to juke the tough guys. I put the okey-doke on them, bounce around, and look for daylight. If I can't find a hole, I won't just slam in there. I'll run out of bounds before I'll run into a wall. All great running backs are insane, but I'm not that crazy."

Insane?

"A great ballcarrier is the most unpredictable guy in sports. The great backs don't know what they're doing. There's no way to explain what they do when they have the ball — there's no rhyme or reason to what they do — and no way to teach it. You can teach a running back to block or catch, but running is completely instinctive. You hear passers, receivers, blockers, pitchers, hitters, shortstops, pole vaulters and everybody else say they've been out working on their thing, but you never hear a great running back say, 'I'm going out to work on this or that.' All he says is, 'I'm going out to work out,' or, 'I've been working out.'"

What three or four qualities have the great running backs, in your opinion, all had?

"They've had blockers, coaching, speed and power — and one more thing: running knowledge, or what some people call instinct. You either have it or you don't."

Who had the most of it? Do you put any one running back at the top?

"Jim Brown is much the biggest guy who had everything a great running back has to have, including blockers, so you've got to put Jim on top. He could run over them or around them, but like me he went around them when he could. That's why he lasted nine seasons without injury. The runner I used to identify with was Gale Sayers. I'm the faking type, and so was Gale."

Comparing yourself to Sayers in his prime, what's the edge you have on him?

"He didn't get to play for the Buffalo Bills."

v

Night. The trip. And O.J. is having more fun than anybody, getting a lot of mileage out of two beers. The ribbing is merciless. In one weekend, Simpson has been struck by two disasters — USC was upset and Buffalo won big without him — and there are forty-six other football players in Buffalo who won't let him forget it.

Linebacker John Skorupan has a new nickname for Simpson, "22 to 7," the score of Arkansas' win over USC, where Simpson won his Heisman. "Hey, 22 to 7, how about another beer?" Skorupan shouts. Skorupan is from Penn State.

"Is Vassar still on your schedule?" Simpson fires back. "Think you can beat Hofstra this year?"

The dialogue, when athletes get together, would never make Broadway, though much of it is obscene enough. But the thing they seem to like best about life on a winning football team is just the "messin' around with the guys," the ribs and pranks, the horseplay. And this they miss the most when their careers are spent. They all say so.

Simpson gets the roasts going in Buffalo, and keeps them hot, playing a part he learned at USC. The two wires that run between Simpson the college athlete and Simpson the pro are his talent — the ability to make a ninety-degree cut at 9.4 speed — and his endless campaigning to make All-Americans and All-Pros out of the people around him, from Ron Yary to Reggie McKenzie.

As president of the Electric Company, O.J. roasts them in the locker room and toasts them in the press. He turns *them* on.

6. Paul Hornung, Golden Boy

SPEAKING OF the Green Bay Packers in 1968, Jerry Kramer, the author who had been an All-Pro guard for the five-time world champions, said: "Paul Hornung was always the star of our team, even after he stopped being the best player." It was a thought I shared. And the year Hornung finally made the Hall of Fame, I flew to his old Kentucky home for another visit.

LOUISVILLE, Ky.: Feb. 24, 1986.

This is Paul Hornung's town. The one-time Golden Boy of Green Bay and Notre Dame was born here a half century ago. And though he has traveled widely for the last twenty-five years, Hornung has always come back to Louisville. "Who wouldn't?" he wonders. "Like the man said, I've never met a Kentuckian who wasn't on his way home."

In the years when Hornung was an All-American quarterback at Notre Dame, he returned to Louisville every month or so to spend a day or two with his mother. He lived at her house until he was thirty. "I always hitchhiked to South Bend," he recalls. "I must have made thirty or forty round trips to Notre Dame in those days, and it was my thumb that did it. Never went any other way."

Later, when Hornung was an All-NFL halfback with the Green Bay Packers, he cruised back to his old Kentucky home each winter in newly-purchased convertibles. "Been tooling new Cadillacs for twenty-eight years," he says, although, this month, he made an exception. He came home from Honolulu in a jet.

Hornung, now a Louisville businessman with holdings mostly in real estate, ventured to Honolulu at the request of a committee from the Pro Football Hall of Fame in Canton, Ohio, a group that proudly introduced him as a new member. It was a long time coming. Nine other Packers preceded him to Canton despite Hornung's 1960s status as the champions' big gun.

The delay was due to a habit he had picked up in his home town. For nearly two centuries, betting on horses has been fashionable in the land of Kentucky Horseman Henry Clay, who for awhile doubled as a U.S. senator. At the height of his NFL career, Hornung was banned from football for a year for betting on himself, and that troubled some members of the Hall of Fame selection committee. Overvaluing what they called Hornung's immorality, they kept him out, year after year.

Hornung's bitterness, if any, isn't evident. "The thing I'm proudest of," he says, "is that I made the College Hall of Fame as a quarterback and the Pro Hall of Fame as a running back."

Was he that good?

The record identifies Hornung as a unique football player, the most prolific NFL scorer the game has known, the only pro who ever scored 176 points in one season. In 1960, in a twelve-game schedule, he kicked fifteen field goals and scored fifteen touchdowns, adding forty-one extra points. The Golden Boy is also the most decorated football player of all time, the only one who has earned all this: NFL MVP twice (1960 and 1961); NFL championship game MVP (1961); top pick in the NFL draft (1957); college football Hall of Fame; pro football Hall of Fame; Heisman Trophy winner (as a member of a 2-8 Notre Dame team in 1956).

The only player from a losing team to get the Heisman since it first went to Jay Berwanger of Chicago in 1935, the Golden Boy was also the only quarterback to win it in the fifteen years between Johnny Lujack in 1947 and Terry Baker in 1962. Thus Hornung remains the leading candidate for recognition as the best all-around football player ever. Consider: At both Notre Dame and Green Bay, he successfully played all three backfield positions, quarterback, halfback and fullback, excelling as runner, passer, receiver, kicker and blocker. He was the blocker for a Hall of Fame fullback, Jim Taylor. Moreover, Hornung punted, kicked off and kicked field goals, and at Notre Dame he returned punts and kickoffs. A sixty-minute player, he also played safety at Notre Dame, where, one season, he was second in total tackles. "Second in tackles," he muses. "I'm kind of proud of that one."

II

The Golden Boy at fifty isn't quite as golden as he used to be. These days he is a gray-toned blond who comes to work in old jeans or old cords and pullover sweaters. The sweaters fit snugly. He admits to 255 pounds, but it's more. The familiar 215-pound athlete disappeared when he quit smoking several years ago but kept eating. "Paul is always on time for dinner," says Angela, his second wife.

Between meals, he travels extensively as a football announcer for WTBS, visiting different cities each fall weekend. The distinctive Hornung trait, most noticeable in airports, is his gait, which is fast-forward. A bundle of nervous energy, he always seems to be in motion. He says he can get in and out of any restaurant in America in twenty-eight minutes. Though his reach reportedly isn't that fast when the check arrives, Hornung is essentially good-hearted, open, unreserved, trusting. Particularly loyal to old friends, he asked one of them, Max McGee, to make his Hall of Fame presentation this summer.

On the Hornung teams at Green Bay, McGee doubled as a wide receiver and fun-loving curfew-buster, but he, too, has settled down, married, and grown rich. He started a Mexican restaurant in Minneapolis and ran it into an extensive franchise operation. A bit sadly, McGee says: "You can't party all your life."

Hornung remembers when they tried. "Max was my roommate on the Packers, and one year at training camp, he was out every single night," Hornung says. "I know, because once or twice I had to get him up and make him come along."

III

The great Kentucky flood of 1937, the year the Ohio River overflowed in Louisville, changed Paul Hornung's life. He was two years old when, terrified, he clutched his mother's hand on the roof of their submerged house while the river rose. Just in time, a man in a small boat came round the corner, rowed up, and rescued them. "That was the start of a beautiful friendship," Hornung says. For the oarsman was Henry Hofmann, a real estate investor-developer and family benefactor known to Hornung as Uncle Henry. Hornung's father, who had been an insurance company executive, left the family early in his son's life, the new Hall of Famer says, a victim of alcohol. Hofmann replaced him as adviser, friend and football fan.

As long ago as the Notre Dame years, Hofmann, who died in 1983, was investing Hornung's savings — exclusively in Louisville real estate — and, at the same time, rescuing another Louisville youngster, Frank Metts. Encouraging Metts to resign as the driver of a milk truck, which appeared to be his destiny, Hofmann put him in business with Hornung. And in Kentucky today, they're still doing business as Metts Company, with Metts in charge. Hornung, vice president, focuses on sales, contacts and contracts. Their holdings include shopping centers, rental properties, equipment manufacturing and oil interests. "Paul has a good business head and gets along with people well," Metts says. "Those are the two big things."

In a corner office, Hornung sits at a big modern desk where he catches the eastern and southern sun. He obviously likes bright colors and mixes of modern and antique furniture. The dominant decoration is an oil portrait of former Green Bay Coach Vince Lombardi, painted by former Ram Receiver Tommy McDonald. Down the street, not too far away, is Muhammad Ali Boulevard, named for another Louisville champion. It is a measure of Ali's clout that no Louisville thoroughfare is yet known as Golden Boy Boulevard.

IV

A tour of Louisville is also a trip into the past for Paul Hornung, who has traveled from the blue collar west end, where he was born, to the more affluent east side, where he lives now. "See that house across the street?" he asks, pointing to a tiny, one-story, white-frame cottage. "Mom and I used to live there. We could only afford to rent one room, that front room there. We had two cots, and not much else." His grandparents, who once ran a mom-and-pop grocery store in Louisville, had died. His mother was just getting started in Kentucky's civil service. After her first promotion, they rented the second floor of a slightly larger, two-story, white-frame house nearby.

"There it is," he says, indicating a house in a low-income Portland Street area once filled with an immigrant group known as the Portland Irish. Hornung is Irish and German. That was his home through high school, and it was to that home that he returned so often from Notre Dame, hitch-hiking as far as possible, then riding up in a Portland Street bus. "That's the Marine Hospital across the street," he says. "As you can see, their front yard is as big as a football field. That's where I learned to play football. Played every day."

His mother was to vouch for that. Speaking as a Hornung fan who saw most of his games at Notre Dame and Green Bay, Loretta Hornung, now eighty, says: "No boy was ever crazier about football."

During his first year in high school, she remembers, there was a September Friday when the coach ended practice early. He was saving the legs of his athletes for a big Saturday game, so Paul dressed and, as usual, made the five-mile trip home on his bicycle. When he got there, he noticed that a pickup game was still in progress on the Marine Hospital grounds. Rushing into the house, he changed clothes again, and played sandlot football until dark. "That gave him an idea," his mother says. "After that, he always hurried home when high school practice ended early. He loved playing football twice a day. The day of the game was kind of a letdown."

Her boy still thinks of his high school years as the best of his life, despite his penniless circumstances, and despite the fame and fun he knew later. "High school is the only time when you can play every day," he says. "I looked forward to basketball so much that I couldn't wait for the football season to end. Then in the late winter, I couldn't wait for baseball. How could you have a better life? Studies came easy. Mom made sure I studied enough to get to Notre Dame."

Hornung's guided tour ends in Louisville's Windy Hill district, where he and Angela share a three-bedroom condominium on a pleasant, carefully landscaped little street in a lush residential area. Two prominent bars, one upstairs and one down, are stocked with the best in gin and Scotch, but the bottles look like rarely touched museum pieces. They're apparently token reminders of a bygone era in the life of a reformed playboy. In his playroom, the many framed pictures on what he calls the wall of fame are dominated by three Sports Illustrated covers featuring Hornung in his Golden Boy decade, the earliest in 1956, one in 1963, one in 1966. The conversation piece in the master bedroom is an oil painting of Angela Hornung, who is wearing, all told, long blonde hair. A bathroom statue and most of the other portraits in the house are also discreet nudes. No Windy Hill resident could ask for more.

V

Hornung was fourteen when he hitch-hiked to Churchill Downs the first time. He has been a regular ever since, sometimes as a track employee. Starting as an usher in his high school days, when he was already a famous Louisville athlete, he hardened up for Notre Dame football with summer jobs at the track as a construction worker. Since Henry Clay's day if not before, fast horses have been part of the Kentucky landscape, and Churchill Downs is a glamour center in the heart of the state's biggest city. You can walk to Churchill Downs from downtown Louisville. To a Louisville boy, the race track is as commonplace as his church or school. The act of betting comes naturally, and from betting on horses it's an easy step to betting on baseball and football.

When Hornung was an NFL player, he knew the league had a rule against betting, but the rule was hardly consistent with life as he had known it and lived it in Kentucky. He didn't change his lifestyle just because he had become a Notre Dame football player, or even an NFL player. Nor would he go underground. It isn't like Hornung to sneak around. He associated with the same people he had known and trusted for years. And eventually he paid for it when Commissioner Pete Rozelle, bringing up the familiar evidence of Hornung's gambling, suspended him for the 1963 season.

A few years later, when Hornung had become a football announcer, pairing with Lindsay Nelson, he was flying to a game one day when another passenger came up and consoled him. As Nelson tells it, the passenger said: "What an s.o.b. that Rozelle is. How could he ban a guy for betting on his own team? Worst thing he's ever done." The Golden Boy would have none of it. "No, sir, you're wrong about that," he said. "Rozelle was right, and I was wrong. When I broke the rule, Rozelle did what he had to do."

The thing that appeals to McGee about Hornung is his friend's horse sense. "He's got me so interested in horses that I've bought eight of my own," McGee says. "In my first first seven races, I've had five winners." Hornung's opinion of that: "He's just been lucky." Other Hornung opinions: On Bill Hartack: "My favorite jockey. Bill never pulled a horse." On Swaps: "My favorite horse. Swaps held five world records at the same time." On Carroll Rosenbloom, formerly president of the Colts and then the Rams: "My favorite owner. You can't knock an owner who bets on his own team."

VI

A fan of 1980s football, Hornung identifies a play in this year's Pro Bowl as the NFL's play of the season. It was a pass thrown for a touchdown by a Raider halfback, Marcus Allen. "As a passer, Marcus is as good as I was," Hornung says. "And he's a better runner." The others who attempt to throw halfback passes these days, including Walter Payton, don't fake the run properly, Hornung says, adding: "Walter and those guys slow down too soon and retreat too fast. Marcus does it just right. He's the best halfback passer since the single wing."

Hornung was talking about his own best play, the one that made him famous. "It's the most neglected play in football today," he says. "Teams like the Raiders should use it all the time. They think it's a surprise gimmick play, but it isn't. It's a game-plan play. In one series at Philadelphia (in the early 1960s), we ran it on every down. It was a regular-season game, but Coach Lombardi thought we needed work on the halfback option. So we ran it for about sixty-five yards. I mean, I was out there throwing or running on six or seven consecutive plays until we scored."

That time, following an old custom, Hornung doubtless spiked the ball flamboyantly. A showman as well as a football player, he was the first to showboat after touchdowns. By the 1980s, spiking and dancing in the end zone have become tiresome, but in the 1960s it was a novelty when, following a touchdown at Chicago, Hornung threw the football high into the stands one day at Wrigley Field. The Bears' coach, George Halas, livid, screamed: "You'll pay for that, young man."

Green Bay Coach Lombardi, grinning, said: "Don't worry, George, I'll pay for it."

It is the view of Hornung's teammates, including Jerry Kramer, that Lombardi got his money's worth. Summing up Hornung's career in his most recent book, "Distant Replay," Kramer put it this way: "Paul was, really, the only player we had in Green Bay who came in a superstar and left a superstar."

The Golden Boy also came and left a playboy. Former Bear Linebacker Bill George, who drew Hornung as a roommate one week in the era when the Pro Bowl was a Los Angeles institution, was asked after the game what it was like rooming with a legend. "I never saw him," George said. "Haven't seen anything but Hornung's luggage. I roomed with his luggage all week."

7. Henry Aaron Catches Babe Ruth

AS A home run hitter, Hank Aaron spent a lifetime sneaking up on people. Though he outproduced Babe Ruth in the end, retiring in 1976 with 755 home runs, he never hit fifty any year, whereas Ruth hit fifty-four in 1920, fifty-nine in '21, sixty in '27 and fifty-four in '28. The thing that made Aaron baseball's number-one home-run hitter was his consistency. Year to year, nobody, not even Ruth, has ever matched him. On the day that Aaron caught Ruth, my assignment was to combine a breaking news story with a personality piece — doing which is a hard way to earn a day's pay for a daily paper.

CINCINNATI: April 4, 1974.

Of the nineteen pitches Henry Aaron saw Thursday afternoon, it was the fifth that had his number on it. The number was 714. Swinging smoothly, Aaron, a right-handed hitter, lifted the ball over the left-field fence with his first swing in his first at bat in the first inning of the first game of the year to tie Babe Ruth.

The right-handed Cincinnati pitcher, Jack Billingham, either shuddered or shrugged — from a distance it was hard to tell — as Aaron's 714th career home run drifted to the left of the 375-foot sign identifying the power alley in left field and dropped out of sight. It was 2:40 p.m. (Cincinnati time) on Aaron's twenty-first opening day as an outfielder for the Braves, whose uniform Ruth wore at Forbes Field, Pittsburgh, in 1935 the day he knocked a ball out of a ballpark for the last time.

No one else has hit 700 home runs. Only Ruth, Aaron and Willie Mays have hit as many as 600. Mays called it a day with 660. Ruth retired a week after parlaying his last three home runs in one afternoon — at the age of forty. Aaron at forty is still looking ahead. "I feel like I can hit thirty-five or more this year," he said Thursday. "My goal is 750."

The Reds, as it happened, won this opener on a wild pitch in the eleventh inning, 7-6, before a crowd of 52,154, including the first-ball pitcher, Vice President Gerald R. Ford. And afterward, Aaron said: "I thought I'd get one in this game." The one he got, a three-run home run for a 3-0 Atlanta lead in the first inning, was his only hit in three at bats.

Billingham, thirty-one, the former Dodger relief pitcher who became Cincinnati's most popular starter last year, said: "Aaron hit a mistake. It was a fastball, low and outside, that didn't sink." Gamely, he pitched to Aaron again in the third inning, getting him on a grounder. But in the fifth inning, Billingham was startled to hear himself booed in his own park after walking Bad Henry on four throws. "That was the smartest thing I could have done," the Cincinnati pitcher maintained. "He was swinging the bat good, and I wasn't having a good day."

Altogether, it was a lucky afternoon for Aaron from two standpoints: Billingham was off and the weather was on. It was ideal, that is, for an old man's bones, the temperature standing at sixty-three on a brilliant, breezy day. Perfect, full sunshine lit things up for all forty-year-olds swinging for 714 with possibly failing eyesight.

The ball Aaron disposed of was worth $2 when he connected and $15,000 or more when it landed. For it's the only one in the world adding up to 714 — the most famous number in baseball for a half century. Ruth's 714 ball has been lost since, probably, the instant he hit it. Aaron's was retrieved by an off-duty policeman named Clarence Williams, who had been hired to stand behind the fence for just that purpose.

In a six-minute ceremony at home plate, the ball was returned to Aaron, briefly, then locked up with the bat that struck it. In invisible ink, the ball had been marked ahead of time with a code number, 14-1. The number Aaron saw on it was a bit larger.

For years it has been assumed there would never be a 715 ball. Aaron promises there will. Referring to the pressure in which he's been living, he said: "I'm glad it's almost over with."

II

The pressure, ironically, has made him a celebrity at last. After years in which he alone could see that he was chasing Babe Ruth's ghost, Aaron has attracted more than two hundred sportswriters to Cincinnati this week. To those who first met him twelve or fifteen years ago, he seems no older. The comparatively close-cropped hair is as black as ever, the face plain and solemn most of the time, the smile still big and toothy when he turns it on. A long time ago, his mother said it for then and now: "He was a quiet boy who just loved to play ball."

Aaron resembles Ruth in no way. Ruth was six-two and 215 or more; Aaron for twenty years has been a boyish six-foot figure weighing 185. Ruth, they say, liked fifty-two-ounce bats; Aaron prefers thirty-four ounces. Ruth lived as big as his bats; Aaron is a quiet homebody. Still, the astrologists have been having a field day. Ruth was born on February 6, 1895, Aaron on February 5, 1934. That's Aquarius.

Aaron's wife, father and brother were sitting behind the Atlanta dugout when Hank homered, and his father remembered not only number one, which Vic Raschi pitched in 1954, but also Hank's original power shows in his boyhood. "He used to roll a ball up on the roof," said Herbert Aaron, "and hit it with a broom handle when it came down." In those days Herbert Aaron made eighteen cents an hour as a rivet bucker in the Mobile shipyards. His son is now a millionaire with a salary of $200,000 a year.

Despite his money, nothing whatever is spectacular about Hank Aaron. Although it will shortly be mathematically proved that he is the most prolific home-run hitter who ever lived, he has never, in any one season, hit sixty — the magic number Ruth and others have flirted with (and reached occasionally). Nor has he hit fifty. Rather it is consistency that has made Bad Henry what he is. He keeps plugging along. He has hit thirty or more home runs fifteen times. He has been in every All-Star game for nineteen years. And in two World Series, he hit safely every day — in fourteen consecutive Series games. Match that, Babe.

Twice married, Aaron is a family man who fathered two sons in 1957. His second wife, Billye, is a television personality in Atlanta. She came to Cincinnati this week after her Wednesday TV show, and Hank met her at the airport just before a tornado struck near the runways. They spent that night quietly at the hotel, where Aaron tried to decide whether he wanted to play here opening day. "I'd like to hit it in Atlanta," he said, "but if I play, I hope I hit one here. I'll swing my natural way." He kept his promise.

III

Henry Aaron's natural way is a whip-like action that powers the fastest bat in baseball. It's mostly wrist movement. His wrists measure eight inches around, bigger than Muhammad Ali's. Thus, with his fast bat at rest, he can stand there patiently, the most relaxed man in the stadium, waiting for the pitcher to do something, anything.

Aaron's quiet career is summed up in his batting manner. "At the plate," Sandy Koufax once said, "Henry looks as if he's sleeping. He looks that way until he swings."

Sure enough, ten minutes after the game started Thursday, Aaron seemed sound asleep waiting for Billingham's first pitch. The leadoff man had walked on four throws and the second man had singled, indicating that something was brewing. And although the next man flied out, perhaps depriving Aaron of a record fifteenth grand slam, Billingham was in more trouble than he may have guessed.

The first pitch was low, the second outside, the third a fastball that surprised Aaron, who took it for a strike. The next one was outside, and then, on three-and-one, the thunder.

Before the game, meeting the press in a beige suit and see-through turtleneck shirt that he could have bought at Penney's, Aaron playfully suggested he might run the bases backward if he got the chance. When the time came, though, he didn't. Having perfected the home-run trot in 713 prior chances, he simply loafed around the usual Aaron way. Impassively.

8. Arnold Palmer, Idol of the Galleries

THE BIG MAN during the five years I covered golf was Arnold Palmer, whose galleries, known everywhere as Arnie's Army, were the largest in the sport's history. Two of the four Palmer pieces that follow were written at the 1966 U.S. Open, which he blew in a bizarre stunner. That was a defining Palmer performance: a loss that resulted from the strengths of a winner.

PALMER AT OLYMPIC

SAN FRANCISCO: June 20, 1966.

In living color, in the living rooms of America from coast to coast, Arnold Palmer, the world's richest golfer, fell on his face yesterday, blowing a five-stroke lead on the last four holes. He fell because he's an unremitting gambler. He wanted a record instead of just another title, even if it is the U.S. Open title, and it beat him.

Though playing with Billy Casper in a kind of match play final that paired the leaders of the sixty-sixth Open, he wasn't playing against Casper yesterday. And, comically, Casper wasn't playing Palmer. In one of the weirdest rounds in Open history, Casper was playing for second place, and Palmer was playing the ghost of Ben Hogan, who set the record in 1948.

On the scheduled last day of the tournament, both men, as it turned out, were guilty of monumental misjudgments. But it is likely that the story of their freakish struggle on the final few holes of the first seventy-two will outlive the details of the anticlimactic playoff, which will be today's feature. For in the end yesterday, Palmer collapsed with a 32-39 (71) — 278 and Casper scrambled to a 36-32 (68) — 278. Each finished the tournament two under in a week when nobody else broke par, when, indeed, nobody else came close. Jack Nicklaus, third, 285, was five over and seven back.

There were, in this tournament, only two golfers.

II

Palmer was undone by his supreme confidence in himself and by a frightening ambition. Combined, these qualities lured him into an overmatch with a vicious golf course, the historic lake course at Olympic, which has humbled the weak and the strong indiscriminately in two Opens since 1955 and which made a mockery finally of Arnold's confidence and his ambition.

It was his deceptively successful 32 on the front nine that broke him.

His first shot of the day had whistled 270 yards up the track. Arnold hurried over, looked at it, peered at the well-trapped little green, and chose a 3-wood. The army gasped, and then broke the forest silence with a roar. Here was a guy starting the last round of an Open with a three-stroke lead. Inaccuracy could cost him it all — on the first hole. But Arnold smashed it aboard, and, with the round barely under way, the three-stroke leader was putting for an eagle. As it happened he made birdie.

He also birdied the second for a quick big five-stroke bulge, and the confidence was in him beyond recall, the confidence that would shatter him. He made the turn seven shots in front of Casper, an advantage that he could have nursed easily into the championship. But he was thinking of something else. "It entered my mind there," he said afterward, "that I could shoot a 274. I realized that I could break the record."

This is Hogan's 276, set at Riviera in 1948, the lowest score in more than a half century of Open war.

So at the short fifteenth hole, still 5-up on Casper, Arnold gambled extravagantly with the U.S. prize, the most valuable in golf, which was then all but his. "I tried to shoot at the pin," he said, "instead of to the left. It was one of those shots that if they work, they're great. If they don't, you're in trouble." What he got was trouble, landing in the sand. Bogey. Casper found the bottom of the cup with a twenty-foot putt, "my toughest and best of the day," he said. Birdie. In seconds, Palmer's lead had been slashed from five back to three.

III

In the competitive and emotional world of golf, there doubtless isn't another pro who would, with a three-stroke lead, three holes to play, the Open in the bag, on a course like this, court disaster. But on the very next hole, the man gambled again. Lost in a forest after his first shot, Palmer, with awesome stubbornness, pulled out a 3-iron. "It didn't get airborne," he said sadly afterward of the shot that television missed in a classic moment of negligence. "I should have taken out a 6-iron," Arnold murmured. "If I had, I'd have been out of there. I was gambling," he confessed.

He needed a wood, astonishingly, on his fourth shot. Bogey. Casper's third shot meanwhile was beautifully placed. So was his putt. Birdie. In consecutive holes, Palmer's once commanding lead had been fried down to one stroke.

At the seventeenth, as the nation watched unbelievingly, the leaders groveled in the rough like two boxers with concussions. But Casper out-boxed Palmer, and suddenly they were even. At the eighteenth, where both short-putted, you would swear both choked, but both made par. And the man who makes par at *this* eighteenth has done something, although, for Arnold, it was done a little late.

IV

Despite his collapse, Arnold might have won it anyway if his luck had matched his ambition. Four times he putted perfectly up to the last inch. Had any of them dropped, the party's over. At both the tenth and the thirteenth, the ball crept up, looked in, and froze. At the fourteenth, it snaked around the rim, but sneaked away. At the seventeenth, it just stopped. The army, four and five deep, dozens with green periscopes poking upward like the eyes of a science-fiction monster, shuddered. Arnie was entitled to at least one of those four putts, the soldiers thought, and said, and will always believe.

V

In the absurd fourth-round climax of this tournament, nothing was crazier or funnier than Billy Casper's earnestness in playing for second money during the same moments exactly that Palmer was blowing apart. "I was never discouraged at any time," Billy said afterward when they asked him how he reacted personally to the four birdies Arnold threw at him on the first nine. "I was trying to make second all day," he said.

He was asked if he knew whom he had to beat for second. "I knew just who I had to beat," Casper answered promptly. "Lema and Nicklaus. I knew I was one over and they were three over on ten."

For Palmer, second is like dying. Why is it so vital to Casper? "If you can't be first," Casper instantly replied again, "absolutely nothing is better than second."

Going all out to beat Nicklaus, Casper birdied two of the last five holes, and what's more he seemed fully capable of a birdie stroke on the eighteenth, except that, by then, to his astonishment, he was no longer out to beat Nicklaus but to tie Palmer, who had busily come back to him with four bogeys in a stretch of five holes through the seventeenth. "It was all very exciting," said Billy.

Next Day at Olympic

SAN FRANCISCO: June 21, 1966.

Billy Casper had one big thing going for him in this tournament. When Arnold Palmer blew, Casper was closest. And so for the next twelve months, the emaciated Peacock Gap, California, veteran will have the pleasure of hearing himself identified as Open Champion Billy Casper.

In the end, he was the only subpar shooter of the week in the pine trees of Olympic, wresting from the lake course one more of this species than it had surrendered in 1955. And in yesterday's playoff, Casper compiled a 69 to Palmer's 73. Yet Casper didn't earn this championship, he inherited it when Palmer, on successive days, on the back nine, blew up twice.

Long after the playoff contest that wasn't a contest, Palmer last night summed up the tournament simply and honestly and tragically. "I'd like to know what happened," he said.

II

What happened yesterday is that Palmer, leading by two walking to the eleventh, lost six strokes at the next six holes as Casper came on to win by four. Palmer's game simply came apart again there at the scene of Sunday's crime — and in Palmer's mind, there must have been a correlation.

On two unseasonal days in San Francisco, mild and sunny, Palmer lost thirteen shots to Casper altogether on the home nine. Even so, the week in San Francisco verified Palmer's skills. It takes a golfer to lead a U.S. Open for three and a half rounds by seven strokes.

III

The precise question has to do with Palmer the man. Did he choke or miscalculate? Did the pressure get him on the last nine holes Sunday and again yesterday or was he beaten by a malicious tree-dominated golf course? Is the army living on the dreams of a bygone era?

It is all too true that Palmer today is 0-3 in Open playoffs. Moreover, in front of Western galleries, he has not uniformly distinguished himself lately on the late holes. He faded, for instance, on the last day of last January's L.A. Open and won it largely because he had come out of the third round with a seven-stroke lead. Then at Palm Springs, Arnold was easy pickings for Doug Sanders in a quick and disappointing playoff.

There are, however, other and better reasons to explain Palmer's recent behavior than to concede that he has at this late hour fallen victim to the strangleholds of pressure. What happened to Palmer is what can happen to John Unitas in a Green Bay game. Bart Starr is no Unitas, but he can outplay him the day John throws three interceptions. Palmer didn't fold in San Francisco. He was beaten by some recklessness Sunday and by the lakeside course yesterday, and Casper stepped forth to become the winner because, in golf, the hot player very often can.

Arnold's offensive style is ill-suited to the corrupted Open courses generally, partially explaining his record in Open playoffs. "Palmer tries to tear a course up," Casper said. "That won't work on Olympic, which is a very demanding course. I feel you can't charge it. You have to romance it. Above all, don't take dead aim at the pin on every hole."

That's like telling U.S. Grant to stay the hell out of Richmond. Palmer plays golf the way Grant and Patton made war, and so he is an idol in a nation of aggressive people. But in San Francisco, on the back nine, it killed him.

Palmer at Rancho

DURING THE great years of Arnold Palmer, he was always a favorite in Los Angeles, especially when he won — which in 1967 he was careful to do after the fiasco at Olympic six months earlier.

LOS ANGELES: Jan. 20, 1967.

On the ridges of the little fairway hills at Rancho Park, Arnold Palmer stood like an Indian sentinel yesterday morning, and again yesterday afternoon, scouting the enemy on the greens below. He carried an aluminum tomahawk, and, from a distance, his yellow sweater looked like war paint. With the Army behind him, he was scouting Gay Brewer of Dallas, the only man who had a chance to destroy him in the last hours of the forty-first Los Angeles Open.

Brewer had pared Palmer's lead from four strokes to two on the first thirteen holes. But when he bogeyed the fourteenth, Palmer saw it from afar, then closed in and scalped the Texan with a birdie.

Arnold's reward four holes later was $20,000, first prize in a $100,000 tournament, which he won by five strokes with his new aluminum clubs. His four-round 269 is one over the L.A. Open record, and fifteen under par.

The aluminum shafts, fitted out with Palmer Company heads and grips, were tooled by a Los Angeles firm, LeFiell Sports Products, which talked him into abandoning Palmer Company shafts for the duration of this tournament — an experiment disclosed exclusively by the Herald-Examiner.

Arnold afterward was by turns coy, mysterious, and reluctant, but, he conceded, the new tools are lightweights by comparison with steel-shaft clubs, which he has always used before; and in any case he was moving the ball farther with aluminum than he does as a rule with steel. His putter was the only holdover from last week's bag. And on the Indian reservation in West Los Angeles, putting was the weakest part of his game. Alcoa can make of that what it will.

II

On the fourth day at Rancho, Jack Nicklaus fired a solid 71 to tie for fifty-first. They only paid off to fifty places, thus enabling Paul Harney, a two-time champion here, to capture $257.50. Palmer, pocketing twenty grand less taxes and airplane fuel to Palm Springs, acknowledged that it happened because he kept his mind firmly on first place instead of a tournament record that was well within his grasp.

This was a switch on his philosophy of last June in San Francisco, where, in possession of a seven-stroke lead with nine holes left, he went for the U.S. Open record and lost the tournament to Billy Casper. "I was shooting for 268," Arnold said last night, referring to Phil Rodgers' best ever here in 1962. "But I wasn't going to be foolish," he added. "I was trying to win. Of course, I always do, but this time I was trying to win a little more consciously."

III

In the chill and damp of a gray morning, Brewer and Palmer left the first tee in contiguous threesomes, next to last and last, and by the turn Brewer had gained one stroke as Palmer, striding up fast from behind, glared at him from every hill. Said Palmer: "I knew what he was doing every time." Said Brewer: "Arnie saw what I had to do and what I did. Every time I made a bogey, he came right in behind me with a birdie."

In this kind of pressure, Brewer not only managed to finish all eighteen holes but somehow saved second with a 69 – 274, worth $12,000. He cracked just once, at the four-par fourteenth. "The best iron I hit all day carried over the flag," he said quietly of his bogey there. "It was the only green I missed."

Palmer, charging up for the kill at the fourteenth, used two of his newfangled clubs, a driver and 9-iron, to whale the ball within twelve feet of the pin, then downed it with his old-fashioned putter. Out on the course, with aluminum, Palmer kept getting distance, even more distance than he'd had earlier in the week. Of his 64 Friday, he had said: "From tee to green, it was a better round than the 62 I had here last year." Yesterday, recalling the 62, Palmer said: "I have never putted that well before or since."

IV

At thirty-seven, Palmer is beginning, close up, to look his age. But the magnetism is still there — in abundance — and he turned it up for the television audience at the eighteenth. When his superfluous five-foot birdie putt rolled down, he reacted in a mood of pure boyish delight. Most of the 20,000 in yesterday's Rancho galleries were not only for Arnie, but with him, although well over half of them missed the big scene at the eighteenth after a wild stampede that overwhelmed the meager facilities there.

A lonely guy at the edge of the crush was asked what it feels like to play eighteen holes when Palmer is charging right behind. "Well," said Gay Brewer, inscrutably, "with some fellows, you feel they may blow it, against others, you know you've got to be exceptional." Although Brewer didn't specify the category in which he had placed Palmer, he will never forget that Indian scout yesterday, up there in those hills.

PALMER AND HIS ARMY

THE FINAL story in this series, written ten years later, was assigned by Times editors who remembered that before the Herald-Examiner dissolved in a disastrous strike-lockout, I had sometimes reconnoitered Palmer's army. The assignment: Why are the soldiers so enthusiastic?

PALM SPRINGS, Calif.: Feb. 16, 1977.

Arnold Palmer, the Latrobe, Pennsylvania, millionaire who has won more golf tournaments than anyone else except Sam Snead and Ben Hogan, finished 115th last year on the national tour. On his best day, Palmer tied somebody for fifteenth. He made but $17,000 playing golf in 1976 — in twelve months. He came in twenty-fifth here Sunday.

Yet Palmer remains the most magnetic figure in fun and games.

Once the greatest of winners in an extraordinarily trying profession, he is still, apparently, a winner in the eyes of his fans, who are still legion. In the Bob Hope Tournament galleries last week, Palmer, forty-seven, starting his twenty-third winter on the tour, outdrew the other pros by large margins — as usual. Why? What has Palmer got? During Hope week, four Palmer fans were asked about that. Their comments:

Golfer Bob Hope: "Arnie has a unique personality for an athlete. No one is more personable. He is a veteran showman who continues to live in the minds and hearts of those who love this game."

Golfer Alistair Cooke: "Palmer was the first TV sports star. His was the first face to become known to large groups of people who don't play golf. He'll represent the magic of stardom as long as he can totter out to the golf course."

Golfer Bing Crosby: "Arnie's a competitor who still plays superb golf. I follow him just to see what he'll do next. He is a power hitter, you know, and in all sports, power appeals to everybody."

Golfer Steve Bick: "When you follow Palmer, you feel like you're watching your best friend play golf."

Bick? Who's Steve Bick? He's a thirty-five-year-old firefighter from Ogden, Utah, who flew to Palm Springs last week to serve three days in Arnie's Army. His reasoning: "Golf is my sport, and Arnie has always been my idol. When your sport is baseball or football, you can't get close to your favorite players. You can in golf. I stood right behind Arnie for two hours last night at the driving range. I walked with him on his practice round. Most of the day we were as close as you and I are right now. And he seems to like that. He always gives me the impression that he is a good friend of everybody in the gallery. He'll stop and visit with anybody."

II

A golf ball just sits there in the grass. You don't have to run for a golf ball, or catch it, or even react to it. And people in their fifties can still hit it splendidly. Golf is almost the only sport that gives a man a chance to be a timeless figure, and Palmer has made the most of that, playing to the crowd, and also playing fine golf, for what seems like most of the century.

Once the master of a game in which hits numbering seventy or seventy-two tend to be par for the course, Palmer, today, comes in only about two strokes a day behind those who finish first or second in the tournaments.

Accordingly, his fans ask, why not stick with Arnie? Maybe he'll get a break or two and win. And if not, the afternoon will be a lot of fun, anyhow.

While some of the players who consistently finish in front of Palmer these days are attended only by their girlfriends, agents and an occasional bill collector, Palmer's galleries often run into the hundreds. Dave Marr, an ABC-TV commentator who as a golfer was for years one of Palmer's good friends on the tour, knows one reason: "When you think of Arnie, you think of a man in the woods. He's always in trouble, and always getting out of it, and the rest of us can appreciate that. All people have troubles. And we can identify with the guy who can overcome."

To Golfer Gene Littler, there's something simpler, more intimate: "I think the explanation is that Arnold simply thrives on people. A lot of us get upset with the spectators when we miss a shot. We sometimes behave badly. But Arnold never gets upset with anybody. He's the best I've ever seen with a gallery. He and they are always looking for him to do something great. Again."

III

Tamarisk Country Club, Palm Springs. Time: one day last week. Place: ninth hole.

Wife (age about sixty-five): "Honey, here's another man who thinks Arnold Palmer walks on water."

Stranger (about sixty): "You bet I do. His picture hangs right in my office."

Husband (about seventy): "It did in mine, too. But I haven't got an office anymore."

IV

Scene: Tamarisk, fourth tee.

Palmer, a relaxed, stocky figure wearing a yellow shirt, brown pants, and, invisibly, contact lenses, has just driven the ball out of sight. He's waiting quietly for one of the amateurs in his foursome to tee off. Suddenly, a voice from the gallery breaks the quiet: "Could I shake your hand, Arnie?" Turning, grinning, Palmer says, "Shhhh. . . ." Then, after the hit, he walks back toward the voice. Still smiling, he shakes hands and talks pleasantly for a moment with three women who have been following him since the second green.

The size of Palmer's army at the Hope tournament ranged at any given moment from a hundred to five hundred. Most were golfers, and few golfers walk anymore, especially here. They aren't used to an eighteen-hole hike. They pick Palmer up for a while, then pick a green where they can sit for a spell and rest.

So Palmer's largest crowds are at the tees. Fewer watch him putt. As he prepares to drive the fifth, a three-par hole, someone feels free to call out: "What you using, Arnie?" His expression softens, but his eyes remain on the ball. "A 3-iron here," he replies.

As he brings the club back, a woman on the front row crosses her fingers, the first two fingers on her right hand. She has been watching him protectively, and crossing her fingers, every time Palmer has hit the ball since 9:08 a.m., when he teed off. A woman in golf shoes, she appears to be in her seventies. The face is as weatherbeaten as an old golfer's, the hair is tied back out of the way. She talks to no one except, under her breath, to Palmer. As he stands in to swing or putt, she says, every time, softly, "C'mon, baby."

v

In both directions, the interaction is almost constant. When not working on a golf ball, Palmer is usually making eye contact with somebody. He looks everyone in the eye, everyone in his gallery, each in turn, male and female. I have never known another athlete who so consistently seeks out strangers in the crowds around him and, while sizing them up, locks eyes with each, one after another. If the stranger smiles, man or woman, Palmer smiles back. If a camera is raised, he holds his pose, whatever it is, until he hears the click. Once at Tamarisk, with everyone waiting for him to putt, he told one dilatory shutterbug, "Well, shoot." But he said it kindly, with a smile that was only a little grim.

The contrast in behavior between Palmer and other golfers perhaps explains, at least in part, why crowds favor him over the others. One day last week, for instance, Palmer bounded up to the eighteenth green laughing and joking with the customers and downed his first putt for an eagle, bringing his total for the round to 68. Johnny Miller, as it happened, came up in the next foursome, more tense, all business, and grimly tapped in the last of his 74 strokes before stalking off. As defending champion, Miller arrived with, seemingly, every advantage over Palmer, including youth, looks, height, and skill. He has everything, in fact, but Palmer's ease, the good feeling about his sport and his life that radiates out from Palmer toward all those around him.

This isn't an accident of temperament so much as it is a systematic approach. As Golfer Rick Massengale says: "Arnold has been cultivating these fans for ten or fifteen years. By now they're all pals. Arnold isn't just playing a round of golf. He's keeping up with old friends."

Palmer agrees with this assessment. And when you ask him about it, he is ready with a believable answer: "I always enjoy meeting anyone, especially somebody I know. Through the years I've become good friends with these people, and at tournaments we have a lot of fun. I've got a warm spot in my heart for anyone who would take his vacation and fly to a tournament to watch me play. Besides, the biggest mistake any athlete can make is to think he can exist without the crowd. Galleries are the one essential. They're more important to pro sports than pro athletes."

In Palmer's opinion, it doesn't disturb an athlete's concentration to jolly with the crowd. "My concentration is only affected by the way I'm playing," he says, "not by what others do."

VI

A ten-handicapper could, of course, have Palmer's personality and demeanor and still attract few soldiers. Palmer was the game's best at one time. He still plays excellent golf, and more than that he continuously reflects the qualities that Hope, Crosby, and Cooke admire. Says Hope: "I would liken Arnie to Jack Dempsey and General William Westmorland. To me, they personify the American spirit. The can-do spirit." Pausing for a moment, Hope adds: "Arnie makes good golf clubs, too. They play better than I do."

At the ninth tee at Tamarisk, a par-four, 440-yard hole with a fairway so straight you could drive the green if you had the strength, Palmer makes the power point that fascinates Crosby. In front of the usual large crowd, Palmer uncoils and pounds out his longest hit of the day as the gallery erupts with a bunch of ooohs and ahhs and then a prolonged cheer that rolls over the land like the rebel yell at Shiloh. Says Crosby: "Arnie isn't the longest hitter on the tour, but when he winds up, he looks like it."

Every time.

"I remember one year on fourteen at Pebble Beach, a par-five hole," Crosby says. "Arnie was leading the tournament but got into trouble with his first shot. He hitched up his pants, and walked over there full of purpose, like he'd planned things that way, and immediately called for a wood. He was going for the green, but hit a tree. So he took the same wood, wound up again, and, by golly, he hit the same tree again. I think he took an eight or nine on the hole — anyhow, it knocked him out of the tournament — and then the rains came. It rained all night, and when we got out there the next morning, Arnie's tree was on the ground. He'd weakened it so much with those hits, it fell down in the rain."

If that's the sort of story you tell about a legend, it doesn't surprise Cooke, the erudite Briton who keeps elegant tabs on all things American. "People are interested in Palmer for the same reason they still like to see Clark Gable movies," Cooke says. "Palmer is a TV star in a TV nation."

And if you like him, he likes you. At Tamarisk, making eye contact with Palmer right now, is a twelve-handicapper named Cliff Sumner, fifty-eight, a retired Lockheed engineer from Mountain View, California, who has followed Palmer every step he's taken on California golf courses for the last nine years. "If I had my choice — if I could see Jack Nicklaus win the British Open, or watch Arnie for two hours at the Indio driving range — I'll tell you what," says Sumner. "I'd take Arnie."

PART 2 FOOTBALL

The thing that most intrigues me about any major league sport is the game itself: the game and the way the best players play it and the way the best coaches coach it. As a point of view, that separates me from many other sportswriters, who are interested in many other things.

For example, there's a lot of interest in the problems and idiosyncracies of the players — the surrounding soap opera. Sports is a big show with a seemingly endless supply of controversies, vendettas and other off-the-field attractions. But for me, the *game* is the show.

All this is particularly true of football, which is the most intricate, comprehensive, and demanding of the team sports.

The attraction of football rests on its uniqueness as both a physical and intellectual challenge. No other sport intimidates, at such depth, on both levels. Indeed, the fusion of mind, body and spirit that football requires may have no counterpart in any of man's other pursuits. I think of football as the most interesting thing that human beings collectively do — as the most absorbing of group activities — in or out of sports, at work or at play.

V

THE BEAT

A reporter's *beat* is his main assignment or area of responsibility — the courtroom beat, for example, or the ballet, or, as in my case for thirty-two years in Los Angeles, the Ram beat. In major league sports, the optimal way for a newspaper to cover such a beat, I have always argued, is with one writer working a seven-day week — for half the year — before working a four-day week the rest of the year. Today's way on most papers, dividing the assignment between two writers, costs both continuity and understanding. It may not help me with St. Peter that during all those years on the Ram beat I was never scooped by any other reporter, but it does at least show a continuous striving for comprehension.

Throughout the 1950s — in the years before the Big Apple and the big media discovered pro football at a 1958 sudden-death title game (New York Giants versus Baltimore Colts) — the NFL was already major league in Los Angeles. By the mid-1950s, Ram attendance frequently exceeded ninety thousand and sometimes hit a hundred thousand — the NFL's first crowds in that range — as year after year the Rams fielded exceptional offensive stars taught by imaginative coaches. Unhappily for Ram fans, those teams were also plagued by a succession of serious personality conflicts between and among players, coaches and competing ownership blocs. With one exception, 1951, the championship years that should have been never were. In 1957, to take a typical season, the Rams had everything they needed to win the NFL title but were scuttled by a typical 1950s feud. And I was there when the vessel went down.

During the seven days when I was preparing the following beat stories for the old Los Angeles Examiner, the running story involved Quarterback Norm Van Brocklin and Coach Sid Gillman, the two big men in the franchise, who were having a monumental misunderstanding. Both of them were then on the way to the Hall of Fame, Van Brocklin as a winning passer, Gillman as the game's leading pass-offense expert. Gillman was a pipe-smoking pianist and famous football philosopher, Van Brocklin a brilliant football technician with a corrosive ego. Their war over play selection — it was mostly Van Brocklin's fault — ruined the Ram season. And because that had from the start seemed likely, I followed the Van Brocklin-Gillman conflict drama closely — unlike most personality-conflict stories, which are usually sideshow stuff.

In addition to the conflicts that sunk the ship, there were always subplots in those unruly days with the Rams; and in that November week, one of them concerned a temporary power outage among NFL offenses that Chicago Bears Owner George Halas tried to exploit into a trend. In another subplot, the oddball alley-oop pass suddenly blossomed in San Francisco, to the distress of defensive coaches everywhere.

Bit players that week included Elroy (Crazylegs) Hirsch, the Hollywood movie star whom souvenir-hunting Los Angeles fans would soon strip to his jock on the day he retired; Jon Arnett, the most inventive open-field runner in Ram history; Tom Wilson, perhaps the greatest unknown runner the league has produced; and Les Richter, the linebacker worth an entire team. And, mind you, this was just another week in the mid-century life of the Rams.

Tuesday: The Second-Day Story

BEGINNING THE endless weekly cycle, my Mondays during the six-month football season forty years ago were devoted predominantly to producing what I thought of as the second-day story — an extended analysis of Sunday's game that appeared the day after the Monday game story. As I still feel sure, such two-day coverage is required, and desired by readers, for football, which is a complex, once-a-week sport. Second-day attention one November week in 1957, after a distressingly low-scoring game, was directed in two ways: toward, first, the defensive emphasis of the coaches and, second, the familiar Ram tendency to self-destruct.

LOS ANGELES: Nov. 5, 1957.

After 80,456 Ram fans, coming out in Sunday's rain, had paid $240,000 to see a pro football game in which nobody made a touchdown from scrimmage, Owner George Halas of the Chicago Bears commented yesterday as follows: "We put all our best men on defense. In the NFL, nowadays, we all do."

In the NFL? Not all, surely. With Hugh McElhenny at halfback, the San Francisco 49ers can, if they choose, do something offensive to the Rams in the Coliseum next Sunday.

But obviously, Halas is proud of his defense. And it's true that the defensive performance by the team known as the Monsters of the Midway was one of two things that led to the most recent unhappy afternoon for Los Angeles. In alphabetical order:

• The Bears placed their best coach as well as their best players on defense. Their defensive leader, Clark Shaughnessy, who converted America to the T Formation a decade or so ago, is now unraveling the gains he made for offense in his favorite sport.

• The Rams, reaching the halfway point of the season with a dismal 2-4 record, threw away their best chance to beat Shaughnessy's defense by again trying to play football with two different game plans. The two signal-callers are the coach, Sid Gillman, and the quarterback, Norm Van Brocklin, whose conflict over play-calling is getting to be serious.

This has put the brakes to a talented group: Van Brocklin and his teammates. Constructed by their front office and coaching staff to be a passing team — with a great passer and such gifted receivers as Ends Elroy Hirsch and Bob Boyd and End-Halfback Jon Arnett — the Rams are spending most of their time running the ball. They are now first in yards gained rushing — and last in title contention — among the teams that began the season as NFL title contenders.

Gillman's assistants say his game plans are full of plays that are rarely called on the field. The head coach was asked about that Monday, when he was reminded that restless season-ticket holders are telephoning the newspapers with complaints. The fans are stuck, they feel, with an unimaginative Ram offense in which there are all too few hook passes and sideline passes, not to mention bombs of the kind that Van Brocklin threw to End Tom Fears six Decembers ago to beat Paul Brown in the NFL championship game.

Said Coach Sid: "If you'd like to examine our game plan with me some time, you'll see that we still have all the pass plays you've mentioned. I'm a great believer in them. We still like them a lot." He paused, then added: "What's more, we work on them every day in practice."

Ram coaches for weeks have discussed ways and means of persuading Van Brocklin to throw more often — but they're still giving their quarterback the option of declining their orders. The objective in all proceedings is to appease the temperamental quarterback because of a question that answers itself: "Where are you going to find another Van Brocklin?"

And so in Sunday's disappointing game, what with one thing and another, the only two thrills came on freak plays: Arnett's ninety-eight-yard kickoff run to a touchdown for Los Angeles and Defensive Back Vic Zucco's forty-three-yard touchdown sprint with a Ram fumble for Chicago. Coliseum football has come a long way — down and back — from the days when colorful Ram teams shot off touchdowns like sputniks and built up patronage to the point where eighty thousand will come out now in threatening weather.

The hero this cheerless day was, unfortunately, Shaughnessy, who deployed his defensive strength to get fast and willing Bears in front of every inoffensive Ram. On offense, by comparison, the Bears were ridiculous. Chicago's revived tight T Formations, minus flankers — an absurd sort of football for 1957 on which Shaughnessy does not even advise — returned pro ball to the days of the buggy and horse. As Ram Owner Dan Reeves said: "The only thing left now is the single wing."

For next Sunday's Ram-49er game, another eighty-thousand crowd is in prospect; but if it's another defensive struggle, in which the home pros keep trying to run the ball, that could be about the last of the big Ram crowds. For one thing, next year, there will be baseball competition in Los Angeles when the Dodgers move over from Brooklyn. For another, it should be obvious to any critical witness that defensive pro football won't sell forever in the land of Hollywood.

If Halas' philosophy mirrors current sentiment in this league, it's time for a new sentiment.

Wednesday: The Ram Pro-File

THE OBJECTIVE each week, when breaking-news developments were placed in separate Ram stories, was to keep the seven-day beat format alive. The objective each Wednesday was a mini-profile personalizing a Ram starter who might otherwise get no attention. The premise: any athlete who can start for a major league club is worth a metropolitan newspaper story.

LOS ANGELES: Nov. 6, 1957.

Kenny Panfil, the towering Ram tackle who won the game ball for a recent ballgame, is warmly respected in the National Football League for two other reasons.

• He once outplayed Gino Marchetti, everybody's All-Pro end from Baltimore.

• His custom-made shirts are equipped with size nineteen collars.

As you unquestionably know, some of the really big necks in the pro league these days measure up to seventeen and one-half. Panfil, addressing a man in that class, calls him "Tiny."

When Panfil marches out to meet the enemy Sunday, you will see an offensive tackle who stands six feet six and weighs 261, wears size fifty-four coats which taper to thirty-eight at the waist, and who concedes that at age twenty-seven, he was only born to protect Ram quarterbacks. "They need help to have a big day," says Panfil. "To an offensive tackle, a football game doesn't seem like a football game. It's just a long fight with a defensive end."

Like every other Ram lineman, Panfil would rather block for Halfbacks Jon Arnett or Tom Wilson than the quarterbacks. For on running plays, a lineman charges with one clean, solid blow, and it's all over. "On pass-protection plays," says Panfil, "you stand there and take a beating. An aggressive spirit is no help. If you lunge at the end, he goes around you and takes it out on the passer. A good pass blocker is like a good boxer who has no hands."

For Panfil, this is year three with the pros after a strange amateur career. When he was graduated from Gage Park High School, Chicago, in 1948, he received not so much as one offer from a college coach. A year passed as Ken took up the trade of his Polish-German father, driving trucks in Chicago, before somebody at Purdue finally offered him a scholarship — as a basketball player.

He lasted for two days of practice on the basketball team, but as a sophomore he was a starter on the Purdue football team which tied Wisconsin for the Big Ten title in 1952, and Panfil has devoted his life to football ever since. "I never want to leave the game," he says. "I think I'll be able to help a college staff some day with the things I'm teaching myself on this team."

As Panfil remembers it, too many college drills are designed to build endurance. "Pro drills aim at perfection," he says. "When I have a college line, I'll do both things with my drills — with emphasis on perfection."

A California-hater who still goes back to Chicago to drive trucks in the offseason, Panfil isn't, however, in a hurry to leave the pros. And Ram Coach Sid Gillman may keep him around for twenty years. Panfil, you see, has only had three football coaches in his life. The first lost his job the day Kenny graduated from high school, and the second lost his job the day Kenny graduated from Purdue.

Thursday: The Next Opponent

DURING THE seven-day rotation, I devoted a midweek story to each new team on the Ram schedule; and my rationale still seems sound. When a football team can fill the largest stadium in America — and especially when television ratings are high for road games — there must be some interest in the teams to be played. A game holds more interest for fans if they have some idea of what to look for on both sides of the ball. Second, I still think that, in a major league sport, starting lineups are news. As assistant sports editor of the Examiner in the 1950s, I could develop the space each week to set the lineups high in a lede two columns wide, where, I held then and still hold, they belong. In a year when wide receivers were still called ends — and when middle linebackers were middle guards, cornerbacks were halfbacks, and safeties were designated left and right instead of free (or weak) and strong — the 49ers introduced sports fans to a fabulous new play, the alley-oop pass, which to this day continues to thrive, though not as successfully as it did that first season in San Francisco.

LOS ANGELES: Nov. 7, 1957.

Quarterback Y.A. Tittle and Halfback R.C. Owens, the two name-droppers who have helped lead the San Francisco 49ers to the top of the National Football League, are making an art form this season of a new play: a long, rainbow pass ending in a seemingly freakish jumping catch by Owens in an end-zone crowd of friends and enemies.

With that tactic, which is befuddling their opponents, Tittle and Owens have in recent weeks pulled out three games for the 49ers, who will face the Rams in the Coliseum Sunday with a 5-1 record. On a team led by Hustling Hugh McElhenny at left half, the 49ers have something old and something new in their starting lineups:

49ERS' OFFENSE
(with uniform numbers, weight, and starting positions)

49ERS' DEFENSE

Clyde Conner, 88, 195, LE
Bob Cross, 78, 250, LT
Lou Palatella, 68, 230, LG
Frank Morze, 53, 280, C
Ted Connolly, 64, 240, RG
Tom Dahms, 70, 250, RT
Billy Wilson, 84, 190, RE
Y.A. Tittle, 14, 195, QB
Hugh McElhenny, 39, 198, LH
R.C. Owens, 27, 205, RH
Joe Perry, 34, 210, FB

Ed Henke, 75, 227, LE
Leo Nomellini, 73, 255, LT
Marv Matuszak, 54, 235, MG
Bill Herchman, 72, 235, RT
Bob Toneff, 74, 255, RE
Matt Hazeltine, 55, 205, LLB
Charles Powell, 87, 225, RLB
J.D. Smith, 24, 200, LH
Bill Stits, 20, 195, RH
Bob Holladay, 40, 175, LS
Dick Moegle, 47, 195, RS

During Frankie Albert's second year as coach of the 49ers — continuing a storied Bay Area career that began at Stanford when he was college football's first T quarterback — his ace is still McElhenny. But Albert is creating more interest now with two other people, Tittle and Owens, who have been changing the purpose and nature of the forward pass.

Their big play, the jumping-catch touchdown, isn't as freakish as it seems, according to an expert on the subject, Harvey Knox, the man who manages the career of his son the quarterback, Ronnie. The play, Harvey said yesterday, was deliberately designed several years ago at Santa Monica High by Coach Jim Sutherland for Knox and Owens.

It's actually a basketball-type pass, the sort they lob toward the basket in the general direction of a six-foot-nine center who is rushing up to tip it in. In the 49er version, Tittle lobs the ball up for grabs, and Owens, an athlete with the ability to leap over an automobile from a standing start, outjumps everyone else to pick it out of the air.

"Everything I've learned about throwing a football I've had to throw away," Tittle said. "We can't score now unless I throw a bad pass."

Owens, who used to practice the basketball play by the hour with Knox in Santa Monica, is the 49er who persuaded Albert to change Tittle's passing style. Result: five Owens touchdowns that, otherwise, surely, never would have been. Said Harvey Knox: "The timing and execution by Tittle and Owens is like a symphony. The best way to play pass offense now is with a guy who stands six-three, Owens' height. You teach him to high jump, and then make sure the passer gets the ball up out of the reach of the defensive halfbacks, who are mostly little guys anyway."

It's all leading to a big year for Tittle, who has completed sixty per cent of 140 passes for, so far, 1,086 yards and ten touchdowns. That compares with Van Brocklin's present forty-seven per cent. In a full season a year ago, Tittle only threw seven scoring passes.

In the mood of the day, however, Albert rates his defensive platoon as the key to his 5-1 record. The 49ers in one goal-line stand in Wisconsin turned back Green Bay with a first down at the San Francisco one-yard line. Last week they twice stopped Detroit on the goal line, Albert said.

It wouldn't be 1957 if one of history's greatest passers weren't bragging about his defense.

Friday: Voice of the People

DURING THE great days of the Rams, their fan club luncheons each week brought in hundreds of partisans from Los Angeles, Orange, Ventura and other counties. The setting was the ballroom of a downtown hotel, frequently the Biltmore Bowl, and it was in the coach's contract that he had to be there, along with five or six players, answering, or at least acknowledging, every question. This week, the spotlight was deflected from the play-calling controversy during the first few minutes of the luncheon by Gillman's announcement of a new starting halfback.

LOS ANGELES: Nov. 8, 1957.

Sid Gillman agreed yesterday that at halftime of 1957, Halfback Tom Wilson is leading the National Football League in yards gained rushing. "But he isn't scoring," the head coach told the Ram Fan Club at the Biltmore. And so, off with his head. Jon Arnett will replace Wilson at halfback in the starting lineup Sunday, Gillman announced.

A part-time end, Arnett, the rookie of the year from USC, earned that honor by, among other things, running ninety-eight yards with a kickoff last week for Los Angeles' only touchdown.

Coach Sid agreed with a fan who told him that substituting Arnett for Wilson for the stated reason — because Wilson isn't scoring — is like taking Hank Aaron out of the Milwaukee lineup for hitting only doubles and triples. But, said Gillman, 2-4, "When you lose a few, you have to do something."

The year's other hot Ram controversy — the one that centers on the club's so-called unimaginative offense and Quarterback Norm Van Brocklin's part in that — was not ignored by yesterday's assembled fans, who as usual came in with a load of questions on this and other subjects. A selection:

Q: Some of the NFL teams I've seen this year have a larger variety of passes than the Rams. Why don't you put in a few of them for Van Brocklin?

Gillman: We have every type of pass action there is in the book — rollouts, straight back, waggle action and so on. But I'm not going to second guess the quarterback.

Q: Wouldn't you have scored at least one touchdown Sunday if you had passed the ball more?

Gillman: We have a set game plan for every game. In practice every week, we work on play passes, out passes, the whole works. We have a regular practice routine. We must work on several hundred out passes each week.

Q: That wasn't responsive.

Gillman: That was my answer.

Q: Why didn't the quarterback call one or two of those plays?

Gillman: He has access to all of them. If he desires to call some of them, we're glad to see him do it.

Q: Soon you'll be on the road again, where the Rams have only won once in two years. Why do you have so much trouble in out-of-town games?

Arnett: We don't score enough points. The other teams score more.

Q: What's the difference between college and pro ball?

Arnett: The pros have more speed, spirit and desire. They don't hit too much harder. The biggest difference is overall speed. The tackler gets you from the other side.

Q: When you retire, will you be available to coach the ends?

Elroy (Crazylegs) Hirsch, end: I have hoped I'd never have to go into coaching. It's a sure way to the grave.

Q: How is your movie career going?

Hirsch: Our new picture is "Zero Hour." I'm an airline pilot. I pass out from poisoned food, so I'm not in it long enough to hurt the picture.

Q: Why do the Rams choke on the road?

Hirsch: At home the crowds are with us, and I think we play with more spirit. On the road, when forty-nine thousand are booing you and throwing things at you, it drags you down a little.

Q: Have the Rams run 238 times this season and passed only 96 because Van Brocklin is worrying too much about interceptions?

Gillman: He doesn't worry. He wants to call the right play at the right time.

Q: Is there something wrong with Van Brocklin's arm?

Gillman: Van Brocklin has never been greater than he is now. I have never seen and never expect to see a better arm than Van Brocklin's. He will go down in history as the possessor of the greatest football arm of all time.

Saturday: Q&A with a Star

MOST GOOD football fans, I've always assumed, would like to sit down each week for a visit with one of the players they've been watching. On TV, those thirty-second interviews slide by too fast. On TV, moreover, few football players are asked to talk about football. A newspaper, however, is a good place for that; and once a week, as a beat writer, I aimed for a Ram player interview. This week the talker was a linebacker with Hall of Fame ability and skills, Les Richter, a player who, it can be proved, was worth an entire team. The Rams in 1954 dealt away eleven players to get him. No other pro has ever been traded for eleven of his peers. Richter responded with an All-Pro career, playing in eight consecutive Pro Bowls.

LOS ANGELES: Nov. 9, 1957.

Les Richter of the Rams, who is playing linebacker these days with a wrenched knee, a depressed rib cage and a broken face, is one of the world's leading authorities on football injuries. He is a self-made man in that field, you might say, having specialized in painful attention to detail.

Richter also acknowledges that many sincere critics, editors and others, are concerned today about the upswing in the football injury curve, particularly in high school games. But he advises the nation not to panic.

"Except in pro football," says Richter, "most injuries are caused by the fact that the boy is not in tip-top, first-class physical condition. He gets a new helmet, for example — and today's helmets are beautifully made — and he thinks he can run through a brick wall. So he tries it. A neck injury puts him out for life because he was relying on the helmet before his body was physically fit for the shock."

How many high school football coaches are negligent in physical training?

"Damn few," says the Ram captain. "But physical condition is a personal thing. You can be told what to do, but you have to do it yourself. Self-punishment is the key to physical fitness."

How dangerous is football for youngsters? After your experiences, do you want your boy to participate?

"It's all right with me if he wants to. Football is not much more dangerous, in my opinion, than playing golf in a hot sun when you're not in shape for it. More people break their necks swimming than playing football — not because they dive into an object but because they didn't toughen up before they dove in. Fundamentally, a pro football player is no more rugged than a bank clerk. We're just normal humans who slaved to get in condition."

Now, speaking of the pros, it's been said that dirty football accounts for most injuries in pro games. How true is that?

"Only a small fraction can be traced to that stuff. You can see in the movies that most pro injuries are caused by loafing, by not running full-go, by pulling up just before the whistle, and by freak accidents."

Loafing?

"You're not paying attention and somebody creams you."

Referring to the current assortment of Richter breaks and bruises, some of them, surely, came in retaliation for, let's say, your aggressive way of playing.

"Not so. Regardless of what you might hear, dirty players don't last in pro ball. If they do last, they change. The two injuries I have now came in pileups with Rams. I was shot by my own men, like Stonewall Jackson."

I thought you had three injuries, not two.

"That's right, I forgot my face. But that's just a few small fractures in the cheekbone."

How long were you hospitalized for the operation that time?

"I went in Monday morning and I was planning to stay overnight, but didn't. They didn't have a portable whirlpool. I had to get out and soak my knee in the whirlpool."

Is football worth all that? Why do you want to play hurt every week?

"Because it hurts more not to play."

A leg injury, I assume, can't slow you down much. You've never been famous for straight-ahead speed.

"True, but in football, you don't measure speed against a clock. The question is, how fast can you react to a situation?"

What sort of situation?

"Here's a simple, obvious example. When a good linebacker sees a bunch of linemen run off to his left, he reads the play as a screen pass. If the linebacker is a fast reader, he'll get there quicker than a slow reader who might run the hundred in 9.7."

A fast youngster who could read might get there quicker yet.

"The worst thing about being young and fast is that it's such a waste. I have never seen a youngster who was fast enough to outrun his own mistakes. A pro football player needs at least three years to learn how to handle whatever speed he's got. And by the time he finally learns, he's been dinged up and some of the edge is gone from the speed he started with. That's the thing that makes this game great — new guys with terrific speed are always threatening to get away from experienced old vets. And vice versa. To me, that's what pro football is all about: Those who can run fast against those who can think fast."

Give us a name. What experienced pro running back is better now than when he was young and fast?

"You missed my point. I didn't say experience is better than speed. Experience *equalizes* speed. A new balance is struck every year. And to me, that's what makes pro football so interesting."

Even with all the injuries?

"What injuries?"

Sunday: Day-of-Game Advance

ON THE morning of the game, it seems to me, the function of the beat writer is to set the stage with old and new scenery. I see Sunday as the wrong day for beat writers to come in with interviews or personality stories of the kind that are sometimes the game-day fare these days. The reader — in particular the casual sports fan, who is in the majority — may only see the Sunday paper. More dedicated sports fans have also seemed to appreciate reminders of the week's principal events and controversies. The threads of these stories should be reassembled in the game-day advance, in my view, and woven into a story that also takes a look ahead.

LOS ANGELES: Nov. 10, 1957.

Frankie Albert's basketball stars will ride a five-game winning streak into the Coliseum today to defend first place in the NFL's Western Division against the cellar club, Los Angeles. A series of basketball passes by his football players has carried Albert, coach of the San Francisco 49ers, to the top of the division with a 5-1 report card that is tops in the league.

It's a game that will for the first time match Halfback Jon Arnett of the Rams against Halfback Hugh McElhenny of the 49ers — Arnett in his first start as an NFL back, McElhenny at his peak — but Albert acknowledges, looking back, that his quarterback has put him where he is.

The quarterback is Y.A. Tittle, who has lobbed five long passes that Halfback R.C. Owens has transformed into five touchdowns with the jumping catches that have brought San Francisco three last-minute triumphs while insuring two others. Though it is sometimes said that there's nothing new in football, it is also almost certain that no other NFL pennant contender ever won three games on three planned plays that looked for all the world like desperation passes.

Nothing that exciting has happened lately to the Rams, who, instead, on their way to 2-4 for the first six of their twelve scheduled games, have been caught up in another controversy. The conflict this time is between the Los Angeles coach and quarterback.

Coach Sid Gillman's game plans haven't seemed to suit Quarterback Norm Van Brocklin, who, calling his own plays, has proceeded along an alternate track to four wrecks in six starts. Ironically, among those in football today, it is probable that Gillman knows the most about passing and that Van Brocklin is the best passer. And so it's easy to conclude that the Rams can win anytime Van Brocklin throws Gillman's passes.

In the warm, sunny weather that is due, the crowd prediction is ninety thousand. The Rams, in other words, are expected to continue one of their new traditions: attracting the largest numbers of spectators in the country for any pro club in any sport. Somewhat surprisingly, the Rams are also a three-point favorite.

McElhenny, the Los Angeles-born 49er with all-time talent, comes in as the NFL's number-two rusher and might go out number one. The present number one, Ram Halfback Tom Wilson, has been benched for a loathsome habit: failing to score enough touchdowns. So Arnett will start in the Ram backfield with Van Brocklin, Halfback Lamar Lundy and Fullback Tank Younger. For the other side, Fullback Joe Perry will join Tittle, McElhenny and Owens.

For both teams, it is their last California appearance in a month. The battles for both in the next three weeks are all in the frozen East, where, historically, neither has played very well. But the Rams, at least, have been consistent this year. They haven't played very well at home, either.

Monday: The Game Story

FOR WHAT we thought of in the 1950s as one of the country's great sports sections, Examiner coverage of big league football was much different from that of other papers — then or now. We always sent five or six working reporters and five or six cameramen to the Coliseum — capitalizing on an interest in pro football that other editors didn't always apprehend. It was a time when, elsewhere in Los Angeles and throughout the country, college football still dominated local coverage; but for our paper, the page-one sports columnist, Melvin Durslag, was at every Ram game. The Examiner locker-room writer, Dan Hafner, quoted the coaches and players at length. My goal as the game-story writer was a game review and analysis. The event we saw that Sunday was memorable both for the size of the crowd and for the football by both teams as — for one of the few times in football history — a coach proved a more adventurous play-caller than his quarterback.

LOS ANGELES: Nov. 11, 1957.

They didn't build the place big enough. At the gates of the largest stadium in the United States, more than ten thousand football fans were turned away yesterday for lack of places to sit inside. That was after 102,368 had forced their way into the Coliseum to watch Sid Gillman and Norm Van Brocklin pull off the first double play in the soon-to-be home of the Dodgers.

Theirs was a play-calling double play. Using Coach Sid's signals, relayed, in a surprise development, by alternating guards, Quarterback Van Brocklin threw the ball for a change to win a 37-24 game for the last-place Rams over the first-place San Francisco 49ers.

Never before, here or anywhere, had there been a hundred thousand witnesses for pro football. And not since the championship year, 1951, had the home pros played such football as this against a championship contender. As Van Brocklin overloaded the San Francisco defense with passes, most of them errorlessly thrown, the Rams moved ahead at the quarter, 14-7, built their lead to 28-17 by halftime, and outscored the 49ers down the stretch, 9-7.

One of Van Brocklin's strikes flew through the air for fifty-four yards to End Bob Boyd, who at the goal line made an overhead catch for a touchdown on a play which measured an even fifty yards from scrimmage. Another strike went to Boyd for a fifteen-yard touchdown. And on Los Angeles' two other first-half scoring drives, Gillman resurrected the famous Ram battery of yesteryear, Van Brocklin to End Elroy Hirsch, on the four pass plays that set up a pair of three-yard touchdowns by Jon Arnett, the celebrated new starter at left halfback, and Fullback Tank Younger, the running star of the afternoon.

In one burst of near-perfect execution during the decisive first half, the Rams completed eight of ten passes, throwing two away to avoid interceptions.

Artistically, Van Brocklin, who completed fourteen of twenty-three for 224 yards, has been capable of bright performances like this regularly through a season that, to the contrary, has been mostly dismal. Even after this one, the 3-4 Rams are far behind the 5-2 49ers. As yesterday's events made clear, the problem has been not Van Brocklin's arm but his generalship.

Gillman stepped into that void in this game, calling the signals himself, for the first time, with dramatic results. That makes two NFL coaches in that business now. Cleveland's Paul Brown has for years felt that play-calling is too important to be left to a player. And on the day of another big

Ram-49er game, when Gillman joined him in that thought, he borrowed Brown's methods, rotating Guards John Hock and John Houser as messengers.

For a change, therefore, Gillman's game plan was in the game. For the first time this year, there was pattern and consistency in the Ram operation along with deception and variation. These are the things, as any football fan can see, which Coach Brown gets as the Cleveland play-caller. And in Los Angeles, the Rams can't seem to get them any other way. Over the protests of his players, it may be — and against the advice of his critics in the press and the Ram Fan Club — Gillman sent in the plays that got an even four hundred yards of Ram offense leading to one touchdown after another.

The Los Angeles defensive team was also in the game — again — and that was another good thing. For there was a resourceful team to beat. To begin with, the 49er coach, Frankie Albert, had suspected that the Rams would be ready for his most feared play — the basketball pass from Quarterback Y.A. Tittle to high-jumping Halfback R.C. Owens — and he was right about that. All four times Tittle lobbed the ball, Ram Defensive Backs Del Shofner and Don Burroughs jumped with Owens, each grabbing an arm midair to mess things up for the 49er basketball team. But because Albert had anticipated all that, after beating three opponents with Owens' jumpers, he could attack the Los Angeles defense with other kinds of tricks which for three quarters kept the 49ers close.

On one series, Albert put his players in field goal formation and fooled Gillman's people with a fake kick. The San Francisco ballholder, Halfback Joe Arenas, jumped up that time on fourth down, circled out, and passed to the NFL's leading receiver, Clyde Conner, for twenty-seven yards. Three plays later, Tittle sneaked in a touchdown.

Next, Albert struck for a touchdown with a fake run, also by Arenas, who reversed to his right after a handoff from Tittle and passed into the end zone to Conner, thirty-three yards away. Thus of San Francisco's three scores, Albert's magic accounted for two. Tittle marched to the other 49er touchdown, throwing the scoring pass twenty-two yards to Halfback Hugh McElhenny, who, in his first matchup with Arnett, held him even in points at six.

If the game had a turning point, the Ram defense turned it in the final seconds of the third quarter at a time when Los Angeles was in command by only four points, 28-24. At the 49er seventeen-yard line, as Tittle dropped back to throw, Ram Middle Guard Les Richter threw him instead. The loss was seven yards. Then, before McElhenny could get secure possession of a Tittle handoff, two other defensive Rams, Linebacker Dick Daugherty and Tackle Frank Fuller, threw *him* in the end zone for a safety. When the Rams took the free kick at midfield and drove it to their fifth touchdown, they had scored nine points in three minutes for a 37-24 lead that stood up as the 102,368 dispersed.

What a crowd. And what an offense. In the afterglow, there was one first-half sequence that said it all for the Rams: Younger's twenty-nine-yard run to midfield and, on the next play, the fifty-yard Van Brocklin-Boyd touchdown. All season, with first down at midfield, Ram quarterbacks had been calling on their running backs. This time Gillman called the long pass, and, as Van Brocklin dropped back, his protection looked awesome. It wasn't his blockers, though, who made the play. It was the call. Not expecting a pass, the 49ers failed to rush. Looking for Younger off-tackle, they overlooked Van Brocklin.

If there were underlying feelings of disappointment this day, they came afterward in the knowledge that the Rams *could* have been doing this all year long. More than any of the world's other pastimes, the game they play is a coach's game.

VI

THE GAME

My most arduous hours have been spent in press boxes attempting, against deadlines, to make written sense out of football games. It seems unlikely that any football writer can ever be completely satisfied with the results of such a brief and pressured process — I know I've never been — but in honor of the thousands of hours I have invested in the process, I am offering a few game-story samples in this chapter.

There is one selection from each of the last seven decades.

I have been covering football games since 1936, when I was at Soldier Field, Chicago, to report on the College All-Star Game. Also in this package is a bonus selection: an account of an American Football League title event in the 1960s, when, representing one or another of three Los Angeles papers, I worked in AFL stadiums more often than did most other NFL writers.

Through the years, there have been many changes in the way football is reported. When I entered journalism in the 1930s, the game-story writer delivered, as the bulk of his account, a simple play-by-play recitation. A brief summary at the top soon led into a chronological rundown, written largely as the game unfurled. You could almost hear the reporter racing for the 5:40 train. A nationally syndicated writer, Damon Runyon, who seemed to be the model for this method, once told me: "The way to write a football game story is to get the first half out of the way by halftime."

I didn't think so.

Watching sports-page readers, I had noticed that most gave up on any football story at the point where the chronology began. The game is over. Who wants to struggle through a written replay?

Thus, years ago, my objective became (and still is) to review and analyze the sixty-minute event as a whole.

If most 1930s journalists considered a football game to be a work in progress, I saw it as an entity that can be explained.

Most games, it's true, should be summarized in a sentence or two early on — indicating the score at halftime and other relevant points. And it's true that the central facts must be there — it is an error to assume, as some journalists do, that people who *saw* what happened also *remember* it. But pro football is a particularly intricate game. It is so complex that a seasoned football watcher can closely study the proceedings in all four quarters, either in person or on television, and still not know what happened — still not know why the winning team won. To the football writer, therefore, the first two challenges are to understand, and to communicate that understanding.

It has accordingly been my settled practice to write only when the game is over — regardless of deadline urgencies — and to make use of every minute.

On the road, in the old Examiner days, that meant moving fast. Travel budgets were tighter in those years, when, in most cities, newspaper publishers told their writers to ride team charters and team buses. I had to hand my last page to the Western Union operator in time to catch the airport bus — meaning that I had less than an hour for the game story.

In Los Angeles, by contrast, after NFL games, making use of the available minutes has often meant writing and rewriting for hours. There have been times in the Coliseum press box when I went on and on until no one else was left — in a dimly-lighted room nearly fifty yards long — except the teletype operator, who retyped each page as I finished it, and the janitor sweeping up Coca-Cola cups.

Years earlier, rewriting had been impossible in Los Angeles' competitive multiple-newspaper era when my wife helped me struggle through the deadlines that came and went during football games. But today's Times is basically a one-edition paper with no competition. There's time today. Why not take it?

In recent years, game-story writers have diverged in still another fundamental respect. They have developed different ways of writing their opening paragraphs — what they call their *lede* paragraphs. Some of the new ways today are indistinct and indirect. My approach is more direct.

My intent each time is to get into the main story instantly, to state concisely, as soon as possible, how and why the game was won. Along the way, I will have more to say on the main themes, often with quotations — if they're relevant — but the first priority is a succinct analysis of the tactics and plays that made the difference, with an emphasis on the players who made the difference.

By contrast, on other word processors these days, many newspaper people compose oblique, leisurely, sometimes languid ledes — often opening with picturesque material far from their main point. It's a trend that began, I recall, with Sports Illustrated magazine writers, who, because of deadline commitments, must write their football game stories *before* the game begins. During the week leading up to it, they fill their pages with background material on the two teams, the coaches, and the stars. At game's end, new paragraphs, covering actual game developments, are created to replace some of the material in their first drafts.

In the view of the reporters who once worked with him, it was the admirably talented Dan Jenkins, writing football stories for Sports Illustrated some years ago, who made the principal breakthrough. Seated in a press box one night, Jenkins discovered that the lede paragraphs he had written in his first draft during the week, crafted no doubt at great cost, were better than anything he could come up with after the game. So in his final draft he left them in — even though they could have had nothing to do with the game as it was played.

Building a magazine career on a deadline problem, Jenkins created an off-the-point lede-paragraph style that newspaper sportswriters presently imitated. And then at many papers in New York, Los Angeles and elsewhere — even on page one — newspage writers began imitating the sportswriters who had imitated Jenkins.

As a result, many newspaper writers today, in their opening paragraphs, carefully avoid any reference whatever to anything they're about to write about. One journalism school professor, reviewing such articles, has rather crudely called this the "era of the assforwards lede."

It's a fashion that can quickly descend to the absurd. For example, the

New York Times was ridiculed in a 1995 New Yorker magazine spoof that exhibited a dozen new-style lede paragraphs. The paragraphs were found, the magazine satirically suggested, on the Times' front page. One example:

> LIMA, Sept. 15 — Field Marshal Hidalgo de Romero glanced at his toes, restless beneath the huge mosquito net that represented his clandestine authority, brushed a *Sarcophaga agricola* fly from his fly with a brutal oath, raised himself on his withered elbow, and cried out, "The revolution has begun!"

Elsewhere, echoes of that writing style are present now in many game-story ledes. The writers are obviously having fun. And what they're proving, among other things, is that there are many ways to write newspaper stories. So the leisurely style flourishes, even in the increasingly competitive video-computer era, when newspapers are full of material that needs to be read in a hurry — if it is to be read at all.

I would personally find that style more engaging, conceivably, if I were less interested in football. But after sixty years of watching football games, I still consider each game, as it comes along, to be a puzzle worthy of attention — despite the plain fact that solving the puzzle in clean, clear prose provides a goal that is ever just out of reach. If Jenkins and his followers are onto something — or if Damon Runyon, with his play-by-play notions, had the right idea in the first place — there is room in journalism for different priorities.

1936 in Chicago

THERE'S A rumor that I'm the only sportswriter who covered the first and last of the College All-Star Games in Chicago. The series, which matched graduating All-Americans against NFL champions, was played at Soldier Field from the 1930s to 1976, when Commissioner Pete Rozelle pulled the plug on the forty-third renewal during a fourth-quarter lightning storm. Then he pulled the plug on the series. Early on, when the game was a Midwest event romantically opening each new season of college and pro ball, Chicago papers called their stadium Soldiers' field, referred to fullbacks as full backs, and wrote about college boys and girls — in the years before they became men and women — and so did I. The following is juvenilia — a 1936 game column written for the Yankton (South Dakota) Daily Press & Dakotan while I was still in school. I can't say it's an exemplar of the game story as I conceive it, and you can hear the country boy in the big city; but even at that age I couldn't stand the play-by-play.

CHICAGO: Sept. 4, 1936.

For the pro league-champion Detroit Lions, Earl (Dutch) Clark scored only one point here Wednesday night. In the fourth quarter, he drop kicked the ball straight into a Lake Michigan wind, and that was just enough to save a tie with the All-American football team of 1935, 7 to 7.

Clark, an All-American quarter back himself four years ago, is Detroit's captain and star. He led the veteran Lions to their first championship eight months ago. But the all-star team, which was organized less than three weeks ago, had the better of the first game of 1936.

Cheered by a Soldiers' field crowd of 76,361, the college boys held the professional team to four yards passing, and until late in the fourth quarter they held a 7-to-0 lead after Minnesota Quarter Back Babe Le Voir's seventeen-yard touchdown run in the first half. The only fumble of the game, at the all-star 20, finally gave the Lions their big chance, and they scored the tying points two minutes before the end.

It was the first game arranged by the Chicago Tribune's sports editor, Arch Ward, between college stars and pro champions. A local team, the Chicago Bears, played the all-stars the last two years, when no touchdowns were scored by anybody. After it was 0 to 0 in 1934, a good Bear team barely won from last year's all-stars, 5 to 0. What it looks like now is that the best of the college players and the best of the pro teams are a standoff.

The crowds have been over seventy-five thousand each year despite the fact that this year's game was rained out Tuesday night and re-scheduled Wednesday. In hardier South Dakota, football is played rain, snow or shine. The oldest Yankton residents can't remember when the Yankton College Greyhounds were ever rained out or snowed out. Also in Yankton, football is played weekends. In Chicago, Ward has to avoid conflicts with the Cubs and White Sox.

But in Chicago, they'll pay more for tickets. Ward sold all the good seats at Soldiers' field for $3.30, $2.20 and $1.10. If that seems like a lot, remember that all-star game parking is free here — as free as it is at Yankton College. You can park wherever you please on all sides of Soldiers' field except the east side. There's a lake on the east side.

Ward said 11,500,000 football fans in all forty-eight states voted for their favorite players, electing a starting lineup of All-Americans including Jay Berwanger of Chicago at left half. The college team was coached by Bernie Bierman of Minnesota's national champions, who has seemed satisfied with his practice program for the last several days. "The boys drilled diligently," Bierman said. "I'm proud of them."

He can take pride in their first half. Three times the college boys started from midfield or farther back and drove down close to Detroit's goal. Fourth-down runs failed the first two times. The third time, on fourth down at Detroit's 17-yard line, the all-stars cleverly ran Bierman's favorite play for a touchdown.

At Minnesota, Bierman features what he calls the buck-lateral series with a spinning full back. And his team fooled the Lions when Minnesota Full Back Beise took a short pass from center, spun, and faked a line buck before lateraling to his Gopher teammate, Le Voir, who had replaced Alabama's Riley Smith at quarter back. The only Lion who wasn't faked out was blocked out by a pulling guard, Danny Fortmann of Colgate, as Le Voir darted into the end zone. The place kicker, Wally Fromhart of Notre Dame, added the seventh point.

"The Lions weren't as tough as Northwestern last season," said Le Voir, whose touchdown was the first scored in an all-star game in three years.

Late in the game, one of the stars of the all-star first half, Tuffy Leemans of George Washington, fumbled a punt as the Lions closed in. The Detroit coach, Potsy Clark, was ready with a fake play of his own, the only play that could have slowed down big Bob Reynolds, the Stanford tackle who was making most all-star tackles. When Detroit Full Back Ace Gutowsky shrewdly faked a line buck from the all-star eight-yard line, Detroit's center instead passed the ball to Half Back Frank Christensen as Wing Back Ernie Caddell reversed behind him. At top speed, Caddell took Christensen's lateral and raced past the off-balance all-stars to score easily.

At the Sherman Hotel later, a reporter, en route to the College Inn to hear the new Benny Goodman band, looked around first for Quarter Back Clark, Coach Clark, and Detroit Lions Owner G.A. Richards. Question: Do you feel you were a bit lucky tonight? No one could say. They had all left for their special train back to Detroit.

1949 in Los Angeles

BY THE 1940s I was covering NFL games in Los Angeles as an Examiner reporter. In those early years, the Chicago Bears were the best theater of the season in Los Angeles, and their coach, George Halas, was the main attraction. His anger-inspired jogging along and onto the field — to harry the officials — drew the loudest cheering and booing of each year. In 1949, when these teams were in the same division, the Rams won it for the first time as a California entry by twice beating Halas, whose club finished 9-3 (.750) to the Rams' 8-2-2 (.800). The 1949 Ram stars, who two years later would lead the team to the NFL championship, were Quarterback Bob Waterfield and two receivers, Elroy Hirsch and Tom Fears, all now in the Pro Football Hall of Fame.

LOS ANGELES: Oct. 30, 1949.

In the dusk that all but blacked out one of California's ideal October afternoons, the Rams won their greatest victory yesterday as a Los Angeles team. They came from behind — the way they've done it so often since Clark Shaughnessy signed on as head coach a year ago — to beat the hard-to-beat Chicago Bears in the last five minutes of play. By 27 to 24 they won, and the largest crowd ever attracted to an NFL game saw them do it.

A multitude of 86,080 all but filled the Coliseum for the decisive game in the NFL's Western Division. That's six wins in a row now for the Rams — without defeat in league games — and all their competitors, including the Bears, are three-time losers at the least.

Ram Quarterback Bob Waterfield's second field goal, the only points scored by either side in the third quarter after a 17-17 first half, made the mathematical difference, and his twenty-four completed passes for 303 yards were too much for the team that lost to the Rams in Chicago three weeks ago, 31-16.

But in the fourth quarter, the Bears fought their way into a 24-20 lead, whereupon a little Ram halfback ran fifty-seven yards with Chicago's last kickoff to turn the tide. In near darkness, young Tommy Kalmanir scooped up the ball. As the Bears crashed in for the kill, Kalmanir swung sharply to his right and took off behind a wedge of Ram blockers. At midfield, he burst into the clear just a step in front of John Hoffman, the speedy Chicago back, who finally caught him on the Bear 35.

Six minutes to play, and thirty-five yards to go.

Waterfield had spent the afternoon successfully throwing flat passes to End Tom Fears — who had caught eleven for 143 yards — and now he pitched immediately to Tom for nine more. Most of the screaming fans were still on their feet as Fullback Jerry Cowhig took two three-yard chunks out of the Bear line, and there the ball was on the Bear 17.

At that juncture, with night closing in fast amid calls for "Turn on the lights," the Rams got the last of a series of breaks which did them no harm this day. As Waterfield threw to Halfback V.T. Smith in the end zone, the officials signaled Chicago's Hoffman for interference. George Halas, coach of the Bears, who had been hiking along the sidelines instructing the officials continuously since 2:30 p.m., capped his little sideshow with yelps that could be heard in Row 63 across the field. But Referee Ross Bowen placed the ball on the Bear one-yard line anyway, conforming with the rule, and Cowhig bucked over.

In the next few minutes, two Bear passes thrown by Quarterback

Johnny Lujack were intercepted on all-out plays by two Rams, Middle Guard Milan Lazetich and Halfback Elroy (Crazylegs) Hirsch, to end Chicago's dying chances to pull out the game. And not until the Rams finally gained possession on the Hirsch interception in the last minute did the Coliseum turn on the lights. At the time this seemed to be an unfriendly gesture to the Bears, who had been trying to pass by night, but afterward the officials said they had asked the captains after each series if either team desired more illumination. Strangely, neither did.

When it was over and Waterfield had another triumph in this year which has seen him emerge as the league's outstanding quarterback, Coach Halas trotted across the field. "To shake the hand of Coach Shaughnessy," a witness predicted. "To beef at the officials again," said Sportswriter Dan Hafner.

Hafner was right. One of the most spectacular games of the decade ended with Halas threatening an official — to be separated by one of his own players, Tackle Paul Stenn. The last anyone saw of the coach of the Bears, threading his way through a mob of players and fans to the dressing-room entrance which sealed him from view, he was still jawing away.

1955 in Los Angeles

THE NFL's most important intersectional rivalry during the mid-century years brought the Rams against the Cleveland Browns in a series of preseason and postseason games that Cleveland usually won from the team that had deserted Cleveland in 1945. Ten years later, when the Rams combined Hall of Fame Coach Sid Gillman with Hall of Fame Quarterback Norm Van Brocklin, the results were excellent until this game, but never as good again.

LOS ANGELES: Dec. 26, 1955.

Like a youngster fixing a watch with a hammer, Otto Graham yesterday smashed the Rams into small pieces. The Cleveland quarterback played his best game on a day when Ram Quarterback Norm Van Brocklin couldn't keep up. And the result was a rout, 38-14, as the Browns won the world championship for the second year in a row and the third time in six years.

It was on a hazy afternoon in the Coliseum that Graham ruined Christmas for the NFL's crowd of the year, 87,695. With a performance that included two touchdown passes and two touchdown runs, Graham put his name on twenty-eight of Cleveland's thirty-eight points.

But it is doubtful if he could have done as much without the involuntary assistance of Van Brocklin, who threw six intercepted passes. Any team making that many mistakes in a Cleveland game is likely to lose by 38-14. One of Van Brocklin's wild throws was neatly converted into a Cleveland touchdown by Halfback Don Paul with a sixty-five-yard runback. And three other interceptions led to more and more Cleveland points. The Browns did not suffer from lack of opportunity.

Los Angeles, which had won the NFL's Western Conference championship this year while Cleveland was winning in the Eastern Conference, in no way resembled the team that had been so formidable in the decisive hours of the long regular season. But as Western champions, the Rams were rewarded with $2,316 apiece as their share of the gross receipts of $504,257.

Never before has there been that much money around for the participants in a football game. Each Cleveland champion collected a record $3,508, and for Graham the check was, he said, the last he'll cash as a football player. At thirty-four, he has announced his retirement after possibly the most successful ten-season career of all time in any sport. During the four years of the old All-America Conference, Graham quarterbacked the Browns to all four titles. During six NFL years, he has quarterbacked the Browns to six Eastern titles and three world championships.

The man seems inhuman. And to the Rams, again, he assuredly acted the part of a ghost. Time after time they got to him only to find he wasn't there. His ability to elude rushing linemen, founded on years of experience as a ballcarrying halfback in the Big Ten, is perhaps his number one asset. Any Cleveland receiver can work his way into the open with the time he gets while Graham, with a football at the ready, is moving and feinting and shifting around.

Completing fourteen of twenty-five passes for 209 yards, Graham threw his touchdowns to End Dante Lavelli on a fifty-yard play in the second quarter and to another end, Ray Renfro, on a thirty-five-yard play in the last quarter. The points he scored himself in the third period on two runs after two Ram mistakes decided the game.

The Browns were a mere ten points ahead, 17-7, when Graham meticulously faked to his fullback, put the ball on his hip, and sprinted fifteen yards around the line on a bootleg play for the big touchdown midway through the third quarter. Five minutes later, he was sliding gently into the end zone on a short quarterback sneak, and Los Angeles, trailing by 31-7, was a certain loser.

These plays and all the others in Graham's arsenal were called, as usual, by the Cleveland coach, Paul Brown, who has built the most efficient organization in football. A champion for all ten of his years in pro ball, Brown, for whom the team was named, directed the Browns in detail from his command center on the sideline. Usually, he alternated guards with his most pertinent messages, but during timeout periods Brown conferred directly with Graham.

Occasionally bringing other members of the offensive platoon into these conferences, Brown personally instructed Tackle Lou Groza on the play before Graham's touchdown sneak.

These orders and instructions, whatever they were, brought nothing but misery to Los Angeles. During the game's opening fifty-five minutes, the Rams negotiated only one creditable play — Van Brocklin's long pass to Halfback Skeet Quinlan for a sixty-seven-yard touchdown in the second quarter. Otherwise, Browns were catching Van Brocklin almost as often as Rams.

The really unusual thing about this year of Ram football is not that the last game was lost but that the Western championship was won. In his rookie season as a professional coach, Sid Gillman put up with an injury jinx that lasted for twenty games and still paraded all the way to the final round. His team didn't look all that good when it got there, true, but there were two reasons for that. Graham and Brown.

1964 in Buffalo

JACK KEMP, the GOP's 1996 nominee for Vice President, quarterbacked the Buffalo Bills to the AFL championship in a game I covered in the 1960s, which are represented twice in this collection of football stories because there were then two pro leagues. Few other NFL reporters regularly covered big AFL games in that decade.

BUFFALO, N.Y.: Dec. 26, 1964.

A 240-pound linebacker and a 250-pound fullback joined with a $100 quarterback this afternoon to separate Sid Gillman from the junior world title on the warmest day after Christmas in the history of the Buffalo Weather Bureau. The temperature never got under forty, and Gillman, the coach of San Diego, never got over seven. He went down, 20-7, as the Buffalo Bills replaced the Chargers as champions of the American Football League.

It happened on a reasonably fast track in a cozy, steamy stadium populated by 40,242, some of whom lost their overcoats, which they didn't miss, and then their voices, which they did, during a snake dance afterwards in which thousands cried, "Bring On the [NFL Champion] Colts."

The senior NFL prohibits interleague competition, and so the exuberant fans of Buffalo will know nothing of despair, remembering, instead, only that Quarterback Jack Kemp and Fullback Cookie Gilchrist were too much for a San Diego team that had Keith Lincoln for six minutes and Lance Alworth for none. The most obvious difference between the two pro leagues is the AFL's lack of depth. On Gillman's bench there was nothing at all behind Fullback Lincoln and Receiver Alworth. When Sid lost those two, he lost the title.

Charger critics will carry the argument further, alleging that Gillman blew this title when he waved goodbye to Kemp two years ago, parting with the bright and disciplined quarterback for $100, the waiver price. The Chargers called that a clerical error. But in any case, Kemp specialized in ball control today, leaving the heavy work largely to the heftiest fullback in America, Gilchrist, 250. On sixteen carries, Gilchrist totaled 122 yards, showing the speed and blocking ability of an NFL back and almost the same maneuverability.

Minus Lincoln and Alworth, the Chargers couldn't match Gilchrist's productivity. "Give me those two," said San Diego Quarterback Tobin Rote, who at thirty-six was playing his last football game, "and I'll take our team against Buffalo or anybody."

II

The two-play turning point was the contribution of another big Buffalo man, Mike Stratton, 240, an outside linebacker who has as much talent as any athlete in his position today in any league. On the sixteenth play of the first quarter, with San Diego leading, 7-0, Stratton went stride-for-stride on a deep pattern with Paul Lowe, the gifted Charger halfback, and deflected Rote's pass when it got there. That made it second and ten, whereupon Stratton, having demonstrated his speed on long patterns, proved his versatility sideways, speeding into the flat to knock Lincoln down and out.

Lincoln had been running a flare pattern when Rote's pass and Stratton reached him simultaneously, with disastrous consequences for San Diego. Smashed viciously, Lincoln was immediately horizontal with a throbbing rib fracture, and that was the ballgame. Stratton's two remarkable plays were followed on third down by the stoutness of defense that Buffalo was to exhibit thereafter. Some of the Chargers' interest in football left them when Stratton hit Lincoln. They lost more than a ballcarrier.

A handful of Charger fans had shuffled off to Buffalo during the week with a small-caliber big-noise cannon that went off only once. Rote performed as well as ever — in spots — but uncharacteristically blooped three horrendous interceptions. Neither Rote nor his relief man, John Hadl, ever quite played back to San Diego's first six minutes, when there was a fullback in the lineup.

The Buffaloes, after scratching Lincoln, keyed on Halfback Lowe and stopped everything San Diego could think of. Rookie Jerry Robinson, seen in Alworth's position, was an unfortunate replacement. Rote put the ball in Jerry's hands three times for drops which interrupted gathering drives. Later, Hadl lost an apparently certain touchdown when Robinson stumbled with the ball overhead.

But afterward, Gillman blamed nobody. "Every team has injuries," he said.

III

Buffalo attacked San Diego with a roughhouse bunch which made up with soundness of execution for certain deficiencies in style. Coach Lou Saban has a solid Green Bay-type backfield. Gilchrist and the 216-pound halfback, Wray Carlton, are both accomplished blockers who selflessly blocked each other about the premises.

Gilchrist slammed away once for thirty-nine yards and again for thirty-one, playing apparently with more emotion than normally. He was a factor in all four of Kemp's long drives in the 13-7 first half, when Buffalo looked the better team by twenty-eight. "We had trouble putting the ball in," Kemp said, "but we didn't have any trouble winning."

In the second half, Buffalo sagely controlled the ball on the ground, secure in the knowledge that San Diego couldn't strike back. Kemp's best play of the last thirty minutes was a sharp fourth-quarter first-down pass to Receiver Glenn Bass gaining fifty-one yards to the Charger one. A veteran who has often seemed to be the closest article to an NFL quarterback yet developed by the AFL, Kemp then jumped into the end zone.

Long forgotten at that instant was a twenty-six-yard touchdown pass for San Diego, Rote to Tight End Dave Kocourek, which had been the feature attraction of the first four scrimmage plays of the game. Buffalo, in the opening minutes, had been jarred off balance by Lincoln's thirty-eight-yard sprint draw on first and ten. During an overcast afternoon, the lights had been on since noon; but when Lincoln disappeared, they went out for Gillman in the first quarter.

1967 in Dallas

TO THIS day, I have never seen a better football game than this one, which, moreover, was as fateful as it was brilliant. Quite possibly, had the Dallas Cowboys won, they would have won the first Super Bowl game two weeks later — with historic consequences for the coaches, Tom Landry and Vince Lombardi, and for Dallas Quarterback Don Meredith, among others. Despite an early deadline, I tried to write the kind of story I'd never now attempt, a story combining the results of two games the same day. But both games were nationally televised and widely watched. And in both games, for the first time, places in the Super Bowl were the winning prizes. For, in both instances, the games decided conference championships — although in those days, toward the end of pro football's acrimonious 1960s civil war, the conferences were called leagues: AFL and NFL.

DALLAS: Jan. 1, 1967.

The football season is ending prematurely. Instead of playing the first annual AFL-NFL title game January 15, they should arrange a three-week round robin for the world championship among the Green Bay Packers, Dallas Cowboys, and Kansas City Chiefs.

The miracle of television let you in on all the drama yesterday: Those were the three most explosive offensive performances yet seen, probably, in one day of championship pro football — in two towns — by three teams, the Packers, Cowboys and Chiefs. It is unfortunate indeed that only two of these champions, Green Bay and Kansas City, will be moving on to Los Angeles shortly for the world game.

What a day:

• Dallas matched Green Bay thrill for thrill, yard for yard and almost point for point in the Cotton Bowl spectacular here for the NFL title, and at the end, as Green Bay won, 34-27, the Cowboys missed a sudden-death playoff by thirty-six inches. Considering the quality of the athletes playing defense down there on a summer day in January, this game was a candidate for offensive show of the century.

• And considering the field on which Kansas City won the AFL title in frozen Buffalo, 31-7, the offensive performance of the Chiefs, with Quarterback Len Dawson throwing and Halfback Mike Garrett running, was nearly as impressive. On television it seemed probable that Kansas City, with that offense, and with the world title on the line in Los Angeles, will score some points on Green Bay.

To the partisan Cowboy crowd in Texas, it was apparent that the catastrophe of the season was yesterday's suicide of the Dallas team, which lost three quarters of a million dollars — $15,000 a man — on two self-destructing plays, a fumble and an offside penalty. For a breathtaking moment, the Cowboys held the NFL title in their hands — and let it slip away.

A defect of football as a sport is that championships are wrapped up in one game instead of, as in baseball, best of seven. Thus the greatness of the Dallas Cowboys this winter is now only a memory. And Kansas City, which may have as much talent as any football team in the land, gets one shot only at the poised veterans of Green Bay. It isn't just — a round robin would be more just — but it's football.

II

Green Bay Quarterback Bart Starr, under orders from Coach Vince Lombardi, beat Dallas by playing Dallas' game. Nine times, a Packer record, Starr threw the ball on first down for what is normally a deeply conservative team. Four times he threw for touchdowns. This was the Lombardi version of the useful cliché which dictates that if you can't beat 'em (any other way), join 'em.

In Western Division competition in 1966, Lombardi, the dominating coach who has now acquired four NFL titles in seven seasons, forced every adversary to play the Packer game, which is a compound of conservative ball control and tough defense. "But we knew today," Vince said afterward, "that against this team, we had to go after them, and keep trying for points."

This was Green Bay's game plan, and absolutely no other would have prevailed.

The difference in the Cotton Bowl between two evenly-matched division champions was that Starr and Lombardi adjusted to the reality of their competition. Starr came to throw. He was throwing the ball in defense of a 21-20 lead in the third quarter, and he was still throwing it to enhance a 28-20 lead in the fourth. If, even once, the Packers had given up and settled for a safe and sane punt, they would have lost this game. And it was their daring strategy, which is not usual or even understood in most of the precincts of football, that won the day for the Green Bay realists.

III

All the same, it took a package of two suicide plays by Dallas to separate these clubs into a winner and a loser. The Packers converted a Cowboy fumble into a 14-0 lead in the first quarter. And with 1:32 left in the fourth, Dallas lined up second and goal on the Packer one-yard line, where the Cowboys blew the tying touchdown when a blocker skipped offside.

The spectacle of Dallas' charge toward a would-be 34-34 in those final minutes will not soon be forgotten by either the packed 75,504 in the Cotton Bowl or the millions who participated via TV. Here was a Cowboy team that (a) had come back from 0-14 to 14-14, (b) had held Green Bay to 21-17 at the half, (c) had survived four Starr touchdown bombs, and (d) had closed to seven points — 34-27 — in the fourth quarter with a bomb of its own, Quarterback Don Meredith to an outside receiver, Frank Clarke, for sixty-eight yards.

And now with only 2:31 left of a surpassingly exciting afternoon, the Cowboy line rushed Green Bay's Don Chandler into an awkward punt that carried only sixteen yards to midfield. In a wink, the Cowboys were on the Green Bay 22, and next, after an interference penalty, they were on Green Bay's two-yard line, first and goal. "I still can't catch my breath," Lombardi said an hour later. "My heart feels like it's coming out of my chest."

The minute that followed was, he said, the longest of Lombardi's life. On first down, Dallas Halfback Dan Reeves gained half the distance to the goal line. And on second down, Tight End Pettis Norman apparently gained the rest on what would have been a Meredith touchdown pass if there hadn't been some movement in the Dallas line. Offside. "It was me," Dallas Tackle Jim Boeke confessed afterward. "I blew it."

On second and six, a pass was dropped. But on third down, Norman took delivery from Meredith and bulled again to the two-yard line. Fourth and goal. Plenty of time: forty seconds showing on the Cotton Bowl clock. Meredith rolling out. Sprinter-Receiver Bob Hayes open. And, suddenly, Green Bay Linebacker Dave Robinson all over the passer. As Robinson mugged Meredith, the ball wobbled toward Packer Defensive Back Tom Brown, who intercepted to bring down the Dallas curtain.

Robinson, a canny four-year veteran, twenty-five years old, graduate of Penn State, bright and tough at 245 pounds, had made the play of the game. "We expected an off-tackle running play," he said. "That was my first responsibility. I didn't look at Meredith, but when I saw the guard pull, I knew it would be a rollout. I changed direction, and ran out there — and there Meredith was."

IV

The most attractive kind of football game is one in which two skilled, disciplined defenses are attacked imaginatively by gifted offensive specialists, and this was the case here yesterday. Prodded by visions of fame and $50,000 each in the NFL-AFL title game in Los Angeles, both quarterbacks, Starr and Meredith, routinely called nearly-perfect sequences of offensive plays. Execution, too, was often faultless, particularly in the lines, where openings were created for four skilled ballcarriers: Don Perkins, a 108-yard contributor, and overachiever Reeves of Dallas, and Elijah Pitts, who averaged 5.5, and roughneck Jim Taylor of Green Bay.

The upshot was a bundle of 418 yards by Dallas and a total of 367 by Green Bay, all artistically developed on a day of comebacks. Unlike the proceedings in most football games, yesterday's scoring highlights are worth preserving in your memory book:

• After Green Bay had opened its 14-0 lead in the first five minutes with a scoring pass and a touchdown run with a fumble, the Cowboys rebounded with two good, long marches: 14-14.

• Starr's answer to this was not a ball-control drive but a prompt fifty-one-yard bomb to Wide Receiver Carroll Dale for Green Bay's 21-17 halftime lead.

• Starr's other pair of touchdown passes went to his other receivers, Boyd Dowler (sixteen yards) and Max McGee (twenty-eight), to keep Green Bay always ahead of Dallas — if sometimes only barely.

• For in the middle periods, Meredith was marching the Cowboys to field goals, holding Green Bay in sight.

• And in the fourth quarter he caught the Packer defense on the move and out of position with the bomb to Clarke that closed Green Bay's lead to seven points, 34-27.

"They hit us with at least twenty different formations," said Phil Bengston, defensive coach of the Packers.

Said Landry: "They never did stop us. We stopped ourselves."

In a Green Bay game, that can happen. It is a fluke indeed if it doesn't happen. As of today, you can figure the world championship game that is now only two weeks off: Kansas City will score on Green Bay in Los Angeles, but it will lose to the poised Packers with a big mistake. And Lombardi wouldn't want it any other way.

1973 in the Rose Bowl

AT THE Times in the 1960s and '70s, continuing to report on the Rams and other NFL teams, I was increasingly assigned to college football games as well. Many were Rose Bowl games; and in the second half of one of them, on New Year's Day, 1973, USC's unbeaten Trojans won the national championship. The losing coach that day was Woody Hayes of Ohio State, a frequent Big Ten champion who, in those years, was often seen in California during the holidays, watching footballs in the air like a tourist gawking at the Goodyear blimp.

PASADENA: Jan. 2, 1973.

There were two parades in Pasadena Monday, including the one USC led in the second half at the Rose Bowl with Ohio State following far behind. To win on a strange sort of day, 42-17, the unbeaten Trojans scored the first five times they had the ball in the last two quarters after a 7-7 struggle in the first two.

The fifty-year-old bowl, home to a record 106,869 for the afternoon, hasn't often seen such a parade.

Nor has the Rose Bowl's winning backfield often proved as productive as USC's this time with Mike Rae, Lynn Swann, Anthony Davis and Sam (Bam) Cunningham. Quarterback Rae's passes, which were to gain 229 yards in all, broke the game open. Flanker Swann's six catches and Tailback Davis' 157 yards moved the ball along. And Fullback Cunningham moved it over.

Scoring a Rose Bowl-record four touchdowns with high dives from the one- and two-yard lines, Cunningham ruined one of Ohio State Coach Woody Hayes' proudest possessions, his goal-line defense.

And so the Trojans finished the season 12-0 as the country's only major undefeated football team, bringing Coach John McKay his third national championship in thirteen years. The 42 points were the most yet scored against an Ohio State team coached by Hayes.

II

The Trojans, who had played only twice since November 4, were plainly out of practice in the first half. This was most noticeable when they tried to tackle the Buckeyes, which quite often they didn't. For two quarters, Ohio State, keeping the game close, whomped away inside the ends in a caricature of its own style.

Still, in their last few tries before the break, the Trojans were plainly getting their timing back; and in the third quarter, as a West Coast entry beat the Big Ten in a fourth straight Rose Bowl, they broke Hayes' heart. The catalyst was Rae, who, with deep sideline bullets, tore Ohio State's defense apart. Flanker Swann made the turning-point play — catching Rae's twenty-three-yard pass on third and seventeen on USC's go-ahead drive — to make Ohio's roughnecks look like kiwis, the flightless birds down under. For, in a graphic contrast with Rae, Buckeye Quarterback Greg Hare threw only eight times all day, completing but four.

It was all over — 28-10 — before the end of the third quarter. All told, USC marched fifty-seven, fifty-six and sixty-seven yards to three touchdowns and scored three others after turnovers in Ohio State country.

Asked if this is the greatest team he's played against, Hayes replied, "Yes, I'd say so."

III

McKay has schooled and polished a deeply talented team.

Fullback Cunningham, for example, who is six-feet-three and 218 pounds, was the weapon McKay used at the end of each drive to take Hayes down. Not long ago on national television, Hayes' goal-line defense twice stopped Michigan to put Ohio State in the Rose Bowl. That day Michigan was much the better team — except on the goal line.

And if you were watching closely Monday, you saw what the Buckeyes do on defense down there. They charge with the ball and submarine effectively. Probably only one kind of play could have beaten them on the one-yard line, the Cunningham dive.

Four times Sam sprinted up to the Buckeye line and leaped over it like a kid diving into the ol' swimming hole. When airborne over the line, Cunningham seemed so large and moved so fast that each of his touchdowns tended to materialize as a mere formality.

In Trojan effectiveness, nonetheless, Cunningham yields to Davis. The man who makes it all go on the Trojan machine is the sophomore tailback who calls himself A.D. Productive all over the field, Davis, in the second half, scored the only touchdown Cunningham didn't, scissoring through the Buckeyes on a twenty-yard burst.

A.D. gives USC the one great back that most of football's great teams have had over all the years. Recalling two Trojan Heisman Trophy winners, he skips around like Mike Garrett, and, in a crowd, drives forward like O.J. Simpson, with the long, high leg action of the game's most effective backs.

The Trojans would have won without Davis, but they wouldn't have won big; and plainly, they wanted to win big. They were still pouring it on with passes in the fourth quarter after Ohio was a certain 35-10 loser. But that's football as it's played today in the era of the polls, and the Trojans are already thinking of next year, when McKay will be aiming for number one again.

IV

The Buckeyes were number three in America going into this game, but they don't pass well enough for a first-class team. Neither do they make a skilled defense against passes.

Hayes is, however, a fighter, and his inside running attack on McKay reflected a sound game plan. As the Buckeyes demonstrated, the way to attack defensive players who are as quick and fast as the Trojans is to run straight at them. Power can neutralize quickness, and for thirty minutes Hayes had enough power to make the game look like a throwback to the era when the Big Ten always beat up on West Coast linemen.

The Buckeyes as they played Monday could have played with any of those old Big Ten winners. But the Trojan can run with running teams now and pass with passing teams. That's the difference. In this second half, no Big Ten opponent could have stopped USC.

1982 in San Francisco

THE GAME that began the long San Francisco 49ers-Dallas Cowboys rivalry in the winter of 1982 is usually identified by two words, The Catch. The 49ers won it, 28-27, in pro football's most significant recent watershed event, ending the Tom Landry era of Dallas dominance and beginning the age of Bill Walsh. When the 49ers won the Super Bowl two weeks later, history shifted as well. During previous winters, from 1969 through 1981, National Conference teams had lost eleven of thirteen Super Bowl games. In a startling contrast, National Conference teams have since then won fourteen of fifteen Super Bowl games in a streak dominated by the 49ers. In the game that started it all, there was much more to the historic 49er victory than Dwight Clark's fingernails, as I tried then to point out.

SAN FRANCISCO: Jan. 11, 1982.

These were two of the better football teams ever to meet in a championship event. And they scrapped most of the afternoon and into the evening Sunday at Candlestick Park, where the San Francisco 49ers finally won it with fifty-one seconds left, 28-27, and saved it with thirty-one seconds left.

The San Francisco quarterback, Joe Montana, won the game with his third touchdown pass — a high, hard one to Wide Receiver Dwight Clark on a six-yard rollout play — to complete a spectacular eighty-nine-yard fourth-quarter 49er drive through the Dallas Cowboys defense.

Then a San Francisco defensive end, Lawrence Pillers, saved it. He did this at midfield with a crashing, second-effort rush at Dallas Quarterback Danny White, who fumbled as Pillers sacked him, the 49ers recovering to win their first National Conference championship and first Super Bowl trip.

They'll play the Cincinnati Bengals at the Silverdome in Pontiac, Michigan, January 24 when San Francisco Coach Bill Walsh will be dramatically reunited with Paul Brown, the Cincinnati chief executive and former coach, who, with a chance to hire Walsh as his successor six years ago, didn't.

II

"Montana's mobility gives us a lot of options," San Francisco Tackle Keith Fahnhorst said Sunday night. "That last big touchdown will go down in history."

So will the last big drive. For the Cowboys had led at the quarter pole, 10-7, at the half, 21-14, and in the fourth quarter, 27-21, as their stars kept making big plays, including two touchdown passes by White and a short, punishing touchdown run by Halfback Tony Dorsett.

But Dallas had one unreal problem: Clark's catch. "When I released the ball I knew it was high, but I was pretty certain he could get it," Montana said of his favorite receiver, who made an all-out, leaping, clawing catch on the end line. Said Dallas Cornerback Everson Walls: "We (Safety Michael Downs and Walls) had Clark inside-outside, but when Montana broke containment, I couldn't find Clark."

Dallas Safety Charlie Waters, after noting that Montana was heavily rushed by Defensive End Ed (Too Tall) Jones and Linebacker D.D. Lewis, said: "It had to be a perfect throw and perfect catch."

More than that, it was a perfect play.

"We've been working on it since training camp," Clark said of what many coaches and fans mistakenly assumed was a broken play. "The pass was supposed to go to (Wide Receiver) Freddie Solomon in the flat while I went to the back of the end zone as an optional secondary receiver."

In another crowded corner of the locker room, Montana said: "It may have looked like Clark was scrambling like I was — but he wasn't. He ran it the way Bill Walsh told him to, sliding back (along the end line). When Solomon is covered, the thing that makes the play is that you hope the defense stays where it is when Clark slides back."

Clark's last move was the trick that fooled Walls and Downs. Starting wide right along the six-yard line, Clark ducked into the end zone, continued with a square-in move to his left, then broke back to his right for the ball. Perhaps only Walsh would have added that last wrinkle.

The late-developing play was obviously designed with Montana's escapism in mind. A nimble scrambler, the former Notre Dame star, who is only in his second year as a 49er starter, is always scrambling to pass (not run), and he can throw as accurately on the run as he does in the pocket. Those are the two traits that make him different — particularly his continuing interest in throwing the ball when out on a scramble. And they're the traits that the San Francisco offense is built on.

III

The winning touchdown was one brilliant example of the 49ers' strategic new approach to football this season. Another was the winning eighty-nine-yard march as sustained with a blend of runs and passes. Of all that Walsh has done to turn a perennial loser into a Super Bowl team, the decisive thing Sunday was running the ball against Dallas Coach Tom Landry's pass defense in that last fourth-quarter drive, a tactic which continuously surprised the Cowboys.

It's true that, afterward, Landry didn't see it quite that way. "On their last drive, we just couldn't get any pressure on Montana," he said. But one of his linebackers had a better understanding of what happened. Said Lewis: "It's hard to get pressure on a passer when he's handing off."

For sure, Montana couldn't have passed his way eighty-nine yards in those final moments against a pass defense as scientific as Landry's. Even though San Francisco's ballcarriers, as a group, are possibly the league's worst, they could and did beat Landry's fourth-quarter defense — which sat linebackers down in favor of six and sometimes seven defensive backs. In their carefully prepared offense, 49er Running Backs Lenvil Elliott and Bill Ring both looked like Tony Dorsett when, on the winning long drive, San Francisco's two guards pulled quickly out ahead of them to block Dallas' little defensive backs on the end runs that set up Montana to Clark.

To be sure, Landry's fear of San Francisco's passes wasn't unreasonable. All told, Montana and Clark alone were to combine on eight plays for 120 yards as Montana completed twenty-two of thirty-five for 286.

Yet it wasn't pass offense, it was balanced offense that made a winner of San Francisco. And that may be the only way to catch up with Landry's players — who for years have dominated the National Conference, and who seldom lose games like this, especially when they force the other side into three interceptions and three fumbles, as they did this time. Other coaches talk *all* the time about the damage that turnovers cause, but in his system, Walsh, apparently, ignores a little thing like six turnovers. When he gets the ball back again, he simply sends his team out to throw it again, or, if the other side wants to play with seven pass-defense backs, Walsh runs it. If a balanced approach is what it takes to beat Landry, Walsh was ready.

IV

Dallas Quarterback White thought the turning point was the Cowboys' aborted last drive in the last minute — with the score already 28-27. The Dallas offense, moving, as usual, after Clark's big catch, had reached midfield on White's thirty-one-yard pass to Wide Receiver Drew Pearson, and there, White said, "If we could have just gotten fifteen more yards, we would have been in field goal range, and we would have won."

The sack by a second-string 49er defensive end, Pillers, ended that dream. Crashing into a Dallas guard, Pillers kept advancing on what seemed to be sheer courage and want-to, pressuring White into the fumble that brought Dallas to the end.

On the day that Walsh, for the first time, became a pro football champion, some of the Cowboys were critical of the coach who has done so much for Dallas. In particular, Wide Receivers Pearson and Tony Hill were unhappy with Landry's play-calling. Pearson: "We didn't go deep enough." Hill: "I think Coach Landry wanted to play more of a ball-control game. I don't feel the 49ers are the caliber of the Cowboys."

Landry agreed with that last sentiment. "San Francisco isn't a better team than us," he said. "Time ran out on us."

Walsh, thinking of something else, said: "We have another game to play."

1993 in San Francisco

FOR FOUR seasons in San Francisco, 1987-90, Quarterback Steve Young mostly sat on the bench, unhappily drawing his $1 million a year, and watching Joe Montana play the position they both coveted. So he had never led the 49ers into a playoff game when, climaxing the 1992 season, he finally did — only to find that Montana, coming back from an injury, wanted to play, too. Consider: In the twenty-four months just ahead of him, Young was to quarterback San Francisco against Dallas in three memorable NFC title games — the 49ers losing twice before they won the one that put them in their fifth winning Super Bowl — but he has never known a pressure day like the day of his first playoff game: the day that Montana was there to take over again. Or so Montana's fans hoped. It was the event of the year in Candlestick Park.

SAN FRANCISCO: Jan. 9, 1993.

On what was probably the most nervous day of his life, San Francisco Quarterback Steve Young won his first playoff game Saturday — with Joe Montana warming up on the sideline and eager to move out to his rescue.

As a quarterback, Young is no Montana, maybe, but he didn't need rescuing.

He took charge in the fourth quarter and, as the 49ers advanced to next week's NFC championship game, Young sent Montana back to the bench and sent the Redskins back to Washington a 20-13 loser. Asked to explain it, Washington Coach Joe Gibbs said: "The 49ers are a team without a weakness."

It was a game of bad plays on a bad field, with eight turnovers, four to each side; and Young made his share of the bad ones, fumbling three times and throwing one atrocious interception. That didn't surprise Gibbs either. "With the mud and all," he said, "those were the worst field conditions I've ever seen."

II

The 49er turnovers would have unnerved some quarterbacks. They seemingly only encouraged Young, who delivered two touchdown passes — to Wide Receiver John Taylor for five yards and to Tight End Brent Jones for sixteen — to push the 49ers into a halftime lead, 17-3, which was the score until the end of the third quarter. Then on two more turnovers, the Redskins scored ten points to close the 49er lead to 17-13.

All of a sudden it appeared to be the Redskins' game if they could complete one more touchdown drive. On two good passes by Quarterback Mark Rypien, who had pitched the Redskins to the Super Bowl championship only twelve months earlier, they moved forty-five yards, prompting 49er Coach George Seifert to say: "When Rypien got going, he was a thorn in our side."

But there, at the 49er 23-yard line, the Redskins came apart. With the turning-point play, they gave possession back to the 49ers when Rypien didn't quite get the handoff to Tailback Brian Mitchell. "I think there was mud on the ball," said Gibbs. Said Rypien: "The ball just came out. Mistakes killed us."

More than ten minutes remained, time enough for the Redskins, if they could force another 49er fumble or interception, and drive again. They couldn't. Young coolly used up more than seven minutes, moving the 49ers fifty-nine yards to their final field goal. And when Rypien got the ball again, there was too little time and too much mud.

III

The fourth-quarter field-goal drive was doubtless the most eventful of Young's life. As Montana loosened up on the sideline, Young began it with a twelve-yard gain on a called running play.

It was, as he said later, a good call (by Seifert and the 49ers' offensive coordinator, Mike Shanahan). Moments earlier, Young's fumble had put Washington in position to score an easy touchdown. Now, Seifert and Shanahan were giving him a chance to make a positive play immediately — on first down — and when he made it, going twelve yards, the most significant drive of the 49er season was underway.

In the next few minutes, Young faced two nerve-racking situations, a fourth and one and a third and ten. But he made both, the first on a sneak and the second on a ten-yard throw to Wide Receiver Jerry Rice.

Later, Young came close to acknowledging that his first playoff start was, for him, nervous time. Montana has won four Super Bowls. And to hear Bay Area football fans talk, most of them — ignoring Young's performance all season, and all day Sunday, as well as the team's 14-2 1992 record — wanted Montana in there anyway. Asked about that, Young merely said: "In the second half, you realize, 'This is it.'" The words were charged with electricity.

Given the circumstances, anyone could be pardoned for dropping the ball a few times. Still, the truth is that most of Young's blunders Saturday weren't blunders of execution. He seemed, rather, to be snakebit. For example, on one fumble, he was running a bootleg when a Redskin linebacker got around one of his teammates and reached him the moment Young turned to throw. Surprised, he let it go straight up. If the 49ers had picked up the blitzer, that wouldn't have happened.

On another Young fumble, a teammate, Center Jesse Sapolu, ran into him. On another, he was blindsided. For Young, the potential for tragedy was there all day. After a brilliant season, his turnovers could have caused him to fall apart. Young's last drive not only saved the 49er season. It probably saved his career.

The game was a rainy-day matchup between the passers, Young and Rypien, because the field was basically unplayable for running backs. San Francisco Tailback Ricky Watters, who churned for a net of eighty-three yards in the mud, said: "I knew I couldn't make my usual moves, so I just had to hit the holes."

When the game was over, three other things could be said about it: The 49ers were the better team. They will play today's Philadelphia-Dallas winner in the conference championship game here a week from today. And Joe Montana will be ready again.

VII

LEADERS

Football's leaders — the coaches and quarterbacks — have more impact on their teams than leaders in any other sport. To begin with, football is a coach's game. It is axiomatic: Great football coaches win, poor coaches lose, those in between win and lose. Earlier in the century, much the same could often be said of quarterbacks, who, when they excelled as play-callers as well as passers, were as influential as coaches — often more so.

Vince Lombardi provided the decisive example of coaching dominance. Before Lombardi arrived in 1959, the Green Bay Packers had struggled through one losing season after another under four other coaches for more than a decade. Then in 1968 when Lombardi left Green Bay — after coaching the Packers to five NFL championships in nine seasons — they resumed losing and stayed at it under four more Packer coaches for another decade.

Lombardi's approach to winning has been well-documented for many years, but nobody copying him has been able to match him. For there is no single way that winning coaches win. Football is a game that can be mastered by leaders who are as drastically different from Lombardi as Knute Rockne was and Jimmy Johnson is.

Of Lombardi, his players could say, with amusing accuracy, "He treats us all the same — like dogs." In Dallas, though, Johnson, in the early 1990s, deliberately followed another course during the years when the Cowboys were winning back-to-back Super Bowl games. "I believe in a double standard," Johnson told his players. "I'm going to treat you all differently. The harder you work, the better you play, the better you'll be treated." Proving his point after two quarterbacks fell asleep at a team meeting, Johnson only cut one of them. Addressing the other, star Quarterback Troy Aikman, he said: "Wake up, Troy."

It is their variations in attitudes and actions, one coach from another, that have caught my attention. How do winners differ? What is there about their different ways that leads to success? What has each man learned, about himself and about his game, that allows him to excel?

Similar questions could once have been asked of NFL quarterbacks, who, into the 1960s, called their own plays. Some were still doing it in the 1970s, and Jim Plunkett continued as the Raider play-caller into the early 1980s. By then, however, most coaches were following the lead of Paul Brown, who at Cleveland in 1950 became the first NFL coach to send in every play every day. In the 1990s, only Buffalo Quarterback Jim Kelly, after long running arguments with his coaches and a virtual on-the-field rebellion, has succeeded in wresting control over play-calling from his elders.

There is a vast difference in quarterbacking when the job requires signal-calling and when it doesn't. In the years when quarterbacks served as their own play-callers, they all rated that as their most important responsibility, with passing second. Even today, when earlier generations of coaches and players are discussing former quarterbacks — Sammy Baugh, John Unitas, Joe Namath, Terry Bradshaw and all the rest — they grade them on generalship first and *then* passing. Thus, it can't accurately be said of any late-century player, even Joe Montana or Dan Marino, that he is the best quarterback of all time, or even comparable with, say, Unitas and Namath. Modern quarterbacks can be compared as passers — as physical technicians — but passing was less than half the job in all the years when, as leaders, quarterbacks were up there with coaches.

1. George Halas: Founder of the NFL

THE NFL began with George Halas. At the outset of his half century and more in pro football, Halas was the principal founder of both the NFL and Chicago Bears. Later, during four decades as coach of the Bears, he won 326 games. In most NFL stadiums, including the Los Angeles Coliseum, Halas was also known for the way he boisterously intimidated game officials.

CHICAGO: Aug. 14, 1976.

George Halas, the eighty-one-year-old chairman of the board of the Chicago Bears, remembers that he was sitting around the house in the 1920s trying to think of a good name for a new organization he was putting together with the help of a few friends. A Cub fan, Halas had picked up the paper that morning to check the National League baseball standings when the name came to him: National Football League.

"If I'd been a White Sox fan," he says, "I guess it would have been the American Football League all these years."

So Halas was there when pro football began. And as the owner of the Bears for fifty-seven years, he has been there ever since. That fifty-seven years is conceivably the world record. No one else in any sport has ever led a team that long — although Connie Mack came close, starting his fifty years with the Philadelphia A's in 1901. And in Halas' case, he insists, the end is nowhere in sight. "I've heard you can live practically forever," he says, "if you work six days a week, and ride a bicycle six miles a day, and that's what I do."

Chicago-born, George S. Halas was a college football star in 1915, graduated from Illinois in 1918, played in the Rose Bowl a year later for Great Lakes Navy, organized an Illinois pro club in 1919, moved it to Chicago in 1920 (when he was twenty-five) and has run it ever since. He has also run a $50 investment into twenty million dollars — the market value of the Bears today. After he and a friend had combined their resources in 1920 to pay $100 for the franchise, Halas bought out his partner in 1932 for $38,000, borrowing the money. He repaid it out of profits.

As coach of the Bears for forty years in four separate ten-year tours, Halas won at least one NFL championship each time. But in football, championships aren't enough to save a man's job even when he owns the club. Halas is the only owner who ever fired himself, doing it four times.

In all, he coached the Bears to 326 wins, an impressive football statistic. The goal in the pro business is 100 wins (which Vince Lombardi, for one, never reached). Bud Grant has won 87 games, George Allen 97,

Tom Landry 126, Don Shula 138. Paul Brown is one of the few over 200. Halas alone is over 300. All this qualifies him, perhaps, to express opinions on the state of U.S. sports today; and he makes two comments.

• Competition is the key to excellence and success. "You don't improve much if you aren't competing," he says. "In addition to talent, you only need three things to play football well: size, speed, and desire. Modern athletes are bigger and faster than we were, but they don't have any more desire."

• Competitive balance is, by extension, the key to the continued success of sports leagues. "The NFL," Halas says, "will last as long as there is a balance of power between teams. The point of the draft is simply to spread the talent around."

Halas in his last decade as a coach won his last game at age seventy-one. "I'll never forget the day," he says. "In the locker room afterward, I was crying a bit when I got the boys together and said, 'Gentlemen, this was my last game. From now on, you're on your own.' Then I went across the hall and told the officials the same thing."

Does he like retirement?

"Hell, I'll never retire. I'm at the office every day, and working at home many a night."

And loving it all.

The hair is thinner and grayer now, but he closely approximates the Halas dimensions the day he played in the Rose Bowl. He is still a bit under five-eleven and over 182. The face is still square and beaming, the eyes thoughtful and probing. Think of Actor Barry Fitzgerald playing an eighty-one-year-old man on a bicycle, and you have Halas today.

In the exercise room of his Chicago apartment, the owner of the Bears rides the bike morning and night, pumping the equivalent of three miles each time. After warming up with a set of heavy barbells, he sets the bicycle's stress levers for a half mile on the flat, then two and a half uphill. "You aren't exercising," he says, "if it doesn't fatigue you."

Regardless of when he gets home, Halas without fail swings the barbells nightly, and rides the three miles. His philosophy is that of an awesome competitor: "Never go to bed a loser."

II

Those calling on Halas today in his office on the twelfth floor of a new Chicago building are sometimes asked to match him lifting weights. The prescribed weight is a table-top statue of Halas in a business suit and snap-brim hat, crouching on a sideline in a fist-waving pose familiar to millions.

He smiles when a California visitor can't budge the heavy little statue, then leans over and, taking hold carefully, raises it waist high. Still smiling, he sets it down gently.

From his elegant corner office, the largest in the Bears' new suite of offices, there is a wide-angle view of the two historic landmarks of Chicago, the lake and the loop. And as Halas glances outside, water-skiing youngsters are speeding in the summer sunlight on Lake Michigan at the same time that taxpayers with briefcases are hurrying through the shadows of the old elevated railroad that loops around the city's downtown area, giving it its name.

A block away in full view is Michigan Avenue, which on its way north becomes Lake Shore Drive, Chicago's gold-coast roadway fronting Lake Michigan. Halas lives eight miles up that road in a lakeside apartment. He has lived there since the era when the Bears beat the Washington Redskins, 73-0, for the 1940 championship.

All this is Halas country. It's true that Lincoln was nominated in Chicago in 1860 and that, sometime thereafter, a Mayor Daley ran the town like a dictator for a couple of decades. But as of the 1970s, this is Papa Bear's place. It was his base when he got the NFL going more than a half century ago, and he's still here, still going strong, still surprising and impressing a new group of Bear rookies each summer. Running into George Halas in Chicago, they say, is like finding George Washington alive and well at Mount Vernon.

A self-made multimillionaire, Halas lives like it. He can see and thrill to wind-driven winter blizzards and summer thundershowers — the elements that make Chicago what it is — without ever having to feel either, game day excepted. Mornings, he takes the elevator down eighteen floors from his comfortable apartment — a big one that faces in three directions, east, north, and west — to a weather-tight garage. There he steps into his blue Continental, and drives it out the door and through the gale into another garage under his air-conditioned office downtown. In a Chicago storm lasting a week, he is never outdoors.

"I live a little differently now than I did growing up," Halas says. "But there is one tie. I have always been an apartment man. Never lived anywhere else. We called them flats in the neighborhood where I was born, an immigrant neighborhood on the west side of Chicago. My dad had come over from Pilsen, Bohemia. That's Czechoslovakia now. He was a tailor, and very early he invested in real estate. He bought a triple three-story flat not far from (Wrigley Field), and we lived on the second floor. It seemed all right at the time, but today it seems like a long time ago."

III

The athletic ability that lifted George Halas out of obscurity took him first to Illinois, where he played end both ways for a football legend, Bob Zuppke, and then in 1919 to the New York Yankees. There, he played the outfield and hit a triple one day off a baseball legend, Rube Marquard, in an exhibition game. Sliding into third that time, Halas hurt his leg, and the Yankees, discouraged, made an offseason trade, replacing him with a man from Boston, a portly left-hander named Babe Ruth.

Returning to his home town, Halas became not only the first coach of the Bears but also their first trainer, first film editor, and first public relations director. The contacts he made trying to get the Bears in the paper led to a brief career as a basketball writer on the old Chicago Journal.

His newspaper background makes him wary of picking an all-Halas team, but he says, "The backfield is easy." He proves it isn't by naming two fullbacks, Bronko Nagurski and Bill Osmanski, and three halfbacks, Red Grange, Gale Sayers and George McAfee, along with one quarterback, Sid Luckman. He also names two centers, George Trafton and Bulldog Turner, two guards, Dr. Danny Fortmann and George Musso, three tackles, Joe Stydahar, Link Lyman and George Connor, and two ends. One is Harlon Hill. The other, he says shamelessly, is George Halas.

As a coach, Halas was ahead of his time for awhile, keeping the Bears in the T Formation twenty and thirty years before it became the thing to do elsewhere. Not often noted as an innovator, he experimented with the single- and double-wing formations, among others, he says, but threw them out in the 1920s. "We kept good records on all the formations we used," he recalls. "And the T was the most productive."

Not until the 1950s did the last of the single-wing holdouts make that discovery.

His greatest contribution to football was, in Halas' opinion, something else. "The thing I'm proudest of," he says, "is a rule recommendation. I introduced the rule that forbids a pro team to take a college player until his class has graduated. The NFL made that pledge away back in 1926. It saved college football — and ours, too."

Teen-agers aren't as a general rule mature enough for professional sports, Halas believes, adding: "Professional baseball and basketball would both be stronger if they had our rule and let their players mature for four years after high school before turning pro. I hate to think of the number of kids whose lives have been ruined by playing pro ball before they were ready for it. The exceptions who make good are the only ones you hear about."

As for the future of the NFL, Halas thinks it depends on two things, the first of which is good high school coaching. "That's a big plus for us now," he says. "The preps have made this a big league by giving young prospects the right start. It wasn't like that in my day. Red Grange told me his high school football coach was his manual arts training instructor. Mine was at least a gym teacher. But it takes football coaches to make football players, and that's what we've got now in the high schools all over the country — good football coaches almost everywhere."

The NFL's other need, in Halas' view, is a continuing interest in new rules. "Our rule changes have made football what it is," he says. "One of the big ones in the 1930s legalized passing from anywhere behind the line of scrimmage. That was the beginning of offensive football as we know it today. Football is the kind of game that can't stand still. The changes we've made in the last fifty or fifty-five years are the reason football has grown faster than any other game. And I predict it will be bigger than ever fifty years from now."

If his bicycle holds up, Halas may be here to check that out personally.

2. The Ram Champions

THE GREAT years for the Rams were the seven at mid-century, when they won four division titles and their only NFL title in forty-nine years in Los Angeles. Curiously, despite a rare mix of talented players and coaches, the 1949-55 Rams experienced seven seasons of almost continuous, self-defeating conflict. One of the most famous of mid-century football coaches, Clark Shaughnessy, won the division with the 1949 Rams and was fired. His replacement, Joe Stydahar, won the 1951 NFL championship and was fired. *His* replacement, Hampton Pool, developed the Rams into (a) the league's first modern passing team and (b) the first wildly popular pro club — one that could attract a hundred thousand spectators at a time in what was a small-crowd era in New York and elsewhere — and was fired. Then Sid Gillman went down in the dispute with Norm Van Brocklin.

In those same seven years, Dan Reeves, the Ram owner who hired and fired all those people, created the television broadcasting patterns that the rest of the NFL soon borrowed to run away from baseball as a crowd-pleasing economic power. For the Rams, in short, those were at once the best of times and worst of times. The two following pieces first appeared in a book I wrote about the club in 1955.

JUMBO

LOS ANGELES: Aug. 1, 1955.

Los Angeles in 1950 was a city converting to television. Fading away rapidly were the days when the owner of the only TV set on the block had to have a warehouse, too, to keep enough beer for the whole neighborhood. Almost overnight, antennas appeared on half the roofs of California, and each antenna was an aluminum tombstone marking a darkened room below where immobile human forms slouched and stared at moving forms on a screen.

The inert wanted action. And two Hollywood television stations united to provide it, contracting to broadcast every Los Angeles Rams game in the Coliseum that season. Thus 1950 was the pivotal year in the rise of pro football in Los Angeles. For a change, the team won a championship; for a change, the coach kept his job; for a change, the owners broke even, and, most significant of all, there was an explosion of Ram interest in the community. Thousands of televiewers were converted into cash fans, stabilizing the franchise in a matter of months after four economically stormy Ram seasons beginning in the club's maiden year in Los Angeles, 1946. Since 1950, the owners have never had a losing season.

Club President Dan Reeves soon settled on the correct broadcasting formula. Each fall, all out-of-town Ram games were screened live in Los Angeles, widening the circle of fans who would report in ever larger percentages for the non-televised Coliseum fare. The Rams thus became in their mid-century years the first major league enterprise in the country to use television intelligently — setting the standard soon imitated in every big league city.

II

The leader who made 1950 unforgettable for all those new Los Angeles fans was Jumbo Joe Stydahar, the Rams' first television star. An ex-tackle who looked and acted like an ex-tackle, the jovial 280-pound giant coached the Rams to a divisional championship in 1950 and the NFL championship in 1951, riding the crest of the team's short wave of spectacular winning football.

Jumbo arrived amid undertones of bitterness and left in the same atmosphere. His predecessor, Clark Shaughnessy, was still accepting congratulations for winning the division in 1949 when Stydahar replaced him suddenly in February, 1950. "I hired Joe," Shaughnessy said angrily, "but when he gets through coaching the Rams, I'll be able to take any high school team in the country and beat him."

As it turned out, Shaughnessy couldn't even do it with a pro team. But his complaint was historic. Alleging that Stydahar, his assistant, had stolen his job, Shaughnessy made that statement precisely thirty-two months before Stydahar said the same of his assistant, Hampton Pool.

III

To his players, Stydahar was a riddle. Most of them loved him, and he loved most of them — proving it by punishing them often. For example, there was a night in Little Rock, Arkansas, in 1951 when he fined no fewer than twenty-six players in an NFL-record crackdown for staying out late. Joe had started working himself into a suspicious mood following a night exhibition game, which ended at 11:30. At 2 a.m., most of the players were still overdue at the hotel where Stydahar sat smoldering in his suite. He telephoned End Tom Fears' room. There was no answer. Temper rising, he called several other players. They didn't answer, either.

The big man tore out of his room and raced to the lobby. There wasn't a Ram in sight. Acting on a hunch, he called a Little Rock night spot he had heard about, and asked for Jack Finlay, the veteran guard. Disguising his voice to resemble that of an injured Ram player, Stydahar inquired brightly of Finlay, "Any Rams there, Jack?" The player shouted back, happily, "Yeah, we're all here. C'mon down."

Jumbo burned. "Listen, playboy," he said, "this is Joe Stydahar, and I'll give you guys thirty minutes to get back here. Tell everybody. You're all fined $100, and it'll cost you another hundred if you're not back in thirty minutes."

He sat down in the lobby and brooded, and when the athletes began trooping in, he bickered with every one who would argue back. Fines ranging up from $100 were assessed on the spot, and Fears eventually hit the jackpot: $500.

In the morning, Jumbo, by an interesting process of jurisprudence, revised the scale, making it a democratic $300 for each of twenty-six players. "And that's on the record," Jumbo thundered during a press conference.

Laboriously doing the numbers, I said, "Thanks, Joe, that's a great story: 'NFL Coach Fines Players $7,800.'"

"What are you talking about? $7,800?" shouted Stydahar. "*That* is *OFF* the record."

Stydahar was a consistently erratic coach, and his teams were as erratic as their leader. In 1950, the Rams were good enough to run up seventy points on Baltimore and sixty-five on Detroit, and bad enough to lose to Philadelphia by 56-20. A year later, they lost six times, suffering two exhibition defeats and — during a twelve-game regular-season schedule — four league beatings. This was an average of one trimming for every three starts, one of the spottiest records ever made by a world-championship team.

The Stydahar explanations for these defeats were always excellent. He attributed one solely to the fact that his players were unreasonably fond of their teeth. "They'd rather keep their teeth than tackle," he mourned. "No guy is a pro until he's lost six teeth."

Stydahar, a West Virginia native, acquired his own six-tooth bridge as a lineman for George Halas in Chicago. He also had two other pertinent coaching qualifications. First, he was immensely popular with the players. And second, he won their respect for a distinguished achievement. He was the only coach in the league who could chew tobacco and smoke a cigar at the same time.

IV

As headman, Jumbo had the privilege of coaching the finest team in Los Angeles history, the 1950 Ram club for which Fears caught an all-time record eighty-four passes. Army's Mr. Outside, Glenn Davis, had his one big pro year in 1950. Most important, a revolutionary new offense, based on the long pass as the key weapon — rather than as a desperation expedient — was making itself felt. Field generals Bob Waterfield and Norm Van Brocklin were throwing the big pass with skill; and otherwise they were operating the machine so efficiently that by the end of the season, it had smashed a record twenty-two NFL records.

This amazing output was largely the handiwork of the assistant coach Stydahar had handpicked as his senior aide in the spring of 1950, Hamp Pool. As offensive coach of the Rams' 1950-51 champions, Pool introduced the NFL to a new kind of offense. In the movies of his first two exhibition games, he had discovered that with the man-for-man defenses then standard in the league, opposing players were unable to keep up with the Rams' contingent of fast receivers. He devised several plays based on this knowledge, and early in the regular season, against the Baltimore Colts, he sprung one, flanking End Tom Fears wide left and Halfback Tommy Kalminir wide right. As expected, two Colts shifted out to cover the more dangerous Fears, leaving only one to watch Kalmanir, and when Quarterback Bob Waterfield threw a forty-five yard pass to Kalmanir, the Rams were on their way to a new kind of football.

Soon they had the highest-scoring team of all time. One touchdown followed another when Hamp flared out Fears, Elroy Hirsch, Glenn Davis and other sprinters in fancy, complicated patterns, spreading them from one side of the field to the other, some near, some deep. No opposing team could double-cover all of them. And when, inevitably, one hapless defensive back wound up guarding one of the Rams' several potential receivers by himself — an almost hopeless task considering their speed, skill, and careful coaching — the quarterback, Waterfield or Norm Van Brocklin, merely passed the ball to this Ram.

Schemes deploying three and sometimes four receivers simultaneously were too much for Ram opponents, and Pool's success with this strategy worked an NFL revolution. Other teams rushed to adopt it at the same time that they labored to stop it. All over the league, conventional man-for-man defenses were scrapped, and new ones, based on a zone principle, were designed and redesigned. The new defenses rarely stopped the Ram offense, but there were times when the Ram defense stopped the Ram team. Most memorably, in the NFL title game that glorious year, against Cleveland, the Rams lost, 30-28. A year later, against Cleveland, again, the Pool offense achieved its all-time high, winning the NFL championship for Los Angeles, 24-17, on a fourth-quarter bomb from Van Brocklin to Fears.

Stydahar and Pool were both giant physical specimens who had been Bear teammates in Chicago before the war. The deterioration of their relationship under the stresses of coaching an NFL team was at once the most influential and the most tragic thing that ever happened to either man — or to the team they served.

All things considered, the coaching job they did together in 1950-51 was the best the Rams had in all the years from 1937, when they arrived in the NFL as a Cleveland expansion team, to the present. Stydahar placed in Pool's hands complete responsibility for both offense and defense. This was unorthodox but compatible with the complex nature of modern football. Jumbo realized this in 1950. The beginning of the end was his inability to steer the course straight. He was increasingly upset by the emphasis on Pool in the newspapers. A victim of his reaction to the consequences of delegated authority, Jumbo didn't understand that applause for Pool was applause for Stydahar.

In 1952, he reclaimed Pool's responsibilities, and, carrying the burden of two jobs, lost his last three of seven exhibitions. After the first regular-season game — a defeat — club Owner Reeves urged him to restore the old victorious balance of power of 1950-51. Joe refused. "Either I go or Pool goes," he said. Reeves selected Jumbo as the one to go.

HAMP

LOS ANGELES: Aug. 1, 1955.

On the training-camp practice field one hot afternoon at Redlands, Fullback Tank Younger frowned when Hampton Pool's name was mentioned. "That man is two men," said Tank. "Maybe more. From January to July, you couldn't meet a sweeter guy. But after football starts, I don't know what happens to him. He hardens up like this here ground."

The multiple personality of Hamp Pool is the central fact about him. As the club's head coach, even his accomplishments added up to a paradox. Though he descended unfailingly in the standings from second in 1952 to third in 1953 and to fourth in 1954, the club moved steadily upward in gate receipts, attracting new fans annually. It was under Pool that the Rams won acceptance by the Los Angeles community: his were the first Ram teams spontaneously cheered in the Coliseum. The championship editions of the three previous years had provided entertainment; Pool's teams added warmth, a sense of belonging, a college-style fan sentiment.

He did for the spectator what he was trying to do for the team — and strangely, he lost in the end because he failed precisely at this point. The last paradox was a player rebellion at the very peak of fan enthusiasm.

As Younger suggested, Hamp was indeed several men. Essentially an intellectual, and assuredly a skilled coach, he passionately believed that intelligence and skill were not enough to produce football championships. And so as a coach he posed, gruff and grim, as a man consumed by a fierce desire to win. This annoyed rather than stimulated his team, which diagnosed him as simply confused.

The emphasis placed on the emotional factor by a man of reason carried him to unbelievable lengths. In his first spring as a head coach, he took his worries to the Stanford University Center for Advanced Study in the Behavioral Sciences, where he learned that human emotions can be aroused artificially by ultra-sonic tones. Reacting promptly, Pool decided that a high-pitched whistle, recorded and piped into the Ram locker room, would be the scientific answer to the pre-game fight talk. In science as in life, however, things don't always go according to plan. Experiments proved that Pool's whistle had a quaint effect on human beings: Instead of stimulating them, it irritated the hell out of them.

The project was dropped in favor of other psychological experiments, but the tragedy was this: Pool was one of the few coaches good enough to have won without undue resort to psychology. He was one of the most intellectually gifted football men the league has had.

He even contrived the first successful defense for his own high-powered offense, winning eight straight games with his 1952 defense to tie for the Western Division title. For the playoff that December in Detroit, the Rams' two key defensive men, Halfback Night Train Lane and Linebacker Don Paul, were out with injuries, and the game was lost, 31-21. The effect of this defeat on Pool was frightful. Through the long ride home, he sat brooding on the floor of the airplane. Sportswriter Frank Finch, studying Pool for awhile, finally inquired: "What are you thinking about, Hamp?" The coach replied dejectedly: "Wouldn't it be wonderful if we ran into a mountain?"

Still alive a year later, Hamp insisted: "Only those who are really scared they're going to lose will develop a genuine desire to win." And that year he sought to build the requisite desire with, among other things, a weekly motto. Ahead of a 49er game, he chose "31 to 30," the score by which San Francisco had won earlier in the year. Imprinting this message on post cards, Pool mailed one to each player special delivery. There was, however, a malfunction. Not until 11 and 12 o'clock the night before the game were most deliveries made by bustling messengers who punched the doorbell and woke up the whole house. One player got his post card at 2 a.m., interrupting a dream in which he had recovered a 49er fumble and was running for the winning touchdown.

Pool's unconventional nature was visible in his early youth. Restlessly, he played football for three different colleges, California, West Point, and Stanford, at six different positions, end, guard, center, quarterback, halfback, and fullback. Following a career with the Chicago Bears, he coached at five places in five years: Fort Pierce Navy, San Jose, San Bernardino, Miami Seahawks, Chicago Rockets. At age thirty-seven, he became the first native Californian to coach the Rams. At thirty-nine, he was out, overwhelmed by a barrage of enemies: antagonistic assistant coaches, discontented players, and captious reporters.

Hamp fought back on the emotional level, ignoring his best weapon, his intellect. One day in a locker room tirade, he addressed his players as quitters, emphasizing the point by banging a table with his fist. The table, unfortunately, was stacked with sliced oranges as refreshments for the players. When Pool's fist came down, oranges spattered his face and clothes, and left him looking like something out of a Mack Sennett comedy.

Repeatedly, as if the pattern were predestined, this man meant one thing and got another. But the record shows that the merest change in a handful of plays would have led Pool to at least two championships. Unlike Paul

Brown or any other NFL leader, Pool was never badly beaten on the field. Any game he lost was still capable of being won long into the fourth quarter. This is the lasting testimonial to his stature as a coach. Caught in a web of emotion he had himself spun, and beset by rebellious assistants and players, Hamp almost plucked the title, anyway.

To the end, he was the faithful nonconformist. Traditionally, departing coaches pound on the desk and demand alimony. Pool asked for nothing. He was offered by way of settlement six months salary. He took it and left.

3. John Unitas: Confidence Man

HIS ABILITY to successfully lead NFL players into action as a quarterback is what made John Unitas a champion. And as he says, it was his confidence in himself that opened all the doors, giving him a commanding presence rivaling that of any football coach in this century. As an athlete, Unitas, who in the 1950s led the Baltimore Colts to two NFL titles, was self-made. During his first year as a pro quarterback, in fact, he wasn't even good enough to make the cut.

BALTIMORE: Nov. 28, 1959.

John Unitas of the Baltimore Colts is a thin, crew-cut blond with watchful eyes, a bashful grin, a long chin, long arms, long fingers, and boundless self-confidence. How does that kind of confidence happen?

"I have learned how to concentrate," the Baltimore quarterback says. "That's one thing I'm really thankful for."

How does concentration build confidence?

"It doesn't exactly build confidence," Unitas says. "It keeps you from thinking about it. I am lucky enough to be able to concentrate so hard on the job to be done that I never think whether I can do it."

Suppose you throw a couple of interceptions. How do you concentrate when the season-ticket buyers are screaming for the quarterback's head?

"I found a long time ago that nobody can do two things at once. It's impossible for a quarterback to hear a crowd of people *if* he's trying to hear himself think at the same time. Maybe I'd be better off to stop and listen to the fans. I'm sure they have some good ideas, but I just can't do it."

I was here the day you threw your first pass for the Colts, which was intercepted. That must have worried you a bit.

"No, I took it in stride. When we got the ball back, I raced into the game, called a running play, and we fumbled — and the Bears scored another easy touchdown. I learned right then it's six of one, half a dozen of the other. I have never worried about fumbles *or* interceptions again."

People say that's how you look — you never seem very emotional.

"The best way to play this game, in my opinion, is calm and collected. Keep cool, and keep thinking — that's the way to win."

Football coaches all talk about the value of enthusiasm or emotion, being up instead of down, and so on. In your opinion, how vital are intangibles like enthusiasm?

"That depends on what you mean. You have to like football, you have to like anything to do it well. But as far as I'm concerned, this is a thinking man's game, not an emotional game."

Many coaches have said that football is sixty per cent to seventy per cent emotion.

"Nonsense."

What is it then?

"It's sixty per cent to seventy per cent preparation — physical and mental preparation. Myself, I work at it all week. I watch film and study and practice. That's my pep talk. I don't need a holler guy around."

But isn't a pre-game nap in the locker room going too far?

"Well, I've done that for many years. It's my theory that getting plenty of rest is beneficial, and that the holler guys and the worriers just burn themselves out. The way I look at it, the coaches should do the worrying, and the fans should do the hollering."

4. Paul Brown: A Coach Takes Over

FROM HIS Ohio State days in another generation to his final days with the Cincinnati Bengals, I recurrently covered Paul Brown, filing, altogether, two dozen Brown interviews. His biggest years were those at mid-century, when he began by coaching the team that was named for him, the Cleveland Browns, to four championships in the four years of the old All-America Football Conference (1946-49). In the next eight years — after the NFL admitted Cleveland — Brown took the Browns to seven more championship games and won three NFL titles. Although the Brown-coached Bengals lost the matchup with John Unitas that is described below, 17-0, Brown subsequently had more influence on football. For one thing, his notion that coaches should call the plays, revolutionary at first, has spread throughout the game.

CINCINNATI: Dec. 25, 1970.

The miracle of the winter in pro football is that Paul Brown is back in the playoffs again as the coach of a team he organized only three years ago, the Cincinnati Bengals, who are playing Baltimore Saturday in a classic: Paul Brown versus John Unitas. Between the two of them, they'll be calling all the plays.

An overwhelming favorite again this week, Colt Quarterback Unitas has nothing to fear but the weight of all the winning games in his opponent's history. Across thirty seasons as a coach, consistency has been the distinguishing feature of Brown's career. He has won, year in and out, about four of every five games. His record for fifteen years with high school, Ohio State, and World War II service teams was 130-21-6. His record for fifteen years with the Cleveland Browns was 152-42-6.

He is a man in his sixties now, and time has rounded off the sharp Brown features, but in bearing and outlook he remains the thin, urbane intellectual of his big winning days at Massillon (Ohio) High School. That was before Ohio State, before Cleveland, long before Cincinnati, at the start of a career that began during Herbert Hoover's presidency, the year before Knute Rockne died.

Part legend, part genius, part humanist, Brown is football's first organization man — the first to arrange matters scientifically under a full-time staff with systematic concentration on movies, playbooks, play-calling, game plans, closely-timed practices, tactics and strategy — particularly pass offense and pass defense tactics and strategy.

His obvious goal — to gain control as completely as possible over a game of challenging complexity — has with some earned him the reputation of an autocrat. And no area of his operation opens itself to that interpretation more easily than his theories of player relations. "The principles haven't changed for forty years," he says, "and the first principle is that you've got to have fun. That means you have to surround yourself with nice people. Good football can only be played by good people — those who are nice people inside."

How do you define nice people?

"I don't know how to define it," Brown says, "but when you meet them, you know them. A clinker can win a game now and then, but they don't win consistently."

What kind of players are your kind?

"They are players who are quick and fast and who love to play football. They are players who agree with me that life is a bowl of cherries."

As you move into the 1970s, is it a bigger problem than it used to be for you to tailor your kind of athlete?

"In Cleveland, we didn't bother to change individuals, and we don't bother now. We try to draft or trade for the sort we want, and we only keep that kind. We don't draft guys that sleep on the beach."

What's the first rule you would give a young coach on how to handle players?

"Never keep a secret from them. Never tell any athlete to do anything unless you are prepared to tell him just why you want him to do it. And never lie. The smartest coach in football couldn't fool the dumbest player."

Can a dumb coach be fooled by a smart player who likes to do his training at 2 o'clock in the morning?

"Drinkers and rounders can play good football for a few years because of the wonderful resiliency of youth. But they represent nothing of what we value in football, so we don't keep them around after we find them out. Like a husband with an errant wife, we learn about it later than others, but we always find them out."

Your attitude leads some people to call you a dictator. How much do you mind that?

"I never do anything about it, if that's what you mean. Vince Lombardi telephoned one day and said it troubled him to be referred to as 'Mussolini' by newspapermen and by some of his former players. He asked me what I did about things like that. I said I ignored them. You have to, because the problem is built into the situation. The two basics that make winning possible are understanding and authority. The players must always understand exactly what you mean. And the authority must be in one person one hundred per cent of the time. There can be only one place for a player to go for an answer. I doubt if any football team can succeed very long unless the coach has the final word on everything from the draft and trades to all the responsibilities of a general manager."

Speaking of absolute authority, what is your philosophy during the exhibition season when you have to cut the squad, depriving so many of a livelihood?

"I put it in the form of a question. In what other business can a man discover in two months whether he's good enough to make it? Let's say another boy wants to be a lawyer. He invests four years in college, three years in law school, and maybe two years in law practice, only to discover, after all that time, that he can't cut it as a lawyer. The break is just as painful in football, but quicker."

Another aspect of total control is play-calling. As the first coach to do that, why did you take the responsibility away from your quarterback?

"Let me ask *you* one. What's the first thing the quarterback does after he takes the ball from center? He turns his back on the defense. Coaches, in other words, have a better view of the defense than quarterbacks. Second, if we've sent in the play, we know where to look when the ball starts to move. On a given pass, if all three receivers are covered, we can see the kind of defense they're in, and what to do about it next time."

It is often said that the coach has a poorer view of the game than any spectator.

"The press box has a better view, and that's why we have a telephone to our assistants there. But the quarterback's view is the worst of all. I played that position, and I know. A quarterback has his hands full. He calls the offensive blocking. He calls the defenses. He manipulates the ball. Then he turns his back to pass. His wife sees more of the game than he does."

The title of (former Cleveland Quarterback) Otto Graham's next magazine article is, 'Why the Quarterback Should Call the Plays.' What is your reaction to this?

"That wasn't the way he felt when he played for us. He never questioned the idea of our calling the plays although he was fully capable of doing it himself — as he proved last August in Chicago at the College All-Star Game. The first chance he got to coach a football team, he sent in the plays just the way his old coach used to do it in Cleveland."

Today's defenses are stunting more than ever. As a play-caller stuck on the sideline, how do you cope with all that?

"Here's what some people don't realize: Our quarterbacks have always been flexible at the line of scrimmage. Otto won a lot of games by changing my calls. (Bengal Starter) Ken Anderson checks off as much as a third of the time."

You're winning with the plays he changes. Some players would say that Anderson has earned the right to be the first-string play-caller.

"Try looking at it like this. If something goes wrong on the field, I'd rather have people blame me than my quarterback. Quarterbacks improve faster and play better when they aren't criticized for everything that goes wrong."

Another factor, I imagine, is that you enjoy play-calling.

"Yes, I can't hide that. I like to be involved. I get more kick out of it than anything else I do, in or out of football."

Here's another way you're out of step. Of the teams that made the playoffs this winter, most have coaches who work around the clock. Nobody ever accused Paul Brown of doing that. How do you get the job done so fast?

"Personally, I fold up every night about 10. I get sleepy, and when Brown gets sleepy it's all over. So, for us, football is mainly a daytime industry. When people call me a man with a fiendishly one-track football mind, I don't mind it at all — as long as I get nine hours sleep a night. And winter vacations in Florida."

Do Cincinnati's assistant coaches take the winter off, too?

"No, for the coaching staff, there are a million things to do between seasons, including thousands of feet of film to study. I fly up and talk to them once in a while."

What do you do the rest of the time?

"Sit. We own a home in Coral Gables, and I try to swim a little one day, and golf a little the next, and maybe fish once a week. But the thing I like best is the beach chair."

How often do you review Bengal movies down there?

"Never. All I do in a football way is think about it. I think football in that beach chair all winter."

Year-round, [former Notre Dame Coach] Frank Leahy used to set aside an hour every day to meditate offense and defense. What does football meditation do for you?

"I would say the best ideas I have had about football have come along while I was relaxing in Florida. The leisure to think is the most productive thing about vacations or days off from any job, I imagine. It would be hard for me to keep up in this fast-moving business without an opportunity for relaxed, easy-going thinking."

You've been through everything: building expansion teams, climbing, winning championships in college and pro ball. What's hardest?

"Staying up there once you've got there. In Cleveland, we were in that last big game at the end of the season eleven times in thirteen years — and each one was harder than the one before."

Speaking of Cleveland, when you left the Browns your endowment was $80,000 a year in severance pay. Why did you give that up to run a new team?

"I can't think of any two or three other things I'd be satisfied with indefinitely, even if two of them are golf and spending money. I went back to football because it's my life. Call it chess in hip pads. Or call it miniature warfare, it's exciting, it grabs you, it's a man's life."

5. Football's Shotgun Formation

MORE THAN a third of a century ago, the San Francisco 49ers, with Howard (Red) Hickey coaching, startled the NFL with a new offense known as the shotgun formation. With ordinary talent — except for their three alternating quarterbacks, John Brodie, Bobby Waters and Billy Kilmer — the 49ers just missed the playoffs after routing the Detroit Lions, 49-0, and Los Angeles Rams, 35-0. In one form or another, the shotgun has been with us ever since — though its first incarnation in San Francisco was the most well-rounded and spectacular. With receivers spread sideline to sideline, Hickey rotated his quarterbacks and ran them — against a spread-out defense — as often as he passed. Here's how it seemed that first year to a 49er rookie who went on to a big NFL career.

KILMER ON HICKEY

SAN FRANCISCO: Oct. 18, 1961.

Billy Kilmer of the San Francisco 49ers, nominally a quarterback, has become the first tailback since Sammy Baugh of the Washington Redskins to rise from the campus to instant stardom in pro football. A few weeks ago, Kilmer was only a draft choice. Today, as a ground gainer, the UCLA-bred 49er tailgunner is in the NFL's top ten. "I wouldn't be up there," he says, "if I had to call the signals like other pro quarterbacks. Our coach, Red Hickey, does that. All I have to think about is running or passing, and that's a full-time job for a rookie."

On game days, what is your relationship with Hickey?

"We huddle with Red after each play," says Kilmer. "But that's a lot different from taking the responsibility yourself. I don't see how any rookie could keep his mind on strategy and execution at the same time. A lot of veteran quarterbacks have trouble. I'll tell you how tough this pro game is. I've learned more about football just since July than I learned in the rest of my career put together."

What do you and Hickey talk about there on the sideline?

"We concentrate on how the defense reacts to the play that was called. Five of us know what play was sent in: the quarterback on the field, the two quarterbacks standing with Hickey, and the spotter upstairs. We get a picture of the play right now. It's like a movie."

How often are you allowed to overrule the coach?

"Hickey is a man who takes suggestions all the time."

How does he act when he's losing a game?

"I haven't known many guys with that much poise. Out on the field when things go bad, it's hard to keep from blowing up. Even veterans blow up. But if the coach is calm and collected, he settles things down, because the quarterbacks are always coming out of the game to talk to him."

The way the 49ers rotate three quarterbacks, you are only in action one-third of the time. Does this cause you to lose the feel of the game?

"It would, I'm sure, if I were calling the plays. But when one mind is responsible for continuity, I'm just another ballcarrier. And I run as often in this system as if I were playing sixty minutes."

What about the criticism that you run too often? An NFL quarterback is supposed to be a passer.

"I throw the ball more often than an (orthodox) T quarterback runs. The defense has to be ready for both."

Are you more vulnerable than T quarterbacks?

"I think those guys are in more danger of getting hurt. They get blindsided. Nothing is worse. I like to size up the man who is hitting me."

Suppose the 49ers change back to the straight T. Based on your observation so far, what does it take to be an NFL quarterback?

"What it takes is years and years of experience. It's the hardest job in sports. I'm not a great passer, but there aren't many of those. Most winners aren't great passers, they're smart passers. They've passed and learned. I'll get there eventually, maybe in four or five years."

In the meantime, I suppose you've noticed that NFL quarterbacks are running the ball more than ever this fall.

"Yes, I have, and that's the Hickey influence. Red shook up the game with a new idea. He showed them that you don't have to baby the quarterback in a rocking chair."

As a Southern California native, how do you stand it up here in San Francisco?

"It's the only place to play football. Other parts of the country have a few days of perfect football weather. We have it every day."

CLARK SHAUGHNESSY

FOR NEARLY a month of 1961, the 49er shotgun seemed unstoppable. Then Clark Shaughnessy, defensive coach of the Chicago Bears, shocked the league again by not only stopping but blanking the 49ers. The greatest of all football strategists in the century's last sixty years, Shaughnessy designed both modern offense and modern defense. His was the biggest contribution to the development of the game-changing T Formation in the 1940s, when the Bears overwhelmed the Washington Redskins for the NFL championship, 73-0. Twenty years later, he moved to the other side of the ball and showed the league how to play defense — using the same principle, player movement, that is the basis of T football. Some of his thought processes shine through in the following very brief interview.

LOS ANGELES: Oct. 27, 1961.

Clark Shaughnessy says he killed the shotgun with a possum. He told us about it Thursday in an exclusive interview set up by A.T. & T. It was the first interview authorized by the defensive coach of the Chicago

Bears since he aimed his possum defense at San Francisco's shotgun offense Sunday and blanked the 49ers, 31-0.

Chicago yielded only six first downs in that upset, the most startling of a football season which had seemed drained of shock value when the 49ers parlayed routs of 49-0 over Detroit and 35-0 over the Rams. "Right off the bat," Shaughnessy says, "I want to tell you that you have to be lucky to beat the shotgun. That's the most original offense in the last quarter century — since George Halas opened up with the T. We were lucky because our linemen executed their possum assignments perfectly."

Exactly what is involved in this defense?

"You fake out the offense instead of letting the offense fake you," says former Ram Coach Shaughnessy, a recognized football philosopher. "Our middle linebacker, Bill George, was a perfect possum in that game. He lined up head-on the snapper, and just before the snap he jumped one yard to the left, or one yard to the right. The blocker assigned to George couldn't find him."

On the Chicago team that day, who else was play-acting?

"Most of us were, all but the (secondary). We were in what appeared to be a six-man line. They all played possum until just before the snap. Sometimes they jumped away at the moment of the snap. You can do that against the shotgun because a shotgun play never starts as fast as a T play. That's the weakness of the shotgun. The reason the 49ers couldn't block us was, they couldn't find us."

What percentage of the time did George and the other linebackers blitz Kilmer, Brodie and Waters?

"George blew in one-third of the time. On the average, he possumed twice and blew once. We always rushed at least two men, almost always three or four, often five, and occasionally all six. The basic defensive alignment was a six-five. Against the [conventional] T, a four-man secondary is usually enough, but you need at least five against the shotgun. They have five speedy receivers coming down the field at you, spread out from sideline to sideline. That's the strength of the shotgun."

Who becomes your fifth defensive back?

"A linebacker, either Larry Morris or Joe Fortunato, moves into the secondary."

Why do you suppose other NFL defenses have had so much trouble with the shotgun?

"It's different, and anything different is tough to handle. Most defenses today are based on keys. A defensive tackle might key on an offensive guard, for example. If the guard goes one way, the tackle reacts. At

Chicago, in our dictionary, there's no if. We have no keys. We substitute responsibility for keys. In each of our defensive (alignments), every man has one responsibility, either an opponent or a zone. Regardless of what the offense does, he's responsible for that one opponent, or that one zone. He plays possum as long as he can — pretending to be reading keys — and then rushes to his assigned man or zone. It's a simple system."

But it's a rigid system. You can be fooled.

"Certainly. Every defensive team in the league exposes a weakness when it lines up. We expose a glaring weakness on every play. You have to gamble that they won't find it. The 49ers didn't — that day."

What are the advantages of shotgun football?

"There are those five ends — that's the main thing. And the three quarterbacks are talking over every play with the coach personally. That's a tremendous advantage. You'll see a lot of shotgun football in this league from now on, not on every down, maybe — but there are a lot of downs when it will be the best offense."

POSTSCRIPT

AFTER THE above interview was printed, Shaughnessy sent me the following letter. Although he makes a valid point about his Stanford quarterback, Frankie Albert, it was the Stanford offense — Shaughnessy's offense — that was emulated nationally in the early 1940s. It was, in fact, so widely used that it took football over. Nothing remotely like that has happened since.

DEAR BOB: George Halas and others, including myself, have often been described as the "inventor" or "popularizer" of the T Formation. I would like to set the record straight. If it hadn't been for Frankie Albert, you nor anybody else would have heard much about the T Formation. It is to him that credit is due, more than any other one individual, for football as it is now played by the high schools, the colleges and professionals.

It is true that before Frankie's time, Sid Luckman was very successful with the Chicago Bears. But no college or high school team attempted to copy Luckman, or the Bears, and I am inclined to doubt if the attempt ever would have been made. It wasn't until an unknown like Albert and a football team that had failed the year before to win a conference game came along in 1940 with a Rose Bowl winner that the rest of the country noticed the new formation.

Looking back on that year, I have often wondered what would have happened if we had lost two or three games. What would football be like today? — Sincerely, CLARK.

6. Vince Lombardi: Five-Time Champion

OF OUR many visits during the years I knew Vince Lombardi, I remember two in particular. The first was in 1960 before he had won any NFL championships, the second in 1969 after he had won all five during a matchless career as perhaps the greatest coach of all time. The emphasis here is on matters that separated Lombardi from less successful coaches — as is the accent in the interviews that follow with two of his former associates, Hall of Famers Tom Fears and Willie Wood.

GREEN BAY, Wis.: Nov. 18, 1960.

As anyone who has spent time in an NFL city this fall will tell you, Vince Lombardi, the new coach of the Green Bay Packers, is the most frequently discussed individual in pro football today. Although this is only his second season as a head coach, he is, except for Paul Brown, already the league's most widely respected leader.

A strangely reticent person, seemingly embarrassed from one moment to another in any private setting, Lombardi in action is a combative, domineering coach with an assertive, dominating approach to football. In a week when such a man is preoccupied with his next opponent, the Detroit Lions, he agrees to a brief interview, and you start by asking him an offensive question.

What's the best thing to do against a team like Detroit — a team with a magnificent, nationally famous defense?

"We'll hit them at their strongest point," he says. "We'll attack their strength."

Most pro clubs attack weaknesses. Why hit them where they're strongest?

"I learned most of my football from Red Blaik when I coached under him at West Point," Lombardi says, "and Blaik believed in giving battle to the best players on the other side. My offhand recollection is that our opponents all try to attack us where we're weakest, but we want to do it the other way."

For what reason?

"To break their morale. If you can beat down their very best men, it's all over."

Suppose you were up against eleven Pro Bowlers. That might be the place for shotgun plays or some other variation on your usual plan.

"No, we believe in keeping the offense simple. We know the shotgun may beat us once in a while. So may the four-end spread. Those two new offenses this year are troublesome, but you can't win with them over a fourteen-game season. Mistakes decide most football games, and the team with the simplest offense and defense makes the fewest mistakes."

Surely there's a time for rollouts or reverses, or *something* livelier.

"I'm not against these things, but to do them you've got to have two offenses. And it's hard enough coaching one offense, let alone two. You must first have an offense that's good all over the field. You've got to be sound on your five-yard line, for instance — and theirs. And you want to be sound in the fourth quarter of a close game. Of course there are times when you'd like to get fancier — but there isn't enough practice time to put in a sound offense and a fancy offense too."

How many hours do the Packers practice each day, on the average?

"You can't practice a football team more than an hour and a half. On Fridays, it's an hour, and next to nothing on Saturdays and Mondays. Time is so limited that we have to spend it all on the few things we do best. If we don't get those nailed down, we're out of business."

Suppose you had been stuck with really inferior personnel at Green Bay. I've heard people say that that's the time to try things that are more imaginative.

"The poorer the personnel, the simpler I'd keep the offense. Let's do what we can do right."

Some people complain that this style hurts pro football as a spectacle for the fans.

"Well, I doubt that. And anyhow, I don't look on football as a spectacle. Fans who go to a pro game to see a show are going to the wrong place."

What should pro football fans expect to see?

"A pro football game."

I think it can be documented that some of the touchdown explosions in the other league this year have been appreciated by AFL fans.

"The pro football fans I know would rather see pro football than basketball."

What specifically attracts them to football?

"First, I think they like to see a well-coached team that makes good plays. They also appreciate individual effort, and they like to watch good defenses. The main reason football is popular with sports fans is the skill and violence they see. If it weren't violent, it wouldn't draw."

One more thing. A number of Green Bay's good players have to spend most of their time on the bench. How do you keep all of them happy?

"I don't worry about that. They better keep me happy."

Might any of them play this week?

"They better be ready."

How can they impress you enough to start? What quality do you most prefer in a football player?

"It's all w-a-n-t in this business. The boy who wants to play is the one I'm looking for. The day I don't want to coach, that's the day I'll quit."

Lombardi at Washington

WITH NINE years in Green Bay behind him, Lombardi took a year off, then moved to the Washington Redskins for his tenth and last season as a head coach. Before his health failed, he turned around another loser, compiling a 7-5 record that matched his first-year 7-5 at Green Bay. Once more, his sole concession to spirited football was the halfback option play, which is still the game's most effective weapon, potentially, though rarely called by any other coach. If any coach had exploited Halfback Marcus Allen's excellent arm, for example, he might have dominated football. Lombardi got results with inferior passers.

WASHINGTON: March 11, 1969.

After five NFL championships in nine years, Lombardi left Green Bay because, he says, he couldn't think of another new way to inspire his team. Resettling in Washington, he has noticed, no doubt, that the challenges are once again enormous. The Redskins haven't had a winning season in fourteen years.

What's it like for football's finest coach to change bases in mid-stream?

"The most difficult part of a new job," he says, "is analyzing and understanding the personality of each player. This got most of my attention in the early days at Green Bay, and it's the top-priority thing in Washington. You can't begin to coach a forty-man team until you understand each of the forty men."

How does that help?

"You can't coach without criticizing — and it's essential to understand how to criticize each man individually. Some can take constructive criticism in front of a group, and some can't. Some will take it privately, but others can only take it indirectly. Football is a pressure business, and on my teams I put on most of the pressure. The point is that I've got to learn forty ways to pressure forty new men."

What other high-priority missions have you begun in Washington? Of the various procedures and policies you followed ten years ago in Green Bay, which ones are you applying to the Redskin problem?

"Broadly speaking, the two main things on a new job are personality analysis and talent analysis. The idea is to make sure that every player is in his best position."

What has your talent analysis shown so far?

"The veterans here are better than they have played to date."

You said the same thing at Green Bay in the spring of 1959.

"Did I? Maybe I'm an incurable optimist."

Overall, what do the 1968 Redskin movies reveal about your new players?

"They show only what the players have done — not what they're capable of doing — and that is the trouble with relying too heavily on pictures of a new team. I'm really not sure yet what I have in Washington. The pictures don't tell you the big thing — the potential of each player."

I'd think they might give you a rough idea.

"Yes, but it's very rough. Football is a game played with emotion, not muscle, and if a man is just playing satisfied, that doesn't come through in the pictures. What can he do under stress and duress? What is he capable of if I push him to the limit? What *is* his limit? Those are the things I have to know, and I can only approximate the answers by grading the Redskins in last year's games."

What other priorities do you have?

"Just analyzing the opposing defenses and offenses, and discussing techniques with a new coaching staff."

Hiring a new staff was easy for you, I'd guess. As an NFL coach, you have won with seemingly all kinds of assistant coaches.

"The point to be made here is that there are no bad coaches in this league. All the coaches are good ones, the head coaches and the assistants. If you have played in this league — or if you have just been deeply interested in what we do, and if you deeply want to coach — you can be a coach, and you can coach for me or anybody."

It seems likely that many assistants have a deep interest because they hope to be head coaches some day. Why does it take so long for some of them to get there?

"The dividing line is on the question of direction. There are assistants who are great at taking direction — but can't give it. Most people need direction. And most fans don't realize that comprehensive football knowledge is not the most important thing in coaching. What I ask of an assistant is that he be a good technique man."

Is that all?

"No, I also demand loyalty — loyalty to the Redskins and loyalty to me. I have worked with many kinds of assistants — but this they've all had. I won't tolerate anything less than complete loyalty. Contrary to what you may have heard, I *will* tolerate practically everything else — if the man can coach techniques."

It has been said that even on techniques, you are something of a dictator in relationships with your staff.

"That isn't true at all. This spring in Washington, I suppose my coaches and I are devoting most of our man hours to a study of techniques. And I'm not dictating anything. At our staff meetings, I might say that on a given play I'd like to have it blocked this way. Then I ask, what do you think? If any coach — offensive or defensive — has a better way, I change. Most definitely, I value assistants with creative ability."

On most clubs, offensive and defensive coaches work apart. Why do you ask them to sit together?

"It's the only way to do it in the spring. First, I want all my coaches to be thoroughly familiar with both our offensive and defensive concepts. Second, I want a defensive coach, for instance, to be familiar with other NFL defenses. And third, when a trained defensive coach puts his mind to offense — or vice versa — he can often help the rest of us find a solution."

Provided he has accepted the overall Lombardi philosophy.

"Well, there are many ways to play football, and it's not too important what you decide on — as long as everybody is in agreement. You call me a dictator. The fact is that I'm reluctant to take any step that doesn't have the wholehearted support of my whole staff."

TOM FEARS ON LOMBARDI

FORMER RAM Tom Fears, one of the club's all-time receivers who was an assistant at Green Bay in the first Lombardi season, 1959, was asked about him a year later when he returned to the Rams as end coach.

LOS ANGELES: Sept. 10, 1960.

When you compare Vince Lombardi to Paul Brown, Hall of Famer Tom Fears says, "you have to remember that Brown had two years to build his team before he ever played a game in 1946. At Green Bay a year ago, Lombardi found himself in the most mixed-up situation in the league. He walked into a hornet's nest, and got them all making honey."

What is your estimate of Lombardi's personnel?

"They're just fair," says Fears. "His best back, Paul Hornung, isn't any better than Frank Gifford (whom Lombardi coached as offensive coordinator of the New York Giants)."

Is that bad?

"Gifford is an average runner and ordinary passer. Every back and end we have on the Rams, except Tom Wilson, is a better receiver than Gifford — and Wilson is a better runner."

How does Gifford make All-Pro every year?

"When Lombardi was the Giant backfield coach, he built Gifford into an All-Pro. Vince put in an offense in which the fundamental play was the halfback option, run or pass. He and Gifford worked on it until that one play was the biggest threat in the [NFL's] Eastern Division. It made Gifford an All-Pro halfback — that and the fact that Gifford is a terrific competitor."

In Green Bay, you're saying, Lombardi deliberately set out to make Hornung into another Gifford.

"Yes, and he got the same results with a back who is just as ordinary."

Otherwise last year, you got a chance to test the theory that strict, stern coaches are not always beloved. How did the players react to Lombardi?

"An unusual thing happened after our opening game. Hornung and the other Packers felt so good about the way things were going that they put Lombardi on their shoulders, and carried him off the field."

What was unusual about that?

"The Packers had lost the game."

WILLIE WOOD ON LOMBARDI

FORMER PACKER Willie Wood, the All-Pro safety who played eight seasons for Lombardi, was asked about him a year later when he joined the San Diego Chargers as an assistant coach.

SAN DIEGO: April 14, 1972.

Vince Lombardi's secret was "getting along with the players," Hall of Famer Willie Wood says. "He wasn't a dictator at all, contrary to popular opinion. He was a conciliator. The thing that made him strong was his ability to solve the personal problems of his players."

What do you mean by personal problems?

"Something wrong at home, financial problems, things like that," Wood says. "Vince was a beautiful father confessor, a man you could really confide in."

He appeared to be the last person anyone would go to with an embarrassing personal problem.

"Ah, you didn't go to him. He went to you."

How did he know you had a problem?

"That's the thing that really explains Lombardi. In the first place, he had so much confidence in his judgment that when he picked a man for a job, he knew he had the right man. Therefore, if the man's performance tailed off, Vince knew it had to be something personal. And instead of letting the problem fester, as a lot of coaches would, Vince went right to the player, and had it out with him."

How about an example of the kind of personal thing he solved?

"If it was personal, how could I know what it was?"

Then how did you know he solved anything?

"Sometimes after a man had been playing badly, he would play well, and I'd congratulate him. He'd say, 'Vince helped me with a little personal thing.' Problems are usually small. There aren't many big problems."

What do you mean?

"When you talk them over with somebody who is sincerely interested in you, they suddenly don't seem so serious. Most people who think they have problems just want to touch base with someone who cares. Vince cared about his players. That's how he kept forty of them playing at their peak, and that's why we won."

If you were lecturing at a coaching clinic, what other attributes of Lombardi's would you bring up?

"I'd mention first that he was honest with his players. Nothing is more important than being scrupulously honest in all matters at all times. Secondly, he demanded our best at all times. Your second best gets you second place. And third, he had a sincere relationship with his players. That's hardest of all. You can't feign sincerity indefinitely. Vince really was sincerely interested in the welfare of the kind of guy who would go out and die for the Green Bay Packers."

Do you suppose Lombardi agonized over players he fired?

"I know he did. He gave this subject more attention than almost anything else, especially in the last days of training camp, when you have to cut the last two or three men. I saw the way he handled it. It was hard on him, but he did it like a man. I don't think one guy left Green Bay bitter in all the years Vince was there."

If true, that's a unique record.

"I think it's true. He would cut or trade a player in such a way that the guy could see it wasn't personal. A traded player is inclined to think the coach has it in for him. You think the coach doesn't like you. Vince made them see otherwise."

How?

"He sat down and showed them the whole picture. If he intended to trade for a receiver, for example, he said so, then he explained how trades work. If you're short on receivers and long on linebackers, you may have to trade a linebacker to get what you need. Vince said this so persuasively that the guy sometimes walked out of camp thinking he had personally delivered us our next championship."

7. George Allen: All Football

FROM THE start of a comic-opera controversy, it seemed obvious that (a) George Halas was fighting to keep George Allen with the Chicago Bears because he wanted Allen as the Bears' next coach, succeeding George Halas; (b) Allen was making it plain that he wanted Los Angeles as surely as the Bears and Rams wanted him, and (c) both clubs were right about his talent. He proved it with twelve winning seasons in the next twelve years, when, continually, many reporters were disturbed by Allen's flaws, real or perceived — in the same sense that, in other sports, Bobby Knight and Charles Finley disturbed them. This has resulted in an injustice: Allen can't get the Hall of Fame votes he earned. In two Herald-Examiner football columns, here he is at the beginning of his coaching career.

LOS ANGELES: Jan. 12, 1966.

Although George Allen has been an important member of the Chicago Bears' football staff for the last eight years, there are an estimated 3,250,000 people in Chicago alone who had never heard of him until yesterday. Throw in the suburbs, and the extent of Allen's obscurity in northern Illinois had become a legend in his own time.

But overnight, George Halas, the owner-coach of the Bears, has transformed Allen into a man of distinction. In both Illinois and California, football fans have been rendered breathless by the struggle of the lovable underdog, Halas, to keep the villain, Allen, from strengthening the already powerful Rams as their new head coach.

Is Allen all that good? What's he got? How does it happen that he is in the middle of a bitter tug o' war between two of the wealthiest franchises in American sports? Who *is* George Allen?

Well, at the moment, Allen is best described as a classically typical football assistant of possibly the highest order in background and accomplishments — a man who has put in eight seasons on a good winning staff, who has developed a talent for human relations, and for whom nothing at all exists except football and family.

One hundred times at least this week in Los Angeles, Allen has been asked: "What's your hobby, George, besides football?" And the answer is always the same: "That's it."

He does have two other interests. Once a year, he throws himself into a mission bettering race relations in South Dakota — between Sioux Indians and whoever else it is that lives in South Dakota — and every night in the year, if possible, he retires to the basement in Deerfield, Illinois, for a fast game of table tennis or billiards with the G-Men: His boys, George, Gregory and Gerald.

"In our recreation room," says Allen, "we don't have a television set. I've got to admit that we don't even have much to read down there. I'm one of those fellows who have to keep active, and the Allens are an active family. Except when I'm working or they're studying, about all we do is play together as a family."

For example, the head of the family keeps a wrestling mat in the middle of the floor of the recreation room. He would like to have it in the living room, but his wife Etty has, so far, won that argument. At Michigan, George was a college wrestler. "It's a fine sport," he says, "I'm a great believer in stretching and limbering exercises, and wrestling takes care of that. No matter how busy I get, the one thing I try to do is work out three times a week — stretching, limbering and lifting light weights."

This is a man who is easy to get acquainted with. One of his friends here from the old days says his number-one qualification for this job, or any job, is that he is "genuinely interested in people."

The first day I saw him, Allen was standing on the sideline of the Ram practice field at Redlands. That was in 1955, on one of those overheated afternoons that killed off generations of Rams out there in those years, but George couldn't have been happier. He was then coaching at Whittier College — and running a boys' camp most of the summer — and this was his vacation: Seven twenty-four-hour days with the Rams.

That first afternoon, he made friends with even the most introverted sportswriters. And, every night, George shadowed the head coach of the era, Sid Gillman, from movie projector to squad meeting to movie projector until Sid retired, sometimes as early as 3 a.m. In twenty years at Ram camps, I have never seen any other college or high school coach who was interested enough, and interesting enough, to come out there on his own and move in with the coaches, living with them familiarly and uninterruptedly.

Gillman finally hired him in 1957, full time. They admired each other's brains. And, of course, this week, you're beginning to get an idea of what

Halas thinks of Allen. The Halas reaction, to be sure, must be judged either sophomoric or senile, but that's another story, to be continued tomorrow.

LOS ANGELES: Jan. 13, 1966.

One thing the country is learning about George Halas this week is that it's always an upset when his way of running the National Football League coincides with NFL policies. Change comes, once in a while, to the league; but to father Bear never. Some say that George hasn't changed since he started the Chicago fire.

Thus when he reports he can't possibly spare George Allen because the boy knows all of the Bears' secrets, Halas is demonstrating that he has plumb forgotten about the invention of movies.

There are great coaches in the NFL and good coaches and lousy coaches, but no secrets. The eye of the camera has brought everybody up (down?) to the intellectual level of the mighty Bears.

The Rams have hired, as their new coach, a man who doesn't know any more about football than Halas, Svare, Gillman, McPeak, McKay or McFurillo. This was emphasized again at Allen's press conference the other day when he sat down at a hotel table and looked into all those television cameras for the first time as club Owner Daniel Reeves' choice as the Ram leader.

"The thing we're going to concentrate on," Allen said, answering a question, "is the elimination of mistakes." Later he elaborated: "Whenever the personnel is about even, the team that wins is the one that makes the fewest errors."

In pro football today, this philosophy is not, precisely, a secret. One of Monday's interviewers, in fact, persisted: "Isn't that what all coaches attempt to do — eliminate mistakes?" Said Allen: "Certainly. We all try to win, to block, and to eliminate mistakes. The only differences between teams are the way they go about it, the techniques."

And there is no such thing as a secret Bear-Allen technique system. Of the four books Allen has written on football, all of them published by Prentice-Hall, two are devoted entirely to techniques. "Those books mean a lot to me," Allen said, "but not because of the money I made. There isn't much money in books. They're important because of what I learned. The author of a book learns more than anybody."

Halas and others wishing to discover Allen's secrets can find them in "The Complete Book of Winning Football Drills," Prentice-Hall, 1960. One of Allen's other volumes is "How to Train a Quarterback."

And it could be that, in putting this to print, Allen defined one of the essential points of difference between him and the last Ram coach, Harland Svare. Both are defensive coaches, but Allen, in the nine years he spent on the offensive side and as a head coach, also specialized on attack.

The Ram appointee expects, nonetheless, to stay with defense this season, as Svare did for three years. "Pro football today," he says, "Is half offense and half defense, but I'll run the defense for two reasons. First, that's what I'm in now. I'm familiar with it. And second, if you don't have defense, you can't win. It's harder for offensive players to get up emotionally than defensive players. But if you're playing technically sound defense, you're always in the game almost regardless of how emotional anybody is. Good defense will get you a win on an off day. Nothing builds confidence on a football squad like a defense that won't budge."

The first coach, of course, who divulged the secret that confidence builds defense was either Lombardi, Howard Jones, or one of their grandfathers. Nor are there any mysteries at all on the Halas-Allen team in Chicago — speaking of football. The only secrets there are are of the non-football variety, and they remain the exclusive possession of Halas — despite the many probes of the Rams and others.

For example, in Wrigley Field, how does Halas tap the visiting team's phone line from the field to the press box? Does he use a hot wire, or is it all electronics? No man in football has more fun than G. Halas.

8. Joe Namath Super Bowl-Bound

ALTHOUGH HE rose to national prominence as football's best passer, a distinction that's still his, Joe Namath, like Vince Lombardi and George Allen, contributed most decisively with his activities as a leader. In the two stories that follow:
• His election as the Jets' offensive captain was first announced.
• A day later, he got their Super Bowl season under way with a cleverly called fourth-quarter game-winning drive.
Here's Namath in Missouri on the eve of his biggest season.

KANSAS CITY: Sept. 14, 1968.

Joe Namath of the New York Jets was described the other day as a "great passer who may never be a great quarterback because he doesn't have the respect of his teammates." The remark was made by a Hall of Fame quarterback, Otto Graham, who continued: "The Jets have never named Namath their Most Valuable Player. They voted him fourth place once, but never higher. That's what his own team thinks of Broadway Joe."

In Kansas City Saturday, Broadway Joe was asked to comment on

Graham's comment. His face darkened for an instant, then he smiled. Setting down his draft beer, Namath turned and said: "I'll tell you what my own team thinks of me. They've just elected me captain. They voted me offensive captain of the Jets an hour and fifty-three minutes ago."

Disclosing that Cornerman Johnny Sample has been elected defensive captain, Namath continued: "We voted in the locker room before practice, and the team gave me the greatest honor of my life. The only thing close to it was the day they elected me captain at Alabama."

So the Jets are closing ranks behind their night-life expert at the start of a season in which they have their best chance yet to make the Super Bowl, even though, on national television today, the talent-loaded Kansas City Chiefs are favored in pro football's Game of the Week. "Maybe we can fool them," Namath said.

On Saturday morning, the Jets had moved from the airport directly to the practice field for a short workout. Then in the early afternoon of a bright, warm day, they checked into their hotel, where Namath, answering a knock at the door, had changed clothes. He was wearing brown silk socks, a white towel, a new mustache, and the well-known Namath smile. Thus, the equally well-known scarred knees were also visible. With a trace of a limp, he turned away immediately to get back to the television set in the only suite, a rather small one, on the team floor of the Hilton. He's usually in a large one — it's in Namath's contract that the Jets must accommodate him in suites at road games — but this is Kansas City. Offering a guest his choice of a beer or Coke, Joe kept an eye on the screen. He was rooting for Jimmy Ellis. "I've got a $5 bet with Milton Gross," he explained. Gross is a New York sportswriter.

As the host hunched over in his chair to keep up with the fighters, he looked as round-shouldered as Stan Musial. A hard, lean, 205-pounder, Namath leads the league in sex appeal — women who hate football love Broadway Joe — but he will never be a West Point poster boy. Namath and a football, in fact, resemble a bow and arrow — the bow is six feet two — and at practice Saturday, as usual, the arrows were launched with impressive accuracy. Namath is the most effortless natural passer the game has known. Norm Van Brocklin matched him for range and skill, but Van Brocklin was a disciplined passer, a trained passer, in the same sense that Zasu Pitts is a trained actress. The Namath talent is innate.

To watch him watch a fight, his feet resting on the coffee table now, one knee terribly scarred, is to make a guess: Namath will go as far in this league as his knees take him. He is the best forward passer some of us have seen yet, but at the same time he is one of the most famous cripples in sports, a survivor of three knee operations in four years. His guest had come to talk to him about those knees, after, earlier in the week, Namath had consented. So when the fight was history, and fresh draft beer was on the table, there was a question for Broadway Joe: Should the pro football establishment be taking more steps to guard and preserve its quarterbacks before it loses them all? Namath tugged at his new mandarin mustache as he considered the question.

"I've thought about that," he said at length. "This year I guess every quarterback is giving it some thought, but I have to hope they don't do anything. A drastic rules change would ruin the game. I'm not in favor of anything that would detract from the essence of the game."

What do you believe that is — the essence of football?

"The fight to get at the quarterback," Namath said. "The fight between the offensive line and the defensive line. As I was telling [Ram Defensive End] Deacon Jones the other night, that's what pro football is today. And if the defense wins, you've got to give them their trophy."

The quarterback?

"Yep, me. Throwing a football is not that tough if you're just standing there throwing it. I know some girls who could do it. In pro football, on practically every play, at least one receiver is open. So when you talk about passing a football accurately, what you're talking about is the ability to throw it straight with seven-footers coming in on you. A few people can, most can't."

It is being said more and more, however, that sports like auto racing and football are too dangerous to continue in their present form.

"Speaking of my sport, I don't agree. I think there's a place for a contact sport like football, and I'll take it the way it is. Deacon Jones has a job, and I have a job. He likes his, and I like mine. Injury and risk of injury are a part of it, that's all. The only thing I fear is losing. I can't stand to lose a game."

In retrospect, what do you think today about the injuries you have had? [Raider Lineman] Ben Davidson broke your cheekbone in Oakland last December, and got off with a fifteen-yard penalty. Did the punishment fit that crime?

"I suppose so, although I've been quoted as saying he took a cheap shot. That isn't quite what I said. I'm very much against anyone hitting me after I've thrown the ball, but my job is to throw it and get the hell out of the way."

They say you haven't spoken to Davidson since.

"I stay away from him. I always have. The first time I played Oakland as a rookie, he went for my knees. No one else ever did that. I'm not what you would call a Raider fan."

A week after breaking your cheekbone, you went down to San Diego and set the pro football record for yards in one season — 4,007. Didn't it bother you to have to play so soon with an injury that severe?

"A fracture only hurts for a couple of days, but I did add a bar to my face mask. I wear a double bar all the time now. If there was room, I'd wear a third one. A nose like mine is some target."

I noticed you limping today, a little. What have you hurt this time?

"I hurt my big toe dancing."

Where?

"Coach [Weeb] Ewbank gave the team an extra day off last week, and three of us went to town and got a suite. It was some weekend."

At this point in your career, would you say that the Namath lifestyle harms Namath the athlete?

"Maybe it's bad for me to say this, but I might be a better football player if I didn't like to stay up and see so many late movies. But I can't change the way I am. In the last ten years, right up to this minute, I've only changed one thing in my operation."

What was that?

"I gave up smoking on April 12, 1967."

What time?

"It was just after 3 a.m."

As a frequent California visitor since the year you signed that first $400,000 contract, have you had an opportunity to make a detailed comparison between California girls and New York's?

"They talk different in Los Angeles. That's a movie town, and in California the girls are all interested in that. But they're all pretty, very pretty."

Have you invited them to Broadway Joe's?

"My new restaurant? That's in Miami. We're going public this winter — a Wall Street company is handling the stock sale."

Can you wear that mustache on Wall Street?

"The mustache comes off when we win the Super Bowl. At least, that's what I told the lady last night."

THE NEXT day, Namath had a game to play. During that storied 1968 season, I was to cover his first and last games. He won the first in Kansas City, 20-19, beating the previous year's AFC Super Bowl entry, and the last in Super Bowl III, beating Baltimore, 16-7. In both games he displayed the leadership and play-calling acumen that, combined with his quicksilver throwing motion, made him the dominant player of his era. Here are the first few paragraphs of my Kansas City game story.

KANSAS CITY: Sept. 16, 1968.

Captain Joe Namath of the New York Jets, their controversial quarterback, began his fourth pro season by upsetting a Super Bowl team here Sunday, 20-19, in a game he ended with an artistic ball-control drive. When the Kansas City Chiefs closed to the one-point margin of the final score, 5:56 remained, whereupon Namath took possession on his five-yard line and ran out the clock.

He held the ball for the game's last fifteen plays. "They were almost all audibles," the Jets' new offensive leader said later.

Before the largest sports crowd of all time in Kansas City, 48,871, Namath had opened a 17-3 halftime lead with two long passes to Receiver Don Maynard, who was asked afterward if he can still run forty yards in 4.6. "It depends on who's chasing me," he said.

Kansas City won the second half by almost the same score, 16-3, because the Jets made one blunder after another, and because Jan Stenerud, the Chiefs' resolute kicker, made one field goal after another until he had a total of four. To a crowd that spent the entire day screaming for the Chiefs or booing Namath, it seemed likely that, before long, Stenerud would finish with a fifth field goal. For, when he kicked off after number four, a Jet halfback ineptly ran the ball out of bounds on his five-yard line. But this was to prove the final New York blunder. More than five minutes were left, and they all belonged to Namath.

"I was handicapped on some calls because I couldn't afford an interception at that stage," he said. "I had to pass safe — and that's something I never do if I can afford it."

On the last big drive, in a number of clutch predicaments, Namath:

• Could have escaped trouble on second down from the New York four-yard line — when he reached Maynard slanting across the middle — but the ball was dropped during a loud collision with the middle linebacker.

• Made his first clutch play on the next play when, on third and eleven, he came back with the identical pass, which Maynard held this time for a net of sixteen yards. Asked why in such a grave emergency he would repeat a play that had failed, Namath said: "I was keying on the safeties, and they left Maynard for the middle guard. No middle guard can handle Maynard twice in a row."

• Survived three more third-down crises with straight throws that were caught each time for not much more than the required yardage.

Stenerud, Kansas City Coach Hank Stram, and the big crowd died one play at a time as Namath marched. He kept marching for fifty-six yards until there was nothing left on the clock but its motionless hands.

9. Sammy Baugh on Passing and Play-Calling

THE MAN called Slingin' Sammy — that's Sammy Baugh — was the league's first dominant passer. He was also the losing quarterback (to Bob Waterfield) in the first NFL game I covered, the 1946 Times Game at the Coliseum, the first Ram game in Los Angeles. Baugh has been a lifelong football student with a keener understanding of the game than most coaches.

LOS ANGELES: Feb. 25, 1969.

During his sixteen years as a National Football League passer, Sammy Baugh also became the greatest punter of all time. One season his punts *averaged* more than fifty yards (51.3 in 1940). On defense, as a safetyman, he intercepted four passes one afternoon, setting a record that has been tied but never surpassed by the specialists of the two-platoon generations.

In what to the oldest of the old-timers is the NFL's fiftieth season, Baugh today is a weather-beaten Texas rancher who rises before sunup each morning to quarterback a thousand mother cows, with whom he shares his twenty-seven thousand acres. But after years of that, he still holds eight major NFL records. One season he completed 70.3% of his passes. One day he completed 85.7%.

At quarterback for the Washington Redskins from youth to middle age, Baugh led the league in passing six times — twice as often as anyone else. On the first ballot for the NFL Hall of Fame in 1962, Baugh and Chicago Bears Owner George Halas were the only unanimous choices. It has been said often that there will never be another passer like Slingin' Sammy Baugh.

Sammy, however, says he has already found one: Joe Namath of New York. "In the next four or five years," Baugh believes, "Namath can go down as the finest passer who ever played the game. Only two things could stop him, his knees."

If he has the talent of an All-Pro, how do you account for Namath's occasional lapses from form?

"Very few people fully understand the value of experience," Baugh says. "Namath doesn't know his job yet. Neither did I when I was his age. Joe has had four years. I have always felt that my best year was my twelfth in pro ball. My best three were the tenth, eleventh and twelfth.

Namath next year will still be making some terrible mistakes — some game-losing mistakes that he will avoid instinctively in 1972."

Provided he is still with us in 1972.

"I sincerely hope that his knees will allow that. A pro quarterback can't be ranked with the great quarterbacks until he's played at least eight years. He has to prove he can handle himself over a distance of time. Playing ability alone doesn't mean that much. There have been a lot of flashes in the pan, a lot of great high school stars who didn't have the self-control to do a man's job over a stretch of time."

What is the quality that separates a great quarterback from a good one?

"The quick answer first: It's the ability to call the right play at the right time. That's all there is to quarterbacking. But wrapped up in that simple answer are so many thousands of things that nobody has ever mastered them all. For example, you have to know every weakness of every player in the league — and the exact strength of each of your teammates in relation to all those defensive weaknesses. There's no sport in the world nearly so involved as football. Automatically, just by living, a quarterback gets better every year."

As a veteran whose sixteen NFL years are second only to [Cleveland Browns Tackle] Lou Groza's seventeen, you must agree that most athletes retire prematurely.

"They used to. I think there's been a better understanding lately of the fact that an extra year of experience more than cancels out some loss of agility. George Allen in Los Angeles is a coach who has grasped this point and convinced his players. I was disappointed that Otto Graham and Norm Van Brocklin both quit so early. As a football fan, I felt Van Brocklin deprived me of his best years."

Van Brocklin was a bomb thrower — which is a reminder that Sammy Baugh has been called a great short passer who couldn't throw long. How much does that disturb you?

"It hasn't bothered me at all because what it shows is a misunderstanding of football. The idea is to throw the ball where you have to throw it to complete a pass in the time you can rely on your protection to protect you. I was neither a long passer nor a short passer. I was a protection passer. And in the nature of things, that usually means a shorter pass. Van Brocklin threw too long too often when he started out in Los Angeles. He finally became a great passer in Philadelphia, at the end of his career, when he shortened down. The 1940 Redskins (Baugh's team) threw bombs about as often as the Eagles did in 1960, Van Brocklin's championship year. That was the year he convinced me that he'd arrived at the top."

Calling on your sixteen seasons in the league, and sixteen more as coach and scout, what would you say is the best way for a young man to develop his football ability?

"Only practice one way — the hard way. If you're a punter, always punt into the wind. If you're an end or halfback and the coach says to run it out fifty yards, run a hundred. If you're a passer, throw off balance in practice. Don't drop back into the pocket in dummy scrimmage. Don't see how accurately you can throw over the top. Throw it sidearm, or off your shoes, or left-handed. The coach knows you can throw accurately overhand with nobody rushing, or you wouldn't be in there. So practice the hard way. Then the games will come easier."

John Unitas told me one time that he makes things as difficult for everyone else as he can in practice.

"Unitas is the example of what I mean. Nobody ever outworked him in practice. As a passer, Unitas has the best touch of all, and in this respect it will be a long time before Namath catches him."

How much does it distress you, thinking back to your wages as a pro quarterback, to read that Namath got $400,000?

"Not a bit. I say more power to him. He has the benefit of television — and also the pressure. I really laugh when I think back to my rookie year in Washington. The three highest paid guys on the team got salaries of $2,750 — and we won the world championship. So one of them, Cliff Battles, asked for a $250 raise, and quit when the Redskins wouldn't pay him $3,000. Namath's taxes are higher than that — but pros don't play for money. They play for pride."

How do you define pride?

"There's something burning deep inside you that drives you to become the best man in the world at your job. I still have the same desire. As a cow-and-calf rancher, my goal now is to raise all five-hundred-pound calves in the six months before I sell them. When I get there, I'll shoot for five-fifty and then six hundred. The only other goal I have is, when I'm through, I hope to leave the countryside better than I found it."

10. George Blanda at 47: Nobody's Older

THE OLDEST big league football player ever, George Blanda lasted twenty-six years before retiring at forty-eight in 1975. The all-time point champion with 2,002, he once threw seven touchdowns in one pro game for a record he still shares.

OAKLAND: Dec. 20, 1974.

Quarterback-Placekicker George Blanda of the Raiders is at forty-seven the oldest man in the National Football League playoffs this year. In fact, no other athlete ever lasted twenty-five years in pro football. Many of his Oakland teammates were born after Blanda began his career with the Chicago Bears in 1949.

At home, however, before leaving for football practice at noon, Blanda is the embodiment of the lazy Californian on a long weekend. "The best part of the day," he says, "is loafing around the house, reading the paper, maybe shooting a little pool, or just looking at the bay or the skyline of the city."

Blanda's apartment edges the broad waters of San Francisco Bay on the Alameda side. Talking about it, he leans back in the recliner, a big man in an old blue cardigan sweater, dark blue shirt, blue plaid plants and old loafers with a hole in one sole, a la Adlai Stevenson. The truth is that Blanda, in appearance, is almost indistinguishable from the millions of other middle-aged Americans who sit in such chairs and watch him kick field goals or throw an occasional winning pass. He grins and says: "You're wondering how an old man of forty-seven can keep up in a kid's game. I think the two keys are relaxation and challenge — in alternating cycles. I believe in long, regular periods of total relaxation to store up the energy needed to meet the challenge of football."

Now he laughs. "Or maybe," he says, " I'm just lazy."

Blanda is the only player who has scored nineteen hundred points in the NFL. The number-two man, Lou Groza, is more than three hundred points behind. "I think of myself as a challenge-meeter more than a football player," Blanda says. "Nothing excites me like a challenge. On the first tee of a golf course I feel exactly the way I do kicking a field goal in the fourth quarter. At night, playing pool or giving a speech, I keep pushing myself to do better than last time. The day I threw seven touchdown passes I wanted to throw twelve. A challenge is all the motivation I need. I'm always up. Play the Star-Spangled Banner and I'm ready."

If this is the attitude that explains Blanda's longevity, he may still be playing football in his fifties. For there hasn't been much erosion of his skills. His 236th NFL touchdown pass last week beat the Dallas Cowboys, the team ranked first in the league by CompuSport going in.

Including high school and college, Blanda has been playing quarterback, blocking back, tailback and linebacker for thirty-three years. Honoring his long career, his wife Betty sent him a Christmas card this week. An art major when he met her at the University of Kentucky a while ago, she made the card herself. The picture is of Santa Claus visiting with Blanda. Says Santa: "You're the only little boy I gave a uniform to that's still using it."

II

The boy Betty married is one of a kind. He not only *is* forty-seven, he looks it. He looks like the only player who has ever lasted a quarter century in pro football. The hair is long and gray, the face lined and craggy. Like the rings on a tree, there is a crease in Blanda's face for every year he's been in football. He is the epitome of the grizzled NFL veteran. At the same time he is the symbol of everlasting youth to the middle-aged. If Blanda can play football at his age, there's hope for every man in the world in his forties and fifties.

Built like a linebacker, Blanda is six-two, 224 and rugged. "He's a tough old man," says a Bay Area sportswriter, Charley Zeno of the Concord Transcript. "Everybody in the organization looks up to him because you can depend on him."

Betty Blanda, petite and charming, thinks of her husband as a moody hell-raiser. "When George went in the bathroom yesterday, there wasn't any soap," she says, "and he bellered like a wounded animal. If I didn't know him so well, my feelings would have been badly hurt. But I knew he'd soon get over it. A Blanda storm only lasts about five minutes. Then he's happy and cheerful again. That's his normal nature."

The Blandas have been married twenty-five years. Their anniversary was Tuesday, when Betty took George to the Japanese Trade Center in San Francisco. "We planned to spend the night," she says. "I wanted for us to soak in those sunken tubs and eat on the floor. So many anniversaries are lost in the shuffle that I wanted George to remember this one. He'd have grumbled, but he'd have done it. Then we got there and it was closed."

They settled for an anniversary dinner across the bay in Sausalito.

George and Betty have been dining out three or four times a week this year, their first without either of their children at home. Their daughter Leslie, eighteen, is a freshman at San Diego State. George Jr., twenty-two, an art major at Northern Illinois, has ambitions to be a sculptor. He doesn't play football. "He's a senior, I think," Blanda says. "This is his fifth year. He'd better be a senior."

III

Blanda has been up since 10 a.m. He has eggs and bacon or sausage every morning, followed by a walk on the beach or a pool game before it's time to go to work. The Raiders practice from 12 to 4:30 at a field five minutes from Blanda's apartment. But right now he's eased back in the recliner, ready to talk. And his natural topic is offensive football.

At practice and in games, Blanda continually studies the Raider offense with the care of a surgeon. "I never run a play in practice any more," he says, "but I know everything they do and why. My greatest interest is offensive football."

He's asked if he misses practicing.

"From a selfish standpoint, I'd very much like to run some plays during the week. But we have two other top quarterbacks [Daryle Lamonica and Ken Stabler] and there's no way a pro team can practice three quarterbacks. So the other two practice and I watch."

Don't you even get in there for a series now and then?

"Yes, last week I got four plays," he says, "but the week before that, I didn't have any."

But wasn't that a week that you won the game?

"*We* won it."

You didn't even practice ball-exchange with your center [Jim Otto] that week?

"At one stretch this year, Jim and I went five weeks without exchanging the ball."

It's about time you lodged a complaint with the Oakland coaches.

"I can't do that because I think they're handling the situation right. Lamonica is number one and Stabler is a helluva quarterback, a great prospect. I have no complaints. During the fifteen-minute warmup period, I get to hand off to all our backs. And I throw the ball every day. And we're winning."

How can an NFL quarterback come in cold and win the game when he hasn't even been practicing the plays?

"One thing is more important than practicing, and that's play-selection. In football, play-calling makes a bigger difference than anything else in winning and losing. That's my opinion. At least I've given it more of my time than anything else in the last twenty or twenty-five years."

What do you mean by the term play selection?

"When, where, and why you throw or run the ball and who gets to run it or catch it."

The four W's, as in journalism.

"I didn't study journalism, but there are a lot of throwers coming out of college these days who can throw the hell out of the ball. They can hit you anywhere on the field — except they don't. Today, you don't win pro games with a passer who can throw straight. You win by getting a receiver four yards open — and that's play-selection. Your sister can hit a target that's four yards open."

How do you get a receiver four yards open against a modern defense?

"The key is to keep the defense off balance. You have to bear in mind that any team in the league can stop anything it expects. The defense will stop you if they anticipate the play. You can only get a man open by surprising the defensive people."

And you can do all that without practicing?

"I have both the stamina and knowledge to run the offense the way (Oakland Coach) John Madden wants it."

Madden is nearly a decade younger than you are. What did he tell you when he sent you in last week against Dallas?

"When John called me over, I asked him, 'What do you want me to call?' He said, 'Do whatever you want to do.'"

What did you do?

"I had been watching the Dallas defense and talking with Cliff Branch on the sideline. I'd been hoping I could go in. I told Cliff I'd call one of two plays on first down, if I went in, and to be ready. He was ready, and the one I called went for a touchdown. That was the first pass I've thrown with the team this year in either a game or practice."

That sounds like an experience call. What can you tell younger athletes to help them last as long as you have?

"I don't think there'll ever be another twenty-five-year man. All my other records will be broken, but it takes a combination of unusual circumstances to last this long in this game. I'm fortunate to be a quarterback and kicker. No running back or defensive lineman could play twenty-five years, and I doubt if a kicking specialist or quarterback specialist could, either. The ability to do both helps you do well at both. Second, I'm fortunate to have been free of injuries. Third, you have to love the game so much you won't give it up voluntarily for any reason. If I were looking for reasons to quit, I've had plenty. And fourth, you've got to be in the right organization. Most football teams start looking to replace you at thirty. Al Davis, who runs this team, thinks about it, too, of course — but he doesn't do it if you're still making a contribution. That's one reason the Raiders keep winning."

What will you miss most when you finally leave?

"The camaraderie. You can't believe how beautiful it is to be around the players and families of a winning football team. The Peter Principle is inoperative in football. Those promoted over their heads don't last twenty-four hours. So everybody has the same goal: winning. In other kinds of businesses, the petty jealousies are enough to drive you into the wall. Everybody wants to be the president of the company or sales manager, and to get there, they'll screw anybody they have to. In a company, the goal is to get to the top personally. On a football team, the goal is to get there together. When I'm out of the game, I'll miss that togetherness more than anything."

More than the money?

"Until 1970 (in Oakland) I never made more than $35,000 in any year. Money doesn't motivate. Don't tell Al Davis, but if he cuts my salary in half next year, I'll take it."

Looking back across your career, which year would you say was your best?

"This year. I reached my peak against Dallas. I'm throwing as well as ever now, and I never kicked better because I'm concentrating more. If you have the physical skills and the right attitude, you don't go downhill much over the years."

What have you gotten out of football?

"Everything I have. My family, a wealth of experiences, a wealth of memories and friendships, a good life and a little prosperity. A football player is looked on as a celebrity and meets the most interesting people. I mingle with presidents. I have also mingled with the lowest guys on the totem pole that is our economy. Most football players are from the humblest of beginnings. They and their families have worked hard all their lives. My father was a coal miner. My first challenge was to get out of that."

When do you plan to retire from the game?

"When they tear off the uniform. Quitting is easy. Anybody can quit."

11. Woody Hayes Does It His Way

ONE OF the most stimulating college football coaches of the twentieth century — he has been called the most colorful if not the ablest — was Woody Hayes, who until the end seemed to enjoy his squabbles with sportswriters. He was another celebrity that many of them objected to — long before Hayes had to resign for an assault on an opposing player. On the evidence it can be argued that Hayes had a character flaw, but you could still learn a lot from the man. And you might rather look at the rose than the thorns. For an uncharacteristic interview in which I was searching for reasons that explained him as a frequent Rose Bowl visitor, Hayes sat around his office so long, in an unbuttoned shirt and his underdrawers, that he was late for football practice.

COLUMBUS, Ohio: Nov. 9, 1973.

You are spending the early afternoon before football practice at Ohio State with Woody Hayes, coach of the nation's number-one team. At sixty, the leader of the undefeated Buckeyes is a driver who has become in appearance the sort of man he most admires: an army commander, erect but heavily built, obviously well fed, obviously in charge. He has been asked to explain why he wins all the time.

"You win with people," says Hayes, author of the new book of that name. "In college football, success attracts the better athlete. The mediocre man won't try it with us. In this respect, college and pro ball could hardly be more different. The pros today are more like the rest of the world."

What is there about college football that is out of step?

"College winners aren't penalized," he says. "In the NFL, they are. Bottom pro teams get the best choices in the draft. The pros, in other words, reward you for losing."

They feel it's necessary to maintain competition. Most pro football divisions are more competitive than most college conferences.

"Regardless of reasons or motives, pro football is like most other things in our society today. It rewards losing. The income tax is another example. So are the rules of football, as a matter of fact: The team that's scored on gets the ball. Except for that, college football is the exception to the way things are going in this country. Success leads to success in college football."

In a successful coach, what quality is most important?

"I would say total dedication. There are some similarities between football and war, as you have doubtless heard many times, and this is one of them. Winners are men who have dedicated their whole lives to winning. The fact that really explains General Patton is that in World War II, he fought his battles where he had spent his honeymoon years earlier. He anticipated."

Football, of course, is less brutal than war.

"The goals are different. It's the strategy that's similar. For example, at Ohio State, we consider ourselves the cleanest team in football. Clean teams play better football, in our opinion. They concentrate better on their assignments. They feel they get more leverage."

As entertainment vehicles, how do you compare college and pro ball?

"College ball is more versatile. That's because we run three or four backs, including the quarterback, and the pros run only two. Secondly, I have to think the pros have hurt their game with all their good field goal kickers. Every time I've had a good placekicker here, our goal-line offense has suffered. It's some kind of mental reaction to the fact that it's so easy to get three points."

In the NFL, a running quarterback is soon an injured quarterback.

"It's been our experience that the only way to toughen up a quarterback is to run him. You certainly don't get tough throwing. A quarterback who runs some does a better job against a tough rush than a passer who just drops back and fires all the time."

At USC, they might not agree with you. They aren't running the quarterback as much this fall as they used to.

"They have better passing there now. And John McKay has some baby in that I Formation. We'd be using it now except for one thing: the fullback is third in the I to the tailback and quarterback, and we decided we didn't want to do that. We'd never relegate the fullback to a blocker. In fact, we'd rather run the fullback than anybody. It tends to make everybody else on the team tough and team-oriented."

The Wishbone T showcases hard runners, including running quarterbacks, and you used it here for a while. Why did you give up on it?

"The year we used it in the Rose Bowl, it only got us seventeen points. We think we can be more versatile in other formations, get more receivers out quicker. The other thing is that you don't do as good a job with the fullback in the Wishbone. It's hard to get a Wishbone fullback off tackle, for one thing — and as a coach, that troubled me."

As a coach, if you were to list your assets, what would you list first?

"I run it."

You're in charge, you mean. You make the decisions.

"Yes, I'm in charge, but no, I don't decide everything. I'd guess that at Ohio State, the assistants and even the players make more decisions than they do almost anywhere else. What I mean is, I don't depend on other people. I'm the first guy to work in the morning. There's no job too small for me. In football, the little things are really the big things. On this team, I make the hospital runs myself."

What hospital runs?

"It's a tough business. We're having two operations tomorrow morning, for instance, and when an Ohio State football player wakes up in the hospital, the first guy I want him to see is me. There's no way you can delegate that — and I have the best staff of assistants in the nation."

I notice that most of your assistants have come aboard in the 1970s or late '60s.

"They keep leaving me — always vertically into better jobs, never laterally. That's because everybody knows Ohio State's success is due to my coaches."

That's what one of your assistants, Lou Holtz, was telling me last night.

"Lou was just quoting me. Recruiting assistant coaches is more important than recruiting players because the assistants recruit the players."

When there's a vacancy on your staff, how do you fill it?

"The nominations come from my coaches. For two reasons. They know the candidates, and they know me. They make a list of about ten guys who have the requirements. Then we sit down and discuss who'll do this better and who that. Finally, we interview about three of them. That's where I come in, and because I know all three are well qualified, I only want to know one thing. I want to know why he wants to come with me. If his answer isn't satisfactory, we don't hire him."

What's a satisfactory answer?

"If he says he wants to be a head coach someday, and this is as good a place as any to learn it, I'll take him. I know I'm dealing with an honest man."

Did you say your staff recruits Ohio State's players now, too? I should think you'd want to get into that.

"The way we work it is, my coaches only come to me if they have a difference of opinion on whether to take a boy. In that case, I usually decide we don't want him. So they bring me fewer and fewer things to decide. One of our starters now dips snuff, for instance. I'd have decided against him if I'd had the chance, but he's a good tough player, and I'd have made a mistake. So I've learned that some good people dip snuff, and you win with people."

12. John Robinson: Change and Win

ONE QUALITY the great coaches have typically had in common is enthusiasm. From Knute Rockne on, most of football's big winners have been dedicated cheerleaders. John Robinson has also shown a sound grasp of modern college football, but it is the warmth of his approach that gives him and USC their edge.

LOS ANGELES: Dec. 31, 1978.

Rounding out his third year as USC's football coach, John Robinson is back in Pasadena, where the Trojans have won a record fifteen Rose Bowls in twenty-one New Year's Day appearances and where Monday's game will be watched by dozens — perhaps hundreds — of future Trojans. It is the pomp and glory and tradition of the Rose Bowl, Robinson believes, that makes USC what it is in football, attracting the most gifted of each new generation.

"The Rose Bowl," he says, "appeals to youngsters who have an abundance of two things — talent and ambition. And that's what we want at USC. We're looking for the player who wants to be the best and dreams of being the best. You have a better shot at greatness if you dream about it. The Rose Bowl provides an ideal showcase for that player. The kids know it and we know it and I think that's why we keep coming back."

Ambition can be measured as readily as ability, Robinson says, explaining:

"When I talk with them [the prospects for USC] about the effort it takes to be great, they tend to react in different ways. Some are turned off completely — some of the better prep players. Other very talented youngsters are frightened by the challenge. And a few will tell themselves: 'Heck, yes, I'm the best, and this cat will give me a chance to prove it.' Those are the ones we want."

At forty-five, Robinson is a big, hearty, affable man — popular with the press and Trojan fans — who has spent half his life in football, including three years with John McKay as a Trojan assistant and one year with the Oakland Raiders.

"I've always been fascinated by football and the way it changes year in and out," says Robinson. "To me this is the most interesting thing about football. Baseball's charm is that it's the same game every year. The charm of football is that it's a new game every year. It evolves continually."

What does this mean to a coach?

"It means you have to be aware of the changes, to anticipate them every season, to stay in business. My philosophy is that you've got to be innovative to be successful in football. You have to keep searching for what's best — or at least what's better. The most successful coaches are full of surprises, mostly little surprises, some big. Who's the most successful active football coach?"

Bear Bryant?

"Yes, I'd say Bryant, and I don't know anyone who's changed more things than Bryant in the last fifteen or twenty years. He's been in every defense known to man. And every offense. The Wishbone he's running today is nothing like the Wishbone he was in a few years ago. He gets more out of it than anyone else because he keeps tinkering with it, improving it."

Isn't it true that fundamentalists — conservatives — win, too?

"Every winning coach believes in the fundamentals. Bryant does. So did Vince Lombardi, but if Lombardi were coaching today he wouldn't be doing what he did ten years ago. He'd stress the same determination and enthusiasm and he'd get great blocking but his offense would be entirely different. He'd also have a dramatically different defense. A successful defensive team today lines up a different way *every* down. If you could bring back the best teams in football in 1971 and leave them in the same defense that worked so well then, they'd give up forty points to Stanford today and fifty or sixty to Alabama."

Other coaches often say football is a simple game of blocking and tackling.

"They're talking about the foundation of the game, the fundamentals. Sure, there is a core of football that doesn't change. We're still running the 28 pitch (tailback around end) that John McKay put in back in 1961 or '62. We haven't changed the foundation — but it's what you build on the foundation that counts. The offseason today is as important as the season. How much research you do, and what changes you decide on, determine your success."

What's an example of a USC play you researched and put in?

"There are a lot of them. Take Lynn Cain's best play this year — the one we've gained so many yards on. This is a straight copy of a Michigan play they used with Rob Lytle — 32 dive. Everybody has a 32 dive — a quick hit by the fullback — but the style of blocking makes it different, and Michigan does it best. We ran it over and over trying to defend it. And during our offseason review we decided we had to have it ourselves."

Is this the way all teams build their offenses?

"The coaches I admire are always researching and changing and adding new things. After our first season here (1976) Joe Paterno came out and spent four days with us. You'd expect Paterno to be *teaching* some place. Instead he was out going to school. When we asked him about it, he said: 'In this business you can't afford to sit on your hands in the offseason.' And I have to agree."

VIII

THE TEAM

The San Francisco 49ers, campaigning in the most competitive era of a traditionally competitive league, have held on as a big winner for a longer period of time than any peer or predecessor. They have won, moreover, with a creative flair based on aggressive passing. These two specifics — the consistency of their success and their stylish approach to football — have made the 49ers the team of the century.

More than that, they represent, for me, the fulfillment of a career-long vision.

For the better part of sixty years, it has seemed to me that most football coaches have illogically feared and undervalued forward passes. Even the connoisseurs who have known the most about pass offense — Clark Shaughnessy and Hall of Famer Sid Gillman among them — have been loath to make a full commitment.

Since football's day one — in 1881 — it has been not the science and artistry of passing but the violence of the running game that has most obviously appealed to most of the most prominent coaches: Hurry Up Yost, Red Blaik, Bernie Bierman, Vince Lombardi, Paul Brown, Bud

Wilkinson, John McKay. Basing their offensive systems invariably on power-running plays, these coaches, along with most of their opponents and most of their successors, have all apparently regretted the 1906 legalization of the forward pass.

And I have regretted their regretting. One theme in the football stories I've written all these years is that in most games, more and better passing would have made winning easier for the winner and losing less likely for the loser. Across the decades, I have remained confident that:

• The way to play football is with a passing team that, secondly, can run the ball when it must.

• The coaches in their standard philosophy, with their insistence on running first to set up passing, have all this time had it just backward.

• Fear is the emotion that has delayed the evolution of pass offense. The coaches have been hamstrung and dominated by their fear of interceptions.

And then came Bill Walsh.

As the 1979-88 coach of the 49ers, Walsh made pro football a different game. For the first time, an NFL team — the novel 49er team — showed itself to be endlessly unafraid to throw the ball. For the first time, a sound and thoughtful NFL coach had his players ready each Sunday to pass first and frequently and effectively.

And the consequence was remarkable. In Walsh's third season with the 49ers, they started winning Super Bowl games; and a decade and a half later, still in Walsh's system, they were still at it. During a fifteen-year run beginning in 1981 — the hundredth anniversary of football's birth — the 49ers won five Super Bowl championships and eleven of every fifteen of the regular-season games they played, setting an all-time NFL record for sustained excellence.

As Walsh says in the accompanying 1996 Times interview, the timed short pass — which in his system replaces the off-tackle smash as football's basic offensive play — made the elemental difference. And the spectacular results achieved with that system made San Francisco the team that I had been waiting for and writing about and urging since the 1930s.

II

Though not widely noted, Walsh's approach has, in many respects, been traditional. It has been surprisingly similar, in fact, to that of Vince Lombardi, the coach who led the 1960s Green Bay Packers to five NFL championships in an even briefer period. Walsh's top priorities are identical with Lombardi's: sound defense and skilled, comprehensively drilled players plus thoughtfully designed offense. Their differences are most visible in offensive philosophy: Lombardi attacked not with passes but with end runs and other conservative running plays.

Significantly, Green Bay's winning era ended after eight years. San Francisco's has now gone on nearly twice as long, reflecting, for one thing, a difference between the emotional nature of running and the much less emotional nature of passing. When he resigned at Green Bay, Lombardi acknowledged that a powerful running game demands highly motivated blockers to root out fierce and aggressive defenders. And he confessed that he had run out of ways to motivate the same old blockers and runners every year.

By contrast, as Walsh and his successor George Seifert have shown, a quick-rhythm passing team can work its way successfully through emotional ups and downs, week after week, year after year — relying on intensively practiced eye-hand coordination rather than emotional, man-to-man battles.

This helps explain how the 49ers have changed their most important leaders — their coach and their quarterback — yet steamed right on to twelve division titles and thirteen playoff appearances in their extraordinary fifteen-year run through the league.

III

Walsh's pass offense is not, of course, the only reason for the long San Francisco streak. A companion explanation is to be found in the 49ers' front office, where Eddie DeBartolo, on his record, is the ablest franchise holder football has had. As the unifying force in a unique organization, DeBartolo has made it a point to foster a climate of comradeship and harmony in the congregation — the only climate in which the 49ers, or any other pro football club, could have flourished for so long.

You can be sure that ego and envy, the forces widely believed to have destroyed the Jerry Jones-Jimmy Johnson partnership in Dallas, are not unknown in San Francisco. In Walsh's heady days as a winning coach, he was the prima-donna type, often prickly in dealings with people who didn't, or didn't want to, understand him. Star athletes such as Quarterback Joe Montana, Wide Receiver Jerry Rice, and Halfback Ricky Watters, among others, have also displayed on occasion the self-centered arrogance that greatness sometimes breeds. Though often ruffled, DeBartolo, working on his self-control, has managed to stay above all that, creating an atmosphere in which his temperamental artists could thrive. This is professional sports the 49ers are in — the NFL is an association of high-strung artists — but the distractions have been controlled with more empathy and humanity in DeBartolo's organization than elsewhere.

Single-mindedly committed to the preservation and enhancement of the company, the owner has also shown other requisites of a big winner. He has twice demonstrated, for example, his mastery of management's most important function in pro football: finding and hiring the right coach.

What's more, he has demonstrated that he can run a creative and aggressive front-office operation. In the most vital instance, in the mid-1980s, DeBartolo joined with Walsh to stabilize the 49er dynasty with a new personnel concept. Stung in their early years, like all other NFL leaders, by extensive sequences of player injuries, they shifted gears. Walsh had been trying to corner America's finest players. Now instead he began recruiting, at great cost, two layers of very good players, starters and backups. And DeBartolo, showing the required insight and financial readiness, cooperated. Not the only NFL multimillionaire, he is one of the few disposed to convert meaningful chunks of his assets into football players.

By the mid-1990s, San Francisco's coaches, charging again, with four Super Bowl crowns already in the vault, were in need of just the kind of front-office help they got from DeBartclo and club President Carmen A. Policy. In the first season with the NFL's new salary-cap restraints, 1994, the 49ers were the first to finance a championship run with rearranged player contracts and delayed but guaranteed bonuses. Strengthening the franchise where it needed it most, DeBartolo and Policy freed up dollars by the millions for a number of high-priced defensive stars, among them Linebackers Gary Plummer and Ken Norton and, for one memorable season, Cornerback Deion Sanders. The result was a fifth Super Bowl trophy for DeBartolo's team. No other NFL owner has ever achieved so greatly.

IV

The three individuals who most obviously got things going and kept things going for the 49ers in the 1980s were Walsh, DeBartolo and Montana, whom I visit in subsequent sections of this chapter. But during the 1990s, two others have been most prominently identified with the club's continued success: Seifert and Steve Young, the new coach and the new quarterback.

In 1989 when as a rookie head coach Seifert won the Super Bowl in his first try, it was difficult to measure him, for, that season, he had been the beneficiary of two pieces of unusual good luck. He had, to begin with, inherited all of Walsh's great players. Second, he'd found that most of them were powerfully motivated: They wanted to prove they could win without Walsh. Thus, winning came easy for Seifert that happy season.

He then bogged down in an extended learning experience — letting such first-class players as defensive stars Ronnie Lott and Charles Haley get away — while simultaneously struggling against a powerful opponent Walsh never had to face: the Jimmy Johnson Dallas Cowboys. During the 1994 season, however, Seifert fought through these challenges to win the Super Bowl again. And it is this second championship that will set him apart from most other coaches for as long as the game is played.

Often described as a born gentleman, Seifert has spent most of his life playing or coaching football in San Francisco. From his first day in his present billet, he has made the biggest impression on football men simply by hanging on and winning as the successor to a legend. In pro football, that hadn't happened before.

Against even greater odds, Steve Young has fashioned a Hall of Fame career in the shadow of the mythic Montana. After Young's first eleven years in the league, he and Montana ranked as the NFL's all-time top two passers — Young first, Montana second. In the history of pro football, only two passers have scored a career 90 or more in the NFL rating system, Young with 96.1 and Montana with 92.3.

The greatness of Montana and Young in the 49er system has, however, tended to obscure the truth that as quarterbacks, both were created by Walsh. The question is whether either would even have been heard from under any other pro coach. In the supercharged NFL world, it's no cinch that a third-round draft choice with a high school arm would have received — anywhere else — the extended opportunity Montana got in San Francisco. As for Young, who was known in his pre-49er career as the world's best white running back but out of position at quarterback, he had failed at his first two pro stops.

Walsh in the early 1980s was a coach with a fresh, full-blown football system that would work with any decent quarterback who was willing to listen to the best quarterback coach of the century. Flexible, far-seeing, Walsh simply adapted portions of his system to a noticeably unusual kind, Montana, who was the best he could find. Then as Montana aged, the 49ers worked Young into the same system.

It was on the 49er practice field — where the Walsh ethic of perfection was like no other in NFL history — that Montana and Young became

NFL passers. No Walsh quarterback was *ever* allowed to throw other than a perfect pass — and to this day, under Seifert, no quarterback is.

Strong-armed and quick of foot, Young is still bedeviled with a sloppy, roundhouse throwing motion, but the results he gets — after years of practicing to perfection in a brilliant system — are second to nobody's. Mentally and physically the toughest of the modern quarterbacks, Young, a determined left-hander, now guns the mid-range pass, feathers the long ball, throws at every distance with almost perfect accuracy, and makes the big play off the scramble. Tiring in the final minutes, he once ran fifty-nine yards to score the touchdown that won a critical late-season game in San Francisco.

The 49ers have clearly prospered lately with Young and Seifert. The record shows, indeed, that it was not Montana and Walsh but Young and Seifert who took the Bill Walsh offense to its peak. That was in 1994, a Super Bowl year for the 49ers, their fifth. For generations, most football coaches had argued that offense sells tickets but defense wins championships. Even Walsh, as his top priority, had built and maintained what he always called a Super Bowl defense. But at San Francisco in 1994, the defensive team was ordinary and the kicking team nondescript. In a championship way, the 49ers that season had naught but offense — but it was offense at a level never seen before. Through a 13-3 season, Young passed his team effortlessly up and down the field to get 42, 38 or 50 points or 37, 41, 42 or 44 — finishing with 505 points in sixteen games. In that symphonic year, Young threw thirty-five touchdowns, only ten interceptions, and set the NFL record for passing efficiency with 112.8.

That winter in Miami, the self-sufficient San Francisco offense reached the top against the San Diego Chargers in Super Bowl XXIX. On a day when the 49er defense surrendered 26 points, the Chargers were never in the game. As Seifert presided over a more dominant offense than Walsh ever had, Young dispensed a better Super Bowl than Montana ever had, and the 49ers, with seven touchdowns, scored 49 points to smash the Chargers with offense alone. On plays called by Offensive Coordinator Mike Shanahan, Young delivered a record six touchdown passes, four to his backs, and two to all-time Receiver Rice.

Extraordinary passing had invalidated the seemingly eternal verities of smash-mouth football. The 49ers had brought to fulfillment the new game they invented.

V

Improbable as it seems, the 49ers could have won — almost certainly would have won — *seven* Super Bowl games in *fourteen* seasons (1981-94) but for Jimmy Johnson. During his brief tour in Texas as coach of the Dallas Cowboys, Johnson overlapped the players and legacy of Walsh to give football two all-time coaches in the same era. That was unforeseen. If the game's top six coaches have been Lombardi, Walsh, Knute Rockne, Frank Leahy, Paul Brown and Johnson, this was the first time that players coached by two of the six had met in big games.

And in these confrontations, it can be said that Walsh — though gone in those days to coach Stanford University — clearly dominated. For Johnson and Seifert *both* played the West Coast or Bill Walsh offense.

Johnson's Cowboys, though often considered a power running team, in fact called their plays in the pure 49er style while continuously using, as Walsh has always taught, the same five assault weapons in a set lineup — the same two backs and two receivers and tight end. Thus, in what were termed the real Super Bowls of 1993 and 1994, Johnson beat the 49ers at their own game. The Cowboys then, in walkovers, twice routed AFC teams in the nominal Super Bowls.

In the years that followed, with Johnson and Walsh no longer coaching at Dallas and San Francisco, the Cowboys and 49ers have split two more Super Bowls. And for both teams, one mystery now remains: Can they keep their dynasties going in the age of free agents and salary caps? The precise question is whether free agency will have the same ruinous effect on the leaders of dynastic football teams that it had twenty years ago on Charlie O. Finley, the 1970s owner of the Oakland A's. Under baseball's old rules, Finley, on a long roll, built a record five consecutive division champions and three consecutive World Series champions before a set of radical new rules took him down.

In the NFL, the Cowboys have lately also had a five-year run; but football's normal internal problems may dissolve their powerhouse, as such troubles have dissolved so many others, long before the new player freedoms get them.

The 49er winning streak, more substantial after an unprecedented fifteen years, will be the better test of the new rules. DeBartolo and Policy must soon replace Young, Rice and nearly everyone else in their historic offense. They recycled smartly once. Can they do it again when bidding for free agents — their own and others — under rules that artificially limit spending?

The answers are still invisible. But in any case, the 49ers have already had their revolution. The future of football is doubtless a passing future. Bill Walsh's future. It seems plain that only those who, like Jimmy Johnson, learn to play pass-first, quick-pass football can hope to beat pass-first, quick-pass teams like those Walsh has pioneered.

And so, personally, there are satisfactions. The pass offense that Walsh created and that others are now emulating has made football what for most of the century I thought it could be. As Young and, now, Troy Aikman and others throw the ball, I like what I see. The passing game can dominate. Brains and beauty can beat brawn.

Moreover, in the context of a tough and physical sport, Walsh's pass-first offense amounts to a triumph of qualities that are distinctly human — a triumph of creativity and intelligence and refined skill.

Maybe Vince Lombardi would call it basketball.

I call it brilliant.

1. Can Joe Montana Win a Super Bowl?

THIS IS a picture of a young quarterback, Joe Montana, before the first of his four Super Bowl games. In time he was to win all four; but in the beginning, the question was how an immature third-round draft choice with an obviously weak arm could have pitched the 49ers *into* a Super Bowl in only his third NFL season. As of that winter, the NFC, Montana's conference, was a famous, chronic loser. NFC teams had blown eleven of the thirteen most recent Super Bowls; and nobody realized that Montana, who was then in residence with his first wife Cass, was about to turn pro football on its head. Nobody knew he would plunge the AFC into an even longer and more devastating losing streak than the NFC's — which was then so vividly in place — and, simultaneously, launch an era for the 49ers. Nobody knew *what* to expect of Montana. Was his early success a fluke? What was this kid like? What made him go? As of that winter, it wasn't routine for newspaper sports departments to seek answers to such questions in a man's past — in the testimony of old friends, his former coaches, his family. But even then, Montana seemed worth the effort.

PONTIAC, Mich.: Jan. 21, 1982.

During the football games of his last ten years — in high school, in college and with the pros — Joe Montana, the San Francisco 49ers' winning young quarterback, has spent less time playing than watching. His coaches have questioned Montana's ability to throw the ball like a Dan Fouts. Or a Ken Anderson. And so they have been a bit reluctant until this season to bet their jobs on him.

As a rule, however, his teammates have been Montana fans.

This was most strikingly demonstrated during his junior year in college, when, as Notre Dame's third-string quarterback, Montana finally showed up late in the third game of the season — a game the Fighting Irish were losing at Purdue. As he ran out for his first play that afternoon, the Notre Dame players, who were huddling in the center of the field, caught sight of him and, incredibly, raised a cheer. "Some of them were so pleased they jumped up and down," a witness recalled the other day. "It was the most amazing sight I've seen in thirty years of watching football."

The witness is Roger O. Valdiserri, Notre Dame's assistant athletic director, who said: "The team thought Joe would pull it out. And, of course, he did."

In California this season, there were quite a few 49er fans who could appreciate how that Irish team felt. Coming from nowhere, the 49ers won their first National Football Conference championship in Montana's first full season as an NFL quarterback — and only his third in pro ball — and not surprisingly, they won it in the last quarter of their last game, when he brought them from behind to knock Dallas out.

And in Michigan Tuesday, stepping from nowhere onto the national stage, Montana became the central attraction of a week that will climax next Sunday with Super Bowl XVI: San Francisco vs. Cincinnati.

At twenty-five, Montana is the youngest star in pro football; and what's more, he is a different kind of quarterback. His is the harum-scarum style of the born athlete who just dropped in to see if it's as tough to play quarterback as people say. Asked about him recently, his high school coach, Chuck Bramski, said: "Joe would be the best six-foot-two guard in basketball — his favorite sport — but his father always wanted him to play football."

Most NFL quarterbacks are specialty passers who can only run enough to stay out of trouble. By contrast, Montana specializes only in athletics. If you were grading him, he'd rate a B or B minus as a passer, if that, and B plus as a scrambler. But he'd get an A plus for quickness, which is probably the definitive trait of a great athlete. The great ones from Babe Ruth to Jim Brown to Elgin Baylor to Joe Namath and Billy Sims have come in different sizes, with differing strengths, and they've dominated different sports, but the quality they've all shared is quickness, or what might be called innate agility. And Montana is in that mold. "He even thinks quick," said former Notre Dame Coach Dan Devine.

Said Valdiserri: "Let me tell you how quick he is: During a telecast at Notre Dame one day, the camera stayed on Montana *after* he'd thrown a touchdown pass. He has such a quick release that the cameraman didn't see him pull the trigger."

That's what Cincinnati is up against Sunday.

II

Joe Montana spent most of his first twenty-five years getting ready to play quarterback for the 49ers — though neither he nor the 49ers suspected it until lately. His father, Joseph Clifford Montana Sr., now forty-nine, never wanted the boy to hold a job when he was growing up in Monongahela, Pennsylvania. "Working is for adults," said Joe Sr., a finance company manager who spent most of his working years as a Western Electric equipment installer. "A kid should be a kid."

Theresa Montana, the quarterback's mother, who is here with her husband for the NFL's first indoor Super Bowl, said: "Joe had Joey throwing footballs when he was four years old. The earliest memory I have of Joey is toddling around the house with a ball in his hand — a baseball in summer, then a football, then a big basketball in the winter. When my husband wasn't home, Joey was always pestering somebody to throw him the ball."

One summer when Joe's boy Joey, by then in junior high, was lounging around the house, his conscience got the better of him, and he hired on as a caddie at the country club outside town, reporting early each day. His father disapproved, but decided, reluctantly, to hold his tongue until the Wednesday night that Joey was scheduled to pitch the 6 p.m. game for an insignificant kids' baseball team. "When Joey wasn't there at 5:45, Joe went after him," Theresa Montana said. "He picked up Joey's baseball uniform at home, drove out to the country club, took him off the golf course, had him change clothes in the car, and got him to the ballpark in time for the first pitch."

That was the last day Joe Montana ever worked. Or probably ever will work.

"That night, Joey's father had a few words with him," Theresa said. "He told him: 'We'll have no more of this, son. If you need money, I'll give it to you. If I can't afford it, you'll go without. You came close to letting your team down tonight. You almost let down your teammates, their parents, your parents, your coach, and most of all yourself.'"

It is a measure of Joe Jr. that he listened to the old man. Polite, quiet, well brought up, he listened, and obeyed. "His humility is the most appealing thing about him," said a former coach, Jeff Petrucci.

There could well be another side to Montana — who really knows about any new star? — but at the Super Bowl this week, he has impressed everyone with the straightforward, uncontrived, soft-voiced approach he takes to his position on the team and in everyday life. "Poised and graceful, that sums him up as a football player," his wife Cass said.

Think of any smart-aleck you've known and you have the opposite in Montana. He has been called a blond Joe Namath, and his smile is as engaging as Namath's, but the image he calls up is very different. Reminded at a round-table press conference here that Namath once predicted the outcome of a Super Bowl game, Montana smiled broadly and said softly, "I'm not going to do that."

Answering questions, he turned and looked directly into the face of each of his questioners, always meeting their eyes. His are bright blue. The full head of hair is as dark as you can get and still qualify as a blond. In a sky-blue jogger suit, he looked thinner but no taller than his 190 and six-two. Put a surfboard under his arm and he's a California beach boy. Asked about the hype of Super Week, he said, quietly, "I enjoy it."

Montana wears a tiny scar just above the mouth on the left side, all that's left of a bloody wound that once required a dozen stitches, and at the round-table discussion I asked him if there's a story about that. "There is," he said. "I was bitten by a dog." Laughter. "I really was," he said. "It was when I was about eight years old. He was my aunt's dog. He wanted to quit playing, and I didn't."

Joe Montana never does.

III

The first sound the San Francisco quarterback remembers from his babyhood wasn't his mother's voice. It was the sound of a Notre Dame broadcast. Every Saturday during the season, his father had every radio in the house tuned loudly to Notre Dame. "Joe never had a chance to go to Pittsburgh [only thirty miles away] or any other university," Joe Sr. said. "He was brainwashed."

As tall and wiry as his son and as white-haired as 49er Coach Bill Walsh, Joe Sr., who played a little football in the Navy, has been a rabid sports fan for years. But he only began to live a quarter century ago when Joe came along as his only child. At that time, Joe Sr. became one of the hundreds, let's say hundreds of thousands, of American fathers who have envisioned a son playing quarterback for Notre Dame. He seems only a little surprised that the fantasy came true. Asked to list his hobbies, he said: "Watching my son."

Although he and Theresa flew to San Francisco for most games this season, they have all the TV tapes, too, and their idea of a big night in Monongahela is putting on a tape and watching their boy Joe pull out another game for the 49ers. Joe Sr., mentioning the team's owner, Eddie DeBartolo, who lives not far from them in Youngstown, Ohio, said: "Mr.

DeBartolo sends us his tapes. Then we make our copies and send his back."

Two generations ago, the Montanas were all still in northern Italy. "The name was either Montagna or Monteni, something like that," Joe Jr. told interviewers here this week. "I think there was a 'g' in there some place. My mother is a full-blooded Sicilian."

His parents still live in Joe's boyhood house. "His room is just the way he left it the day he left," Joe Sr. said, "except it's kind of a trophy room now. We have all his trophies and the newspaper clippings there — more than ten thousand clippings before the Super Bowl, and I'd judge another ten thousand soon."

In a Montana family footnote to the country's deepening recession, Joe Sr. said he's hired an out-of-work former high school teammate of Joe Jr.'s to paste the clippings into scrapbooks. Of the teammate, who only recently was laid off, Joe Sr. said: "He was a helluva kid and a good athlete himself. There isn't that much difference between the National Football League and standing in an unemployment line."

IV

When Joe Jr. was a year old, his father left home. Wanting more for his family than he could get in a workingman's town near Pittsburgh, Joe Sr. left the boy and his mother in Monongahela and found a job in California at Northrop Aircraft. "The first week I was out there, I went into a restaurant and ordered steak and onions," Joe Sr. said. "The waitress told me the onions would be twenty-five cents extra and I said: 'Back where I come from, you get twenty-five pounds of onions for twenty-five cents.' She said: 'This here's a desert. It's harder to grow things here.' I told her: 'Skip the onions.' And I told myself: 'The hell with this. I'm going back where there's some green grass.'"

He is a Monongahela fan. "My roots, my friends, are all in Money-go-to-hell," he said, meaning the town that is also known as Mon City. "You do what you want to do here. You do things together. We all went to Joe's games in midget football, and of course to all his high school games."

Theresa interrupted at that point to correct the record. "I went to every game but one," she said. "We'd had a week of bad weather, and the question was whether to take two cars out of town or one. I told them one car is safer, I'll stay home." She was to regret that decision. "Joey came home with a hole in the forehead of his helmet," Theresa said. "I was so frightened I said never again, I'll never miss another game. We went out the next morning and bought him a new helmet, one of those one-size-fits-all water-and-air helmets. He wore it through midget football and junior high football and all the way through high school football. I don't know if it helped him, but it sure helped me. I felt a lot better."

The big, expensive helmet helped give rise to one of the few tales or truths or rumors or myths about Montana the football player. "We used to think that Joe didn't like to get hit," said a next-door neighbor, Stan Robin, who played midget football with Montana and still lives in Monongahela, where he is a factory maintenance man. As recently as this week, under questioning at the Super Bowl, Montana said he used to beg off as a baseball catcher because, "I don't care for foul tips." Asked if he gets a thrill out of running the football downfield, he said, frowning, "Oh, no. You're live bait. That's why you see those quarterback slides."

Montana's high school coach, Bramski, said: "Joe isn't as strong as he ought to be, and never has been. He'd be a better quarterback by thirty per cent if he'd concentrate on building up his body. He just didn't want to go into the iron house [weight room], and his father didn't want him to hurt his arm lifting weights — but it's the only way to go these days."

Bramski's wife, Theresa, said: "I used to hear the men say: Joe Namath played with pain, will Joe Montana? If he's not hurt, they said, he'll surpass every quarterback who ever lived. Joe never played defense in high school. Defense makes you tougher, and Coach Bramski made everyone else play defense, but Joe's dad didn't want him to."

Asked about all this, a veteran football coach, Tommy Prothro, said: "Montana is every bit as tough as any quarterback in the league. They don't *any* of them like to get hit." An NFL scout, Dick Steinberg, said: "I'll tell you what this comes down to: Montana is a great athlete, and great athletes don't have to play guard in football or catcher in baseball. They don't even have to run the ball — if they can play quarterback. They can scramble and throw it away. A great athlete can pick and choose *when* they're going to get hit. And Montana is just that smart."

v

When his friends talk about the San Francisco quarterback, the two things they mention first are his passion for sports and his competitiveness. There isn't a game Montana doesn't like, apparently, and he plays them all to win. "Except skiing," his wife Cass said. "That isn't as competitive as some sports. The reason I like to ski with Joe is that he doesn't say, 'Last one down does the dishes.' When you play golf with Joe — that's something else. That's one of his favorite games — and he doesn't like you to win a hole."

Last July, Cass and sports fan Montana got up one morning and played eighteen holes of golf. Then they went home and got married. "Joe wanted an afternoon wedding," she said, "and didn't see any reason to waste the morning."

They had met a couple of years earlier on an airplane. A tall, effervescent brunette with expressive brown eyes, Cass is a United Air Lines flight attendant. When he first saw her, she was on the plane taking Notre Dame home from Montana's last college game. Like many other people whose jobs enable them to live anywhere, Cass was living in California at the time, in a Manhattan Beach apartment, and Eastern-born Joe could see the advantages of that. At the conclusion of his college career, to the consternation of his family and friends in Pennsylvania, he moved to Manhattan Beach and became what he appeared to be anyway, a beach boy. He stayed in shape for the NFL's 1979 draft by running in the sand at the beach and trying out for the Rams, who rejected him for the usual reason. "Nice guy, no arm," they said.

After the 49ers drafted Joe, he and Cass moved to 49er country. There, on an acre of a hill thirty miles south of San Francisco, they live in a little old three-bedroom ranch house, where, once in a blue moon, they'll welcome a visiting reporter if he promises not to stay long. From one side of their home they have a splendid ocean view, and from another they can see San Francisco. Theirs is horse country. Said Cass: "Right out of our backyard, there are six miles of trails down to the ocean at Half Moon Bay."

The Montanas have their own barn for their two horses. "They're papered Arabians," Cass said. "We call them Mac and Asim, but their real names are El Makata and Ghafad Asim."

During the late summer and fall, homebody Joe gets the short stick at his place. "He doesn't ride during the football season," Cass said, "but Joe and I are still equals in the barn. We feed and groom the horses together, year-round, and he does his share of shoveling the, ahem. . . ."

Said Joe: "Not from choice."

An animal fan, he still likes dogs despite his experience long ago with his aunt's fierce face-biter. But possibly because of that experience, Joe's own two dogs today are runts. They are miniature dachshunds named Broadway for Namath and Bosley for a TV character. "Joe practices his passing with Bosley," Cass said. "Pine cones, tennis balls . . . that dog will bring back anything you throw him. We call him the league's smallest receiver. One day last year, when Joe was out nine hours repairing the fences, I think he spent most of the time throwing to Bosley."

In the lives of Joe and Cass, this is about to become their biggest winter ever. After the Super Bowl, win or lose, they're going to the Pro Bowl in Hawaii, where Joe will start for the NFC All-Stars (and where Cass Montana was born Cathleen Castillo). Then they're off with her parents on an African safari. "It's something Joe has always wanted to do — he can't get enough of animals," she said.

"No guns of course," Joe said. "It's a photo safari."

But first, there's one more 49er workday. There's this championship game; and regardless of what he's saying this week, Joe has, for many weeks, expected he'd be here to play it. "He knew I'd be with him in Michigan," Cass said. "He got me a fur coat for Christmas."

2. Eddie DeBartolo, Model Owner

OF THOSE who have owned sports teams in this century, Eddie DeBartolo of the San Francisco 49ers resembles most in one respect. He started as a loser. Then, painfully, he learned about football; and armed with that knowledge, he became its biggest winner. What follows was written in New Orleans a day or two before his players won the fourth of their five Super Bowl championships.

NEW ORLEANS: Jan. 28, 1990.

Eddie DeBartolo Jr., who has owned the San Francisco 49ers since 1977, isn't much like anyone else in pro football. For one thing, his is the richest NFL family. He and his father can put their hands on $1.4 billion. Second, although he has been in California long enough to know better, DeBartolo keeps going back to Youngstown, Ohio, to live. And third, shockingly, he's in football to win. Whereas the profit motive drives some of his opponents to "maximize our financial potential," as more than one NFL club owner has said, DeBartolo, who builds shopping malls for a living, is in football to maximize his Super Bowl appearances.

So when there was a fight over former Los Angeles Raiders Linebacker Matt Millen last summer between the 49ers and the Los Angeles Rams, it only lasted about thirty-five seconds. The Rams dropped out of the Millen bidding as soon as DeBartolo made his first offer.

A knockout puncher who is feistier than most other owners, but also friendlier and more candid, DeBartolo is a fighting man who knows what he wants. And today, of course, what he wants is victory in the Super Bowl. At 2:15 p.m., in the packed Louisiana Superdome crowd, he will be one of the two spectators who want it most. The other is the owner of the Denver Broncos, Pat Bowlen, forty-five, who got his law degree from the University of Oklahoma in 1968, the year that DeBartolo, forty-three, graduated from Notre Dame.

That DeBartolo already has three Super Bowl rings — to Bowlen's none — hasn't kept him from striving for more. "It isn't much fun if you don't win," DeBartolo said at his New Orleans hotel this week. "The only reason you're in football is to win the Super Bowl."

II

In addition to this daunting competitiveness, three things about Edward J. DeBartolo Jr., careful critics point out, distinguish him from his peers:

• He hires coaches and front office people who make good player decisions — good decisions, that is, on how to spend his money.

• He creates a harmonious, winning atmosphere by treating his players as valuable human beings.

• He is an expert in an owner's most important job — how to choose a winning coach.

On some NFL clubs, the reasoning and the logic behind all that are not really understood. So there has been grumbling that DeBartolo merely uses his fortune to buy Super Bowl championships. One of the league's most widely shared perceptions is that teams owned by some of the NFL's poorer millionaires don't have a shot against a billionaire.

And it's obviously true that, whenever he gets a chance, DeBartolo lays out large sums for more talent — even though the 49ers have lost money in each of the last two seasons while fielding championship teams that sold out Candlestick Park in sixteen consecutive games. Ten months ago, for example, DeBartolo was a big player in the convoluted free-agency market known as Plan B, paying more than $2 million to a group of five NFL castoffs. Then he outbid rival owners who, along with the 49ers, wanted two useful, available veterans, Nose Tackle Jim Burt, who played for the New York Giants in the 1987 Super Bowl, and former Raider Millen.

But is DeBartolo taking advantage of the NFL with his wealth? "If you'll think it through," he said, "I think you will agree with me that the other clubs can compete this way, too, if the desire is there."

DeBartolo argues that pro football's really astronomical expenses are the ones that are more or less fixed — the basic payroll, for instance. Around the league, these costs are similar. "The free agents and the other extras we get don't add that much," DeBartolo said. "It's like buying insurance. But I'll tell you this. If it weren't for Millen and the other depth we had this season, there's no way we're in this Super Bowl. We'd lost some really great defensive starters to injury."

In trading cash for second stringers, DeBartolo is executing a policy formulated by Bill Walsh in his final years as 49er coach, when San Francisco began stockpiling gifted backups. "We don't have the NFL's highest paid starters," said 49er General Manager John McVay. "[Free Safety] Ronnie Lott is the only guy we have who leads the league in salary at his position. But we have the league's highest paid backups."

If that helps explain how and why the 49ers could hold on at or close to the top through the 1980s — defying the maxim that such a thing can't be done in pro football — two examples are Steve Young and Terry Tausch. As Quarterback Joe Montana's backup, Young sits around collecting $1 million a year. Tausch is a talented offensive lineman who came to San Francisco this year after a bidding war involving, altogether, six teams. Talking about it here this week, Tausch, a guard who has sometimes played as a 49er regular this season, said: "The 49ers called and said to go and see the five other teams and then see DeBartolo at the end."

At the end, DeBartolo topped them all with a $1-million offer, including $350,000 this season in salary and signing bonus. That's where DeBartolo's money goes. And as he said, that's why he's here. Said Millen: "In the short time I've been with the 49ers, the thing that's struck me is he way they go out and get anything they need."

Former NFL Coach Sid Gillman said: "But that's not the same as *buying* a pennant. You can't buy a pennant. The Boston Red Sox and the Angels and some in the NFL have tried that, and failed every time. That's because winning takes more than money. The 49ers have made the Super Bowl by identifying the right personnel to go after — *not* by throwing money around. Getting the right players is everything. The 49ers waste less money on bad decisions than most teams."

III

But why would DeBartolo live in Youngstown?

In his view, it is perfectly understandable: He was born there, went to grade school and high school there, married a high school girlfriend there, and has always lived there. "It's home," he said. "Youngstown, Ohio, is a small midwestern city, a good place for raising children, a place where you can appreciate the change of the seasons. My oldest friends are my neighbors. The best guys I know I went to school with in Youngstown. Some of them still live on my street. They say you can't go back, and I guess you can't, but you can stay — and I've stayed."

It was in high school that DeBartolo began dating Candy Papalia, who was to become his wife and the mother of his daughters. A half century ago, Candy's father ran a grocery store in a Youngstown suburb. A century or so ago, DeBartolo's grandfather was a paving contractor who put in many of the streets and curbs of Youngstown. In time, DeBartolo's father — E.J. DeBartolo Sr., age seventy-eight — branched out, first into the construction of duplexes and houses, and then after World War II into shopping malls. "My father got into malls at just the right time, just when America was ready for such an evolutionary development," DeBartolo said.

Over the years, their corporation has built about one hundred million square feet of retail shopping space in malls from coast to coast. It's a cash-rich family, financing its own projects. "We own and operate everything we build," DeBartolo said.

His father, who preceded him to Notre Dame and recently contributed $30 million to Notre Dame, still heads the company from an office in Youngstown, where at fourteen Eddie began at the bottom, shoveling snow and mowing lawns at a Youngstown mall. He joined up full time after college.

And at thirty-two he advanced, at the will of his father, to president and eventually chief administrative officer of a corporation with fourteen thousand employees and associates, many of them engineers, architects, and lawyers. Said the head of the DeBartolo family: "Eddie and I, the two of us, run the company together."

IV

When the earth began shaking not long ago in the Candlestick Park area of San Francisco, Lisa DeBartolo, the proud possessor of a book of World Series tickets, had just pulled into the parking lot. The oldest of the 49er owner's three daughters, Lisa had driven across from her Oakland apartment less than fifteen minutes before the Bay Bridge collapsed.

It was two and a half hours before Lisa could telephone her family that she was safe and well. "Let me tell you," Eddie DeBartolo said, "there are easier ways to spend two and a half hours."

He is known as a family man. Nothing is too good for Eddie's daughters. Everyone around him says that. And, apparently, nothing is too good for what he calls his other family, the 49ers. Everybody says that, too. Montana, identifying one of DeBartolo's most welcome winning traits, said: "With Eddie you go first class all the way."

Wherever the 49ers stay on the road, each veteran gets his own room in a fine hotel. And, aloft, the 49ers move about only in wide-body jets. Two or three seats are provided for each player; and at mealtime, all players get first-class dinners. Such treatment is not at all routine in other NFL cities, where management not infrequently expresses open disdain for its players. On such teams, the players are viewed, and treated, not as partners, but as competitors and enemies. DeBartolo, however, seems to be genuinely kind as well as sophisticated enough to realize that players treated well fight harder for their club — in good times and bad.

He pays well, distributes perks lavishly, and talks with players as peers. On his record, it is possible to say that, contrary to rumor, nice guys do finish first — over and over.

The 49er club was priced at $17 million when he bought it. DeBartolo and his team both turned thirty that year. Thirteen winters later, *that* family is worth an estimated $100 million. A more important statistic, DeBartolo said, is that his team has made the playoffs in each of the last seven years. His is the only team that has.

Can he keep it up? One trait will help him. He knows a good coach when he sees one.

During his first three seasons in the NFL, DeBartolo went through five coaches, including the one he could have kept around when he bought the 49er franchise in early 1977. Though other owners usually take three to five years to judge a new coach, fearing to appear capricious, or failing to learn the game, or both, DeBartolo kept pulling the plug — in one instance twice in one year — until he had coach number five, Bill Walsh. Then, proving that he was anything but capricious, he stuck with number five through two more disastrous seasons (2-14, 6-10) before Walsh suddenly delivered the first of San Francisco's series of Super Bowl rings.

Clearly, DeBartolo recognized greatness instantly. What's more, when he had to replace Walsh, he hired another winner, George Seifert. By contrast, the Green Bay Packers weren't heard from for twenty years after Vince Lombardi retired.

The 49ers minus Walsh have come right back to the Super Bowl — and the quarterback who holds the all-time comeback championship smiles when he thinks about that. "Eddie was here before Bill Walsh or any of us were here," Joe Montana said. "He had some tough years at first — but he learned how to win."

3. Walsh on Walsh Football

WHEN THE Dallas Cowboys were getting ready for Super Bowl XXX (a game they won), I visited with the inventor of the offensive system they've been using, for the most part, in the 1990s: the West Coast or Bill Walsh offense. Walsh has a rare mind, both creative and systematic, and it took both qualities to remake football. A few days after this story appeared, San Francisco rehired him to serve as an advisory coach.

TEMPE, Ariz.: Jan. 20, 1996.

This is another Bill Walsh year. The 1980s innovator who won so often in San Francisco has retired from coaching except, as he says, for several advisory roles. But he is still being represented in the NFL by his offense. It is called the West Coast offense now. Fifteen years after Walsh first sent Quarterback Joe Montana out to win 49er games and championships with that offense — with quick short passes to backs as well as wide receivers — many others were doing it that way this season.

Ten 1995 pro clubs in all used elements of the Walsh or West Coast offense. Five made the playoffs. And two, the Dallas Cowboys and Pittsburgh Steelers, reached Super Bowl XXX, in which they will be seen here Sunday.

By reputation, the Cowboys and Steelers are both tough-guy teams with a yen to run the ball. But in fact they owe their present eminence in great part to passes by Quarterbacks Troy Aikman and Neil O'Donnell.

That is most noticeably true of the Cowboys, who, under two different kinds of coaches, have been winning since 1993 with the essential play of the West Coast offense: the quick ball-control pass. As a Dallas play starts and opponents stiffen for a jolt from Tailback Emmitt Smith, Aikman throws sometimes to Smith or Fullback Daryl Johnston, sometimes to Tight End Jay Novacek, and sometimes to a wide receiver racing in on a quick slant pattern.

Like Walsh, the Dallas coaches frown on four wide receivers; and they avoid shotgun football as well. They prefer to keep their base unit in the game — their starting running backs, wide receivers and tight end — with the quarterback under center. And like Montana used to do it, the Cowboys throw often on first down. When Aikman won his first Super Bowl game with four touchdown passes, each was delivered on a first-down play.

As for Pittsburgh's coach, Bill Cowher, who for years has been trying to run his way into the Super Bowl, he finally got here this season when he switched over to O'Donnell's arm. At times, O'Donnell threw 49er-like quick short passes, but the Steelers are newer to the passing game, and arguably less sophisticated. Going to extremes on many plays, the formerly macho Steelers, lining up five wide receivers, don't even use a running back.

That's not Walsh's way, nor the Cowboys'. The Walsh or West Coast offense is a balanced and integrated approach to football; and lately, there has been a lot of talk about it.

But as an offense, what is it?

The best source is Walsh himself. And in a conversation with the man who led the 49ers to three Super Bowl championships, you hear that West Coast football is a system based on three principles in particular, of which the first and most important is "a willingness to pass on first down."

Second, he says, "You have to complete a bigger percentage of your passes in this offense than most football teams can. You're trying to keep possession throwing the ball — you're trying to move down the field — and the best way to do that is with closely timed short-to-medium-range passes."

Third, says Walsh, "You want the other team to keep using most of its base defensive people instead of situation specialists. So you attack them the way Dallas does: with a base set that threatens everything, everywhere, on every down. That means a possession receiver, a speed receiver, a good receiving tight end who is also a very good blocker, and two running backs who are also good receivers." Thus, in the pure West Coast system, Walsh says, there are "very few plays with four wide receivers" — or even three — even though it's a pass-oriented offense.

Isn't it true that the West Coast objective is to establish the pass in the same sense that most coaches try to establish the run?

"No, our objective is to establish the offense," Walsh says. "On first-down plays, we want to establish the fact that we can move the ball either passing or running — and that means being ready, able and willing to do either. The big thing on first down isn't throwing — it's a *willingness* to throw."

Football players since boyhood have tried to grind it out on first down. How do you make them willing to pass?

"You need a pass offense that they can count on," Walsh says. "What it takes is a sound way to throw the ball that will make the assistant coaches as well as the players feel confident that they can do it."

Why is it so important to throw on first down?

"Because that's one time when the defense can't gear up against passes. On first down, they always have to be ready for the run, too."

So there's less blitzing on first down?

"Usually much less. And the linebackers aren't cheating back into pass coverage either."

Critics say the West Coast offense is just a bunch of short passes and long runs after the catch. Why do they think of it that way?

"Because that's what they see."

But that isn't what it is?

"Not quite. We call as many long passes as any other team. We might call a particular deep pass five times and not throw it once. What we do in every game is go to the outlet receiver quicker than other teams. If the deep pass isn't open right now, we go immediately to the tight end or a back."

What is the basis for your assumption that ball-control passes are more efficient than a ball-control running game?

"We've learned that it's too difficult to go head to head against today's defensive linemen and linebackers on a running play that they anticipate. They're too quick and mobile. When was the last time you saw a good offensive line block seven guys to the ground? A well-designed pass offense is more reliable for ball-control — especially against highly motivated defensive teams."

NFL defensive players are very often highly motivated. Don't such players rush the passer more aggressively?

"Sure, but if you're ready to throw a short pass quickly, you can throw over them."

What theory are you advancing here?

"Offensive football is like this: If a team is trying to establish the run, emotionally charged-up defensive players will climb through good blockers to get your ballcarrier. And there goes your rushing game. But when you're throwing the ball, motivation doesn't help defensive players that much. Pass offense is skill, not muscle. An effective pass offense neutralizes emotion. That's one of the great things about it."

Moving along to your third aim or principle in West Coast football — the need to perfect a base offense — why are starting lineups more productive for teams like Dallas and San Francisco than, say, specialist groups of four wide receivers?

"When you leave your base offense on the field — with the quarterback under center — the defense has to account for every run and pass you have [power plays, traps, sweeps, draws, quick passes, deep passes]. We're not against formations with four or five wide receivers provided you're using them for two reasons: to see if the defense makes a poor adjustment or gives you a major mismatch. But we think it's counterproductive to bring in three or four wide receivers just to confuse the defense by giving them a different look."

What's wrong with that?

"Timing is critical to pass offense. And the more people you have milling about, the harder it is to get your timing down. I think all cosmetic things hurt offense more than they help. Take a play when a team has excessive motion, and then just runs up the middle. That leaves the offensive line sitting too long in place."

What theory is involved with this example?

"Perfecting your own timing is more important than trying to confuse the other team with motion plays, shotgun formations, situation specialists, or any other gimmick."

In West Coast football, how do you perfect a base offense: an offense with two backs all the time, two wide receivers, the same tight end?

"What we recommend is going into training camp knowing every play that's going to be called in the first six regular-season games. We simulate game-time conditions for every play we practice — everything we do — both in training camp and in a regular-season practice week. We isolate every possible game-time contingency — first and goal, third and fifteen, the four-minute offense, the two-minute offense, and so on — and we practice every play in one of those situations."

How many such situations are there altogether?

"We isolate four kinds — time on the clock, position on the field, down and distance, and field conditions — and no offensive or defensive play is ever practiced except in one of those contingencies."

Is one contingency more important than another?

"We think the four-minute offense is the most underrated or overlooked part of the game. The NFL is so competitive that most games are won or lost in the last four minutes of the half or the game — when too much or too little time is too often taken off the clock."

What's most important in down-and-distance planning?

"We have distinct plays for, say, third and five, or six, or seven, or eight. The most difficult down is third and three."

Why?

"That's a long way to pound the ball on a running play, and the defense knows it."

Do you always expect to win?

"We approach every practice as if we're a one-point underdog. To a winner, complacency and overconfidence can be destructive. To losers, desperation and despondency are just as harmful. So on the practice field, we're always slight underdogs with a chance to win."

What does this sort of planning accomplish?

"People concentrate better in practice when they're in a game situation mentally. If you visualize the game all the time you're working out, you're better prepared."

Do pass plays or running plays get most of the practice time in West Coast football?

"During every regular-season game, there are occasions when you absolutely have to be able to run — you're in short yardage, you're ahead in the fourth quarter, you're on the opponent's goal line, times like that. So you work on it. But in the NFL today, it's very difficult to line up and run early in the game, or relatively early, when both teams are fresh and inspired, and thinking clearly, and determined to win. The only thing you can rely on to circumvent the strength of today's defensive teams is the timed short-to-medium pass. We allot more practice time for that."

How do you define timing pass?

"You drop back, say, three steps and throw to a man who will be there when the ball arrives."

The 49ers have had a fifteen-year run at the top of the NFL, winning it all every three years, on the average. No other team ever did that. Is the way you time the short-to-medium pass a principal explanation?

"It's the elemental difference in what we do. But I'd say the explanation for why the whole thing works is our attention to organization and detail. We have a format to do everything, a role for everyone, a plan for scripting every moment of practice as well as the first fifteen or twenty plays on Sundays after the opening kickoff."

What's the theory behind scripting early plays?

"We want to show the defense a lot of formations and read their adjustments; we want to get in our basic runs to set up play action for later; it takes the pressure off the coaches to make critical early decisions; it helps the players to know ahead of time what plays are coming."

Other teams are also scripting the first fifteen or twenty plays these days as the West Coast offense spreads around the league.

"Yes, there are things about this offense that can be and are being used now by many coaches. It's an offense that is a little different everywhere. Everybody including me revises it every year. The aim is constant improvement. The emphasis is on developing the skills of the athletes and giving them a platform to play on."

But why is it called the West Coast offense? Why not the Bill Walsh offense?

"Some of the people who used to play for the Cincinnati Bengals wonder about that. When I was Paul Brown's offensive coordinator there [in the 1970s], we were doing pretty much what the 49ers do now. This is an offense that originated in Cincinnati — which doesn't even have a suburb on the West Coast."

IX

REASONING

*Quand la fermeté suffit,
pourquoi la témérité?*
—BONAPARTE

Football in its strategic sense is often compared to war. There is, however, one major difference: They don't sell tickets to a war. And inevitably, football fans in large numbers mean conflicts between those who run the war on the field and those who pay to see it.

For decades, most football coaches have lived by the maxim of Napoleon Bonaparte, "When firmness suffices, why be reckless?" Most fans, however, yearn for *la témérité* in spades — or at least a long bomb once in awhile.

I must say that I am partial to recklessness myself, speaking of football; and so I have been heartened by the recent triumph of inventive passing attacks. But, in truth, every style of football holds considerable fascination for me. For after a century of American creativity, the game in all of its manifestations is now a daunting mix of brute force, refined skill, and subtle strategy. And uniquely among sports, the evolution of football goes on every year.

While Babe Ruth's New York Yankees could doubtless beat any baseball team operating today, and while the 1972 Los Angeles Lakers of Wilt

Chamberlain and Jerry West might be favored against the 1995-96 Chicago Bulls — who broke their single-season victory record — there is no way that the 1940 Chicago Bears or the 1967-68 Green Bay Packers, playing football as they did in their time, could hold their own in a matchup with a good modern NFL team.

Although the players are pumped up today — remade in the weight room — the decisive difference lies in the game's improved tactics and strategy. Like experts in computer technology, football coaches keep turning out a better product.

It has for years seemed to me that because tactical and strategic superiority is typically decisive in an NFL game between roughly equal opponents — as demonstrated especially in the playoffs — tactical and strategic matters should be covered regularly, along with football's personalities and Sunday's events, by newspaper writers. But few daily journalists see the world that way. And though I agree with them that you lose some readers when you start talking about influence plays and roll-up zones, the topic is nevertheless as intrinsically interesting as any other creation of the human intellect.

Personally, I never had a chance with quantum mechanics or nonequilibrium thermodynamics — football is more my speed — and with that in mind, here are some of my football-analysis stories.

1. Movies but No Replays in 1950s

INSTANT REPLAY was still in the future in when the Los Angeles Rams, on one of the great days in the club's history, went into Detroit in 1958 to defeat the defending NFL-champion Lions on five end-run touchdowns, 42-28. Thus, as was usual four and five decades ago, I had to wait a day and view the movies before the final analysis. On 1990s TV, big plays are replayed dozens of times during and after games. In 1958, the following analysis was for the sports fans who on TV saw the five big plays only once.

DETROIT: Oct. 13, 1958.

Ram Coach Sid Gillman acknowledged today, as he leafed idly through his new contract, that the club's running game looks even better on film than it did yesterday when the Rams were beating the NFL champion Detroit Lions, 42-28. Sid came out of his dark room in Henry Ford's colonial-era hotel, the Dearborn Inn, and, shuddering in the bright sunshine of a typical autumn day in Michigan, said: "That's the greatest running we ever had. On any one of the five scoring plays, if the field was a thousand yards long, we'd still be running."

The distance requirement for the first touchdown, Tom Wilson's, was eighty-two yards, following which Jon Arnett scored three times and Joe Marconi went twenty-four yards — all on sweeps around end. Three different backs, five similar runs, five scores.

"They were all team plays," Wilson said, speaking a partial truth.

His was a class-by-itself gem. Wilson skillfully outmaneuvered three Lions, the movies show, before picking up downfield blocks by Guards Bob Fry and John Morrow. Forty yards from the scrimmage line, End Del Shofner flew up to apply the key block, leaving only one enemy in Wilson's way, Lion Safetyman Gary Lowe. Tom survived a head-on collision with Lowe and scored.

First to last, the Wilson touchdown run was the best ever made by a Ram, in my opinion, considering (a) the distance; (b) strength of opposition, one of the toughest of recent defensive teams, the one which won the NFL title last year with defense; (c) persistent Ram blocking from the scrimmage line on down the field, and (d) Wilson's ability to evade or run down so many tacklers over so many yards.

Since the Rams transferred to Los Angeles in 1946, only two scrimmage runs have covered more ground. Kenny Washington went ninety-two yards in 1946 and Tom Harmon eighty-four in 1947.

En route to the end zone, Wilson made many Lions miss — the way Arnett does it — and those he couldn't miss he ran over, the way Jim Brown does it. Even so, Gillman, calling all the plays, gave Wilson the ball only three other times — and jerked him after Tom's second fumble. For reasons that defy analysis, Wilson gets short shrift from this team.

All the same, it has heartened the club's owners to win two in a row on the road. They feel they guessed right in extending Gillman's contract for another year.

2. The Rams Become a Winner

STARTING IN 1959, the Rams lost for seven seasons in a row, finishing 4-10 in 1965. Under a new coach, George Allen, they began to win immediately; and in Allen's second year, 1967, they pulled away to 11-1-2. My natural interest in winners and their ways was sharpened by the contrast; and, continuously, I was intrigued by how a new leader could do that. Burnishing a young star, Deacon Jones — the next several paragraphs commemorate Jones' coming out as a superstar — Allen also played intelligent football on both offense and defense, as I set out to explain by talking to his players for analysis columns like the following.

ATLANTA: Nov. 21, 1967.

Those who saw Sunday's game on television might well agree that the Rams are now a team with a genuine superstar. He is David (Deacon) Jones, the defensive end whose value to Los Angeles is beginning to parallel that of Quarterback John Unitas to Baltimore.

There are many other Ram stars this winning season. And in the league today there are a few other superstars, although not many after you have named Unitas, Jones, and Chicago Halfback Gale Sayers.

But the important thing about Jones is that he has made it on defense, at the edge of the spotlight that is always on the men with the ball. Sunday, in a game that was still 7-3 in the last period, he made the big play again, deflecting the throw that was intercepted to set up the go-ahead touchdown. Jones was playing, moreover, with an injury. "That's the only way to play for Coach Allen," he said. But that still isn't easy. And it's Jones' attitude toward the game — his enthusiasm and energy coupled with superior physical and mental endowments — that have made him a superstar.

II

In Detroit Thursday the Rams can complete an undefeated road schedule — a rare thing in pro football — if they are again attacked on the ground by an efficient passing team. Ram opponents have seemed astonishingly anxious lately to hit the strength of Allen's Assassins with running backs.

We were talking this over today with one of Allen's All-Pros, Tackle Merlin Olsen, who said: "The best way to handle a good passer in this league is to put your linebackers in the pass defense with the deep backs. We did this as usual against the Falcons Sunday. Anybody can see it — so the Falcons knew they couldn't pass. And that's why they ran the ball. But we're confident they can't beat us on the ground. What they're actually doing is just spinning wheels. They're using up the clock. They're cutting down on their chances to throw enough passes to hurt us."

The lesson seems to be: don't fret if you see them making a few first downs running against the Rams.

III

After ten games Allen's team is still averaging four touchdowns a week, the best in the league west of Baltimore. This remains the most surprising thing about an offense that could hardly score a year ago. What's happening?

Well, here's how the Rams produced six of their thirty-one points Sunday on third and goal at the Atlanta two-yard line in the second quarter:

First, in the movies, Allen's offensive coaches sized up all three of Atlanta's short-yardage defenses. Second, they designed a play to break one of them — the defense that uses a seven-man line with the middle linebacker (Tommy Nobis) on one side and a blitzing linebacker on the other. Third, they schooled Quarterback Roman Gabriel in the look of this defense and what to do about it. Fourth, Gabriel spotted the blitzer and routed Fullback Dick Bass behind him in the area away from Nobis. And fifth, as Gabriel threw the touchdown ball to Bass, the nearest Falcon might as well have been sitting with you in California.

The Rams this year are illustrating two things about offensive football that Vince Lombardi proved long ago: (1) No pro quarterback can be much better than his teachers. And (2) with careful coaching, a fine quarterback, a Gabriel or a Bart Starr, can get the ball in the end zone against almost any defense.

3. Pancakes for a Sunday Afternoon

MY SUPPOSITION is that football fans are interested in an occasional inside-football analysis. I originally wrote this story near the end of the first great age of middle linebackers, but the 1990s return of the four-three defense means that middle-linebackers are back in fashion. Among the revelations in this story, to me, was the definition of "to pancake."

LOS ANGELES: Dec. 6, 1973.

The football player who will doubtless be remembered as the finest middle linebacker of our time, Dick Butkus of Chicago, says there is one major qualification for the job: "The thing I want to know about a linebacker is his dedication. You can wrap it up in that old word, desire. Other things help — intelligence, size, strength, instinct for the ball — but what's he really like inside?"

Every good pro team these days has a good middle linebacker. It has to. This is the key position in defensive football today.

In a typical NFL defense, the middle linebacker makes most of the tackles. As a rule, he is also the defensive quarterback — calling both the signals and the audibles (the last-second changes shouted in code). "This is the nerve center," says Kansas City Coach Hank Stram. "Defense begins and often ends right there."

How long has this been so? What makes it so? What exactly does a middle linebacker do, and why does he do it?

Most football coaches will tell you, to begin with, that there's no other position like it in sports. Baseball catchers have somewhat similar leadership responsibilities — but not the same kind of physical contact — and though hockey players sometimes experience the contact, they don't play a linebacker's role in the decision making.

In offensive football, quarterbacks make decisions, but they don't often hit people. A Butkus or a Willie Lanier, the Kansas City middle linebacker, is first of all a hitter. Or is he? Isn't he first of all a commander?

"Those are the two things, brains and brawn," the Rams' former All-Pro middle linebacker, Les Richter, says. "A middle linebacker should be a guy whose approach to the game is like a football coach, intellectually, and like a kamikaze pilot, spiritually. He actually offers himself up as a sacrifice on every play. Everybody is shooting at him."

It was Richter who established the cash value of a middle linebacker several years ago when the Rams landed him in a trade with Dallas — trading eleven players for him. A full team. His interest in the game remains.

II

A distinctive thing about middle linebacker is that it is easily defined. Whereas quarterbacks are not a quarter of the way back of anything — and ends today are seldom ends — a middle linebacker is just that. He stands in the middle and backs up the defensive line. Says Lanier: "You're the only man on the team who can see all eleven of the other guys — and by the same token, you're the only guy that ten of those eleven can block. Usually it's the center, a guard, a tackle or the tight end. But sooner or later they all get a piece of you. You've first got to dispose of whoever comes out after you."

Even this physical aspect of the middle man's assignment is more complicated than it might seem. Lanier, for instance, prefers one or another of four techniques. "I'll often begin with a forearm shiver," he says, "or, if the run is coming at me directly, I might pancake."

Asked to define his terms, the Kansas City linebacker says: "A forearm shiver is just that. You shiver them with your forearm. Pancaking is backing up quick and falling flat out — as the blocker rolls over you — and getting right back up."

On other occasions, Lanier takes the backdoor to the ballcarrier or merely fills the hole. "The backdoor," he says, "is going behind the blocker, chasing a play that's angling away from you — off tackle, say. Filling the hole is going forward into the line, clogging the point of attack.

You might not make the tackle, but you don't leave the runner any place to run."

On the contact level, Butkus, during his long and eminent career, has considered his role to be fundamentally a duel with the ballcarrier. "You've got to put your label on them," he says. "I want the guy to know he's been stung by me, personally. After I've left my trademark, he won't feel so much like coming around for more. I don't care who the runner is, or how brave he is, when he's been stung a couple of times, he starts thinking about his own well-being. He forgets about the ball, and then you've got him. He'll cough it up, and that's what you're after. The definition of defense in football is getting the ball."

Butkus for years has been the most feared of the NFL's linebackers. An arthritic knee is apparently bringing him to the end of that career, prematurely. But he will be remembered. Pittsburgh Quarterback Terry Bradshaw says: "Playing against Butkus is like playing with a thumb in your eye. He intimidated me before we even played the game." In Detroit, Quarterback Greg Landry says: "Butkus is the last carryover. He gambles, breaks his own defenses and is so physical he can put the fear of God in you across that line when he growls." A running back, O.J. Simpson of Buffalo, says: "I fear no man on this earth — except Butkus."

III

Their opponents tend to discuss linebackers in physical terms. Coaches, however, point to their intellectual contributions. "It doesn't really matter whether the plays are called on the field," says Butkus, "or sent in by a coach. Somebody out there has to call the audibles — and the less experience the signal caller has on the field, the less you can do in the way of audibles and defensive changes."

During the George Allen era in Los Angeles, the defensive signal caller, Maxie Baughan, knew, and used, more than two hundred audibles. For most linebackers, particularly those with only two or three years in the league, just understanding the signals is a challenge. Here are two Butkus examples of audibles he might call:

Fifty-Six Crash Buck-I: "That's a blitz by the weak linebacker. 'I' means blitz. Buck is the weak side linebacker. The strong linebacker is Stub, the middle is Mac. Anytime they hear 'I' they blitz. Crash means the ends come down tight."

Forty-Six Double Burn with a Sticky Sam: "The middle linebacker blitzing between the center and the weak guard, and the strong linebacker between the center and the strong guard."

Butkus doesn't of course, shout: "Double Burn with a Sticky Sam." The Bears have an audible code word or two meaning all that. The intellectual challenge to him and his teammates is to remember exactly what's meant and to react on the instant. After a lost game, when a coach says his team "made too many mistakes," he usually means someone didn't instantly remember to act on a code word that stands for a phrase that isn't even in English to begin with.

IV

Twenty years or so ago there was less of that to remember. Football's original middle linebackers are not only still alive but only recently retired. The inventor of the position may have been Bill George, a recent Bear operative. "In the early 1950s," says George, "I played what the colleges call nose guard today. But they kept completing little passes over our middle. George Connor captained the Bears at that time, and one day I told him they wouldn't be able to complete those passes over me if I stood up. 'So stand up,' Connor said."

When he stood up and backed away from center, presto, George became a middle linebacker, maybe the first one on the planet.

The more football changes, however, the more it stays the same. The new way of playing the game, as popularized in the AFL before it spread to the NFL, is with a tackle on the center's nose — the very position Bill George played before he turned into a middle linebacker. They're calling it the three-four defense, which is the four-three turned upside down. As devised by John McKay at USC and adapted by Don Shula in Miami, the three-four has three linemen and four linebackers, with two middle linebackers.

"Can you think of anything worse," Quarterback Bradshaw asks, "than *two* middle linebackers?"

4. USC Power versus UCLA Veer

WHEN TWO disparate strategic styles are on view in the same college football game, I've sometimes used a three-part series: pre-game (Friday), game story (Sunday), post-game (Monday). In the following series, my game story is represented by only a few paragraphs.

The Planning

LOS ANGELES: Nov. 19, 1976.

When UCLA meets USC here Saturday in a football game matching the nation's second- and third-ranked college teams, something more than bowls and titles will be on the line. This one is also an uncommon matchup of styles. Throughout the country, coaches may be influenced for some time by what they see when UCLA's Veer-T team confronts USC's Power I.

The uniqueness of this game rests on two things:

• The importance of the competing offense systems. As of 1976, the two dominant ways of attacking a college football defense are with option plays (as executed in the UCLA system by Veer Quarterback Jeff Dankworth) and with power plays (as quarterbacked for USC by Vince Evans and run by Ricky Bell and Charles White).

• The strength of the defenses. Many pro scouts think the real matchup here Saturday pairs the one-two defensive teams of college football. What USC and UCLA do to each other offensively with power and triple-option plays will therefore have a national impact.

Each of the coaches is confident of his approach. "The Veer system gives you the edge," says UCLA's Terry Donahue. "We can attack you in three different places with one snap of the ball."

"Perhaps, but tradition is with power," says USC's John Robinson. "In my lifetime, most of the great teams have been power teams: Green Bay, Don Shula's Miami Dolphins, John McKay's USC teams."

So it's deception versus force — though the stereotypes aren't, of course, absolute. UCLA fields some good, tough blockers, and the Trojans complement their muscle-running with a fine passing game honed by Robinson and assistant Paul Hackett, and operated by Quarterback Evans. But the ground-game contrasts are pronounced, and, in this game at least, paramount.

II

Even in appearance, the Trojan I and Bruin Veer are distinctively different. The Trojans station their fullback and tailback in single file behind the quarterback; and as the play begins, the fullback blocks for the tailback, achieving instant power. The Bruins start with their halfbacks side by side behind the guards. On each play, one halfback dives into the line (first option) while the quarterback swings out (second option) and pitches or fakes a pitch to the trailing halfback (third option).

Coming out of the I, the Trojans will attack UCLA's defense in a time-tested old-fashioned method reminiscent of the way their old coach, Howard Jones, used to go after UCLA, that is, by massing blockers in front of runners. "Every team in the country is in the T Formation now," Robinson says, "but at USC we're still using single-wing principles. We're out to attack you on every play. We're going to double-team. You know we're coming — we don't rely much on finesse or deception — but we think we'll outman you."

At UCLA, by contrast, Donahue bases his whole offensive approach on the finesse and deception that are never more than a part of the Trojan show. The essence of UCLA's Veer-T Formation is the triple-option machinery that keeps defenses guessing. "Once Dankworth has it and starts down the line," says Donahue, "our blocking is exactly the same whether we're hitting the middle, the corner or the outside."

USC's running game is likewise equipped to strike at those three places — but not without changing its blocking assignments. This is sometimes a cumbersome thing to do in I-Formation football. On a sweep or pitch play, for instance, the Trojans pull a guard or two. The Bruins don't have to. "We stretch the defense laterally," Donahue says. "We're trying to find a crack. On every play we stretch you until we see a crack and attack there. An I team tries to pound a hole open. We just run along until we *find* one."

III

The Trojans have three basic running plays: 22 blast (up the middle), 25 power (off tackle to the weak side) and 28 pitch (the sweep). As for USC's running backs, Bell follows Fullback Mosi Tatupu into the 2 or 5 holes if it's a blast or power play; if it's a sweep, Bell takes Evans' pitch and swings outside behind Tatupu and pulling Guard Donnie Hickman.

In his first five games this year, before he was hurt October 23, Bell gained well over a thousand yards for the Trojans running those three plays over and over. He was assisted, to be sure, by the strategy of the USC offense, which on most plays threatened with its polished passing attack. And on each rushing assault, Bell was assisted by a tactical piece of deception: At the instant Evans took the snap from Center Gary Bethel, USC's opponents couldn't know which of the three ways Bell was coming. But they were never deceived for long. All they had to do was watch the fullback. In the USC system, wherever the fullback goes, the tailback can't be far behind.

Veer football is much more complicated, both in design and execution. Any of UCLA's three backs might wind up with the ball on any play. In the Veer, as in the Wishbone, the three options can be either predetermined or read by the quarterback. "With a good quarterback like Dankworth," says Donahue, "we mostly read. Whether he hands off, keeps or pitches depends on what two defensive linemen do — the first man outside our offensive tackle (usually the defensive tackle) and the defensive end (or outside linebacker) on that side."

These two people, the defensive tackle and end, aren't blocked in Veer football. They are optioned, as the Bruins say.

So that's the difference between power and option football. Whereas the Trojans are likely to double-team the key man in the other side's defense — hit him with two blockers — the Bruins won't bother to block him at all.

THE GAME

LOS ANGELES: Nov. 21, 1976.

The USC defense has kept five teams from scoring touchdowns this season and shut out three. But it is plain now that the Trojans have been underrated. When their biggest game was on the line, their defense played nearly perfect football Saturday as USC took a 24-0 lead into the last four minutes before winning eased up, 24-14.

On a sunny afternoon before a crowd of 95,019 at the Coliseum, UCLA scored a couple of late touchdowns imaginatively to remove some of the pain. But this was a game that was all USC's after Safetyman Dennis Thurman recovered a Bruin fumble in the air and returned it forty-seven yards to the touchdown that made it a Trojan first half, 7-0.

Thereafter, as Coach John Robinson's USC defense took charge of UCLA's Veer machinery, his power offense took charge of the game. The Bruins failed to get a first down during the third quarter and for half the fourth quarter as the score mounted slowly but irresistibly to 10-0, 17-0 and 24-0 on Glen Walker's forty-two-yard field goal, Halfback Ricky Bell's one-yard touchdown, and Quarterback Vince Evans' clever, scrambling run to a thirty-six-yard touchdown.

THE REVIEW

LOS ANGELES: Nov. 22, 1976.

Taking a few minutes from his preparation for Notre Dame this weekend, USC's football coach reflected on the results of Saturday's controlled experiment in football theories. Said John Robinson: "The game was philosophically a commentary on the success of power football."

Watching the UCLA Veer this season, viewers sometimes got the feeling that the Bruins were going to score every time. But against the USC defense, that didn't happen.

Robinson summarized the game as follows: Faced with a cute offense, USC found a cute defense to stop it. Facing well-trained power, the Bruins had no recourse but to meet it head-to-head. Over the course of the afternoon they couldn't do that successfully.

But this, in Robinson's view, doesn't mean simply that USC had the bigger, stronger people. "We don't beat people with brute force," he said. "We're not just a bunch of gorillas. To play the power style, players have to be deeply committed and intensively coached. When you play against SC, it isn't just the big guys against the little guys. Our players work very hard and they're very well trained in the techniques."

The creativity of Trojan thinking on Saturday could be most easily seen in their defensive plan. Opposing the Veer-T, which is designed to option a defense into hesitancy and confusion, the Trojans played a complicated combination of power and non-contact techniques that gave each of their players a definite assignment (no options) while thwarting each of the several Bruin threats.

The Trojan defense was anchored on the muscle of Defensive Tackles Gary Jeter, six-four, 255, and Walt Underwood, six-four, 225. For most of the game, they eliminated UCLA's first-option runners, Theotis Brown and Wendell Tyler, on the halfback dive or line buck that begins every Veer play. With that option thus blocked, Quarterback Jeff Dankworth, on a typical play, only faked a handoff to the dive man and proceeded laterally into phase two of the triple-option series. Out there the job was done for USC by outside Linebackers Rod Martin and David Lewis, who, lining up as defensive ends, had one primary responsibility: the quarterback rolling out after faking an inside handoff. More than any other Trojans, these two broke the Bruin option. Robinson: "Our game plan was to slow-play Dankworth, to keep him going sideways. We didn't want to give him the easy decision whether to keep or pitch."

When Dankworth slid toward Martin, for example, Martin didn't commit himself. He neither attacked Dankworth nor tried to flank him. He merely moved laterally with him. Robinson: "It was like one-on-one basketball — with one guy trying to drive and the other staying in front of him." Inasmuch as football's triple-option series is based on defensive reaction — on taking action only after the defensive tackles and defensive ends have committed themselves — Dankworth was rendered helpless by the Martin and Lewis stall.

USC's defense was thus executed as well as it was conceived. For in Veer football, defensive tackles and ends aren't blocked by offensive players, they are optioned. And in Saturday's game USC's tackles and ends were required to respond in two different ways: Jeter and Underwood attacked, blunting the first option; Martin and Lewis stalled, delaying the second.

That left phase three. Robinson: "We kept Dankworth going laterally until he pitched [to Brown or Tyler]. By then, as a rule, the halfback getting the pitch was pinched between the pursuit and the sideline."

As for the Bruins, Robinson didn't say it — he would never say it — but he thinks UCLA's problem is the Veer. Finesse can't beat well-coached teams, he would say. He likes power.

5. How to Win a Rose Bowl Game

SIX WEEKS later, Robinson's Trojans taught a related lesson to the University of Michigan. Rose Bowl games were for several decades instructive contests between Midwestern teams attached to the running game and West Coast teams enamored of the pass. In the 1990s everybody passes, but it wasn't always so, and in this game the limitations of the option running game were further defined, as I tried to show in this analysis.

PASADENA: Jan. 3, 1977.

When the game was over and USC had won again, 14-6, a Michigan defensive player named Greg Morton best explained Saturday's Rose Bowl: "It's so rough to defense USC because if you try to key on [Quarterback]Vince Evans, the tailback will hurt you, and if you try to key on the tailback, the fullback will hurt you."

USC, in other words, is a team believing in an equitable division of labor. Against Michigan, generally speaking, when it was time to run the ball, the Trojans ran simple power plays with Tailback Charles White and Fullback Mosi Tatupu. And when it was time to pass, they passed effectively with Evans.

The Wolverines, on the other hand, built their entire offense around Quarterback Rick Leach, who on pass plays was the passer and on running plays a runner, sometime keeping the ball, sometimes holding it an instant before handing off to the fullback, and sometimes exercising his other option: pitching out to the tailback. And on the evidence of the sixty-third Rose Bowl, Leach had more to do than he — or perhaps any quarterback — could learn to do well.

In an age of specialization, in other words, Michigan lost because it didn't specialize enough. Put another way, option teams like Michigan have shown an Achilles heel. It takes their quarterbacks such a large quantity of practice time to master the intricacies of the option that they don't have time to polish a pass attack.

Coach John Robinson, who brought the pass back to USC this season, and who, as a result, finished 11-1 with a Rose Bowl victory in his first try, believes strongly in specialization as a way to proceed in college football. "In our practice periods," Robinson says, "we divide the offense into two parts. The quarterbacks, split ends and flankers spend eighty to ninety per cent of their time on the pass offense. Vince Evans, for instance, has worked on his passing and almost nothing else since practice began last September. As for our flanker [Shelton Diggs], we used to have him do both, but we've practically taken him out of the run offense to keep him concentrating on the pass offense."

Quarterback Evans' practice schedule at USC compares strikingly with that of Michigan's Quarterback Leach, who in Wolverine drills must work on three things: option plays, power plays and pass plays. Not surprisingly, his passing on game afternoons is less effective. "I'd estimate we've practiced half the time on passing since we've been in California," Leach said the other day.

Earlier in the season, however, when Michigan was facing other gravity-bound running teams in the Big Ten, it was more like one-third of the time, if that. The rule of thumb in option camps is that the quarterback divides his practice time seventy per cent to runs, thirty per cent to passes. Mastering the option process is a time-consuming matter for the quarterback, who can only learn by doing whether to keep or pitch, and precisely when to make the decision.

And so it is that Leach, a dropback passer in his prep days, hasn't progressed into a Joe Namath type in college. He has, of course, learned the option well enough to beat up on Navy and Wisconsin. But when it takes a serious passing threat plus a running threat to hassle a team like USC, Leach doesn't have the drill-field background to bring it off.

"Some people have the wrong idea about passing," said Robinson. "They think it's just a matter of sending out a guy who can throw and a guy who can catch and hoping for the best. The truth is that passing has to be carefully organized, and it has to be practiced over and over. If you're going to have a sound pass attack, I don't think the quarterback and the receivers can do much else during the week but work on it."

The conclusion is that USC was too strong for an option team to beat in the Rose Bowl this year because (1) you have to pass to beat the Trojans and (2) you can't run the option and pass in big league style.

6. Three Kinds of Greatness

THE FOCUS of my Times football columns is on the game itself and on the different ways that players play football — rather than the different ways they rave or behave. In the next three selections, for example, there are analyses of the varying styles of three very different athletes: Dan Marino, Herschel Walker, and Marcus Allen. The Allen story became a football tragedy: After the fumble play described below, Raider Owner Al Davis first sat Allen down for several years, then let him go.

DAN MARINO

MIAMI: Nov. 18, 1991.

The quality that distinguishes Miami Dolphins Quarterback Dan Marino as a passer is his rare quickness. He's like a snake striking. He does everything in a great hurry: read, decide, release. That was evident again the other night when Marino, one of the NFL's all-time finest passers, was seen in an almost flawless performance.

His opponent, the improving New England Patriots, whatever their problems on offense, manage to line up a playoff-caliber defense with Andre Tippett and Vincent Brown at linebacker and, among others, Ronnie Lippett in the secondary. And in defeating this team, Marino was unfailingly on target, reminding everyone that when the players around him are playing as well as they can, he's like someone from a more refined universe.

He got his passing power in his customary way, with a fast, easy centrifugal motion that is a cornerback's bane but a football fan's delight. Instead of bringing his arm back and then forward — and stepping forward to throw, as many passers do — Marino merely twisted his hips and upper body around and whipped the ball out in one stroke. It's a motion not unlike a shot putter's, or a golfer's, enabling Marino to uncoil so fast that, as usual, no viewer could really see it unless the picture was slowed down.

That is the Joe Namath passing motion, a form of which is also used by Dallas' Troy Aikman, Chicago's Jim Harbaugh and others.

No one today, however, comes closer to the pure Namath style than Marino, who, in fact, releases the ball faster than Namath could. Said Patriot Cornerback Lippett after three Miami touchdown passes won the game, 30-20: "They say Marino has been struggling, but we sure didn't see it. Nobody's sharper."

Nobody playing today, that is. As a passer, Namath, overall, was probably more effective. And at the short and middle ranges, the Joe Montana of 1988-89 was a match for any quarterback.

But to see the ball thrown with exceptional grace and precision this year, you must tune Marino in. Of the greatest passers of all time, he's the only one now playing.

HERSCHEL WALKER

LOS ANGELES: Oct. 23, 1990.

Herschel Walker, the 225-pound sprinter who has been turned into a jogger by the Minnesota Vikings, continues to be the most misunderstood football player of our time. A preposterous rumor — that Walker lacks courage — was brought into the open on national television Sunday by NBC Commentator O.J. Simpson. The truth is that as a running back, Walker has all the courage that Simpson ever showed in his NFL career. And to allege otherwise is to slander a veteran athlete irresponsibly.

Walker's problem is his style, or lack of style, as a ballcarrier. He could be an asset to any coach who knows how to use Walker's assets: his great speed and his aptitude for catching the ball. But as a conventional running back — on slashes or sweeps or when cutting in a broken field — he never has been more than ordinary.

Except for his extraordinary speed and sure hands, Walker, to give him the best of it, was no better than mediocre on conventional offensive plays at Georgia, or at Dallas, or in the USFL or anywhere else he has played football. Always faster than any defensive player on the field, he has often gained a lot of yards when loosed in the open, although, to this day, he doesn't know how to cut, change pace, hit a hole or attack a defensive player.

In short, he isn't an instinctive football player. Thus, when confronted by a defender dead ahead, Walker doesn't know what to do. And his indecision in head-to-head confrontations makes him *appear* to be flying a white flag.

The appearance is a lie. Nobody catches passes in a crowd more courageously than Walker. And no ballcarrier has ever carried more tacklers on his back, play after play, while struggling on. Virtually defenseless because of his style, Walker has taken more shots than probably any other active NFL player and has always come back for more. Simpson, one of the best running backs of all time, should know all that. His assault on Walker was shocking and embarrassing.

MARCUS ALLEN

LOS ANGELES: Dec. 17, 1986.

Halfback Marcus Allen's slashing twenty-eight-yard touchdown run to beat the Chargers in overtime November 20 at San Diego brought the Raiders to the high point of their season. It was one of Allen's greatest runs. It might have been a candidate for pro football's hundred best runs, or even the fifty best, considering Allen's bad ankle, and considering what it meant. For it put the struggling Raiders snugly on the heels of the Denver Broncos, who lost that week.

But since the night they left San Diego, the Raiders haven't won a game. They have been upset three times — by Philadelphia, Seattle and Kansas City. What happened? Here's an explanation that may fit:

The Raider team has been in a state of shock since Allen fumbled in overtime against the Eagles ten days after he had beaten San Diego in the same circumstances.

That was a gut-wrenching fumble, twisting almost certain victory into certain defeat, and putting Denver beyond reach in all but a mathematical sense. Before that fumble, the Raiders had overcome their 0-3 start this season. They had overcome the injuries that are still bothering their best offensive player, Allen, and their best defensive player, Howie Long.

In overtime against a team with a hot young quarterback playing his hottest game of the season, Randall Cunningham, the Raiders had overcome third and twenty at midfield. Quarterback Jim Plunkett, making a typical Plunkett clutch play, had scrambled and thrown to Allen twenty-seven yards down the sideline at the Eagle 20.

As of that moment, the Raiders had put their season back together. And, led by their persevering thirty-nine-year-old quarterback, they had gained the momentum for a final run at the fading Denver team.

It wasn't to be.

On second and six at the Eagle 16, when Allen fumbled, the Eagles brought it back eighty-one yards to the Raider four-yard line, using a rare, last-minute, tide-changing, long-distance fumble return to win with shocking ease.

The Raiders haven't been the same since. They can't rush a passer, they can't pass-block, they can't run, they can't even hold onto the ball. The bright future they glimpsed when they lined up on the Philadelphia 16-yard line that afternoon — in the enchantment of overtime — has been replaced by total darkness, indicating that the Raiders are as human as the rest of us. One play tore their hearts out.

7. Game XVIII: The Last Time the AFC Won

SINCE THE early 1980s, I have focused on tactical and strategic analysis at most big games, leaving the basic game story to other Times writers. Of the Super Bowl analysis columns I've written in that time, four are reproduced in this chapter. The column from Tampa, which examines the AFC's last Super Bowl winner, was, like the others, written immediately after the game for Monday's editions.

TAMPA, Fla.: Jan. 22, 1984.

For nearly three years, the National Football League's best-informed citizens have been saying this about the Washington Redskins:

They have built the league's finest team.

They've done it with mostly mediocre players.

It developed Sunday, however, that the Redskins are now no more than second best. In Super Bowl XVIII, the Los Angeles Raiders blew Washington's journeyman talent out of Tampa Stadium, 38-9.

As impeccably directed by Coach Joe Gibbs, the Redskins had incredibly won thirty-one of their most recent thirty-four starts with a unique combination of togetherness, enthusiasm and smoothness. They had led the league in these significant intangibles — making, by far, the NFL's fewest mistakes and turnovers — but when the Raiders could match them in the intangibles Sunday, it was all over. For the Raiders have the superior talent.

Their advantage in ability appears almost everywhere:

• Cornerbacks Lester Hayes and Mike Haynes are incomparably more gifted than the Redskin receivers they covered, Charlie Brown and Art Monk.

• Raider Receiver Cliff Branch is clearly more talented than Anthony Washington, the cornerback he beat on an important early touchdown.

• Marcus Allen of the Raiders is a halfback with multiple skills: he runs inside and outside, blocks, and catches passes. His opponent, John Riggins has only one skill: plugging.

• Raider Punter Ray Guy is an outstanding athlete who may have saved fourteen points with two plays that few other NFL kickers can make — leaping for a high snap (which he somehow held one-handed before getting the punt away) and making a last-man tackle on a punt-returner in the clear. By contrast, the famous Washington kicker, Mark Moseley, is an ordinary athlete who in the Super Bowl had the kind of trouble he's had all year.

• Finally, Quarterback Jim Plunkett of the Raiders has the ability to stand in the pocket, read the field, and, when his receivers come open, throw accurate bombs and touchdowns. His opponent, Joe Theismann, is a quarterback deficient in reading skills who must scramble to be productive — which tends to take his team out of its game plan. And when behind on the scoreboard, Theismann loses effectiveness by comparison with Plunkett or, say, Joe Montana.

In short, at almost every position, the Raiders have better football players than Washington's. Except for Riggins, who would team marvelously with Allen in anybody's lineup, there probably isn't a Redskin who could start for the Raiders.

II

It was the athletic excellence of Cornermen Hayes and Haynes that allowed the Raiders to blockade a high-scoring offense. The point is not that the Raider pair, playing Washington's receivers man-to-man, took them out of the game. The Raiders could have shut down the Redskin pair even more certainly with zone and combination coverages; even Raider Owner Al Davis, an incorrigible fan of man-to-man defense, will tell you that it isn't the best form of pass coverage. The real damage was done to the Redskins elsewhere. As Hayes and Haynes handled Washington's receivers single-handedly, the Raider defense immediately became immensely stronger overall.

On the plays when Brown and Monk were in the exclusive charge of Hayes and Haynes, the four of them, as Davis said, might as well have been sitting in the stands. Instead of an eleven-man game, it became a nine-man game. And because, on running plays, Quarterback Theismann merely handed off, the Raiders were bringing up nine defenders to fend off seven Washington blockers and converge on Riggins.

That's a two-man disadvantage, which for the Washington team was overwhelming. The Redskin running game excels in concept and execution, but it couldn't overcome a continuous two-man disadvantage at the points of attack. When the Raider rushing defense, thus fortified, could keep Riggins from gaining his usual yardage on first-down plays, the Redskins were thrown into a confused state that prevented them from playing their game.

The pressure went onto Theismann, who, it developed, is not skillful enough to carry a team against a Super Bowl opponent.

III

The difference between the quarterbacks was shown on two pivotal plays in the second quarter. First, Plunkett broke the game open with a fifty-yard bomb to Branch, setting up the touchdown that made it 14-0. Second, struggling to get back into the game, the Redskins marched seventy-three yards to the Raiders' seven-yard line, where, on third and three, Theismann unadvisedly threw down the middle to a Redskin who was double-covered, Halfback Joe Washington.

Two months ago, Theismann had delivered the same pass to beat the Raiders — but they have since changed their coverage on that play, placing two defensive backs on Washington. Because Theismann has difficulty reading defenses, he didn't see the second Raider. And when his pass fell incomplete, the Redskins settled for the only three points they were going to get until the game was clearly over.

It was also in the second quarter that the Raiders capitalized cleverly on the multiple talents of Running Back Allen for the decisive 21-3 touchdown. On that play, when the two Raider wide receivers both lined up left, Allen, the day's MVP, shifted forward to play wingback on the right side. Allen's move prompted Redskin Safety Mark Murphy to slide to that side, leaving Washington Cornerbacks Anthony Washington and Darrell Green to single-cover Branch and the Raiders' other wide receiver, Malcolm Barnwell. This was too much for, at least, Cornerman Washington, who had the closest view as Branch took Plunkett's twelve-yard slant pass for the touchdown.

One conclusion: Washington can't single-cover Branch. Another: as a pass receiver, Allen strikes fear into an opponent's heart, by comparison with Riggins, who on pass plays plainly doesn't.

The Redskins, one of the NFL's smartest teams, had won sixteen of eighteen this season by playing uninterruptedly smart football — but in Tampa Stadium, the Raiders took away their usual advantage in intellectual and strategic approach. And because their players are mostly discards from more richly stocked NFL teams, the Redskins proved easy to beat.

In defeat nonetheless, Washington Coach Joe Gibbs gained stature. For three years, he has been beating almost everyone else with this motley crew.

8. Super Bowl XXI: Coaching Wins Again

THE MAN who coached the New York Giants successfully in two Super Bowls, Bill Parcells, is famous for running the ball off tackle, for playing tough defense, and for talking tough football to win in the snows of the NFC East. The myth that the NFC owes its Super Bowl dominance to its toughness owes much of its currency to Parcells. The reality is that run-and-defense teams haven't won Super Bowls since the mid-1970s, and Parcells, though always a macho talker, knows that. It takes two things today — passing effectively and performing imaginatively — to make your way past the best teams in the playoffs and in the Super Bowls. In the two times that he has reached that eminence, Parcells, using his imagination overtime, has talked macho and won smart.

PASADENA: Jan. 26, 1987.

The truth is that the Denver Broncos lost a title game Sunday that they could have won from the better team — if they'd had a better plan. The decisive difference between these organizations, this time, was that the New York Giants were ready with the plays that had to be made to win it — the right passes and the right runs at the right times — and Denver wasn't. That settled Super Bowl XXI, which New York won, 39-20.

To be sure, the Giants went in as the stronger team, keying on a powerful defense led by Linebacker Lawrence Taylor. But they won not because they were stronger but because, as coached by Bill Parcells, they were smarter.

This was evident as early as the first quarter, when the Giants, on a long drive, came down to the Denver six-yard line. Though an off-tackle team this season, basically, on the goal line, the Giants, on the biggest play of the first quarter, passed the ball there. Passing on first down — when every Bronco on the field anticipated a run — they were ready with the play that virtually guaranteed the six-yard touchdown that swiftly materialized.

To encourage Denver's run expectations, Parcells that time sent in a second tight end, Zeke Mowatt, who lined up on the right side of their line and went in motion left. Then, as Quarterback Phil Simms faked a running play, Mowatt broke into the end zone and cut sharply back to his right. The Broncos, mystified, had nobody on him when Mowatt caught Simms' easy touchdown pass.

That's football. That's the kind of play good teams bring to the goal line of a big game.

In a similar spot later, by contrast, with time running out in the second quarter, the Broncos suffered a strategic brownout. After reaching the Giant 21, they ran predictably and futilely, on both first and second down, into the rough Giant defense. Left with third and five, the Broncos then threw a routine pass to Tight End Orson Mobley at the predictable five-yard distance, where the Giants had him routinely surrounded. A Denver touchdown there would have left the Giants in arrears, 17-9, at halftime. Instead, they trailed only 10-9.

II

In the third quarter, the Giants were again at the ready with the right play, the play they had to make to overhaul the Broncos. This one was a fourth-down quarterback sneak — not a garden variety sneak, but a special one: a sneak not previously seen in modern playoff history. It wasn't even the gamble that it seemed to be when Coach Parcells gave his team the green light to go for it. For it was a play with three essential components, all carefully executed, and, as a series, guaranteed to befuddle the Broncos:

• First, on fourth and one at the New York 46, the Giants lined up in punt formation with backup Quarterback Jeff Rutledge on the field as a blocking back.

• Next, Rutledge moved up under center, and, playing quarterback now, began a long count that made the Broncos, and almost everyone else, believe he was trying to draw them offside.

• Proud of themselves for adjusting to Rutledge's surprise move without flinching, the Broncos were still standing flat-footed when, just before time ran out, Rutledge took the snap and easily gained the needed yard.

Against a sophisticated pro defense, only the three steps, combined, insured success.

The change in momentum created by this one crafty play is hard to overestimate. After Rutledge had made his yard, the Giants drove easily and smoothly on to the go-ahead touchdown, 16-10. And, soon, en route to a rout, they were driving again as Parcells continued to reap the benefits of ingenuity.

For one thing, he introduced the Joe Morris role-change play. Positioning themselves for a helpful field goal, the Giants, who almost always run Halfback Morris to their right, ran him left — on a passing down. That time they anticipated, and got, a particular Denver nickel defense — one with a defensive back playing linebacker in the hole Morris hit. Defensive backs playing linebacker don't bother Morris. They don't, that is, until he has run for at least a first down. Morris' nine yards on that run made that field goal inevitable.

Then there was the Giant flea-flicker. Parcells still didn't have the game won when, on the next New York drive, he chose an ideal moment for a Morris-to-Simms-to-Wide Receiver Phil McConkey flea-flicker production that gained forty-four yards to the Denver goal line. The touchdown that followed put the Broncos on the airport bus. They'd still had some kind of chance when Simms unloaded. Afterward, they were through, 26-10.

All of this creativity on the part of the New York coaches contrasted sharply with the things that Denver's coaches did and didn't do. In the most dramatic moment of the first half — after Denver Quarterback John Elway had passed the ball to a first down at the New York one-yard line — Bronco Coach Dan Reeves chose to run the ball on three consecutive plays. In all there, as one of the greatest passers in NFL history kept handing off the ball, Bronco running backs lost five yards. Then their kicker missed the field goal.

This was a game that Elway played well enough to win. His passes in the first half alone earned what should have been a 24-9 lead at the break. It was only 10-9 because the Broncos, when in scoring position, kept taking the ball out of his hands, calling unimaginative runs that went nowhere instead of the imaginative passes that have made him famous. It could have been different in one critical respect: At momentum-changing time in the third quarter, the Giants, had they been two touchdowns behind, might not have had the courage to call that fourth-down quarterback sneak.

III

The change in Phil Simms in the last fifty-six days is probably the story of the year for the Giants, who have won seven straight times since December 1. That night in San Francisco when their quarterback turned the corner, they had dropped behind in a devastating first half, 17-0, before Simms' passing pulled it out, 21-17. Since that hour, intercepted only four times, he has delivered sixteen touchdown passes. "We've gotten a lot better in the last six weeks," Parcells said.

What happened?

"He's a very supportive coach," Simms said of Parcells, thinking, no doubt, of the early-season weeks when he was a five-for-twenty passer — when, that is, he was completing nearly five of every twenty passes. "He came up to me one day, and during the conversation said: 'I think you're a great quarterback. I know you're a great quarterback.' I was looking for support, and he gave it to me."

Simms had been wondering about that through the Giants' first twelve games, when, ignoring Simms, they usually gave Morris the ball on third and six or seven. But in the thirteenth game of their season, that wouldn't work. The Giants desperately needed Simms after falling behind San Francisco by seventeen. And when they called for him, he knew — or at least he believed — that he had Parcells' confidence. Hadn't Parcells told him he was a great man? Thus, in that blackest hour of the season for the

Giants, on the other team's field, the notorious Candlestick Park, Simms confidently pulled it out. And he has been playing All-Pro ball ever since. "Sure I told him he was a great quarterback," Parcells said. "And I meant it."

Whether he meant it is really irrelevant. For, as many coaches seem not to understand, self-confidence is much of the job for a quarterback, as much as half the job, some have said. So this was Parcells' Super Bowl. The difference was Parcells' coaching, his strategy, his tactics, his trick plays — and his understanding of the quarterback psyche. All the Broncos had was Elway.

9. Super Week XXVII: The New Cowboys

A PORTION of my Super Bowl XXVII report is the central section in the following three-story analysis of the 1992-93 champion Dallas Cowboys — the briefly dominant team that was coached by Jimmy Johnson and owned by the general manager, Jerry Jones. The first and third stories were written several days before and several days after Johnson's first Super Bowl. He and Owner Jones started closer than most, but split faster. The focus here is on the heights Dallas reached when they were a pair.

JOHNSON AND JONES

DALLAS: Jan. 11, 1993.

As the San Francisco 49ers head into another National Conference championship game this week in Candlestick Park, the surprise is that they have a new rival now, the Dallas Cowboys, who in the last three years have risen from a league-low 1-15 to a club-record 13-3. How did that happen so fast in the town that hasn't been heard from since Tom Landry was a youth? There seem to be three things to think about:

The coach who replaced Landry in Dallas, Jimmy Johnson, appears to be the NFL's best college talent scout since Bill Walsh (Exhibit A: Dallas Halfback Emmitt Smith).

Johnson is also proving to be an astute tradesman (Exhibit B: Dallas Defensive End Charles Haley, formerly of the 49ers).

The Johnson partnership with Owner Jerry Jones is working. (Exhibit C: Dallas 34, Philadelphia 10 in their playoff opener last week.)

Says Hall of Famer Sid Gillman: "It isn't every coach who can look at large groups of faceless college boys and say, 'We've got to have that guy,' meaning Jerry Rice, or, 'We can't get along without that one,' meaning Emmitt Smith."

Former 49er Coach Walsh chose Rice. Johnson chose Smith.

II

If talent evaluation is Johnson's edge, as it was Walsh's, there are two obvious personnel threads in the new Dallas organization, speed and youth. Johnson plainly wants fast men: His is already the fastest team in the league. And he isn't afraid of beardless youngsters: His is the youngest team in the league.

And so despite San Francisco's 14-2 this season, the 49er-Cowboy playoff Sunday has the look of a tossup. And if you want reasons to pick the Cowboys, here's one: Johnson has made more improvements in his team this season than 49er Coach George Seifert has made in his. At one position in particular, Johnson has jumped far ahead of the 49ers — who traded him their ablest, if angriest, defensive end, Charles Haley.

The 49ers would be an obvious favorite if Seifert still had Haley and Ronnie Lott, the safety who left for the Raiders when the 49ers failed to protect him in Plan B free agency. And it is Haley, an aggressive pass rusher, who gives the Cowboys a chance this year.

III

Last summer, shortly before the Cowboys' first game, Johnson made the two trades that gave him a Super Bowl defense, bringing in Haley and Pittsburgh Safety Thomas Everett. Any other coach could have done the same. It was Johnson who got it done, relying, as usual, on Owner Jerry Jones for the actual deal-making.

For in the larger perspective, it is the unique Johnson-Jones partnership that has given the Cowboys their advantage — so quickly — over most NFL opponents. No other team enjoys their unusual division of labor:

• The coach, Johnson, decides what new players he wants or needs.
• The owner and general manager, Jones, goes out and gets them.

From their first days with the franchise, Johnson and Jones have run the Cowboys with uncommon collegiality. Unlike any other coach in the league, for example, Johnson routinely accompanies Jones to meetings of club owners — even during training camp.

Player-acquiring general managers on other teams — though they have long backgrounds in pro football — are often plagued with doubts during the procurement process. They worry about whether they might be drafting a college player too high or too low, or whether, perchance, they are offering too little or too much in trade. On occasion, they back off when they should be bold, or plunge ahead when they should hold back.

Johnson, sometimes, might well have those doubts himself; but once he has come to a decision on any player, he is out of the loop. The rest is Jones' job. The owner, who puts his trust in Johnson's decisions, can put all his energy into getting results without worrying about the validity of those decisions.

In the Dallas organization, their working relationship helps take the insecurity out of trades. During any negotiation, when a proposition lands in Jones' target area, bingo, it's done. There was no possibility, for example, that Jones would be carried away by impetuosity in the days when he was dealing with Raider Owner Al Davis for Quarterback Steve Beuerlein. Sources close to that deal suggest that, well ahead of Jones' preliminary discussions with the Raiders, he and Johnson had decided on the upper and lower parameters of what the Cowboys would finally accept. That is their usual practice. In this two-stage system, happily for the Cowboys, Johnson never has a chance to second-guess himself, and Jones never has to adjust on the fly.

The basis for the partnership's success is the Johnson acumen, even though, as a former big-time college football player, Jones knows his subject. He knows as much about talent as many other general managers. His input is always in the study process in the Cowboys' front office.

But when you have Jimmy Johnson sitting there with his feet on the table, chewing a pencil and staring into space, why butt into the decision making?

HALEY'S DAY

ON THE eight-man panel that chose the Most Valuable Player of Super Bowl XXVII, there were six votes for Dallas Quarterback Troy Aikman. The two votes for Dallas Defensive End Charles Haley came from Sports Illustrated Writer Paul Zimmerman and me. What follows is the first section of my game analysis.

PASADENA: Feb. 1, 1993.

Some big games have to be saved before they can be won. And that's what happened in Super Bowl XXVII Sunday when Dallas Cowboys Defensive End Charles Haley made the turning-point plays in the first quarter.

In his most conspicuous effort, Haley moved from his usual station at right end to attack the Bills from the left. Confounding a good Buffalo offensive tackle, Howard Ballard, who apparently hadn't expected to see him on his side, Haley sacked Buffalo Bills Quarterback Jim Kelly into the fumble that was to put the Cowboys in front for keeps, 14-7.

But more than that — much more — Haley's aggressive play throughout the first quarter steadied the young, nervous Dallas team in the game's critical opening minutes. Although the Cowboys were a runaway winner eventually, 52-17, the Bills played the better football for most of the first quarter, when the Texas visitors, jumpy in their first Super Bowl, tried to give the game away.

It was in the game's fifth minute that the Cowboys suffered the blocked punt that led to a 7-0 Buffalo lead. They also drew two early penalties for fouling Buffalo unnecessarily. And otherwise, for nearly a quarter, they were still performing much the way you might expect of the league's youngest team in such a game as this.

Then Haley said, "Watch me."

He was the only Cowboy on the Rose Bowl field with extensive Super Bowl experience, which he had acquired as a San Francisco 49er. And, playing as alertly as he ever had in San Francisco, he provided the example that the Cowboys followed to victory.

Dallas Coach Jimmy Johnson had traded for Haley last summer just before the season began, when he also traded for Safety Thomas Everett, who made two sure-handed interceptions to help smash the Buffalo team in the second half. Everett helped. But without Haley the Cowboys might not have been in the game soon enough, or long enough, to win.

Seldom has an NFL trade meant more to two clubs than Johnson's for Haley. At the same time that it knocked the 49ers out, it eased the Cowboys in.

AIKMAN'S FIRST-DOWN PASSING

WELL BEFORE their first Super Bowl victory, the 1990s Cowboys were widely thought to be a power running team — and they've been known as that ever since. The national perception is that with Tailback Emmitt Smith pounding into opposing defenses behind a monstrous offensive line, the Cowboys rely on football's most intimidating running game. But the reality is something else. Since the day that Jimmy Johnson first brought this team to prominence, the Cowboys have been a West Coast, first-down passing team that only masquerades as an Eastern Division slogger. It is by combining quick, cheap, first-half passes with crushing second-half runs that they've won and achieved their reputation for devastating offense.

LOS ANGELES: Feb. 9, 1993.

The 1993 pro football season is closer than you think. There are only 155 days until training camp. And when the coaching staffs begin their serious planning this month, their role model could well be the NFL champion. To sports fans preferring lively football, that is a happy prospect. For the new champion is a Dallas Cowboys team that has developed one of the league's most aggressive passing offenses.

Thus, in last week's Super Bowl, when Dallas Quarterback Troy Aikman threw four touchdowns, he threw all four on first down. That was surely a big-game first — college or pro. Traditionally, football coaches have hesitated to be that assertive — or that rash, as they call it. They like to establish the run first, and *then* pass. The Cowboys don't establish anything. They just do it.

"That is the style of our coach [Jimmy Johnson]," Dallas Offensive Coordinator Norv Turner said recently. "His style is to be aggressive. We feel that you have to pass aggressively to pass successfully. You throw the ball on early downs to keep the heat off the quarterback — and to keep the defense from anticipating run or pass."

Other teams spend a lot of time practicing special offensive sets and substitution packages for second or third and long. Widely favored are shotgun formations with three or four wide receivers. But the Dallas coaches rarely substitute specialists. They play no shotgun, and, instead, spend their time and energy making sure they rarely get into third and long.

"As an offensive team," Turner said, "what you want to do is dictate to the defense. You want to throw the ball on a lot of first downs when the defense has to play the run *and* the pass, *both*."

Cowboy passes, which are usually short slant-in darts to Wide Receivers Michael Irvin and Alvin Harper or dumpoffs to Tight End Jay Novacek and Tailback Smith, are typically as simple as they are quick-hitting. Whenever the game is still on the line in the first half, half or more of Aikman's strikes are thrown to areas near, or even behind, the line of scrimmage.

"We're trying to stay out of second and ten," Turner said. "If a big gain isn't there on first down, we want Troy to dump it off to Smith or Novacek for four yards or so. That's as good as a run. People are always asking us why we bother to throw to Smith for a yard and a half. Our answer is that it's better than an incomplete. If the primary option isn't there, we dump it immediately because it's a chance to get some positive yards. Any time the ball is in Smith's hands, you have a chance at a big play."

When there *is* a first-down incomplete, Turner, on second and ten, often calls a run. Second and ten is a passing down; and with the defensive line rushing the passer, the Cowboys can usually wangle a few yards with one of their favorite plays, the lead draw. "You want Emmitt Smith running on passing downs," Turner said. The objective with such calls is to stay out of third and long. Turner argues that football's third-down conversion statistic is overrated. "The percentages are heavily against you when your quarterback is throwing on third and long," he said. "That is no measure of a team's passing ability. On third and long, the defense dictates to the quarterback."

The Johnson-Turner theories were showcased in the Super Bowl against Buffalo when the Dallas offense, en route to a 52-17 rout, produced five touchdowns — four with passes on running downs [first down] and one with a run on a passing down [third and ten]. They were scored in this order:

• First quarter, first down at the Buffalo 23, on the play after Smith gained eight yards: Aikman to Novacek, touchdown.

• Second quarter, first down at the Buffalo 19, on the play after Smith gained thirty-eight yards: Aikman to Irvin, touchdown.

• Second quarter, first down at the Buffalo 18, on the play after Buffalo Tailback Thurman Thomas fumbled: Aikman to Irvin, touchdown.

• Fourth quarter, first down at the Buffalo 45 on the play after Smith gained eleven yards: Aikman to Alvin Harper, touchdown.

• Fourth quarter, on *third* and goal after Buffalo Defensive End Bruce Smith sacked Aikman: Emmitt Smith, fake-pass draw play, touchdown.

"Even other coaches around the league don't seem to understand what we are doing," Turner said. "Maybe Emmitt Smith will gain 130 yards in a game, and I'll hear from people how we pounded another team on the ground. They don't seem to notice that Aikman had 195 yards in the first half while we were building our lead and Smith got 105 in the second half while we were protecting it."

As a pass-offense coach, Turner traces his lineage through Ernie Zampese to Don Coryell and Sid Gillman. But what he believes in is not passball but balance. "At Dallas," he said, "our players are capable enough in enough areas for us to be either a pure passing team or a pure power team. Both are our strengths. Everything we do starts with the threat of both."

It is a fact well-recognized by Turner and Johnson, however, that a well-balanced offense can hit the scoreboard faster with passes than with runs — faster and more often. "We pass a lot," Turner said. "And the best time to take a shot at a big play is first down."

That was illustrated most memorably in the most recent NFC title game, two weeks before the Super Bowl, when the Cowboys wrested from the San Francisco 49ers the honor of being the NFC's (and thus the NFL's) best. The Cowboys led that game by four points in the fourth quarter, but the momentum, after a long San Francisco touchdown drive, had switched to the home team.

After the kickoff, on first down at the Dallas 20, the 49ers had no idea that the Cowboys would throw aggressively. They foresaw a blast or two by the redoubtable Smith in defense of Dallas' small late-game lead. Accordingly, the 49ers lined up an eight-man defensive front, leaving the three remaining 49er defensive backs in man-to-man coverage.

"Aikman and I had just discussed such a possibility," Turner said. "We called a curl [hook] pass to Irvin, but I reminded Troy to take a shot at Harper if he got man coverage. To be honest with you, I expected the curl, but a slant to Harper is built into the play if the defense changes from zone to man. When Aikman saw the eight-man front, he immediately threw it to Harper."

The rest is very recent history. Harper, slanting in front of a 49er cornerback, caught Aikman's short, straight pass at about fifteen yards and continued on for another fifty-five to put Dallas in the Super Bowl. A 49er safetyman has been faulted for misstepping on the play, but in truth it was the first-down call that left the 49ers defenseless.

The quick-hitting nature of that pass was also typical of Dallas football. Johnson and Turner, from one end of the field to the other, aim for mostly one- to twenty-yard completions — rather than bombs. The short throws require assets which Aikman possesses in abundance. As Turner said, "We need a quick quarterback who can drop quickly, set up with urgency, and quickly deliver the ball."

That's Aikman.

10. Game XXX: First-Down Passing Wins Again

MOST OF those who in 1996 watched Super Bowl XXX in Arizona concluded that Pittsburgh Quarterback Neil O'Donnell blew it with interceptions. I saw something much different and said so the next morning in this Times analysis. To those who read the column, it couldn't have come as a surprise four days later when the Steelers fired their offensive coordinator.

TEMPE, Ariz.: Jan. 28, 1996.

Don't blame those interceptions on the passer. And don't credit the Dallas Cowboys' defense for winning Super Bowl XXX. What happened was this: The Pittsburgh Steelers' coaches asked more of their players than any football team could give.

Surprising almost everybody, the Steelers demonstrated Sunday that although the NFC has dominated the NFL for fifteen years, AFC players are at least as gifted as the NFC's. And as coached by Bill Cowher, the Steelers became a Super Bowl rarity in the game's second half: They never gave up.

Down by two touchdowns, they fought back wildly, and they could have won, should have won. Cowher's heart kept them in the game. But his head took them out.

On a 27-17 day, the Steelers lost because they're an unsound team offensively. They lost because in a comparatively short season, it's impossible for a pro club to master the multiple offenses their coaches want and used: a five-wide-receiver offense, four-wide-receiver offense, shotgun offense, power-running offense, quick-passing offense, dropback-passing offense.

And most obvious of all, they lost because, from first to last, their play selection was incomprehensibly faulty. This was a team that, for awhile, ran almost all the time. Then it tried to pass almost all the time. And the Cowboys, catching onto that pattern, eventually won easily with those intercepted passes.

Pittsburgh Quarterback Neil O'Donnell threw three interceptions on plays that were so certainly going to be passes that the Cowboys blitzed recklessly each time, destroying his aim. The first was a third-and-ten pass after the Steelers had sought unsuccessfully to run the ball. The second interception, materializing on second and ten, came as O'Donnell attempted to complete his sixteenth pass in a sequence of nineteen plays. On orders from his coaches, he kept going to the well, in other words, and Dallas, finally outguessing him, blitzed him into the game's decisive error. The last interception came on the game's meaningless last play.

II

The Cowboys won on the momentum and memory of what they used to be. They weren't the better team in this Super Bowl, but they called the better game, and they executed well enough because they have so often practiced the simple plays they still use in their same simple, repetitious system.

Scorning multiple formations as usual, Quarterback Troy Aikman took every handoff under center and, in the clutch, completed the first-down passes that were just enough to win:

- In the second quarter, he threw the first-down pass that Wide Receiver Deion Sanders carried into scoring position, where Tight End Jay

Novacek caught Aikman's touchdown pass — also thrown on first down.

• Then in the third quarter, after the first of Cowboy Cornerback Larry Brown's two interceptions, Aikman threw the first-down pass to Wide Receiver Michael Irvin that set up a short touchdown run that was to prove sufficient, 20-7.

On a day when Pittsburgh was as usual calling ground plays on first and other running downs — and calling passes on third and long and other passing downs — the Cowboys were as usual mixing up their plays admirably. That's the way they did it under former Coach Jimmy Johnson to win their first two Super Bowls. And they still remembered enough of that same sound system to win again.

And a good thing, too. For the Pittsburgh defense played well enough to bring the Cowboys down, taking Dallas Halfback Emmitt Smith, among others, out of the game. Nor was Dallas' coaching memorable. No self-respecting team is ever fooled on an onside kickoff.

III

It is clear now that the Steelers have the talent to come back next year and win this game provided, in the meantime, they improve their understanding of offense. If they don't blame O'Donnell for losing this one, if they bring him back, if they give him a more modern offense, they can in the next year or two end the NFL's Super Bowl monopoly. If in Miami Jimmy Johnson doesn't beat them to it.

The Steelers showed that any cornerback, even Deion Sanders, can be beaten on an inside pattern. All you have to do is get between him and the ball. They showed that O'Donnell has the pass delivery of a winner. And they showed that with Yancey Thigpen and others, they match most NFC teams in wide receivers. They've learned all that.

But they haven't learned that when you send out five receivers, you don't have anyone left to pick up the blitz. They've got to do something about that offense.

PART 3 MEDLEY

There is more to athletics than big games and prominent people. On another level, the interest in twentieth-century sports has led to all kinds of questions: Why does anyone want to climb a mountain — a killer mountain, say, the Eiger? What is football like on an Ivy League campus? What is fox hunting like today in California?

Happily, I have worked with a number of editors who thought about such things. One was Bud Furillo, a sportscaster now who, as sports editor of the old Herald-Examiner, first sent me to Europe.

Later, at the Los Angeles Times, I was for years privileged to work with a sports-assignment editor named Jack Quigg — whose curiosity was wider-ranging than that of anyone else I've known — and with other concerned editors: Bill Dwyre, Mike Kupper, Bill Shirley, Leonard Riblett.

The chapters that follow in Part Three reflect the variety of their interests as well as the assignments I initiated myself during this greatest of centuries for American newspapers.

X

EUROPE

Aboard airliners, Times reporters for many years were always ticketed first class; and after thirteen hours of front-cabin cocktails, breakfasts, cocktails and dinners, and a nap, my wife and I touched down in Athens, Greece, one day in April, 1975, to begin four and a half months on assignment in Europe. We had crossed the Atlantic occasionally in earlier years, but this time I had a story to write each week. The series was on sports and recreation in Europe, from dry-fly fishing at Winchester to dueling at Heidelberg, twenty-six installments in all. It was a series that continued for half the year, the longest in my time, and each story was featured on the front page of the sports section in the Sunday Times.

The first two installments were written on a little Greek Island — pretty, hilly Hydra. We took an apartment for a week on the second floor of a small hotel overlooking the bay; and as I worked there on the balcony each day, punishing the portable typewriter that was the computer of its time, my wife went out and got acquainted with the natives.

Starting in early May, I was based for three months in London, where the Los Angeles Times office was then on Fleet Street, a pleasant walk past St. James's Park from our summer home — or, in the rain, a pleasant ride on a big red London bus. For those spectacular three months, our home was a three-floor flat on Eaton Square, in Belgravia, near a similar household where a British production company was then making a popular TV series about an English lord, his family and their servants: "Upstairs, Downstairs." Like theirs, our butler's room and the kitchen were in the basement.

That summer I worked a seven-day week. Starting each Monday, Marnie and I spent five days on research missions, taking the train to Wales or Heidelberg or Scotland or the bus to Wimbledon. On Saturday, back at Eaton Square, I struggled through a first draft in an upstairs bedroom that I had converted into an office. As always, the research was great fun, the first draft was hell, and the final draft each Sunday was a breeze.

Mondays after breakfast were for walking the finished draft to the Belgravia post office three blocks away. There, before taking off on a new research excursion, I mailed the copy to Los Angeles in care of the Times editor in charge, Jack Quigg. In a summer when I used the Fleet Street office only for interviews and long-distance research calls, Quigg and I relied on the mails exclusively and never missed a deadline.

For recreation that summer, in the daylight hours, we inspected London. After dark there were plays and, quite often, dinner-dancing, usually at hotels near the Thames, once with overnight house guests from Los Angeles, tennis-playing friends Bob and Jeanne Mueller. We found one thing not to like about England. No paddle-tennis courts could be found.

1. Ancient Greece: Where It All Began

AS WESTERNERS, we originated in Greece. The question is, in fact, have we caught up with our origins?

DELPHI, Greece: April 12, 1975.

Let's say you're planning to spend four or five months in European countries comparing their sports with America's. Where would you begin? One likely place is Greece. This is where organized sports began.

The world was all work and no play until twenty-eight or thirty centuries ago, when, surprisingly, the people of this land originated a remarkably sophisticated program of competitive athletics. At about the same time, of course, they originated many other things. Greece was the beginning of nearly all that is worthwhile in Western civilization: the first democracies (including Athens), the first great scientists and philosophers (Pythagoras, Socrates), the first sculptors (Phidias), the first literary giants (Homer, Aeschylus), the first orators (Demosthenes, Pericles), and more.

Unhappily, the full flowering of ancient Greece — in sports, arts and politics — was a brief phenomenon compressed into not much more than two hundred years, 600 to 400 B.C. All too soon, the many splendid athletic stadiums of the Greeks were wrecked, one after another, by the religious fanatics who for centuries blacked out the world.

Not until 1500 A.D. was there a revival of Greek ideals and refinements, which, that time around, were visible first in arts and literature with the European Renaissance. Democracy, the imaginative political invention of the Greeks, returned next, distinguishing the final decades of the eighteenth century.

Only in the late nineteenth century did the world begin to play again, when, once more, it was inspired by ancient Greece. Indeed, it still is.

II

At a museum in Olympia, home of the original Olympic games, there is a reproduction of the Olympia that used to be. Incorporating temples, theaters and many other structures, the model is necessarily large — but not large enough to include the Olympic stadium, which as the guide notes laconically is "off to the side." Clearly, games were only part of what they had in old Olympia.

Outdoors on the historic Olympic grounds, however, the visitor makes a blithe discovery: Behind the ruins of all the statues and the many colonnaded structures, the old stadium is still there, doubtless looking much as it did when the last sprinter pulled up in 394 A.D.

The place was built without seats. Around the field, earth is still piled up on four sides to form sloping embankments where crowds of up to forty thousand once sat on the grass. As a stark reminder of the action that once was, the old, long, thin marble starting and finishing lines are still in place — with carved incisions for the toes or heels of twenty starters abreast.

The field is a narrow rectangle, twice as long as an American football field and half as wide. The basic event, a sprint on a 200-yard straight, was first won in 776 B.C. by a chap named Koryvos. The distance is a chance result of the planning (or lack of planning) by the first stadium architect either at Olympia or Delphi. In any case, the distance was soon known as a stadion (hence stadium).

Longer races were multiple stadions. Modern racing around a turn is a refinement, or handicap, due to the shorter soccer and football fields of a different era. The oldest measured mark in track and field, as chiseled into an Olympia stone, is the equivalent of 23 feet, 1 1/2 inches, the winning long jump of Chionis. That was in 656 B.C.

Koryvos, Chionis and their rivals and descendants moved onto the Olympic stage through a ground-level tunnel that resembles the Coliseum tunnel in Los Angeles, passing on the way small statues the Greeks called Zannes — models of the god Zeus. These were built with money exacted in fines from the handful of athletes who cheated.

The athletes entered the stadium nude. All competition was in the nude. On other kinds of fields, Greek infantry — encouraged by the friendly, California-like climate (Athens enjoys three hundred days of sunshine annually) — fought their famous wars nude. Except for shields. The Greeks, it is plain, were the first streakers — male Greeks, that is. Only two groups were forbidden participation in the annual festivals: undesirables (slaves, convicts and the like) and women. There were times when women had their own Olympics, but they weren't allowed even as spectators at men's events.

In those centuries it was the male body, not the female, that was glorified. Shocking Americans raised on Playboy magazine, the marble representations of girls and women on extant Greek statues, columns, friezes and coins are clothed with overwhelming decency from throat to ankle. By contrast, the men in the statues are everywhere nude. That was an age when the male body was admired and celebrated as never before or since.

Individuals winning Olympic events were also admired and celebrated. As winners, they became, in fact, instant professionals. For, monetarily, it was immensely rewarding to be an Olympic champion in ancient Greece.

Though the contestants lined up as amateurs, competing for wreaths of celery leaves and other native foliage, the athletes who won were embraced royally in their native city-states by grateful neighbors. Winners rode home in white chariots pulled by white horses, trappings of a champion, and went on the state's payroll for life.

Thus it was inappropriately misleading to call the ancient Olympics amateur festivals, as the late Avery Brundage and other American Olympic officials did for years, financially injuring generations of twentieth century athletes. The Brundage view of history is both revisionist and incomplete.

A major league athletic contest in the ancient era was an amateur event only for the losers — which is about the way things are today.

III

You can still see the playgrounds of the ancient Greeks up and down the length of Greece: in the Nemean valley, at Corinth and Olympia, at Athens — then as now the first city of Greece — and elsewhere. On a panhellenic scale, the old Greeks had four great quadrennial festivals, one each year, but only one at Olympia. Most impressive are the playing fields of Delphi, near the Gulf of Corinth, which separates Greece into a mainland and a large island-like peninsula to the south, called Peloponnesus.

Some twenty-six hundred years ago, Delphi was built into the side of a graceful, forested mountain on the northern shore of that gulf. With a moderate climate and mountain vistas, it is one of the world's most favored places. Reportedly, in the beginning, the god Zeus loosed two eagles with instructions to find the "center of the universe" and both landed here.

A short six miles in from the water, Mt. Parnassus rises majestically and, today, tier on tier, the stately ruins of Delphi rise with it. At the bottom, in a valley, the citizens of old Delphi and their neighbors alternately raced horses and chariots. On the first tier of the mountain, they worshipped at the temple of Apollo. Up the road on the next tier, they strolled to the theater of Delphi, a handsome semi-circular outdoor bowl whose seven thousand white-stone seats are mostly still in place. On the highest tier is the sports stadium, seating five thousand in rows of stone seats that have also, for the most part, incredibly survived.

The most significant thing about all this, and the most unusual when compared with life in twentieth century America, is that life in ancient Delphi was extensively integrated and coordinated. Religious and cultural activities were synchronized with sports events both here and in all the old Greek city-states. And it is this integration of their affairs that most certainly sets apart the ancient Greeks from modern Americans.

In a 1970s U.S. community, the Santa Anita race track is in one suburb, the Hollywood Bowl in another. Spotted in other neighborhoods are Dodger Stadium, the city hall, and the cathedral. Here, by contrast — as at Olympia and the other Greek shrines — the religious, cultural, governmental and sports sites were combined in a setting about the size of Exposition Park in Los Angeles. The three largest Delphi structures, church, theater and stadium, are physically and thus symbolically linked.

In part, this merger resulted from travel imperatives. An Athenian who made the long trip to Delphi for the theater, or to hear great religious music, might as well stay for the races. He didn't worry about hotel space because most visitors camped out.

But travel factors were never the prime cause of the cultural synthesis. The central reason, as the inscriptions on numerous old monuments make plain, was the character of the citizens of old Greece. Their objective was full participation: the well-rounded man.

It's a commentary on the nature of their fairs or festivals that they were called games, a Greek term meaning contests in poetry, music and other arts as well as athletic and equestrian contests. And at game time, routine life in the city-states virtually stopped.

For years, any citizen assaulting another during the Olympics, except in prescribed contests, was barred from the games ever after, a fate worse than death.

Plato and Aristotle were regulars at Olympia. As late as 63 A.D., after the Roman conquest, Emperor Nero won the Olympic chariot race. He liked the place so much he built a house there. Attending as contestants, citizens of the various states became spectators when eliminated in the early rounds of the flute, javelin, or other contests, or the races, foot, horse, or chariot.

During the festivals that were the Olympic games of the ancient era, sports weren't the only attraction or even the main event. At Delphi the attention-getter was the oracle, the voice of a priestess presumably speaking the mind of Apollo, whose prophecies influenced Greeks for centuries. At Olympia the principal attraction was Phidias' ivory-and-gold statue of Zeus, father of the gods, a statue so perfect that before cracking up under the blows of religionists of other persuasions, it made the most famous of the all-time teams: the seven wonders of the world.

The Greeks wanted it all at once, and, by prominently coordinating their sports and cultural facilities, they were encouraging all free men to participate — in everything, including politics — on the major league level.

Willingly, joyfully, until age sixty sometimes or even longer, most Greek citizens competed in everything. Most entered playwriting contests, read poetry aloud to one another, sang to one another, competed in flute and lyre, built and raced boats, played chicken in speeding chariots, boxed, wrestled, bred and raced horses, and raced on foot. They threw the javelin and discus together, boxed and wrestled, and invented the relay race, one of their few team sports.

In an interview at the University of Athens, Dr. Spyriden Papaspyropoulos, the director of studies, tells you: "The ancient Greeks believed that human beings are three things in one — mind, body, and spirit — and that all three should be developed equally. Therefore, in school, they spent as much time on music as mathematics, and they boxed and wrestled as often as they competed in words (debating).

"Their ideal," Papaspyropoulos says, "was the man of well-balance: the sound mind in the sound body. They loved sports, they played hard, but they also studied hard. Many of their best poets, musicians, and writers of plays were also great soldiers and great athletes. Their best writer of history (Thucydides) was an Athenian general."

To UPI Bureau Chief John Rigos, an Athens-born student of the ancient era, there was also a key political extension. "The games were the United Nations of antiquity," Rigos says. "City-state councilmen all got together every time. They went to compete, and stayed to talk. The annual festivals at Delphi, Olympia and other places were a substitute for war, not always, but often."

IV

Why Greece? How did it happen that the Greeks invented games? And why, after a run of a thousand years, did the Olympics disappear?

Most explanations take politics as well as religion into account.

To begin with, the Greeks could develop into major leaguers — the world's first — because they had the first leisure class of sufficient size. Until 1000 B.C. or thereabouts, every human society, including theirs, had been structured as a despotism, with a tyrant and a few nobles plus untold thousands of workers and slaves. Most nations continued in that condition. Some are still there.

Ancient Greece, however, for various reasons that aren't all fully understood even in modern Greece, evolved differently. By 800 B.C., it was becoming a land of sovereign city-states, each ruled not by a monarch but by a group of citizens — aristocratic citizens who had wrested power from the despots. In many of these city-states (Sparta notably excepted) the political evolution continued until a democracy enfranchised all adult male citizens.

With a sound economy and an abundance of slaves for all their mean and repugnant work in an otherwise egalitarian society, numbers of Greek citizens were left with time on their hands. Energetic, creative, affluent and fun-loving, they wanted to play, and they had the means to play magnificently.

Even so, they were not, in their world, the only people with the energy and means for games.

In the decades when the Greeks first started racing for celery and other plant life, the Egyptian civilization was already thousands of years old. Why didn't the Egyptians make time for sports?

At the University of Athens, Dr. Minos Kokolakis, professor of ancient literature, has a one-word answer: Religion. "If you go back far enough," Dr. Kokolakis says, "Egypt and Greece started along the same path — with religious games honoring their heroic dead. They chanted funeral dirges and so forth. And when the Greek path diverged from Egypt's, both peoples continued to honor dead heroes. But the Egyptians had strong kings (pharaohs) and powerful priests who wanted to build better tombs (pyramids) for their kings. The Greeks wanted to sing better songs.

"In Greece," Kokolakis notes, "they began competing to see who could sing their gods and heroes the best songs. From there it was a short step to who could run fastest and jump farthest in tribute to the gods." The UPI's Rigos sums up: "As they say, a tomb in Egypt, a stadium in Greece."

The Egyptians were apparently never in any danger of inventing competitive sports. For centuries, their whole population, highborn and low, was preoccupied with a religion of death. Thus, the Egyptian hoped to find the good life in the next world, whereas the Greek rejoiced in his life in this one.

The Egyptian was subjugated by a mighty despot supported by a large, single-minded organization of aggressive priests, whereas the Greek, putting his faith in democracy, put his priests as well as his athletes in their place. "There were so many gods in ancient Greece," Rigos says, "that they couldn't all be offended by sports events."

Kokolakis' research shows there was never any all-powerful church establishment in ancient polytheistic Greece as there was in Egypt and other civilizations earlier, and in Rome and other civilizations later. A modern visitor walking idly among the ruins of the old Greek city-states can see that it didn't much matter to their residents whether gods or athletes were in the center ring. In some cities, as in Athens, the temple was geographically and symbolically the crowning edifice, relegating the stadium and a theater or two to a lower road. By contrast, at Delphi and other places it was the stadium or a theater that crowned the community.

Moreover, inscriptions on the beautiful old Greek temples, many conceived by the philosopher Plato, are secular, not religious. Two have come ringing down the centuries: "Know thyself" and "Nothing in excess." Those were the scriptures, the reminders, the challenges that encouraged the ancient Greek to shape up for the discus throw as well as the poetry competition — to know himself in as many dimensions as possible, but to go overboard in none. For as long as it lasted, it made for an exciting little world.

V

As the visitor can tell by standing on the blank spot at Olympia where Phidias' great golden Zeus once stood, the polytheistic Greeks couldn't keep their civilization going. Their Olympics spanned a millennium in various forms, but the heyday was the two-century period ending in 404 B.C., when Athens, the spirit and symbol of ancient greatness, lost an ill-advised war against Sparta. For awhile, Greece's sporting traditions were continued in a derivative, sometimes degenerate, style by the old Romans, who, too often, promoted and enjoyed sporting contests that were contests in cruelty, frequently to the death. And, shortly, even these ceased.

Says Rigos: "The church in the early Christian era — the monastic establishment especially — was opposed to bodily things like sports. The monks didn't go along with the earlier Greek ideal of mind-and-body soundness. That had a heathen ring to them, and they opposed whatever they considered heathen."

It was in 394 A.D. after Rome conquered Greece — and Christianity conquered the Roman Empire — that the remnant versions of the ancient Olympics finally ended. Suppressed by a succession of Roman emperors and other authority figures, the games, from one century to the next, were hardly a memory.

For more than a thousand years, no organized athletic activity, anywhere, could withstand the world's all-powerful establishment forces.

Significantly, the eventual rebirth of sports was accompanied by the rise of the modern university in England and America. In recent decades, university emphasis on intellectual inquiry over religious faith has paralleled the revival of interest in physical prowess. The underlying explanation for the sports boom of the twentieth century is that the modern world has reproduced two essential components of the old Greek world: enough free thinkers to successfully challenge established beliefs and a free society with the leisure for games.

On the present massive U.S. scale, sports are approximately as new as airplanes, having originated in the 1920s. Though the age of American baseball, football, and basketball seems timeless to us, and endless, it effectively began only about the time of Babe Ruth. Brief as it is, there has been nothing to compare with it anywhere, since humanity emerged from the caves, except for one short spell in the land of Zeus.

2. Vienna: Sports in a European City

THE GREEK ideal of the well-rounded man has, in modern Europe, shattered into extremes of specialization. Academic learning and skilled sports on the European continent have now become completely separate activities carried on in widely different subcultures. The European approach to sports helps, in fact, to make America's uneasy marriage of academics and athletics seem more civilized.

VIENNA, Austria: May 4, 1975.

Major league football in both Europe and America begins with what happens on the playgrounds of the elementary schools. The best of those who star in pickup games rise eventually to the majors. But the way they get there is radically different on the two continents:

• An American pro football player is almost always a high school graduate with a background of four years in college. For most of his life he has been — if incongruously — a celebrity in the academic world.

• In Vienna — which is typical of Europe, where football is what Americans call soccer — the professional player is a career athlete whose years of formal education cease in the eighth grade. After age fourteen he seldom sets foot in a classroom. Indeed, the high school graduate on a European soccer team today is about as rare as the high school dropout who makes good in American football.

"Our athletes are all undereducated," Ferdinand Wimmer, an Austrian editor, observes. "For example, Austria's leading skiers and soccer players all lack higher education. And these are the nation's favorite athletes. Franz Klammer, our best skier, was fourteen when he finished school. Anne Marie Proell-Moser, the finest woman skier in the world, finished school at fourteen. It's the system."

Wimmer, a veteran of more than twenty years on Vienna news desks, defines the problem this way: "For youngsters of average intelligence, there isn't time in an Austrian high school for both homework and sports, particularly fussball (soccer) or skiing. So instead of high school, which we call gymnasium, athletes attend Hauptschule — a vocational school. Among the boys and girls of high school age in Austria, about half go to Hauptschule and half gymnasium — unless they want to become athletes. Virtually all of those take the vocational way."

In all, eight grades of education are compulsory in Austria. The first four are called Volkschule. Then after competitive examinations, Viennese students diverge to spend either eight years in gymnasium or four years in Hauptschule. If they qualify for gymnasium, they can still choose Hauptschule, instead, and learn typing, perhaps, or printing, as well as football.

In either case, while still in fourth grade, they make an all but irrevocable life-determining decision.

"On school days," Wimmer says, defining the old-world system, "classes end at 1 or 2 p.m. A gymnasium boy must go home and study. He has much more homework than any Hauptschuler, or any American. A Hauptschule boy can play soccer all afternoon, if he wishes, and if good at it he probably does."

Thus by the fifth grade at the latest, when he is ten or twelve years old, an Austrian with either a talent for or an interest in athletics is already spending his time learning to be a pro athlete — or at least aiming for a career as a pro athlete — with no real understanding of what that means or what's ahead.

II

Though they may be heedless of their environment, Vienna's boy athletes work out in one of Europe's most beautiful cities. One-time capital of the Austro-Hungarian empire, Vienna is a city of clocks, castles, music, and streetcars, of tree-lined boulevards and winding streets. The beauty of the inner city is in the graceful trees and the many large baroque stone buildings of the former empire, including the palace and opera house, which are linked to Vienna's suburbs by one of the most efficient streetcar systems in the world.

It is the fleet of streetcars — narrow-gauge, electric, red, fast and numerous — that brings the young athletes together. Within thirty minutes after school is out, regardless of how far they have to come, they're on the city's soccer-football grounds. And to those watching them in action, it is evident that soccer is already a way of life for many ten-year-old Vienna Hauptschulers.

No organized sports are visible in or near the gymnasiums or Hauptschulen — and this is another striking difference between Austria and America. The pomp and circumstance of high school athletics in the United States, involving a high percentage of non-athletes, are entirely absent here. There are no marching bands or manly yell kings or short-skirted song girls or attractive cheerleaders and majorettes or big, noisy teen-age crowds. To a European man or woman, sports and school plainly go together like sausage and candy. It never occurs to a citizen of Vienna to connect the two.

III

The Viennese of this century have developed, instead of high school football, a multiple-division web of soccer teams that may either be pro or amateur but are unrelated to any school system. On the lowest levels (or divisions) of Austrian soccer, the color and excitement of American football are sometimes missing. But athletically, the clubs, which resemble the sports clubs in other European cities, are effective. Here are some aspects of their way:

Some fifty soccer clubs lie within the city limits of Vienna, which, housing one-fourth of the country's seven million residents, dominates the flat east end of Austria. There are also swimming clubs here as well as handball clubs, ski clubs and others for athletes age ten to sixty. Of the soccer clubs, which enter teams in both the major and minor leagues, three play first-division professional soccer in Austria's ten-team federal league. Others compete in second, third and lower divisions.

Most clubs are amateur, but all, including those competing professionally in soccer, enter teams in all soccer leagues at every age level from ten to over-thirty. For instance, Vienna's best pro team (Rapid/Wien) is represented by farm teams not only in the federal soccer league but also in every Austrian youth league. Scouts for each club, Rapid particularly, recruit aggressively on Austrian playgrounds, signing players ten years old and up. Thenceforth, as regular members of the club, these youngsters practice football under professional coaches four times a week. This means, among other things, that a European soccer scout has one of the worst jobs in sports. Picture an NFL coach, Chuck Knox, say, evaluating ten-year-old guards and tackles. Or think of the Dodgers drafting their 1990 catcher this summer out of grade school.

At an age when American boys are just going out for fullback or defensive end in high school, Viennese youths are skilled veterans who, besides, keep improving faster than Americans. An Austrian lad has year-round coaching and training that appear to be more intensive and extensive than that offered in America by most Pop Warner and other youth programs.

This year, the captains of three first-division European soccer teams — one of them based in Austria — are eighteen, the age at which American athletes are beginning four years of college football.

IV

If, for qualified athletes, sports are overemphasized in Austria — and in Europe generally — life is much different for Viennese high school students whose athletic ability is average. Although they take some exercise in gym class, prep students here play few games, and compete in few sports. And this may account for a nationwide sedentary tendency among those not actively involved in any sport club. In Austria, it often seems, the national pastime is sitting, talking, eating, and imbibing beer. As a way of life, that has its attractions — but not if accompanied, among overweight people, by a lack of respect for those who appreciate physical activity and physical fitness.

A century or so ago, this was discovered by Austria's Empress Elizabeth, an accomplished horsewoman who was roundly criticized in Vienna for two eccentricities: her rigid, low-calorie diet and her morning exercises at the bars and rings. In her dressing room here in the Hapsburg family's massive palace, her exercise bars and rings are still in place. They helped the beautiful Elizabeth to be for a time the best woman athlete in her realm — and doubtless always the slimmest. When assassinated at age sixty-one, she was wearing a dress which, as laid out in her bedroom today, appears to be about a size six or eight.

Much of the Viennese population needs at least twice that much dress today, and, in fact, the Ministry of Education has lately isolated two major Austrian problems: the athletes are undereducated and the nonathletes are out of shape. "We know what's wrong," says Dr. Robert Mader of the ministry, a former professor whose office is across the street from that of another former Vienna University professor, Sigmund Freud. "The dichotomies aren't good. We're trying to find the best possible combination of school education and physical education."

One experimental new response is a Sportsschule, in which students get the regular Austrian gymnasium (high school) education plus intensive instruction in one sport, usually skiing. They live at school and concentrate on books and skis. In a Vienna suburb, one Sportsschule offers swimming. In time, such schools may well benefit the saddest of Vienna's lost souls, the failed soccer players who at age ten opted for sports and against high school. Today, they are neither educated nor athletic.

A vote for Sportsschulen comes from Norbert Hof, thirty-one, a career athlete who captains Rapid/Wien after beginning his soccer career at eight and turning pro at thirteen. Hof is an Austrian anomaly. Because his older brothers strongly urged him to choose gymnasium over Hauptschule, Hof is one of the few high school graduates in European soccer. Tall, slim and serious, he also attended Vienna University for awhile. "In gymnasium," he says, "it was a bit difficult playing football and keeping up with my studies. But college worked out nicely. The hours and opportunities are such that a lot of professional athletes would go to college if they could go to high school first. They're bright enough. It's too bad they must leave school in the eighth grade to have a professional career." In sports today, that is Europe's challenge.

3. Switzerland: Climbing the Eiger

I'VE NEVER really understood mountain climbers. And that was long before I ever saw the Eigerwand.

KLEINE SCHEIDEGG, Switzerland: July 5, 1975.

Were an impartial observer to compile a list of the seven wonders of the modern world of sport, he or she might start with a half dozen American phenomena — Dodger Stadium, no doubt; the Augusta National golf club, perhaps; the New Orleans Superdome, the Indianapolis Speedway, Muhammad Ali, and, of course, the Pittsburgh Steelers' defensive team. The seventh wonder of sports, however, is possibly in Europe. It's the Swiss mountain known as the Eiger.

Though not the tallest mountain in the Alps, the Eiger is the angriest. From the 1930s, when it first was climbed, to the late 1960s this was one of the most dangerous places on earth. The Eiger's mile-high north wall, which rises abruptly out of the back yard of a hotel here in this Alpine village, has killed forty-one mountain climbers in the last forty years.

In the 1970s, happily, life tends to be safer here. Improved tools and techniques — particularly the more general use of strong pitons, metal hats, and other metal — have lately made a perilous sport less hazardous on all continents. The Eiger has been conquered more than a hundred times in recent years, and, theoretically, it has come within the range of an estimated two hundred to three hundred of the world's top climbers. Even so, only a few are ever seen in Kleine Scheidegg. They tend to keep their distance for two good reasons: the bizarre local weather problem (sudden, mighty blizzards all year round) and the geological problem (the peculiarities of the Eiger's north wall.)

German climbers call it the Mordwand — murder wall. To the Swiss, it is the Eiger Norwand, or Eigernorwand, or, simply, the Eigerwand. And like Dodger Stadium or Mean Joe Greene, it has to be seen to be believed. As inspected from a respectful distance, the Eigerwand stands erect, the only grim, black mountain in a sea of white mountains: a high, wide, concave thing measuring six thousand feet up from a seven-thousand-foot shelf.

The closer you get to it during a walk through the Alps, the tougher it looks. The top half bulges out like the eye of a monstrous fish, and the bottom half, winter or summer, is normally glazed with ice. It's a freak of nature that faces almost due north, so the ice doesn't melt. And the wall drops straight off, so the snow doesn't cling, except in a few gleaming streaks.

Everything you can see seems to be telling you: don't touch.

II

On the eve of another climbing season in Europe, some Eiger tales:

• In the 1930s, the Eiger killed the first nine men who attempted to climb it. No one even tried until 1934, when the late Adolf Hitler offered a gold medal at the 1936 Olympics to the first man up. The medal was never claimed. Not until 1938 was the Eiger conquered, and the score, as recently as 1947, was still Eiger 9, man 1. In 1965 there was a 1-1 tie (one climb, one killed). The 1966 result was also a tie, 1-1. Tipping the scales at last, the human race scored a clear-cut 1968 win, 2-0, and it has won annually since.

• As the highest limestone mountain in Europe, the Eiger is unavoidably unstable. One of last year's climbers said: "The rotting limestone keeps breaking loose, and it falls on you in torrents." Said another: "You risk death from falling rocks just standing at the base looking up."

• The worst hazard is the weather, which is moody and mercurial. This is the 1970s deterrent. On a bad day, the Eiger offers perhaps the worst weather in the civilized world. On a beautiful summer afternoon, it can become dead winter in less than an hour. Tactically, the problem is that the north wall can't be traversed laterally to areas of safety. If a sudden turn in the weather traps an Eiger climber after he has passed the point of no return — whence there's no safe way back — he's dead, literally. Left or right, there's no way to go. There's no way down, of course — and no way up through the avalanches, the chill waterfalls, and the falling rocks that distinguish a heavy snowstorm here when the wind is blowing fifty miles an hour.

• The reason for "Eiger weather" is the Eigerwand's exposed position as the northern terminal of the famous Swiss Alps. A storm blowing down onto this continent from the Arctic north breaks first across the Eiger, often without warning. The best place to be at such a time is the hotel bar. The worst is at the end of a rope, dangling off the Eigerwand.

• In the Eiger community, mountain climbing becomes a spectator sport. It is this aspect that, finally, makes the Eiger unique. From the meadows near the foot of the great wall, the crowds can watch a climber all the way up — if the weather holds, and if he gets there. The possibility of a hand-to-hand war in a storm attracts visitors from throughout the world each summer.

III

In Zurich, a Swiss mountain-climbing expert named Constant Cachin, an army captain, acknowledges a mild distaste for the people called Alpwatchers or Eiger-birds. "Occasionally," he says, "you get the feeling they're simply waiting for something to happen. Like they say about people who go to auto races, they're hoping, but not daring to say it out loud, that a car will go into a wall or flip over."

The accuracy of the analogy is to be doubted, but not the show. An Eigerwand climb is unmistakably good theater. And it's likely to remain so indefinitely because the auditorium is unique. The Eiger's north wall rises sharply, vertically, a stone's throw from the back windows of an old hotel. Kaspar von Almen, the man who owned the hotel earlier in the century, built here because: "The north wall is the classical Alpine theater, a vertical stage open to anyone with normal eyesight and a pocket telescope."

This describes his place today. The wall is still a perpendicular stage, and the audience still gathers on the terraces and the lush, green yards of von Almen's hotel to watch the climbers through telescopes. Except for the quirk that the view is up instead of down, it's much like watching a play through opera glasses from a top row in the Vienna opera house.

With the naked eye the actors are fleas, but they're there.

IV

The Eiger modern modus operandi:

On a clear day, the expedition gets up and on the road at 2 a.m., and, using the latest metal equipment, the climbers proceed carefully to a level just below the point of no return — which is about halfway up. At that point, mountain climbers have learned, it is more dangerous to turn back than carry on. Nobody who turned back there, in a storm, has ever lived to talk about it. So that's the place to pause for a final evaluation of the weather.

If it's fogging a bit, or sometimes if there is just a cloud or two in the distance, they retreat to the hotel, order a round of beers and wait for another pleasant morning. If it's clear, they race up the piton road as fast as they can, hoping to reach the summit before the weather shifts.

The trip takes about two days, overall, a good long show for the crowd below.

V

For mountain climbers, the Eiger is one of many venues — the world's most challenging, it may be, but otherwise just another hill. For the spectator, however, it provides a spectacular weekend. At an elevation of 7,010 feet, the village of the Kleine Scheidegg — which means little pass — is a mountain complex of five buildings, including the railroad station. And getting here is half the fun. You have two choices. You can walk or board the cog railroad. That's the only way to ride the fifteen miles up the mountain from Wengen, a pleasant Disneyland-like town so entrenched in the Alps that automobiles can't get there, winter or summer. What a blessing.

Switzerland indeed is the last best refuge of the train freak. There are, for instance, 241 railroad trains a day in and out of Interlaken, a typical Swiss city. From Zurich to Kleine Scheidegg through Interlaken, a distance of a hundred miles or so, you change trains three times. Each time a new train crew is waiting to whisk you past a new series of cool streams, delicate lakes, quaint villages, and quiet forests. The only scenic constant is far away: the majestic Alps. Mainly white-capped, the mountains provide a continuous backdrop for the shifting scenes of Switzerland outside the train window.

The Eiger comes into sight as one of three peaks in what is possibly the most picturesque area of the Alps, the so-called Jungfrau region between Wengen and Kleine Scheidegg. From right to left as the train clatters up the hill like a San Francisco cable car, these peaks, comprising a three-pointed, thirteen-hundred-foot tower, are the Jungfrau, Monch and Eiger. In English, Jungfrau and Monch are the virgin and the monk, and the Eiger is the ogre.

Sublimely named, the ogre has seemed both irresistible and formidable to generations of climbers. Comparing it to other mountains, Captain Cachin says: "I believe the Eiger is the most difficult peak to climb." He was including American as well as European peaks. In California, Yosemite's El Capitan is about as high and flat as the Eiger, but there are few weather problems in Yosemite Valley during the climbing season. And few rockfalls. As for the Rocky Mountains, Cachin says: "Climbing the Rockies is mostly rock scaling. This is the easiest kind since it's a solid climb. In the Alps, the climber confronts ice. Even in summer, the shadowy sides of the high mountain peaks are covered with a glaze of ice."

Thus, the weather is still a hazard in climbing, but mountaineers tend to agree today that it is the only serious one. Height isn't the obstacle it used to be. Without exception, the highest mountains have been conquered. Women are now climbing Mt. Everest, at 29,000 feet more than twice as tall as the Eiger. A thirty-five-year old Japanese housewife was on Everest last month. And this month, a ten-man party of Americans and Canadians is taking a leisurely walk 28,000 feet up K-2 in the Himalayas, a peak once considered impregnable. In the group are three or four photographers.

This isn't to say that climbing mountains has become as simple as playing gin rummy. It remains an arduous and deadly sport. All over the world, climbers are still falling dead, four of them this year on the slopes of Nuptse, a killer in the Everest triangle. But, clearly, mountain climbing is safer than in the years when Hitler was urging young Germans to challenge the Eiger. And equipment changes have made much of the difference. In Wengen, Kurt Schlunegger, fifty-five, a survivor of the third successful expedition against the Eigerwand, is asked how much metal he used that week in 1947 on his way up. "We only had three pitons with us," he says. "Now they use fifty or sixty."

Pitons are metal spikes pounded into cracks to support the ropes and pulleys that support the climbers. A climbing expedition today can race straight up the wall of a ninety-story building on a grid of ropes and pitons. There have also been recent improvements in clampons, head lamps, ice daggers and, especially, hard hats. Says Schlunegger's son Tres, twenty-eight, a fourth-generation climber and guide who, however, hasn't yet chanced the Eiger: "My dad climbed in a woolen ski cap. The new hard hats have made the biggest change in climbing because falling rocks are the biggest danger."

Kurt Schlunegger's brother, Hans, who went with him to the top of the Eiger twenty-eight years ago, was killed the following summer by a falling rock. Most of Kurt's boyhood companions died young, many on the Eiger. He survives, lean, hard and weather-beaten, to live out his days peacefully as the owner of a Wengen cafe. There, with his son interpreting, he says: "No climb in the world is hard any more — on a sunny day. There's nothing to worry about except the weather."

Even now in the Eiger country, all the same, I'd rather be a spectator.

4. Heidelberg: Dueling is Still in Fashion

DUELING HASN'T died, though in its contemporary official European form it's hard to get dead dueling. Risk there is, risk and comradeship, and the two are a powerful human combination.

HEIDELBERG, West Germany: June 8, 1975.

When a Heidelberg University graduate signs his name formally, he might end it with a few numbers, thus, 57:33. There's a message there. And to those who understand it, the message is clear: The gentleman is a damn good swordsman. He has fought many duels in which he has been cut up thirty-three times — but you ought to see the other guys. He has cut them open fifty-seven times.

Nicks and scratches don't count. The mere drawing of blood isn't enough. In a duel between Heidelberg students, a cut is defined as a sword wound requiring at least one stitch. And, happily, the boys get the best of care. Dueling isn't allowed unless a doctor is present to sew up the wounded and vouch for the cuts that enable a fighter to progress from, say, 52:32 to 57:33.

The most unusual sport in Europe today — and possibly the most dangerous — this kind of dueling is called mensur fighting. The duelists, be assured, almost never fight in anger. What's more, crossing swords high, they are restricted to one target: the other fellow's head. Such a duel is, literally, head to head.

Continuing an ancient practice, dueling is not only still allowed at Heidelberg, it's a way of life in thirteen of the university's thirty-two fraternities. The thirteen are referred to here as the fighting (or dueling or fencing) fraternities, and, uniformly, they have one membership qualification: dueling is a required subject. Students pledging to join a dueling fraternity must fight at least once, and to continue as active members, they must, as undergraduates, fight at least two more duels.

From choice, most students fight often. The opponents are mainly drawn from other dueling fraternities at Heidelberg, and after a typical bout the antagonists sit down and drink beer together. They drink the rest of the night.

Matches occasionally are arranged with students from other German universities. Though many Americans thought dueling died when Aaron Burr killed Alexander Hamilton more than a century and a half ago, it survives in West Germany today not only at Heidelberg but also at such universities as Hamburg, Bremen, Munich, Frieburg and Mannheim.

There is nothing quite like it in America, where, for one thing, Greek is the language of the fraternities. Latin is favored here. Heidelberg's dueling fraternities include Rhenopalatia, Allemagnia, Danubia, Normania and, among others, Rheno-Nicaria, whose members, in a friendly letter written earlier this year in reply to my letter, agreed to let me in for a day or two.

Their fraternity is legally the Corps of Rheno-Nicaria, which is Latin for two German rivers, the Rhine and Neckar. Broad and sparkling, the Neckar has lazed through Heidelberg for hundreds of years. And on the road leading up from one bank, there is a tavern, the Hirschgasse, where Heidelberg students fight every Thursday night throughout the school term. It's an old tavern. They have been dueling at the Hirschgasse since 1472.

The university itself is on the other side of the river. A series of weathered stone buildings, some dating to medieval times, the old university is laid out on the main street of Old Heidelberg, the Hauptstrasse, which parallels the river. At one end of the Hauptstrasse, with a commanding view of the river, is the Rheno-Nicaria house, which also overlooks the Hirschgasse on the opposite bank.

A square, stone, multi-story structure going back two hundred years or so, the RN house is a Teutonic version of the old Sigma Chi house on the USC campus — the Trojan football fraternity of its day — and, inside, the RN fighters don't appear to be that much different from Trojan athletes. Minus their swords, they seem amiable, hospitable and clever, representing a variety of college majors from economics to medicine. Sons of businessmen, professors, doctors and government officials, all have some knowledge of English. A working knowledge, anyhow. Some might say a fighting knowledge.

II

Seated casually in their dark-paneled library, four Rheno-Nicaria members discuss their hobby with obvious pleasure and pride. A med student, Edgar Stahl, slight and soft-spoken, wants to make one point first: "This kind of fighting isn't as dangerous as boxing. We've never had a fatality. You can get hurt, but in boxing you can get killed." Black-haired Harold Bill frowns, ruffling a high, wide forehead, and comments: "You mustn't think mensur fighting is simple. A duel is the best way I know of to get to know yourself, to get the measure of your character." A slim, reticent, almost languid student in metal-rimmed glasses, Klaus Thieme, says a West German university duel differs from the classic French epée variety in these particulars: "We fight with the blades above our heads. French fencers thrust and parry. We chop. They wear much armor and padding. We fight with our heads uncovered."

Nico Dienst, six feet three, one of the few really tall Europeans you see on a 1975 trip, is asked to assess the advantage of height in dueling. "It doesn't help much," he says. "We give the shorter fighter a platform to stand on. The council is the matchmaker — the interfraternity council, which announces the pairings on Mondays, ten days before the fights — and the idea is to match opponents exactly in every way, experience, skill, physically."

On fight night, the public is excluded from the dueling room, a large, second-floor room in the Hirschgasse, so two RN members offer to show you how it's done. Descending to the fraternity's training room (the paukkeller, or hit cellar) they put on their gear. Included in a mensur uniform are a leather collar, a padded leather vest like an umpire's, a heavy leather skirt like a butcher's, a broad metal nose guard with tiny slits in front of the eyes, and a metal glove for the right arm. The left arm is held behind the back.

So far as it goes, the uniform is first rate. It would discourage a bullet. But there's a missing link — no helmet. The cheeks and head are exposed to the sword, which is much heavier than a rapier. More than three feet long, a mensur sword comes to a point that is as wide, and as sharp, as a razor blade. Moreover, the weapon is two-bladed. It can be legally honed and sharpened for twelve inches on one side and six inches on the other. A fraternity boy occasionally skips class on the day of a fight to make sure his sword is as sharp as he can whet it.

Because the match is Bill versus Thieme, pal against pal, blunt swords and training helmets are being used today. Otherwise, it's classic mensur, in which these seem to be the main elements:

• The combatants stand the length of a sword apart, no more and no less, throughout the fight. (Mensur is a unit of measure, about three feet, approximately the span of a sword.) At the start, they cross blades above their heads. And at a signal, one chops down at the head of the other, who, during Round One, can use his sword to block the plunging blade but not to attack his opponent. In Round Two, their roles are reversed.

• A round is five chops. A fight to the finish, so-called, lasts thirty rounds, and takes twenty or thirty minutes. There is a halftime.

• Only the right arm can be moved. Head and body must be immobile and erect. Fighters aren't allowed to duck or evade a blow. The duel ends if either man moves his head — perhaps prudently, but disgracefully. Those who flinch are guilty of a mucken, which brings disqualification.

• Officially, neither fighter wins or loses. Nobody keeps score. Nobody keeps track of anything but the cuts, which are inflicted when the offensive fighter chops away the defendant's sword. A sword prick that draws blood is often decisive in other forms of dueling but not in mensur fighting. It must be a measurable cut.

• The goal is simply to hang in. A lifetime cut score of 5:20 is as good as a 20:5. "A 1:20 wouldn't be an embarrassment," says fighter Thieme. "It shows you've given your best, and this is the result. The whole point is not to mucken."

III

German duelists fight with seconds who also carry swords and crouch on the floor between the fighters. If either fighter drops his sword or falls off balance, his second rises up immediately to protect him from harm. The seconds, who wear heavy leather helmets and uniforms, also start and end each round, counting the blows. There is a referee, of sorts. He may not take part unless appealed to, in which case his decisions are final.

The duelists apparently don't worry much about serious injury. Asked about that, Stahl, the med student, answers carefully: "The reason these fights sometimes seem so bloody is that the cuts are many. But they aren't serious. The doctor lets them fight unless the cut is so deep he can't repair it without stitches. There is basically only one difficult injury for the doctor. The little artery in the temple might be severed."

In former days, the badge of a German university education was a scar on the cheek, but that part of the mystique has succumbed to modern medical methods. Reaching into a pocket, Stahl exhibits a color picture of himself made after a fight last year. One cheek has been ripped raw from ear to chin. Today his cheeks are pale but unmarked. "Medicine marches on," says Dienst, the tall one.

The duelists are in it apparently for the camaraderie. "We're very warm friends," Dienst says. The fiancee of a Rheno-Nicaria member says, with some indignation, "They're an incredibly close family with only a few interests: sword practice, duels and beer. On Monday, Wednesday and Friday they practice and drink. On Thursday they fight and drink. And Tuesday is their night to get together for a party."

The details are a little warped, but the comradeship is like that on a good American professional sports team. This could account for the fact that West German fraternity boys stay in school longer than many students in other countries. Most RN members seem to be in their mid-twenties. People who like fighting, drinking and loving are loath to give it up. There's nothing like merry company to remind a man that if he's on a short trip to a sure fate, at least it's a common fate. The huddle-up instinct was well understood by the late Vince Lombardi, the champion Green Bay coach who likewise emphasized loving and hating, and even beer drinking, so long as his players drank together, and never on Wednesday (or Thursday, Friday or Saturday).

IV

This is the last European country in which dueling is legal. Of the three hundred thousand students in West German universities, nearly half approve of mensur fighting, polls show, and some twenty per cent join dueling fraternities. Efforts to abolish student dueling in Germany are made from time to time, but federal courts still support it. Frankfurt University, the most recent to ban mensur fighting, was overruled by the courts a few years ago. Some of the best-placed and most influential figures in West Germany are products of the dueling fraternities. There are believed to be more than two hundred thousand of these mayors, judges and businessmen, known collectively as "alte herren." The old men keep it going.

Elsewhere, the fascination with dueling also remains. Since the invention of swords, it has always been popular with some people in most countries. And, outside the law, duels are sometimes still staged, or threatened. In Copenhagen recently, a theater publicist and set designer dueled (over theater credits) with old cavalry pistols. Wearing white ties, top hats and tails, both missed. There have been two known duels in the last ten years at England's Oxford University. One pair kissed swords and lunged at each other at dawn, flailing around for ten minutes before the loser retired with a slashed arm. They were fighting over a girl. Two other Oxford debaters settled it with umbrellas. The duel was judged over when one forced the other to his knees.

America is the home of the political duel. Treasury Secretary Alexander Hamilton and Maine Congressman Jonathan Cilley were both shot dead by political opponents in the early 1800s — Cilley at eighty paces in a duel of rifles. The most famous duelist of Andrew Jackson's term as president (1829-37) was the president himself. Old Hickory engaged in a number of pistol fights, including one against the best shot in his native Tennessee. In that duel, Jackson showed that early Americans knew how not to mucken. Letting his opponent shoot unchallenged, the future President absorbed the ball in his chest near the heart, where it remained until his death forty years later. Then, with no further chance that an incoming missile would upset his aim, Jackson measured his man, and dispatched him to another world.

A decade later, Kentucky Congressman John J. Crittenden saved two lives, including his own, when offered his choice of weapons by an insulted Texas political opponent. He chose howitzers on opposite banks of the Rio Grande.

V

Germany is a little different. Beer, duels and bonhomie have been central to life at Rheno-Nicaria and other houses here since the first Heidelberg fraternity was organized in 1388. On the university side of the river today, in the older areas of the city, the fraternity houses look much as they did then. They can be identified by their flags. Each flies its distinctive colors prominently. Resembling small palaces — many with red pitched roofs, leaded panes and dormers — Heidelberg's fraternities are scattered through town on the hill from the river up to massive Heidelberg Castle, whose ruins dominate the scene.

In the lives of most fraternity members and other students, and indeed most other Heidelberg residents, music is central. This is a city of music. Most students, when they venture out, take in an opera or symphony concert downtown. With a population of a hundred and fifty thousand, Heidelberg is one of the smallest cities in the world with its own opera company and symphony orchestra. And, as Germans, Rheno-Nicaria members like music, too.

But they'd rather fight.

5. *Everybody* Plays Soccer in London Town

THIS IS the greatest city in the world, I discovered as a young man, years ago. As a discovery, that, of course, is more exact than profound. For, during many centuries, many others have cherished London, too. In my century, the twentieth, I have returned many times to the quaint streets and structures, the pubs, parks and theaters, the open-air buses of a marvelous old river town.

LONDON: May 18, 1975.

A public opinion survey in a large American city last fall turned up a composite picture of the modern American sports nut as a man who goes bowling Tuesday night, plays golf or tennis Saturday, and spends Sunday watching pro football on television.

What does this individual's counterpart do in London? Is the Englishman a sports fan?

The best place to ask about that is in a London pub, and not just because the best food in England is served in its pubs. In addition, much of the social life of the old city centers there. And, there, you learn that Londoners enjoy three national pastimes: watching soccer, playing soccer, and talking soccer over a glass of warm beer. The English call it football — a better name than soccer for what it is — and in all the pubs, as well as all the polls, it ranks, singularly, as both the number-one spectator sport and number-one participant sport in England. Three out of four Englishmen watch or play the game or both.

In America, as Americans all know, most persons compartmentalize their sports. For watching, there is football or maybe baseball. For doing, there is tennis, golf, or swimming. In Britain, by contrast, Saturday is for watching soccer and Sunday for playing soccer.

This is a rather simple game you can play for much of your life, into your fifties at least, on any flat street or vacant lot, with any or all of your friends, skilled or unskilled. And by 9:30 on a characteristic Sunday morning, London is alive with thousands of amateur athletes kicking a ball around, or trying to. From a helicopter, the entire city seems to be covered with soccer players. By 11:59, they're dispersing. And by noon, they're gone. There isn't a kicker in sight. Promptly at noon, London's pubs open for two hours of Sunday drinking, and the athletes are all in there. That's England.

II

As in other lands, there are other things to do here:

Motoring for pleasure is a favorite pastime for millions. Climbing out of a new MG one day last week in Leadenhall Street, a young businessman, Bradford Kirk, said: "We're near the continent here, you know, and on a holiday it's jolly good fun to put your machine on a boat and go buzzing through Holland or Austria. An American can't do that."

Most Englishmen consider gardening their "second hobby" regardless of what they name first, motoring, drinking or soccer. On a recent train from a London commuter town, Robert Swaffam, a well-dressed electrical engineer, said: "I have a boat and a garden that get every minute of my free time. Boating gives the most pleasure, but it's a painful pleasure. You're either freezing or soaked to the skin all the time. Gardening is the most relaxing thing a man can do. This year I have three hundred square yards of cauliflower, cabbages, radishes, shallots, beans, lettuce, tomatoes, potatoes, onion, corn and Brussels sprouts."

One of the most ornamental aspects of Europe in the spring is its abundance of gardens, both vegetable and flower. Fresh gardens are everywhere in every country, in the villages, in the countryside, on the few parcels of open land in the cities. South of the Dover Road near Sidcup, on the edge of London, a young gardener, Mavis Wilson, her hair in a kerchief, knees on the ground, removed her hands from the dirt and said: "Motoring is a bit too dear for every day, and the television is bloody awful. That leaves gardening, now, doesn't it? Besides, who can afford to *buy* vegetables?"

For those without a patch for gardening, London maintains probably the greatest municipal park system in the world. Within a short walk of Big Ben, three dozen parks of various sizes have been laid out among the buildings and row houses of Europe's first city. Each is a synthesis of manicured trees, flowers, rich green grass, and usually a pond or two.

In other respects, London sometimes seems the Los Angeles of Europe — a spread-out, understated series of towns with mostly small buildings, a mild climate, and an enormous population. One difference is that Los Angeles is a collection of modern suburbs, architecturally undistinguished, whereas London is continuously medieval, Gothic, Georgian, and romantic. Another difference is that this is a river city. After a game of tennis at Battersea Park, it's only a half block to the Thames, where you can order a beer at a riverside table and watch either the traffic on an historic waterway or the wildflowers on the riverbank or, more likely, the girls of London in their short tennis skirts standing or strolling nearby.

III

For economic and other reasons in this year of rising prices and unemployment, England's fastest-growing sport seems to be brewing beer. The other day in Rugby, a retired butcher, Harold Nelson, said he has three interests — gardening, soccer and beer — and added: "Everybody's brewing up beer now, and I don't know why not. It only takes six weeks to make a batch, and you can brew twenty-eight gallons at a time."

Though a native of the town that invented rugby, Nelson said he was born into a large working-class family whose members think rugby is for upper-class snobs. Along with most of his countrymen, including most of Britain's famous soccer pros, he left school in his mid-teens and, therefore, identifies with the pros. He can name every starter on England's twenty-two first-division soccer teams.

In the small living room of his old-fashioned row house in Rugby, the old butcher sat down heavily in his favorite chair by the side of a coal fire and rested tired blue eyes on a ten-gallon beer tub in the corner. "There are two ways to make your own," he said. "You can buy the hops and malt and give it the full go, or you can bring home a beer kit. I started the proper way but soon transferred to a kit. It's rather good that way too, you know."

He drinks at home five nights a week, visiting his pub the other two nights. When he was working, he said, it was the other way around. For nearly a half century, he has patronized the same pub, sat in the same chair, and talked to the same people about the same things.

This is the English way. Recently an American visitor passing through Wallington, on the Oxford road out of London, saw the same faces on successive nights in the same chairs at the sixteenth century pub in the George Hotel. It was like going to the same play on consecutive nights. Even the lines were the same. There seem to be only four subjects of conversation in a British pub: soccer, sex, movies and money.

Like most pubs, the George looks like it was built in the thirteenth or fourteenth century, surely not as late as the sixteenth. Oak-beamed, heavily paneled, it is a complex of dark heavy furniture, crooked walls, and sloping floors that creak slightly, invitingly. In foggy London town, the colder it is outside, the friendlier inside. But the beer is better in Rugby. Just ask for the butcher.

IV

One thing that makes England greatly appealing to sports fans is that its amateur soccer teams, incredibly, have a chance each year to win their way through all the pro tournaments to the last big round at historic Wembley Stadium for the equivalent of America's Super Bowl. Picture the Duluth Eskimos in the Super Bowl and you have it. And, occasionally, England's amateurs do make some advances, as some did in tournament play this winter, when an amateur side defeated two pro clubs and lost to a third by one goal. This is something like USC beating the Rams and 49ers before losing to the Chargers by one touchdown.

An Englishman can see when an amateur side has a bit of a chance, for he is a soccer player himself. He understands the nuances. "I'm ecstatic when Arsenal win," a fan said not long ago at an Arsenal-Liverpool game, "but I'm just as thrilled to score the winning goal myself."

Soccer's pull to the London masses was illustrated in Fleet Street recently when an unused building was torn down near a newspaper office. The vacant lot, as large as a football field, was appropriated for lunch-time soccer by the newspaper's employees, who formed a new league for the duration, and played with forty-two eleven-man teams in four divisions — staggering their lunch hours for more than a year — until construction began on the new building.

Adding to the attraction of soccer is that the underdog team very often has a chance, making it a lively betting game. Gambling is legal here, and the average Englishman likes to have a few pence riding on himself, if not his favorite pros.

As a sport, here and everywhere east of America, soccer remains uniquely competitive for still another reason: It is played by young men of normal size with normal nervous systems. To play well, you don't need the eyesight of an American baseball player, or quite the courage and intelligence of American football players or English rugby players. And if you weigh fourteen stone (200 pounds) that might be too much. The premium is on quickness, reaction, enthusiasm, and the ability to anticipate, diagnose, and inspire.

In both England and America, a lot of 160-pound printers and bank clerks have all that. But in America, they can only prove it in tennis or maybe volleyball. There aren't enough pitchers to make baseball a game of public participation in America, and, as for football, who wants to play guard?

In London, anyone can be a star in his nation's pastime, locally if not nationally. The friendly neighborhood druggist is both a professional soccer authority and a great amateur soccer player, and that's what's great about England, that and the pubs.

6. Eton College: Bonaparte Lost Here

IF YOU ever wanted to go to school in a building six centuries old while wearing a bow tie and tails, Eton is for you.

ETON, England: July 13, 1975.

Launching nearly a hundred years of peace for England, the Duke of Wellington beat Napoleon at Waterloo in 1815. And it was after this decisive fight that Wellington reportedly said: "The Battle of Waterloo was won on the playing fields of Eton." He meant his officers were tempered, shaped and proved in Eton College sports. A private high school for boys thirteen to eighteen, the institution has been known as a college since the day classes began in 1440, a half century before Columbus took off for America.

On any list of the world's most famous schools, Eton belongs near the top — along with Harvard, perhaps, as well as Oxford and the Sorbonne. For hundreds of years, Eton men have played major roles in British government, particularly in the more responsible billets, including prime minister.

So this is a school that can be identified first by its history as an academy for British leaders and second by its exceptional playing fields, whose layout, physically, is unsurpassed anywhere. Wellington linked the two, reasoning that leadership is learned in teen-age sports. A novel thought for its time, it still isn't universally accepted, although it has had a wide appeal throughout English history to the individuals known in this country as gentlemen.

The upper crust of this hallowed island has always had a complex attitude toward proficiency and excellence, in sports and every other endeavor. To begin with, an English gentleman scorns all professionals — the grubby, upwardly mobile experts in any field who have to sell their skills. Second, an English gentleman hopes to display great accomplishment himself in one or more fields. And, third, he wants the world to know that if he *doesn't* excel — if, that is, he loses a game or two — it doesn't affect his self-esteem or social standing in the slightest.

One inspecting this part of England today can, accordingly, understand why sports seemed so important to the most successful British soldier of the last several hundred years, and to those of his station, then and later. During a visit here, one senses that the Eton sports experience has been a foundation for that peculiarly English characteristic: a personalized dedication to both excellence and the stiff upper lip. Win if you can, stand tall if you don't.

As an attitude toward life, that, possibly, can best be instilled in sports. At Eton in any case, it seems to be the goal.

II

Laid out in a bend of the River Thames, Eton College is surrounded on three sides by its playing fields. More than three hundred acres of choice English real estate are here devoted exclusively to games, a wide variety of games, and the twelve largest fields are each larger than an American football field. A dozen structures the size of the Los Angeles Coliseum could be accommodated comfortably. Yet there isn't a grandstand in sight, or even bleachers.

The playing fields of Eton are strictly for playing.

Grouped in a massive semicircle around a cluster of ancient school buildings, Eton's many sports grounds are sited in such a way that it is a walk of less than five minutes from any of them to the heart of campus. There isn't a comparable athletic plant in any American university, and probably not in the world. A half dozen rugby games and thirty or more soccer games can be, and often are, played simultaneously here.

And when they feel cramped at Eton College, they convert a nearby farm to a playing field. The school owns the surrounding countryside as well as most of the town of Eton, a medieval community that straggles along both sides of narrow High Street an hour west of London. The castle-like school buildings are tucked in behind. A foot bridge leads across the Thames to Windsor Castle, the most famous of the country homes of the kings and queens of England.

During the Eton College sports season, which lasts nine months, its 1,230 students swarm over its fields and rivers all at the same time competing in every sport known to Europe and a few that aren't. Heading the latter are three games known as Eton fives, the field game, and the wall game — which as a group do much to define Eton and its effects.

Eton fives, a form of handball, is played against three walls that are rife with obstacles, including brick ledges and a protuberance that looks like the foot of a buttress on an old church. This is because it's a replica of the foot of a buttress on an old church, which just happened to be there, very much in the way, the day the game was invented. Enshrining England's veneration for both tradition and eccentricity, all Eton fives courts since — both here and in other British cities — have been built with the same crazy obstructions that can, by the way, still be seen on the original church wall.

The sport referred to as the field game is also called Eton football. A form of soccer, the field game is the great intramural sport of Eton, played competitively by teams representing the twenty-five student-residence halls. It was during a field game one day in the eighteenth century, or maybe it was the seventeenth, that the ball got away from both sides and rolled toward a fourteen-foot brick wall, where the spectators began fighting for it, pushing one another into the bricks as they wrestled on the ground. Thus the birth of another peculiar and famous English pastime, the wall game, Wellington's favorite during his undergraduate days at Eton.

The wall game is an outlandish form of competition in which a dozen students, groveling on the ground, frequently in mud, try to prod a dozen other students and a little round ball the length of a fifty-yard wall on a field only five or six yards wide. To numerous Etonians, the wall game is as exhilarating as it is exhausting. To non-Etonians, it is the definitive Eton sport, symbolizing a school where dogged perseverance and giving one's all are often admired above intellectual qualities. At Waterloo eventually, Wellington persevered until he won. And, perversely, British perseverance led the same British army, in the same year, minus Wellington, on a disastrous straight-ahead charge against America's Andrew Jackson at the Battle of New Orleans, where Jackson's frontier marksmen, ensconced behind a fence, won lopsidedly. On a day when, tragically, neither side knew the War of 1812 had already been settled, the difference in fatalities was 2,000-13.

Resolute perseverance is a British trait for good or bad. Nourished at Eton, it led later to another disastrous charge — by the Light Brigade in the Crimean War — and then to England's glorious performance in the Battle of Britain against Hitler in World War II. The unifying quality in all of these operations has been not intellectual vigor but plain tenacity, the bulldog bottom line for an Eton athlete.

III

So Eton is different. Even sitting still, Eton boys look different. They dress with unvarying uniformity — as if on their way to a wedding — in formal morning suits with long black swallow-tailed coats, dark pants, white shirts with cuff links, stiff white collars and little white Eton ties. Seniors wear white bow ties. Morning, noon and night, the students dress that way, both in class and on the streets of Eton Town, startling strangers. The 130 members of the teaching faculty, known as masters, are a sight, too. They wear dark suits, white shirts with wing collars, white bow ties and long black gowns. When a master rides his bicycle to school, the gown streams far out behind.

In the jeans era, the boys of Eton finally made one modest change a few years ago, dispensing with the black silk top hats that used to crown their dress clothes. But they didn't dispense willingly. Their tailors simply ran out of silk, and that ended that.

Oddly enough, in a continuing small argument over whether to keep the boys in their morning coats, both sides use similar reasoning. School officials want a more modern uniform, fearing the present one is socially divisive. Most boys like it the way it is, hoping it *is* socially divisive. Snobbery here isn't unheard of. Eton was, after all, founded by a king, Henry VI, whose century was the fifteenth, a turbulent period if there ever was one. Henry VI was the Englishman Joan of Arc opposed, and, in the tragic climax of their argument, it was Henry's troops who burned her. Henry himself was strangled in the Tower of London.

For Eton, the good news is that he did launch this college, and at the time that was some achievement. It even antedated the invention of printing. Eton had been a going concern for thirteen years when Gutenberg's first bible appeared. The dark, heavy-beamed classroom used here that first winter (1440-41) is still in use, its wooden benches and tables scarred with the names and initials of centuries of schoolboys.

There are older schools in England. Winchester is older and, academ–

ically, more prestigious. Millfield is more expensive, and stronger in varsity sports, having produced many Davis Cup players and international rugby stars. Harrow rivals Eton in most respects, including annually in cricket on a celebrated London field, Lord's. But it is Eton that has the name and prestige. And a principal reason for that, no doubt, is its curious approach to sports. Eton is a school with no interest in either awkward amateurs or world-class professionals.

IV

David Townend, twenty-nine, teaches chemistry at Eton and coaches track and field. Bright, bearded, genial, he is in some respects a typical Eton master. Talking about his school and its goals, Townend, plainly pleased with both, says: "We hope the boys will enjoy winning. But even more, we want them to play games well enough to enjoy sports if they happen to lose. Here's an example of school policy," he adds, pointing toward the Eton swimming pool. "When they built this, they deliberately designed it to make competitive swimming almost impossible."

The pool is in the shape of a giant S. It is so large that the entire student body can be accommodated at one time, yet the narrow straightaway isn't Olympic-sized, and no diving board has Olympic height. On a warm day last week, the fifty or sixty swimmers were in there just having a good time. "Our policy," Townend continues, "is to give the boys any sport they want — from the wall game or mountaineering to beagling." A seemingly typical English pastime, beagling is like fox hunting without foxes or horses. The boys participate on foot, chasing hares with beagles. They breed their own beagles.

"The idea is to have so many different sports," Townend says, "that every boy can learn at least one game well enough to play it acceptably. That, in one sentence, is the sports philosophy of Eton College."

Regardless, therefore, of how many students go out for any given sport, the school fits them all in. This year when eight hundred Eton boys signed up for rowing, the school provided each boy with his own boat. Rowers are called wetbobs. Cricket players are drybobs. Rowing and cricket are the principal spring sports.

Socially, Eton is still mainly for those from upper class homes. Most boys are enrolled by wealthy parents at the age of two or three months, if not earlier. They won't know it for awhile, but they're about to spend most of their lives looking forward to, or back on, the privilege of wearing long-tailed coats and little white ties with good Eton friends.

Athletically today, the school isn't quite what Henry VI had in mind.

He authorized just two sports, the two that would strengthen him militarily, jousting and archery. Happily for the Duke of Wellington and his soldiers, and for England, jousting and archery were outdoor sports. Requiring large playing fields, they generated a way of life.

7. Wales: The Star is a Doctor

ON A TOUR of Europe, one seldom meets anyone who can place Johnny Unitas or Babe Ruth or any other U.S. athlete except Muhammad Ali. Most sports stars everywhere are home-side heroes. Americans never heard of J.P.R. Williams, either.

CARDIFF, Wales: June 1, 1975.

The most famous athlete in Wales is a medical doctor. That says something about Wales, and also about the doctor. He is J.P.R. Williams, and at twenty-six he is the greatest rugby fullback in the world. Or so they say here. And they ought to know. Rugby is the national sport of Wales.

In only three other places on earth is rugby played as well and loved as much: South Africa, New Zealand and Tonga. How a chill-weather game like this took root in Tonga, a warm-weather South Sea island, may remain a mystery forever. Nor did it figure to take root here. Wales is the western sliver of the ancient island of the Angles and Saxons, and in recent years the English have gone raving mad over soccer. Before they did that, however, they invented rugby. And there are those in Wales who think that's the only good thing England ever did.

From one side of Wales to the other, a Welshman today never misses a chance to watch or play rugby. And his devotion to the game is the reality that has made it possible for Dr. Williams to become a national legend.

A reason it happened is that rugby is essentially a sport for amateurs. Though pro rugby exists in northern England and Australia, the game doesn't seem to be as much fun when played for money. Thus in a world of expanding professionalism and commercialism, Wales stands out as a stronghold of amateurism. This is one of the few remaining lands where the national pastime is an amateur sport. As a consequence, schoolteachers, engineers, bank managers, coal miners and firemen can double as idols of the Welsh masses in the national rugby league, a sixteen-team association that is the counterpart of America's National Football League.

And because the compact geography of Britain is favorable, a Welsh boy can study medicine in London and also play beautiful rugby in Cardiff. Through the 1970s, J.P.R. Williams has been doing just that.

After many years in medical school, he is now interning in a London hospital and playing rugby here regularly and well. This spring he led Wales to another title in the world series of rugby, the annual five-nation tournament bringing Wales together with France, England, Ireland and Scotland.

In Williams' six years on the team, the Welsh have won the series five times. And they have usually followed by beating, in turn, South Africa, New Zealand and Tonga. They have yet to lose in Cardiff Stadium during Williams' career as their fullback. "Thank God for J.P.R.," a reporter in Bridgend, Wales, wrote after the clinching game this year. "He's a lovely player to write about, if you have the vocabulary."

II

Bridgend is J.P.R.'s town. A clean, wind-swept community of thirty thousand, it's an industrial town near the Atlantic Ocean twenty miles west of Cardiff (population two hundred thousand). Williams' father is a Bridgend doctor. His mother is also a doctor. So is his wife. "I didn't make a conscious decision to go into medicine and play rugby," he says. "As long as I can remember, it was all settled."

A bit over six feet and 200 pounds, Williams is a taller, huskier, Vin Scully with long reddish hair, alert blue eyes and a ruddy, open face. And in every situation, he shows the poise of a world traveler. He has in fact played rugby on every continent except Antarctica.

As a medical practitioner, Williams specializes in sports orthopedics, a result of a lifelong interest in broken bones, his own. On rugby fields, he has broken his jaw twice, his ribs and fingers often, and his nose five times. He has sprained both knees, pulled both hamstrings, and depressed both cheekbones. "There are hazards in any game," he believes. "I always figure that if I can breathe through both nostrils, I'm all right." In orthopedics, he says, "The hardest problem is finding out whether the injury is serious. Athletes are prone to worry. They have a lot of psychological problems. Rugby is a good research area."

Williams has been a research casualty somewhat more often than others in rugby because of the position he plays, and the way he plays it, according to Cardiff Sportswriter Brian Wall, who says: "J.P.R. has revolutionized fullback in the last six or eight years. It used to be a defensive position. He has made it an attacking position with his audacity running the ball. He stands under a high kick without flinching, and he likes to run." A veteran journalist, Wall has covered rugby eight months a year, home and abroad, for twenty-three years. "In that time," he says,

"Williams is the bravest athlete I've seen. The people here have an enormous admiration for him."

III

Like Joe Namath in America, J.P.R. Williams has become a household name in his country along with fellow Welsh stars Richard Burton, Tom Jones and Shirley Bassey. Politically, Wales is no longer a nation. As a British principality, it bears a relationship with England similar to that of Texas in the United States. And, similarly, it feels inferior. In a downtown Cardiff stationery store, Betty Roberts, a shopper, says: "We like J.P.R. Williams because he beats England. We can bear losing to others. We can't stand losing to England."

To measure Welsh interest in rugby, Roberts suggests crossing the street to look at the Cardiff playing fields, which are a stone's throw from Cardiff Castle, a charming relic whose sculptured fireplaces were built into walls that go back to Roman times. The two big rugby stadiums stand incongruously side by side. One is the home of the national league's Cardiff rugby club. The other is reserved for international matches. The tenderly-cared-for international park, used only a few times a year, has the best playing floor in the world, reportedly, for any sport. Certainly its grass surface is the greenest, thickest, lushest.

The city stadium, which is used all the time, and lofty international stadium seat twenty thousand and seventy-eight thousand respectively, although seat isn't the right word. Both stadiums are ringed halfway up by terraces without benches or chairs. On game day, half the crowd stands throughout. "Standing is a Welsh rugby custom," says Brian Wall. "These are hardy people. They don't like to sit." Wales favors rugby over soccer "because it's the rougher sport," Wall adds. "Many Welshmen look down on soccer-mad England as a bit effete." Says rugby star Williams: "This is coal-mining country, a man's country, and rugby is a man's game."

There are three other good things about their national pastime, Cardiff men and women say:

• Rugby is regularly played by pro and amateur athletes of varying talent and size. On the good Welsh teams, forwards range up to six-feet-five and 260 pounds. Backs and ends start at five-six and 140, even on the better clubs, meaning that it's a game that can be enjoyed simultaneously by the ponderous and the quick.

• As an amateur sport, it's a college man's game. Amateurs are encouraged to stay in school and compete internationally on the various junior and senior teams. Playing international rugby for Wales this year, nine of the fifteen starters were college graduates, and most others had a college background.

That never happens in England or other European countries, where soccer, the national pastime for most, makes its strongest appeal to the undereducated. As a sport, ironically, soccer is much less physical than rugby. A British cliché makes the point: "Soccer is a gentlemen's game played by hooligans. Rugby is a hooligans' game played by gentlemen."

• Rugby is more social than soccer. Says Williams: "In a professional sport like soccer, you have to win at all costs. In rugby you run and tackle hard, and give it a hundred per cent, but if you lose, it doesn't really matter, does it? You socialize with the other team, anyway, have a few beers and a few laughs together."

IV

A social being, Williams is still close to his family. "Dad is a G.P.," he says. "Mum is in family planning." In Bridgend, his parents live on a cool, quiet street that has a typical Welsh name, Merthyrmawr Road. Theirs is a large black and white Georgian house with an office attached. They work at home. As an intern whose hobby is a nonrevenue sport, J.P.R. lives less elegantly. In Wales, home is his parents' home.

In London, he and his wife have invested in a small, old three-floor flat on narrow York Road in suburban Teddington. The bright red Ford Escort parked in front of Williams' house has a prominent sign on the windshield: "Doctor on Call." In a crowded city, that saves him a fortune in parking fines.

When in London, he and his wife ride to work together to a hospital near Heathrow Airport. Dr. Priscilla Williams, who says she "met J.P.R. in med school," is in obstetrics now with an eye on a career as an anesthesiologist, the better to partner with Dr. J.P.R. in orthopedics. He wants an office eventually in Canada or America. "Rugby is all that keeps me here," he says. "I won't want to stay without changes in the National Health Service. The NHS theory is good one — my father was for it at first. But a $20,000 income for a doctor is unrealistic."

Asked how well his patients like the British health system, Williams says: "Very well. I've been in many countries, including America, and nobody gets better medical treatment than British patients. It's the other end that's wrong with NHS. Doctors' wages are below what they should be." Americans often suggest that a flaw in socialized medicine is that one can't choose one's own doctor. "I don't think that's a flaw," Williams says. "When you start out with a doctor in any country, you go to one you don't know. You choose a doctor you've never met before, now, don't you?"

He seems content that his parents pushed him into medicine, although, growing up, he was an all-around athlete. As a teen-ager, Williams was a Wimbledon singles champion who regularly beat today's Davis Cup stars, and he briefly considered a career as a tennis bum. Lifestyle decided him.

"The trouble with tennis," he finally concluded, "is that from the age of fifteen, you have to give it all your time. You don't learn anything else playing that cutthroat game. In rugby, you can have two careers, and I honestly can't tell you what appeals to me most, rugby or medicine."

8. Scotland: Vacation in the Moors

SOME OF the letters that came in after we printed this one weren't totally complimentary. But this is what I saw when I went to the Scottish moors.

BRECHIN, Scotland: Aug. 25, 1975.

After a long, hard summer in Greece, Austria, Switzerland, France, Germany, and England, anybody would need a vacation. And for the discriminating tourist, there's only one place to go: to Scotland for a grouse shoot. Americans call it hunting. To Britons, grouse shooting is an adventure. If you have the money for this, it's an experience of unparalleled magnificence.

Each year, prosperous Englishmen by the hundreds and Americans by the dozen spend more than $10 million in Scotland pursuing a little bird. Weighing barely a pound, the grouse is a plump, reddish-brown game bird that can fly fifty miles an hour.

Matching guns worth $9,500 each aren't required, exactly, but they're recommended. In any case, you need a pair. And don't take jeans. The proper livery is a plus-two tweed suit — meaning a matching jacket and knickers — and if you make London first, any Savile Row tailor will be glad to fit you out for about $400.

On the firing line in Scotland, there's no such thing as the free and open hunting that characterizes many areas of America. The Scottish landlord charges you about $300 a day to shoot — for each individual, that is, in a hunting party of eight — and you're expected to stay four or five days. Transportation is extra. The approved way to get from southern England to the grouse moors of Scotland is by plane or helicopter. Meanwhile, your chauffeur drives up from London with the guns and ammunition in the Rolls Royce.

Headquarters is a plush hunting lodge, where Land Rovers pick you up each morning and drop you off in the middle of the action. Hired beaters and drivers tramp through the heather, scaring the birds in your direction. As soon as you fire, a hired loader hands you your second gun and reloads the other. For lunch, they bring a white tablecloth and white turkey sandwiches with fine white wine. The Land Rovers, standing by to carry you home, are heavy with champagne, beer and ice. And back at the lodge, two cooks and six other domestics — eight willing servants for eight hunters — are fixing dinner, mixing cocktails, laying log fires and getting out the poker chips and backgammon boards and brandy.

Now and then you feel a little sorry for the grouse, but it's a cold world. If the birds had the upper hand, they wouldn't feel sorry for you.

II

An American with the time, money, and heart for a grouse shoot undertakes a ritual of four movements: shopping for the right guns, buying proper clothes, leasing good land and, finally, the hunt. The weapons come first, and there are two or three places in London that will take your $10,000 or $20,000 for guns and ammunition, among them Bost and Co. and Holland and Holland.

Holland's is a calm, quaint little shop in Bruton Street, and you're met at the door by a salesman with discouraging news. You'll have to wait three years for your $9,500 pieces. "It takes ten months to put a gun through our factory," he says rather tartly. "The rest is the queue." In other words, you aren't the only one who wants to go grouse hunting. While waiting for your $9,500 number, the salesman suggests his "competition gun," priced at only $1,000. You shrug, and order a couple.

For any hunt in Scotland, you also need a game gun, an ordinary double-barreled shotgun, so you pick up one of those, too, ignoring three other Holland's specials — duck guns, deer rifles, and $11,000 big-game rifles — because you don't need that much firepower. Since the birds are driven directly at the hunters, a gun range of fifty or sixty feet is enough. But the birds come like the wind, at low altitude (eight or ten feet), so the gunnery requirements are inflexible: accuracy and perfect balance. Grouse hunters must be able to bring their guns to the right height swiftly, and swing them smoothly, and nothing but a $9,500 weapon really does it, though you'll try to get by.

The cartridges are $16.50 a hundred, and the salesman thinks $250 worth of ammunition will get you through a few days. No. 6 shot (270 pellets) is recommended for the Scottish moors. At fifty feet, as fired from a pitiful $1,000 gun, these leave some gaps in a thirty-five-inch circle, but it can't be helped. The shot stream is seven feet long, and against the fastest grouse in Scotland the salesman guarantees you a ninety-five per cent chance with your first pellets and thirty per cent on the second wave. Those aren't bad odds.

III

With a proper arsenal, a hunter could afford, you might think, to dress a bit casually out in the country. But with $1,000 guns, you'd better not look like a cheapskate. Before leaving London, accordingly, if either your chauffeur or your wife has some taste, you can send him (her) to Edinburgh to buy a bolt of Scottish tweed for your new plus-two suit. Your tailor will be impressed, though he'd rather sell you his own.

The jacket is belted and pleated, and the outfit is worn with a hat, either a Bear Bryant tweed hat or a Sherlock Holmes deerstalker. "Never wear loud colors," says a London realtor, Major F. (for Francis) Holdsworth-Hunt. "The tweeds should be inconspicuous."

Other people poke fun at Englishmen for dressing up to go hunting or to play games. But at red-carpeted Buckingham Palace one day this summer, while some of us were waiting for Queen Elizabeth to come downstairs, one of her aides, Ronald Allison, said: "An English sportsman is just being practical when he dresses up. We live in a cold climate, don't you know, and a coat and tie are really more comfortable for us than sports shirts."

IV

In the opinion of various European gourmets, the grouse, as a table delicacy, is "superb," or "rare and tasty," or "not bad." But most British chefs surveyed this summer ranked grouse no higher than second to pheasant, a delicacy that is hunted in South Dakota each fall by thousands of hungry Ohioans and other Easterners.

Grouse shooting is a no-limit activity in Scotland, which appeals to most chefs, according to a Scotland-based hotel manager. "This is a small bird. It takes a lot of them to make a dinner," says Capt. S.G. Gorsline, a former U.S. Naval aviator who owns and operates the Panmure Arms Hotel in Edzell, Angus, Scotland. At the Panmure Arms, grouse is never a featured entree. "We offer it as supplemental to any entree," Gorsline says, "and we have many takers. Grouse have a lovely aroma. There is a distinct heather flavor."

In London, an executive with the gourmet food store Fortnum and

Mason, declining to be quoted by name, says grouse is "a favorite" in most good London hotels and restaurants. His store also ships grouse to America and other countries throughout the world, he says, adding that he selects only birds shot through the head. In season, they are flown to London from Scotland twice a day.

V

Your friend Holdsworth-Hunt, the retired British Army major who has become a real estate expert, knows a land agent in Brechin, Scotland, named J.T. Sutherland. And Sutherland knows John Durant, who manages an eighty-thousand-acre estate near Brechin for Simon Ramsay, the sixteenth Earl of Dalhousie, whose grouse moors are excellent, reportedly, for this kind of action. So you contact Holdsworth-Hunt, who contacts Sutherland, who speaks to Durant, who speaks to Lord Dalhousie, who approves a lease arrangement. It's a tad under $300 a day for each hunter, board and room included.

Fearing helicopters, you take the night train north from London to Aberdeen, which, perhaps, was named for Aberdeen, South Dakota.

There's not much to see from a night-train bedroom, but when you wake up the next morning, it is daylight in Scotland. And as viewed from the train, this proves to be a cool, pleasing and beautiful land of firths, lochs, moors, glens, birks, kilts, highlands, lowlands, stone buildings, stone fences, stony soil and thousands of sheep, lambs, black cattle, blackface rams, and what might even be a few red grouse.

On the motor trip from Aberdeen to the Brechin area eight miles in from the North Sea, the scene gets wilder and rockier until, for miles on end, there is nothing but chilly, hilly wasteland coated with heather. This kind of land, open, uncultivated, forbidding, is by definition a moor. Heather is a low-growing bushy plant whose hard stems change color with the seasons from green to brown to a picturesque purple.

For grouse, heather has two functions, providing both food and hiding places. A grouse is territorial, non-migratory and monogamous, the only game bird in which the hen chooses the cock, leaving the bachelors to shift for themselves. And as nourished and sheltered by heather, a little grouse grows with unbelievable speed, hatching in May, and attaining nearly adult size three months later in time for what the hunters call the "glorious twelfth of August," opening day of the shooting season.

In the hills of a heather-coated moor, the hunters line up in blinds called grouse butts. These are rectangular enclosures which, from a distance, look like bumps or mounds on the hillside. Each rectangle is roughly seven by three feet. Each has stone walls, which, covered by turf and heather, are between hip and chest high. There are no roofs. A line of butts includes ten blinds forty or fifty yards apart. The line extends vertically up the hill. In a typical grouse moor with twenty-five thousand to fifty-thousand acres of heather, there are thirty or forty lines of butts.

The idea is to drive the birds with the wind, and so butt lines, like airport runways, run in various directions. Only five lines are used in any one day because a grouse moor can survive only about five drives a day.

VI

For both prey and stalker, the hunt starts peacefully enough. A shooter and his loader are hiding in each butt; and in the surrounding hills, in the stillness resembling the calm before a great battle, the grouse are lying low and quiet in the heather, hoping for the best. They must be scared into flight, a big job for which Lord Dalhousie is employing twenty college boys for this one action. Setting out a mile or two from the inhabited butts, the cream of Scotland's university youth marches noisily through the heath, each lad waving a white flag. The boys are called beaters, although they look more like a line of skirmishers surrendering to General Grant.

In truth, the whole grouse shooting look is military. On a gray, misty morning, the grouse butts could be battlefield pillboxes. And with the flushing of the birds, the soldiers open fire, shooting out of the pillboxes with an intensity that soon covers the battlefield with the fallen and with the smoke of battle as well as the smell of gunpowder.

On a good morning early in the season, two hundred to three hundred birds race toward the hunters at once, going forty-five to fifty miles an hour at an altitude of no more than ten feet. The excitement, to those who love it, is unmatched in any other pastime.

There are of course other ways to hunt grouse. One means is called walking-up. On the smaller Scottish moors particularly, the hunters and their dogs, walking in line, march up on the birds. This is cheaper (under $100 a day) but more rigorous, requiring a younger man's constitution.

In general, by the time a hunter is old enough to afford grouse shooting, he is too old to walk.

Indeed, as a sport, the shooting of driven grouse was invented by those who had tired of walking up and down the hills in these desolate wastes, or could do it no longer. This was about a century ago. The hardy pioneers of that era were filled with the spirit of the men who invented golf carts — among other spirits. Scots know how to live. If you like log fires, good Scotch, stud poker and guns, take a vacation in the moors.

XI

FITNESS

Otherwise civilized people in ever increasing numbers these days seem to be seeking the E-ticket ride — E meaning extreme, as in high-risk sports. Maybe the current vogue is a revolution against long sits in the computer chair; but there is nothing new about the urge. Third President Thomas Jefferson, who recommended three hours of exercise a day, took most of his in the risk sport that brought down Actor Christopher Reeve, horseback riding. In the stories that follow, there is some E-ticket riding, some conventional exercise and fitness, and a couple of original takes on living healthy and stress-free. Across the years, few topics have interested me more than these.

1. A Fox Hunt in California

THE INFINITE variety of man's (and woman's) taste in sports is visible on a fox hunt, which isn't for everybody. A strenuous, physically demanding activity — gravely demanding if you miss a jump — fox hunting can be dangerous to your health, not to mention the health of the fox. In a recent Harris poll, fractions at least of the American public expressed an interest in thirty-six different sports, and fox hunting makes thirty-seven.

PINE VALLEY, Calif.: March 29, 1973.

On the wall of an art gallery in Paris, Louis XVIII is still riding to hounds. The scene is a pageant of lords and ladies in colorful costumes on galloping horses chasing a pack of hounds through a meadow. The pack is chasing a fox.

Across an ocean, on a wall of the state capitol in Virginia, a horseman in a similar resplendent uniform is mounting up.

He is the president of the United States, George Washington, and the scene is the courtyard of his home, Mt. Vernon, where a dozen riders have gathered to meet Washington's hounds. They are about to hunt the fox — an ancient sport, one of the most persistent in man's history.

Centuries after fox hunting became the favorite pastime of the kings of France, as well as the English nobility and the first American president, among others, this most aristocratic of sports persists even in Southern California. In the hills near Los Angeles, a disparate crew of twentieth-century types, gathering in full regalia, rides to hounds in the early daylight hours of each Wednesday and Saturday through the six-month hunting season, which in this state peaks in spring.

The riders are members of the Los Angeles fox-hunting club known as the West Hills Hunt, which is a look-alike for almost every other formal, organized fox hunt in the world this year, last year, a decade ago, a century ago, since 1690 at least.

The techniques and traditions and customs of the centuries stand almost inviolate when West Hills mounts up. The hunters are still outfitted in an excess of elegance with colorful, long-tailed coats and shiny boots, and the hounds and horses are as sleek and aggressive as their ancestors. But the horsemen do make one concession to their time and place: All they can find to chase in Southern California are coyotes. In these precincts, unhappily, the indigenous western fox is a gray-coated wise guy who insists on running up a tree. Thus a fox hunt here is actually a coyote hunt.

Coyotes lead the hounds a longer race than foxes, and "almost always" get away, according to the master of the Los Angeles hunt, a downtown businessman named Harold C. Ramser, who founded his upholstery company forty years ago. "We haven't caught up to one in the last three seasons," says Ramser, the moving force in West Hills, and master for twelve years.

"The sport," he says, "is in the chase — galloping through the canyons, riding across country, watching hounds work, listening to them. As they pick up the line (of scent), hounds speak. A horn blows, and we're off at a gallop through elegant countryside we'd never otherwise see."

This kind of lyrical analysis comes easily to fox hunters, even if all they can't catch is a coyote. They're romantics who for these hundreds of years have hunted the same way, sung the same old hunting songs, blown the same notes on their hunting horns, and strictly observed the same rules of dress.

East and West, their traditions endure today in more than a hundred American fox-hunting clubs.

II

West Hills riders get up before dawn on a hunting day and turn themselves out impeccably in top hats or derbies, pink or black riding coats, white or tan breeches, white shirts with white stocks (scarves), yellow waistcoats, yellow gloves, black boots and spurs. The master and two or three others are in velvet hunting caps.

The wardrobe is out of the eighteenth century. In the years when they weren't making war, both sides in the American Revolution — Washington and his officers here, and King George and his advisers there — went fox hunting in riding habits that weren't significantly different except for the affectation of their era: the tri-corner hat. Indeed, the long pink coat signifying status in a fox-hunting club (it is actually a red coat) is descended from the regulation jacket worn at that time by British Army redcoats.

So far as the eye can tell, it could be either 1773, 1873, or 1973 when the West Hills Hunters meet at precisely 7 a.m. on a misty Saturday morning in rural California. They've gathered on the low-lying hills of a rocky, wooded ranch of forty thousand acres in Pine Valley, forty miles east of San Diego.

Thirty-four horsemen and women, veterans of 5:30 reveille at a nearby inn, have come together in a clearing edged by oak trees and a stone wall. And as they exchange greetings in the saddle, their colors are as fresh and spotless as if this were the first dance at the Hunt Ball. The first gallop will be something else, raising the dust that changes the picture, but at this instant this could be a roofless display room in the world's biggest costume store.

As the hunt begins, some two dozen hounds appear and move off in front of the horses. The pace is leisurely, and it is immediately apparent that this is a unique kind of sports event. The exquisitely-groomed participants carry no weapons. They are observers — not hunters — and though most are skilled horsemen or horsewomen, they aren't even in competition with one another. The competition is between hounds and quarry. This is a hunt in which the hounds do the hunting.

For those in riding coats and breeches, a fox hunt is a spectator sport on horseback.

III

The ritual each Wednesday and Saturday is as simple as it is timeless. There are three components of a hunt: a pack of hounds (usually numbering twenty or twenty-five), followed closely by a group of four or five riders (collectively termed the staff), followed at a distance of twenty to three hundred yards by the rest of the riders (known as the field).

On the staff are a huntsman and several whippers-in. A huntsman is a professional hunter responsible for the year-round care of the hounds; a whipper-in is a veteran horseman, usually amateur, who helps the huntsman keep the hounds to their business.

All other riders are in what's termed the field. These are the mounted spectators whose director is the fieldmaster, who is usually the club's master — more properly master of fox hounds (or MFH), an elective office. From their observation posts to the rear of the staff, members of the field proceed casually until the hounds pick up the scent of the quarry.

The fox and coyote are both nocturnal animals who themselves have been out hunting, and the course traveled by one of them — and the scent he leaves as he runs off — is known as the line. When the hounds come across it, they give chase — baying and barking, or speaking — as the tempo shifts abruptly in the field.

The spectators must gallop now to keep up with the hounds. If there's a fence, they must jump it, and if the coyote streaks uphill, they must follow, though their preference is for open country and a hot line. The nearer the fox or coyote, the hotter the line, the faster the chase.

It ends when the quarry is captured, or escapes temporarily or permanently. The chase might have lasted five minutes or an hour and five minutes. It might be measured in yards or miles. It might be succeeded by a two-hour walk, or by another race before you can catch your breath. The chase is known as a go — and goes are the essence of fox hunting: the touchdowns, the home runs, the birdies or aces.

Fox hunting is not, to be sure, all that romantic to the fox or his West Coast surrogates. On the occasions when the hounds run down their quarry, they kill him. But in this kind of hunting, the contest is at least animal versus animal, which to a fox hunter seems more equitable than animal versus gun. And on a West Coast hunt, the sport is even less bloodthirsty due to the creative elusiveness of the coyote. He's so successful, in fact, that you surmise he may even enjoy giving those sluggard hounds the slip. Time and again, in any case, that's what seems to be happening here.

IV

The riders say the objective of a fox hunt is to view the fox or coyote. And in California, even a view is so rare, by comparison with a kill in England, that the cry of "tally ho" rings louder and more vibrantly here than anywhere else in the world. Or so the West Hills people all say.

"Tally" is a synonym for quarry. The expression (pronounced tally'O) announces a sighting. On this week's hunt, during the longest go, the coyote got away after a twelve-mile chase by climbing to the highest rocks, where the hounds lost the scent. This is a frequent coyote ploy. Kills are few in California because coyotes can outspeed hounds even though the latter have more endurance.

Members of the hunt say two coyotes have been known to take turns leading the hounds, one resting while the other runs.

West Hills' second-ranking officer, J. Edward Martin, secretary, says: "We are people who like to ride horses, but there isn't much zest in trail riding, or hacking through the park. In fox hunting, the hounds decide the itinerary, and you can't let any obstacle stop you. The excitement is in keeping up, keeping going, and in feeling the horse's excitement. It's the most thrilling way to ride."

Board member Robert C. Daigh: "The horse is our common denominator. There are a lot of other things to do on horseback, of course, but some of them aren't very challenging. We think of a fox hunt as the main event."

Mrs. Janice Daigh: "It's exhilarating, the same vertigo as mountain climbing and skiing. And it's a family sport. Most of those who ride with us are married couples. In golf and other things, the wives stay home."

As a fitness activity, they all say, fox hunting tends to be more beneficial than many other vigorous sports. "It's not as strenuous as tennis, but it's more exhilarating," their leader, Ramser, notes. Tall, erect, dignified in bearing, Ramser, who both looks and acts the part of a master, adds: "There's nothing like galloping side by side cross-country, coming to a wide jump, and jumping side by side. It stirs the blood."

Asked why he schedules hunts on Saturdays instead of Sundays,

Ramser says: "Over the centuries, Sunday hasn't been much of a fox-hunting day. Sunday is for love."

V

Ramser's is a sport that for hundreds of years has addicted many. There have been long-lived members of the English nobility who hunted almost every day into advanced old age. One lord rode to hounds, his own pack among many others, every morning for a quarter century, finally missing a jump on the day of his fiftieth birthday party, when the fall killed him. To this day, Britain's Princess Anne regularly rides in fox hunts, seeking to perfect her equestrian ability despite notices from the League Against Cruel Sports that forty-eight per cent of the English public disapproves.

An American enthusiast rode until he was ninety-one though blind the last years of his life. He died on his horse. "A master in Maryland is seventy-six years old," Ramser says. "The Denver master is eighty-six and still going out to hounds."

At the other end of the scale, there are riders aged nine or ten in several U.S. and English hunts, most of them girls (boys today lean toward the mechanized sports). Often chosen for its fitness benefits, fox hunting may be the only international sport in which it is possible to participate with skill from nine to ninety.

It's also an activity in which males insistently discriminate against females. No matter how talented, women can never qualify for a pink coat — the sport's badge of excellence, awarded only by masters, and usually only after five years of demonstrated excellence. Fox hunting's dominant male chauvinists extend their female stars only a dark-blue coat which is all but indistinguishable from the journeyman black. The wife of the secretary, Mrs. Betty Martin, puts it this way: "This is the last stronghold of chivalry. They won't let us close gates and things. There's some advantage in that."

Discrimination is perhaps most obvious at the annual Hunt Ball, where the best of the female riders wear evening gowns, competing on that level against girls who can't stay on a horse — whereas the best of the horsemen change like peacocks from pink riding coats to pink, swallow-tailed evening coats.

Hunt Ball tickets cost $60 a couple. Like the sports it replaced in the seventeenth century — stag hunting and falconry — fox hunting is for men of means. The major cost item relating directly to the sport is support of the hounds. West Hills maintains its own kennels in Chatsworth.

California's only master of fox hounds, Ramser, whose sons, Harold Jr. and Philip, both work and ride with him, can I.D. all of West Hills' forty-five hounds, calling each by name. After five of the fastest were lost in San Diego the other day, every hound was quickly retrieved when the master, cooperating with the San Diego Police Department, could identify them all.

Ramser concedes that his sport isn't for the masses. Indeed he agrees that a primary attraction of the hunt is its exclusivity — its tradition-soaked status for those who aspire to costly traditions. The pageantry, for example, is irrelevant to the essence of fox hunting. "The pageantry is simply a colorful link with the past," he says. "It isn't important. It just makes the whole thing more fun. Iconoclasts can go do something else."

2. Risk Exercise (RE) is Essential

ON THE fox hunt, I rode with a man from Illinois who told me that swimming and gardening are commendable exercises, but that wilder sports like horseback riding and skiing are essential to physical and mental well-being. Later, I pressed him on what he meant.

PINE VALLEY, Calif.: April 2, 1973.

To live a full life, you must participate regularly in a sport that provides an element of danger — surfing or skiing, perhaps, or horseback riding. Golf doesn't do it — nor do tennis, calisthenics, or jogging.

Those are the conclusions of a research scientist, Dr. Sol Roy Rosenthal, professor of preventive medicine at the University of Illinois. His M.D. is from that university. His Ph.D. is from Germany's University of Freiburg.

Rosenthal, who divides the world into RE (risk-exercise) sports and non-RE sports, makes these further judgments: Tennis (non-RE) is exhausting whereas skiing (RE) exhilarates; men and women are more efficient and creative after RE; all this being true, risk sports should be subsidized by someone on some level: city, county, state or nation. "Somehow, we must find the time and money," says Rosenthal, who earlier in his career in preventive medicine helped prove the link between cholesterol and hardening of the arteries. He is here on sabbatical this year working on a book and seeking a producer for an RE documentary.

"To do it right, risk exercise takes time," he says. "Once a week isn't enough. You should ski or play polo several times a week, and it needs public financing for two reasons. It's expensive, and there aren't that many places to go. In a city like Los Angeles, there should be hundreds of places where you could rent and ride horses inexpensively. There should be hundreds of places to surf and sail inexpensively — and hundreds of inexpensive ways to get to ski resorts."

What do you have against tennis and golf?

"Not a thing. They're both commendable exercises. So are hiking, gardening, carpentry, and the like. These things complement RE. All forms of exercise are excellent — but RE is essential. For it's in man's inheritance, in his history. During most of the years of his evolution, he has engaged in physical activities associated with risks. Throughout most of his days, man has risked himself to procure food, to protect his territorial rights, and to protect his family as well as himself. Long ago, he became attracted to these dangers, if not addicted. He was happiest under their influence. And today, if they're absent, he's left with a void. He operates on low voltage. The lights grow dim."

You seem to be saying that danger leads to happiness.

"It does, and the dangers were carefully calculated long ago. Risk became sport as well as necessity. Natural risks evolved into challenges and physical feats. They helped mold man's codes of honor, his pride, and his loyalty. They also prolonged his youth and prowess. In time, the old stimuli were deleted, but the need for risks persists. The body craves risk. Man is still happiest when physically threatened."

In today's world, that's hard to arrange.

"Let's be sure we understand each other. I'm not advocating recklessness. There was nothing foolhardy about the risks your ancestors took. They were calculated risks, well calculated. Early man developed great skills in procuring food under dangerous circumstances. By the same token, skiing is a calculated risk requiring considerable skill. The thing I advocate is attaining skills in RE sports."

What particular RE sports do you advocate?

"It depends on the individual. Some give more stimulation than others to some people. For my wife, horseback riding is enough. I need fox hunting on horseback — jumping fences and the like. In all, there are three categories of RE sports. At the top are skiing, surfing, mountain climbing, and so on. Perhaps flying and auto racing. In the second category are things like horseback riding, outdoor living, water skiing. Third are swimming, fencing, hunting and sports of that kind."

What about people who can't develop much proficiency in any sport?

"If they have their health, they can do something — sail, perhaps, or fly airplanes."

Those are expensive.

"The alternatives are not attractive: sunken chest, flabby muscles, dull eyes, frustration, quiet desperation, depression. Risk exercise is not only a basic evolutionary need but it also gives exquisite joy and vigor. It also helps us maintain our sense of humor and perspective. And on the evidence I have from fox hunters to football coaches, RE appreciably improves the participants' sex life."

For these benefits, is the explanation chemical or evolutionary?

"Probably both. Reaction to fear followed by the liberation of adrenaline is a commonly known phenomenon. For RE people, the height of enjoyment in any activity, sex or otherwise, comes after performance in sport — perhaps as a reaction to the adrenaline."

What if you can't take the time to ski three times a week?

"Try it. You'll accomplish more the rest of the week."

3. Lost in the Wilderness? How to Stay Alive

IT'S NOT often, in the sports pages, that you get to write about life and death matters.

YOSEMITE NATIONAL PARK: June 30, 1976.

So you like to hike off the beaten path. You enjoy life at the edges of civilization — not too far out, but definitely out — and you've just sprained an ankle. It is almost 5 p.m. What now?

Well, don't panic. Facing an unexpected day or two in the wilderness, any stranded traveler can manage in any kind of California weather — if he thinks he can.

This is the collective opinion of the faculty of the Yosemite Mountaineering School, where classes in Alpine survival are taught each summer. "Surviving is first of all believing you can survive," says Loyd Price, the school's Alaska-born director. "That's half the battle. There are cases of injured persons living for days in the mountains without food or water, and over a month without food if they had water. One guy," says Price, referring to a historic case, "was out there in rain and sleet for seven days with a broken back and one box of raisins. When they asked him how he did it, he said: 'I had a few raisins every day, and I sang a lot.'"

Two members of Price's twelve-man faculty, Craig Patterson and Doug Wiens, specialize in how to live when lost in California or when incapacitated in the Western wilderness. On the average, a dozen nature lovers each year lose their lives in the Yosemite area, and most of the losses are needless, in the opinion of Price, Patterson and Wiens.

They recommend ten commandments for survival:

1 — Don't get lost.

Price: "Put yourself in position not to get in trouble. You might be missing for a while — but not really lost — if you tell someone the general area where you're going to be hiking, skiing or riding. Tell your parents or a friend or the rangers. And the more specific you can be as to trails, the better." Wiens: "Plan what to do if you have trouble. Plan for a longer hike than you expect. If you're just thinking of going out for the day, plan for overnight. Take an extra candy bar or two and a small survival kit."

2 — Know yourself.

Price: "Make a realistic appraisal of your ability. Don't forget you're eight thousand feet up. Don't assume you can walk over that mountain if you've never done it. Remember, a kayak can kill you if you're inexperienced on rivers. Set realistic goals." Warning strongly against hiking alone unless on a marked trail, Price says: "A majority of those who aren't found until too late are single people."

It is nonetheless true that those drawn to the wilderness probably like the solitude particularly. "I like to walk alone," says Patterson, professor of survival at the Yosemite school and author of a forthcoming book ("Practical Mountain Survival"). "It should only be done by persons who understand they're taking a much greater risk."

3 — Know the area.

Price: "Do three things before you start out. First, learn to read a topo (topographical) map and take it with you. Get an expert to explain those contour lines and you'll remember how to read a map forever. Second, have a short chat with someone who knows the country thoroughly. A ranger will be glad to discuss it. Finally, get the latest weather forecast."

4 — Prepare for the worst.

Price: "Carry minimum survival equipment whenever you think you might be off the trail. In addition to a map, knife and flashlight that means a plastic water bottle, first-aid kit, repair kit (for fixing boots, etc.), survival kit (waterproof matches, compass, etc.) and survival food (candy, nuts, instant energy food, etc.)." Patterson: "It's good to carry your own shelter — a small tarp and a plastic space blanket — and keep your watch wound. If set on standard time it can be used as a compass in sunlight after about 6 a.m. Hold it level — and point the small hand toward the sun. Due south will be roughly halfway to the 12 on your watch."

5 — Concentrate on being found.

Patterson: "The first thing to do if you're incapacitated or think you might be lost is analyze your resources. There's no reason to panic — in California, at least — if you'll concentrate on being found. Check your food supply, water bottles, clothing, and shelter possibilities. The inventory will affect all your subsequent decisions. Then decide whether to stay put or travel back to civilization. Either way, your chances are better when you make a decision you can stick with."

6 — Don't wander aimlessly.

Patterson: "Point yourself in one direction and stay on course — if you decide to go — and it's usually better to go if you know the extent of your injury and which way to go. I've been lost a dozen times and only waited once to be rescued. For those who have been in a plane crash, of course, or who might not have proper equipment, it's best to stay, but I'd rather hobble out."

Price: "It is often said: 'When lost follow a stream' — or, 'Follow drainage downstream' — but not in the Sierra. If you do that in Yosemite or Sequoia or other places in these mountains, you might go over a waterfall." Patterson: "In Yosemite last winter a lost hiker followed a stream to the top of Bridalveil Fall and died there of exposure in sight of traffic on the road below."

Price: "Topographically, the Sierra runs from northwest to southeast. You can get out from most places in a couple of days by following the sun or going away from the sun." Patterson: "Head east or west for a road or highway. If it's cloudy and you don't have a compass, the moss on the trees is unreliable in this area. But most of the year, the snow melts faster on the south side of a snowbank. The north side just looks colder. I've used that a lot."

7 — Build a home. A forest is a lumber yard.

Patterson: "If you decide to stay put when lost or injured, the first thing to do is find suitable shelter. To stay alive you must above all minimize body-heat loss. Hike around for a cave or a boulder you can crawl under and attach a front door. Forests are lumber yards, with slabs of logs, bark, boughs and branches, and you can put a roof over your head without touching a living tree. Make a fire outside, and put a roof over the fire, too. Direct the heat inside."

Wiens: "Proper shelter and clothing are vital to human beings caught in the wilderness because their greatest danger there is hypothermia (body-heat loss leading to subnormal body temperature). Malnutrition is almost never a killer in the mountains. The real threat is hypothermia — or 'dying of exposure'. You don't have to freeze to death. You can die at 55 degrees if you're exhausted or if the weather is wet and windy and your body isn't producing enough heat. Normal body temperature is 98. If you gain 2 degrees, you're miserable. If your temperature gets down to 80 you die — and 80 is the temperature of a nice summer day."

Price: "When hiking or skiing cross country, if there's the slightest possibility you might be lost or spending an unscheduled night or two in the open, plan for the worst possible weather. Always wear wool pants and shirt. In cool, wet, windy weather you lose body heat if you're wearing cotton clothes. Normally, a human being is surrounded by a quarter-inch of warm air. But if it's windy, this warmth is blown away — and if it's wet, cotton makes the condition worse. Cotton wicks the outside moisture toward the body. By contrast, wool repels moisture. Wool doesn't wick. It dries from the inside out."

Patterson: "Wear or carry a little wool cap. The head is like a steam radiator. Half the heat that escapes from the body is lost from the neck up. And except in midsummer, it doesn't hurt to carry a knit face mask." Wiens: "Hypothermia is insidious. Once you start losing body heat, it affects your mind and judgment."

8 — Conserve your energy. A forest is a lousy grocery store.

Patterson: "The best survival food is the extra food you've stored in your own pack — those two candy bars or whatever. In recent years there's been an edible-plants craze, but edible plants are overrated. During storms, the Indians didn't go out looking for food. Better to hole up and conserve your energy. You'll be hungry, but in the California wilderness the chances are you won't live long enough to die of starvation. You'll die of hypothermia first. If you're shivering and exhausted, don't ration your food too carefully. Eat that candy bar, even the last of it, because if you're in the first stages of hypothermia and aren't found, the next stage is death anyway."

Survival food is the opposite of what you want when dieting. Patterson: "Animal food is better than plants because it has more calories. In a survival situation, try to catch a frog, lizard, mouse, rattlesnake, porcupine or fish. A porcupine is the largest animal you're likely to catch with a club. If you're starving, carry a three- or four-foot club. Price: "It helps if you know how to catch fish with your hands. In a shallow stream, build a rock barrier and chase them into the rocks, catching them with your T shirt. In waters where fish hide under banks, you can immobilize them with your hands by reaching under the bank and tickling them in the tummy. This is a sport in Scotland. It's called cuddling."

Water isn't the problem in the Sierra mountains that it is in typical wilderness areas. There are many streams, springs and other sources.

Patterson: "When I need water, I head for a valley bottom and make a five-minute side trip in one direction or the other, and usually I find water before I've walked five minutes. Maps are helpful. The blue stream lines on a USGS map identify year-round water. A third alternative is to look for lush green plants, the sign of a spring. In summer you'll often find a stream running down from a snow patch on a north-facing slope. It may be there in winter, too, and if so, that's better than eating snow — which uses body heat to melt. Don't eat colored snow, although the stream from a colored snowbank is OK. The algae stays in the snow."

9 — Signal.

Patterson: "In the wilderness, you're the quarterback. If you're lost or hurt and waiting for help, nothing is more important than food, clothing, shelter and signaling — and it's up to you to call the signals for your searching party. Walk or crawl to the nearest meadow or open space and make a big X — thirty or forty feet long — using anything that will do it: pine boughs, log slabs, bright pieces of clothing, pieces of canvas, sleeping bags, anything. In military code, an X means *Unable to Proceed*, and if written large and clear it will get the attention of planes or helicopters. Use contrasting colors. If the field is snow-covered, use pine boughs. In a green meadow, white rocks or white logs." Price: "When lost or in trouble and trying to hike out, leave signals. Stack up rocks. Repeating three of anything means *Help* — three stacks of stones, three wooden stakes or logs, three fires. You can also make an arrow with stones and leave your initials."

Patterson: "A black column of smoke rising in the mountains is apt to be investigated. Try burning wet leaves. But remember that white smoke is no good in snow. In a stalled car, stay put. A car is a good survival shelter, windproof, rainproof. Burn crankcase oil or the tires to signal for help. If you're without matches, you can strike the terminals of the car battery and get a fire going with a gas-soaked rag." Wiens: "You can signal a passing airplane with the rear-view mirror or the shiny bottom of a can, assuming the sun is out. Extend one arm as a sighting device. Point it at the plane, and, holding the mirror in your other hand, shine it on your pointing fingers."

10. Don't get hurt.

This is worse than getting lost. Survivalists say an incapacitating injury is more likely to prompt an unplanned night or two in the open than anything else. Therefore, the faculty of the Yosemite Mountaineering School stresses safety, illustrating, for example, the right way to ford rivers and cross snowfields.

A snowfield — meaning, usually, a broad, icy, snow-covered hill — frequently stands in the path of a Sierra hiker, lost or not. Large ice patches remain through most of the summer in many California mountains and there's a trick to crossing them safely. The method is called glissading — an intentional small slide. It's something like skiing in hiking boots. One should proceed with small steps — toes pointed up, heels dug in. An essential is a pole to serve as tripod and brake.

Yosemite school students also practice falls on steep icy hills. They are taught to roll over when tumbling, to bury their face in the snow and dig in with their elbows and knees — arching their backs to get a better grip.

As for fording streams, Patterson says: "There are several things to remember. The most important is knowing when not to cross. If the current is swift or there's a waterfall near or you're uncertain about the depth, take no chances. Explore up and downstream for two hundred yards or so. A log may have fallen across or there may be stones or boulders you can use as a bridge. If not, look for a wide place. As a rule, the wider the spot in the river or stream, the more shallow it is and the easier to ford. Next, find a stout stick — a long pole — and use it as a tripod to help you keep your balance."

Always wear shoes when crossing a stream. Price: "You have less traction barefoot and there's more danger on slippery boulders — but take off your socks before stepping into the water. Putting on dry socks after you get across is better than having everything wet. Finally, if you're fording a stream in a group, cross as a unit, with everyone linked and the taller persons upstream. A rope can be dangerous unless you anchor it solidly far away from the stream."

Survival, in other words isn't just a matter of chance. You have to work at it.

POSTSCRIPT

A survival kit can be a man's best friend in the California deserts or mountains. And the rule is that any person venturing far enough to strap on a backpack should carry a survival kit. Hence it must be small so there's no temptation to leave it home.

Commercial kits are available at outdoors stores but can be assembled in your kitchen — using an empty pill box or adhesive bandage box or, as recommended at the Yosemite Mountaineering School, a Planter's (or Scudder's or Fisher's) peanut tin — one of those round containers, about three by three inches, with a plastic top.

Remove most of the peanuts and, for surviving in the Sierra, insert:

Waterproof matches (book matches in a plastic bag).
Butane lighter (change annually to keep fresh).
Candle (for sustained flame under wet twigs).
Compass (a small dime-store model will do if checked for accuracy).
Space blanket (fifty-by-eighty-four-inch waterproof aluminized plastic folding into a package the size of a cigaret box).
Several sugar packets (salt is a luxury but think about it).
Water purification tablets and two plastic lunch bags.
Some forty feet of ten- to fifteen-pound test line on a small sewing machine bobbin (to use when lashing together branches for shelter or when fishing).
A small pocket knife (if you don't carry one regularly).
Adhesive bandages (if you don't carry a first-aid kit).
Needle and thread (if you don't carry a repair kit).
Think about insect repellent, fish hooks, leader line, treble hooks (for snagging animals), bouillon cubes, parachute cord, safety pines and candy.
Wrap some waterproof tape around the outside.
Water purification tablets are seldom needed in the Yosemite area; but they don't weigh much — and nothing is more important than water.

4. Relax and Run Faster

TWO EXPERTS in physical education have their say in the next two pieces. Both men are coaches of champions, and both believe that optimum foot speed isn't inborn. Anyone can be trained to run faster, they say — even a slow football player — but their focus is different. To Bud Winter, the key is relaxing. To Jim Bush, it's striding uphill.

SAN JOSE, Calif.: May 21, 1974.

Would you like to run faster? You can, you know. All you have to do is relax. "Well," says L.C. (Bud) Winter, "that's maybe not quite all. But relaxing is the main thing. The way to run faster is with a four-fifths effort. Just take it nice and easy."

But what about George Allen? He always says to give 110 per cent.

Says Winter: "He's wrong about that. Going all-out is counterproductive. Our greatest athletes have been the sleepy-looking guys. Joe Louis, for example. Joe DiMaggio. John Unitas."

Fair enough, but who says so? Who is Bud Winter?

He's a veteran track coach, a specialist in sprinting. For many years, Winter has rated as the most consistently successful coach of sprinters on the planet. During his three decades at San Jose State (1940-70), Winter's sprinters broke or tied the world record at all distances: 50 yards and meters, 60 yards and meters, 100 yards and meters, 200 meters, 220 yards (on both curved and straight tracks), 400 meters and 440 yards. For a period in the late 1960s, Bud Winter's students held all ten records at the same time.

But he is a fan of all sports, and Winter is depressed these days by the fact that football and baseball players remain so slow. "Everybody can learn to run faster," he says. "And most people can improve a lot. Your inherent speed is just part of it. The trained sprinter is much faster than that. And what counts is learning to relax under the pressure of combat — learning to move with a four-fifths effort. An athlete who wants to die for dear old Rutgers, or San Jose, misses the point. He's no good dead."

What's wrong with the all-out try?

"Your antagonistic muscles mess up your performing muscles," Winter says. "A clenched fist is the mark of a loser. So is a set jaw."

What are antagonistic muscles?

"The reverse of performing muscles. It takes one set of muscles to extend the arm, for example, and another set to draw it in. Under conditions of tension, antagonistic muscles drag you back. To get full efficiency of the performing muscles, you have to fully relax the antagonistic muscles. The thing you want is leg speed — the legs moving faster — and relaxation achieves this because you stop fighting yourself."

In addition to sprinters, what other athletes might improve with a four-fifths effort?

"Have you ever stood next to a shot putter who, after coming close to a record, says: 'That seemed easy.'?"

Not recently.

"I have. He's thinking: 'That was so easy I'm going to gun it this time.' The guy wants to set a shot-put record that will last forever. But when he guns it the second time, it falls three feet short of the first one."

How do you explain that to the shot putter?

"I tell him what I'm telling you — but most people find such things hard to believe. Here's another example. At San Jose, to get a man's inherent speed, we measure him at thirty yards with a running start. If he's any kind of athlete, he'll do it the first time in about three seconds. Then we talk it over, and I tell him to have two things in mind next time: Keep your hands loose and your jaw loose. And when he runs it again, invariably, he takes from one-tenth to two-tenths off his time. But even when we show him the watch, he can't believe it."

To relax properly, what's necessary besides keeping a loose jaw?

"It's a long story that I'd rather not go into now except to say that our relaxation program takes six weeks. During (World War II), I was chairman of relaxation research in Navy Pre-Flight, working with all kinds of people. We took guys who failed in gunnery, who froze at the controls when they had to shoot bullets, and made them into some of the best shooters in the Navy. We had one hundred per cent results. After six weeks in our relaxation program, they could fall asleep if they wanted to in two minutes."

To be a great sprinter, what does it take besides the ability to relax?

"It takes perfect form. You've got to have that to reach your full potential. Most athletes — and many sprinters — don't have it. Bob Hayes runs like he's pounding grapes into wine. What we've learned at San Jose is that with perfect form, anybody can run faster."

What do you mean, precisely, by perfect form?

There are a half dozen or more essentials, starting with high knees. A man doesn't walk with his knees up, so first you have to develop the muscles for that. The second and most important essential is foreleg reach. The knees have to be pumped high, but they can't be pumped straight down unless what you want is to run in place. A long stride is obligatory. Watch a whippet sometime, or a race horse. They're extending their legs as far as they can."

What makes you so sure that humans should do the same?

"You can prove it mathematically. If your stride is only one-quarter inch longer than the next guy's, you'll beat him by eight inches at a hundred yards, other things being equal. The only problem is that foreleg reaching is hard to learn. The human tendency is to bring the knees down like a drum majorette. They're pretty to watch, those girls, but confidentially, they make lousy sprinters."

What are the other essentials?

"Good arm action, lean forward, run tall, and dig a hole in the track with each foot as it comes down. Run as high on your toes as you can. You can't sprint on a flat wheel. And bound forward, not up. One foot should always be on the ground and working."

What's meant by good arm action?

"Relaxed hands. Elbows bent ninety degrees. Pump the air back with your elbows, not your hands. You should be pumping your arms faster than your legs. Swing them as fast as you can. One mistake most football players make is that they think a man runs with his legs. They would be faster if they ran with their arms."

What else does a top sprinter need besides talent, good form, and the ability to relax?

"Only one more thing: the ability to sustain top speed. Which means to sustain form. In the crunch, when everybody is tiring in the last twenty yards, the champion pointedly emphasizes his form. Very often, the difference between winning and losing is the ability to reaffirm the fundamentals near the end of the race. A loser's form deteriorates in the last fifteen or twenty yards. Champions are able to emphasize their form there because we have drilled them on it every day for nine months."

How hard do you work them?

"The question is not how long you work, but what you do when you're working. And the key is the right kind of exercise. Two or three hours of aimless running accomplishes very little. A sprinter can sustain his form with an hour and a half of proper exercise a day, five or six days a week."

That sounds like a lot of exercise.

"But on the [major league] level, it's all you need — if you've learned to relax."

5. Run Uphill to Quickness

THE JOGGERS who litter the streets of the world are more than a public nuisance. They also harm themselves, this coach says, and his campaign has doubtless caused many people to (1) run faster or (2) quit running. He advocates hard, uphill striding to maximize quickness.

LOS ANGELES: March 4, 1975.

As a track coach, Jim Bush, who has led UCLA to four national titles in ten years, raises two hypothetical questions: First, what physical quality is the most prized today in football, basketball, tennis, hockey, and most other sports? Everybody's answer: quickness.

Second, what does it take to develop or improve quickness? Bush's answer: strong legs.

Accordingly, he is a leg man. A veteran physical fitness expert, Bush has worked with thousands of pairs of legs — including basketball player Jerry West's, tennis player Kathy May's, and film player Elke Sommer's — recommending in each instance a program based on running up hills.

A track specialist to begin with who has become a man of all sports,

Bush has found that traditional jumping-jack calisthenics are of limited value to any athlete — pro, amateur, or duffer — building neither speed nor quickness. And for conditioning, he stands squarely against both jogging and sprinting — preferring a gait in the middle that he calls striding. To stride is to move at three-fifths to four-fifths speed.

Surprisingly, he advocates more or less the same things for all athletes. There isn't much difference between the training schedules he draws up for tennis and basketball players. "When I become involved with an athlete I haven't met before," says Bush, "it usually starts the same way. The coach will come to me and say: 'I'd like to help his quickness. What can I do?' I tell the coach: 'If it's quickness you want, we've only got one choice. We'll have to strengthen his legs and lower body.'"

A program of hard running is then specified. "To build up the legs," Bush says, "you have to run — regardless of whether your game is tennis, basketball or hockey. The only variances are individual. One athlete will train by running up a hill every day. Another might run it three times a week, and go to speed work on alternate days — or perhaps long, easy runs on a flat surface."

The hill used by most Bush clients rises five hundred yards from the UCLA landscape, but any hill will do. Jerry West used to run one at the Bel-Air Country Club. Says Bush: "There is a climb of thirty or forty degrees on our hill at UCLA. It isn't steep until you go to run it. The reason I prefer it to a flat surface is that running a hill is a resistance-type exercise. It fights you. When you tire, it's harder to keep your form, so a workout like this is more valuable than, say, lifting weights. I got the idea some years ago watching (Olympic runner) Peter Snell train on a hill in New Zealand."

Athletes working with Bush aren't allowed to jog up the hill. "I hate the word jog," he says. "It's a word we ought to get rid of. When I hear it, I immediately think of a guy plodding along, pounding the ground, and jarring his whole body with every step. Joggers jar their spine, their knees, their hips, their ankle joints, everything."

According to Webster's, to jog is to move at a slow, leisurely, or monotonous pace. Bush: "I've been with men and women who bragged that earlier in the day, they jogged two or three miles. They'd have been better off to run a bit faster and not so far. When you move faster, it's easier on your body because you're brushing your weight over the feet — distributing it quickly over various portions of each foot." By contrast, he says, "joggers come down with all their weight at once. That's what I have against jogging."

Moreover, in his opinion, the optimum training distance is one mile. "That's enough," he says. "It's enough to give the cardiovascular system a good workout — and also the respiratory system. They work hand in hand. But don't start out running a mile. Experiment. Run until you're tired, then stop and walk awhile, staying at it till you get in a full mile each time."

It doesn't hurt to carry a stopwatch. Bush: "Your first goal should be to break seven minutes, then six minutes, then see how close to five minutes you can come. Few people can run a mile that fast, but *think* about five minutes. The greatest thing for a man's — or woman's — physical fitness is to run a mile at least three times a week, five times if you can handle it."

A running program should always be supervised by a specialist, Bush stresses, and never undertaken except after consultation with a physician. "Some people in their seventies can run a mile, and some in their thirties shouldn't," he says. "Don't go out on your own. See a doctor first."

There is no optimum way to run. To the contrary, according to Bush, there are almost as many ways as runners. "You can't learn running in a book," he says, although he has turned out one book on the subject and is writing another. "The problem is that humans come in all sizes: short and long torsos, short and long legs, short and long arms. The key to coaching is to respect individual differences, and the key to running is to relax. But what might be relaxing to one person isn't to another."

In learning to run, experimentation is advisable in all aspects. For instance, says Bush: "There are at least three ways to hold the arms — high, low and halfway between. To arrive at an individual's most relaxed position, we first have him let the arms drop. Then as the arms are hanging, bend the elbows up to an angle that feels good."

The most important equipment is the right shoes. Bush recommends training shoes. "Tennis shoes don't provide enough support," he says. "What you need is a shoe with good arch support, a secure top, and enough sole to cushion some of the shock of landing."

Of the many kinds of exercises recommended by doctors and trainers, walking ranks down the list for Bush. "There's nothing wrong with a brisk hike," he says, "but if your doctor allows running, you get more out of running. It builds more strength." Bush thinks any healthy man or woman can profit from a course of instruction with a track coach. And the example he often uses is Actress Elke Sommer, whom he taught to hurdle and put the shot for a role as a Soviet track star. "She's a very well-coordinated woman," he says. "She could be a great athlete."

Says Elke: "Coach Bush is a stickler for correct form. In one scene when I was running away from the secret police, I had to hurdle a baby buggy — and Jim made them turn the buggy around so the handle would be on the other side. He said the way they had it the first time, it would be impossible for me to hurdle it properly."

Says Bush: "I never paid so much attention to form in my life."

6. Stretch and Reach for the Gin

MY FRIENDS Jeanne and Bob Mueller introduced me to Laurence Morehouse, whose advice I try hard to follow, day and night. I think of this as one of the most important newspaper stories I've ever worked on.

LOS ANGELES: April 1, 1976.

Does it worry you that you don't have the time to keep yourself in condition physically? Do you wish you could exercise more often and play more games? If so, you're in the majority, UCLA Professor Laurence E. Morehouse suggests. But don't worry about it.

An exercise physiologist, Dr. Morehouse says:

"The average normal man or woman can get most of the exercise he needs just by being as active as possible, all day, every day. When you walk into the bedroom, for instance, walk briskly. Avoid elevators and escalators. Walk upstairs — and down. Park several blocks from your destination — and walk. Avoid car washes — wash your own. Don't have the boy carry your groceries out of the market — and don't push them out on a cart — carry them."

And another thing. "Stand up," Morehouse says. "Always stand when you're talking on the phone. But don't stand on a chair to get the gin down. Always reach for the gin. Or any container. Reach, stretch, twist, bend. And don't take your sex lethargically. During the sex hour, be vigorous. Be the one who volunteers to carry the trash out, or to lift the typewriter, or to move the chair. Keep the furniture well polished, and the windows washed. Jump, yank, move, sweep, mow, hoe, be active."

The author of the standard textbook on his subject as well as a best-seller, "Total Fitness in Thirty Minutes a Week," Morehouse has served as a physical conditioning adviser to the astronauts. He has also written the sections on physical conditioning in the Encyclopaedia Brittanica and other encyclopedias. Connecticut-born, an Iowa Ph.D., Morehouse at sixty could be a mellowing, prematurely-gray Marine sergeant. Tall, trim and athletic, he has the closely cropped hair — and the health — of his youth. Plainly, he practices what he preaches. "Like anything else," he says, "an active life is just a habit. But most people aren't active enough to keep from decaying. Surveys show that at least eighty per cent of adults in this country aren't exercising enough to arrest physiological decay."

What does that percentage tell you?

"That most people are like me," Morehouse says. "I hate to exercise myself. My bias is strongly against structured exercise. But I do force myself to face the truth, and the truth is that an inactive life is a slow form of suicide. Activity, on the other hand, is the means to an alert, vigorous, and lengthy life. The fountain of youth for which Ponce de Leon searched was right inside his body."

If he could have searched there, what would he have found?

"He would have learned, first, that body tissues and functions are improved by physical activity, and, second, that use delays the aging process. Use makes the organ. There are two kinds of aging, and while chronological age is invariable, physiological age has a variability of up to thirty years. On your fiftieth birthday, you can have the outward appearance and internal system of a sixty-five-year-old or a thirty-five-year-old. It's up to you."

What should I do?

"How fit do you want to be? There are three levels of satisfactory fitness. On one level, you need specific conditioning to play football, for instance, or to ski well. For the second level of fitness, we suggest our thirty-minute exercise program — ten minutes three times a week. The other fitness level is that of minimum maintenance. Below this irreducible minimum, you're going to experience degradation of function and structure. How fit do you want to be?"

The minimum.

"All right, you can achieve it by meeting a group of five simple requirements every day. Stand up every chance you get. Stretch and twist once in a while. Lift something heavy. For a period of three minutes, walk more briskly than usual. And make it a point to burn up three hundred calories a day in physical activity."

How much activity equals three hundred calories?

"Three miles of walking. But that doesn't necessarily mean three miles continuously. Going out to get the car is walking. Walk fast. Shopping is walking. Shop fast. Activity calories are burned whenever you make ordinary motions more vigorously than you ordinarily make them. If you stretch, stand, lift and move briskly all during the day, you're almost surely burning your three hundred calories."

Why should I be especially brisk for three minutes?

"The body doesn't fall back on its oxygen mechanism until the third minute. The muscles benefit in the first minute, but it takes a three-minute burst to stimulate the cardiovascular system."

Why do you recommend stretching?

"It's a mobility exercise. Reaching or stretching for groceries on the top shelf helps. So does bending for things on a bottom shelf. When you feel like yawning and stretching, make a big deal out of it, like a cat does. These things keep you from stiffening up. The idea is to be as active as possible all day, and the general maxims are simple: Don't lie down when you can sit, don't sit when you can stand, and don't stand when you can move."

How heavy is the package you want me to lift?

"For a fairly strong person, lifting an electric typewriter may be about right. Or you can lift a child, or even an adult. For many people, lifting a chair is an overload. That's what we're trying to get with all these things. An overload is an effort just a fraction greater than you're used to exerting, and we're trying to overload the system a bit."

Why?

"The human body is different from a machine. If a machine is continuously overloaded, it breaks down quicker. But when the human body is loaded, it improves. At the moment of the overload, it's fatiguing, but at the same time the body is getting signals that it better build up some muscles, and improve the circulation, and so on. The body adjusts itself to the load it has to handle. You decide what body you want to have, and load it — and the body will build up to that. It's better than a machine."

Should I avoid machines?

"They're often counterproductive, physiologically, in human terms. That's the fact. You're losing a lot when you have an automatic garage door, or automatic transmission, or a modern washing machine. If you're shopping for a new car, think about a stick shift. If you're in the bathroom, think about your wrist muscles when you're wringing out the wash cloth. Wring it hard."

Is raising the pulse rate desirable — speaking of exercise in general?

"A good general rule is that if you feel the heart beating in your chest, it's good. If you hear it beating in your head, you're being too vigorous."

Some overweight people worry about exercising too much. They think it makes them hungrier.

"Think of it like this: The way to make money running a ranch is to keep the cattle quiet and inactive. Then all they do is eat and get fat.

Human beings have a further problem. When they aren't active, they have to eat so little to keep from getting fat that they don't eat properly. Activity makes the man. Activity makes the woman."

7. How to Fight Stress

A WINNER in any human activity is an individual who can handle stress and pressure. In or out of sports, talent is never enough to guarantee success — as professional coaches all know. For, invariably, they have themselves experienced stress. Here's a man with some answers:

SAN JOSE, Calif.: July 3, 1989.

Stress and pressure are poisons that sting coaches and athletes more often than spectators, San Jose State Psychologist Bruce Ogilvie says. Yet Dr. Ogilvie is sure that for other men and women, too, his prescription for reducing tensions can be useful.

As a student of football and basketball coaching, he identifies a well-adjusted, reasonably contented coach as one with realistic goals, a personal physical fitness program, a concerned family, and a healthy sex life.

And if Ogilvie has a similar prescription for everyone else, he sees the problem in sports as more acute. "Stress in coaching is a given," he says. "And stress is very much like a poison. The pain and discomfort continue to build until you find a release. Running and swimming are particularly good releases, but hardly anything is more important than a good relationship with an attentive companion."

A veteran of thirty-five years as a psychology professor, Ogilvie has found that the NFL and NBA are the country's two most traumatic places to work. "Big league coaches are subject to two kinds of stress or pressure that don't much bother the rest of us," he says. "First, the performance demands by owners, fans and the press are unreal. Making the playoffs is now a minimum requirement, and if you don't get there, regardless of how ordinary your players are, you're made to feel that your job is in jeopardy. That's a hell of a way to have to live."

Second, most NFL and NBA coaches, Ogilvie says, "have been winners most of their lives — either as athletes or on lower coaching levels — or else they wouldn't be where they are. Suddenly, they're in a situation where they *can't* win no matter what they do. The result is a feeling of helplessness, anxiety and pressure — enormous pressure."

The antidote is finding a way to cope. Or as Ogilvie says: "You have to develop a defense. To go on living, you've got to drain the poison off by, for example, running to exhaustion. Or by involving yourself closely in a caring family, or with a loving wife. The world's greatest tranquilizer is a rumble in the hay. Coaches and others in stress-filled jobs need to return to the warmth and shelter of a loving partner after each workday."

San Jose State research has shown that *all* creative persons know extreme pressure — painters, architects, writers, editors and others as well as coaches — and many of these people are most effective when working against the stresses of rigid deadlines. Still, when the pressure comes to a boil, Ogilvie sees a wide gulf between, say, newspaper editors and football coaches.

"Creative people on magazines or newspapers and in other fields don't work in crowded stadiums," he says. "They can hide. They can make a mistake or two without losing their job. For a coach, there's no place to hide — and one wrong decision is career-threatening. That is real pressure."

8. Big Leaguers Don't Choke

THIS EXPERT has been worth visiting over and over over the years.

SAN JOSE, Calif. March 11, 1973.

San Jose State Psychologist Bruce Ogilvie has a new take on an old wives' tale:

• When an established major leaguer fails in a stressful situation, it is nonsense to say he choked. An athlete can be said to choke only when the pattern of his failure under pressure consistently exceeds mathematical expectations.

"You can't draw meaningful inferences from a major leaguer's mistakes — his occasional instances of failure — in the pressure of big games," Ogilvie says. "What usually happens is that against great players, professional athletes are fighting at the limit of their ability. You tend to make more errors when the threat is overwhelming and you're fully extended over a period of time. This is an example of a situation that is frequently confused with choking."

• The pressure on a quarterback in a third-down crisis is similar to that on a surgeon in the operating room, or a newspaper writer on a deadline.

"Surgeons, quarterbacks, first basemen, journalists, dentists, university professors, individuals of that type all are seeking recognition or the approval of society," Ogilvie says. "These are the people who have to learn to live with pressure."

What group exactly is Ogilvie defining?

"Those who feel socially pressured to achieve as individuals," he says. "Such people are making an ego investment. A man under pressure derives an ego satisfaction out of expressing himself in an area where society makes judgments."

As in sports.

"Yes, when an athlete invests his identity in a talent or skill or ability that is evaluated by society, the possibility of non-achievement becomes a threat to his ego. His performance as an athlete is inseparable from his performance as a human being. If he were a machine, he would feel no pressure, but men don't function like automatons."

In how many different ways does pressure originate or evolve?

"There's really only one way. In each instance, the pressure that any person feels is related to the needs of other persons — to a desire for their approval or recognition. The man who doesn't feel much pressure is the one who is satisfied with a small salary or who settles for a modest performance. Those who feel pressure are individuals who seek to be above the average."

What should they do about it?

"Athlete or not, make sure your goals are reasonably realistic, plan regular physical exercise, and marry well."

XII

1981

Of the two hundred stories I wrote in a typical Times year, 1981, there is room in this chapter for only a few. But as a chronological cluster, they may give some flavor of my yearly routine as well as some idea of the itinerary of a late-century U.S. sportswriter with national assignments. As usual that year, I looked for baseball topics in the spring before returning to football in the summer months, although, every year, month in and out, I never stop writing football if something's there.

For me, 1981 began in January with a different kind of human interest story — one featuring Super Bowl Quarterback Jim Plunkett — and rounded out twelve months later with the story of The Catch. The turning-point play for his generation, Wide Receiver Dwight Clark's leaping catch that day in San Francisco began the 49er era. On consideration, however, I have moved the account of that game out of this package and placed it with the other football game stories in Chapter VI. There are more 1981 pieces in the Rockne package (Chapter I). Here, Jim Plunkett is up first.

1. Jim Plunkett: Up or Down?

DURING THE thirteen years they represented Los Angeles, 1982-94, the Raiders seldom played as well as they had in Oakland. Their 1983 team won a Super Bowl for Los Angeles, but thereafter they were generally erratic — most noticeably in the eight seasons after Jim Plunkett retired. In their Los Angeles years, Plunkett was the Raiders' only great quarterback. He was, in fact, the best they had in their first thirty-five years in two towns. Of the three Super Bowls the Raiders won in that time, he won two — one for Oakland, one in Los Angeles — although at first, nobody predicted any such thing, least of all Plunkett.

NEW ORLEANS: Jan. 20, 1981.

The biggest man in the South this week, speaking in a football context, is Oakland Raiders Quarterback Jim Plunkett. A tall, quiet, smiling flamethrower, Plunkett is the central figure of Super Bowl week for this reason: the premise of the game is that Oakland will win from the Philadelphia Eagles here Sunday if this is the real Jim Plunkett. Two hypotheses have emerged:

• It is possible, first, that a physically and emotionally battered Jim Plunkett, permanently damaged by a decade of pro football disgrace in which he lost his composure and failed conspicuously in both New England and San Francisco, will fold again in the pressure of the Super Bowl.

• The other possibility is that, to the astonishment of the NFL, Jim Plunkett has been born again — his damaged arm rebuilt, his shattered confidence restored — and that the prepossessing quarterback who led Stanford to a Rose Bowl victory in 1971 will dominate Philadelphia in Super Bowl XV.

Not since Joe Namath in 1968, in those long ago days before Super Bowl III, has an NFL quarterback engendered such controversy and confusion. Who's right?

There appears to be a good chance that Plunkett's admirers are right. This group includes his former coach at Stanford, John Ralston, his present coach at Oakland, Tom Flores, and several others up there who, having followed his career for years, agreed the other day to talk about him openly but privately. These are the old, old friends who know him best. And their story — an intriguing, different kind of sports story — creates a portrait of the controversial quarterback that differs greatly from his public image.

This is what's in their sight lines when these people look at Plunkett:

They see a veteran quarterback who at thirty-two is "incredibly shy and sensitive, almost neurotically sensitive." They see a gifted athlete who, after leaving Palo Alto with the Heisman Trophy in 1971, was "all but ruined" at New England and San Francisco by "insensitive coaches and executives." At the same time, partially forgiving the Patriots and 49ers, they see a "deeply insecure young man" with a kind of split personality.

They say that Plunkett, on the one hand, carries a negative self-image so deeply ingrained that he has trouble functioning. On the other hand, he is fueled by an ambition to succeed that "amounts to an obsession." This continuous conflict between a self-image that "repels" him and his driving ambition to be a great quarterback is a trauma that "has almost torn him apart."

They say that Plunkett, an undeniably able quarterback, needs a football team that above all understands him "and cares for him as a person." Surprisingly, they say, he seems at last to be a member of such a club. And because the Raiders need Plunkett as much as he needs someone like them, his friends see a "player and an organization that were meant for each other."

They see a team that is on the brink of a big victory in Super Bowl XV. They could be wrong. They think they're right.

II

If the person and the team were meant for each other, there is a ready explanation. To the Raiders, who play football with a consistent long-ball philosophy, Plunkett brings the arm for the very long ball as well as the quick feet to stay out of trouble while Oakland's long pass patterns are developing. To Plunkett, the Raiders bring an attitude of patience and understanding, the off-field prerequisite for success for one of the nation's most complex and unconventional sports personalities.

The team is apparently putting Plunkett back together after his fall from the very top pedestal in football to the very bottom. More miraculously, the person, improving steadily through a season that finally brought him to the championship game as a wild-card quarterback, is apparently resurrecting the team after its two-year non-playoff skid.

The Plunkett turnaround is the more remarkable. With the Raiders' help, he has become the first quarterback in NFL history to complete the full circle from first player drafted in the league to waived out of the league to the Super Bowl. Reclaimed from football's junk heap by prescient Raider Owner Al Davis — who has done things like this before — he is already the comeback champion of the year, win or lose the Super Bowl.

The most baffling aspect of the strange Plunkett story to the NFL in general is that, this season, despite all he's gone through in so many disappointing NFL years, he seems to be the same great quarterback, artistically, that he was at Stanford. There hasn't been much change, Flores says, "except for the improvement you'd normally expect." NBC Commentator John Brodie, also a former Stanford quarterback, says: "He still throws with that powerful overhand motion you saw in the Rose Bowl." Ralston, now a 49er executive, says: "He was a great passer then and he's a great passer now. He has that same strong arm, he throws with the same accuracy, and he has the same great sense of timing."

Still, physical ability is only part of football. Cleveland Quarterback Brian Sipe has said: "It's probably the smallest part. There are dozens of kids who have the physical ability of an NFL quarterback." It is the psychological ability, the mental strength of a great quarterback, that is the possession of the few. And, says Ralston, "This is where Jim has always walked a tightrope. He has what it takes to be an NFL star, but his self-doubts are always a threat to bring him down. It's literally impossible for him to play for a coach who doesn't understand him. He has taken so many blows from life that he just can't get hold of a normal view of the world."

What Super Bowl XV is about, then, is whether the star stays on or slips off the tightrope.

III

The blows that have all but crushed him began to strike in Plunkett's earliest childhood in San Jose. From the day his parents were married, after they had met in a school for the blind, they lived mostly on welfare. Says Ralston: "The first time I was in his home, they had a football game on the TV, and his father sat there with his face three inches from the screen. And he complained he couldn't see a thing. And this was the parent who could see. His wife was blind." Plunkett recalls that he "never had $5" to his name until he had grown up and left home. Ralston: "That kind of background doesn't give you a chance to develop much self-expression."

Slowly, however, Plunkett conquered, in part, his feelings of inadequacy. At San Jose's James Lick High School, where he became student body president, he "was voted most popular boy," a high school friend remembers. Moreover, as a successful senior quarterback in high school, Plunkett was invited to the North-South Shrine game in Los Angeles, where, his friend says, "the coaches took a half-hearted look at him and told him: 'You're a defensive end. We've got a quarterback who's better than you.'"

And, that year, Plunkett played all but two minutes of the Shrine game for the North — as a defensive end.

"Those coaches were right," Ralston says. "At the time, the other kid [Mike Holmgren] was the better quarterback, but you can imagine what it did to the self-esteem of a fellow like Jim Plunkett. It ruined everything he had slowly built up about himself in high school. What he did next shows you the kind of man he is. He went out and *made* himself better than the other guy—and everyone else."

He did this at Stanford, where, "obsessed to be the best, Jim would throw the football until his arm fell off," Ralston says. And, gradually, under Ralston's coaching, the honors began to accumulate for Plunkett in college as they had in high school: All-Coast as a Stanford sophomore, All-American as a junior, the Heisman Trophy as a senior, then recognition as the number one football player in the country when the first team to draft in 1971, the New England Patriots, picked him first.

Arriving in New England at the top, Plunkett again spun dizzily to the bottom, and in 1976, the Patriots, disgusted, decided to trade him off. Surprisingly, when the deal was made, the 49ers gave New England three first draft choices and a second for Plunkett—plus a backup quarterback who is still on the Patriot roster. "I don't guess any other NFL player ever brought four first-stringers and a second-team quarterback," a Palo Alto friend says, naming the NFL names that materialized from the numbers in that draft as a consequence of the Plunkett trade: Stanley Morgan, Tim Fox, Mike Haynes and Raymond Clayborn, each an All-Pro. That helped Plunkett regain, in part, his sense of self-worth. But not for long. Within two years, the 49ers were to put Plunkett's name on the waiver list.

He was then only twenty-nine, but nobody picked him up. There were twenty-seven other clubs in the league, but nobody could use Jim Plunkett. Nobody wanted a castoff quarterback who couldn't play for two of the worst teams in pro football. Beaten again. Down again. "I marvel that Jim kept his sanity," Ralston says.

Yet in Louisiana this week, it's Super Bowl time again, and here's Plunkett again. "Millionaire to bankrupt to millionaire to bankrupt to millionaire," Ralston says. "I don't think it's ever happened before in football."

IV

During Plunkett's first season with the Raiders, in 1978, Tom Flores remembers they were at practice one day when he called across the field for his new backup quarterback — and the man didn't respond. So far as the eye could tell, Plunkett didn't realize he was being paged. "Maybe it was the way I asked for him," Flores says. "I called: 'Hey, rookie.'" When Plunkett eventually caught on, it was because he remembered finally that he and Flores had agreed he would be handled that way in Oakland — as if he were a rookie, as if New England never happened, nor San Francisco, as if 1978 were his first in the NFL, as if the Raiders were the first to employ him.

"When he came to us, I could tell he'd had enough of pressure to last awhile," Flores says. "Everybody expected him to produce immediately at New England as a kid out of Stanford [in 1971]—and as a veteran in San Francisco [in 1976]—even though neither team had enough players to play NFL ball. It seemed to us that the best way to let him know the pressure was off was to treat him as a rookie. He learned the [Oakland] system at his own pace. We wanted him to be eager to play before he had to play."

That finally happened last September. When Dan Pastorini got the first chance to succeed Kenny Stabler as the Raider passer, Plunkett was so eager to play that he asked to be traded to a coach who would play him. "I loved that," Flores says. "That was the signal that we had a quarterback."

V

At Raider practice, Plunkett is the most conspicuous athlete in sight. All about him are teammates dressed in the Raiders' colors, the defense in black, the offense in silver, but the quarterbacks are in bright red shirts and pants—red meaning don't touch—and Big Jim Plunkett is the biggest of the men in red. He is six feet two and 205 pounds with massive arms, shoulders and head. He could be the hero of a Zane Grey novel, black-haired, black-eyed, high cheekbones and all the rest. Although he is of German, Irish and Mexican descent, there isn't much German and Irish in his appearance. Put him on a white pony and he's a Sioux chief.

He remains, nonetheless, a reluctant chief. Asked if he is (as many are calling him) the key to the Super Bowl for the Raiders, he replies, promptly, "I hope not." After thinking that over, he says: "I doubt it. I'm one of the keys, along with the defense and our receivers." Then: "In my opinion, one of our receivers will be the key to the Super Bowl."

That is the genuine Plunkett. And if his self-effacing approach to football is unusual in a quarterback — awkward, actually — it is consistent in him. In his habits and preferences, he is, in fact, consistency itself. He still lives near his old friends in Atherton, near his old school in Palo Alto, not far from where his mother lives with his sister in San Jose—an hour or so by car from the Raider practice field in Oakland. He refers to his roommate as Gerry. He knew her in New England. He has known everyone else in the Atherton area for a thousand years. He is only comfortable there. In his 1973 BMW, he will drive two hours a day to spend his free time among people he has known always. No sense making new friends when the old ones are perfectly good enough.

The trouble is, this denies the rest of the world access to a man worth knowing. Bright, warm, compassionate, Plunkett graduated as a political science major from Stanford, with an above-average grade-point average, and to this day he maintains an interest in politics and books, mostly best sellers. He runs several miles a day, in season and out, and sponsors an annual Fourth of July race known as Nuts to Zotts. Those are taverns owned by friends. In the Palo Alto area, it's about seven miles from Nuts to Zotts. Some four hundred runners compete each year for Plunkett T-shirts (the first hundred competitors into Zotts) and gift certificates. As a rule, the gift certificates go to those who, understandably, are a little slow getting away from the taps at Nuts. This is Plunkett's idea of a ball. He knows them all, the swiftest runners and the slowest drinkers.

For many years, Plunkett did another kind of running — carrying the ball on the college option play for the New England Patriots — a play that kept him in touch with Stanford. He had to keep flying back and forth to the Stanford hospital for shoulder examinations and operations, three operations in all. This worried his Zotts friends, who thought he was killing himself. And he did have some tough moments. "I'm not the option type," he says.

Why didn't he ask the Patriots to stop calling such a play? "My feeling," he says, "is that when they employ you, you should do what you're called on to do."

Analyzing himself, he thinks he's a more physical package today than in the days before he was injured. "Everything I've hurt has healed stronger than it used to be," he says. "You work so hard to strengthen an injured area, it's better than new."

The Raiders agree that despite Plunkett's various shoulder operations and other miseries, he has never been sounder. After a fast start as Pastorini's replacement last October, followed by a slump in November, he has come back like an All-Pro in the playoffs. "First he showed us something," says Flores, "then he worried us, then he came on tougher than ever."

For any good rookie, that's usually the way it is.

2. Raiders Win XV with Big Jim

FOR MOST sports fans, there were two surprises at Super Bowl XV. When they arrived, there was a gigantic yellow ribbon around the Superdome honoring a contingent of U.S. hostages who were just then out of captivity, in another corner of the world, a long, long way off. Second, inside the 'Dome, a second-place team, known as a wild-card team, won a Super Bowl game for the only time yet. Some game-story excerpts:

NEW ORLEANS: Jan. 25, 1981.

When Super Bowl XV began here Sunday, the Oakland Raiders came out throwing and the Philadelphia Eagles came out making mistakes. And with remarkable consistency, both stuck to it until the Raiders had won easily, 27-10, before a Louisiana Superdome crowd of 75,500. The numbers tell it. Oakland Quarterback Jim Plunkett threw three touchdown passes as Philadelphia Quarterback Ron Jaworski threw three interceptions — all to Raider Linebacker Rod Martin — and so an American Conference team won the Super Bowl for the eighth time in nine years and the eleventh in fifteen.

Going in this winter as the longest shot on the board before the playoffs started, Oakland has been the underdog in three straight playoff games. But against Philadelphia, as Plunkett took charge immediately, the wild-card Raiders opened a 14-0 lead in the first quarter. It was 24-3 before the Eagles awoke in the fourth quarter to score their only touchdown.

Plunkett, completing an amazing season that took him from the Oakland bench to Most Valuable Player of the championship game, threw two touchdown passes to Wide Receiver Cliff Branch (two and twenty-nine yards) and one to Running Back Kenny King (eighty yards). As Philadelphia Coach Dick Vermeil said later: "Plunkett did it. When we pressured him, he scrambled out and came up with the big plays."

The Raiders made Tom Flores a winner in his second season as their coach in his first Super Bowl try. "He's the most underrated coach in the league," said Commissioner Pete Rozelle.

To their Oakland associates, the winning coach and the winning quarterback are known as the Chicano Connection. Both are Mexican-American products. And they are clearly proud of one another. Plunkett: "I think now it's obvious that he (Flores) was overlooked for all the coaching honors. This team was picked by many people to go 4-12."

The 1980 season was more than a month old when Plunkett replaced Dan Pastorini, who suffered a broken leg in the fifth game. Asked what he thought then, Flores said quietly: "I knew we could win with Jim."

II

The Eagles nearly matched the Raiders in the statistics, totaling 360 yards to Oakland's 377, but as between these teams there were two major differences. Putting a finger on one, Oakland Tackle Art Shell said, "Our quarterback played steadier than their quarterback." Second, the Raiders had come in with the more big-game experience. This was the third Super Bowl for Flores and Raider Owner Al Davis, and ten of their players had appeared in at least one of the first fourteen.

Oakland Guard Gene Upshaw, noting that this was the first big game for most of the Eagles, said: "The difference between the first time and the second time is that you're proud to be in the Super Bowl the first time. The second time, if you're lucky enough to get back, you know that winning the (conference) isn't enough."

Emotionally, the first time was much too much for the Eagles. Said Vermeil: "I couldn't believe it when they (his players) came out after their first drive. They acted completely exhausted."

But of course they weren't. It was big-game pressure that left them breathless.

III

Some of those watching the game thought the Oakland line was giving Plunkett more protection than Jaworski got. And up to a point, that was true. But mainly, the Oakland coaching staff was buying time for Big Jim with a winning game plan. Most of his key passes were thrown on first down when the Eagles were looking for ground plays. And at clutch moments, the Raiders slowed down the Eagle rush with play action.

Philadelphia's prize defensive end, Claude Humphrey, explaining what happened to his side, said: "They kept us off balance throwing on running downs, and running on third down."

Nobody could have been happier about that than Plunkett, who, after beginning as a college winner at Stanford, had been nothing but a professional loser until Sunday. Described by his friends as a quarterback with a split personality — "incredibly shy and sensitive," on the one hand, and, on the other, "wildly ambitious to win" — Plunkett had begun his NFL career with eight profoundly unhappy years.

One problem at New England, which, long ago, made Plunkett the first pick in the draft, was that the Patriots asked him to be a macho quarterback and inspire their inept team by running the ball. Result: three shoulder operations in five years and a trade to the 49ers.

At San Francisco, he was asked to carry the franchise on his back. But an introverted quarterback can't be made to feel he must carry any football team on his back, let alone a bad football team. Result: when the 49ers offered him around the league for a humiliating price, the $100 waiver price, no team would pay it.

In time, Raider Owner Davis decided to take a chance on Plunkett, and it is Davis who gets the credit for leading the rescue operation. Of the NFL's twenty-eight chief executives, he alone could see the possibilities in Plunkett — and, as well, in Flores. The Chicano Connection is Davis' ornament. In all the years since the NFL began playing championship games, Flores is the first coach of Mexican descent to win one — or even play in one — and Plunkett the first quarterback.

3. Inside Super Bowl XV

THE EMPHASIS of the second-day story is on the kind of leadership the Raiders had as a Super Bowl winner in 1981 and again in 1984.

NEW ORLEANS, Jan. 26. 1981.

The fifth New Orleans Super Bowl in fifteen years will be remembered as a dual rescue operation. This was the season the Oakland Raiders brought Quarterback Jim Plunkett back to life, after which he brought them back to life. But more than that, Super Bowl XV was a triumph of human decency.

A nice guy named Tom Flores, the velvet-gloved coach of the boisterous Raiders, made the decisive contribution, recognizing the sensitive nature of another nice guy, Plunkett, and providing the only climate in which the former Stanford quarterback can flourish — warm and sunny. To use the language of the day, Flores in his relationship with Plunkett was continuously positive and supportive. And that is what it took.

After he got up to talk about it Monday, Flores, asked to list his assets, named two or three conventional things, and then, thinking of his pirate crew, said: "I don't panic. And if I don't, they won't." As he spoke, Flores smiled only rarely, and never raised his voice to make a point. He also coaches that way. And on a team that's full of players no one else wants — Plunkett, John Matuszak, Burgess Owens, Kenny King, Bob Chandler and so many other Al Davis specials — Flores is a continuously soothing presence.

For Plunkett — this year's Exhibit A on Davis' hard-to-handle list — the results have been extraordinary. Plunkett's Super Bowl performance was as close to flawless as a quarterback's can be. "He didn't throw a bad pass," Raider Wide Receiver Cliff Branch said after Oakland's 27-10 win over Philadelphia.

From start to finish, Plunkett was solid, controlled, continually calm, on target, and both active and alert under a rush.

His first series was typical. Facing three little crises in Oakland's first seven plays — after Philadelphia Quarterback Ron Jaworski turned the ball over with an interception at the Eagles' thirty-yard line — Plunkett found a different answer each time. On the Raiders' key first third-down play of the game, Plunkett first pulled the nervous Eagles offside with a long count in their first jittery moment of Super Bowl pressure. Then on first down, he made an ideal call for the time and place, the Philadelphia 20-yard line — a safe pass to Branch running a delay route across the middle in front of the Eagles' linebackers. This gained fifteen to the five-yard line. Then to get the touchdown on third and goal at the two-yard line, Plunkett stood in against the Philadelphia rush and kept looking and moving until Branch was open, whereupon he neither overthrew nor underthrew — although, early in the day, in those circumstances, moving quarterbacks often do one or the other.

The 1981 Super Bowl was probably Plunkett's best game since the 1971 Rose Bowl (in which he was also the winning quarterback), and those looking for a tie to the two events can find it in the quality of the coaching he had both times. In upwards of ten years as a big-time quarterback, Plunkett has played only twice for caring, understanding leaders, John Ralston at Stanford and now Flores, and the record is plain that he can perform for no other kind. He couldn't be more different from the ego-driven great quarterbacks of another day — Norm Van Brocklin, say, or Joe Namath or John Unitas.

Artistically, Plunkett isn't that far behind those three. But what he has needed in pro ball is what he had in college, an appreciative and supportive coach, a civilized coach, and Flores appears to be one of the few. The irony in the dehumanizing world of pro football is that Flores is the leader of the league's most conspicuous ring of bandits and pirates. Wondrously, in this atmosphere, Plunkett has found warmth, compassion, understanding and happiness. And the Raiders have found a quarterback.

4. Hubbell's Screwball Comes Back

FOR MOST of the century in Los Angeles, from February until summer, there wasn't much football. And so, during the spring months, I often turned to baseball. The game's 1981 phenomenon was rookie Dodger Pitcher Fernando Valenzuela, whose art seemed to be based on Carl Hubbell's. One day I looked up Hubbell.

MESA, Ariz.: April 20, 1981.

On a July day this summer, it will have been forty-seven years since a left-handed pitcher named Carl Hubbell struck out Babe Ruth, Lou Gehrig, Jimmie Foxx, Al Simmons and Joe Cronin, one after another, in baseball's 1934 All-Star Game at an old ballpark in New York, the Polo Grounds. The hitters were the five best in the American League. All were headed for the Hall of Fame. And so was Hubbell.

Known as the Meal Ticket of the New York Giants, Hubbell, who lives in Arizona now, fooled them mostly with his screwball.

The pitch was one he developed in 1925, and named himself, and it has to make him one of the dominant athletes of his generation. Even so, from that day to this, organized baseball has known few other masters of his pitch. The pure Hubbell screwball indeed seemed to have passed out of the world of fun and games until just the other day, when, suddenly, a southpaw from south of the border started throwing it with extraordinary success in the National League. At age twenty, Fernando Valenzuela plainly brought back the screwball this month, throwing it better than anybody since Hubbell.

By definition, a screwball is a reverse curve — a curve breaking away from instead of into a right-handed batter when thrown by a left-hander. And it foils managers as well as hitters. Managers like to send right-handed batters out to face left-handed pitchers, but the screwball, when thrown properly, is difficult for baseball's many right-handed batters to hit. No matter how often they see it, they can't quite believe that a breaking pitch from a southpaw will behave that way — especially when he's a rookie southpaw.

And that leads to two questions: Why have there been so few screwball pitchers? And how does Fernando Anguamea Valenzuela happen to be one of them? The brief answer to the first question is that it is anatomically almost impossible for human beings to throw a screwball. Second, Valenzuela not only has the anatomy (and disposition) for it, he isn't good enough without it. His fastball isn't quite fast enough.

"When Freddie came to us, he was already a pitcher with excellent rotation on his curveball," Pitching Coach Ron Perranoski says, using the Dodgers' abbreviation for Fernando. "And he had a good, moving fastball — but his velocity was below average, quite a lot below average. He's a screwball pitcher today because a year ago last fall, the organization thought he needed another pitch. With the surprising control he already had as a teen-ager, if he'd been real fast, I don't think he'd have ever thrown a screwball."

II

An Arizona-based Giant scout might have something to add to that. He is Carl Hubbell, at seventy-seven a well-preserved six-footer, who says: "The first time I saw him, I knew Valenzuela was a natural screwball pitcher. His delivery is just about perfect — he has the right screwball formula exactly. In fact, he's the only pitcher I've seen in forty years with the right formula — the best since mine."

As a pitch, the screwball has recently been associated with two others, Tug McGraw and Mike Marshall, but Hubbell says: "Marshall's comes too fast to be a real screwball. And McGraw doesn't come over the top. The ball slithers off over the side of McGraw's hand, and Marshall kind of slides it out. I have a high opinion of both of them as pitchers — but nobody throws the screwball quite right except Valenzuela."

That and his control and composure are the three factors in Valenzuela's success, Hubbell says, adding: "It isn't the way a screwball breaks that bothers a good hitter — it's the change of speed on the screwball compared to a fastball. The trick is to throw it over the top with exactly the same motion you use on the fastball. What a hitter looks at is the hand on the ball. And what crosses him up is the last surge of the pitcher's arm and wrist. The hitter has got to protect himself against the fastball and can't adjust to the slowdown of the screwball. What beats him is that it isn't coming as fast as he thinks."

III

When Hubbell first threw his new pitch more than fifty years ago, the motion of the ball, as it spun up to the plate, reminded him of a turning screw — hence screwball. He threw it (as does Valenzuela) hardly more than fifty per cent of the time in a typical game, mixing it in with fastballs and curves.

In terms of the human anatomy, delivering screwballs is out of the question for most pitchers. "Most aren't loose-jointed enough to throw it," Hubbell says. "They can't get the wrist turned over. The action of the arm and wrist as you come over the top putting spin on the ball is what makes it break. So it's an unnatural pitch to throw — just the opposite of a curve. The ball comes out of the back of your hand with a wrist snap. You're going against the grain, in other words — throwing out of the back instead of the front of the hand. It's a hard pitch to throw even when you have the body for it — and few people have that kind of body construction."

A six-footer, Hubbell held his weight under 175 as a pitcher, and has it under 170 now. Valenzuela is an inch shorter and lists at 180 though he looks heavier. "If he came to me for advice, I'd warn him about eating too much," Hubbell says. "The right weight is the key to a long and happy life as a pitcher." The other hazard to Valenzuela's future is the toll the screwball takes on a screwballer's arm. "Nature never intended a man to turn his hand over that way throwing rocks at a bear," Hubbell says. "All those years of evolution developed a body construction that encourages you to throw fastballs when something is gaining on you. The screwball is such an unnatural pitch that I've often wondered how I lasted as long as I did (sixteen years in the majors ending at age forty). I was abusing my arm all that time."

Although Hubbell has spent thirty-five years in the Giant farm system, specializing in player development, he says it has been more than forty years since he taught anyone the screwball. It isn't hard to learn, he says, it's just hard to throw. But as a teacher, he had an "unfortunate experience last time," he says. "We had a new kid on the Giants then — this was 1938, I think — a big left-hander, Cliff Melton. The year before he'd won twenty games for us — a hell of an achievement for a rookie — but he wanted to be even better. He begged me to show him the screwball, so I did, and by the Fourth of July he'd won ten or eleven games — well on his way to twenty again. But against Boston that day, breaking off a screwball, he grabbed his arm and kind of stumbled off the mound in great pain. He finished 14-14 and never did have another twenty-win year. I don't think he lasted but five or six more years. A great shame. I've been reluctant ever since then to work on the screwball with anybody."

IV

The best way to train for a career as a screwball pitcher, it could be, is to luck into a harsh boyhood. "My father had a cotton farm on the Missouri-Oklahoma border," Hubbell says. "And I've often thought it was the farm work I did throughout my boyhood that gave me the arm to withstand the rigors of the screwball. I was either chopping cotton or picking cotton or getting in the wood all the days of my life until just the year before I graduated from high school. The one thing about farm work is that you never get done. I know I had a well-developed arm when I started playing ball."

Moreover, Hubbell entered baseball by way of the Oklahoma oil fields, where he worked a year or two after high school. After signing first with an oil field semipro club, he originated the screwball while pitching for Class A Oklahoma City. "It was easy," he says.

On the afternoon in 1934 when he struck out Babe Ruth and four other future Hall of Famers, Hubbell got them all on screwballs after setting them up with fastballs and an occasional curve. "You can't win with one pitch," he says. "Even Walter Johnson couldn't. When I saw Johnson (in the early 1920s when Hubbell was still in the minors) he threw what would be called a slider today, and mixed it with his fastball."

Alluding to John McGraw, who managed him in his first four major league years, Hubbell says: "He was the only man I ever knew who thought you could win with one pitch. McGraw wanted us to throw a curve every time. Any day you threw a fastball on McGraw's team and it beat you, you got fined." Hubbell concedes that "against hitters like Ruth or Gehrig, you've got to throw a lot of fastballs. But you never give them a fastball over the plate. First the speed, outside or inside, up or down, then the screwball. The only strikes I ever threw a good hitter like Babe Ruth were screwballs. I think Valenzuela does the same. It looks that way."

5. Tommy Lasorda, Emotional Winner

DURING THE 1980s in Los Angeles, there was a conspicuous contrast between the leaders of the Raiders and Dodgers. In the presumably emotional world of pro football, Tom Flores and Jim Plunkett were stoics. In the presumably unemotional world of baseball, Tommy Lasorda has always been, first of all, a cheerleader — and as of 1996, his philosophy and successes had kept him in command of the Dodgers for twenty years. In the spring of 1981, I spent a few days visiting with Lasorda and baseball's five other Western managers.

LOS ANGELES: May 5, 1981.

Tommy Lasorda, manager of the Dodgers, has a clear idea of how to get where he wants to go. "What a player in a slump needs is his teammates in his corner," Lasorda says. "What the team needs is a manager with an understanding heart who won't turn his back on anybody who's struggling. What the manager needs is the support of his general manager and owner. When you have all that, you have togetherness, and it's togetherness that wins baseball games."

Not all the time, of course, but nothing works all the time.

In baseball, Lasordaness works more often than most things, he insists, suggesting that it starts with the manager's attitude. And so, he says, "No matter how depressed or dejected I might feel, when I go in that clubhouse, I go in with a happy face, a winning face. There's nothing as contagious as an emotion."

At first, that didn't help too much, Lasorda concedes, when he was a pitcher. A lefty, he appeared in only twenty-six games in his three years in the majors and started only once. His lifetime record as a big league pitcher is sort of embarrassing, so we won't embarrass him.

His prescription for success as a manager, however, seems to be getting results. In four years with the Dodgers, Lasorda has two firsts and two seconds as one of the newer members of an exceedingly select group: the few who manage America's major league baseball clubs. Six of these organizations are now based in the Far West, and in the last few days each of their managers was asked the same question: "What does it take to win?" Lasorda's thought — "pull together and be happy" — appeals to at least one observer, Angel Vice President Buzzie Bavasi, who says: "Tommy is proof that a college atmosphere on a ballclub *does* pay off."

If, at fifty-three, Thomas Charles Lasorda remains the personification of the contented man getting precisely what he wants out of life, he is also the case example of a man who doesn't make reckless decisions. He has lived in the same house in Fullerton for seventeen years, and he is now third in Dodger seniority after thirty-two years in the organization. Father of a son and daughter, he was one of five sons in the family of a Norristown, Pennsylvania, truck driver.

II

The probability is that, nationwide, all baseball people agree with Lasorda on the importance of what seems a simplistic notion, sticking together. Yet it's a first-priority matter for few other managers — and among the six West Coasters, for none. The thing that's distinctive about these six people is what they emphasize. And in recent interviews, they focused on six very different things: Frank Howard, repetition; Frank Robinson, self-sacrifice; Billy Martin, aggressiveness; Maury Wills, fundamentals; Jim Fregosi, effort, and Tom Lasorda, togetherness.

Asked the same question ("What is your philosophy in terms of what it takes to win?") each manager curiously started talking immediately and spontaneously about six wholly dissimilar aspects of the game:

• At San Diego, Howard of the Padres: "I can put it in one word, repetition. It's the same in medicine or plumbing or baseball. As a player I kept repeating my basic skills in practice until I could do it. Even the great ones have to polish their skills."

• At San Francisco, Robinson of the Giants: "It takes a much stronger commitment today because of high salaries. A winner is a guy who will sacrifice his own best interests for the team's best interests."

• At Oakland, Martin of the A's: "Aggressiveness is what wins ballgames — and a daring attitude can be taught. You have to eliminate the fear of being wrong, and the manager does that by taking the blame for aggressive plays that fail."

• At Seattle, Wills of the Mariners, making the point that the most important thing in the game isn't hitting or pitching but learning the fundamentals: "Every team in baseball is weak on bunting, throwing, running and all the others. The best and fastest way for the Mariners to compete is to master the fundamentals."

• At Anaheim, Fregosi of the Angels: "There's only one way to play this game right. Every time you're out there, you've got to bust your rear end."

Even more curiously, when each of the Far West six was asked for his second priority, they promptly named six *other* things.

• Howard: "My second goal is to maintain an open, consistent, honest line of communication with the players."

• Robinson: "Managers used to rule with an iron hand, but today, far and away, the main thing a manager needs is the respect of his players. His job is to get twenty-five players to play up to their capabilities, and I don't think he can do it today unless his players respect him."

• Martin (whose second priority is a major voice in personnel): "When the manager's way is the only way, your minor league coaches can concentrate on just one thing: improving the players."

• Wills (who has abolished all fines): "I'm not going to police you. My attitude is that you are respectable, reasonable persons."

• Fregosi (who frets about mental fatigue): "You look for signs of fatigue, and then look for breaks in the schedule to do something about it."

Lasorda: "Togetherness and having fun are one-two."

III

Quite possibly, Lasorda is reacting to a somewhat different personal background. As a marginal player, he must often have experienced rejection. Hanging by one's fingernails as the last Dodger to make the roster (which was Lasorda's fate in both 1954 and '55) can be educational.

It doubtless reminded him that pennants are won not by stars but by twenty-five man teams. "Nobody wins these days with eight ironmen and a few stars," Lasorda says. "I need every man I have, and that's why one of my main jobs is to make them all feel wanted."

What's a good way to do that?

Lasorda: "Give them all some playing time. If you want to keep a car in working order, you can't just let it sit in the garage. You have to run it once in awhile. The human voice, remember, is a great tool. Be honest with them, but tell them you need them. When a guy is in a slump, some managers avoid him, and some of his teammates do, too, but not me. That's when he needs a pat on the back and some friendly words, not when he's in a streak."

Suppose there are several players on the roster who don't get along. How do you make them love one another?

"If you don't like somebody, chances are it's because you two don't have much in common. So if you're on my ballclub, don't bother to go over to his house. You don't have to visit him socially. When the club is on the road, you don't have to go out with him. But when we're at the ballpark together, we do have something in common. We have a common goal, and it's the greatest goal there is: winning. That should bring you together. Togetherness starts in the clubhouse, and ends when you jump in your car to go home. That's all I ask, and I don't think it's too much. Togetherness moves mountains."

From a strategic standpoint, what's the most important thing in managing?

"Probably the big thing is to know the strengths and weaknesses of all your players, to know them exactly, particularly the attributes of the pitchers. If pitching is seventy-five per cent of baseball, it should get that much of your attention."

What's hardest about managing?

"Keeping everybody happy and producing. In my opinion, the greatest baseball slogan ever was: 'It's great to be a Yankee.' That's a happy thought, but we have a happier one: 'I'm proud to be a Dodger.'"

6. One Hundred Years of Football

LEGENDS DIE hard. When in 1969 Princeton and Rutgers celebrated what was termed college football's centennial, they should have identified it as a soccer centennial. As documented in 1869 newspapers, the athletes who played for Princeton and Rutgers that year were unquestionably soccer players who called their game football — as soccer players do to this day in Europe and Latin America. Not until 1881, my research shows, did American football become a reality. And a hundred years later, I reported on my findings in the six Times stories that follow.

LOS ANGELES: June 20, 1981.

With the first games of a new season in September, including USC-Tennessee at the Coliseum and UCLA at Arizona, college football will reach a previously inconspicuous milestone. It will be one hundred years old exactly. The anniversary should be celebrated sometime this fall, somewhere, by somebody, yet that apparently won't happen.

It has already happened, twelve years prematurely, and mistakenly.

In 1969, Princeton and Rutgers observed what they called the hundredth anniversary season of collegiate football — but it wasn't football they played that first year, it was soccer. With twenty-five players to a side, they used a round soccer ball in the two-game 1869 Princeton-Rutgers series, and there was no way to score a touchdown. Accruing one point at a time, they could only score by kicking the ball under a crossbar.

Football's authentic anniversary year is this one. The basic rule changes that severed football from soccer and rugby — installing the game that American sports fans know as football — were all made in 1881.

You learn about that in the minutes of the meetings of the late-nineteenth-century college football rules committee, as mostly chaired by a Yale student-athlete, Walter Camp. His generation had inherited soccer and rugby from European forebears, and played both, but didn't like either. Most Americans then and later, and now, have never liked either game.

Lacking a choice through most of the nineteenth century, Americans kept going out for soccer and rugby, but hoped for something better, and, finally, sitting around a conference table, Camp and his friends got it. They got it by inventing a new game.

"It took two clever new rules to convert rugby into American football," rugby Historian A. Jon Prusmack says, speaking from his New York office. "Everything else followed naturally from those two changes. The first was reducing the number of players to eleven on each side. Previously, they'd had twenty, twenty-five, and sometimes more — but eleven made their game more manageable. The second change was more drastic. That was the scrimmage concept guaranteeing possession of the ball to one side or the other for a set number of plays. This was a really sharp break with the rules of both rugby and soccer. There is nothing remotely like it in either sport. Nobody is guaranteed the ball in either."

To trigger the plays in their new ball-possession game, the Camp committeemen invented centers. They were needed first, Camp wrote in 1910 in "The Book of Foot-Ball," because, "The first thing we had to do was get the ball out of scrimmage." Soccer doesn't have to worry about that.

On each play, Camp authorized the center to deliver the ball to his team without hindrance from members of the opposing team, and much of the American difference was to result from that imaginative change.

For U.S. players could then develop football into a game of sophisticated plays and play-calling and warlike strategy — the aspects that differentiate it from the other sports — as Princeton Historian Parke H. Davis wrote in his 1911 book, "Football." Of the ball-possession concept, Davis wrote: "This is the device which introduced the principle of an orderly retention of the ball by one side at a time, thereby making possible the use of prearranged strategy, the most distinctive and fascinating characteristic of the American game."

In European games, by contrast, the players still scramble for the ball. And the continuous flow of action in soccer and rugby deprives their coaches and athletes of the leisure to plot strategy once the match is under way.

The game-transforming ball-possession and eleven-man rules were accepted by Camp's committee in the late fall of 1880, passing unanimously. And they were implemented in 1881, changing the American game for all time wherever it was played. For these reasons, historians have determined that 1981 is correctly year one hundred of American football.

"This should be celebrated as your centennial," says Prusmack, the nation's leading rugby authority who wrote the best-selling sports book of the same name, "Rugby." "When people come up with a game that lasts a century, they've done something."

II

The story of football's first hundred years in America is a story of almost continuous change. Astonishingly, it has been a different game — usually a strikingly different game — in every decade of football's first American century. The differences have been made by upwards of seven hundred rule changes since 1881, including legalization of the forward pass in 1906 and 1910 and the authorization of free substitution a half century later.

Simultaneously, football has continued to change in dozens of other ways from the shape of the ball to the shape of offense and defense. The original first formation, the T, was erased in time by single-wing football, and then made a dramatic comeback. One-platoon football yielded to two. Wide receivers replaced ends and halfbacks. Blitzing linebackers and other exotic new players appeared, and, most radical of all, some coaches even decided that passing is as trustworthy as running.

Nothing is now as it used to be except the name of the game. During football's awesome hundred-year revolution — a revolution that is still happening — the changes in any one year have been so comparatively few that a new name has never seemed necessary. And that, no doubt, would please Walter Camp, who is identified in a 1926 book by Biographer Harford Powel as "the father of American football."

According to Powel and other contemporary writers, Camp, a halfback at Yale before he was a coach there and elsewhere, proposed and wrote most of the game-changing legislation of the nineteenth century, including the ball-possession and eleven-man rules as well as the rules providing for three and eventually four downs. In 1881, Camp's committee gave the offensive team three plays to make five yards, then improved on that thought in 1882, awarding the offense four plays to make ten yards.

As a member of the rules committee continuously during the thirty-three years in which the American game was most noticeably tailored (1877-1910), Camp also wrote and introduced the early blocking rules legalizing the interference plays that rugby had so insistently forbidden. But his first changes were more historic.

Powel on Camp: "Some of his friends regard the scrimmage as the greatest single invention in any game in the memory of man. The distance to be gained in three or four downs is a detail. Blocking is a detail. The scrimmage is the cardinal, essential feature of American football."

One way to trace the evolution of American football is to inventory the game's numerous scoring changes. As of 1883, a touchdown was only worth two points. That year, the goal-after (now known as the conversion or point after touchdown) was valued at four points. Field goals earned five points. In 1884, the value of a touchdown was doubled to four points. In 1897, when touchdowns were raised to five points, the conversion finally became the point after.

Not until much later did field goals (1909) and touchdowns (1912) achieve their present values, three and six points, and even those numbers aren't sacred. From the turn of the twentieth century on, at least one college or critic has proposed to change one or the other every year.

III

Throughout the first century of football — a hundred years of ferment and change — America's other major entertainment attraction, baseball, has remained basically static. The two games couldn't, in respect to change, be more different. Baseball's most important new rule of this century, which allows designated hitters for pitchers, is still being opposed by one of the two major leagues. Otherwise — since increasing the pitching distance eighty-eight years ago from fifty to sixty and one-half feet — baseball has put on a show almost every summer day that has looked nearly identical to such diverse enthusiasts as the trolley Dodgers of nineteenth-century Brooklyn and the freeway Dodgers of twentieth-century Los Angeles.

If it seems unusual that the sports fans and entrepreneurs of the same country should have two entirely different attitudes toward change in their two favorite games, it is. Though both grew out of English games, the one has virtually stopped growing in America and the other, fantastically, can't stop growing.

Asked to explain this, a baseball spokesman, Joe Reichler, assistant to the commissioner, says: "These are games in which different things are important to sports fans. In baseball, it's tradition. In football, it's excitement. The baseball fan wants to relate to everything grandpa told him at his first game twenty years ago, forty years ago, sixty years ago. Baseball sells nostalgia. Football sells spectacle. It means a lot to the baseball fan to compare Pete Rose as a hitter to every great hitter of the last hundred years. That can only be done with statistics which mean what they used to mean. The football fan doesn't much care about Red Grange. He's only interested in what's happening now. He doesn't oppose *any* change that makes football more exciting."

A football spokesman, President Tex Schramm of the Dallas Cowboys, says: "Baseball is a game of precision, with a rigid number of strikes, balls, outs, bases, infielders, outfielders. There is nothing rigid about football. A baseball play can only start one way, with a pitcher throwing a ball. In football, plays start many ways, with short passes, long passes, end runs, line bucks, kickoffs, punts. In football, an offensive coach can deploy his eleven men any way he wants to, sideline to sideline, as long as he keeps seven men on the line. The defense doesn't even have that restriction. In baseball, there are rigid places for all nine players to line up. Football lends itself to change, baseball doesn't. To keep their game in balance, all baseball has to do is keep the right amount of rabbit in their ball."

All football has to do is change a rule.

IV

Along with baseball, strangely, the two big international pastimes, soccer and rugby, have also remained substantially unchanged during the same one hundred years that American football has continuously evolved and progressed. A 1981 spectator deciding to watch two sports the same week, soccer one day and American football the next, finds it all but impossible to believe that both descended from the same game, British soccer. In Europe as well as the Americas, that's the game that most of our ancestors were playing during all the decades leading up to 1876, an historic year in sports.

Camp was a freshman at Yale in 1876 when the United States finally abandoned soccer and officially adopted England's Rugby Union rules.

Shortly, however, the Americans lost interest in rugby, too. At a time when, from one year to the next, Englishmen went on playing soccer and rugby in the old familiar ways, as they do to this day, America's rebellious 1870s-1880s college students rebuilt the two games into one game — one that is wholly different from either.

Before the close of the nineteenth century, Americans were regularly blocking their opponents (illegally by British standards), they were snapping the ball with the center's hands (instead of his feet), they were lining up in set plays from scrimmage (instead of flinging the ball into a crowd of players from a sideline), and, most heretical of all, they were soon even throwing forward passes. What the Americans were after, clearly, was a more sophisticated sport than the intellectually undemanding games that still satisfy their neighbors on other continents.

As in any revolutionary era, some of their innovations were blunders, but the Americans never stopped tinkering with the rules, and eventually they got it right. Which raises a question. Why did the country's nineteenth-century college athletes destroy and remake a game that continues to entrance others in Europe, Latin America, and almost everywhere else?

The answer is a commentary on the ingenuity and spirit of the American people, who were mass-producing automobiles at a time when a horse was still good enough for an Englishman. There is a comparison to be made between Camp's creation of a lively new game in the era that Henry Ford was creating the flivver.

Britons for decades have put up with rugby's rule against blocking simply because the rule is in the book. The American attitude is, the hell with the book. After America's early athletes had widely ignored the no-blocking rule (as, in another decade, they ignored Prohibition), they presently got a rule they could live with. An Englishman can't make himself do things that way.

As a Texas football coach said: "Don't quote me as knocking Europeans, but the fact is that they will accept authority where an American resents it, tests it, attacks it. The U.S. form of government, for better or worse, encourages people to think for themselves. In the old country, you wonder what the lord or the noble in your neighborhood might want, either that, or you don't think at all."

There are, of course, nobles here, too. In America, a noble is any person in any field who plays by the rules and wins.

V

Football is a candidate for world's oldest game. Since at least 28 B.C., men and boys have been playing forms of football, sometimes kicking around the skull of an enemy instead of a ball. The barroom toast, "Skoal," lingers as a reminder of those heady days. Until 1640, however, all such games shared one fate: They were repeatedly banned by the authorities. Football was too disruptive for the kings and queens of England and other lands, or it was too brutal, or not military enough, or not serious enough for Sabbath afternoons.

Some of these same complaints were in time to be heard in America, and some are still being heard, although genius has usually appreciated football. A female character asks in Shakespeare's "Comedy of Errors":

> *Am I so round with you as you with me*
> *That like a football you do spurn me thus?*

If, as a sport, the game that everyone calls football was recurrently banned before 1640, it has been consistently played, somewhere, ever since — most frequently in its British versions. Looking back from the end of the first century of the American version, historians see three landmarks:

• One day in 1823, when soccer had the field to itself in England, and running with the ball was illegal, a Rugby School chap named William Webb Ellis picked it up and ran with it — pleasing his peers so much, after they'd thought about it awhile, that they added this dimension to their game, launching rugby. A Rugby School plaque still commemorates Ellis' big run.

• Somebody somewhere kicked the first ball over a crossbar (for a field goal) instead of under (for a soccer goal), establishing a scoring method that has become integral to American football. But the time and place of this inspired innovation and the name of the kicker have disappeared into the mists of time. A recent survey of researchers in America and England has been profitless. If anybody out there can identify this guy, this is the year to speak up.

• After football had been alternately played and banned from 28 B.C. or earlier to 1640 A.D., it took hold in the latter year, at last, with a number of games in a London church that's still there, Westminster Abbey, where it was called cloister football. The 1640 turning point was made during the reign of a different kind of leader, young Charles I, who dissented from the views of the intolerant monarchs who had preceded him. In allowing the games to go on, Charles set a precedent that has bound his descendants down to Elizabeth II.

The only serious threat to football since Charles' day was felt during the tenure of an American president, Theodore Roosevelt (1901-09), who said the game would be outlawed unless the rules committee outlawed the flying wedge, a popular if lethal formation. He said it was maiming too many players. The committee agreed, if belatedly, and changed a rule — making another improvement.

Yet on the whole, football owes more to Charles.

In 1649 when he was hanged by his enemies outside his London banqueting hall, a place that still stands, the football or soccer players of Westminster Abbey went on playing their game as usual. It's a hardy game. It even reached America about that time. Though it failed to last out the nineteenth century here in its British form, it's still prospering in this country in the U.S. version.

To be sure, in what is mostly a soccer-playing world, American athletes are out of step. But the usual explanation — that they grew up with football and don't know soccer — is inaccurate. They know it. They used to play it. They kicked it out.

WALTER CAMP

LOS ANGELES: June 20, 1981.

At Yale a century ago, when he helped invent the game that became American football, Walter Camp was a twenty-year-old Yale halfback. Precocious, persuasive, persistent, but patient, he had started his thirty-three-year term on the rules committee as a college sophomore. That was *before* football coaches.

Student-athletes ran the football program on every campus, in fact, until the game began paying off at the gate, when, predictably, the various college administrations seized control and put the students in their place, where they remain today, still overworked and underpaid.

Happily for football, students were very much in charge during the late 1870s and early '80s, when Camp, an early Yale football captain, sponsored most of the legislation that tore football out of rugby, which had succeeded soccer as the dominant campus pastime.

As a freshman athlete, Camp had begun as a Yale soccer player in 1876 just as his college and the others in America were giving up on soccer and turning to rugby as their official game. Before the end of his sixth Yale season (in an age when graduate students were eligible for U.S. varsity sports), Camp had willed rugby into American football. It was one of the great achievements in sports history.

Inexplicably, Camp has received hardly any credit for his achievement. In baseball, ironically, Abner Doubleday has been extensively honored for inventing a game he may never have played. In football, John Heisman (of the trophy Heismans) is considerably more famous than Camp although he was neither the athlete, the coach nor the man that Camp was. Truth is, Heisman was the greatest pour-it-on coach ever. One of his efforts (222-0) is still an American record.

In contrast, Camp was the sort who, in the 1920s, led the campaign for municipal golf courses in this country. After discovering that the annual dues at a private English golf club cost less than one round at an American country club, he decided it was time for those who enjoy golf to do something for the average American.

Compassion, indeed, was the quality that helped Camp get his innovations through the rules committee that he chaired for so many years. Thus he won the gratitude and support of Harvard (then and now Yale's great rival) by establishing the official width of a football field at the odd distance of fifty-three and one-third yards. Under pressure to reduce injuries by opening up the game with a large field, Camp settled for fifty-three and one-third because that was the largest that would fit in Harvard's new stadium, now Harvard's old stadium.

Camp was of English descent, soft-spoken, they say, as well as mild of manner, and lean, physically fit. In appearance he could have been an English country gentleman. Son of two New Haven schoolteachers, he married the daughter of Yale's most respected professor. He is still warmly remembered in his hometown. "His spirit still lives here," New Haven newspaper Editor Bruce Reynolds says.

Best defined as a winner, Camp also knew how to lose with grace and purpose. He once said: "When you lose to a man in your own class, shake hands with him, do not excuse your defeat, do not forget it, and do not let it happen again."

Acting on his own advice during the years when he was the football coach at Yale and then Stanford, he became the biggest winner of his time, the 1890s. Among the coaches who have lasted eight or more years, Camp is the leading percentage winner ever: 79-5-3 (.940). Even so, his careers as football legislator and coach were only two of his five in a lifetime of urgent versatility.

Primarily a businessman, Camp put in forty years with the New Haven Clock Company, rising to sales manager, treasurer, president and chairman. He wrote twenty books (fiction, history and sports) and became possibly the highest paid nonfiction magazine writer in the country. His Colliers file each year included the Walter Camp All-American, which, in the first twenty-four years of this century, was college football's universally accepted All-American team — preceding the present era of uncertainty and controversy inspired by wire-service and other competitors.

In 1914, a world war launched Camp on his fifth career as the nation's most prominent physical fitness expert. Originating the exercises known as the Daily Dozen, he promoted them nationwide. In his final years, continuing to excel in tennis and golf, he also composed passable poetry, and played cards with great skill, writing one of the early bridge manuals.

In 1925, at sixty-five, he died in his sleep. "It can truly be said of him," a biographer wrote, "that even death, last enemy of us all, came to him like a friend."

Harvard's Dean Briggs, summing up an era, said: "I knew Walter Camp as the great master of football whose advice — if the Yale captain would listen to it — meant inevitable defeat for the college I loved best."

Flying Wedge

LOS ANGELES: June 20, 1981.

The most infamous play in football history, leading the game down a long blind alley, was the flying wedge. As developed in the late nineteenth century, the wedge was an outgrowth of American football's changing rules and their effect on the fertile minds of the game's early era. Commenting many years later, football Historian Parke Davis said: "No play has ever been devised so spectacular and sensational as this one."

It was a mass-momentum play, or, more exactly, formation. In effect, guards and tackles played in the backfield behind a line consisting of other guards and tackles. The most famous of football's All-American guards, W. W. (Pudge) Heffelfinger of Yale, gained much of his fame carrying the ball in the flying wedge. He was Yale's leading ground gainer one year.

At the same time, flying-wedge players and opponents were getting killed and maimed in such numbers that a U.S. president, Theodore Roosevelt, warned the colleges to abolish either football or the wedge.

They chose the latter. But as the rules committee changed one rule after another, it proved hard to kill, enduring for years.

As first used, by Harvard against Yale, the flying wedge was a kickoff play. Later, Harvard, Yale and others developed ways to use it as a scrimmage play based on the original flying-wedge machinery, which had these six components in an era when it was legal for the kickoff team to retain possession:

First, the Harvard quarterback (or kickoff man) stood with the ball on his 40-yard line. Second, the other Harvard players, who had been divided into two five-man sections, were deployed twenty yards behind the quarterback near each sideline. Third, at a signal, the two sections sprinted toward the quarterback, gathering momentum as they advanced. Fourth, when they reached him, the quarterback put the ball in play (that is, conforming to the rules of the day, he touched the ball with his foot and handed it to a sprinting halfback). Fifth, at that moment, one of the five-man sections executed a quarter turn and fell in behind the other to attack the Yale team with a moving mass of great weight and velocity. Sixth, the ballcarrier, proceeding untouched behind the flying wedge, reached Yale's 20-yard line before he could be found and tackled.

In 1906, the rules committee moved to get rid of all that for once and all by legalizing forward passing. But by then, coaches had succeeded players in charge of most teams, and the coaches didn't get the hint. Being coaches, they feared the pass. They simply continued to refine, embellish and rely on the flying wedge as usual. Not until 1910 did the rules committee finally knock it out with some drastic changes including, primarily, these three: Only four players were permitted to line up in the backfield (behind a mandatory seven on the line). Offensive linemen were barred from using their hands. And the kickoff man, instead of merely touching his foot with the ball, was required to kick it at least ten yards. Over the screams of the coaches, the game progressed.

SINGLE-WING DAYS

LOS ANGELES: June 20, 1981.

Football's single-wing era, which ended in the late 1940s, is still recalled nostalgically by old coaches and fans. But in the full hundred-year sweep of the game, it represented, like the flying wedge, merely a long detour growing out of a rule change.

In single-wing football, the team's center, instead of handing the ball to a quarterback, snaps it directly to any of the four backs much as he snaps it in today's shotgun formation. But that wasn't legal before 1910. Until then, forms of T-Formation football were standard because, on scrimmage plays, the first two players allowed to touch the ball (known as center and quarterback) were ineligible to run it.

The first man remains ineligible to this day. But in 1910, as the rules committee fought desperately against the flying wedge, the second man won the legal right to carry the ball forward. And that rule change had an unintended consequence, creating a position that came to be known as single-wing tailback (or, as he lines up today, shotgun quarterback).

By definition, a football team's wing is a backfield area several yards to the left or right of center. A wingback lines up out there. In a double-wing set, there are wingbacks left and right. A tailback usually stands several yards behind center as the play starts.

For some three decades, from, roughly, one world war to another, the T Formation all but disappeared as the coaches warmly embraced the single wing and other new offensive formations, including the double wing and Notre Dame box. All were based on bypassing the quarterback with direct passes from center to other backs.

Of the nation's major football powers, only the University of Chicago, coached by Clark Shaughnessy, and the Chicago Bears, owned and coached by George Halas, resisted the stampede away from the T Formation. The Bears' old-fashioned T was, however, nothing like the Shaughnessy T, until, in the late 1930s, Shaughnessy moved across town to join Halas as an adviser. Then, persuading Halas to modernize, Shaughnessy proved that the nation's single-wing advocates had all been on the wrong track for the better part of three decades.

The features of the Shaughnessy T that distinguished it from the early-century Halas T were quick hitters, counter plays, players in motion, widely spaced receivers, and, among other things, many more passes than the Bears had been throwing.

In the winter of 1940-41, when Shaughnessy was both advising the Bears and coaching a Stanford team that for years had been failing under single-wing coaches, the results of two dramatic games laid out the picture for all to see. These were the Bears' 73-0 win over Washington for the NFL championship and Stanford's 21-13 Rose Bowl victory against a strong Nebraska team. As a pair, these events doomed the single wing, led to the nationwide T-Formation revival, and restored the quarterback to his ancient role as the initial ballhandler and director of offense.

THE NFL EVOLUTION

LOS ANGELES: June 20, 1981.

College football came first to America — the pros were a distant second — but the National Football League has been either gaining on or ahead of the campus establishment ever since Walter Camp died in 1925. And one reason for its steady improvement is that the NFL, emphasizing that football is a game created by rulemakers, has been more innovative for the last half century than any other group in football or any other sport.

The pro league's many changes — in league procedures as well as in the rules of the game — have kept pro football vibrant and moving.

Some of the more historic NFL innovations:

1926: College players ruled ineligible for the pros until their class graduates. (This rule stabilized both pro and college ball.)

1933: Small (Eastern and Western) NFL divisions established and a national championship game authorized. (The colleges have yet to agree on implementing a championship program that could have limitless revenue possibilities. And baseball has yet to agree on a small-division structure that would expand public interest.)

1933: Passing legalized from anywhere behind the scrimmage line. (This was the landmark passing rule opposed for so long by so many college coaches).

1934-35-36: Chicago's first College All-Star Games. (This was the making of the NFL at a time when college football seemed dominant.)

1936: The first annual NFL draft of college players.

1946: Transfer of the Rams from Cleveland to Los Angeles. (This established the NFL as the first national league in any sport. Baseball was to remain a provincial eastern sport until 1958, when the Dodgers moved from Brooklyn to Los Angeles.)

1951: Equal split of TV revenue among all NFL franchises. (This rule and a rule awarding forty per cent of all gate receipts to visiting teams have built the economic foundation of pro football. The ominous financial imbalance of baseball arises from a rule allowing each team to keep its TV income, thus enriching baseball's already-rich big-city franchises, and further weakening the poorer small-city franchises.)

1952: Home-game TV banned. Full road-schedule television mandated. (This was a response to baseball's financially harmful home-game TV policies in eastern cities, which nicked ticket sales. At the same time, the NFL's road-game TV policies became the major factor in building up public interest in pro football until it became the nation's favorite spectator sport.)

1967: Super Bowl. (The nation's biggest sports event.)

1970: Monday night football. (The colleges could have had this plum for themselves but NFL Commissioner Pete Rozelle visualized if first .)

1977-78: Bump-and-run defense ruled illegal. (The landmark modern change opening up the passing game.)

ALL-TIME TEAM

LOS ANGELES: June 20, 1981.

Who were the best football players of the game's first century? Who earned places on the all-time All-American team? The answers are necessarily subjective, leaving little room for agreement over a period that long, although, for reasons that will presently be apparent, it's possible that my team will be readily accepted here and there.

The first great football player I saw was Bronko Nagurski, a 1920s tackle and fullback for the University of Minnesota. Of the three best I ever saw, two played at times for Los Angeles teams, David (Deacon) Jones, a Ram defensive end, and USC Halfback O.J. Simpson. The third is Dick Butkus, a linebacker for the Chicago Bears.

In the following all-time team, the athletes selected were the eleven best at their positions, in my view, irrespective of whether they played offense, defense, both ways, college, pro, two years, or twelve. Although I never saw Pudge Heffelfinger or Ernie Nevers, I am willing to take the judgment of earlier spectators that you can't have an authentic all-time team without them. Others say you can't have one without Elroy Hirsch, Red Grange, Paul Robeson, Brick Muller or George Gipp, and they may be right, too, but I don't think so. Mine:

End Deacon Jones, Rams, South Carolina State (1960s)
End Don Hutson, Packers, Alabama (1930s)
Tackle Bronko Nagurski, Bears, Minnesota (1920s)
Tackle Jim Parker, Colts, Ohio State (1950s)
Guard Pudge Heffelfinger, Yale, (1890s)
Guard Danny Fortmann, Bears, Colgate (1930s)
Center Dick Butkus, Bears, Illinois (1960s)
Quarterback Joe Namath, Jets, Alabama (1960s)
Halfback O.J. Simpson, Bills, USC (1970s)
Halfback Jim Brown, Browns, Syracuse (1950s)
Fullback Ernie Nevers, Cardinals, Stanford (1920s)

7. Joe DiMaggio Gets Around

MY OFFSEASON objective in 1981, the fortieth anniversary of Joe DiMaggio's fifty-six-game hitting streak, was to find him. He doesn't much care for newspaper reporters. Allowing what I thought was plenty of time, I got on the telephone in November, 1980, between football games, leaving word every week or so at his San Francisco restaurant. His family has since sold it, but at that time the restaurant was the only place that friend or stranger could even think of a DiMaggio sighting. He finally called back in April, when I was working on the NFL draft, and he was working on his next trip. He looked at his calendar, and agreed to meet me for thirty minutes on a morning in June — if I could get there at 9:30. Over straight shots of Sanka, he showed an interest in some of the things we talked about. And at 1:30 he wound up driving me to my next appointment.

SAN FRANCISCO: July 10, 1981.

As of this month, it has been forty years since Joe DiMaggio, the Yankee Clipper, hit the ball safely in a record fifty-six consecutive baseball games — from May 15 to July 16 — for the 1941 New York Yankees. It has been thirty years since the smooth center fielder retired, ending an historic career in which he always seemed more at home on the road than at Yankee Stadium, the ballpark built for Babe Ruth, who swung from the other side.

All these years later, DiMaggio is still on the road, and he still loves it.

He has spent more than half his sixty-six years as "America's Mystery Guest," as a San Francisco friend calls him, mentioning the Clipper's frequent disappearances and numerous travels to the hometowns of many friends and the golf courses of many states. When asked about his vocation today, DiMaggio says, happily, that he's a traveling man.

Talking about his former career and present lifestyle during a mid-morning interview at his Fisherman's Wharf restaurant, he says: "I spend less than four months a year at home now, and seldom more than four or five days at a time. The rest of the year I'm off playing golf or visiting some of my good friends. Sometimes I stay at hotels, sometimes with friends. When I'm on the road awhile, I look forward to relaxing in San Francisco. After I've been home a few days, I get restless. I start to ask, where am I going next? I can't wait to get back, and I can't wait to leave."

One on one, he seems pensive but thoughtful, not too friendly, maybe, but polite. Nobody has ever seen all of Joe DiMaggio. At one time his wife was Marilyn Monroe, the late actress, but since their divorce he has not remarried. Aloof, regal, tall, trim (he skips breakfast and lunch when going out to dinner), he looks like a Roman emperor. A thin Roman emperor.

An unusual ex-athlete, DiMaggio was for years an unusual athlete. As a 1933 rookie with the Coast League's San Francisco Seals, he had a sixty-one-game hitting streak, still the all-time professional baseball record. After hitting in fifty-six major league games in 1941, he went hitless one day, then launched a new streak — hitting in sixteen additional consecutive games. During thirteen seasons in the majors, he struck out only twenty-eight times a year, on the average, and in his magical season, 1941, he struck out but thirteen times. He was a three-time American League MVP, batted .325 lifetime, produced 361 home runs, led the league twice in RBIs and twice in home runs, and led the Yankees to ten pennants and nine World Series championships in thirteen years.

As ever in the retelling, it seems beyond belief; in particular, the hitting streak is still the most improbable achievement in sports.

When DiMaggio is asked what he thinks of as the most difficult problem he had during the two months he needed to break Willie Keeler's forty-four-game record (later tied by Pete Rose), he replies, promptly, "It's difficult to get a base hit any time." Asked what it will take to break his record, he says: "A charitable scorer."

That's one thing, no doubt. The other essential is a hitter who loves the road. That, DiMaggio agrees, was his secret weapon.

II

The Clipper is still thinking that over, and inspecting the last of his first cup of Sanka, when a waitress walks up. "Excuse me, Joe," she says. "Your son is on the phone." His only child, Joe Jr., thirty-nine, lives nearby in Walnut Creek. "Nothing serious," DiMaggio says when he comes back. "Joe's in trucking, and likes it. He likes being an owner-operator."

Joe Jr.'s mother was Actress Dorothy Arnold, DiMaggio's first wife. Although, altogether, he has been married for a total of fewer than three years, he can look back on relationships with two of the most attractive women of his time. The end of his marriage to Marilyn Monroe and her subsequent death at age thirty-seven in 1962 — a suicide, the authorities reported — marked him for life. He doesn't like to talk about it, but their friends say the famous actress and the famous athlete remained fond of each other to her last day. His flowers, bouquets of fresh roses, still arrive three times a week at her grave in West Los Angeles, and, at intervals, DiMaggio still drops by.

Their storybook romance and the tragedy that followed have left a question that still lingers: What happened to their marriage? DiMaggio

Biographer Maury Allen quotes two witnesses, one of them Monroe's last press representative, Lois Weber Smith, who said: "I know she cared very deeply for him but Marilyn had the idea she could have both lives, the private and the public. She deceived herself in that." The other witness, Phil Rizzuto, the former ballplayer and now Yankee TV announcer, said: "Joe loved her but he didn't like all the men looking at her."

The week they were married, Joe brought Marilyn to San Francisco to live with him for a time in his old brownstone home on Beach Street. And to this instant, the neighbors well remember her sunbathing in the courtyard. "The Arthur Gordons lived next door," San Francisco Writer Art Rosenbaum says, "and Marilyn became quite friendly with Mrs. Gordon. One day when they were having tea in the Gordons' bedroom, Mrs. Gordon left Mrs. DiMaggio sitting on the bed and went down to answer the doorbell. When it turned out to be her husband, she whispered, 'Arthur, have I got something for you in your bedroom.' She led him upstairs and said, 'Arthur, this is Marilyn.'"

III

Born in Martinez, a nearby fishing town, DiMaggio has resided since infancy in San Francisco. The sandlot where he first played baseball is only a couple of blocks from his restaurant. "It was a place called the Horses Lot," he says, pointing. "It belonged to a dairy, and they brought their horses in there at 5 in the morning after they had finished delivering the milk. We used to move the horses all to one side of the lot, and play on the other side with a taped-up ball and a bat or two. One or two guys had gloves, but there was no mask for the catcher. I can't remember when I didn't love every minute of every ballgame, there or anywhere."

That affection, he says, made it easy for him to keep hitting the ball until he had a record that long-ago summer of 1941, six months before Pearl Harbor, when, at age twenty-six, in a stretch of fifty-six games, he scored fifty-six runs, drove in fifty-five, totaled ninety-one hits (including fifteen home runs) and batted .408. He is a little hazy on the details of the fifty-six games in which he hit safely, but he is an expert on what would have been the fifty-seventh. "Ken Keltner stopped me," he says, naming the Cleveland third baseman who threw him out twice on two almost identical ground balls that sizzled down the third base line. "Keltner was playing in short left field, right on the line. I could never understand why he was there. I didn't know until four years ago when we met at a banquet and he told me: 'I was giving you first base. I was just trying to avoid the extra-base hit.' I've always felt I'd have had two hits that night if it hadn't rained in the afternoon. Both were bang-bang plays at first base. I'd have beaten the ball both times on a fast field."

It was only the fourth night game for the Yankees in two months. But had the Clipper beaten out either grounder, he might have run the most impressive streak in sports to seventy-three. For after Keltner stopped him at fifty-six, DiMaggio went two more weeks before he was stopped again. In other words, for nearly half the season — in seventy-two of seventy-three consecutive games — he hit the ball safely in every game at least once. Asked whether the sixteen-game streak would have happened if he'd made it through fifty-seven, he says: "The only way I can answer that is to tell you they were all legitimate hits. The New York scorer (the late Dan Daniel) didn't give me anything that summer after the streak was under way. He leaned way over backwards — we had some discussions about it later — and on the road, the Yankees never did get anything (from the scorers). Every hit was legitimate. I take some pride in that."

IV

DiMaggio is speaking in a voice so soft that sometimes it's hard to hear him in the quiet, second-floor tap room of the restaurant that bears his name. It is after 10 a.m. now. Known for conservative suits, he is dressed for the morning in a checkered jacket with blue pants. Across the street in the sunlight, the fishing boats are coming in or putting out, whatever fishing boats do on a cool summer morning at Fisherman's Wharf. Fifty, sixty years ago, DiMaggio's father, Sicily-born, had one of those boats. Indeed, Joe might be on it himself right now, pulling in fish like his father used to do, if it hadn't made him seasick, and if, long ago, he'd had trouble with the curveball.

Instead, he's made it to the Hall of Fame — although the thing that pleases him most is not that he earned that distinction, or that he once hit the ball in a record number of games, but that he was a complete ballplayer. "I worked hard at it," he says, looking back fifty years. "I was a good base runner because I worked to become one. In the Coast League one year, I stole twenty-four bases in twenty-five attempts — but the Yankees weren't that kind of team."

After chronic seasickness turned him away from his father's trade as a fisherman, he vowed at an early age, he says, to master baseball as if it were a trade. "I was never one to hang around the batting cage," he says. "I just worked at baseball — on every facet of the game. Maybe the hardest thing I worked on was getting rid of the ball. A very high percentage of games are lost because an outfielder lets a runner take an extra base. In a close race, that's always the difference in the pennant. You can look it up."

DiMaggio has a theory on why the sportswriters of his time often described him as the smoothest and most graceful outfielder ever — the Julius Erving of the 1940s, so to speak. "At first," he says, "I didn't understand what they were talking about when they called me nonchalant and graceful. There I was, busting my insides to get the ball, and the next morning I'd read: 'The Clipper made another nonchalant, graceful catch.' Then one day I saw a movie of myself making a catch and throwing home, and I realized what they meant. I was always looking for the best and quickest way to get to the ball, and get rid of it. And in this game when you do that, it's bound to look streamlined."

At the plate, hitting thirty or more home runs most years, DiMaggio usually made contact. He might have been the best ever at getting a bat on a ball, at least for a power hitter. Young athletes are always dumfounded to read that in the year of his hitting streak, DiMaggio struck out only thirteen times. "My strength and my weakness was that, normally, I put the wood on the ball," he says. "That worked against me sometimes. I'd have often been better off if I'd missed the ball clean. That would give me another shot. Too often, I got a piece of it, and dribbled it to somebody. That's what happened in my last at bat the night my streak ended."

As his fans all know, the Yankees won the pennant again that season. In the DiMaggio years, they usually did. "We were always a winning team because we always played as a team," he says. "I remember a ninth inning during my streak when (Outfielder) Tommy Henrich, batting ahead of me, asked (Manager) Joe McCarthy if he could bunt in a one-on, one-out situation. I hadn't had a hit, and Tommy knew a double play would end it before I came to bat one last time. We weren't that far ahead, but McCarthy said sure, and Henrich bunted, and I finally got a hit. We were that kind of team."

V

If his active career identified him as one in millions, DiMaggio's later career has been even more unconventional. He is a flying gypsy who, from choice, logs tens of thousands of miles annually in commercial jets. His full-time vocation or avocation now is visiting his dozens of friends, most of them golf enthusiasts he has met over the years. He has never held a job, unless, as some believe, baseball is work. Frequently the houses and hotels he visits edge top-of-the-line golf courses. To get there, he always flies first class, and at a hotel, he always engages a suite. Smiling, he says: "If you're a traveling man, you've got to have those little luxuries."

The bills are no problem. He was baseball's first $100,000 player, and he still watches his money, and, according to some estimates, he makes a million a year as the television spokesman for a bank, a coffee company and other businesses. But regardless of cost, what he likes about first class, in or out of hotels or jets, is the relative privacy.

"I enjoy myself on airplanes no matter how often I fly," he says. "For one thing, I sleep very well up there. The music in those earphones puts me to sleep. And as you can imagine, I don't have a lot to say to the passenger in the next seat." DiMaggio is just along for the ride. "I look forward to every trip," he says.

What seems a trip to DiMaggio seems a disappearing act to others. He confides in no one. His acquaintances and even some of his friends think of him as a phantom. He can only be found when he wants to be found. "I don't know why I'm the way I am, but I like it this way," he says. "Because I'm a loner doesn't mean I'm a lonely guy. I've never had a lonely day in my life."

From one year to the next, the Clipper doesn't need much excuse to hit the road. He simply accepts a few of the invitations that roll in from sponsors of old-timer games or sports banquets or golf tournaments or pals. "A lot of my dear friends live in small towns all over the country," he says. "It isn't easy to get to them all, but it's always enjoyable."

Just in the last six weeks, DiMaggio's travels have taken him to New York, Miami, Panama, Pittsburgh, Boston, Las Vegas and Chicago, where, more often than not, he holed up awhile in hotels. Cold and impersonal to many, a hotel is a haven to DiMaggio, who prefers to stay each time in the same suites of the same good hotels. "In New York," he says, "the people at the Sheraton Center, the old Americana, have been very good to me. They've had the same suite for me every time I've been in New York for the last ten years. All I have to do is let them know I'm coming."

He draws a distinction between hotel rooms and lobbies. "I've never been a lobby sitter," he says. "What I like about hotels is the luxury of a big, nicely furnished suite, with the lights of a big city down below, or maybe a beautiful golf course. Hotels give you a lot of privacy. If you shut off the phones they'll take all the messages, and if the room service is good, a hotel is a beautiful place to relax."

Of course he wouldn't want to live there. "A few days anywhere," he says, "and I've had it."

8. Hacksaw: Rams to 49ers

BY MID-JULY, I'd had it with baseball and the other subjects a 1981 football writer had to get into in the offseason. And even though the San Francisco 49ers were in a thirty-year slump, I thought they'd made two major improvements with Jack Reynolds and Ronnie Lott, and I headed for their training camp. That was the year, surprising the league, the 49ers went to the Super Bowl for the first time, and won it. Reynolds had starred for the Rams, who will do anything to make money — even cutting him and Eric Dickerson and other high-priced talent. The 49ers, who will do anything to win, wouldn't have won that first championship without Reynolds. Moreover, with Reynolds, they won both 1981 games against the Rams.

ROCKLIN, Calif.: July 19, 1981.

The San Francisco 49ers prudently stationed a tackling dummy instead of a quarterback in the backfield here the other morning before asking their energetic new linebacker, Jack (Hacksaw) Reynolds, to practice rushing the passer. On the line of scrimmage, at the snap of the ball, it was one on one: Reynolds against a big, young blocker, whom he attacked, rolled back, knocked down, and jumped over. Then, reeling but still on his feet, Hacksaw bowled over the dummy. It all happened in about two seconds. "Those were some hits," Coach Bill Walsh, awed, said later.

Reynolds plays football furiously. He also practices that way. He enrages so many teammates in scrimmages that for the last eleven years, unofficially but undoubtedly, he has led the league in practice-field fights, some of them two-a-day fights.

All that time (1970-80) Reynolds was an employee of the Los Angeles Rams, for whom, last year as usual, he was first in tackles, first in fights, and last in the hearts of management. Between seasons, getting even with him, the Rams let him go. They didn't get anything in return. They didn't even trade him for a seventh-round draft choice, or a tenth, or even two elevens. After Reynolds came home from the Pro Bowl, where he played middle linebacker for the National Conference, they just said goodbye.

And, declining offers from other clubs in other divisions, in both conferences, he signed with arch-rival San Francisco.

"The Rams were making an example of Hacksaw," a National Football League club executive says. "He was working on them for a new contract and asked for a long-term, no-cut three or four years. They didn't want to do it, and decided to signal their other veterans to quit thinking about guaranteed contracts." Reynolds is thirty-three. Is it true that at that age, he wanted a three-year no-cut? "When people are negotiating contracts," he says, "they always ask for more than they expect to get. All I wanted was to be wanted."

Asked if in the course of the negotiations (presumably with General Manager Don Klosterman) he was ever able to reach the club owner, Georgia Frontiere, for a one-on-one discussion, Reynolds shakes his head slowly, the familiar face clouded with unhappiness. "In a lot of ways, I'm glad to be out of there," he says, meaning, almost certainly, that in most ways he isn't happy to be out of there.

Being Jack Reynolds, he will give the 49ers everything that's in him. He is a San Francisco man now, but he is rewriting the song. Hacksaw left his heart in Orange County.

II

This is a new training-camp site for the 49ers, who have moved into Sierra College, twenty miles east of Sacramento, where the temperature never gets under 105. Or so it seems. But nobody's knocking Rocklin yet. Or even the Rams. "You guys probably want to talk to me about the Los Angeles situation," Reynolds told San Francisco Writer Frank Cooney one day. "And I'm not going to do it." When CBS Commentator Brent Musburger sent up a cameraman, sound man and announcer last week for a few words with Reynolds, he turned them down. He was polite, but immovable. His attitude has been so puzzling that San Jose Writer Mike Antonucci urged him to change his name from Hacksaw to Jigsaw.

Turning to a reporter from Los Angeles, Jigsaw asks: "What good would it do me now to stab (the Rams)? The only thing I tried to do was help those people, and it wasn't good enough." He may talk about it someday. "And again I may not," he says. "The truth may never be known." Asked about Pat Haden instead of Vince Ferragamo for the Rams at quarterback, Reynolds says: "What the (Rams') offensive line feels about who's at quarterback will have the most to do with how well the quarterback plays. They have so much talent down there. Their problem is that they can't get the ability out of all that's there."

Reynolds seems a flake to many of those meeting him here for the first time. Always something of a loner, he is one of the shy ones who would rather be known by actions than words. In Los Angeles, to insure that he was rightly understood on those terms, he spent most of his free time inspecting game films and studying football (a habit he has resumed here).

The thing that angers and frustrates him the most, after those long years of above-and-beyond service to the Rams, is that they didn't make an effort to get to know a valued employee and cajole him into staying. He seems to be saying that a big outfit like the Rams should learn how to deal with the shy ones, with their really talented people, that is, of any stripe.

His insistence on appealing to Frontiere and Klosterman without an agent — he was one of the few modern-day athletes doubling as his own agent — was probably a cry for attention. (As a 49er, he has finally hired one.)

A 1970 first-round Ram draft choice out of Tennessee, Reynolds isn't exactly the dumb athlete. His father, a chemical engineer, is an MIT graduate, and Hacksaw might have followed engineering himself except that his mother, a socialite from Marblehead, Massachusetts, was a New York Giants fan. She introduced him to the wonderful world of Sam Huff–Jim Brown collisions, and he found, early on, that football is more exciting.

Some of the excitement has faded in recent months, and he is searching for an answer. "Most people don't know me," he says quietly, as if to himself. "The only two Rams who know what I've been through are Nolan Cromwell and Fred Dryer."

III

Reynolds is one of three exceptional players the Rams cut loose in the offseason to avoid paying high salaries to veteran talent. The others are Ferragamo, who went to Canada, and All-Conference Linebacker Bob Brudzinski, now of the Miami Dolphins. "Bob is a sensitive, studious, team-oriented player," says Reynolds, who thinks the loss of Brudzinski will be devastating to the Rams.

In Los Angeles, they're saying the loss of Reynolds will be worse.

In San Francisco, they're saying he belongs at weak-side inside linebacker, and Walsh has shifted him there from the strong outside. As a rule, strong-side linebackers get more ballcarriers to tackle; and because Reynolds sees himself as primarily a tackler of ballcarriers, he is concerned by the change. Any middle-aged man forced to change jobs, in a different city, for a different firm, would be concerned, but it is possibly harder on an athlete. "I'll have to wade through more garbage now to get to the ball," he says of the increased traffic he expects to contend with as a weak-side linebacker. He doesn't seem to be complaining. But he is plainly worrying about the extra hits on his legs, which are now thirty-three years old.

To Walsh, the Reynolds change is wholly in the player's benefit. "This gives him an opportunity to extend his career," the San Francisco coach says. "In a four-three defense like the Rams use, middle linebackers take an awful beating, and it gets worse toward the end of their career, especially in the longer sixteen-game schedule. As we go along, Jack will find that he has more access to the runner from this (inside weak) position. He will be unblocked more often as he comes across from the back side. He will get into the pursuit faster, and that's one of the best things he does."

Complicating Reynolds' life in a new environment, he will be going it alone here for awhile. His wife Pat stayed in the Bahamas, supervising construction of their new house on the island of San Salvador. "It's an island with a population of eight hundred," he says. "Our house is forty yards from the water."

On San Salvador, he concedes, rather sadly, there are few cars to cut in half with a hacksaw — should he get the urge again — although there are quite a few boats, including his. And, all in all, carving up a boat should be easier for a man in his thirties. He was twenty-one and in the prime of life when, during a prior frustration, he sawed a Chevrolet in two. The nickname he's had ever since seems a good fit.

"We love the clean water and clean air of the Bahamas," he says, indicating that, henceforth, he plans to spend only a month a year at his house in Huntington Beach. "San Salvador was the first land Columbus saw in the new world. The only industry we have is arguing over where he landed. It was either on our beach or down the path or across the island." In the meantime, with more relish than most men of thirty-three, Reynolds is looking forward to his next birthday, November 22, a Sunday. (He denies this — he has to try to deny it, but he can't do it, convincingly.) He will be in Anaheim Stadium that day with the 49ers.

9. Ronnie Lott, Football Student

STARTING EARLY in Coach Bill Walsh's tour with the 49ers, I spent a week or so in their training camp each summer. And during a July week in 1981, the year they went to the Super Bowl for the first time and won it, I visited two or three times with their top draft pick, Ronnie Lott, a safetyman who became a cornerman before moving back to safety. Even then, Lott had all-time talent and toughness, but my main interest has always been in his mental focus. Here's Lott at the beginning of his NFL career.

ROCKLIN, Calif.: July 25, 1981.

When the San Francisco 49ers drafted USC Defensive Back Ronnie Lott on the first round three months ago, his life was about to change rather drastically in two ways that have since set him apart from other athletes. In chronological order:

• Lott graduated from college. Four years after entering USC, he graduated with his class. This made him something of an educational rarity, at least in America. Of the thousands of athletes and nonathletes enrolling as freshmen in four-year colleges today, fewer than half stick it out to get their degrees on time. Increasingly, if they finish at all, they spend five years in college. Of the football players who graduate, more than ninety per cent take five years or more. "You can only do it in four," Lott says, "if you make it your first priority."

• He changed positions. An All-American strong safety at USC, Lott became San Francisco's left cornerback, playing the most difficult position in a National Football League secondary.

Most NFL backs, receivers and linemen play their college position, and benefit by the continuity. But for defensive backs, it's different. In both college and pro ball, the best defensive backs are asked to play the hot spot wherever that might be. In college it's safety. In the NFL it's a corner, and in pro ball left corner is the hot corner. The league's fastest runners and receivers appear more often on that side — on Lott's side — than the other side. At San Francisco's new Rocklin training camp, which is near Sacramento, he says, "I have a lot to learn."

"Ronnie has a lot to learn," third-year 49er Coach Bill Walsh says. "But he's so bright. He's learning fast. He's coming every day."

II

The 49ers, who open the exhibition season against the Seattle Seahawks in the Kingdome tonight, fielded one of the world's worst defenses a year ago. They expect to improve, eventually, with their young, new personnel (including three rookies in the secondary, all top draft choices) and a new defensive philosophy much like that of the Oakland Raiders.

Thus, in some of San Francisco's basic defenses this year, Walsh is planning to assign Lott to the offensive team's fastest receiver with instructions to "follow him everywhere," thereby freeing the rest of the 49ers to gang up on slower opponents. The formula as formulated by Raider Owner Al Davis: "If your best man stops their best man, the rest is easy." For many years, Oakland has won with this strategy, most recently with All-Pro Cornerback Lester Hayes, a former college safety (at Texas A&M). Says Lott: "Assuming I can keep up, it's a great defense, but it's sure different."

Last year, USC, too, could have employed Lott at cornerback. After all, he was to be the eighth player chosen in the 1981 draft. If it makes sense in pro ball, why not on a college team? "There's nothing our opponents would rather have seen than Lott on a corner," USC Coach John Robinson says. "Everybody knows he's one of the toughest guys the Trojans have ever had. They'd simply ignore him, and we'd lose Lott from our defense. We wanted Ronnie near the ball at all times, and on a college team that means safety."

It also means that when the pros draft a top college safety, he must enter a new world. A Ronnie Lott, say, arrives at his first pro training camp at a development stage comparable with that of a college sophomore running back. "Ronnie won't be as good right off as people are saying," 49er Safety Dwight Hicks said after watching him for a few days. "But he will be." In other words, the 49ers will eventually get what they paid for, and it might be sooner rather than later.

For, at Rocklin, Lott's great natural ability has been shining through from the start. On a typical twenty-yard 49er pass pattern the other day (Quarterback Steve DeBerg to Wide Receiver James Owens) Lott was the star, knocking the ball away. Said DeBerg: "Owens had about three yards on him, (and) I threw a bullet right on his stride. Lott made an All-Pro-type play." That didn't surprise Robinson. "Lott is the kind you can count on," the Trojan coach says. "He's what you want whether it's a football team, a war, or a business."

Analyzing his new cornerback, George Seifert, who coaches the 49er secondary, places his emphasis on the way Lott keeps coming on. "He'll get himself in position *and* make the play," Seifert says. "A lot of guys get in position, and figure they've done their job, then the play gets away from them. But that's when Lott accelerates: right at the critical moment."

III

In his spare time, Lott still studies like a college student. The study habits he got into as a Trojan will be particularly helpful, he's sure, in his first pro season, for he has a whole new league to learn. During his USC years, Lott's willingness to spend some time with his nose in a book won him a B.A. degree in business administration. "More football players would graduate if they could see how vital it is," he says. "That's surprisingly hard for an athlete to grasp. He knows he's in college because he's a good athlete. He has a scholarship to prove it. So he thinks football is what's important."

In Lott's opinion, any youngster with enough on the ball to be admitted to a college can get an education if he goes to every class and reads the assigned books. "It isn't that difficult to pick up a book and read it," he says. "You just have to want to. I keep hearing that a lot of kids can't read today, and maybe that's true, but the ones I knew at SC could read and read well. To play football, you have to be able to read a playbook, and playbooks aren't all X's and O's. The terminology you need to play and compete is in there. It's pretty sophisticated stuff, and if you can read a playbook, you can read a history book."

One problem, Lott discovered long ago, is having to concentrate on football one minute and biology the next. "Take your average businessman," he says. "I wonder if he could focus his whole body and mind on something as dazzling and demanding as football for three hours and then turn around and focus on the stock market. I think there's an insufficient realization of what college football players have to go through to be college students. The critics think they're just a bunch of lucky kids, but the truth is, they're under more stress than most people."

The stress takes many forms. "Suppose you're in college on an athletic scholarship and you're not playing," Lott says, remembering some of his schoolboy friends. "You were a high school star, but now nobody notices you. You keep going out for practice, and going through those same hard three hours the starters go through, but they're not using you in games. That's a big worry. It's very stressful. But as worried as you are, you're supposed to go back to your room and study. You're nineteen or twenty years old, and you're supposed to handle a crushing disappointment as if you were an adult. Your big dream of a pro career is disappearing, and you're supposed to carry on bravely in the classroom. That's just unrealistic."

For Lott, the big dream is still alive. He's one of the lucky ones. Well adjusted, self disciplined, self motivated, and greatly talented, he still seems to be on his way to a big career. But for the overwhelming majority of America's prep and college athletes, the future, as Lott knows, is past. And his compassion is for them. "The least we can do is understand," he says. "People who knock lazy athletes for not going to class don't make allowances for all the stressful things that can happen to young guys under twenty-one."

10. Dan Reeves: Born to Win

AS A football player, Dan Reeves lasted nine years with the Dallas Cowboys, spending his last season as a player-coach before entering coaching full time. To most sports fans today, after Reeves' careers in Denver and New York, he is known only as a coach. But to the old friends who have been with him all along, he is still the athlete who, given his choice between winning and dying or losing and living, would ask to think it over. This story was written at the start of his coaching career.

DENVER: Nov. 18, 1981.

Dan Reeves, the one-time Dallas Cowboys halfback who joined the Denver Broncos as their new head coach this season, was playing golf in Texas several years ago when, as he tells it, rain drove him into the clubhouse. There, the golf pro gave him a lesson that would be hard for anyone to forget. Bouncing a golf ball on a barroom table, the pro caught it on the back of his hand and said: "Bet you $5 you can't do that."

Reeves, an inconceivably intense competitor, replied: "Give me five practice shots and you're on."

An hour later, frustrated and still failing, having lost more than he wanted to lose, Reeves packed up and grumped home. "The rain had stopped, but the temperature was under thirty," he remembers. "I put the car in the barn, and went straight out to the patio with a bag of golf balls. It was so cold I almost froze to death, but before midnight I could catch that little old ball on the back of my hand every time I bounced it. And the next day, I went back to the golf club and got my money back."

That's Dan Reeves. A close friend from his Cowboy days, Cornell Green, the former All-Pro cornerback, says: "Danny wasn't much of a running back, no speed, no size, but he outhustled everybody, and he memorized every assignment of every player on every play. He knew exactly where every player was going to be, and that gave him his edge. Made him look good. He even led the league in touchdowns one season."

Walt Garrison, the former Dallas fullback who roomed four years with Reeves, says: "He'd sit up night after night going over (Coach) Tom Landry's plays in the playbook until he had a complete understanding of the old man's philosophy. I've known a lot of guys who loved to win. The thing about Danny is that he *worked* to win."

It has been clear for a long time, in other words, that Reeves is a football-wise competitor — clear, that is, to those who knew him at Dallas, and before that in college at South Carolina, and even earlier on the farm in Georgia. And this year, the Broncos confirmed it when they brought him in as the NFL's youngest head coach. He is thirty-seven. The only curious thing was the club owner's reasoning. "I wanted a guy about my age so we could grow up together," said their eccentric new chief executive, Edgar F. Kaiser. Said a Reeves friend: "Getting Dan Reeves for his age is like getting Bo Derek for her age. On the whole, it's irrelevant."

In Dallas today, what they mostly talk about is Reeves' competitiveness. He can't even go to a party without trying to win. "When time starts to drag," a Reeves associate, Steve Perkins, says, "Danny will pull out a dime and bet you $5 you can't blow it into a glass of water. Funniest thing I ever saw — Danny leaning over and blowing a dime off the table into a cup or a glass."

Reeves estimates he has paid a tuition of several hundred dollars to learn such stunts from various other competitors. "One of the tough ones," he says, "is moving an egg from one shot glass to another without touching it — and without cracking the eggshell. You have to *blow* it across. I'll bet you five bucks you can't do it."

II

As in many Southern towns, football is a religion in Columbia, South Carolina, home of the University of South Carolina, whose two leading performers in the early 1960s were George Rogers, a Heisman Trophy winner, and Dan Reeves, their quarterback. They'll never forget the play that made Reeves famous. "We had the ball on our own one-yard line," Marty Rosen, one of Reeves' teammates, recalls. "I don't think Danny even looked at the defense when he went back to pass." Just as he threw, an opponent stepped forward and tackled the receiver in the end zone. "It's still in the book as the only forward pass ever completed for a safety," Rosen says. "We're all very proud of Danny."

At Carolina, Rosen and Reeves were best friends. They studied, played and double-dated together. "He was the first Baptist I ever knew," says Rosen, a Brooklyn boy who went back to Brooklyn and is now in the import business. "He was a pure down-South cracker, and I was the only Jewish football player they'd ever seen in South Carolina. The first six weeks I knew him, we couldn't understand a word the other said. We had to use sign language."

It was in those days that Reeves' friends started calling him "Frog," a tribute to his posture as a football player. He regularly lined up low, like a frog. As nicknames go, it's hardly elegant, but it's Reeves'. He can't shake it. And, in fact, he kind of likes it. For years, he has worn a silver necklace with one small ornament, a silver frog.

He also favors expensive jeans, expensive boots, and, especially, expensive long-sleeved sports shirts. He always seems to be in a fresh shirt. Bespectacled, baggy-eyed and round-faced, Reeves wears his dark hair nearly to the eyebrows. Women like him. To Denver Writer Marjie Lundstrom, he is "down-home friendly, muscular, rugged. He's a looker, all right."

After eight knee operations, Reeves "can't stand completely up" and "I don't walk right." But he's still a five-handicap golfer, and he still plays backyard basketball with his three children. And he still plays to win. His wife, Pam, says: "Our younger daughter (Laura, eleven) came in the house crying last night. She and Dan had been playing basketball against the other two. And Laura said Dan wouldn't pass her the ball any more because they were losing." Nonetheless, single-handed, Dan went on to beat daughter Dana, sixteen, and son Lee, fourteen. "He came in smiling," Pam said. "The kids knocked his bridge out, and loosened a tooth, but he was smiling — so I knew he'd won."

III

To preserve the official papers of Lyndon B. Johnson, a library was erected not long ago in Austin, Texas, and a similar structure is now under consideration in Georgia for another former U.S. president, one of Dan Reeves' old neighbors, Jimmy Carter. Accordingly, last year, a delegation from two Georgia cities, Plains and Americus, flew to Texas to check out the LBJ complex. The travelers were met at the Dallas airport by Reeves, then a Dallas assistant coach, who discovered that there were two hours before the next Austin flight. "Would y'all like to see where we play football here?" he asked. "Sure," they said, faces brightening. "Then pile in," Reeves said. "All I've got is this little old pickup truck, but I think y'all will fit nicely in the back end." And that's how the Georgia dignitaries saw Texas Stadium—clutching their straw hats in a pickup truck while their seersucker suits flapped in the breeze.

The ties between the Carters and the Reeveses in Georgia go back a long way. The large Reeves family settled around Americus early in the century when the large Carter family was digging in around Plains. The first game Dan ever played in, a grammar school basketball game against a team of other seven-year-olds, was at Plains, and as usual there were Carters on the other side. "We beat them 65 to 2," Dan remembers proudly.

Born in north Georgia, he was six weeks old when the family moved to the farm where he lived until age eighteen. The farm is outside New Era, near Americus, which is just over the horizon from Andersonville and Plains, "As a kid, Dan could plow a mule," his father, C. E. (Edd) Reeves, says, reporting from his 275-acre Georgia farm. "He didn't like it much, especially night plowing, but he could do it." Says Dan: "I didn't even like night plowing with a tractor. It was too scary. I was always afraid I'd meet an escaped convict (from Andersonville). When very young, I learned to turn the tractor around so fast I set a county record for plowing peanuts."

The old record, he thinks, was held by a Carter.

Some of Dan's friends believe his passion for the active life is a reaction to a sickly childhood. "He was in bed most of the time until he was six years old," his mother Ann says. "I remember getting down on my knees and praying he'd live. It was an unusual fever of some kind, and they finally got it with a new antibiotic." Dan also remembers it. "They put me in the hospital to get a needle every four hours, day and night," he says. "Every shot, the nurse gave me a new car for the plastic train I got for my birthday, and eventually that little old train ran around my bed three times. It wasn't easy, but I set another county record. Most needles in the rear end."

As soon as he could walk, Dan was playing football, basketball and baseball, and from the start he played to win. Talking about those days, his sister Joanne says: "That came natural. His daddy didn't want any good losers in the family." Says Marty Rosen: "A remarkable man, Edd Reeves. Even when we partied all night on a Saturday night, he'd get Dan and me up for church. Made us wear coats and ties, too."

Dan's unreal dedication to sports awed his mother. "I felt for him so," Ann Reeves says. "When he was in high school, football practice went on for half the year, it seemed, and Dan wanted to do so well so badly he was always a mass of bruises when he came home. I'd put hot pads on the bruises every night, and soak him in a hot tub, just like a trainer, so he could go back and get bruised up again tomorrow."

By his senior year, Dan was a three-sport star, pitching Americus to the Georgia state baseball championship. "As a pitcher, Dan was very fast and very wild," says his cousin Jerry, now an Americus banker. "It was pretty funny, the headline they put in the paper one day: 'D. Reeves Pitches No-Hitter as Americus Wins, 15-13.'"

Early on, Dan developed the time and energy to also date Americus High School girls. "He was a cute boy," says one of them, Pamela White, who was to become Pam Reeves, mother of his children. "When he was a junior athlete, I was a freshman cheerleader, and one night he asked me out." On their first date, when they went to a sock hop, Dan didn't add too much to the evening. "He said he'd really rather be hunting," Pam says.

Assuming that one of Dan's best games was football, it wasn't immediately apparent. As a high school senior, he wasn't even in the family's top ten. That was the year that cousin Jerry was the Americus MVP, so when South Carolina offered Dan a scholarship, he snapped it up. A week later, quarterbacking the winning team at Atlanta in the annual state high school all-star game, Dan had a big night and was voted MVP. In a wink, he was a sensation far beyond the peanut country. "Talent scouts came to our farm from universities all over the South," his mother says. "Dan had always wanted the state university, and now they and everyone else wanted him."

His father remembers that one night after finishing his chores, Dan, troubled, wanted to talk it over. "Like to see you here at Georgia," said Edd Reeves.

"I'd like for that, too, daddy," said Dan.

"By the way, son, wasn't Carolina the only school that came after you last month?"

"Well, yes, daddy, that's sure enough true."

"And didn't you give your word to those folks?"

"Yes, daddy, I surely did."

"Well, then, son, where you reckon you're a-going?"

"I'm going to South Carolina, daddy."

IV

During his years as a football player at Carolina and, later, for the Cowboys, Reeves' goal was to be a football coach. And that remained his goal until 1973, when, after three years as an assistant on Tom Landry's staff, he abruptly resigned and accepted a job selling real estate. "Probably the best thing I ever did," he says now. "Coaching is a hard life, but real estate is harder. Try it sometime. A big reason I quit football was to spend more time at home and make my family happy. What I learned was that I can't make anyone happy unless I'm happy."

His year off prompted Reeves to work out a compromise lifestyle that might be unique in the NFL. Arising early each morning, he hangs around the house until his children leave for school, whereupon be spends all day with the Broncos, after which he comes home for dinner and works evenings in his den with a movie projector. Workaholics like Philadelphia's Dick Vermeil cringe at the thought of Reeves going home nights for dinner. Even Minnesota's Bud Grant spends more hours at the office. Asked about that, Reeves says: "I doubt if many coaches outwork me. A projector is a projector anywhere."

The Reeves family lives on a new street in Denver in a new two-story four-bedroom house in the Inglewood section of the city. "Dan stays up with that projector of his until all hours," his wife Pam says. "He often isn't with us mentally, but the important thing is that he's always available. If one of the children has a math problem, he'll come out and help them."

Like any other pair, the Reeveses have been through a storm or two. They've thought of separation, a time or two, since his senior year in college, when Dan brought Pam to Carolina as a bride. Their friend Rosen, who was served by Dan as a marriage groomsman one day, "when Dan wore that little hat, the yarmulke," says from Brooklyn: "As a divorced person, I can't say enough for these guys. Marriage isn't the easiest relationship, but Pam stuck by him, and Dan stuck it through."

Pam says that she and Dan live by only one fixed rule: "We never go to bed without the other. I sit up reading or knitting as long as I hear the projector, then we go upstairs. That gives us a bit of time each day to talk and be alone together." Pam Reeves' game is tennis, and in Dan's offseason she tries to get him out for mixed doubles. "It would be good for him," she says. "Tennis is a social game — you compliment your opponent for a well-hit ball."

That poses a big problem for Dan Reeves. "He doesn't have much fun," Pam says, "because it hurts him so much to say, 'Good shot.' He'd rather bet you $5 that he can bounce a tennis ball over the clubhouse."

11. Amos Alonzo Stagg Has 314

THE MAN on the spot in college football's story of the year in 1981 was Alabama Coach Paul (Bear) Bryant. The issue that year: In lifetime games won, can Bear catch Stagg? Of the Bryant articles I wrote during the 1981 season, three are reproduced in the pages that follow. The overriding first question: Who is Stagg?

LOS ANGELES: Sept. 1, 1981.

Although college football has been played in America for a century, it was only twelve years ago that NCAA researchers discovered that a man named Amos Alonzo Stagg had coached his teams to a record 314 wins — with Paul (Bear) Bryant far down the list at 187. Stagg, an early twentieth-century coach, never knew he was the champion. Nor did fellow Coach Pop Warner ever know he held the record at 313 until Stagg broke it in 1946. For, in college sports, keeping comprehensive statistics is a relatively new science.

Stagg was thirty years old when the automobile came in. He was eighty when the atomic age arrived. But he never had time for cars, bombs *or* statistics. By vocation, and avocation, Stagg was a football coach, and, first to last, he had but two other passions, plain food and clean living. "The greatest pleasure one has is keeping and feeling fit," he said one day.

He was ninety-nine when he said it.

Long before he died sixteen years ago at the age of 103, Stagg, who coached his first football team in 1890, was a 314-game winner. His is the record that Bear Bryant is going for as the coach of Alabama this season after winning 306 so far. But even when Bryant gets there, Stagg will still have a leg up on him as, say, an inventor.

For one thing, it was Stagg who invented the tackling dummy in 1889, when he was a divinity student at Yale. That was the first of his many innovations, which later included, reportedly, baseball's batting cage as well as the overflow troughs that line most swimming pools. Yet even though he swam like a fish, batted like a champion, and was known as the deadliest tackler of his generation, Stagg couldn't make an effective sermon. So he left the field of religion in 1890 and took a job as a football coach, accepting an offer from the International YMCA School at Springfield, Massachusetts (now known as Springfield College) where he started 11-10 in 1890-91.

More than a half century later, he was still coaching, and still winning, at Stockton's College of the Pacific (now UOP). His biggest year was 1943, when Pacific beat UCLA, 19-7, and Cal, 12-6, to finish in the nation's top ten as Stagg made Associated Press Coach of the Year. He was then eighty-one, and nowhere near ready to retire.

His whole career was an advertisement for the clean living he valued and pitched. He never smoked anything and, except for water, never drank, not even coffee, never gambled, and never cussed. His angriest epithet was jackass. He called himself a stoic. And according to Miami Herald Sports Editor Edwin Pope, Stagg celebrated his eighty-ninth birthday by dining on pea soup, two ears of corn, peaches, and milk. "I never ate a hot dog in my life," he once said.

Those who didn't like him too much called him stuffy. They recalled that at the University of Chicago, where Stagg coached for forty-one years starting in 1892, he once refused an assistant's suggestion to send in a substitute with a play that his staff thought might win the game. "The rules committee," the old man said disdainfully, "deprecates the use of a substitute to convey information." Chicago lost that day, 21-18.

In the same spirit, Stagg, in 1898, produced football's first clean-shaven team, using his own razor on the last man himself.

Stagg was Eastern bred. He had been born in poverty in 1862 in a neighborhood of Irish laborers at West Orange, New Jersey, where his father began his career as a shoemaker's apprentice at age seven. As it happened, young Alonzo was a good athlete, and even then, in the 1870s, that got him to Phillips Exeter Academy and eventually Yale. Though a stocky 150-pounder who would fatten up to 166, Stagg was a Walter Camp All-American end who in the spring months doubled as a pitcher, leading Yale to five national baseball championships.

Focusing on football, he coached forty-three years at Springfield and Chicago before Chicago fired him. He was then seventy-one. Sorting out the six job offers that came in immediately, Stagg went to Pacific, where, after fourteen more years as a coach, he still wouldn't quit, and *Pacific* fired him. He was then eighty-five.

At 101, looking back, he said he was always proud of his contributions to football, not only the tackling dummy but also the reverse play, the huddle, lateral pass, cross blocking, man in motion, wind sprints, knit football pants, the numbering of plays and players, and, among other things, the awarding of letters or monograms. But he never changed personally. To the year he was 103, Stagg never had a hot dog.

12. Bear Bryant Has 307

THIS MAN was the most unusual and, ultimately, the most successful college football coach of his time. As a rule, longevity records and statistics aren't as meaningful as one-year or one-day achievements — but in 1981, millions of Bryant fans thought otherwise.

TUSCALOOSA, Ala.: Sept. 9, 1981.

By many high school people, Alabama football Coach Paul (Bear) Bryant is ranked as the college game's most persuasive recruiter. And here's what he had to say at a prep-school coaches' banquet one year in California: "I want to talk to you gentlemen about your real good football players. If there are any 'A' students among 'em, I'd like for you to send 'em to Stanford — the Harvard of the West. Your 'B' students, I'd recommend Southern Cal or UCLA. Yes, suh, I'd send my own kin theah. Your 'C' students — put them in the other great schools of this great state. But let me also say this to y'all. If there are any gin-drinkin', hell-raisin', meaner-than-hell 'D' students on your team, please send 'em down to the old Bear."

Nobody else today can be compared to the old Bear. In a few short weeks, he is going to become the winningest college football coach yet, passing Amos Alonzo Stagg, who won 314, and Pop Warner, 313. Bryant reached 307 the other night, impressively starting his thirty-seventh coaching season at Baton Rouge, Louisiana, where, forecasting another big 'Bama year, his new team sped past LSU, 24-7, silencing the animals in a famous zoo.

Still, it's who he is rather than what Bryant's team might be that interests other coaches.

Says former Arkansas Coach Frank Broyles: "Bryant is so dignified that I'm always expecting him to say, 'Let us pray'. But there's another side to him. When he was at Kentucky, he was the only coach who found out that a good young high school player in Texas was a Catholic. The prospect had about decided on Notre Dame when Bryant got him by dressing up one of his assistant coaches as a priest — black suit, white collar and all. The boy was overwhelmed when Bear's assistant dropped by and told him: 'Young man, the Pope wants you to go to Kentucky.'"

LSU Athletic Director Paul Dietzel, who coached on Bryant's staff for a number of years, remembers, "Even at parties, Bear would do anything to win." One night after a night game, Dietzel says, when the coaches were playing charades with their wives, Bryant's team won although he had never, until then, heard of the game. "Bear beat us when nobody could guess the name of a book he called a real book," Dietzel says. "He told us it was 'Fordyce on the Cotton Belt.' Who's going to act out Fordyce? I found out later that's where he's from — but not in time to call him a liar at 3:30 in the morning, not after a few beers."

Fordyce, Arkansas (population 3,206), is indeed where Bryant went to school. He's actually from a suburb of Fordyce called Moro Bottom (population 37). He was born on a farm there. They were already calling him Bear in high school, where he played tackle for the Fordyce Redbugs. He became Bear after a wrestling match. "A promoter with a real live bear came to the Lyric one year," says former Redbug Quarterback Ike Murray. "The guy offered $1 a minute to anyone wrestling the bear, and Paul volunteered." Murray doesn't remember who won, Bryant or the bear. But, he says, "I do remember that half the crowd was pulling for the bear."

To earn his way through high school, Bryant drove a grocery truck after school and lived in an unfinished room on the top floor of the Kilgore Hotel, where Murray, later attorney general of Arkansas, was the night clerk. "If I'd been writing the class prophecy for our senior class at Fordyce," Murray says, "I'd have written this about Bear Bryant: 'He'll be lucky to stay out of the penitentiary.'"

II

For the LSU game, Bryant flew his team over from Tuscaloosa in two planes. He also brought along his wife, Mary Harmon. They left two children at home, a boy and girl, and so at the airport, someone asked Bear if he and his wife were always careful to fly in separate planes. "I'm always careful to fly with the starters," he said.

He was in a seersucker suit with white shirt, blue tie and one of his four hundred plaid houndstooth hats. A closet businessman, a millionaire, he owns part of the New York firm that makes those hats. The familiar sunbaked face seemed more deeply etched than ever. It is the face of a heavy smoker and drinker who has defied the odds and lived to be sixty-eight. Doing his weekly television show last year, Bryant reached for an ash tray one night, missed, and put out a cigaret in the upholstery of a nearby chair. As he droned on, smoke and then flames were visible on almost every TV screen in Alabama. Just in time, the producer rushed in with a bottle of cola, said, "Excuse me, coach," and put out the fire.

A show-must-go-on professional, Bryant never dropped a stitch.

On either television or in person, Bryant, six feet two, 206, could be the aging grandfather of the Marlboro man. During a short walk on the LSU campus, he exchanged smiles and a few casual words with a young woman student, who, afterward, told a reporter: "Mr. Bryant knows how to talk to a lady, and how to look at a woman."

She also said he seemed shy, which may account for the rumbling, growling, low-volume monotone of Bryant's normal speaking voice. "Half the time we can't understand him," one of his players said. But they always know what he means.

Two hours before the Alabama-LSU game, driving up to the stadium behind two wailing police cars, Bryant and his players got out of the bus and slowly walked around the field from end zone to end zone. It's a ritual they follow at road games, testing the turf, and acclimating themselves to the taunts of the enemy.

In this case, thousands of LSU students hooted them all the way around. Though the boys and girls were in shorts on an eighty-two-degree night, Bryant and his players were all carefully groomed in jackets and ties. In an Alabama-red jacket, Bryant led the parade, and to Boston Writer John Powers he was just "a tired old man, shufflin' along, trying to stay out of the hospital." But New York Writer B.J. Phillips said: "The message is clear: "Alabama is checking things out. Alabama will be ready."

And it was.

III

As a football coach, Paul Bryant has worked out a unique formula for himself, one that separates him from other coaches. The formula: Accept the responsibility, invariably, for everything that goes wrong. Listen to him after any game, read his quotes, it's always a set formula piece in which Bryant is blaming himself for any Alabama problems, and crediting others for any successes.

A former Bryant assistant, New Orleans Saints Coach Bum Phillips, says: "Here's how Bear runs a players' meeting. He starts talking about all the good things everybody did, individually — each guy's blocking, tackling, whatever they did good. Pretty soon he's got all the players nodding and agreeing. Then, gently, he brings up a few wrong things. A guy sitting there will tell himself: 'The old man's been bragging on me, and I know he's right about that. Maybe he's right about this, too.'"

At coaches' meetings, the formula is similar. "He blames himself for so much," Phillips says, "that pretty soon he has the other coaches saying to themselves, 'Hey, wait a minute, maybe I could have done something better myself.' It's only human to resist when somebody is bawling you out, so Bear does just the opposite, and gets everybody leaning with him."

It's clear to his staff that before a big game, Bryant runs the strangest coaches' meetings in football history. "He might sit around for an hour or more offering little bits of ideas," Phillips says. "Eventually, one of his assistants will catch the drift and make a suggestion. Then Bear will slap the table and say: 'Damn, why didn't I think of that? We'll do it.' Next thing, he's bragging on the guy in the newspapers. Everybody who knows him well is surprised out of their head every time Bear loses."

But what keeps the old coach going?

Bear says it's fear. "The thing that's motivated me all my life," he says, "is the fear of going back to driving mules in Arkansas for fifty cents a day." That could explain how Bryant has managed to avoid the worst hazard to longevity in coaching, fear of changing football styles and routines. Most of the great ones, back to Bernie Bierman, Bob Neyland and beyond, mastered one way of playing the game, and retired prematurely when they couldn't or wouldn't adjust to new and better ways.

Bryant alone has won, and won big, with all the variations: the single wing, Notre Dame box, T Formation, Split T, Pro Set, and Wishbone. And in recent years, typically, he has made the formerly rigid Wishbone into a formation of infinite flexibility.

What's more, Bryant has closely studied and won with crew-cut kids, bearded kids, white kids, black kids, the sons of a disciplined generation, the sons of a permissive generation, with those who couldn't think for themselves, with those who questioned all authority, with those who weren't allowed a water break all afternoon, and with those who when Bear learned better — he is always learning — get a water break every ten minutes. Thus he may reach his goal. Former Coach Charlie McClendon says that after all these years, Bear still has only one goal: "He wants to coach forever."

18. And Now the Bear Has 315

SEVERAL MONTHS later, Bryant had the longevity record all to himself, and he got there, appropriately, against next-door rival Auburn, which put up a fight, but couldn't match the high morale of Bear's players.

BIRMINGHAM, Ala.: Nov. 29, 1981.

When, years ago, Amos Alonzo Stagg became a winner for the 314th time in his long career, he didn't know — was never to know — that he was the only football coach who ever won that many games. Sports longevity records are somewhat artificial. But Paul (Bear) Bryant will take the one he set here Saturday night when, as Alabama came from behind in the fourth quarter, he and his players beat Auburn, 28-17, and Stagg, 315 to 314.

Even in his hour of triumph, the old coach was thinking of next year. "I liked coming from behind," Bryant said. "Give me my druthers, we'll do that every time. It proved to our players that they have class and character, and it showed them what can be done in the future."

There'll be a future, he's pretty sure about that, but in the meantime he's enjoying what is. To win number 315, Bear's team sustained two dramatic, beautifully coached touchdown drives in the last ten minutes after Auburn — which outplayed Alabama much of the time — had opened a 17-14 lead at the top of the final period.

"This was one of the greatest games ever played," Bryant enthused shamelessly, standing bareheaded, for a change; someone had pilfered his familiar houndstooth hat in the instant the game ended. "I feel like I ought to go back and check the scoreboard to make sure we won."

Staying in character, Bryant praised Auburn and thanked everyone he has ever been associated with in football: his players everywhere he's coached, his assistant coaches, even two "deceased coaches who coached me as a boy." Asked if it was a relief to finally overtake Stagg and extend Alabama's 1981 record to 9-1-1, Bryant said: "I think so. It's been a hard year. I haven't been strong enough, or bright enough, not until the last few days."

On the afternoon that Bryant, sixty-eight, reached 315, his new intrastate adversary, Coach Pat Dye of Auburn, forty-two, was reaching for 60. And in a tense Wishbone duel, they fought to 7-7 in the first thirty minutes. Even after the first fifty, it seemed possible, maybe probable, that the new record would elude Bryant until New Year's Day, if not later. For Auburn seemed slightly the better team.

But Bryant's players wanted the record more than Auburn wanted the game. As one of the old coach's young players, Berry Perrin, said afterward, "Every time we lined up in the fourth quarter, we would say in the huddle: 'We can't give up. This is for 315.'"

Accordingly, after compiling but ten first downs in the first three quarters, Alabama reached back to win the game with two big drives. Backs to the wall, down three points, ten minutes remaining, thinking about the old Bear, Alabama was unstoppable in the three minutes it took to alter the score from 17-14 Auburn to 28-17 Alabama. Reflecting on the tension, Tight End Jesse Bendross, one of Alabama's stars with two touchdowns, said: "It got to the point at one time (in the second half) when we were very nervous. But Coach Bryant tells us to keep the faith and not give up. If you don't think you can get beat, you won't."

The Bear's skills as a leader, developed through more than a third of the twentieth century, shone through all four Alabama touchdowns. No other college or pro coach, for one thing, routinely and deliberately uses as many players each week as Bryant, who is always getting ready for next year, and the next. Even though it was his last regular-season shot at 315 this year, he had all three Alabama quarterbacks on the field as usual, and each of them had a hand in at least one touchdown:

• After Alan Gray's unusual sixty-three yard quarterback sweep to the Auburn 21-yard line, Alabama powered it over on six runs, the last a one-yard Gray keeper — thus showing Auburn its strength first.

• Bryant next showed the Tigers some finesse. At the Auburn 26, ending a fifty-five yard drive, his number-two quarterback, Ken Coley, shoveled a little pass on second and fifteen to split end Bendross. Circling back to catch the ball at the line of scrimmage, Bendross broke for the end zone, and got there just ahead of the Tigers.

• In the fourth quarter, down 17-14 with ten minutes of 1981 left, Alabama came with a first-down play-action pass to score the go-ahead touchdown easily on number-three quarterback Walter Lewis' throw to Bendross from the Auburn 38-yard line. To their dismay, and sorrow, the Tigers went for a running back's fake.

• For Alabama's final touchdown, Bryant called on his best runner, Linnie Patrick, whom for some reason he doesn't call on often. During a forty-nine-yard drive, Patrick carried the ball twice, first taking Gray's handoff and breaking four tackles on a first-down thirty-two-yard run. Then, speeding up as Auburn's spirits fell, he swept the final fifteen yards around end. The last half of the last game of 1981 was thus the biggest of Bear's year, leaving only one question unanswered. Do you suppose he planned it that way?

XIII

JOURNALS

For the Christmas issue each year, Bill Shirley, when he was sports editor of the Times, always sought a long, different kind of story on a subject that personally interested him. After taking pains to explain exactly what he wanted, he sent me to New York one year in the early 1970s to inquire into the inner workings of a magazine, Sports Illustrated.

Before leaving Los Angeles, following a settled practice, I had made appointments with Managing Editor Andre Laguerre and other Sports Illustrated personnel. But when I got to their New York office at the appointed 11 a.m. on a cold November day, I found that Laguerre, unilaterally changing plans, had taken off that morning for Paris. So I took off for Los Angeles, checking out of the Essex House without staying a night. In a similar crisis in Chicago, I'd have found an excuse to stick around awhile, but New York isn't my favorite town. Not until Sports Illustrated displaced Laguerre did I go back, two years later, to complete the assignment.

In the early 1970s, Laguerre had pioneered extensive use of full-color photos in late-breaking, weekly-magazine stories — the huge expense of which helped cost him his Sports Illustrated position. The weeklies, along with most daily papers, are all packed with color now, but Sports Illustrated set the pace. It also set the pace with bylined articles, winning, then and later, the applause of writers at Time, Newsweek, and other magazines where the editors eventually followed suit. Few editors are ecstatic about that policy — few at Sports Illustrated particularly — because, as devout rewrite men, they radically recondition so many articles that the bylined writers are more like contributors.

On any level, it is difficult for most sports journalists to consider Sports Illustrated other than ambivalently. During its first decade, when it lost big money each year, I was a Sports Illustrated rooter because in a sense, it was carrying the ball for all of us. As an assistant sports editor seeking more space for our section, I was then skirmishing constantly with managing editors; and I feared that if Sports Illustrated went down, the fight would be lost. That's one side.

But on another side, Sports Illustrated people have at times cribbed quotes and angles from the nation's sports sections without crediting either the writers who did the original work or their newspapers. As an Associated Press member, the magazine has a legal right to do that — but neither are newspaper editors legally obligated to mention Sports Illustrated. And the truth is, they give the magazine more helpful publicity than any other source.

In person, the people at Sports Illustrated are as friendly and cooperative as they are talented. But they have little in common with a British sportswriter I ran into one day at a London newspaper except that they're all in this chapter. After these two stories appeared originally in the Times, I condensed and edited both for other publications.

1. Sports Illustrated: In the Ess-Eye of the Beholder

NEW YORK: Dec. 24, 1975.

One of the magazines on your coffee table — that slick, sporty one with all those athletes in living color — shouldn't be there. Its most remarkable feature *is* that it's there. From the day it was born in 1954, Sports Illustrated lost money each year for ten consecutive years, blowing an estimated $20 million. By the 1960s, its rivals for the national advertising dollar were cheerfully reasoning that SI Founder Henry Luce (1898-1967) had at last found a trustworthy way to go broke. But he never did.

Sports Illustrated exists today in memory of the Luce genius and as a monument to his stubbornness, proving once a week that in America, a national magazine can be a spectacular decade-long failure and still make good.

This one is now making conspicuously good. SI's weekly circulation exceeds two million. It has earned as much as $12 million a year. And SI readers seem basically content with what they get for seventy-five cents a week: a sports magazine that aims frankly to provide entertainment rather than interpretation, or even information, in prose that is turned out with a flair and, often, humor. It is edited with a strong sense of style. The accent is on lively, full-color photos. And the result is an incongruous weekly ornament in the sweaty world of sports.

Irrefutably, SI (the help all call it ess-eye) has won a solid place for itself in a country that got along very well without it for two centuries.

II

Born again each Tuesday, SI is conceived weekends at its Manhattan headquarters in the sixteen-year-old Time and Life Building, a thin fifty-story skyscraper at Fiftieth Street and the Avenue of Americas. In an area of tall buildings, short trees and narrow streets, the Time and Life temple shares a windswept intersection with Rockefeller Center and the Radio City Music Hall, where the long-legged Rockettes are currently and satisfactorily, if somewhat impertinently, starring in a production of "The Nativity."

The twentieth floor of the house that Henry Luce built is the size of a football field. Called SI country, it has an office for each member of the editorial staff, which numbers 137 men and women. The layout is like that of a cruise ship with exterior and interior staterooms for first- and second-class passengers. In the SI caste system, there are three-window writers, two-window, one-window, and windowless rookies.

In Senior Writer William Oscar Johnson's office, you notice not the windows but the ceiling. There are fifty or sixty thin yellow pencils hanging by their points up there. Each time Johnson finishes a story, he sharpens his pencil one last time and throws it into the ceiling. One wall of Associate Editor Pat Putnam's office is covered with a world map that is all but obscured, in places, by hordes of red-headed pins. Each identifies a neighborhood where Putnam has traveled on assignment.

SI country is the nerve center for a bustling and plainly prosperous undertaking, but in the beginning it was only bustling. Says Time Inc. veteran Andrew Heiskell, who is now the company's chairman of the board: "In the early days [the 1950s], we put all our publishing knowledge together, and did everything wrong." In the 1960s, he says, three relatively small changes turned Sports Illustrated into the mint it is today. First, its advertising salesmen began selling it as a newsweekly like Time or Newsweek instead of a specialty magazine like Esquire. Next, its editors began focusing on major rather than minor sports. And finally, its pages started blooming in color, leading the newsmagazine business into a full-color world.

Of these changes, the first two were pushed through by Heiskell and Hedley Donovan, now editor-in-chief, the two who, not surprisingly, have since risen to the top of an empire whose three most profitable properties are Time, SI and Time-Life books. By selling itself as a newsweekly, SI opened a money faucet. "A weekly newsmagazine has a lot of leverage," says Heiskell, who at sixty is a tall, hearty extrovert. "There are ten times as many advertising dollars in the weekly field as in the specialty field."

By emphasizing major sports, SI overcame, in part, the whimsical, country-club image it had earned in the early years when its pages were brimming with unread stories about lacrosse, sailing, croquet and the like. Nearly as tall as Heiskell but thinner and more scholarly, Donovan, sixty-one, is the executive who sits at Luce's desk as his handpicked successor. "Henry Luce was interested in sports magazines but not sports," he says, confirming that SI's founder knew what he wanted, and thought he had it, but didn't. "Company opinion (during SI's ten-year losing streak) was that it had a wonderful magazine which for some reason wasn't selling."

Donovan didn't see it that way. "I thought it was the magazine itself that needed changing," he says quietly between pulls at a very thin cigar. "So a change was recommended — a shift of direction away from the soft literary approach toward better coverage of the hard sports, the so-called bread-and-butter sports."

Thus in 1964, almost overnight, SI started to make sense — and money. But not for another half dozen years did it make a major impact on the publishing industry. The biggest change was wrought by color photography, which is a commentary on the importance to modern Americans of visual information. Increasingly in the 1970s, SI's main stories have been illustrated with full-color photos, most of them action photos. Other national weeklies also have the capability to do this, as well as the desire, but not (until recently) the courage to spend the money. The thing that made Sports Illustrated a winner was its willingness to part with large sums of money to publish news pictures routinely in full color — in the time crunch of a weekly periodical. (In monthly magazine features, the technical problem is simpler.) Rival editors at Time and Newsweek say it costs an extra $15,000 a page to transform black-and-white news pictures into color.

In any case, to thumb through Time magazine and other SI competitors these days is to realize that they're all shockingly drab. Confesses Newsweek Senior Editor Robert V. Engle: "I don't look at black-and-white pictures much any more. The life quality in a four-color picture makes you think you're really there."

III

The great challenge to those who write, edit and publish Sports Illustrated is to create quality at great speed. Readers who realize that daily papers are constrained by time limitations expect a lot more of magazines. They want a magazine to look good, and to read smoothly, and they make no allowances for what it takes to reach these goals every seventh day in a publication handling late-news stories. The SI solution to the problem stands as its major procedural contribution to sports journalism.

This is a magazine that routinely handles two kinds of stories, fast-breaking and slow. In the second category, it is like any other national magazine with a six-week deadline. No problem. The hassles begin with the many stories that break on deadline. On Sundays, for example, there are only a few hours between the last out — or the last minute of a football game — and SI's deadlines, which are 8:30 or 9 p.m. EST for writers, midnight for pictures, and 2 to 4 a.m. Monday for editors. In other words, SI people are producing a sports magazine at about the same time that newspaper people are putting out the sports section of the Monday paper.

The question: how to get magazine polish and depth that fast. The answer: a writing team. On a fast-breaking news story in the field, a Sports Illustrated writer is actually four people, a writer, reporter, researcher, and senior editor, who, if they're assigned to a Sunday afternoon football game, don't stand around waiting for the kickoff. For four or five days before the game, the writer and senior editor work together, the writer at the site of the event, the editor in the New York office. Most Sundays, to make SI's rigid deadlines, much or all of the story has to be written *before* the game, requiring the writer, with his editor contributing, to develop the story lines that are most likely to stand up. The story is then filed to New York on Saturday — and changed Sunday night when the event is over.

SI's senior editor for pro football, Arthur L. Brawley, says he devotes eighty per cent to ninety per cent of his time to the direction of the magazine's three pro football writers — Dan Jenkins, Mark Mulvoy and Ron Reid — although only one game a week is normally covered. On that day, Brawley watches the event on television, receives the play-by-play and statistics at the end of every quarter on a Xerox telephone copier, and keeps up with the Associated Press file from the stadium: the running story, the early ledes, rewrites, locker-room stories and others. He is almost as familiar with the game as the writer on the scene, and is, thus, in position to make suggestions, additions and subtractions, all of which he does — sometimes at great length.

The writer, meanwhile, confers on game day not only with his editor but with the reporter assigned to him for the day. The reporter is either sent out from New York or hired locally, depending on whether a good local man is available. When the game ends, the reporter's job is to talk with the athletes and their leaders and provide the writer with quotes, notes and anecdotes.

Finally, the team's number-four man, the researcher, is at work on the story back in the New York office. He had been assigned to it when the writer was assigned, and, in addition to the prior research he may have completed at the request of the writer or editor, he has acquainted himself with the sources (human and written) he will need when the manuscript is in hand. There is a researcher for every SI article, and it is his responsibility to make the manuscript error-free. Accordingly, an SI baseball writer who can't remember Walt Alston's first name can safely call him Harold or Joe, knowing it will come out Walt (or Walter) in the end. Nor is it necessary for an SI writer to have the vaguest idea how many touchdown passes Fran Tarkenton threw as a rookie. The SI writer at his typewriter can speed along without looking at record books, statistical sheets or even his scorecard. Every fact and figure he uses will be challenged by a faceless researcher in New York, and, if necessary, changed.

Sports Illustrated's two secrets, and hence its two strengths by comparison with the sports department of any daily newspaper, are the senior-editor writing system and the accompanying research checking system — both based on methods originated at Time magazine. They are costly luxuries that newspapers don't have, adding hundreds of thousands of dollars to the budget, but also adding credibility. Says SI veteran Joe Marshall: "If an Eastern writer carelessly notes that the Los Angeles Coliseum is north of the Harbor Freeway, it destroys him with California readers, who wonder about everything else in the article."

It's no surprise to find that SI writers find the research system a godsend but generally abhor the extravagant editing. Says Senior Writer Mark Kram: "The first canon of good editing is don't, unless you have to." On workdays at SI, when the editors are through with his copy, Kram goes over it again, and challenges their changes. "I stalk around at midnight," he says, "looking for every comma they've taken out. The hardest thing for an editor to understand is that what he thinks is an improvement is usually destructive to the article as a piece of writing."

In varying degrees, all SI writers seem to feel that way. Frustrated by what they see as an abundance of unnecessary editing changes in their copy, some say they don't even read the magazine. Good editors are probably right, however, more often than good writers imagine. Though Jefferson fumed in 1776, every verbal change that other congressmen made in his original draft of the Declaration of Independence left it better than Jefferson had it. Particularly on the planning level, the SI system obviously works. When, in addition to the writer, an editor is specifically responsible for, say, a hockey game, the story becomes the product of not one but two well-trained journalists — plus their assistants — who look at it from different perspectives, and who have given it most of their working time over a period of days or weeks. The reader is the beneficiary.

IV

The crunch at Sports Illustrated comes on Sunday night, most noticeably in the handling of Sunday afternoon stories. Each writer is represented on the twentieth floor by his copy, which typically has arrived by telephone. Because SI is set in lines that average out to thirty-eight characters (letters) or seven words, the writers had been assigned to file not two thousand words or five pages but, say, three hundred lines. These are first edited lightly, then retyped, run through a computer, and edited again. The senior editor edits with a black pencil, the assistant managing editor with red, and the managing editor with blue. Each story is also worked on by a copy editor responsible only for style (e.g., ten becomes 10).

By now the photos are in and ready for editing, having arrived by commercial airline or (if it's an NFL game) by chartered jet. Says Assistant Managing Editor Gilbert Rogin: "We tell the people in the photo department what to look for — maybe number eighty-two has caught three passes — and they pre-select twenty-five or thirty slides. These are projected on a screen for the senior editor and other editors, and if we're planning to use four pictures with this article, ten pictures are selected."

The managing editor refines the ten to four, and these are sent to the art department along with a rough dummy of the story layout as prepared by the editors. Artists refine and alter the dummy into a complete, detailed photostat, inserting dummy headlines, and plugging every line on each page with dummy type. All this gives the editors an exact count of text lines, caption lines, and headlines. Senior editors write all headlines and picture captions (subject to revision by superiors), and count the lines allocated to each column. When the real headlines and real text are finished, they are slipped into the package, displacing the dummy type.

Rogin and the senior editors of the fast-color (late-closing) pages then read things through one last time. It is they who are responsible for exterminating the last errors, typographical and otherwise. They have been working since 10 a.m. Sunday, and it is now nearing dawn Monday. Tired time. The wrong time to edit a national magazine well, but somehow they usually do.

V

Most Sports Illustrated writers started as sportswriters on small daily newspapers, typically south of the Mason-Dixon line. Possessing more talent or ambition than those with whom they worked in Texas or Florida, they sent samples of their stories (their best stories, of course) to the magazine's editors, and were eventually hired. What they wanted, in most cases, was national-magazine exposure. The magazine's wages aren't that impressive. An SI veteran's salary is similar to that of a veteran staff writer for one of the top two or three American newspapers.

A principal difference between SI and newspaper work is the work load. For a periodical that comes out fifty-one times annually, a Sports Illustrated writer averages twenty stories a year. A newspaperman writes twenty a month. On smaller dailies, some turn out twenty a week. "On a daily paper, you can have two or three bad days in a row and make up for it the rest of the week," says SI Senior Writer Dan Jenkins. "Around here, there are fewer editions, so you try to maintain a higher standard."

A self-assured, fun-loving Texan with a satiric sense of humor, Jenkins changed last year from college football to the pro football beat, where, conforming to SI routines, he has to write much of his story before gametime Sunday to make the Sunday night deadline. That's the hard way, and, understandably, Senior Writer Kram prefers other kinds of assignments. "I have to begin at the beginning," says Kram, a bearded pipe-smoker who, after the Ali-Frazier fight in Manila, wrote his story in New York following a twenty-two-hour flight home.

Like those they write about, and for, SI writers are bound by their foibles and habits. Whether doing books or SI articles, Associate Editor Mark Mulvoy, a large, ebullient Boston Irishman, is a man with a clean-copy foible. "I never turn in a page with a single mark on it," he says. "If I make a mistake on the last line, I type the whole page over." His copy is as perfect, at least technically, as that of a centuries-ago predecessor. In extant copies of Shakespeare's first drafts, there are no insertions, no writeovers, no changes. "Willie never blotted a line," Ben Jonson once said enviously. On an acre of Rye, New York, there is, however, a difference in the *way* Mulvoy works and lives. His home is on a golf course, and his office is a converted bedroom. He plays golf during the day and works at night, starting at 8:30 "after the kids are in bed."

Kram writes at 6 a.m. Rising at 5, he hurries to his cubicle at Time and Life, gets the coffee on, and gets to work hours before the rest of the staff checks in. Managing Editor Roy Terrell, in his working days, wrote at midnight. Tex Maule writes his articles and books in two-hour stretches each day, from 6 to 8 p.m., having got in the habit of writing football stories at that time during twenty years of Sundays. Jenkins doesn't watch clocks. "I work when I'm moved," he says.

For most SI writers, as for most writers everywhere, the process is not easy. Says one: "I'm not a fast writer. After a college football game on Saturday, I often write all night to meet a Sunday morning deadline. Usually I get my copy off (by wire or telephone copier) in a blind stupor."

A handful of SI writers live and work in the provinces. They get their assignments by telephone and report in to New York six to ten times a year. The company pays their travel and hotel expenses on New York trips. They and other SI writers on assignment almost always fly coach class. They stay in good hotels but are limited each day to $3 for breakfast, $4.50 lunch and $10 dinner. Says SI Editor John Tibby: "We're liberal on everything but entertainment. If a writer has to fly first class to work on a story against a deadline, that's all right. But he better get his story some way besides entertaining in a bar."

SI's John Underwood, a tennis player, lives ten minutes from his tennis club in Florida and five minutes from his twenty-eight-foot boat on Biscayne Bay. Few writers in America, sports or otherwise, can match his lifestyle. For one thing, he doesn't seem to be overworked, averaging once a month or so in the magazine. One year he was only in six times. But he pays for his lifestyle. As a deadline approaches, Underwood, who calls himself a bleeder, says, "I'll work all day and most of the night, carrying the typewriter blindly around from room to room."

VII

As a sports journal, SI has always had some failings, and at times it still annoys its readers. "The text is often too cutesy," Miami Sportswriter Bill Braucher says, speaking for most other U.S. journalists, including some at SI — where Kram says: "Unhappily, yuk-a-minute writing is contagious. Young writers think that's the road to success, and pretty soon they all sound alike." There is also a lack of magazine depth in some articles. "On breaking-news events," one SI editor complains, "some of our pieces are surprisingly shallow." Other critics charge that SI stories often lack a sharp angle — a well-thought-out, well-defined, interpretive approach. Too often, the lede angle amounts to little more than a cleverly worded assumption that, in a story appearing four days after the fact, the score must in no case be on the writer's first page.

Most maddening of all, SI editors use their mail page for fundamentally only one purpose: to applaud their writers (and by extension themselves). This is a bush-league practice, which, in a publication of this quality, is as amazing as it is disappointing.

And so if you were given a few days to run SI, you would change a few things. But examining the magazine as a whole, your starting base would be remarkably substantial. As any reader can see, a typical issue of SI is distinguished by the rhythm and pace of the prose, by the perceptiveness of experienced reporters, by the effectiveness of the editing mechanism, and, most unusual of all, by the abundance of full-color photographs. It seems worth the six bits.

2. Traveling Headline Writer: On the Job in London

THEN THERE is sports journalism in London, which is something else again. Be sure they don't pay you by the word.

LONDON: Aug. 24, 1975.

Nigel Clarke is a thirty-five-year-old London sportwriter who makes about $20,000 a year, counting expenses. This is his job, as he explained it to an American visitor this summer: Four times a week he turns in a news story with six to sixteen paragraphs. The maximum words allowed in any paragraph are twenty-five. On the average, his stories are about the length of a one-page telegram.

His assignment each day is simply to develop an angle that will translate into what he calls the "splash headline" on the back page — which is his newspaper's main sports page. Thus essentially, Clarke is a traveling headline writer. Like most London journalists, he takes only a quick look at the big picture, the what happened and why. The thing Clarke needs, and has, is an instinct for the most dramatic kernel or nub of the day's sports news. At his writing table, he doesn't have to reason it out sensibly or amusingly. He merely has to recognize it — and get it down telegraphically.

Clarke's job is what it is because the most popular London dailies are what they are: incomplete digests of trivia, preferably sensational. Repeatedly, in London newspapers, attractive women are shown without their clothes. The Playboy centerfold theme is reprised with large photos on page three each morning in one paper, the Sun, which assigns two photographers to look for young women who will sit still and take off their shirts.

There are eleven daily newspapers in London, including a racing daily and financial journal, and the commitment of most to sensational and frivolous news — or what they *call* news — brings a different top-headline treatment some days in each of the eleven newspapers. Crime, sex and money are the favored themes.

These are two kinds of general-circulation dailies in London, serious (Times, Guardian) and popular (Mirror, Sun), and they all have five things in common: they suffer from red-ink problems (they're all losing money), they have large circulations (up to four million daily), they're competitive, they accent sports, and they're small. The prestigious Times of London averages twenty pages a day. The five tabloids average thirty-two pages (the equivalent of sixteen Los Angeles Times-size pages). And Nigel Clarke's job as a globe-trotting composer of sports telegrams or headlines is rooted in all that: the fights to lose less, sell more, and compete on sports pages that are both few and loud.

II

He spends several months abroad each year covering English sports teams. On a trip, Clarke gets $70 a day for expenses from his paper, which pays for his airplane ticket (first class) and hotel (same). He works a thirty-five-hour (four-day) week divided as follows on trips with London soccer teams: Monday travel, Tuesday practice day, Wednesday game day, Thursday travel home. For such a week, he draws his $280 expenses in advance. His airplane and hotel bills are sent to his employer, the tabloid Daily Mirror.

The kind of story Clarke brings in is one that might be headlined, "I Blew It: Bobby Moore." In his dispatch that day, which particularly pleased his editors, Clarke drew an admission from England's most popular soccer player that he was at fault on the big play of a big game. It was good reporting because athletes seldom make such confessions. In a Fleet Street poll three months ago, Clarke was named London's best back-page writer. The voters were his competitors on the six back-page papers — the five tabloids and the Express, a standard-size daily made up to look and sound like a tabloid.

There are, of course, other kinds of work in London sports departments. Half of those on the forty-man Mirror sports staff, for example, are editors. The lower-circulation, more upscale dailies (Times, Guardian, Telegraph) also have some essayists who resemble, at least faintly, American sportswriters. Their stories are longer than Clarke's though generally shorter than an American's. There is a humorist or two in the London press, and the best prose in at least two papers, the Sunday Observer and the Daily Mail, is written by sportswriters. Yet on the whole, even in the serious dailies, sports stories tend to be sketchy and esoteric.

III

Like most other institutions in England, journalism is organized around a caste system. Each newspaper has a chief sports correspondent, who gets more space than other writers, and who has as much freedom and power as the sports editor. The chief correspondent, who answers basically to himself, makes his own assignments. Normally he covers the game of the day in England, regardless of sport, and tells the desk how many words he'll file and when. The sports editor is responsible for displaying the chief writer's story as attractively as possible. The editor's principal role is not to supervise writers but to produce a paper that will look and sound better than its competition. And usually, the layout is better than the story. London's newspapers are better edited, by their standards, than written.

The caste system extends to all ranks. There is a chief football writer on each paper and a deputy chief football writer along with chiefs and deputies for the other sports. On this level, the writers also make their own assignments — unless bumped by the paper's chief writer. The lowest man in the hierarchy, usually the newest and youngest writer, a man called the dogsbody, can be bumped by anybody. At the Mirror, Clarke made deputy chief football (soccer) writer two years ago. He has some standing and authority in his department because football is the country's principal sport, but like the other writers, from chiefs to dogsbodies, he is restricted to a handful of words, and is under continuous pressure to produce.

The maximum number of twenty-five-word paragraphs allotted to the Mirror's chief sports correspondent each day is thirty. No other writer can have more than twenty-four — or two sheets of paper — but they seldom get that much, and can count on less than half that if their stories are placed inside instead of on the back page.

In the field sometimes it seems a strange kind of job. A London sportswriter in Paris, Melbourne or Liverpool may be represented in his sports section, under his byline and a one-column headline, by only four or five paragraphs. You wonder why, with an Associated Press correspondent on the scene, his paper spent the money to send him for that. "The paper expected more," says Clarke. "On a sports trip, you never know what's out there. If your competition staffs it, and it turns into a big story, your paper is in trouble if it isn't there. But just because you have a man in Melbourne doesn't mean it's worth six paragraphs, or even four."

Reporters who fail to bring back their share of headline stories are demoted or replaced. "There's a lot of tension," Clarke concedes. "On a London newspaper, the biggest hour of the day is 5 p.m. — the 5-o'clock editorial conference — and you better have something they can splash on the back page, especially at the Mirror, especially if they're expecting it. We have the biggest circulation in the world, four million, after Pravda, which has ten million, and for our reporters it's dog eat dog. A lot of chaps on my paper are after my job, and frankly, I'm after theirs, if it's better than mine."

IV

It's after work now, and Clarke is sitting on the lawn in his backyard, thinking about his big day and, he hopes, a bigger tomorrow. A thin man in big, tinted glasses, he looks as harmless as his wife and young daughter, who are seated with him, hanging on all the words. They're an engaging family, handsome, open-faced, prone to laughter, and permanently slim. "No one I love — including myself — will ever be fat," Clarke says, smiling. "All you have to do is eat lightly and order champagne. There's no beer in this house and no booze." The house is in the country. An older two-story place of no particular style, it has a curving driveway in front that gives it a small-mansion effect. There are six sunny rooms, three upstairs and three down.

In Clarke's salary bracket, you can't afford a London flat. Only two Mirror sportswriters, both bachelors, live in the city. But on $20,000 a year, a family man can live comfortably in, say, Kent, where Clarke's $45,000 house sits on a wide lot that's more than two hundred feet deep.

It's ripe with orchards and rose gardens. He pays a gardener $15 a week. His village, Chiselhurst, is twelve miles southeast of London, forty miles from the nearest beach, and forty-five minutes by car from the Mirror office.

At the moment there are millions in London worse off than Clarke, who finds himself in a curious industry. It pays well for England — some Mirror printers make $500 a week — yet its future is precarious. Whereas most European newspapers are subsidized by their governments, London's, which lose up to $3 million a year, are subsidized by men of great wealth who may not be around tomorrow. The press in London seems to be living on borrowed time, but Clarke feels he can't control his destiny, and in the meantime he's living well.

The $20,000 his paper pays him annually includes only $12,000 salary. The rest is perks, his word for fringe benefits or perquisites. For instance, his car, a Ford Escort, is owned by the newspaper, which pays all of the car's expenses — even petrol costs on family vacations. "They also pay the upkeep on my wife's car," says Clarke, who bought her an Austin. He gets a minimum of $120 a week expenses when he's just driving back and forth to London. Some say British corporations put their best men on big expense accounts in lieu of salary for tax-avoidance purposes, and Clarke doesn't deny this. "We live on the expenses each week," he says. "The salary check just goes in the bank."

Before leaving on four-day foreign excursions, he brings the $280 expense check home. He agrees that a $70 daily allowance on road trips, which most London papers pay, is excessive — even in France, where you can't spend that much for meals unless you eat out five or six times a day.

Overall, Clarke thinks he's worth what he gets, and he thinks his editors realize it. His byline is often displayed in big type, and on a particularly good story they include his picture, too. London's papers promote their writers extensively. The editors of the Sunday Times began their main eight-column sports headline one day with the two words, Dudley Doust. Doust is their golf writer, and the headline capsuled his opinions on a golf tournament. "It's just good business," Clarke says. "If you're trying to compete, it helps grab the reader's attention, and brings him back another day. I'm sure it would be good business in America, too. The competition there is television, and the faces of the TV news people and commentators are all over the screen."

V

Clarke can remember the day when he seldom saw his name or face in the paper. Like most British athletes (both good and bad athletes) he left school at sixteen to begin, as he hoped, a professional soccer career. A year later a torn-up knee ended that dream — but in the British system, he couldn't go back to school. Having opted at age twelve for vocational schooling that came to an end four years later, he lost the privilege of changing his mind when he matured. "My father was also a failed football player," Clarke says. "Like most of them, he got a job eventually on the docks, but he didn't make enough to help me."

Unskilled, undereducated, Clarke at seventeen took the only job he could find. He became a messenger on Fleet Street, where London's newspapers are mostly concentrated, at $7.50 a week. That was in 1957.

"When my shoes wore out," he says, "I patched them with cardboard. That was all right if it didn't rain. For lunch, I stole apples and oranges at Covent Garden. But as a kid, I'd always been good at English. When they sent me to football games, I watched the writers all the time, instead of the game. I studied everything they did. Later, I began writing my own stories — practicing at home — and when I got to where I could write them as well as they did, I started writing to London papers and news agencies for a job. I wrote a hundred letters a week."

Just ten years ago this led to work at $50 a week for a news agency, where, instead of servicing all clients, he sent his best stories to the Mirror exclusively. "It was unethical, of course," Clarke says, "but I couldn't think of any other way to get through to the Mirror's editors. I knew that's where I wanted to work."

Eight years ago, on his twenty-seventh birthday, they finally hired him. Clarke estimates that in the seven years before they did, his letters of application to the Mirror totaled ten thousand words. He hasn't written that much since.

XIV

Campus

As Gertrude Stein might have said, the many colleges and universities of America are all alike and all different. They look much alike, most of them, but differ in what they emphasize. And as both student and visitor, I have always been particularly drawn to both aspects: their similarities and their differences. I never saw a campus I didn't like. No editor of mine has ever needed more than a hint at a college sports assignment to get me on the plane and gone to the University of Chicago, Harvard, Texas — or Seminole.

Seminole? It's in Oklahoma: a small white town with a small junior college that, surprisingly and suddenly, sprouted an all-black basketball team that became a big winner in the early 1970s. This set up one of my most unusual assignments, and my description of the whys led to the strangest aftermath of anything I ever wrote. In a page-one story, I had started it all with some uncharacteristically unkind comments about the physical appearance of Seminole, the town. This brought in, unsurprisingly, a barrage of heated letters to the Times decrying the brutal misperceptions of a big-city reporter.

It also brought about, astonishingly, a new civic group in Seminole called Operation Pride. A few years later, out of the blue, the operators of Operation Pride sent me a report on their accomplishments: their hundreds of remodeled homes and businesses, their hundreds of condemned and demolished structures, their refurbished lake, golf course, and Little League parks, and their dozens of other improvements — including a landmark new program of semi-monthly litter removal by Boy Scouts, Girl Scouts, men's clubs, and even jail-house trustees.

The litter-removal concept is the one that took off, spreading presently to the rest of Oklahoma, and shortly to the rest of America. I've been pleased to see that in most states, it is still being celebrated in roadside signs promising litter-free highways.

Fourteen years after my original story, responding to an invitation from Seminole's city fathers, I went back in 1986 to find an entirely different town. The junior college had expanded from one to nine buildings, the downtown area had been carefully landscaped and lined with brick sidewalks, most storefronts were new, and at great taxpayer cost Seminole's unsightly tangle of telephone and utility wires had been repositioned underground. Only the basketball team was familiar. It was still black, and still winning.

A three-page Seminole Chamber of Commerce report, tacked to a downtown bulletin board, noted that although Operation Pride wouldn't have happened without the Los Angeles Times, "I don't think we ever looked as bad as Bob Oates saw us."

Though my forays to other campuses have not produced similar revolutions, anywhere, I have seen a link between Seminole and all others: the fascination displayed by America's educators with intercollegiate sport. It was first asked nearly a century ago: What does a Saturday afternoon battle between outsized young men in plastic armor have to do with a college education? Yet the uneasy relationship between higher education and sports in America continues. It keeps getting, if anything, chummier — and it is most visible in college football, which, fortunately for me, combines my favorite sport and a favorite environment. Over the years, this topic has evolved into a multi-part essay on the variety of the educational experience, ranging from universities where football has been banned to universities that football has made great. In Europe (Chapter X) there is also a report on an English school where sports are big, Eton College.

1. Seminole Junior College

AS A sport, basketball doesn't do much for most people, including me. But it's something to see in Seminole.

SEMINOLE, Okla.: Feb. 7, 1972.

Things have always been a little different in Seminole. One night in 1931, Wirt's Pig Stand was robbed of $43 by two desperadoes who also stole a carton of chewing gum. Alert police soon discovered the flavor: Juicy Fruit. What's more, according to the files of the local paper, the Daily Producer, "pigs of all ages, also brood sows" could be bought openly on the Seminole market as recently as six years ago.

Seminole, in other words, bears few of the earmarks of a major league town. So it may not come as a complete surprise that when the Seminole Junior College basketball team turned into an impressive winner this year with a group of new players, almost nobody went to see them play. The gate was $67 the other night for arch-rival Northeast A&M Junior College. "The referees cost us $60," says Bailey Vanzant, head coach and athletic director. "And cokes for the players came to $4.50. We made $2.50."

As of that week, SJC had a 13-1 record and ranked fourteenth nationally in the junior college polls. After smashing Northeast, Seminole moved to eleventh, and, in an effort to broaden appeal, scheduled a doubleheader. With a prelim that matched two girls' teams, the gate rose to $94. The top ticket: $1.50. Average crowd this year: 160 (paid).

Plainly, something is wrong in the city of Seminole (population ten thousand) and one clue comes instantly into focus when the junior college team runs out onto the floor. The nine players, though differing in height from six-two to six-nine, are all black. In general, residential Seminole is white — as is SJC. Of the school's seven hundred full-time students, only thirty-five are black, including the athletes.

So how did a black basketball team spring out of a white settlement? Is this what the junior college people want? If so, why don't they support the team? Why doesn't the town support it? The answers seem to be sociological as well as economic, and they help explain some peripheral but significant things, among them: How do college sports get to be big business in other, bigger schools? Why do certain kinds of people elect to live out their lives in places like Seminole, Oklahoma?

II

During the winter, this is a town that sits like a wart on the dead brown plains of central Oklahoma. The downtown architecture is 1930s desolate.

And though the streets are paved, he train no longer stops at the crumbling stucco station that brings Main Street to a sudden dead end. Nonetheless, Seminole satisfies most of the people who live here. They are the hardy remnants of the fifty thousand who swarmed in during the boom days of the Seminole oil strike forty years ago, and they like things the way they are.

More exactly, they liked Seminole the way it was until last year, when the junior college sent to Louisiana and New York for nine big black basketball players. "Today this is nothing but a basketball training ground for the four-year colleges," says Seminole Realtor W.G. Lynn, a graduate of Oklahoma State University. "I won't go out and root for a bunch of dumb bucks from somewheres else. If these were local colored boys, I'd root for them."

If this isn't a majority sentiment, it seems to be shared by a large minority, although the Seminole optometrist, Dr. Hubert Callaway, cautions that the problem is not wholly nor even mainly racial. "Junior college basketball here is a new idea," says Callaway. "We've only had a team two years, and it takes longer than that for a rural community to cotton to anything new. They also have a lot of competition — high school sports are big in this county — but the main thing is that the junior college players are outsiders, black strangers. Nobody knows them."

This is a fact that doesn't bother Callaway, one of the thirteen Seminole citizens who bought junior college season tickets this year. He is a slender, warm-natured man in his forties whose highly polished spectacles advertise his profession subliminally (if inadvertently), and he is the town booster. If it's good for Seminole, Dr. Callaway is for it, and the junior college would have it made here if there were twelve hundred others like him instead of twelve.

The irony of SJC is that the school's administrators have kept pressing for better and better basketball teams in the face of galloping apathy downtown.

Last year, with a half-black, half-white team, the junior college won 19 and lost 14 basketball games before crowds that often swelled to a hundred or more. By contrast, Seminole High School crowds averaged, and still average, about a thousand. Between seasons, accordingly, the SJC president, Elmer Tanner, asserting that a 19-14 record isn't good enough, ordered Coach Vanzant to come up with a "stronger basketball program" this year. In the Vanzant translation, never opposed by the administration, every white player was quietly dropped, and a new and better black team recruited from up to fifteen hundred miles away.

Commenting on the new product, Ted M. Williams, publisher of the Seminole Daily Producer, says: "There isn't a high school player in Oklahoma this year good enough to make this team."

So we have an American anomaly here: a talented winning team that's a bust at the gate.

III

Following SJC's first basketball season last year, when school President Tanner opted pointedly for a winner, was he simply reacting like a rooter? If so, any out-of-control alumni supporter of any of the nation's great football-playing universities would understand.

One place to search for answers is in the stately office of the president, where the president himself sits comfortably behind a big desk.

A cool, dapper professional historian, Tanner, forty-five, says: "When I came here, I wondered what I was getting into, so I stopped in several places on the outskirts of town, and even downtown, asking directions (to SJC) — just to hear what they'd say. Many of them didn't know they had a junior college. They directed me to the high school. We used to have a couple of rooms there before they built this."

And he waves a hand proudly, almost possessively.

At the moment, his junior college is one large rectangular building, with one floor, sprawling, brick, "modern," new. The seventeen airy classrooms, the stuffy offices, the labs were opened for the first time last year. "We have a beautiful school," Tanner continues, "but before we had a basketball team, there were people ten miles away who didn't know there was a Seminole College. I don't care how good you are academically — and we think we've made a fine start in two years — it takes activities, as they call them, to attract attention. And I know of no finer activity than intercollegiate sport."

Larger crowds would be preferable, but "they aren't necessary," the SJC president says, adding: "You don't need a sellout to get some attention. The word gets around. Regardless of the size of the gate, an athletic team is an advertisement for the school — provided it wins. A loser does nothing for morale on campus, and it's just something to joke about downtown. You must be competitive."

The presidents and chancellors of the major U.S. universities where football and basketball are stressed (Notre Dame, USC, UCLA, Michigan, Texas and all the rest) couldn't agree more. The surprise is that intercollegiate sport is considered indispensable by the administration of a back-country commuter college where three-fourths of the students have never seen their own team play. "We have no residence halls here yet," says Tanner. "Everybody drives to school, some from miles away, and sixty-five per cent of them have full-time or part-time jobs. They don't get to the games, but basketball gives all of us a common bond, something to discuss, to pull the student body together."

Most of the school's other leaders also approve. "An athletic program is especially necessary at a commuter college," James Colclazier, SJC's academic dean, says. "It draws people together, students and faculty. As for the athletes, most of them would choose four-year colleges if they had the grades. They came here to get the specialized individual attention that only a school like this can give."

Proud of the personal attention SJC provides, Colclazier says: "We're the fastest growing junior college in the state. There are one hundred and seventy in this year's class, and ninety-five per cent are going on to other schools. Those who receive either of our degrees (Associate of Arts, Associate of Science) are accepted wherever they want to go." This largely explains why the New York-born basketball players chose Seminole, the dean believes. "We're glad we can help them," he says, "because they help us."

There is room to grow at SJC. The building is two miles out of town, on the main highway to Bowlegs and Shawnee, and for those arriving from either place, it looms into sight as a pile of light-brown bricks surrounded by the acreage where a student union, gym and dormitories will be planted eventually. But even without these appurtenances, things are going well, the school's president believes — both athletically and academically. "We graduated fifty-seven in our first class last spring," Tanner says. "And all but two went on to four-year colleges."

IV

It should not be assumed that the desire for a winning basketball team here led automatically to a winner. Behind all successful sports teams, from the preps to the pros, stands a master recruiter. And Seminole's is Bailey Vanzant, coach. To analyze Vanzant's contribution is to conclude that he should be hired as the chief recruiter for the slumping Big Ten conference — or at least by one of the teams slumping.

Consider his problem: "We have no training table," he says. "We don't even have a cafeteria. There is no place to stay, no dormitories. There's no place to practice. The nearest gym is at the high school, two miles away. There are no fans, nobody is interested. It's a new program, with all the strains and handicaps of any new program. There's no place to play our games — except on the nights when the high school can't think of anything to do. And lastly, there's no money."

During his prep career, Vanzant was once named coach of the year in Oklahoma. That's why SJC went after him. A former basketball player himself standing several inches over six feet, he is well preserved at fifty with a broad, handsome face topped by a field of gray hair. But his financial problems are all but beyond solving. "I have $5,000 for each scholarship," he says. "After tuition and rooms, that means $3.50 a day meal money for each player in a downtown cafe. Who can eat on $3.50 a day? Who the hell wants to come to Seminole?"

He answers the question himself, smiling. "A hell of a team," the coach says. "I have a lot of friends around the country, particularly in New York and the Southeast, and this year I sent out three hundred letters. I also ran up a $120 phone bill, and I made a trip or two. We got fifteen players in from Louisiana, Texas and New York, and nine stayed."

The miracle is that any of them stayed. The downtown place they call a dormitory is on the second floor of a sagging, peeling tenement that has been condemned by the Seminole Fire Department — prematurely. It could easily be used to house Seminole's better quality livestock. "You should see where they stayed last year," says Vanzant, and the emotion that now plays over his face is compassion. "Last year's dorm was a motel — an abandoned motel," he says. "And they chased us out. The rats chased us out."

Greg McDougald, nineteen, doesn't remember that night. This is his first year here. He is the star of the rebuilt team, and the basketball experts of Oklahoma believe that McDougald, six feet seven, can write his own ticket next year, anywhere, if he comes out of Seminole with the grades he has never been able to make anywhere else. "I'm just an average student," he says, using the euphemism of the poor scholar. (There are nine of them on this team.) "My goal," McDougald says, "is pro ball, but before that I've got to play college ball. And my only chance is better grades. That's why I'm here. This is such a small school they can give you a lot of individual attention." Verifying Dean Colclazier's assessment, he adds: "And they don't mind giving it to you. This is all that keeps me in Seminole."

He is not surprised that the spectators are few for SJC games. "It's a little, narrow-minded town," Greg says, without bitterness. In fact, the eyes are twinkling under the massive Afro cut that makes him seven feet tall. "We and Oklahoma aren't made for each other. But I'd put up with worse to reach my goal."

This ambitious Bronx-born basketball player is Exhibit A in recruiter Vanzant's stable. As a high school senior, McDougald had been Player of the Year in New York City. But he couldn't keep his grades up at Virginia Commonwealth University, and when he sought to transfer he couldn't find a college or junior college that would take him. Vanzant, through one of his Texas contacts, tracked McDougald down at the Dallas airport just as the discouraged youth was boarding an airplane for New York and the end of the line — the end of his basketball career.

"I can think of a lot worse," McDougald says again, looking at one shabby wall and then another in his condemned-dormitory room. "The hardest thing at first was eating on $3.50 a day. I didn't think I had ordered a big breakfast the first day, but it came to $2. Now I've learned to pace myself. Food isn't important. At the junior college, they treat me as a person. That's important."

v

They may or may not be the best minds of Seminole, but on the basketball floor McDougald and the other members of the team (who all share McDougald's ambitions and some of his talent) are putting on the best show ever seen in these parts. Says Publisher Phillips: "They're more like the Harlem Globe Trotters than a college team. It's great entertainment — and they win." His sports editor, Robby Trammell, says: "If the people would just come out and see one game, they wouldn't be able to stay away. There'd be big crowds from then on." But getting them out is tough going, and one reason is economic. "These are hard times," says W.D. Graft, a retired oil driller. "I think $1.50 for a basketball game is too much."

Moreover, the lack of a college tradition in Seminole is a constant drag. "It doesn't matter how good their team is," says Barber George Hays. "It's a *new* team. People don't move that fast around here."

Mack Gillham, who runs the Gulf station down at the corner, says: "Honestly, I don't think it's a racial thing. The big problem is that it's basketball they're playing. That's a lousy sport. Who wants to pay to see basketball? I don't even watch it free on television. Now, if they played football, I'd never miss a game."

In one other major respect, Gillham is typical of the members of the Seminole community. "The junior college," he says, "is the best thing that ever happened around here. Most boys and girls don't have the means to go away to school. Every county in Oklahoma should have its own junior college. It's just a great thing."

Bob Jones, manager of the chamber of commerce, adds: "The junior college is so popular here that the people of Seminole voted a sales tax on themselves to support it."

The one-cent tax raises a monthly $17,000, which, with some state aid, keeps the school going.

But just keeping it going isn't enough for President Tanner. "The health of any college," he says, "depends on two things that have little to do with education as such: morale on campus and public relations beyond campus. By morale, I mean togetherness. And by public relations, I mean advertising. Without advertising, the best product withers and dies. A winning basketball team is the finest thing we have going for us at Seminole College in the areas of morale and advertising."

The black men are here to stay.

2. USC, Football Champion

FOR MOST Americans, the rise of college football as a big-time activity in the 1920s coincided with the rise of radio broadcasting, which is to say that both began during the Howard Jones era at USC, which kicked off in 1925. Jones was the first football coach I knew well as a sportswriter for the Los Angeles Examiner, and his university was the first I came to know intimately. On campus in those years before World War II, Jones went by a singular title, headman. The role but not the title was inherited in subsequent years by two other winners, John McKay and John Robinson, who coached the Trojans to further heights at a time when two dynamic presidents, Norman Topping and John Hubbard, leveraged excitement of football to make USC scholastically and architecturally exciting and impressive. Before football helped make USC excellent, it made it famous — as this 1942 story attests. (See the final story in this chapter for the sequel.)

LOS ANGELES: July 27, 1942.

This is a day for remembering at the University of Southern California, where he had won nearly eight out of ten — 121-36-13 (.771) — before it all ended for Howard Jones a year ago today. On a quiet 1941 Sunday, the coach whose football team made the Trojans nationally important died of a heart attack at fifty-five.

Nationally important.

That isn't easy, but Southern California is there now. It has become one of the five most famous universities in the land, along with Notre Dame, Harvard, Stanford, and a state school, Michigan. All are national football powers, past or present, and it was during Jones' fifteen years as SC's headman, 1925-40, that the Trojans came on.

They did it with a football team whose Notre Dame series (beginning as Rockne versus Jones) has become the most popular annual intersectional event in sports. And they did it by keeping their Rose Bowl record perfect. On summer-like California afternoons in the dead of winter, the headman led SC into the Rose Bowl every third New Year's Day, on the average, winning all five games, as hundreds of thousands of frozen fans huddled around their radio receivers in the frozen East.

With radio's help, football went from a regional to a national pastime during Jones' years, when major league baseball also earned the support of millions of sports fans. But major league baseball is a provincial eastern pastime. Its western border is the Mississippi River, emphasizing the plain fact that it ignores half the country. No other sport has football's nationwide big league appeal.

The sportswriters who first called it king football hit a pertinent cliché, and the kings of the kings have been the football coaches, Knute Rockne, Bernie Bierman, Amos Alonzo Stagg, Pop Warner, Fielding (Hurry Up) Yost, Clark Shaughnessy lately, and a few others, most of them distinctive stylists. Jones was a leader of this fraternity as well as a spirited individualist. Unlike coaches like Rockne and Warner, he stressed power plays and hard-running quarterbacks.

Best of all for SC, Jones was a spectacular winner. After a career as Yale player and Iowa coach, he reached Los Angeles at the century's one-quarter mark, when he was forty, and began winning immediately. In his first nine years at Southern California (1925-33), Jones won and lost as follows: 11-2, 8-2, 8-1-1, 9-0-1, 10-2, 8-2, 10-1, 10-2 and 10-1-1.

At the same time, the headman turned out one Trojan All-American after another from Mort Kaer, Morley Drury and Marshall Duffield to Orv Mohler, Erny Pinckert, Ernie Smith, Harry Smith, Johnny Baker, Jess Hibbs, Nate Barragar, Francis Tappaan, Garrett Arbelbide, Cotton Warburton, Aaron Rosenberg, Gaius Shaver, and my roommate at SC one summer in Los Angeles, Grenville (Granny) Lansdell.

In the United States, of course, a great football team isn't an isolated phenomenon. Champions and All-Americans surface in many places to catch the attention of many sports fans. But the excitement has always seemed a little richer and fuller in the city of the Trojans. That's partly because they win so often, but also because of the Southern California climate, plus the proximity of Hollywood and the Pacific Ocean, plus the abundance of coeducational opportunities. It has been said that most Americans of any age, given a choice, would choose the life of "a student at Southern Cal with a convertible automobile of their own."

Howard Jones' role was to provide a winning football team for this beautiful university and for the people of the nation's most desirable city. And he did it with style. He made possible, for one thing, the most glamorous biennial autumn appendage of our times, the special trains from Los Angeles to Notre Dame via the Grand Canyon and New Orleans. And in the 1930s alone, climaxing one big season after another, Jones' teams won Rose Bowl games from Pittsburgh, 47-14; Tulane, 21-12; Pittsburgh again, 35-0, and Duke, 7-3. In 1940, beating Tennessee, 14-0, Jones made it a perfect five for five in the Rose Bowl.

His teams weren't the first to win football games for SC, as all of Los Angeles knows. The university had been gathering steam for several years before Jones, and it had done well in other sports, too. The Trojans won their first national track title a few months before Jones put his first Trojan football team on the field. But the public in general doesn't pay a whole lot of attention to the other college sports, baseball, basketball *or* track.

Listen carefully to SC's track coach, Dean Cromwell: "Before we won that first championship, two New York reporters came up to me asking to know what the 'SC' stands for on our jerseys. They thought the Trojans might be from South Carolina."

That is a mistake that hasn't been made, East or West, since Troy's 1925 football season. That is the legacy of Howard Jones.

3. University of Georgia

COLLEGE FOOTBALL resolves, in most areas of the country, to a way of life. Although the game and its milieu aren't identical everywhere, a focus on any single regional variation brings out the underlying unity of the whole.

ATHENS, Ga.: Nov. 13, 1973.

A college football game, it has been said, is America's most characteristic ritual event. Nationwide, for millions of those who are deeply interested, college football has become an autumn weekend habit. It regularly attracts both national and sectional as well as local attention, and, from coast to coast, from region to region, state to state, village to village, the pageantry, the game, and the ritual each week are similar if not quite the same.

On Saturday mornings all over America, numberless old grads get up early and pack a lunch, mix cocktails in a mason jar, load up on ice, throw in a few blankets and sometimes the kids, and take off for the football stadium. There they pull into a parking lot, meet the friends of their youth, lunch together, cheer together, boo together, and join the traffic jam afterward, often getting together again for dinner somewhere down the road.

From Hanover to Ann Arbor to Athens to Austin and on West, the attraction is the same game played by the same rules and arousing the same passions, thrills, joy, tears. Only the details differ. At the tailgate picnics in New Haven, the tablecloths are mostly white. In Texas, they are checkered red and black. At USC, the song girls are prettier, but at Purdue there are more of them, many more. At Oklahoma, the variation is Wishbone football, which gives way to the Veer in Georgia, the I at Nebraska, and quarterback-in-motion plays at Harvard.

From the twang of New England to the drawl of the South, it is the accent that changes in college football. Thus at the Georgia-Auburn game here Saturday, on the University of Georgia field at Sanford Stadium, the largest flag on view was the American, but the largest number of flags were Confederate. The South is both aggressively and ambivalently loyal to its two favorite countries. As the Stars and Stripes went up the Sanford pole, the Georgia crowd sang the Star-Spangled Banner with more gusto and, on the whole, more affection than Northern crowds normally muster. Nevertheless, eleven decades after the surrender of Robert E. Lee, Georgia fans hailed every touchdown by waving the stars and bars of the Confederate States of America.

Over the public address system before the game, the invocation was delivered from the playing field by a Georgia divinity student. Invocation? There is almost always one in Southern football.

II

The details can be delightfully different. At the University of Georgia, instead of a galloping white horse, the mascot is a dog. Georgia teams are called Bulldogs. Had it originated the other day, this nickname couldn't have stuck. In the 1970s, the worst thing you can call a man, almost, is a dog — except at Georgia and Yale. Indeed, Georgians seem particularly proud of their canine relationship. In the brief stillness following the final words of the invocation Saturday, as the Georgia team remained bareheaded in silent prayer on the sideline, a gravel-voiced alumnus across the field shouted: "Go, Dogs!"

With such for a mascot, the students, some of them, can be expected to major in scatology. One of Georgia's largest athletic symbols, which on game day is frequently drawn across the football field like a chariot by four red-striped cheerleaders, is a massive red fire hydrant. It's an imitation hydrant, to be sure. It's so big, looming into the Georgia sky, the dog doesn't know what it is.

The dog's name is UGA IV. Two of his predecessors, UGA II and UGA III, lie buried at Sanford Stadium in a little cemetery behind the goal posts in the eastern end zone. One marble headstone reads: "UGA III, 1966-1972, 2 SEC Championships, 5 Bowl Teams: Not Bad for a Dog."

Veteran Georgia observers say it's strictly a coincidence that the president of their university, Dr. Fred Davison, is a veterinarian.

III

Comparing football North and South, Coach Pepper Rodgers of Georgia Tech, formerly of UCLA, says: "Football is exciting in the South because this is such a masculine-oriented country. What's that word? It's machismo country. The kids are brought up to consider it an honor and a privilege to play football. In a Southern high school, you have to play football to be accepted as a man. It's like fighting for your country."

Rodgers thinks that over, then adds: "It's just the style here. They love the hard work of football. They love the contact. Do you know what it's like to shake hands with a Southern-born man? He looks you straight in the eye, and likes to break your fist."

Quite possibly this explains, at least in part, why the South is a stronghold of Wishbone and Veer-T football, in which the emphasis is on running the ball like a man instead of throwing it like a bunch of kids. Both Auburn and Georgia are Veer teams, and both played lively football Saturday, blocking recklessly, and running up and down the field at will, until they fumbled the ball. The fumble is apparently one of the basic Veer plays.

The Bulldogs won, 28-13, on a field that was a dense forest when their university was chartered in 1785. The oldest chartered state university in the nation, Georgia was set down in a wilderness area by men who feared and distrusted cities. In time when a village grew up around their campus, the ambitious but undereducated old Georgians named the place Athens because the community centers on seven hills. The name persisted even after they learned it was Rome, not Athens, that had the seven hills.

In general, these are like the gentle, red-clay hills that Scarlett O'Hara might have worked at Tara. But Athens is not really that picturesque. Its main street, Clayton Street, one block over from the university, is a three-block jumble of architecturally indifferent two- and three-story buildings, all but indistinguishable from those in any other Southern or Midwestern hamlet.

The university, however, being a university, is a handsome assortment of white-trimmed, red brick buildings. And Sanford Stadium is one of the best viewing stadiums in America, built as it is in two facing sections, each seating nearly thirty thousand. The east and west ends are open because the stadium was placed in a ravine over a river that still runs through culverts under the playing field.

A bridge crosses the stream as it emerges from one end of the field, and at gametime Saturday this bridge was crowded with fans. Enjoying one of the best free viewing sites in American football, they had gathered the night before, bringing folding chairs, blankets, breakfast, beer, flags, and police dogs. Crime in America, like football, is boundless.

Hundreds of nonpaying fans also had good views at the other open end of the stadium, where, standing on a railway embankment, they occupied the same ground from which their forebears shot at the Federal Army's left wing in 1864 during Sherman's march through Georgia to the sea. The Confederate flags waving from the embankment made time stand still.

And on the playing field, as a matter of fact, so did the football teams. Both Auburn and Georgia scorned passing as if this were 1910 and it hadn't been invented yet. The goal in the South is plainly to run the ball, to run it down your throat, if possible. Even so, it's football they play here. It's the same game they play everywhere else, except it's different.

4. Texas versus Oklahoma

SUPPOSING THE Southern game summons the romance or whatever of the undying Confederacy, Texas football can amount to a Wild West brawl, which it often was in the years when I was covering Texas versus Oklahoma. Any generalization is likely to be an overstatement, yet the weekend of the biggest game in Texas each year usually seemed to be the weekend of, as they often said, "The Biggest Game in Football."

DALLAS: Nov. 11, 1975.

As the Texas-Oklahoma game ended here in 1947, the players were arguing over a touchdown. And when the argument spread to the stands, Oklahoma alumni and students began throwing whiskey bottles at the referee. That was too much for the Dallas police, who, driving a patrol car onto the field in a bold rescue operation, picked up the officials. "As they drove off," an eyewitness remembers, "the Oklahoma guys threw everything they could get their hands on at that police car. This was before cans, you know, and Dallas set the record that day for most beer bottles in the air at the same time."

Shuddering at the memory, the witness recalls: "Beer bottles and whiskey bottles were smashing off the patrol-car windshield like rain."

Although that was twenty-eight years ago, many in Dallas still remember the day warmly. For one thing, Texas won. For another, the Texas-Oklahoma football game was the biggest thing in town that year, as it is every year, bigger than the state fair or the Cotton Bowl or the Dallas Cowboys, or even a sale at Neiman-Marcus. With usual understatement, Texans call it, simply, "The Biggest Game in Football." And truthfully, it often is.

This year, for instance, both teams are 4-0, and today's winner will be in the fight for the national championship. In the last twenty-three years, that honor has gone to the Texas-Oklahoma winner no fewer than seven times.

II

The "Biggest Game" takes a two-day running start. And, again this year, Dallas police and the fans of both teams began gearing up simultaneously on Thursday, when thousands of college students set out from their dormitories and fraternities at Norman, Oklahoma, and Austin, Texas. The event is like a home game for both schools. The campuses are each two hundred miles from Dallas, close enough to make the students possessive, and far enough to help them slip easily and smoothly into a party mood.

By Friday noon, following ancient custom, the kids had installed themselves in Dallas and were taking over the town. And by Friday evening, following another custom, many of them were drunk. At least they looked it. And sounded it. This is the noise capital of the nation on the long Texas-Oklahoma weekend. Modern Dallas has a full complement of hotels and motels, and there, in every lobby and suite, and in the streets outside, old grads and undergraduates from both schools have been sipping bourbon and beer and shouting at one another for hours.

The eye of the storm is in downtown Dallas, where a narrow street named Akard knifes into one named Commerce and makes an end run around the historic Baker Hotel, which is catty-corner from the historic Adolphus Hotel. In this small, intimate, famous intersection nearly a half century ago, in the white-flannel era before students had cars, the Texas-Oklahoma game began every year — on the night before — and here it still begins. The principal difference now is that through the long hours of noisy, shoulder-to-shoulder marching and noisier bumper-to-bumper parading, the police confine pedestrians to the sidewalk, and cars to the street. Unhappily, you can't walk up and down the streets anymore, or drive up and down the sidewalks.

Everybody in Oklahoma red, however, is still insulting everybody in Texas orange. There is still a drink in almost every hand. The managers of the Baker and the Adolphus still issue identification cards to their guests, say their prayers, and lock their doors. And on a weekend day or night, helmeted Dallas police, before opening those hotel doors to anybody, still demand identification.

What's more, on a sidewalk near the Baker, there is still a mobile police station, with, to keep things moving, a municipal judge in residence. Armed guards sit right behind in two police vans, climbing out only to book drunks under the trees, which they continue to do throughout the hot night. Hour after hour, the troublesome are separated into two clusters — not red and orange, as you might imagine, but plain drunk and aggressive drunk. The quieter types are held at the mobile station until they sober up. The fighting drunks are hauled off to proper Dallas jails in paddy wagons that leave the Baker at intervals of ten or fifteen minutes, like airport buses. They make the return trip with sirens screaming, for no useful purpose, apparently, except to raise the holiday noise level.

It is at the jail houses that Texas and Oklahoma alumni, students and fans — and/or their wives, girlfriends, or boyfriends — are carefully segregated. There are Texas drunk tanks and Oklahoma drunk tanks. "If we threw them in together," a police sergeant said, "they'd fight all night. They'd be too tired to make the kickoff, and that would be a shame. We haven't declared war here. We just want them sober enough to see the game."

An alcoholic sports event is not, of course, unique to Dallas. College football traditionally has been a hard-drinking game from the Ivy League to the Big Ten to, most recently, this weekend's UCLA alumni invasion of the Bay Area. What's strange about Dallas is that the police don't seem to mind. A Dallas police lieutenant, asked if the department favored the removal of the Texas game to Oklahoma or, better, Nova Scotia, said: "Hell, no. It's a lot of fun, and it's good for business."

III

As a matchup of state universities, Texas-Oklahoma football is a little different in four other respects.

First, the series is the nation's longest lasting at a neutral site, having continuously defied the tradition that college games should be played home and home. Today's meeting of Longhorns and Sooners is their seventieth since 1900 (Texas leads, 45-25-2) and their forty-seventh at the Texas State Fair (which is billed, naturally, as the nation's biggest state fair). For a game that has played to capacity since World War II, this will be the thirtieth consecutive Texas-Oklahoma sellout at the Cotton Bowl, which seats 72,032.

Second, the geographical foundation of the game is that Oklahoma sits squarely on top of Texas, as if it were the former republic's northernmost county. Accordingly, the Sooners feel free to recruit throughout the state of Texas, which seems to them like going into the next county — a hell of a big county to be sure. The thousand or so prep schools that play football in this state are the chain teams for both universities, and, often, ten or twelve Texans start for Oklahoma. Some of today's contestants have been playing against each other since the first grade or earlier, a fact that adds to the intensity.

Third, recruiting hassles over the years have made the coaching rivalry more intense than most. The opposing coaches, Darrell Royal of Texas and Barry Switzer of Oklahoma, have spent a number of unpleasant months recently calling each other names and demanding lie-detector tests. Down the years, this has been a coaches' graveyard, defeat claiming at least three Texans and one Oklahoma coach. Losing seems intolerable to citizens of contiguous states.

Fourth, there are curious personal differences. Quaint as it may seem to most other Americans, the average Texan thinks he's more sophisticated than any Oklahoman. Whereas Austin (home of UT) is acknowledged to be the most civilized city in the Southwest, Norman (home of OU) is a small, inward-looking college town. All this brings more tensions. Says Times-Herald Sportswriter Blackie Sherrod, "They have a bunch of free-thinkers in Austin. On the day of a football game there, all the tennis courts are full."

Texas' enrollment, however, is forty-two thousand. For the Oklahoma game, it can fill every tennis court and library and still turn out as many football fans as the Sooners can — about thirty-five thousand each.

IV

In any Texas-Oklahoma crowd, the rooting sections include students and former students from every county in both states. Hundreds commute to the event by private plane. For, on Texas and Oklahoma ranches, there are still two kings, oil and football, and alumni wealth and interest in the game are such that scalpers can get their hands on few tickets.

There are years when you can't find a scalper in the Cotton Bowl area to let you into the Texas-Oklahoma game at any price. This is the only sports event I've attended anywhere (including Super Bowl and World Series games) where on game day, scalped tickets have been unavailable on the sidewalks outside.

The natives know this and proceed accordingly. One Texas alumnus who had to be out of town this week placed a classified ad in the Times-Herald offering to trade his pair for either "a citizens band radio, a fishing boat, or a cement mixer." Hours later, reportedly, he chose the boat. The next day, a Fort Worth citizen advertising for a pair offered to trade "my color television set" or "a date with my wife." By failing to submit the lady's picture, he no doubt cut his chances significantly.

If he does get into the game, he'll never have the fun his Texas forebears used to in the days of bottled beer. It's much harder to hit a referee with a paper cup.

5. University of Wisconsin

WITHIN YEARS after I filed the following report, Wisconsin pulled out of a long football slump and made the long trip to the Rose Bowl, where Badger fans set all-time records for extraordinarily enthusiastic behavior. That came as no surprise to anyone who ever saw Wisconsin *lose* at home.

MADISON, Wis.: Oct. 7, 1987.

At the Wisconsin football game here Saturday, the crowd was entertained in the fourth quarter by a troupe of high-heeled, high-kicking college women in short red dresses. Dancing around the edges of the field, the young women were accompanied, as usual, by twenty rock drummers from the university's marching band.

As always, however, a token four drummers were kept in their seats, along with the two hundred other Badger musicians, "in case of an emergency," Band Director Mike Lekrone said.

What emergency?

"We might score a touchdown," he said.

Not to worry. This is a century in which Wisconsin's football players have won less than half the time. It has been twenty-five years since they last represented the Big Ten in the Rose Bowl. In the last seventeen years, they have only had five winning seasons.

That is a record for futility rare today even in their conference, whose football teams have been losing respect for some time. But nobody around here seems to mind. To the contrary, the game is still a smash hit in this area, where Badger football attendance has averaged 70,410 since 1970. Despite years of disappointment, the average Badger crowd since 1974 in a stadium seating 76,293 has been 72,017.

What's going on here?

The strange answer is that although the billing is football, the attraction is the marching band. Wisconsin fans live on the music and color of college football. "It's the band that brings us together," Badger fan Peder Culver II said after Saturday's big show, in which the marching musicians were largely responsible for the unique holiday ambiance. The trombone, tuba, and trumpet players made most of the big plays on the day of another Badger defeat, and as usual they were the high scorers. This is a place where the band is bigger than the game. Purdue graduate Mary Jane Culver, alluding to Wisconsin's musically creative post-game programs, said: "At Madison, they always win the fifth quarter."

A Wisconsin football fan, she added, can be identified as anyone who will gladly miss a third or fourth quarter if you'll guarantee to have him here for what everyone calls the fifth quarter. That's when the world's largest rock band, two hundred strong, plays for thirty or forty minutes after the game while the musicians gyrate madly on the field.

In the big crowd, nobody sits and nobody leaves as the band plays on. The bandsmen and -women play on the run or while lying down — some standing on their heads — or while dancing about the field, the trombone section perhaps dancing with the tuba section, the trumpet section with the cheerleaders, the drummers with the pom pon girls. "We're a very physical band," a student musician said. "At preseason rehearsals, we spend seventy-five per cent of our time on physical conditioning."

The massed students and alumni at Camp Randall Stadium, site of a Civil War training camp, now home to the Badgers, are very physical, too. Rocking the upper decks as they sing along with the band, they dance with dates or with neighbors — or by themselves — dancing in the aisles, or on their seats. The music is "On, Wisconsin" or "Beer Barrel Polka" and the other drinking songs, and everyone is singing or shouting the familiar lyrics.

Commenting on the phenomenon of a big rock band with seventy thousand lead singers, University of Wisconsin Sociologist Dan Parks said: "It's a nonsensical outlet of a kind that appeals to most people. What so many of us want is something to do in common with other people."

Band Director Lekrone, who sees it as all of that and more, said: "I've always doubted that people take winning and losing as seriously as we're sometimes led to believe. I think we're showing at Wisconsin that a good time can be had by all as an alternative to winning or losing." As a point of view, that is doubtless taking the Badger phenomenon too far. On the other hand, maybe, the problem elsewhere is that few people have the Badger alternative.

II

At a Minnesota game here some years ago, a grade-school basketball player, age about seven, tore a football program apart and bunched the pages into paper balls. Then as the Badger band marched by, the youngster completed one jump shot after another into the tubas.

One day, reportedly, he slam-dunked a tuba carried by a bandsman standing six feet six. And this was to have colorful consequences.

First, the university, foiling the grade-school shooter and his many imitators, bought a light-weight, bright-red, form-fitting cover for each tuba.

Next, the band's twenty tuba players, proud of their musicianship and improved appearance, took off occasionally on marches of their own, leaving the rest of the band behind. They paraded along the edges of the field and into the crowd — single-file — to create a series of musical game-day diversions. For, as they paraded, they played the old marching songs in soft, deep, mellifluous tones.

As they do to this day.

At all home games, periodically getting up from their seats in the band, the tuba players transform themselves into uniformed visions in red and white — carrying big red and brass tubas — as they snake about the field, marching in step, playing beautiful close harmony. Thanks to a nameless, long-forgotten kid basketball player, there's nothing like it anywhere.

III

Wisconsin people seem to have a special talent for partying:

• In 1985, the most recent year for which reports are available, they drank 153,492,563 gallons of beer.

• In a state that stands sixteenth in U.S. population, Wisconsin ranks third in total beer consumption.

• Whereas Americans consume a per capita average 24.2 gallons of beer annually, according to the industry magazine, Beverage World, it's 35.9 gallons in Wisconsin.

On the average, that includes every man, woman and child in the state, although there is scant evidence that Wisconsin kids are holding up their end.

"UW (the University of Wisconsin) is the place to go for a party," said a Madison-trained lawyer, James Lindgren, who expressed pride that his school also stands high academically. He added: "We may be the only university that ranks in the nation's top ten in both partying and academics." Choosing to emphasize the more important of these values, Lindgren said: "(At Wisconsin), the drinking starts at 4 p.m. Fridays."

Although that puts a heavy load on the long weekend, it's also characteristic of this state that falling-down drunks are almost never seen at football games. Most Badger fans seem orderly and well-mannered, now that body-passing is against the law. The Madison Police Department is only a little busier on weekends. "The (drinking and party) problems are negligible," said an MPD spokeswoman, Maryanne Thurber, niece of the writer. "Intoxication isn't an arrestable offense in this state."

Down the road a few counties, the Green Bay Packers, who won five world championships in the 1960s before sliding into a long slump of their own, seem to attract a larger percentage of serious drinkers. But that's only because they're professionals, a Clintonville, Wisconsin, farmer, Alvin Suehring, said at a recent Packer game. Observing sadly that "my team has been losing for as long as the university team," Suehring still comes to town once a year to see the Packers. Asked why Green Bay crowds remain at capacity for consistently losing teams, he said: "There are two reasons, loyalty and liquor. Some of these people don't even know they're here."

At Madison games, most college football fans take it a bit easier. They have to pace themselves for a fifth quarter.

6. University of Chicago

TO MANY critics, football and academia are, or seem to be, a set of extremes nearly impossible to reconcile.

CHICAGO: Oct. 25, 1974.
Question: What do you do when you feel an urge to exercise?
Answer (by Robert M. Hutchins): I lie down until the feeling passes.

This is an anniversary season in intercollegiate athletics, and especially for campus football, on two counts:
• Fifty years ago, on November 21, 1924, the University of Chicago won

a precedent-setting sixth Big Ten football championship under Coach Amos Alonzo Stagg.

• Thirty-five years ago, on December 27, 1939, the University of Chicago, by order of Robert Maynard Hutchins, president, abolished football.

Not many events in the history of college affairs have caused more commotion than these. In 1924, Chicago stood alone as the only Big Ten university with six undisputed conference football championships — a record which, all these years later, few others in the Big Ten have exceeded, or even matched.

Yet, in 1939, within fifteen years of Stagg's finest hour, intercollegiate football perished at his university. "Unbelievable," Chicago fans said that winter when Hutchins liquidated their most popular sport. "Incomprehensible," the alumni said. "A sellout," students said, noting the time frame of the Hutchins' announcement: Christmas Week. Nobody was around to protest, or even dissent.

Then and ever since, the questions have been the same. By giving up football, what did Chicago prove? Was it a good idea? Did it portend the eventual end of big-time college football everywhere?

To those spending their days on the university's old-world, graystone-Gothic campus in the 1970s, the answers are still elusive. Chicago, some students know, had been a pioneer in two major if disparate American achievements: the evolvement of football and the release of atomic energy. Indeed, World War II was won at the University of Chicago football stadium. It was there in 1942, three years after the football team left, that a physics team found the key to nuclear power.

The nuclear workshop was under the stands of Stagg Field.

Years earlier, Stagg and his players had built that stadium with their own hands, devoting their summers and weekends to the project. Simultaneously, they had helped build football into a modern game on the insubstantial foundation laid at Rutgers and Princeton by two soccer teams in the nineteenth century. Stagg's teams introduced, among other things, quarterback keepers, draw plays, reverses, lateral passes, knee pads, tackling dummies, huddles, placekicks, linebackers, cross-blocking and many of the other tools and techniques of twentieth-century football.

Then suddenly at Chicago it was all gone. And that shook college people everywhere, for, if one of the game's most successful and innovative powerhouses could give up football, could the rest of the country be far behind?

A third of a century ago, that was plainly the hope of UofC administrators. But today, it is just as plain that at least until now, they have failed. The number of college teams in the big time has increased substantially since 1939. And as of this year, national interest has never been higher.

The game's critics have, of course, also multiplied in recent years, warning ever more loudly against overemphasis. But in the country at large, those who disapprove of college football seem still to be in the minority. Says Robert Feltes, president of Chicago-based Container Corporation, "What it all comes down to, I suppose, is this: College football doesn't belong, but it's with us."

They say football builds character. But is it the business of the university to mold the character of a few football players? Character-building is a function of church, family and state.

— Hutchins

As the "boy president" who in 1939 led Chicago off the football stage, Hutchins condemned the game as an "object of irrelevance" that was not only alien to an academic community, but injurious. He believed this when inaugurated UofC president at age twenty-nine, he believed it at fifty, and at seventy-five he still believes it.

In Santa Barbara, California, where for many years he has administered the Center for the Study of Democratic Institutions, Hutchins says of Chicago's action in giving up football: "It was one of the few totally successful things we did. At Chicago, and in the Midwest generally in the 1930s, the emphasis on winning football games tended to preoccupy the constituency — alumni, trustees and students — in a non-educational enterprise that prevented us from getting on with the business of an educational institution. And at the universities where the game is still valued, this is still true. Everything that has happened in college football since 1939 has confirmed the wisdom of our course."

As a view, that still gets both support and criticism on Hutchins' old campus. Among those in the support group is Mary Ann Lynch, a psychology major from Lockport, Illinois, who says: "In high school I was incredibly into football, but in college there are different focal points: classes, music, movies, conversation, and many other things. It is vital to be involved in something — but in the first year or two I was here, I never heard football mentioned. And I haven't missed it."

A college racing stable makes as much sense as college football. The jockey could carry the college colors, the students could cheer, the alumni could bet, and the horses wouldn't have to pass a history test.

— Hutchins

Even though the Hutchins logic seems irrefutable, his performance as a salesman has disappointed his best friends. In Chicago and its suburbs as well as on campus, those favoring football are still as earnest as ever. And among the anti-Hutchinses, there is one pervasive point of view: In discontinuing intercollegiate football, the university took the fun out of campus life.

More than one visitor has reported that Chicago's students lack the fire that seems to radiate out from the football team at other universities. On this campus, students move from class to class and home again in a distinctively solemn style. By comparison with USC, or elsewhere in the Midwest — or even at Harvard, where the Yale football team is still an object of conversation and obloquy — Chicago seems, quite simply, dull.

This is conceded by many Chicago scholars, professors and alumni. Med student Jeff Trantalis of Norwich, Connecticut, says he only has one complaint against Chicago: "There's no school spirit here." Leslie Mason, a UofC administration employee, recently hired, says: "I was a cheerleader at Ripon. Football was a diversion, and everyone needs a diversion." Business major Howard Bimson: "Football encourages mingling. If you don't mingle, you aren't human."

James Vice, Chicago's assistant dean of students, concedes: "I think we can agree that the average Big Ten campus is livelier. Or at least the gusto is more evident. Life is more adult here. The fun is not so structured. Instead of a Big Ten game against Purdue, a student may be thinking of a chess club meeting, or a pizza trip with a few friends."

Hutchins, unmoved by the heresies, takes an uncompromising view: "To the serious student, the curriculum is what's exciting. The one thing most clearly established when football was discontinued at Chicago was that this is a serious educational institution. There was no thought that anyone was deprived of the joys of football. You can always watch the pros."

To Willie Davis, a pro, this argument begs the question. A Los Angeles businessman now, Davis earned his master's degree at Chicago after a long career as a Hall of Fame defensive end for Vince Lombardi in Green Bay. "For either an undergraduate or graduate student, going to school at

Chicago is like going to work on a real job," says Davis, who at graduation sifted sixty-seven business offers with the help of the business school dean, George Schultz, later secretary of the treasury. "This is the only college in the country where the library is the busiest place on campus."

It's also the only college that ever tore down a football stadium to *build* a library. Chicago's Joseph Regenstein Library, erected in 1969 on the site of Stagg Field — smack in the middle of campus — has been called the nation's finest.

Still, the suspicion lingers that there were more laughs in the days when the place was a football field.

> *American higher education is unique. In no other nation does the university tangle up academic and athletic programs to the confusion of both. In England, the difference is that winning a boat race doesn't establish the merits of one university over another.*
> — Hutchins

It should not be supposed that in its modern guise, the University of Chicago has entirely given up athletics. On intramural and minor league levels, games are still being played here — even football games, of a sort. Once the scourge of the Big Ten, Chicago's football team tied the Wheaton Junior Varsity last year, 6-6, then dropped six in a row — failing to score in five games against Class D opponents.

The new product is emphatically amateur. There are no locker room speeches at new Stagg Field — it seats a thousand — principally because there are no locker rooms. After home games, the players of both teams must walk three blocks to the showers.

There would be no games at all except that five years ago, thirty years after football was last played here, a group of students petitioned for another chance and won. But except to the players, on-campus football interest is clearly minimal. A graduate student from New York, Pete Keers, has a typical comment: "I can't take the time to watch Chicago play Oberlin or Lake Forest."

On the major league level, however, the argument continues unabated. Dean of Students Vice, who sees both sides, says: "The academic strength of the university today is shown in many ways. No class is taught by a student teaching assistant. We don't even have student assistants, except in some of the labs. Full professors teach freshmen. The average class has seventeen or eighteen students. Three-quarters of the faculty live within walking distance of campus. But there *is* one negative aspect without football. We suffer in national publicity. Some of it may be the wrong kind of publicity, but a football game does provide an occasion for people to hear about your school and come to your campus."

Chicago isn't a very good university. It's just the best there is.
— Hutchins

What do you for fun here? What *can* you do?

This is a thought that occurred last year to D.J.R. Bruckner, Chicago's vice president for public affairs. So on February 19, Bruckner threw a birthday party for Nicolaus Copernicus. The occasion was the five hundredth anniversary of the astronomer's birth. More than seven hundred students showed up to share a gigantic eight-layer cake on which each layer had been labeled, in Latin, with Copernicus' descriptions of the sun and its satellites.

Instead of a marching band and drum majorettes, there was medieval music by an ensemble of specialists in the oldies but goodies of 1473. Instead of a traditional pep talk, there was a toast by Astronomy Professor Subrahamanyan Chandrasekhar. Says Bruckner: "At Chicago, it's hard to shake the students out of the library. The party was a response to the feeling that there should be more mirth on this campus."

Thus today's Chicago. Although they no longer fear Purdue here, and although they can no longer beat Ohio State, this is the one place with the wit to appreciate — and the lassitude to need — a big-time party for a Polish genius who never played football.

7. Football at Dartmouth

FOOTBALL SEEMS different, feels different, and looks different in the Ivy League. It also means something different — notably at Dartmouth College, where my guide on a football weekend was a student reporter named David Shribman. Subsequently, Shribman moved to the Boston Globe, where, shortly, he rose to assistant managing editor/Washington bureau chief.

HANOVER, N.H.: Nov. 18, 1974.

Of the eight Ivy League schools, Dartmouth is farthest north. It often snows here in October. Accordingly, there was no objection some years ago when members of the Dartmouth senior class decided to build a giant bonfire at a football rally the night before the Harvard game. As college seniors have done before and will do again, they left the details to the freshman class. The kids were told only to tear down an abandoned barn at the edge of town and bring it in as firewood. On a dark night in rural New Hampshire, however, one barn looks very much like any other. The freshmen ripped up a new one by mistake; and although it made a hell of a fire, the university had trouble balancing the budget that year after paying off the angry farmer.

Despite such setbacks, it is a measure of Dartmouth's interest in freshmen, bonfires, rallies and football that all are still flourishing here on a campus that for twenty decades or more has pleased generations of students and visitors. In the years after World War II, when General Eisenhower was president of Columbia, he once made a speech at Dartmouth, where everybody remembers only the remark he made on a campus tour: "This is just what I've always thought a college should look like."

Ike had it right.

The college, like a small New England town, is built on three sides of a town green; and in the beginning, someone happily insisted on devoting an entire city block to this open space. The dominant structure, Baker Library, whose front lawn is the enormous green, is a stately brick building topped by an unusually tall, slim, white clock tower. The rest of the campus is a park rolling through many of the wooded acres of Hanover, a village that is just across the broad Connecticut River from Vermont. Before the American Revolution, Dartmouth was carved out of a forest.

During football weekends, this idyllic tract becomes the setting for some of college football's most enthusiastic pageantry.

On the night before this year's Harvard game, for example, the Dartmouth band, blaring "Dartmouth's In Town Again," paraded smartly through the park and straight into the library. Gathering, as they marched, a train of more than a thousand students, the musicians burst down the main hall of the library — rattling walls covered incongruously with the angry Marxist murals of Mexican Painter Jose Clemente Orozco — and spun through the revolving front door onto the green, launching a pep rally. For awhile, there were two main events, the band and the bonfire, and then the fire took over, the flames leaping seventy feet above the green and attracting a crowd estimated by the fire department at four thousand.

An annual tradition, Dartmouth's big-game bonfire is one of the last remaining such spectacles in college football. Over the years, Big Green freshmen, called Pea Green, have found and trucked in marvelously combustible hen coops, shanties, barns, trees, and telegraph poles, but the best fires are still laid with railroad ties. The disappearance of American railroads may soon end this sport, and even now, in Avis trucks, freshman scouting parties must forage into Maine and Canada. But again this year, they collected enough abandoned railroad ties to keep the fire going all night.

The ties were stacked as high as a two-story building before the blaze was lit by four Dartmouth seniors holding red highway flares. When the top half of the flaming structure collapsed into the middle, it resembled a settler's log cabin fired by the Indians.

It's hard to say what effect a thing like this has on football players — the Big Green team was introduced at the pep rally, and a few hours later played well against a better team — but the effect on others was profound. The pyromaniacal urges of hundreds were surely assuaged for another year. Half the crowd was still there at midnight, four hours after the fire began. And at 1:30 a.m., a Hanover father instructed his three children, the oldest about twelve, "One more walk around the fire, and then we go."

At dawn, as the Hanover Fire Department was hosing down the embers, the Ivy League's reputation for rapscallion ferment was also upheld. The big Harvard marching band, with barely enough light to see, tip-toed out to the Dartmouth residential area, formed up in full regalia, and started blowing. On a parade past dormitories, fraternity houses, and, unfortunately, the downtown Hanover Inn, the band woke up every Big Greenie (and every visitor) playing "Fair Harvard" fortissimo.

The morning, cold and clear and enchanting, climaxed with, among other things, punch parties at the fraternity houses, where the entertainment was the sing-along at the house piano: "And if I had a son, sir, I'll tell you what he'd do. / "He'd yell 'TO HELL WITH HARVARD' like his daddy used to do."

The punch was the perennial, effective screwdriver, served out of a cafeteria garbage pail. A clean garbage pail, I hope. The game was almost an anticlimax.

II

On a fall weekend at Dartmouth, student-athletes and other students, as Ivies, do it their way. Thus, the most recent Harvard-Dartmouth freshman game was delayed two hours while thirty-one members of the Harvard team took an economics test in a Dartmouth classroom. The examination had been scheduled for 1 p.m. by the Cambridge profs, who made only one concession, moving it to Hanover so the game needn't be canceled altogether.

Earlier this season, Harvard's best defensive back, Mike Page, accompanied the team as usual to New York for the Columbia game but didn't play. He was excused to take the state law-board examinations.

Other Ivy League students appear to be equally ambivalent. On the morning of the big game against Harvard — three hours before the kickoff — scores of Dartmouth underclassmen were still hitting the books in Baker Library. Yet of those questioned, most said they intended to make the opening kickoff, or at least much of the game. And this may define intercollegiate football Ivy-style. It isn't the biggest thing on campus, certainly not as big as the bonfire, but like math classes and rock concerts it has a place. It belongs.

Deemphasis indeed seems to be the wrong word for what's happened to Ivy League sports in recent years. Football hasn't been deemphasized here, just decommercialized. Items:

• There are no athletic scholarships. Athletes pay their own way unless they qualify for aid on a basis of need.

• Pro football scouts in this neighborhood are as rare as the great-tailed grackle. In the NFL's intercollegiate farm system, the Ivy League is Class D.

• The pressure to win has been relieved somewhat by a decision to exempt football and other Ivy sports from gate-receipts funding. The athletic department, along with the history department, biology department and the others, is financed out of general university funds.

Dartmouth Athletic Director Seaver Peters, noting that the school's athletic budget this year exceeds two million dollars, says: "If intercollegiate athletics are worth having, they're worth being supported like any other university program."

So this is what's *really* different about Ivy League people. They like football so much they're willing to pay for it.

III

How good is their game? It is competitive, well-coached, reasonably well-played and colorful. The score was 17-15 Saturday when Harvard's Crimson ended a five-year domination by Dartmouth's Big Green.

Of the eight seventeenth-century schools in the Ivy League — Brown, Columbia, Cornell, Dartmouth, Harvard, Penn, Princeton and Yale — Harvard has the most modern football team. And against Dartmouth,

Coach Joe Restic's Crimson offense took command with a number of smart, subtle plays. The game's decisive run, measuring thirty-three yards, was made by Harvard's left-handed Hawaiian quarterback, Milt Holt, from a strange-looking formation that seemed to be a variant of the Power I.

Harvard uses more formations than possibly any other team in football, college or pro. The Dartmouth offense, less flamboyant, embraces a sophisticated mix of modern option plays, spread formations, and clever passes. The other Ivies also play imaginatively. In terms of intrinsic football interest, it could be said that Ivy teams put on the best show in the country. At Yale, Coach Carmen Cozza notes: "Our teams are exciting because none of the offenses is stereotyped." Columbia's Bill Campbell adds: "It's a very creative and innovative group of coaches."

The academic bent of the players apparently dictates Harvard's kind of football. "Our athletes are a special type," Coach Restic says. "They're inquisitive, well-rounded, highly motivated. They have to be challenged, so we put in a lot of motion plays, a lot of different formations and changeups, a bunch of defenses." This approach tends to enliven Ivy football at the expense of the smoothness the NFL gets with continual repetition of simpler plays. "But," their coach says, "what you lose in polish, you more than make up for in surprise value."

Ivy leaders admit to some unique problems. Says Restic: "The difference at a school like this is that we practice around the players' lab schedules. Sometimes we're out there early in the afternoon, sometimes we don't start until 5 p.m. Football takes more time than many of them can really afford. They're in class or studying every day before I get them, and after practice they go right back to their labs and libraries. What you need to play football here is the ability to turn it off and on. You turn it on going out of your last class, and you've got to turn it off in the shower, and that isn't easy." But they do it.

IV

The official Ivy attitude toward intercollegiate sports is expressed in the charter of the league that calls itself the Ivy Group. In one of the strongest endorsements ever given college football, the eight Ivy presidents announced in 1954: "The Group affirm their conviction that under proper conditions, intercollegiate competition in organized athletics offers desirable development and recreation for players and a healthy focus of collegiate loyalty."

On a typical football Saturday in the Ivy League, that focus is sometimes as strange as it is healthy. Five minutes before halftime, the public address announcer at the Harvard-Dartmouth game came on to report a few scores, and as a visitor wondered about Ohio State against Illinois, the announcer said, a bit breathlessly, "Here's an upset. In field hockey this morning, it was Dartmouth 3, Radcliffe 2."

The cheering rocked the stadium.

Ivy League sports fans live in a world of their own. At New Haven, a Yale student from Los Angeles, Frank Jones, says his roommate told him how to behave at football games the first time they went to the Yale Bowl: "Pretend you're not interested unless we get ahead. Then yell like hell." And at Cambridge, Coach Restic, a big winner, maintains that losing can be more instructive than winning. "Winning doesn't put you to a test," he says. "You might know in your heart you played a lousy game, but it's overlooked because the team won. If you're a player on a losing team, what are you going to do about that? You must measure up in spite of losing."

At Dartmouth, in either case, what they're mostly after is a good time. Before the kickoff Saturday, the entire Dartmouth freshman class was on the field. And as the Big Green team entered the stadium, it jogged through two long files of jumping, cheering, Pea Green rooters. By the fourth quarter, much of the capacity crowd was on the field, too, thronging both sidelines in a scene resembling pictures of turn-of-the-century football before the stadiums were built.

For Big Green football, there are ticket-sellers, but no ushers. Those vending hot dogs and soft drinks are Hanover children aged eight to twelve. The waterboy is a girl. The cheerleaders have also changed: They're still energetic — the men in long green pants, the women in short green skirts — but not quite with it. In the last thirty seconds, with Harvard on the march, Dartmouth's yell kings called for a round of "Hold that line" instead of "Get that ball." Not that it mattered. What really mattered was the Dartmouth band, the Harvard band, and the bonfire.

8. Stanford Pursues Preeminence

THEN THERE is Stanford's way: Do it all, and do it all first class. Though in recent years teams from Palo Alto have infrequently reached the Rose Bowl, the Stanford way has remained much as it was before, after, and during 1974 under many different academic leaders and athletic directors.

PALO ALTO, Calif.: May 14, 1974.

Joseph H. Ruetz of Stanford is the athletic director of a unique university that strives each year for number-one recognition nationally in both scholarship and sports. Academically, Stanford continues to rank among the country's four or five leading universities as surveyed by the American Council of Education and other organizations. And athletically, Stanford's thriving program has developed the defending national-champion tennis team and two of the last four Rose Bowl winners.

Asked if there will be another Rose Bowl trip soon, Ruetz (pronounced Ritz) says: "We're shooting for this year. Our goal is the same as ever: excellence in many different things. Football is still in there with geology, pharmacology, and tennis."

Although, in the last half century, Harvard, Yale, the University of Chicago and other great institutions have deemphasized or abandoned football, Stanford doesn't see the point in such a retreat. "Variety," says Ruetz, "is what a university is all about — variety of learning and experience. Isn't that what you face in life? The athletic field provides another place for excellence to show itself."

His university is nothing if not diverse, having produced, in this century, a remarkable balance of thirty-nine Rhodes Scholars and thirty-six All-American football players. Some of Stanford's best are in the NFL — Quarterback Jim Plunkett among them — but for a quarter century, more Stanford football players have gone into graduate school than pro football.

Fred E. Hargadon, dean of admissions, affirms that pursuit of excellence in many forms is a result of deliberate choice at a university where only 1,450 of 9,400 applicants were accepted this year "although ninety per cent were qualified." The emphasis, he says, "remains on a diverse student body representing many kinds of geographic areas, backgrounds, and talents."

Thus, good biologists, musicians, and athletes are consciously recruited each year.

But the athletes must also be able to make it in political science or perhaps economics, Hargadon says, because there is no physical education major here. And though at most universities, contrary to popular belief, a higher percentage of athletes than non-athletes graduate with their class, at Stanford it's ridiculous. Of those completing their athletic eligibility last year, 100 per cent of the basketball team graduated and 91.8 per cent of the football team. Fifteen of the nineteen Stanford players in pro football last fall were graduates. All six drafted by the NFL this winter will graduate this month.

So Stanford is different. Of course, it has always been that. One of its athletes, Hank Luisetti, revolutionized basketball, discarding the two-hand set shot of the game's early years for today's ubiquitous one-hand shot. And one of its coaches, Clark Shaughnessy, revolutionized football, bringing in the modern T Formation in 1940. Over the years, Luisetti, Shaughnessy and three kinds of champion quarterbacks — left-hander Frankie Albert, precise passer John Brodie, and strongman Jim Plunkett — have done a lot to characterize this most diverse of universities.

As Sociology Professor Sanford Dornbusch has found, there is no typical Stanford man. Instead, he says, "There is an enormous variety of persons all of whom think they're in the majority."

II

Even with the stipulation that variety is a virtue, doesn't the sweeping attention football gets detract from the educational purpose of a university such as Stanford?

That is a popular assessment — but don't number Athletic Director Ruetz among those who agree with it.

"When you think it through," he says, "I don't see how you can conclude that college football is detracting. On Saturdays if there were no games, some students would adjourn to a pub, some would go to the beach, and some, naturally, would study. They do now. To assume that without football, the whole student body would focus on studies is unrealistic."

Nonetheless, big-time football as an entertainment item does seem to do more for the public and alumni than for college students. What's wrong with that statement?

"At Stanford, the athletic program is well supported by all three of those groups," Ruetz says. "With a student body of 11,500, including 6,500 undergraduates, we sell about 8,000 student season tickets — on a voluntary basis. On some campuses, football tickets are tied into a mandatory package — but not here. Our student support is voluntary and excellent."

What do Stanford's professors have to say about that?

"With 1,110 faculty members, we sell 3,500 faculty and staff season tickets to football games. Most of the faculty are warmly in favor. An esoteric science club reunion, for instance, can only get a quorum on a football weekend."

Isn't Harvard superior today in the minds of some academicians precisely because it doesn't fool around in big-time football? Stanford's jock image must at times be harmful.

"On balance, a sports image is more helpful than harmful — that is, it gives you a better-rounded image — if you keep your academic and athletic programs sound and consistent with the university's goals and demands. In short, we think an intercollegiate athletic program is a good thing provided the coach maintains athletic integrity and the school maintains academic integrity. We make a point of both."

III

Insofar as football players and other athletes are concerned, Stanford measures academic integrity in four ways. It keeps track of grade-point averages, academic majors, athletes graduating, and those going on to graduate study.

Last year, Ruetz says, "Our athletes maintained grade-point averages of 3.3 to 3.94 on a scale where 3.0 is a B and 4.0 an A. Thirty-five of our athletes majored in political science, thirty in economics, twenty-three psychology, nineteen English, nineteen history, eighteen engineering, and sixteen biology. Some 86.3 per cent graduated with their class compared to the university-wide average of 85 and the national average of 50. And 83 per cent of our student-athletes went on to graduate school."

With student-athletes oriented so seriously to classwork, why shouldn't Stanford trim down to Ivy League-type football and quit trying to keep up in a conference as difficult as the Pac-Eight?

"First, we really don't have a choice. There aren't enough schools in our geographical area willing and able to compete in an Ivy-type conference. We can either accept the challenge of major intercollegiate competition or get out, and we think there are more than enough values in the challenge to meet it. Second, from a financial point of view, it would be disastrous for us to deemphasize football. Receipts from football support seventy per cent of the Stanford athletic program in all sports at all levels — intercollegiate, club, and intramural."

If that's the case, shouldn't college players get paid? They're the lowest salaried workers in the country considering the revenue they generate.

"That's one way of looking at it. Another way is to realize that college football players don't generate all the money themselves. The crowds come to see the teams — the Stanford football team, or the Notre Dame football team. If Notre Dame's players all quit school and played as the South Bend Tigers, they wouldn't draw five thousand for a game against the Palo Alto Reds."

You're saying the pro emphasis is on excellence only in the won-lost columns.

"I'm saying the Stanford emphasis is on excellence in everything. That's where Stanford is different."

9. USC, Academic Champion

BEGINNING EARLY in the Howard Jones era (1925-40), the Trojans have reversed the usual college football pattern in America. Elsewhere, as a rule, high-quality universities have, at one time or another, created great football teams. At USC, by contrast, a great football team has helped create a high-quality university. The big academic changes happened during the two decades when Norman Topping and John Hubbard headed the university administration, and near the end of Hubbard's presidency I asked him about it.

LOS ANGELES: March 4, 1980.

Dr. John Hubbard has come to two conclusions about the University of Southern California during his decade as president of an institution that has become both academically and architecturally important in the last half century — particularly in the years since he and a predecessor, Dr. Norman Topping, stepped up administration efforts to recruit eminent scholars, enrich the libraries, and build delightful buildings:

• A successful fifty-five-year run in intercollegiate football has, in Hubbard's view, largely made this university what it is. "Frankly, I have no idea what SC would be without football," he says. "It might now be an ordinary small college at best."

• For all their success, USC athletic teams today "are no more than a handsome auxiliary" to one of the nation's fine academic institutions. "The greatest thing we have going for us now is our increasing academic reputation," Hubbard says. "We have become in recent years one of the major research institutions of the United States. And this progress has been accompanied by steadily increasing quality in the three ingredients that make a university: faculty, students, and library."

The changes have been nationally recognized. "Any impartial observer looking at SC's total academic picture would have to say we've made a very significant improvement," the university's eighth president believes. "I'd use the word dramatic, but that would be immodest."

A jovial, outgoing Texas transplant, Hubbard, who is in his office having breakfast with a reporter, gets up to pour another cup of coffee. On his feet, moving around, he looks a great deal more like a football coach than a college president. Although he has spent most of his life studying

British history, or teaching it, he has the rugged features and the expansive bearing of an old grad who went to college on an athletic scholarship.

A World War II naval aviator, son of a college president, father of three daughters, a regular at football practice each fall — and an ex-officio assistant coach who routinely rides the bench at USC games — Hubbard plans to step down this summer as head of the Trojans, whose football team has been to seven bowl games in his presidency.

"And of the seven, we lost only one," he says, beaming.

How did that happen?

"It was Woody's best team," Hubbard says, identifying a Rose Bowl winner coached by Ohio State's Woody Hayes.

In the beginning, what got you interested in football?

"I have always been interested in all sports," he says, thinking of his boyhood in Texas and his school days there at the state university. "As far back as I can remember, sports have been part of my daily affairs."

What was your game as a boy?

"I tried to play every game there was. And I made one important discovery. I found that team sports are more enjoyable than anything individual — at least for me. I have felt since then that nothing people do is more beautiful than some kind of disciplined activity in unison."

In or out of athletics?

"Either. I love to see teamwork of any kind. I find soloists less appealing than symphonies — or big bands. The old Benny Goodman and Tommy Dorsey name bands were examples of brilliant teamwork. In education, too, it's the cooperative aspect that is the most exciting. The way I look at this university, we have a lot of great academic stars — some magnificent individual performers — but what attracts me is the collegial atmosphere: the group sense of purpose, the team effort, if that's not too corny a term."

What's your idea of collegial?

"I'm speaking of the interaction between and among students, faculty and library. The academic word is synergism."

Where does football fit into all that?

"A good athletic program is indispensable as a kind of adhesive that holds the university and community together. It keeps the alumni and our other friends interested in the university — *actively* interested."

But does big-time football really belong in an academic setting? When Robert M. Hutchins was at the University of Chicago, he threw the football players out. What's your view of that?

"I understand it. But I can't say Chicago has been a greater university without football. It was already a great university when he took that step. Secondly, the fiscal picture on the college administration level is so much different now. Just ten years ago, my first SC budget was seventy million dollars. The next one will be three hundred million. For whatever reason, football is the activity that does the best job of attracting those who can help us. And the task of the administration is to channel interest in sports into other areas of the university."

How much exactly does football mean to USC in dollars and cents?

"There's no way to quantify it. Nobody knows how many friends we would have been able to make — or even what would have happened to SC — without sports. But we are sure that it's football that gets their interest now — ergo their generosity. And they are generous."

How can a mere game play such an energizing role in the affairs of a group of scholars?

"To a college administration, football is more than a game, it's an event. It comes under the rubric of tradition: the pre-game parties, the band marching across Exposition Park to the Coliseum, the song girls, the card stunts, the horse. On a Saturday morning at SC during the football season, as many as ten different support [fund-raising] groups will gather on campus for brunch. The fiscal well-being of the university is tied up with these people. And their appearance on campus is tied up with the spectacle that is a Saturday-afternoon football game. The catalyst is the game."

As the architect and chief fund-raiser of USC's multi-million-dollar Toward Century II project, how do you measure the importance of winning in football?

"By and large, I'd say athletic success leads to a meaningful increase in the resources of a university. I get a far better reception after we've beaten Notre Dame or won a game that's put us in the Rose Bowl. People know what I'm after, but almost invariably their opening gambit is, 'Great game.' After a defeat, those who represent a college feel like apologizing. Winning puts everyone in a better mood. People become proud of their institution. It makes for a more congenial atmosphere."

If football success is so vital to USC as a whole, choosing the football coach has to be one of the administration's most important decisions. When John McKay left several years ago, why did you choose John Robinson?

"What I liked about Robinson was his broad and curious intellect. During our recent fund drive for KUSC — the classical music station — the most effective speaker I heard on the subject of what good music means in his personal and family life was John Robinson."

As to your personal future, you have decided to resign the presidency after one decade. That seems to be in line with what most college presidents are doing these days. Why is ten years about the limit now for those in what used to be a lifetime vocation?

"The explanation is in the complexities today. A college president used to be an academic statesman, essentially. Today, the fiscal pressures make him a jack of all trades. It requires an energy level that is unbelievable."

What are you going to do next?

"I decided that a long time ago. In my next incarnation, I'm going to come back as a sportswriter."

XV

COMMENT

Along with other people, I have opinions on subjects that interest me. And of all the ways there are to express those opinions daily or weekly in a newspaper, the most satisfactory, I've found, is the three-subject column limited to seven- or eight-hundred words.

At present, most commentary columns, in sports and other sections of the newspaper, run about that long; but most are one-subject essays. And to me, a seven-hundred-word essay — particularly on a sports subject — usually feels padded. It would be more readable, I often feel, if trimmed in half.

The advantage of the three-subject column is that it gives the writer an opportunity to hand off three quick, strong judgments, wasting no words, while, in a channel-surfing era, keeping his readers engaged. If they don't like one segment, there'll be another along in a moment, they know, and maybe they'll like that.

The problem with a three-subject sports column, the essayists say, is that it requires three arguments with three ledes and three endings, meaning that it's three times harder to generate than a one-subject essay.

Unquestionably, essays are easier; but in choosing journalistic forms, laziness hardly seems a compelling criterion.

If seven hundred words are too many for daily or weekly one-subject newspaper essays, they aren't enough for the sound, thorough think pieces that commonly appear in the best magazines.

Harper's and Atlantic Monthly live on comprehensive commentaries extending to thousands of words — and Sports Illustrated also finds places for them.

For awhile in the 1990s — before losing advertising and column inches — the Times, too, made occasional room on its sports pages for long point-of-view pieces. For awhile I wrote one a month; and some of those are in this chapter, too, along with a few shorter one-subject essays as well as examples of the three-subject columns I've written for three different papers.

SECTION ONE: The Three-Subject Column

1. In the Examiner

THE FOLLOWING, a 750-word sports column written for the old Los Angeles Examiner nearly forty years ago, exemplifies the three-subject approach. Although this particular column has baseball themes, each of the three is different.

LOS ANGELES: March 12, 1957.

Otherwise reasonable men have for years been putting up with the Florida view that "it's going to take a little time, suh," to accept Negro ballplayers as card-carrying Americans. But how much time is enough? Nine decades after Florida rejoined the union, what's it like now in spring training to be a baseball-playing black person down there?

Says Chicago Reporter Wendell Smith, himself a Negro: "If you are a Negro, you cannot get a cab in the morning to take you to the ballpark, unless it happens to be Negro-driven. You cannot go to a movie in the heart of town. You are horribly embarrassed each day when the bus returning the players from the ballpark deposits you in 'Colored Town' and proceeds to the plush hotel where your white teammates live in splendor and luxury."

Baseball players, like artists, musicians and scientists, display a talent highly prized in our society. But an arbitrary subset of this talented group, despite achievements and fame, is submitted each year to months of what Smith calls "humiliation and ostracism."

Shouldn't this be the last year for all that?

If the Southerners honestly believe they can't integrate Negro talent into their communities by next February, the ballclubs should immediately announce that they are moving their spring camps to Arizona, Nevada or California. First-class citizenship, for all, is surely more important than pennants or dollars or the white freaks of Florida.

II

The grapefruit circus is coming to Los Angeles again this year to play Wrigley Field Friday night, when nobody will particularly care that last year's Chicago Cubs and Baltimore Orioles finished behind the champions of the big leagues by thirty-three and twenty-eight games, respectively. Last year was long ago.

Nonetheless, the uneven distribution of strength in the majors, as reflected in those figures, is another disheartening peculiarity of baseball today. Ten or more of the sixteen clubs have no chance whatever to reach the top, now or ever, so far as the eye can see.

The missing link here is the first and crucial link: Those who run baseball won't make an equitable distribution of their talent. This is the defect that cripples the national pastime as a game. And it can be remedied only with an arbitrary apparatus — a draft like pro football's, say, or a time limit on the reserve clause.

Casey Stengel's New York Yankees have, of course, been the chief beneficiaries of baseball's intransigence, winning seven of the last eight World Series. During the same period, helped along by the NFL's annual draft, five different teams have won football's world championship.

Nothing serves the public interest like competition; and in sports, competition must be artificially induced. The wise and the wealthy, if unfettered, prevail. In too many cities, baseball fans are unjustly discriminated against regularly because their teams are owned by persons without means or brains. That is a fact, and that should be changed.

III

Some people were upset the other day by a reference in this space to the artistry of pro football. These folks believe that, along with football players and jazz musicians, a third group, baseball players, should be included among "the most distinctively American artists."

The question is whether baseball is an art form. If jazz musicians and football players are artists, aren't baseball players?

My answer is, not quite. Probably the key word in a definition of art is creative. The key word in a definition of science is knowledge — and essentially, baseball is applied knowledge.

Most decisions by baseball managers are rooted not in creative urges but in a study of percentages. They choose between taking and rejecting the percentage. Hitting and pitching are obviously sciences. Fielding brings to baseball its closest brush with art, although rarely, in the more spectacular plays of an outfielder like Willie Mays.

Football today, on the other hand, is the product of years of creativity. Imaginative coaches have made and remade their sport as surely as Artie Shaw and Duke Ellington revised and upgraded the quality of music.

During the violence of a pro football game, the knowledge of what to do is transcended in every clutch instance by the art of getting it done somehow. Improvisation is as necessary and exciting in football as in jazz. It's true that most of the cultural expressions of this country were imported from abroad — but not jazz, and not football. These, it seems to me, are the U.S. art forms.

2. In the Herald-Examiner

SEVERAL YEARS later, my three-part, seven-hundred-word columns were in the Herald-Examiner. In those days, the Pro Bowl game was always played in Los Angeles, so Ram mistakes were always coming back to town. (Actress Jane Russell was the wife of one coach one year when one trade was made.) In later years, when the Pro Bowl was moved to Hawaii, Ram coaches and owners were much happier.

LOS ANGELES: July 14, 1964.

Their many recent trades have not only brought waves of draft choices to the Rams but have also provided their opponents with starting players in every position. If a playoff game were arranged for Christmas Day, with all proceeds going into a charity fund for the owners, ex-Rams would be 2 to 1 over Rams.

In retrospect, it is plain that the club spent years thinking up the bad deals that have taken away Norm Van Brocklin, Night Train Lane and a dozen others who have either gone on to play in NFL title games or returned as Pro Bowl all-stars.

This isn't to say, however, that every Ram mistake has been unfailingly recognizable the day it was made. At the moment of decision, the average Ram deal has in fact been defensible — the 1961 Del Shofner trade being a prime example. That one turned out to have everything: It fetched a draft choice, it made Del an All-Pro, and it put him in three title games as a New York Giant.

Was this trade necessary? Your name is Bob Waterfield, you're the Ram coach, and here are the facts you saw at the time: (1) Shofner has ulcers, (2) he has been injured off and on for two years, (3) he has been dropping the ball, (4) he is slower than the Rams' other receivers, Red Phillips and Carroll Dale, who are also better blockers, (5) Jon Arnett is available in an emergency, and (6) the Giants have offered you, in exchange for Shofner, a first draft choice.

The background: NFL teams must trim inflexibly each year to thirty-six players. My name is Waterfield, it's up to me, and what do I do? I go home to think it over, and there's Jane Russell.

II

In the age of color television, wide-screen movies, and the instant Kodak, it came as a shock the other day to learn that Sandy Koufax — after losing his touch as a pitcher this spring — had regained it only upon coming across some old magazine pictures of himself, presumably at the dentist's.

The pictures told Koufax that his slump last month was due to a slight flaw of technique. Considering the plight of the Dodgers at this time, even with Sandy back in business, it is a bit frightening to reflect that club President Walter O'Malley rested his pennant challenge this season on the even-money proposition that Sandy's dentist would be the stodgy type pushing sports magazines instead of Playboy.

The fact is that baseball is among the least advanced of modern sciences. It may be the only twentieth-century activity still operating with nineteenth-century customs in America — outside of Congress.

At a time when every NFL coach is photographing every move that every football player makes from the Fourth of July to Christmas, baseball's leaders are still denying the existence of the motion picture camera. The enormity of this oversight can be measured against the fact that most slumps involving pitchers or hitters are due to small lapses from form, to what Koufax calls flaws. They are sometimes visible to the naked eye — but the camera never misses.

Koufax, it's true, might still prefer to look at magazine pictures of Koufax. But there is really more to see in Playboy.

III

The day of July 15, 1932, was like all the days of summer three decades ago in South Dakota: dry, dusty, windy, cloudless, 105 at noon and hotter presently. I happen to be sure of that because I spent it on the road, hitch-hiking to the eastern border of the state for a night of music at a dance hall in Browns Valley, Minnesota.

Perched on the shores of Big Stone Lake, Browns Valley was then the only stop between Minneapolis and Denver for the name bands of music's greatest era — the big-band era — and the attraction that week, at the early dawn of the era, was Ben Bernie. For those of us who were old enough at last to hitch-hike out of South Dakota, Bernie's was the first name band we ever heard in a ballroom.

In the marvelous summers of the 1930s on Big Stone Lake, they all played Browns Valley: Duke Ellington, Benny Goodman, Artie Shaw, all of them, even Guy Lombardo — and I bring the matter up today for a rather special reason. As of tomorrow night, when Count Basie plays Disneyland, it will be thirty-two years that I've been tooling around to hear the big bands. On a night off, with one's druthers, who'd do anything else?

3. Times Football Column

LATER, AT the Times, I continued with three-subject columns on pro football. We had a little more space then, and I took it. This was written in the week of a Los Angeles Super Bowl.

LOS ANGELES: Jan. 26, 1993.

The degree of Super Bowl hype this week is coming as a surprise to some in the Los Angeles area. The NFL's traveling show didn't seem so all-encompassing when it passed through here six years ago. How did the Super Bowl get so big? What makes it the biggest event in the country? Some possible answers:

• This is a one-game event. By contrast, baseball has a long World Series, and basketball has a sequence of series and tournaments.

• The Super Bowl is the championship game of a contact sport. A twenty-game winner pitching to a .300 hitter can be absorbing on a certain level. Watching Defensive End Bruce Smith go after Quarterback Troy Aikman is something else. Will he get him? Will Aikman get up?

• The Super Bowl is played the same week every year. A heavyweight championship fight can be bigger than the Super Bowl — but it might be staged in June or November, and a big one might not happen at all for several years. There's a curious, stimulating rhythm to the annual Super Bowl hype that is lacking for big fights.

• Most significantly, the Super Bowl climaxes a half year of regular-season pro football. All fall, NFL games are followed closely not only in NFL markets but elsewhere in the fifty states. Pro football's in-season national attention is missing in other sports. There is no longer even a network game of the week in baseball.

Year-round in baseball, basketball and hockey, stadium crowds for regular-season games are large almost everywhere these days, indicating significant local interest. But in these sports — all but football — the nation as a whole normally snaps to attention only for the playoffs.

Week in and out during pro football's regular season, there is a national focus on the results and on the various races leading toward the Super Bowl. TV ratings are high on Sundays and sky high on Mondays. "The Super Bowl is like the last chapter of a hair-raising mystery," former Commissioner Pete Rozelle said.

Strangely, it doesn't seem to matter that the earlier chapters are usually better.

II

As another Super Bowl game approaches, two Raider records are in danger:

• Al Davis' team was the last to beat an NFC champion in the Super Bowl. That was nine long years ago.

• The 1980 Raiders, who won as a wild-card entry, are the only wild-card team that ever did.

If Dallas is upset by Buffalo Sunday — by the first wild-card group to make it to the Super Bowl since the Raider people — the Bills will usurp the Raiders in one distinction and tie them in the other.

The Bills, however, are not likely to match the Raiders in performance. In their most recent three Super Bowl starts, Davis' hands dominated Minnesota, 32-14; Philadelphia, 27-10, and Washington, 38-9. Davis has ruined more Super Bowls than the NFL's other owners put together. At halftime, the Raiders were walloping their last three Super Bowl opponents by a combined score of 51-6.

III

Speaking of domination, a Dallas victory Sunday would extend the NFC's winning streak to nine straight over the AFC, which has lost ten of the last eleven. The twenty-six-year series, throughout, has tended to be that one-sided — but it wasn't always the AFC on the bottom.

For fifteen years, the AFC — known part of the time as the AFL —

was the dominant league. Even during the Super Bowl's first two seasons, the AFL, top to bottom, was probably better than the NFL. The Green Bay Packers' two-year sweep in games I and II falsely implied NFL superiority. The Packers won principally because of the personal leadership of Vince Lombardi, who was off by himself as a football coach.

But AFL-AFC teams won eleven of the next thirteen. And as AFL quarterback Joe Namath said at the time, they earned it. Namath wasn't taking any risks with his game III guarantee. He was simply the first to recognize a fact.

It was innovative coaching that pushed the AFL in front of the NFL — ahead of everyone but Lombardi — in the late 1960s. Sid Gillman ran a spectacular air attack in San Diego, Hank Stram a moving pocket in Kansas City, Al Davis a bomb-happy offense and an in-your-face bump-and-run defense. On the Jets, with scant coaching, Namath led a brash offense from the line of scrimmage. At that time, by contrast, most NFL organizations were hidebound, self-satisfied, and lazy. Dallas was the only NFC team that could break the AFL-AFC monopoly between the late '60s and early '80s — and that was no coincidence. The Cowboys, as led by Tom Landry in the '70s, had the NFC's only innovative coach.

By 1980 there were others. And, shortly, the NFC drove ahead with leadership that was generally more imaginative than the AFC's. As creatively coached by Bill Walsh and Joe Gibbs — and, in the playoffs at least, by Bill Parcells — the San Francisco 49ers, Washington Redskins and New York Giants made the NFC the dominant conference. And so it has remained for a dozen years.

NFC teams have had the same edge since 1981 that the AFC had before 1981 — and for the same reason. It's a myth that football is a game of cycles. It is a game of innovation.

SECTION TWO: *Fragments*

1. Dodgers Didn't Blow It

THE FOLLOWING selections were written in the last thirty-five years within the three-subject format at different times for different papers.

LOS ANGELES: Sept. 29, 1961.

The most neglected baseball fact is that the top clubs only win about six games out of ten. The bottom clubs win about four out of ten. We mention this today in an effort to scuttle the notion that the Dodgers somehow blew the 1961 pennant. They didn't. They played well enough this year to win.

They're second now because, for the second year in a row, another fine team played slightly over its head, like the Dodgers of 1959, as a matter of fact. And in baseball that does it.

Although Cincinnati finished eighteen games ahead of Pittsburgh this year, it isn't eighteen games better. Nor was Pittsburgh twenty-five games better than Cincinnati last season. The 1960 Bucs used up two years of luck pulling out the close ones. So did the 1961 Reds. This isn't the same as saying the Bucs and Reds were lucky. The whole point is that their fortune came in bunches.

As for the 1961 Dodgers, General Manager Buzzie Bavasi says he "brought on our collapse," failing to uncover the right right-handed hitter. Others blame (a) platoons; (b) the ten-game losing streak; (c) one error in Ohio.

But these explanations would be neither pertinent nor necessary nor voiced if Cincinnati had played its normal game this year. Speaking as one fan, I enjoyed watching the Dodgers win their six out of ten in 1961 and I'll expect the same in 1962. That's par in the National League. Nobody else, including Cincinnati, does much better.

2. Why Sit Out in the Cold?

LOS ANGELES: Dec. 22, 1964.

There are three reasons why the NFL ought to make sure that Sunday's championship football game in Cleveland is the last ever played north of Mason and Dixon. First, logic demands a neutral field for an event of this importance. Second, sanity dictates something better than Arctic weather and frozen ground. And third, the isolated camera has rendered live audiences obsolete on a cold day. Everybody elsewhere will have a better view of the action than anybody in Cleveland.

CBS, which has paid a record $1.8 million for the program, can be expected to focus four or five isolated cameras on the principals at the beginning of each play. And inasmuch as the I.C. has now become a football-coverage integral, the NFL at last has a choice gimmick to force its annual championship match out of the laps of the season-ticket holders in the northern cities.

As you know, the game is scheduled on icebergs each December solely because of the club owners' desire to please the local patronage. This was understandable in the days when the players paid for their own uniforms and passed a hat at halftime, but pro football has outgrown its rustic beginnings, and the championship game now belongs to the country.

In a sport in which the hometown advantage is impressive, the final round should be scheduled in a neutral warm-weather setting. Television's numerous cameras can now be relied upon to keep most of the home folks happy.

3. Cousin Larry Wins and Wins

MY WIFE'S side of the family, being Irish, isn't as illustrious as ours, of course, but in time it developed a Southern League basketball coach, Larry Hanson. During a distinguished career in South Central Los Angeles high school sports, Hanson became the biggest winner in any sport in the city's history. As a winner he's worth part of a column, I told my editors in that more informal newspaper age, though, frankly I wouldn't have covered either basketball or high school if it weren't for the family connection.

LOS ANGELES: Jan. 28, 1965.

Cousin Larry won another title the other day. You probably saw the headline: "Jefferson High School Wins Again." Across twenty years of basketball, that has happened regularly at Jefferson, whose general, Larry Hanson, has never finished worse than second in any league in thirty-two seasons of coaching.

Remarkably, under Hanson, Jeff has won 92.8 per cent of the basketball games it has played in those twenty years. Although Los Angeles is loaded with high schools, some forty-five of them, Hanson won the city title Tuesday for the fourth time.

Afterward, his friends agreed that this is a coach with only one fault. He makes a lousy picture. And so if you see a family resemblance between the man in the corner and your friendly correspondent, it is merely a shattering coincidence. For one thing, Larry is much older than I. Second, he is my wife's cousin, not mine. And to put all the cards on the table, Cousin Larry doesn't look like her, either.

But the Collins family of South Dakota, which produced them both, was and is one of the fine old families back there. Their grandfather, E.E. Collins, was South Dakota's first superintendent of public instruction, and his sons were all educators. Thus, it was ordained that Larry enroll at the University of South Dakota, where in his spare time he was a pole vaulter. And on a day that will forever live in infamy at Yankton College, Larry beat our man with a vault of 13-10. Before scoffing at 13-10, consider that the world record at the time was 14 1-2. Worse yet, 13-10 is still the USD-Yankton meet record.

The Collins heritage is most visible in Hanson's contributions as an innovator. He was the first in basketball to use the full-court press — a winning idea that has spread to UCLA and elsewhere. And long before there was a hand-raising rule, his players were the first in the nation to lift their arms automatically and smile at the referee when charged with a foul. There is still no smiling rule in basketball — except at Jeff. "Show me your teeth," Cousin Larry shouts. "Make like you enjoy it."

He is also the inventor of an imaginative set of training rules. Unlike other coaches, Hanson posts no curfews, and bans no vices. "You can't do *anything* bad and play winning basketball," he says, "and that's all I have to tell a Jefferson player."

Listening closely, his teams, in the last twenty years, have won eight city championships, four A and four B, and thirty-five of a possible forty Southern League titles. So in South Dakota's Hanson County, they're as proud of Larry as ever. The county was named for his other grandfather. He won it, possibly, in a poker game with a Collins.

4. Those Super Bowl Blowouts

LOS ANGELES; Jan. 24, 1987.

Most Super Bowl games of recent vintage have been alike in one respect. They've figured close and ended as blowouts. Going in, the point spread is three or four points. Coming out, the score is 27-10 or 38-16.

This is an unlikely phenomenon. The National Football League's two conference champions should be a better match, at least some of the time. Why aren't they? Two possible explanations:

• This is a passing era, in contrast with the early days of NFL title games. When a good passing team gets on a roll, it can score a lot of points quickly. In former days, good running teams sometimes dominated good defenses, but they couldn't often roll up a bunch of points.

• Psychologically, the growing importance of the Super Bowl is beginning to work on the players' minds. When one side sees its life's goal slipping away in a public place, before millions, the disappointment and humiliation drain it of energy.

At the same time, stirred by the nearness of an NFL championship that might have seemed remote not long ago, the winning side gains confidence, energy and a sense of irreversible momentum.

Result? Blowout.

SECTION THREE: The Essay

1. Identity Conflict: Reeves and Allen

BREAKING NEWS occasionally calls for an extended commentary, up to 1,500 words sometimes, to get at the complexities of an issue like the George Allen-Dan Reeves conflict in Los Angeles. On Christmas Day, 1968, Ram Owner Reeves shocked the city when he fired his coach, Allen, after three winning years — which had followed seven losing years. For the reasons mentioned below, among others, Allen was consistently controversial. But in a city that had just got used to winning, and liked it, Reeves' action seemed extraordinarily high-handed, stirring his players to open revolt. The situation was without precedent until, a quarter century later, Dallas Owner Jimmy Jones fired a Super Bowl winner. There were good reasons for Reeves and Allen to get back together, which they did a few days after this commentary.

LOS ANGELES: Jan. 5, 1969.

On a weekend when the Rams and their coach are discussing a reconciliation, it can be seen that they were never actually the principals in a fight or feud in the common definitions of these words. Rather, as between the owner, Daniel F. Reeves, and the man he hired in 1966 as his football coach, George Allen, it is likely that there has been an identity conflict.

Quite unintentionally, Allen has been destroying what Reeves built — and therefore what Reeves is. The background for this supposition is in three parts.

I

Like most men, Reeves defines himself in terms of what he has done. His life has been the Rams. It was Reeves who, to begin with, launched the coast-to-coast era of major league sports when he moved the franchise west from Cleveland. It was also Reeves who originated the Ram television plan that undergirds pro football financially to this day — live home TV of all road games.

Most significantly, it was Reeves who developed both the theory of the modern draft and a large organization of scouts to implement the theory. Few other teams have drafted as well.

Today he identifies with these triumphs, and with his lifestyle through all these years. Win or lose, he is only content when participating, and he has been a successful participator.

II

If Reeves' life is the Rams, Allen's is winning. Though he happens to be a football coach, he was born and exists to beat other men on whatever battlefield. And he pursues this goal with a rare singlemindedness that is often mistakenly interpreted as ruthlessness.

Few other football teams — and no prior Ram teams in the era with which Reeves has been long identified — have been led by a more determined one-purpose coach. He is virtually incapable of any thought pattern disassociated from winning football games. His trademark is the 110 per cent effort, and this, almost literally, is George Allen.

It is chance that he happens to be coaching in Los Angeles for Dan Reeves. It is also a most fortunate break for Los Angeles fans and football players. They may perceive only dimly all the machinery, but they fully understand that with Allen, they have a winner. They have risen to his support in unprecedented numbers because winning is the natural way of Western Civilization and because they correctly understand that if they lose this man who wins, they will lose, too.

Now, the essential means by which Allen built a winning team here are not only new to Reeves but new to football. He did it first by building a wall between his players, his assistants and himself, on the one hand, and the rest of the world — including the Ram organization itself. Second, he did it by constructing an intensely personal relationship with each of his forty players. He has sought to convert each of them into a personal friend in defiance of the theories of football and war, and in this effort he has been enormously successful, as his record shows — 11-1-2 in 1967 and 10-3-1 in 1968, the second time with a crippled team.

The rule of thumb is that coaching is at least fifty per cent in the winning of football games. It has been far more than that in Los Angeles. As the players themselves comprehend, Ram personnel is hardly of a quality to dominate the league, particularly in the injury year of 1968.

III

Allen's coaching style — cheerleading forty players individually — took up to eighteen hours of his time on many days of the year. Thus the third part of the background story is that Allen seldom had another hour for Reeves. He did not deliberately affront the owner. What coach ever expected to be working for an owner who wouldn't be happy winning? Because winning is Allen's life, he only thought of Reeves in one of two ways: as a means to get something he wanted — possibly a new training camp site — that would make winning more certain, or as an obstacle to be hurdled to get what he wanted, for the same reason.

So in their first three years, neither man was really capable of dealing with the other, given their two strong and separate identities. When Allen, for example, in pleading for a new practice field, described the old quarters as "the facility of a last-place club," it never crossed his mind that he was attacking Reeves personally.

More centrally, Allen's singleminded drive to win prevented him from seeing that when he scorned draft choices, and built his team by trading for veterans, he was breaking one of Reeves' legs.

Reeves only revealed himself to Allen when he said he had more fun losing with former Coach Harland Svare than winning with Allen. There were times when Svare fielded ten or twelve rookie draft choices — Reeves' draft choices. But Allen has been winning with age rather than youth, often by trading *away* players drafted by Reeves.

Over the years, unlike almost all other owners, Reeves has shown the wisdom to grant most of the requests made by any Ram head coach. He usually yielded to Allen in the end. But it is also Reeves' nature to think through new ideas. Customarily, he first balked at Allen's new ideas — and in balking, he reinforced Allen's image of Reeves as the leader of an incompetent front office.

Thus the identity conflict has seemed total:

• The thought that a football owner *is* the front office cannot be held in the head of a coach whose only thought is winning.

• The thought that Allen is "really winning for Reeves" can't be held by an owner who sees the coach rejecting — destroying — everything he has built. As Reeves believed, it wasn't Reeves' team that was winning, it was Allen's.

There has lately been some evidence that both men are beginning to view their problems with more clarity. They have hurt each other badly, but pain, at least, is communication, and they never really communicated before. From the wreckage they may gain mutually in recognizing each other as persons.

2. Rich Players Help Rich Owners Win

THE NFL's club owners won a lopsided victory over the NFL Players Association in 1987, when the selfishness of a few veterans — combined with the great wealth and intractability of the owners — beat down the union majority. In the 1990s, the players, led by Gene Upshaw, finally won; but they could have succeeded in 1987 by sticking together.

LOS ANGELES: Oct. 16, 1987.

The last time the players, fifteen hundred of them, struck against the National Football League's twenty-eight ownerships, Ed Garvey was their leader. That was five years ago. And when that fuss was over, Garvey, who later resigned to enter politics in Wisconsin, was asked for his assessment. "Never bet against the richest men in a fight," he said.

In pro football again this week, with the apparent end of another strike, that is a representative aphorism.

So is another that has doubtless occurred to many player representatives — among them Lineman Dave Puzzuoli of the Cleveland Browns. "With friends like these, who needs enemies?" Puzzuoli asked.

He was talking about the union members who have crossed picket lines in recent days to play footsie with non-union teams — respected members such as Defensive End Howie Long of the Raiders, who mentioned a responsibility to his family. "I guess this is an association of bachelors," Garvey, a satirist, said a few years ago when another ex-striker entered the same plea. "I guess nobody else has a wife or family."

The unwillingness of such influential players as Long and Dallas' Danny White to hang tight was the undoing of the union. The strike failed for one overriding reason: The very rich owners had more courage and solidarity than the merely rich players. The union's lack of solidarity was fatal.

II

This was a strike that most NFL ownerships could have financed for years; and it was their great wealth that gave these people their sense of fraternity and solidarity. They are one of the wealthiest groups in the country.

Seven NFL owners are on Forbes magazine's 1987 list of America's richest individuals, and the top three have a net worth averaging more than $1 billion each. They are Jack Kent Cooke of the Washington Redskins, W.C. Ford of the Detroit Lions, and Edward J. DeBartolo, who has installed his son, E.J. Jr., as president of the San Francisco 49ers.

Other prominent NFL owners and their net worth as estimated by Forbes editors: Leon Hess, New York Jets, $625 million; H.R. (Bum) Bright, Dallas Cowboys, $600 million; Alex Spanos, San Diego Chargers, $500 million; Hugh Culverhouse, Tampa Bay Buccaneers, $250 million.

Several other pro football owners — the Kansas City Chiefs' Lamar Hunt among them — were on the Forbes list last year and are believed to be in the $200 million category again, although Forbes imposed a limit this year of $230 million.

There must be a few NFL rookies who will eventually ask themselves: "You mean we were fighting *that*?"

III

It is the club owners who invariably set the NFL's goals, and their goal in this dispute was to cripple the union by breaking the strike. They weren't trying to break the union. For they must have the approval of the players to maintain their illegal devices — the NFL waiver system, for instance, and the annual draft, which various federal courts have held to be unconstitutional unless mandated by collective bargaining.

So how do you break a strike without breaking the union? The owners chose a simple means:

• Stonewall the issues. Don't bargain on anything important.

• Divide and conquer. That is, play the regular-season schedule with strikebreakers — and count each game in the Super Bowl races — thereby pressuring the players to cross the picket lines one by one, two by two, four by four.

It was the most divisive policy the NFL has adopted in the sixty-eight-year history of the league — probably the most divisive ever initiated by any league. And with extraordinary consistency — with a sense of solidarity that was surprising even for this group — the owners stuck to their guns until the end. In the language of football, they poured it on.

3. The Year With No World Series

THIS WAS a Times baseball assignment in 1994, when, by late summer, there had been more than enough games for the owners of the clubs, who canceled the rest of the season. Their mindless reaction to the possibility of a player strike — in some unknown future — reminded me of a sign I once saw during Super Bowl week in Florida. The sign, which went up at sundown on the beach behind my Miami Beach hotel, read: "The Ocean is Closed."

LOS ANGELES: Oct. 22, 1994.

For millions of us, this is a special time. This is World Series time. *Show* time. If the club owners hadn't killed it during an argument with their players, another show would have opened today, unless it rained, or the earth moved. It's been like that for years. Every October from one decade to the next, the World Series has been a hit attraction even in

America's small towns — where in the 1920s, far from any ballpark, the defining structure was often a giant World Series scoreboard. The inning scores were about a foot high.

If you were watching, you saw it in Ken Burns' recent baseball documentary. As an awestruck schoolboy, I saw it in Aberdeen, South Dakota, where our scoreboard stood in front of the granite-faced building at Lincoln and Fourth that was home to the Aberdeen Morning American, my future employer.

That was before television. It was before *radio*. So in South Dakota, *our* reporters kept score. The sports editor of the American, monitoring the telegraphed play-by-play report, worked smoothly with the scoreboard operator. And every half inning, there it was: another zero, or maybe a one, a two, or a three. A man with a megaphone told us about the home runs. Invariably, the intersection in front of the newspaper office was alive with baseball fans, many of them in from the farm, or off the train from Ipswich, and the roar of the little crowd as the numbers went up was a distant echo of the thunder at Yankee Stadium or Sportsman's Park.

II

By the 1950s, the downtown scoreboards were gone, radio was going, and live pictures of the action in Brooklyn or the Bronx were actually coming into my new house in Los Angeles. That was the era of daytime, weekday World Series television. Every day was like an NFL Sunday now. And for students, preachers, writers and others with their own working hours, it was the best era yet. On my street in the Baldwin Hills, after my friends left for work, I entertained their wives. And one day in the third inning, Jane Gaynor, a New York Yankees fan from across the street, predicted that her pitcher was on his way to a no-hitter. My wife, a Brooklyn Dodgers fan, said you can't no-hit a World Series team — especially the Dodgers. But that day, as Gaynor ran screaming out the door, Don Larsen did.

It was three years later that the show came to California for the first time. The memory that lingers of that bright, sunny day in 1959 is simply being in a World Series dugout *in Los Angeles* before the game. Later that afternoon, I talked with Dodger fan Mary Heaton Dowling and some of the ninety-three thousand other spectators in a dozen sections of the Coliseum, which, we all concluded, was the best baseball park ever built. And because of its unique features — among them the fascinating left-field screen and so many thousands of unobstructed view seats — I still think it is. Dodger Owner Walter O'Malley, the brightest man I've known in sports, once told me that he felt compelled to build a perfect Dodger Stadium to avoid comparisons with the Coliseum.

The light-hitting Dodgers survived an 11-0 blowout in the first game and won the 1959 Series from the Chicago White Sox in six games. But O'Malley didn't seem to enjoy it much. He didn't respect the opponent. He knew the Dodgers had lucked into the championship in a rare down year for the Yankees, who in that era won ten pennants in twelve seasons for Manager Casey Stengel.

III

Memories breed comparisons. From the '20s to the '90s, during the World Series of my time,

• Stengel was the most effective manager. The man who brought football's platoon system to baseball once used a record seven pitchers in one game — and won that Series, too. Turning seventy the year he won his last pennant, Stengel said most people his age were dead.

• The two most overpowering plays were by Outfielders Willie Mays and Kirk Gibson. An over-the-shoulder catch by Mays in deep center — reminding Ram fans of Elroy (Crazy Legs) Hirsch's over-the-shoulder Coliseum catches — won the 1954 World Series for the New York Giants in the *first* game, demoralizing the Cleveland Indians, who had won a record 111 regular-season games. In 1988, Gibson's ninth-inning pinch home run — in the only at-bat he was physically able to make in that Series — also won the championship for the Dodgers in the first game, demoralizing the Oakland A's.

• My achievement award winner is Reggie Jackson of the Yankees, who in 1977 hit four World Series home runs on four consecutive swings. He started with one home run one day and hit three more the next. No other hitter, not even Ruth, ever got in a comparable groove. Jackson's streak might have been the hottest in sports history.

• It was about that time that I first heard the best of the World Series stories, the one about the two old pitchers who gravely discussed the future one afternoon while seated side by side in the bullpen. "Do you think they play baseball in heaven?" Lefty asked.

"I hope so," said Rip, who tragically died later in an automobile accident, but got in touch with Lefty again as soon as he could.

"Well, *do* they play baseball up there?" Lefty demanded.

"I'll give you the good news first," Rip said. "Yes, they play baseball in heaven. The bad news is, you're pitching Sunday."

COMMENT

SECTION FOUR: The Long Long Commentary

1. Michael Jordan: Why Go Out on Top?

THE NEXT commentaries contrast strikingly with the three-subject columns I favor when the assignment is two or three 750-word columns a week. In the early 1990s, my principal Times assignment was a once-a-month 2,000-word commentary. The subject of one piece in 1994 was Michael Jordan, who had just then retired from basketball. After unretiring, Jordan eventually helped the 1995-96 Chicago Bulls win their fourth NBA title, whereupon he said: "I'm sorry I left for eighteen months, but I sure am glad I came back." All that was highly predictable. In fact, it was predicted in the following commentary.

LOS ANGELES: Nov. 7, 1994.

A wealthy football player, Joe Montana, thirty-seven, says he wants to play forever, through any number of injuries. He has never considered retirement. Neither has Marcus Allen, who, going on thirty-five, is another wealthy football player on his way to the Hall of Fame. Nolan Ryan, forty-six, a wealthy baseball player, appeared to be immortal until a shoulder blew out in Seattle last September, and, at last, he had to give up.

It was his competitive fire that kept Ryan going into his mid-forties, and the same fire burns in Montana and Allen. So what's happened to Michael Jordan? As gifted as the others, as competitive, as wealthy, and strikingly younger, Jordan, thirty, made the mistake of his life when he decided last month to quit pro basketball.

He'll regret it.

And he'll be back.

But he'll pay for it.

A layoff of even one season takes a year out of the best life that any athlete will ever know — a year of more gratification than anybody else can expect doing anything else.

"When you're on a winning team with congenial teammates, it's a great way to live," a former NBA star, New Jersey Senator Bill Bradley, told me one day in his Washington office. Though he had long dreamed of a political career, Bradley said, "As a player, the way I looked at premature retirement was: Why stop doing something you love?"

Jordan is doing just that. And he's going to miss the life of a ballplayer. He may not know it yet, but he will.

Nolan Ryan missed nothing. Along with Willie Mays, Johnny Unitas and the others who played all the way to the end, Ryan tasted the last drop. He won the last game that was in him. He got the last thrill — not the next to last, not the fiftieth from last, but the last.

That is the way to go. The time to retire is when they throw you out.

II

The more popular way to retire is mentioned repeatedly on the talk shows, where most fans and commentators advise going out on top. They are right only when they mean fighters, who, to protect their brain cells, should all retire at twenty-eight, if not twenty-three. Unhappily, most fans mean other athletes as well. "I wish Willie Mays had let me remember him as he was at the top of his career," a characteristic caller said recently. "I hate remembering him as he was at the end, a broken-down old ballplayer."

Distressed by Mays' kind of decline, reporters as well as fans continue to applaud aging athletes who, overvaluing image and pride, needlessly steal away early into the night. Thus, they're still enthusiastic about the departure of Ted Williams, the only .400 hitter of the last sixty-nine years, who at forty-two hit a home run one September afternoon in 1960 and immediately retired. "Ted would never let himself be remembered as an old ballplayer who hung around after his time," said a close friend, Bud Leavit.

So Williams never came back. In a sense, he was anticipating Jordan, who reportedly said the other day, "My pride wouldn't let me come back." Pride, in this context, means worrying about what other people think. And, sadly, it ended Williams' career prematurely. He hit twenty-nine home runs that last year, when he batted .316.

As a rule of thumb, any old big leaguer who can hit .316 should plan to hang around at least until he can no longer hit, say, .265. Instead, Williams, for no good reason, missed out on the pleasure of walloping nobody will ever know how many more home runs.

III

It seems obvious that the many who are counseling Jordan not to come back are insufficiently informed. They see only the athlete in the arena. They can't fathom the whole life of the man: his good-humored interaction with the guys on the team; the delight that wells up with each point or run scored or set up or denied; the inexpressible joy of simply putting on the uniform; the excitement of the major league lifestyle. "If I could still play the game, I'd still be playing," said former NFL star Hugh McElhenny, who retired thirty years ago at thirty-five when "my legs gave out."

McElhenny and other great athletes who have stayed on to the bitter end — Ryan, Mays, Unitas and Warren Spahn, most noticeably, but also Babe Ruth, Kareem Abdul-Jabbar, Jimmy Connors, Elgin Baylor and

Steve Carlton — all discerned two simple truths about professional sports in twentieth century America:

• For an adult with the requisite skill, life in the big leagues beats whatever is second best — a life of fishing or golf, gardening, travel, playing cards, playing the horses, a businessman's lifestyle, you name it — as most former athletes discover sooner or later.

• In their fifties or sixties, most of them, if they had a choice, would instantly return to the playing fields of their youth. The decision to choose between retirement and playing competitively can be made only at an age when both options are available.

Why go out before you have to?

IV

No fan can know what a blow it is to break away from the supercharged life of the professional athlete.

Willie Mays knows. Fading at forty-two, out of a job but still hopeful, Mays said, "All I ever wanted was to play baseball forever."

Warren Spahn knows. To get rid of Spahn a quarter century ago, they had to kick him out of the majors at age forty-four after an extraordinary twenty-one-year pitching career in which he had been a twenty-game winner thirteen times. And even then, Spahn wouldn't retire. He was forty-seven when he finally pitched his last game, after three more seasons — all in the minor leagues. At forty-eight, he learned the worst: Nobody would hire him. "I loved the life of a ballplayer," he said. "The only thing I've ever regretted was the end of the baseball season — any season."

It all seems different to other people — to those watching veteran athletes from the grandstand and press box or on TV. "Fans want stars to retire on top in part to protect their fantasies," Bradley said. Spahn said: "You feel like the whole world is pressuring you to quit. My attitude was: 'Drop dead, this is my life.' But it's hard to resist."

In "Life on the Run," his thoughtful basketball book, Bradley notes that many stars are "naively vulnerable to the quixotic tastes of strangers." Billie Jean King, queen of Wimbledon for so many years, was bowing to such quixotic preferences, she acknowledges, when she retired at thirty-one after winning there in 1975. "I could still have won Wimbledon (in 1976)," she said. "I made a mistake when I quit. I was listening to others, trying to make them happy, instead of myself."

Recognizing her mistake in time, King came back to win competitively until she was forty — showing the way, it could be, to Michael Jordan.

"Every person should listen to herself or himself and nobody else," she said. "It's only a myth that champions have to go out on top. That's just other people trying to make up your mind for you."

Steve Carlton, the four-time Cy Young Award winner who hung on to the last, asked the right question: "Who cares what other people think?"

V

As a pro athlete, Jordan, in almost every sense, is a special case. His talent is spectacular. His understanding of the game is remarkable. And quickness has been his defining characteristic. At his peak, he was the quickest athlete I've ever seen.

In the playoffs last spring, though, he was plainly a bit past his peak. He was plainly adjusting to a new style. He was going more often to his turnaround jump shot, having found, obviously, that it was no longer possible to drive to the basket any time he wanted to, in the style he preferred as a young man. Elgin Baylor, Julius Erving and other aging drivers had previously made the same transition to jumpers, but Jordan last spring, with his superior talent, seemed to be making it more effectively, throwing more strikes.

The smoothness of Jordan's transition did not, however, conceal the reality that the world's greatest basketball player was slowing down. Some predicted that he might soon be second- or third-best in the world. But is that any reason to retire at thirty? "I don't think so," King said. "The fifth- or eighth- or tenth-best brain surgeon in the world wouldn't quit."

Bradley, the Rhodes Scholar who went to the Senate from the New York Knicks, contends that a ballplayer has a full career only when he feels how it is to go all the way up and all the way down. In "Life on the Run," Bradley, a starter on two NBA champions, writes, "The decline (of an athlete) is sad but human. To miss it makes a pro's experience incomplete." To miss it, voluntarily, is running away.

VI

Ryan's major league career lasted eighteen years *longer* than that of Jordan, who in time is likely to see that his retirement reasoning wasn't at all logical:

• If Jordan retired "to get back to a normal life," as he said last month, he will soon discover that he should have stayed in the NBA. He will never have a normal life, whatever that is. He will be a celebrity the rest of his days, as NFL Hall of Famer Joe Namath could tell him. "I still walk around in disguise sometimes," Namath said, laughing about it — twenty-five years after Super Bowl III. Jordan's fame, unluckily for him, will last well into the twenty-first century, when, like other burning-out meteors, he will be famous simply for being famous. Those longing for a normal life should avoid the temptation to become the world's best basketball player.

• If Jordan retired, as he said, "to spend some time with my family," he will discover that he could have accomplished that by staying in the NBA and cutting down somewhat on golf and other hobbies.

• If the tragic loss of his father was a factor in his retirement, as he has indicated, Jordan will have the sympathy of all well-meaning people as he takes on a serious problem: contending with grief during his sudden idleness. "Most doctors recommend keeping busy if there is a deep well of grief," said Bruce Ogilvie, the San Jose sports psychologist.

One danger for a rootless, aimless Jordan in the wake of two shocks — his father's death and his abrupt departure from the thrills of pro basketball — is substituting gambling activities for the fast life of the NBA. "I have no knowledge of Jordan's tendencies, if any, toward compulsive gambling," Ogilvie said. "But in his present circumstances, if the tendencies are there, they raise a whole range of worries."

VII

Jordan last month said also: "I've reached the pinnacle. I don't have anything else to prove." But in this, he was simply wrong. As a basketball player, he still has a great deal to prove. Count the ways:

• At his age, Jordan can't possibly have reaped his allotted quota of honors and records. To take a football parallel, Jim Brown, who retired at twenty-nine, must fight off challenges from supporters of O.J. Simpson, Gale Sayers, Hugh McElhenny and others that he was the greatest running back of all time. Had Brown stuck it out for a few more seasons, his record yardage total, which Walter Payton ultimately surpassed, would have been beyond anyone's reach. Ever. In basketball, with Jordan on the sideline, his reputation as number one doesn't figure to survive the present decade in a sport that creates new stars every year.

• Jordan hasn't yet proved, even to himself, that he loves the game of basketball — as distinct from enjoying his status as the world's best basketball player. Only by continuing in the NBA from year to year with diminishing skills — and by experiencing a progressive decline to pure outside shooter, then perhaps playmaker, and finally even non-starting captain — could he learn what all other basketball players, on every level, already know: It's the most enjoyable of all team games even for those who don't dominate it. Basketball indeed is more enjoyable than golf — for a young man. The transition to a different kind of player would be salutatory, helping Jordan focus not on taking pride in his greatness but on taking pleasure in the rich everyday experiences of life in basketball.

• Jordan has yet to prove how much basketball wisdom he has. By retiring now, before his skills have eroded far, he is missing the satisfaction of becoming at least as valuable for what he knows as what he does. Not too long ago, an aging Wilt Chamberlain went down that road to a new life. Once the NBA's leading scorer, Chamberlain became a defensive standout. And in his mid-thirties, though he retired a year or two too soon, he was proudly fighting to lead the league in assists.

• It is incorrect for Jordan to reason that he can do no more than repeat himself after playing on three NBA champions. He has yet to prove that as he ages and matures, he can be an important championship force as an elder statesman. The fact is, the "pinnacle" he talks about is really no more than a steppingstone. For, in a nurturing role in his mid-thirties, letting go of his ego involvement in personal conquests, Jordan would find that it can be equally fulfilling to live in the sunshine of others' success — provided he has played a vital part in that success. In short, Scottie Pippen and young Toni Kukoc need him.

Best of all, while aging gracefully on an NBA team, Jordan could continue as a participant in the great drama of major league sports. He could extend one of the world's most desirable lifestyles two to ten more years. Such was the intuitive understanding of Warren Spahn, Willie Mays and Nolan Ryan. Such is the perception of Joe Montana and Marcus Allen and Ronnie Lott. Such could be the realization of Jordan if, shortly, he sees that playing basketball beats taking pride in having played basketball.

Of what real value, it might be asked, is pride?

Who cares what other people think?

POSTSCRIPT: Two Ways to Retire

"Needlessly premature" is my description for those who retire voluntarily when still in demand for their skills as an athlete. In the following parallel columns are the names of some of the stars who, in my view, departed either too soon or after a considerably more fulfilling career:

Needlessly Premature	*Much More Fulfilling*
Michael Jordan: 30	Nolan Ryan: 46
Jim Brown: 29	John Unitas: 41
Ted Williams: 42	Willie Mays: 42
Sandy Koufax: 30	Warren Spahn: 47
Bjorn Borg: 26	Jimmy Connors: 40
Billie Jean King: 31	Billie Jean King: 40
Doak Walker: 28	Hugh McElhenny: 35
Magic Johnson: 32	Ben Hogan: 60
Wilt Chamberlain: 36	Steve Carlton: 43
Bill Russell: 35	Babe Ruth: 41

Although Williams and Mays left at the same age, Williams hit .316 his last season, Mays .211. The New York Yankees and others wanted Williams. An arthritic elbow led Koufax to early retirement — but as friends suggested, he could have played longer. A more serious health problem, HIV, stopped Johnson. But had he continued to play NBA ball — demonstrating, before others began to worry about it, that it could be done safely — Johnson might still be with the Lakers. Football player McElhenny was through at thirty-five, when basketball player Russell wasn't. Football player Walker, at twenty-eight, hadn't even reached his peak. King left at thirty-one, caught her error in time, and came back.

2. Hey, Coach, Sit Down

THE MOST widely reprinted of my long Times commentaries is next. Good editors all seem to know that when a newspaper commentary theme is revolutionary but credible and thought-provoking, it should be canvassed thoroughly, and sometimes at considerable length.

LOS ANGELES: Nov. 20, 1994.

Two things can be said today about the people who coach big-time basketball and football in America, college and pro alike:

• They have too much power. All coaches have more power than they need — and more than they should be allowed to keep.

• They belong in the stands. On game day, every coach should be removed from the field, or from the basketball floor, and seated in the crowd with the other spectators — far from the players.

In nearly every instance, the present role of America's football and basketball coaches is incompatible with modern trends in leadership. Most other U.S. businesses have in recent years welcomed their employees into the decision making, thereby improving production. Sports teams, by contrast, appear to be ever more autocratic. In football games, coaches increasingly intrude into the moment-by-moment action. And in basketball, coaches scream instructions even as a player is going for the basket.

Large changes are due. Overdue.

At the university level, that seems self-evident. To bring sports into line with other campus and classroom customs, college coaches should depart at game time for the duration while their players demonstrate what they learned all week in practice. The coaches wouldn't, to be sure, like that. "A (sports) team is not a democracy," Indiana basketball Coach Bob Knight has said.

But why isn't it? In a nation that has strenuously opposed kings and dictators for more than two hundred years, thousands of Americans have shown that democratic measures are more rewarding than an autocrat's. It is the American way, when you think about it, for athletes to elect their leaders, and for coaches to instruct, not rule.

On campus, there will always be an honored place for coaches: teaching athletic strategy, tactics, techniques, and two kinds of leadership procedures — how to be effective play-callers, and how to be effective captains. But on game day, a seat in the stands seems just the right place for the college coach. And for the pro coach, too, for that matter. With more democracy, the pros as well as the colleges would have a more human game, a more varied, more entertaining, more popular game.

Players Can Learn

On the campus scene today, from one school to the next, the real surprise is that so few college presidents seem to realize that football ought to be a learning experience for their students. As should basketball. It's a given at any university that activities such as debate teams and, say, school plays are for learning. Although play directors are also university employees, no school president expects to see the director up on the stage managing Juliet's big love scene with Romeo.

Yet the next day, he *does* expect to see the football coach running the school team as if it were his own personal property: ordering the players about, calling all the plays and defenses, and blaming failures on execution, which means, "I had a good idea and the players screwed it up."

College authorities apparently assume that football and basketball are without educational purpose even though, plainly, student-athletes have a lot to learn about living — about the values that matter to civilized adults — lessons they can get playing a game. For there are no born leaders. Nor was any athlete ever born knowing *when* to lead, when to follow, when to speak up, when to pipe down, how to think under stress, how to interact with teammates.

Most 1990s athletes aren't learning any of that. Standing in the huddle between plays, instead of thinking and talking together, today's football players wait like dumb animals to be led around.

The symbol of what's really wrong now with big-time sports is the NFL's radio in the helmet — the tool that finally reduces the quarterback to an automaton, even in the two-minute drill, which used to be his. Although, happily, the helmet radio hasn't yet reached the universities, they still don't see that coaches should be judged the way math profs are judged: on how well they prepare their students for periodic examinations.

In basketball, quiz time is game time. And at a learning institution, while his students are taking a test in basketball, should the coach be stomping around, waving his arms in anger, yelling at his team, insulting the referees? What do players learn from that? Such coaching excesses result from an overemphasis on winning that could be curbed by converting the autocrat in charge into an educator. Presumably, basketball crowds aren't there to see a coach rave and bluster. They've come to see a game, and so at game time the coaches should be out of there.

They've worked hard all week. They've earned a good seat in the stands.

Players Can Lead

If a college sport is construed to be an educational experience, it follows that student-athletes should be involved in game-day leadership. In fact, they once were. As a game, football was invented in the last century by players, not coaches. And for many years, the players remained in charge. Indeed, coaching by non-students in the early years was forbidden. An explicit rule punished any team that brought in a coach. The penalty: game forfeiture.

Suppose today's student-athletes were to make the game-day decisions, replacing coaches, who replaced yesterday's student-athletes. That would mean superior leadership experience on each team for two or three basketball captains at a time and a half dozen football captains. Different sets every season. Possibly every month or two.

The captains would be busy. There's a lot to do: make substitutions and adjustments, keep each player's head in the game, keep everyone's emotions right on, calm down the guys who need that, rally the team in adversity, verbalize effectively in crisis situations. Majoring and maturing in such subjects is the kind of educational experience that in some respects beats classwork.

And not long ago, American college students were into it. Even today, "The captains are the coaches at Oxford and other (European universities)," says Pat Haden, the Rhodes Scholar from USC, who, before his days as a downtown Los Angeles lawyer and Turner-NFL TV analyst, was a winning Rose Bowl quarterback. "It's a system that works well, too," says Haden, who went from USC's national champions to Oxford's blue (varsity) teams in several sports. "You elect the captain-coach. As a player, you respect the coach because you voted for him."

In America, could captains take over? Says Seattle SuperSonics Coach George Karl: "The game of basketball wouldn't suffer a lot if the coaches were (absent) on game day. If the coach does the job right during the week, there isn't much he really has to do in games." Karl was replying to a question about college coaching, but in his view much the same holds in the NBA. "The big thing in a (pro) game," he says, "is simply recognizing early on who's hot and who's not."

It isn't every captain who can do that. But, then, it isn't every coach, either.

Players Can Call Plays

Play-calling, offensive and defensive, is the other major function of sports leadership, and there's good reason to believe that most games would be more entertaining if players instead of coaches made the calls — as they did in the days of Sammy Baugh, Sid Luckman, John Unitas, Joe Namath, Terry Bradshaw and, among others, Ken Stabler and Jim Plunkett. When coaches are out of the signal-calling process, what's lost in formal organization is more than made up by player spontaneity and creativity.

Here's the difference:

• Coaches, most of them graying conservatives, call plays from a computer list. You see them reading their printouts every Sunday.

Each work week they compute the best percentage play for every situation — on every down — and then at game time, rather than think about what might be going on out on the field, they simply check the printout and make the highest-percentage call. Thus plays sent in by a coach, many of them decided upon last Tuesday, are mostly mechanical, conservative, predictable, and not responsive to sudden change — which exactly describes the Raider calls that have angered Quarterback Jeff Hostetler this year. In recent seasons, the only two NFL coaching staffs excelling as signal-callers have been those organized by Bill Walsh and Jimmy Johnson, both now out of the league.

• Players, most of them young and adventurous, make calls that tend to be more enterprising, more aggressive, and more responsive to what happened a moment ago.

Play-calling quarterbacks, focusing on the here and now, proceed on the evidence of their own eyes and the input of their teammates. Is an opponent winded, or suddenly limping? Is a defensive tackle charging too hard — asking to be trapped? Is there a previously unforeseen opportunity to do something special? Players aren't buried in the ritualized history of a computer printout. They are caught up in the action on the field. They are immersed in *today's* challenge, not last Tuesday's. What's more, their quarterback is doubtless a believer in Unitas' golden rule: "Take what the defense gives you." Quarterbacks are more inclined than any coach to pass the ball aggressively on first down, when defensive teams, both pro and college, nearly always play the run.

Divergent motives make much of the difference:

Coaches, whose concern is not to lose, think about interceptions.

Quarterbacks, whose concern is not to get killed, think about getting hit.

The quarterback is acutely aware that there's less chance of a body-shattering sack on first-down plays, when defensive coaches are worrying more about runs than passes. The quarterback is also aware — if his coach isn't — that most of the head-snapping sacks that make the highlight films come on third and long. "I've never been sacked on second down," a veteran NFL quarterback once told me, praying I wouldn't use his name.

Jim Kelly knows.

The Buffalo quarterback is the single active example today of a play-calling player. It's a distinction he first got four years ago when, disgusted with Buffalo's ground-based game plans, he wrested signal-calling away from his coaching staff. He did this by simply keeping the Bills in their no-huddle two-minute offense for most of every game, throwing early and often, and disorienting defenses with an up-tempo attack. The tempo was so fast that his coaches couldn't send in the plays — which was obviously Kelly's hidden agenda.

Most pro teams wouldn't have stood for any such thing. When in 1977 Namath tried to do it for the Los Angeles Rams, he was benched by the coaches, and never played again. But Buffalo's Marv Levy, the NFL's resident Phi Beta Kappa scholar, has been called the league's smartest coach. It is a measure of Levy that despite his personal conservatism as a football man, he let Kelly have his revolution. The result was four years of Buffalo overachievement, an unprecedented four straight Super Bowl appearances by a team that isn't deeply talented (as it proves year after year.) Overwhelmed by much better talent, the Bills have lost at the Super Bowl all four times.

Elsewhere, ignoring the lesson of Marv Levy and his annual excursions to the Super Bowl, NFL coaches are still tightening their grip on the controls, still calling conservative, unimaginative plays. As are college coaches. Game day still belongs to them. And that will continue for as long as the nation's college presidents, NFL presidents, and NBA presidents will it.

But someday, with any luck, in a more perfect world, game day can be a more democratic day, a more interesting day, a players' day.

Would that end the coaches' usefulness? To the contrary, coaches would still be indispensable as, for example, teachers of techniques. In a more democratic era, moreover, they would have to be out recruiting a different kind of player: a thinking player. Size, speed and motor skills are only enough in a robot world: today's football and basketball world. The new premium would be on thinking under pressure. So in time there would be livelier minds on the field and on the basketball floor. On game day, meanwhile, the coaches would be somewhere else. On game day, sports teams can do without coaches.

SECTION FIVE: What Kind of Century Was It?

1. The NFL Hall of Famers

AS A voting member of the Pro Football Hall of Fame selection committee since the beginning, I endorsed only four players and a coach for the first class in 1962. Of the seventeen selected that winter, I voted against twelve for the reasons given in this segment of a column that was written more than thirty years ago.

LOS ANGELES: Dec. 19, 1962.

For those disposed to consider a Pro Football Hall of Fame today, it will come as a shock of pure delight to learn that Herald-Examiner readers have been asked to submit a slate of candidates. Any number from one to ten will do, and the period under study is merely the twentieth century. Sports fans generally know more about these things than sportswriters, and a lot more than coaches or players, so all suggestions will be warmly received and forwarded to Dick McCann, the executive who is organizing the hunt for the new Hall of Fame in Canton, Ohio.

My position, which could well differ from yours, is that five pro football pioneers stand out from all the others who have ever played or worked in the NFL. They're so far ahead that these five should be the only Hall of Famers inducted in the charter class: Sammy Baugh, Washington's model passer; Don Hutson, Green Bay's model receiver, and three Chicago Bears, Owner George Halas, Tackle-Fullback Bronko Nagurski, and Halfback Red Grange.

This has so far been a minority view on the fourteen-man selection committee, which has a football writer or representative from each NFL city. The committee, which met in Chicago December 3 to do some preliminary arguing, will convene again in New York on December 29; and writers for the Chicago Tribune and New York Times are leading the charge for a first-year Hall of Fame membership of eighteen or twenty persons. Although a gang that large would dilute the importance, meaning, and value of a smaller and more exact charter class, I don't seem to be winning. In fact, if I'm the only holdout in a process that requires unanimous approval, I'll probably vote in the end with the majority. This isn't war or peace, and I'd like to be home for New Year's.

Let's hear what you would do. What handful of names best symbolizes pro football? Don't give me any back talk. Get to work.

2. The Century's Top Ten Athletes

AS THE century lurched toward a close, I began thinking about the most remarkable winners and happenings of my time as a sportswriter: the biggest days, the finest athletes. My nominations are in the following newspaper stories written originally for the Times in 1995. Although some of those named have also been mentioned elsewhere in this book, it seemed like a good idea to gather them here, too, in order of impact.

LOS ANGELES: Feb. 5, 1995.

Only five years remain before they begin playing ball in 2000, when, looking back, some will ask one thing about our times: Who were the greatest athletes of the twentieth century? To this hour, Babe Ruth is first and Muhammad Ali second, I'd say — after watching most of the good ones for most of the century.

It is a subject that came up recently in a different context. A guy in a locker room was wondering if Deion Sanders is in anybody's top ten. Well, he's in mine. He's there for these reasons:

In baseball, Sanders, a Cincinnati Reds outfielder, has been a disruptive presence on the basepaths while hitting .283, .276 and .304 in the last three seasons for the Reds and Atlanta Braves.

In football, Sanders, a San Francisco 49ers cornerback who was probably the NFL's Most Valuable Defensive Player in his early years with the Atlanta Falcons, finally won the title this season almost by acclamation.

Ruth and Ali stand alone all-time. Sanders will doubtless never catch either, but in one respect he's similar: They had multiple talent and so has he. Consider Sanders this way: Michael Jordan of the NBA, a modern two-sport legend, hasn't been able to hit *minor* league pitching. As for consensus legend Jim Thorpe, who was most prominent, worldwide, as a decathlon winner, his six years in baseball's National League ended with a career batting average of .252. He couldn't hit the curveball. Moreover, when Thorpe played football, it was in the game's pre-history era.

Here are two subjective criteria for all-time excellence:

• Although the world's best athletes are not and never have been decathlon winners — who simply do many things fairly well — most of the greatest have done at least two things very well.

• Most of the century's best athletes have helped reinvent or redefine their sport or position.

The ten leaders:

1. BABE RUTH.

Beginning as a superior pitcher with a 3-0 World Series record, Ruth finished as a superior hitter, averaging a home run for every 11.8 times at bat — or one every couple of days for twenty-two years. That transcendent versatility qualifies Ruth as best-of-century. In 1916, defeating Dodger Sherry Smith in the most remarkable of all World Series pitching duels, Ruth pitched the full fourteen innings to win, 2-1, for the Boston Red Sox. Sold to the New York Yankees in 1920, he changed the sport's accent to power hitting — dramatically revising a seemingly changeless game. That was Ruth's most historic achievement during a career in which, batting .342 lifetime, he hit forty-one or more home runs eleven times and fifty-four or more four times.

2. MUHAMMAD ALI.

Most intellectual of the boxers since Gene Tunney, Ali packed everything but a wallop, and that he didn't need. By inventing or mastering three ways to fight, Ali won the heavyweight title three times. In his youth, relying on an unprecedented dancing style, he could hit people when he had both feet in the air. Next, after an unnecessary exile for declining to participate militarily in Vietnam, Ali changed styles to regain the title with perhaps the most imaginative defense in sports history — backing himself continually into the ropes as George Foreman punched himself into exhaustion. Finally, in Manila, an aging Ali beat Joe Frazier with the only thing he had left, the guts to take more than four hundred punches in fourteen rounds.

3. O.J. SIMPSON.

The best football player I have seen, Simpson was, uniquely, the accepted best of class among both the college and pro players of his time. Most other Heisman Trophy winners have faltered as pros. Simpson, a respected team player and team leader, ran USC into the 1968 national championship, then became the first NFL back to rush for two thousand single-season yards. As ballcarriers, Gale Sayers and Hugh McElhenny had more moves, and Jim Brown more power, but Simpson did it all faster. Nobody could keep up with Simpson's cuts. A 9.4 sprinter, he was on the USC 440-yard relay team that broke — and still holds — the world record.

4. JACKIE ROBINSON.

The most gifted of America's four-sport stars, Robinson was a mid-century Hall of Fame second baseman for the Los Angeles Dodgers after a UCLA career in which he was less effective in baseball than any other sport. In basketball he led the conference in scoring. In football he set records for punt returns and average yards from scrimmage for the undefeated 1939 Bruins. And in track, with a jump of 24-10 1/2, he was the 1940 NCAA long jump champion. Even though his best sport was football, he became the first of the great all-around athletes to choose baseball. And after fifty years, he remains *the* all-around athlete of the twentieth century.

5. JOHN UNITAS.

On the short list of football's greatest quarterbacks, Unitas belongs at the top, just ahead of Joe Namath, whose bad knees beat him prematurely, and Joe Montana, who is still untested in the science of play-calling — traditionally half of a quarterback's job. In and after 1958, Unitas, the leader of the old Baltimore Colts, was on three NFL champions — one fewer than Montana, two more than Namath — and he got there by two means: thinking and throwing. For eighteen years, in fact, the question was whether Unitas was winning with his arm or head. He was the wisest strategist in the game before Bill Walsh, the coach who built four Super Bowl champions in San Francisco. Football's greatest defensive players have been End Deacon Jones of the Los Angeles Rams, Linebacker Dick Butkus of the Chicago Bears, and Cornerback Sanders.

6. MAGIC JOHNSON.

Playing beautiful basketball in multiple ways, Johnson, who took the Los Angeles Lakers to five NBA championships, enjoyed everything about a game in which he could do everything — lead the fast break, manage a deliberate half-court offense, drive the lane, catapult no-look, smart-bomb passes, shoot post-up hooks, and nail the coffin-closing three. The greatest of all basketball players, many believe, was Michael Jordan — but I think of Jordan as a gifted hot dog who needed strong coaching to win. He was, in fact, halfway through his NBA career before he got that, from Phil Jackson, his Chicago coach. By contrast, Johnson, right off, willed the Lakers in — as a twenty-year-old rookie and as the strategic leader of that and every other team he played on. The extra dimension Johnson added was winning with joy, winning with a smile.

7. TED WILLIAMS.

Exhibiting two phenomenal skills, Williams was, first, unsurpassed as a hitter. Second, as a fighter pilot, he flew thirty-nine missions one year in the Korean war. Few young men have the nerve, eyesight and reflexes of a fighter pilot, and even fewer can do what Williams routinely did to a pitched ball. When it was anywhere in the strike zone, Williams, a left-handed hitter, pulled the ball to right almost every time up for nineteen years — even against the so-called Williams shift — and still batted .344 lifetime with 521 home runs. If he had been hitting toward Ruth's short porch in Yankee Stadium instead of the depths of Fenway Park, Williams might have had a thousand home runs. He is the all-time leader in what is perhaps a hitter's most meaningful statistic, on-base average, with .488 to Ruth's .474.

8. DEION SANDERS.

An NFL triple-threater — defense, offense, special teams — Sanders is America's best active two-sport athlete. Nobody else has ever had the speed and skill to lead the National League in three-base hits en route to the NFL's Pro Bowl. As a defensive player, he has had more impact on football than any of his contemporaries or predecessors. He is, by common estimate, the best pass coverage specialist in NFL history, changing any game he plays in by taking each opponent's most feared receiver out of the game. That enables teammates to gang up on the others. Probably the fastest good player in football, Sanders is also the NFL's most underrated kick-returner and open-field runner.

9. BOBBY ORR.

This continues to be my idea of a hockey player. Orr played hockey the way O.J. Simpson and Jackie Robinson played football — at a tempo that made it seem a different game. Before Orr's day in Boston, most defensemen brought the puck out halfway, bowed pleasantly, and said good night. By the 1970s, Orr was taking it end to end — eluding some players with his speed, some with power, some with finesse — and when he got there, he could make the shot. And so doing, Orr redefined both defense and hockey, a sport in which Wayne Gretzky has lasted longer and, with his singularly cerebral style, has accomplished more. Orr, quicker and bigger, was the better athlete.

10. JESSE OWENS.

Unequaled in track-and-field history, Owens' 1930s' achievements are unlikely, as a package, to be surpassed in any sport. First, at a Big Ten meet in 1935, Owens *in a single day* set three world records and tied a fourth, advancing the long jump record to 26-8 1/2, where it remained for a quarter century. Then at the Berlin Olympics in 1936, Owens dismantled Adolf Hitler's Aryan-supremacy showplace, winning four gold medals — at 100 meters (10.3), 200 meters (20.7), in the long jump (26-5 5/16) and as a 400-meter relay team member. Although others have been faster — Bob Hayes and Carl Lewis would, for example, finish one-two if matched at the same age at one hundred paces — Owens remains the ultimate big-game performer of the twentieth century.

3. Ten Biggest Days in Sports

LOS ANGELES: March 5, 1995.

By comparison with any other century since the ancient Greeks started playing games in 700 B.C. or thereabouts, the twentieth has been the most athletically active ever. No previous century had wall-to-wall sports. No other people have known interscholastic, professional, and Olympic competition in a continuous parade led by throngs of individual achievers.

The parade began, in one sense, ninety-nine years ago with the revival of the Olympic Games after a lapse of fifteen centuries. But even with the flash and dash of such an opener, it was a parade with few spectators until after World War I, when, suddenly, revealingly, everyone seemed to be applauding the 1920s as the golden age of sport. Since then, there have been so many big days — hundreds of them — that this has become, more exactly, the golden *century* of sport.

Looking back, even so, an all-time top ten can be identified — ten matchless individual athletic achievements — plus two that seem close.

The two are Pitcher Don Larsen's perfect World Series game in 1956 and Bob Beamon's long long jump in 1968, when, flying 350 1/2 inches, he broke the world record by nearly two feet. Yet on his historic day, Larsen, who finished with a real-life won-lost record of 81-91, was simply out of character — as was Beamon, a good athlete who was only magnificent once. That doesn't diminish their accomplishments, but it does diminish my interest.

The intention here is to measure individual achievements in major events by athletes who had careers of excellence. The question: On the top ten days of twentieth century sports, who stopped the world?

1. REGGIE JACKSON: One Day, Three Swings, Three Home Runs.

In New York on October 18, 1977, Jackson hit three World Series home runs for the New York Yankees on consecutive pitches. That extended his streak to a record four on four consecutive swings — counting a final-at-bat home run the game before. Driving in four sixth-game runs with his three home runs, Jackson made the difference as the Dodgers lost game and series, 8-4 and 4-2. It was the century's peak achievement given these three circumstances: No athletic feat is more difficult than hitting a pitched ball over a big league fence; the single-game, three-swing masterpiece came in the decisive game of a World Series; and Jackson hit all four in the pressure created by his own reputation as Mr. October. Because of all he had accomplished as a World Series winner in Oakland, Jackson, just that year, had been brought East to do it in New York. And he did it spectacularly, hitting a fifth-game home run in his last turn, beginning the sixth game with a walk on four Burt Hooton pitches, then hitting first-pitch home runs off Hooton in the fourth inning, Elias Sosa in the fifth, and Charlie Hough in the eighth.

2. JESSE OWENS: One Day, Four Events, Four World Records.

In forty-five minutes on May 25, 1935, Owens, twenty-one, Ohio State's sophomore sprinter, broke three world records and equaled a fourth in the greatest one-day performance in the recorded history of the world's oldest sport. Winning events pioneered in ancient Greece, Owens, during a Big Ten track meet at Ann Arbor, Michigan, tied the world record for the 100-yard dash and set new records in the 220, 220 hurdles and long jump. As usual, he was running on an old cinder track — without the aid of starting blocks — yet he raced the 100 in 9.4 seconds, the 220 in 20.3, the hurdles in 22.6, and jumped 26-8 1/4, setting four Big Ten records that, incredibly, have never been broken.

3. FRANZ KLAMMER: Gold Medal for a Wild Ride.

At Innsbruck on February 5, 1976, Downhill Skier Klammer won an Olympic gold medal for Austria by throwing himself off a mountain. Shocking everyone who saw it, Klammer, racing down the hill recklessly, seemed to ignore all pretense at technique and common sense. At times he hit speeds nearing a hundred miles an hour, and he rounded some turns with one leg sticking out at right angles. Nothing in a century of competitive sports has been as wild and exciting as that run. It was a response to two kinds of pressure. First, the defending champion, Bernhard Russi of Switzerland, had just come down in 1:46.06, a time that appeared insurmountable that day on that course. Second, all Austria was praying for an Austrian to beat an Austrian mountain. In 1:45.73 he did.

4. RED GRANGE: Four Touchdowns, Twelve Minutes.

For Illinois on October 18, 1924, Grange scored four long-distance touchdowns against Michigan in the game's first twelve minutes, scoring the first four times he touched the ball. He returned the opening kickoff ninety-five yards, then added three touchdowns on runs from scrimmage, going sixty-seven, forty-five and fifty-six yards. Unbeaten Michigan, which hadn't lost since 1922, was on a fifteen-game winning streak when it arrived at Urbana, Illinois, where the Illini extended their own winning streak to eleven. After sitting out the second quarter, Grange, on the biggest day a football player ever had, came back with three more big plays in the second half. Playing both offense and defense, he intercepted a pass, scored a fifth touchdown, and threw a pass for Illinois' other touchdown as Michigan fell, 39-14. A year later, Grange rescued the struggling NFL. He was then the magnet for the first big pro crowds, seventy-three thousand in New York and seventy-five thousand at the Los Angeles Coliseum.

5. KIRK GIBSON: How to Beat a Better Team.

On October 15, 1988, the Dodgers were losing to the Oakland A's in the ninth inning at Dodger Stadium, 4-3, when, with one on, Pinch Hitter Gibson limped out to become the only man to win the World Series with one first-game swing. The A's, greatly talented that year, were also full of arrogance, understandably, and with the dominant closer of the era, Dennis Eckersley, they were heavily favored. But the Dodgers had Eckersley well scouted. Although Gibson's knee and hamstring injuries were so severe that he couldn't run — and couldn't even bat again that Series — he was ready for Eckersley's two-out, 2-and-2 pitch, a hard slider that hit the low outside corner. Leaning far out over the plate, Gibson flicked his wrists and astonishingly pulled a perfect pitch into the right field stands. As the ball rose into the night, the air went out of the A's, who realized, sickeningly, that now they'd have to beat the Dodger ace, Orel Hershiser, twice. They couldn't do that. For Hershiser, in his biggest year as a pitcher, was well rested, having been held out opening night. And in five quick games, the A's lost to perhaps the least talented of all World Series winners.

6. MUHAMMAD ALI: How to Win Without Fighting.

At 4 a.m. on October 30, 1974, near the River Zaire in Africa, Ali, forsaking his fists, used his great knowledge of boxing to upset a 1-3 favorite, George Foreman, then and now the heavyweight champion, and then and now the deadliest one-punch destroyer of them all except Joe Louis. To recapture a title that had been unwarrantedly stripped away seven years earlier, Ali perfected a surprise game plan, backing smartly into the ropes instead of fighting the champion, who wore himself out swinging wildly. For seven long rounds, there Ali was, right in front of him, and Foreman couldn't find him. And in the eighth, Ali rose up and knocked him out. The scholar of the century in boxing — in all of sports, it may be — Ali based his game plan on the sometime tactics of Sugar Ray Robinson and two early-century fighters, a welterweight, Young Jack Thompson, and Heavyweight Champion Jess Willard. In 1911, Willard needed twenty-six rounds to wear out Jack Johnson before, like Ali sixty-three years later, knocking his man out. One difference: few saw Willard, the world saw Ali.

7. ARTHUR ASHE: Mind Over Man at Wimbledon.

On July 5, 1975, illustrating the place of the intellectual in competitive sports, Ashe upset the world's best tennis player, Jimmy Connors, by making him run for the ball in the Wimbledon final, 6-1, 6-1, 5-7, 6-4. Connors was, at 2-11, the heaviest favorite in Wimbledon history. He could have demolished Ashe in a heavy-hitting duel. Forestalling that, Ashe, carrying the weight of his lineage as the only black man to win Wimbledon, invented a new style just for the day — a style designed to defuse the hard returns and ground strokes in the arsenal of a classic counterpuncher. With wide serves, and with soft slice shots dropped into the center of his opponent's court, Ashe destabilized Connors by making him come up — or go out — for the ball, where he lost power. Or as Connors said: "He didn't give me much to hit at."

8. MAGIC JOHNSON: Point Guard? Center? Whatever.

On May 16, 1980, with all-time Center Kareem Abdul-Jabbar out with a sprained ankle, Johnson, twenty, a rookie point guard, took Jabbar's place — making the most drastic position switch in basketball — and imperturbably and improbably led the Lakers to the championship in Philadelphia's Spectrum, 123-107. Though never an NBA center before or since, Johnson demonstrated his mastery of the sport that night, scoring on skyhooks, tips, drives, whatever it took, and producing forty-two points on fourteen of twenty-three shots and fourteen of fourteen free throws. He was also there for fifteen rebounds. With 5:12 left, after Julius Erving's six consecutive points put the 76ers close, 103-101, the Lakers scored twenty of the game's last twenty-six points for Coach Paul Westhead, and Johnson, smiling all the way, had eleven of the twenty.

9. ROGER BANNISTER: One Mile in Four Minutes.

On May 6, 1954, a British runner showed a surprised world that what human beings do is what they think they can do. Uncounted thousands of athletes had dreamed about it. Medical student Bannister *believed* it, running the first four-minute mile. In a minor track meet at Oxford, England, before a crowd of about a thousand, he won in 3:59.4 — a time that instantly made a major psychosocial impact on the world. Indeed, it still has a meaning beyond track. As Bannister, now a medical doctor, was to say later: "Most of the barrier was psychological. For hundreds of years, nobody could run a four-minute mile. In the last few years, it's been run hundreds of times."

10. TED WILLIAMS: From .399 to .406 in One Day.

When he got up in Philadelphia on the morning of September 28, the last day of the 1941 baseball season, Williams, twenty-two, was batting .39955. Had he taken the day off, his average would have been rounded up to .400 — an accomplishment so rare that nobody has been there since. But he never considered that. Instead, needing a one-for-one game to reach .401 that afternoon for the Red Sox against Connie Mack's A's, Williams tried for it, and got it. And after 449 at bats that season, after 180 base hits, he had at last earned the right to sit down. In 1950, Joe DiMaggio was to sit out the last game of the season after climbing to .300 in the next to last game — but Williams, doing it the hard way, played boldly on. Putting the .400 in jeopardy, Williams played through a doubleheader into the September twilight, and, achieving with a magnificence that matched his valor, hit .750 that last day — six for eight — lifting his 1941 batting average to .406.